DICTIONARY
DREAMS-SIGNS-SYMBOLS

THE SOURCE CODE

DICTIONARY
DREAMS-SIGNS-SYMBOLS

THE SOURCE CODE

KAYA

UNIVERSE/CITY MIKAËL (UCM)
NON-PROFIT ORGANIZATION

universe/city mikaël (ucm)
Non-profit organization
Publishing House
53, rue Saint-Antoine
Sainte-Agathe-des-Monts, QC
Canada J8C 2C4

Administrator: Jean Morissette, lawyer
Email: org@ucm.ca
Websites: www.ucm.ca & www.kayadreams.com

To organize a lecture, seminar, or workshop: org@ucm.ca
Discover Kaya's webinars on dreams, signs, and symbols:
webinar@ucm.ca & www.ucm.ca

English translation: Blánaid Rensch
Restructuring, correction, final revision and main coordinator of original French version: Rita Haidu
Research and proofreading team: *cf.* next page
Editing coordinator: Martine Thuillard
Editing and graphics: Christophe Guilloteau
Cover: Anthony Di Benedetto, Kasara
Photo: Anthony Di Benedetto

Dictionary Sponsor: Dr. Nancy Smithers, Yeiayel Holdings Ltd.

1st edition: 4th term, 2013
Legal deposit: 4th term, 2013
National Library of Quebec
National Library of Canada
National Library of France
National Library of Ireland

ISBN: 978-2-923654-25-6

Printed in Canada

Printed on Rolland Enviro 100, which contains 100% recycled, post-consumer fiber, and is certified Ecologo, Processed Chlorine Free and FSC recycled, as well as manufactured using biogas energy.

AUTHOR'S THANKS

Heartfelt thanks to all those who contributed to the research, re-structuring, proof-reading and final revision:

Restructuring, correction, final revision and main coordinator
Rita Haidu

English translation
Blánaid Rensch
with deep gratitude to her beloved husband for his faithful love, constancy, support and help.

Proof-reading/correction/final revision team: Christiane Muller, Nancy Smithers, Miguèle Bittar, Andrée Brassard, Maryse Moffet, Isabelle Moran, Sophie Delmonico, Josiane Pauli, Marie Hélène Ruaux, Maryse Fiat, Catherine Cohadon, Monique Langlois, Lise-Berthe Villemure, Pierre Lambert, Huguette Lessard, Marie-Laure Lemal-Stubenitsky, Maryvonne Denis, Danielle Guilloteau.

Re-structuring team: Andrée Brassard, Patrick Thomas, Isabelle Moran, Éloi and Sophie Delmonico, Marie Hélène Ruaux, Caroline Chabot, Josiane Pauli, Maryse Fiat, Catherine Cohadon.

Coordination and file management: Sylvie Camiré, Michel Boisvert, Miguèle Bittar

Editing coordinator: Martine Thuillard

Computing: Jean-François Bohémier

Research team: Jacline Allard Martin, Véronique Andrieu, Louise Beaudoin, René Belliard, Catherine Beyssier, Christine Bienvenüe, Julie Bisaillon, Miguèle Bittar, Josée Blais, Sylvie Blanc, Michel Boisvert, François Bouchard, Sylvain Bouchard, Joan Boux, Mireille Brasseur, Florence Bricchi, Sylvie Camiré, Myriam Célestine, Caroline Chabot, Laurence Chambon, Rita Cormier, Jean-François Côté, Isabelle Coucogne, Claudia Courchesne, Eloi and Sophie Delmonico, Jérémie Denir, Maryvonne Denis, Charles Dichamp, Marie-Claudine Dumas, Johanne Egglefield, Guillaume Favre-de-Thierrens, Marie-Noëlle Favre-de-Thierrens, Thibaut and Claire Favre-de-Thierrens, Carole Forest, Nadine Fortin, Denise Fredette, Karin Gétaz, Marise Gourde, Pascal Guérard, Danielle Guilloteau, Rita Haidu, Petra Hallenberger, Cécile Hancart, Claudette Harvey, Pascale Héraud, Valentin Héritier, Sophie Hitter, Patricia Hoël, Geneviève Houde, Roméo Jacques, Lise Johnson, Agnès Joly, Yves Koll, Danièle Kremer-Wagner, Billy Labelle, Rachel Labelle, Solange Labrie, Brigitte Lafuente, Claudia Laplante, Joceline Laprade, Caroline Lavoie, Sandra Lavoie, Catherine Leblanc-Faury, Isabelle Lepeytre, Lorraine Lequin, Simone Luciani, Pascal Manzano, Sébastien and Laure Manzano, Francis Marcil, Madeleine Marleau Bossé, Jacqueline Masse, Louise Matte, Maryse Moffet, Chantal Monette, Brigitte Monge, Isabelle Moran Huteau, Chantal Osorio, Sylvianne Pellerin, Bertrand Petitgas, Florence Pichonnaz, Laure-Anne Pierson, Isabelle Ponsot, Michèle Potvin, Maryse Raymond, Anne-Marie Régimbald, Aude Richard, Dominique Rieg, Ian Robert, Lysiane Rolot, Adeline Roussel, Chantal Roussel, Guylaine Samson, France Sarda, Jeannine Sieg, Marlyse Sonnay-Cordonier, Patrick and Régine Thomas, Martine Thuillard, Jean-Yves Urien, Denise Villeneuve, Pauline Villeneuve

JOIN US!

All the profits from the Dictionary, *The Source Code* and the volumes to follow, go to the non-profit organization, Universe/City Mikaël (UCM) to help its diffusion among the generations of today and tomorrow.

You can contribute to its diffusion and translation into other languages by making a donation and/or joining our team of hundreds of volunteers from countries all over the world. If you feel that this Knowledge is important to you, please visit our website **www.ucm.ca**, go to the section entitled Join us! and see its various sub-sections, including *Become a volunteer* and *Donation*, or contact us at **goodwill@ucm.ca**

Heartfelt thanks for your help and goodwill,

UCM Team

PREFACE

by KASARA

When we receive the *Source Code*, our whole life changes completely.

Shortly after my birth, my father's life completely changed. From one day to the next, he started having 10-50 dreams per night. He studied dreams in his dreams. At times, he couldn't tell the difference between dreams and reality. Much to everyone's surprise, he gave up everything. He seemed to have become an incomprehensible hermit, and everyone looked at him as though he were crazy or weird. He accepted all this with humility so he could deepen his research to become a better person, to increase his capacity to love humankind unconditionally. People either laughed at him or didn't understand. I experienced this change alongside him: those first years of change when we feel other people's fears and mistrust because we are not like them. The greatest wise men and philosophers of the past often lived as visionaries before being truly understood because they traced a new path, a path that called into question our ways of thinking and understanding the world we live in.

My father, a public figure in his native country, was ridiculed, rejected and excluded due to a lack of understanding regarding his transformation, which he himself couldn't explain. I remember one Saturday morning when I was very young, I turned on the television to watch a children's program. But just as I was changing channels, I stopped to listen to a program that had caught my attention because it was talking about my father. I sat there listening with all my love and admiration, but what was said about him was quite the contrary to the feelings in my little girl's heart. All I remember is seeing my mother come in, just at the right moment, to gently turn off the television and help stop the flow of tears running down my face.

My father went through many ordeals to offer us this unique reference book. It is hard for anyone to imagine how psychologically difficult it was. I used to console him sometimes, holding him in my arms, hugging him, and telling him it was going to be all right, everything was going to be all right.

I have such admiration and love for my father. He sacrificed a most promising career, gave up everything many people dream of accomplishing in order to follow his inner guidance, that wind of transformation that was taking shape in his dreams. Above all, he had the courage to turn the page, to completely change his life, all to learn, to better understand himself, to understand the *Source Code*, and to transmit it to us today. The great change he undertook now becomes completely meaningful with this revolution of Knowledge for the science of conscience. By surpassing all the research on dreams up to now, Kaya opens up new paths for our autonomy of conscience; he helps us understand the multi-dimensions, the metaphysics we all have within ourselves. He may have been ridiculed and denigrated as a man, but this whole path was worth all the courage it required for Kaya to be able to offer The *Source Code* to people all over the world who are on a spiritual path. This Code, which helps us better understand how our conscience and our unconscious works, is already used by therapists, psychologists, psychiatrists, and doctors in many fields.

The present volume represents 15 years of writing, but, in actual fact, it embodies an entire lifetime of research and study. It is also the fruit of the collaboration of over 100 people, who, in recent years, helped my father regarding research and editing. I've seen my father work on The *Source Code* all my life. And when I say that, I don't say it with any ounce of suffering from a possible absent father syndrome, because my father was always there for me. And, along with Christiane my stepmother, it was as a family that we studied, experimented, and applied The *Source Code* daily, as though in a laboratory. As a very young child, I wanted to be like my father, so I bought a little notebook so I could write too. Instead of sending me outside to play, my father played with me. And every single night, he would tell me a deep, symbolic story. It was magical! I'd choose 3 characters, and he'd take a few seconds to interiorize and invent the story he was going to tell me. To my little girl's mind, it was pure magic! In fact, he was already talking to me in symbols; he was teaching me The *Source Code*...he was speaking to my soul. He used to take something that had happened during the day and he'd retell it all in the form of a story. I remember one evening he told me a story about Winnie the Pooh who didn't want to share any of his honey with his friends. Through this apparently ordinary, banal story, just through his intention, my father managed to give me all the necessary keys to help me rectify my behavior. Through symbols that he animated so well, he very gently explained to me my sharing dynamics, and the negative consequences of my acts or thought concepts, without my noticing that Winnie was me. Like in a dream, he helped me travel within myself, while simultaneously positively programming my life and conscience.

A symbolic understanding of our existence modifies the way we conceive life. It prevents us from going in the wrong direction, from committing ourselves to difficult paths with no way out. The capacity to understand our dreams and signs gives multi-dimensional meaning to our life and reveals the deep meaning of our existence. People often dismiss dreams saying, "Oh, it was just a dream." Yet, since we spend almost half of our life sleeping, don't you think it might be important to pay attention to the quantity of information that flows through our cells every night? Personally, understanding my dreams has changed my life. My dreams often showed me the young woman I could have become if I continued in such and such a direction. I could have made many detours, but instead, I took a shortcut. I've had the privilege of being able to integrate the *Source Code* from my earliest childhood. I am convinced this reference book, this work of a lifetime, will still be talked about in thousands of years from now as a new platform for symbolic language, the *Source Code* of Conscience. It helps us get to know ourselves deeply, truly, and allows us to realize that we are on Earth to develop Qualities and Virtues so as to become better souls, to understand that the metaphysical, the *Source Code*, is the root cause, is the very origin of our physical reality, that the metaphysical level is always the cause, while the physical level is always the application of the consequence(s).

It is a great honor for me to write the preface to this Dictionary. I'm both moved and deeply touched. I am convinced this reference book is of fundamental importance for Mankind and all of the future generations, because dreams are reality, and reality is a dream, a space of conscience to which symbols representing us gravitate, symbols which define us as people, as human-beings. A simple dream has the power to change a life. Hence The *Source Code* is a key that will provide you with the answers to your questions, give meaning to the incoherencies in your life, and keep the Light alive and glowing, even in your darkest nightmares.

In my humble opinion, it is truly vital for all of us to receive the *Source Code*, and to share it with those who wish to know about it. This Code reveals the intention inscribed in matter and in each and every one of us. This essential reference book represents a new stage, a quantum leap in the evolution of Humanity. Thanks to the man who has devoted his life to this cause, who continues to spread this knowledge, the first volume of this work – The *Source Code* – is now available. The *Source Code* II and other volumes are under preparation and will be published in the years to come.

Dreams are the reflections of our past, the reasons for our present, and the probabilities of what we may become one day.

Kasara

INTRODUCTION

This Dictionary, *The Source Code*, which represents one of the greatest advances in the field of dream, sign, and symbol interpretation, reveals to us that the dreams and signs we receive are not merely abstract, incoherent, unfounded information, but that they are conceived in accordance with a completely logical, universal code that is to be found in each of us. In actual fact, a dream is a collection of symbols, each of which has its own precise meaning. Thanks to our dreams, we can visit regions of our unconscious and deeply understand that *everything that exists in the outside world, also exists within us, and manifests in states of mind, soul and conscience. The symbolic language of dreams and signs is in fact mathematical: it is composed of equations of conscience* that show us who we really are in the very depths of our being, and what we are to experience and experiment in order to evolve. This language helps us discover that the symbols composing our dreams and signs define structural dynamics that are fundamentally logical. Indeed, they represent parts and aspects of our being, forces, atmospheres and ambiances, programming, and patterns of behavior and functioning; they help us understand the situations, encounters and events that make up our life-plan. Symbols are the basis of the universal parameters and equations Cosmic Intelligence uses to elaborate and activate our learning programs, our apprenticeships in life. Knowing symbolic language allows us to recognize the *Source Code* inscribed in us and in all that exists, thereby opening the door to understanding the multiple manifestations of Life, both in the outer world and within ourselves.

The *Source Code* is our experience – past, present, and future – that dwells in our conscious and unconscious memories, which, in coded form, informs us about what we thought and did in the past, how what we think and do in the present time affects our life today, and activates what will happen to us tomorrow if we don't change our ways of thinking and behaving. This unique Dictionary is entirely based on the capacity to translate a symbol from its logical basis, i.e. deducing its spiritual, metaphysical meaning from its concrete, physical meaning. The profound reflection on the positive and negative aspects of each word helps us see the different angles of the manifestation of a symbol and hence helps us understand its multi-dimensional meaning. The *Source Code* contains Knowledge that comes to us from the heart, the essence, the very core of Creation, and reveals to us the deep meaning of our existence: the development of Qualities, Virtues, and Powers in their purest form. Thus it is a key that guides us toward the discovery of our Divine nature. The metaphor of an Angel is one of the most beautiful symbols to represent a human-being who has developed his capacity to dream, his spiritual dimension that surpasses the limitations of his body and physical senses and allows him to travel in the multi-dimensions of conscience and the Universe. As human-beings, we experiment and experience life and action in matter and in the exchanges we have with everyone and everything around us, and other forms of life. Whether we are aware of it or not, the one and only aim, the true aim of human life and living, is to unfurl our angelic potential and to recognize and acknowledge our divine essence.

Our spirit takes on a physical body in order to experiment, and *via* our choices, *via* the positive and negative, to gradually discover the infinite potential we have within ourselves. Symbols mostly give perspective to this perpetual dynamic of research, development, and experimentation that is present in different forms and situations. In symbolic images, dreams show us the beginning of our life; they show us multiple, positive and/or negative scenarios of evolution and experimentation related to memories of our past, aspects of our present, and the probabilities of our future, of what we may become, or are in the process of preparing or materializing in our individual or collective life-program.

Through studying and working with dreams and signs, we learn to consciously accelerate our evolution by cleansing the distorted memories within us that prevent the manifestation of our spiritual potential. Simultaneously, we learn to anticipate our future and rectify our future selves. To better understand the multi-dimension of our dreams and signs, we need to know that we all live in a *Living*

Computer, that we call God or Cosmic Intelligence (it doesn't matter what we name we give to it) because it is impossible to imagine dreams, symbols, scenarios, situations, events that we have never seen or experienced. We live as *individual computers* permanently connected to the Great Whole, the immense *Cosmic Computer*, and thus we can understand the Law of synchronicity whereby there is no such thing as coincidence in life, that everything has a reason for existing, that everything has a deep, evolutive meaning.

To analyze and interpret dreams, signs, and symbols well, it is essential to know certain rules. Here are the most important ones:

1. **A dream must always be analyzed chronologically.** Like a story, there is a beginning, a middle and an end, that may be complete or incomplete. Whenever the conclusion is incomplete, it means that the behavioral dynamic(s) shown in the dream hasn't been resolved, or that the dreamer is at the learning stage.

2. It is advisable to begin with a general analysis of the dream as a whole, seeking to understand its **general, global theme**, to which we can then add the details. Basing ourselves on the atmosphere, ambiance and events presented, we **first define if the dream has a positive or negative tendency.** We try to understand the main outline of the dream, and if we have difficulty interpreting or seeing the link between the symbols – which is perfectly normal at first – we are happy to reflect on the general, global theme. We can also work with a symbol or aspect that stands out in the dream; e.g. dynamics of aggression, hyperactivity, feelings of embarrassment, envy, or an intense need to please, etc. In this way, we manage to decode the global essence of the dream, which already allows us to do great reflective work on our behavior, and to improve our attitude by transforming the blockages and negative aspects that the dream unveiled and revealed to us. Likewise, when a dream highlights positive aspects, such aspects help us discover our latent, underlying, dormant potential. Generally speaking, the deeper our knowledge and understanding of the *Source Code*, the more precise, the more correct our analyses and interpretations.

3. It is also important to **determine which of the four elements – fire*, air*, water*, earth*– are present** in the dream or situation we wish to analyze because they are the fundamental basis of symbolic language. In one dream, several elements may interact so as to present different parameters of our conscience. (*cf. Dictionary definition of these terms.)

4. The presence of **symbols representing or related to the five kingdoms – mineral*, vegetable*, animal*, human, divine** – is also an important element to consider. (*cf. Dictionary definition of these terms.)

5. **For a symbol to be truly positive, it must be in its right place, and in good condition** (harmonious, non-aggressive, clean, beautiful, radiant, etc.); e.g. a snake in a bed, even if it isn't aggressive in the dream, will indicate a negative dynamic related to what the snake represents symbolically. We make the following equation: bed (intimacy) + snake (sexuality) = the person has too strong a need for sexual intimacy.

6. **Whenever a distorted element is present in a dream, it often confirms that the general atmosphere of the dream has a negative tendency,** depending on the degree of importance of the symbol in the dream; e.g. *There's an aggressive cat in a beautiful, big sitting-room.* This indicates that, on the level of the dreamer's social intimacy (sitting-room symbol), he has beautiful potential for expansion in his social behavior, but at the same time he is very independent, slightly haughty, a little anti-social or distant, difficult to get close to (negative aspects of the cat symbol).

7. **Everyday objects always have a universal symbolic meaning.** Hence, from a positive point of view, a chair is a symbol of receptivity, calm, well-being, rest, and relaxation; from a negative point of view, it symbolizes a lack of receptivity, laziness, indolence, a lack of motivation to be active, to take action, to set things in motion, to advance, etc. The positive or negative symbolic meaning of a chair will be defined in detail

by its shape, color, place where it is found in the dream, etc., but all of these details will always be related to the original (general) meaning of the object.

8. **There are no *tourists* in dreams.** When we receive a dream where we see another person in his home or workplace, etc., even though we may be visiting his soul, we are never simply onlookers, *tourists*. There is always something for us to understand. It's no coincidence that person is in our dream. Generally speaking, all of the elements that appear in a dream symbolically represent parts of the dreamer. We can receive dreams about our past, our present, and our future. Sometimes our dreams can give us very precise details regarding the material level, but also about our personality traits. First and foremost, it is important to always seek to understand the evolution lesson contained in the dream in terms of Qualities, Virtues, and Powers in their purest form.

9. **The Law of resonance.** We always attract what we are in terms of memories, both positively and negatively. Understanding this law is essential for us to be able to accept that in an assault or aggressive situation, we are as much the aggressor as the victim, we are both the person who aggresses and attacks others as we are the person (or people) attacked. Understanding the Law of resonance in dreams as well as in concrete reality is fundamental for the correct interpretation of dreams and signs. However, since we only know an infinitesimal percentage of ourselves, we don't realize the resonance we have with a person or situation that attracts or bothers us. That is why it is important not to identify 100% with the negativity that we experience – disturbances, ordeals, difficulties, etc. – but always remind ourselves that we also have beautiful qualities and potentiality. Nevertheless, we have to be prepared to accept that, to a certain degree, on a certain level, we do indeed have similar aspects to the person or situation in question. The will to apply the Law of resonance in all circumstances is a key element in the evolution work we can accomplish with the *Source Code.*

10. **A recurring dream is an alarm signal.** If the dreamer doesn't change his behavior and cleanse his memories related to the situation presented in a recurring dream, then, sooner or later, he will attract a similar situation in concrete reality. A recurring dream wants to call our attention to the fact that we have accumulated a great number of distorted memories in our inner computer, which often manifest in the form of **nightmares**, which will end up manifesting in a concrete event if we continue to ignore them.

11. **The Law of balance.** Whenever there is excess anywhere – in a concrete situation, in a dream, in an attitude or behavior, etc.– there is necessarily a lack, and vice versa. Very often, we are not aware of our excesses and lacks because they are repressed, hidden in our unconscious. Hence, if we are too patient, consciously or unconsciously, we seek to compensate for those parts of us that tend, or tended, to manifest impatiently; if we lack calm and interiorization, we are sure to have parts that are too absorbed by the social, collective side of life; if we lack confidence, it's a sign that somewhere in us there is too much insecurity, etc.

12. **Evil is educational.** Another essential key we need to integrate is being able to recognize and acknowledge the educational, evolutive role of evil, wrong-doing, hurt. Whether it manifests in our dream world in the form of a nightmare, or in the form of an ordeal or human tragedy in concrete reality, it is important to learn to de-dramatize, and to recognize the stimulating, evolutive effect of every difficult experience or situation. Accepting evil as educational allows us to react differently when faced with conflicting, trying, disturbing situations.

13. **Karma and Divine Justice: *We always reap what we sow; Divine Justice is absolute.*** Work with the *Source Code* leads us to integrate both these Divine Laws, which help us understand in depth the apparent injustices that we see in different areas of life, everywhere on Earth. Indeed, if certain situations seem unfair to us, it's because the people going through them have memories within them, from this life or past lives, where they

themselves engendered unfair thoughts, feelings, and deeds. Thus, a difficult situation always serves as a reminder to the person affected; it invites him to rectify his distorted attitudes and to repair his negative karmas on the causal level so as to be able to continue his evolution.

14. **Spiritual autonomy.** Work with the *Source Code* to understand our dreams and everyday life gradually leads us to spiritual autonomy, because it enables us to find our own answers and to receive them within ourselves.

The study of dreams, signs, and symbols is a field of development that leads us to discover and penetrate the secrets of the physical and metaphysical Universe. To continue your apprenticeship and deepen your capacity to analyze and interpret dreams, signs and symbols, we recommend you follow the Internet courses, the international webinars given by Kaya via the Universe/City Mikaël (UCM) website*, which are a very deep, rich and enriching source of education that will help you attain your autonomy in the understanding of the *Source Code*. You can either attend these Webinars live, or discover them in our web store, where they are available for downloading. They constitute a reservoir of supplementary knowledge to the *Dictionary, Dreams-Signs-Symbols, The Source Code.*

*For more information and registration, please visit the Webinar page on our website: **www.ucm.ca**

Note: To facilitate reading, the masculine pronoun has been used when referring to a person who, of course, could be either male or female.

A

ABUNDANCE

Abundance is a natural state of conscience that corresponds to a universal principle. It concerns all worlds and all levels of existence – physical, emotional, intellectual, and spiritual – and it represents a condition where resources on all levels are continually available and surpass the needs of the moment; the idea or feeling of any lack is inexistent. The resources we may have access to can be situated on different levels: we can refer to abundance on the health level, in personal relationships, love, material wealth, mental or manual capacities, etc. However, ultimate, true abundance is essentially spiritual: it is a representation of merits accumulated in this life and others, that a person has earned through his understanding, acceptance and application of the Divine Laws, through all of his right, positive, altruistic, qualitative behavior, as well as the reparation, the settlement of his karmas. These merits may translate as a profusion of dreams wherein the person receives constant guidance on his path, an ability to understand symbolic language, extra-sensorial capacities, such as clairvoyance, clairsentience, and clairaudience, a clear, enriching, stimulating life mission, understanding his life plan and the facility to accomplish it, etc. It is important to understand that having material abundance does not necessarily mean the person has the same abundance on the spiritual, intellectual, and emotional levels. The experience of universal abundance, i.e. on all levels of our being, is the consequence of right usage of resources on all levels in this life and in past lives.

Spiritual, universal abundance can manifest on the concrete level in the form of beautiful emotions, great intellectual faculties, and material wealth. Depending on which stage a person has reached in his evolution, his life plan may be more focused on material dynamics, thereby offering him an opportunity to make good, right, altruistic use of matter. If he fails to make good use of the abundance at his disposal, then it will be withdrawn from him in this life or a future life, where he will be given a different learning, experimentation program regarding abundance. E.g., he may find himself in a context of poverty, unemployment, destitution, etc., so as to allow him to repair past errors and develop the necessary conscience, virtues, and qualities to deserve and manage resources well. It is also possible that a person may not have material wealth in a life, not because he needs to repair karmas related to wealth, but quite simply because he needs to experiment a new program to develop new qualities and virtues, such as patience, the transcendence of envy, covetousness, desire, submission, etc. Furthermore, having material abundance in a dream doesn't particularly mean we will have access to it in concrete reality. For instance, seeing ourselves discover a treasure at the bottom of the sea and bringing it up to the surface refers more to emotional riches because of the water element. All the factors in the dream need to be analyzed for a correct interpretation.

As a person evolves, he receives signs and dreams that guide him toward the right use of abundance on all levels. He also receives the necessary resources to be able to fulfill his life plan and mission here on Earth.

⊕ Understanding the fact that abundance is a natural, universal state of conscience inherent to Creation, which manifests in our life if we live in accordance with Divine Laws and Principles, and if we cleanse and transform our distorted memories related to abundance, wealth, and prosperity. Feelings of prosperity, plenitude, fulfillment, expansion, peace, gratitude, appreciation, and acknowledgement. Access to important resources allowing us to fulfill our life plan and help others. Work on ourselves to learn how to make good, right, altruistic use of resources, to transform those thoughts, emotions, and behavior that incite us to make poor use of any sort of resources (health, gifts, talents, mental and manual capacities, intelligence, material wealth, etc.), to waste, be unaware of, ignore, and destroy them; or, repress, retain, accumulate, and refuse to share them. Transcendence of miserliness, cupidity, greed, covetousness, jealousy, etc.

⊖ Poor use of resources on several levels, waste, excess, abuse and misuse of all sorts. A feeling of superiority engendered by the presence of abundance in our life, arrogant, haughty, vain, egotistical behavior; or, an envious, jealous person who covets other people's abundance. Feelings of worry, insecurity, constant fear of lacking resources. Accumulation of material goods in order to feel reassured. Poverty of conscience. Lack of generosity, sharing, altruism. Ignorance of the fact that abundance is a universal principle, a natural state of conscience in all of Creation, that it enters and exists in our life if we respect Cosmic Laws in our thoughts, emotions, and acts, and that it will be withdrawn from us if we abuse and misuse it. Absence of abundance, limitations, deficiencies, lacks, poverty, misery, which manifest as the karmic consequences of erroneous ways of thinking, behaving, manifesting that the person has engendered through egotistical, greedy, mean, miserly behavior, only using abundant resources for personal ends, and living with a superficial, materialistic conscience.

ABYSS

An abyss indicates a soul-state of intense despair, a very deep chasm that corresponds to our visiting a region in the unconscious inhabited by memories of no hope, no faith, no foundation whatsoever on which to re-build our life, no perspective of a future at all. An accumulation of doubt, uncertainty and misfortune gives rise to intense existential fear and an extremely negative vision of life, thereby creating the feeling of being on the brink of an abyss. At the root of such a soul-state are memories of atheism. It is normal to see the symbol of an abyss in our dreams at the beginning of initiations, which are characterized by the opening of the unconscious. We mustn't be afraid of an abyss. Whenever we go through soul-states of deep despair, it is essential to fill the emptiness with a more elevated, more global, more universal conscience, as well as new ways of thinking. This will give our life a new foundation, a new structure, and the state of despair will gradually disappear.

⊕ A period of great initiation in which we visit the depths of our soul and memories of a great void, despair, and overwhelming sadness. A new stage, a rebirth is under preparation, just like the popular truism, which says: *When we've hit the bottom, there's only one way to go and that's up.* Incitement to work on ourselves so as to transcend existential fear and states of deep distress and discouragement.

⊖ A lack of spiritual knowledge and faith, which causes us to sink into despair and sadness. The soul is overburdened because of values and principles that are over-focused on matter and social success. A period of intense depression and existential anguish. A lack of confidence in ourselves and others. Fear of the unknown. A situation of inner disaster that can lead a person to commit suicide. The appearance of this symbol indicates that it is time to take ourselves in hand, to work on ourselves, to reflect and meditate on deep, profound values, and on the meaning of life.

ACCELERATE, ACCELERATION

Action consisting of increasing the speed of a movement or activity already started so as to reach a desired goal more rapidly. Acceleration is justifiable when it is a question of advancing more rapidly so as to respect synchronicity. However, it may designate a distortion when it results from an inner impulse that corresponds to a conscious or unconscious need to compete, a feeling of insecurity, fear of arriving late, or of missing something.

⊕ Our life-plan accelerates and progresses faster than planned. A dynamic of correct motivation and willpower to achieve our goals. Good timing. Synchronicity is in place and allows rapid, easy progress.

⊖ A person filled with impatience, desires, and needs that push him to go too fast. Haste because of insecurities, lacks, or fear of not succeeding. A compensatory impulse because there are inner memories which slow down evolution. Ambitions causing harm and accidents if such behavior is not rectified. A tendency to push and force to reach our goal more rapidly. The need to learn to advance calmly, without stress or excessive willpower. A lack of synchronicity caused by feelings of insecurity.

ACCIDENT

An accident is an unexpected event that results in damage to ourselves, others, material goods, the environment, etc. It is caused by conscious or unconscious negligence or irresponsibility. To understand the symbolic meaning of an accident, we need to know that we create every situation we experience in our life, even though we may not be responsible in the eyes of the law here on earth. An accident, whether in a dream or in concrete reality, always stems from an accumulation of negative memories, thoughts, emotions, which, sooner or later, if we don't rectify our attitude, take on concrete form. Seeing an accident in a dream reveals to us that we have memories within us that can engender difficult situations. It does not necessarily mean that we will actually experience an accident in the next few days, but it is important to meditate on the contents of the dream so as to become aware of and transform our memories and energies that can engender such an event. By working on ourselves in this way, we can change our destiny and the events we could have experienced.

On the symbolic level, causing or seeing an accident in a dream, is a warning to us to keep a close watch over our thoughts, emotions and/or behavior the following day so as to avoid creating misactions[1], and/or clashes on the individual or collective level. Because after such a dream, we tend to attract or create all sorts of conflicts, difficulties or little accidents in our lives. When this happens, it is good to study our mood, our state of mind, our state of conscience, our soul-state when it occurred; i.e. to study the thoughts and emotions that dwelled in us at that moment to be able to learn from the experience, to understand the lesson in it for us. It is important to repair any damage done without feeling guilty, without complicating things. When a situation is too subtle, too difficult to understand or explain, we can rectify by apologizing and sincerely asking for the other person's forgiveness on the inside, within ourselves.

From another point of view, accidents can lead to surprising revelations. Many inventions were *accidentally* discovered thanks to unexpected events. The Divine can take unimaginable pathways to

---

1. Misaction is our translation of the French expression 'acte manqué' and it encompasses the idea of a slip-up, a mishap, a mistake, a blunder, an oversight, forgetting to do what we'd intended to do, a lapsus, an act of omission, any act or non-action that is not right, that is not divinely harmonious.

bring forth life. An accident provides us with evolutive, beneficial teaching (lesson(s)) for all humanity. A positive or negative action is always multidimensional.

⊕ Allows awareness, consciousness, surprising discoveries and an opening onto new horizons. Helps us integrate the fact that evil, wrong-doing, hurt is educational and that we learn from our errors. A period of reflection, self-questioning and soul searching where we seek self-improvement. Intense initiation.

⊖ Period of trials, ordeals and limitations caused by an accumulation of negative memories. Lack of foresight due to being *center-less*, scattered and distracted by our personal needs. Disturbing, perturbing behavior that leads to negative consequences and karmas. Turbulent energy and careless behavior. Presence of forces that can cause accidents on the intellectual, emotional and physical levels. Need to meditate and be vigilant so as to avoid the materialization of accidents.

ACCOUNTANT

Symbolically, an accountant represents a part of us that is learning, or has learnt, to manage resources, giving and receiving, **+** and **–**. It is a symbol of equity, a search for balance, rigor and fairness, for what is right.

⊕ Integrity, honesty, rigor and fairness in the management of resources. An understanding of the need to balance giving and receiving and to act wisely and altruistically when using resources.

⊖ Either a lack or excess of rigor in the management of resources. Greed, thinking only of profit, motivated by the lure of gain. Material insecurity. Abusive use of resources. Financial disorder, theft, fraud. Poor planning. Difficulty materializing and fructifying projects honestly. Bankruptcy. A lack of resources. Thinking we are indispensable. Corruption, selfishness, materialism. A self-centered attitude, seeking recognition, acknowledgement and social notoriety. A tendency to want to control and manipulate. Abuse of power.

ACNE

Acne is an inflammatory skin infection caused by an incapacity to transform negative soul-states. The accumulated emotional burden manifests as more or less widespread skin eruptions which generally affect the face and back, often de-stabilizing personality and lowering self-esteem. Several factors can engender acne: stress, unhappiness, negativity, repression, things left unsaid, anger, sadness, feeling rejected, feeling unloved, as well as poor food and hygiene habits. Although acne usually appears in adolescence, during periods of uncertainty and emotional difficulties, of hypersensitivity and a quest for identity; it can also manifest in adults. Its manifestation indicates that the person affected is going through an important opening of the unconscious and is having to face an awakening of powerful needs and negative memories dating from this life or past lives.

⊕ A period of transformation, purification, and healing of memories and soul-states that create tension, stress, inner conflicts, ill-being, lack of self-esteem and deep unhappiness.

⊖ An incapacity to transform memories and negative forces that emerge from the unconscious and affect well-being and self-esteem. A period of stress and hypersensitivity. A lack of discernment. Difficulty distinguishing between good and evil. Emotional blockages. Feelings of rejection. Anger due to an incapacity to please and be accepted. Shame. Isolation. Repression. Rebellious behavior. A lack of love for ourselves and others.

ACTOR, ACTRESS

All the actors and actresses that appear in our dreams, as well as those we like in concrete reality, symbolically represent facets of our personality through the roles they play. From a positive point of view, acting a role is a form of learning, an apprenticeship. The acting profession allows actors to experiment new potential they bear within. Through the roles they play, they discover aspects of themselves, which enable them to deepen their knowledge and visit multiple facets of the human consciousness. Acting is a profession that can awaken a great many unconscious, positive and negative memories in both the actors themselves and in the theatre audience, or film viewers too. It is important to analyze in depth the characters, the roles that attract our attention, that cause us to vibrate – positively or negatively – because we can thus discover different facets of who we are. When we see a famous actor or actress in a dream and they are not playing a particular role, we should think about what they represent for us on the human level, as people, through their lifestyle, behavior, etc. To be able to interpret the dream correctly, we should also analyze the type of films they usually act in. Through their great social notoriety, the actor or actress in question can also reveal to us aspects related to the way we experience and consider fame and celebrity, on both the personal and collective levels.

⊕ Represents facets of our personality that we are beginning to develop or discover. Experimentation and development of renown, fame, celebrity. A capacity to convey, to transmit soul-states, ambiance, emotions, with the aim of helping people understand something, opening their conscience, conveying an evolutive, evolutionary message to the soul.

⊖ Hiding behind various masks, playing roles, a lack of authenticity, over-identification with characters, at the risk of losing our own identity, living vicariously, seeking to please at all costs, self-renouncement, idolatry, disguising reality, agreeing to live in illusion, and to continually play roles in concrete reality in order to be loved and acknowledged. Lack of self-confidence. Superficiality, unnaturalness, behavioral problems, multiple personalities, schizophrenia. Ready to do anything to become rich and famous.

ACUPUNCTURE

Represents a capacity to heal ourselves that comes from ancestral knowledge based on the circulation of vital energy. Through the application of needles to certain points situated along the meridians, this originally Chinese medical discipline, stimulates, in a very precise manner, the energy in those areas of the body where there is stagnation or a lack of energy, thereby favoring harmonious circulation.

Seeing this symbol in a dream indicates that we are committed to a process of energy healing. The liberation of blocked energy will help transform the effect of negative memories on our well-being and general health. In order to understand those aspects of our life and being that we need to work on, it is important to analyze in depth the concrete situation experienced at the time of the dream, as well as the symbolism of the body part(s) the needles are applied to, where the energy therapy takes place.

⊕ Allows precise rebalancing, re-harmonization of vital energy. Heals blockages and accumulated tension. Revitalizes body and soul. Self-healing work. Relieves aches and pains. Helps transform and heal memories.

⊖ Problems related to energy imbalance. Blockages, retention, multiple tensions. A lack of inner and outer harmony. Illness. Bogged down memories. Medicine without conscience. Mistaken diagnosis due to lack of knowledge. A person who seeks to heal but who has a prickly, stinging, needling, inappropriate attitude toward himself and others.

ADD, COUNT

The act of adding or counting up represents a dynamic of expansion, additional resources, facts, data, or supplementary elements. When adding or counting up becomes a need or an obsession, it reveals the presence of profound insecurity and fear of lacking resources.

⊕ A period of expansion, a soul-state of prosperity. A good manager and planner. A feeling of abundance and wealth, riches, or enrichment.

⊖ A period of insecurity, fear of lacking things. Excessive thirst for expansion. Memories of greed and avarice.

ADDRESS

A collection of information allowing us to locate or find a person, a company, or an institution. An address is an important means of communication as it is a means to identify a person, a place, or a form of energy that we can visit in terms of consciousness. The location of a place allows us to analyze the atmosphere emanated, the mentality and temperament of the people who live there, as well as our reasons or motivation for going there. If we do not know the exact address, we analyze the symbolism of whatever details we know; e.g. the country, the name of the locality, the neighborhood, the street, the number and postal code, because all of these details correspond to states of conscience we have visited. We never find ourselves at an address coincidentally, just by chance; it always reflects aspects of ourselves.

⊕ A well-organized, well-structured person who knows where he is going. A state of conscience related to a goal to attain, a situation to be experienced, integrated or discovered. A feeling of being well guided, of receiving good directions.

⊖ Difficulties related to organization, to the capacity to direct ourselves toward our goals and objectives. A person who is not on the right path, who is not going in the right direction, or who has a problem with the place, the address in question. May awaken soul-states of confusion and feeling lost, not knowing where to go. A lack of direction and motivation in life. A tendency to get lost. Difficulty directing our life, our actions.

ADOLESCENCE

Adolescence represents a stage of evolution that engenders great inner and outer changes and upheavals. When it is an experience that is well lived, it allows the person to develop, among other things, a sense of responsibility, a sense of his own identity and autonomy regarding decisions concerning good and evil, wrong-doing, what hurts. During this period, the awakening of the senses and the emergence of memories related to instinctual needs are sometimes so intense that they transform the teenager's behavior to such an extent that we no longer recognize the child that he was. However, adolescent characteristics may also manifest in adults when their inner adolescent, rebellious forces and instinctual needs are activated, thereby creating discrepancies, conflicts, and dualities with their values, opinions, and adult behavior.

The phenomenon of adolescence reactivates positive and negative aspects of former lives, as well as a program of social experimentation that in some cases is very concentrated and unstable. This program also concerns the development of global thought and the apprenticeship of the right management of vital energy and sexual impulses. It is often a period of difficult apprenticeship, because the forces that are set in motion are of great emotional power. The person may feel like a long dormant volcano waking up after years of calm. This intensity of memories is not easy to *tame* or master, because the person is confronted with simultaneously opposing memories, which leads to continual variations in mood and personality. This initiatic passage is characterized by a strong development or growth of personality, an aspiration for autonomy, as well as great openness on the conscience level. Adolescence corresponds to the period or phase of our life-plan when autonomy is set in motion, when the potential of our previous lives emerges, and when we are offered choices in accordance with what we were in our past lives.

⊕ Personality transformation. Positive self-assertion. Confidence in our capacities. Apprenticeship of the management of vital energy. Taming and mastering instinctual needs. An intense development period. Construction of our personality in accordance with our life plan. Preparation of a person in view of life choices to be made. Emergence of potential from past lives. An initiatic period allowing us to develop maturity and true autonomy. Activation of great force, great intensity, great vitality. Experimentations that are rich on every level, leading to the discovery of new energies, ideas, and possibilities, as well as new feelings and sentiments, and a whole potential to develop. Apprenticeship of social life. Activation of a desire to learn from others and to understand life. A need to be listened to, to talk and discuss matters, to receive and to give ourselves second chances.

⊖ Over-intense, exaggerated needs; or, repressed needs and withdrawal. Predominant ego. Over-confidence or lack of confidence. Excessive emissivity. Considerable duality on all levels, extreme needs for sensations. Deep misunderstanding of ourselves, others, and life in general. A period of rebellion and confrontation. Very changeable moods, going from good humor to depression or anger, from kindness to aggression, etc. Intense moral suffering. An existential crisis. Destructive, suicidal tendencies. Exacerbated feelings. Refusal of existing authority, laws, and structures. Rejection of parents, teachers, and all or many of those who have taught us. A lack of listening and receptivity. Letting ourselves be influenced by negative forces. An awakening of negative memories stemming from former lives. Hyperactivity. Seeking illusory consolation and well-being.

ADOPT, ADOPTION

Adoption is a legal action that establishes a filial relationship between two people. Adopting a child means we commit to loving, protecting, supporting, and helping him in his evolution. Adoption reveals a potential for altruistic love and devotion. It involves our soul and our conscience and is a commitment on all levels. By becoming an adoptive parent, we take on the responsibility for providing the child with his essential needs, educating him, ensuring that he develops well, and accompanying him along his path until he grows up, or until life decides otherwise.

Figuratively speaking, we can also adopt a country, a project, a law, an alliance, a contract, a point of view, certain behavior, etc. Adoption then means that we accept and globally approve what the object of adoption represents. Depending on the case, it is a conscious choice to submit to it, to identify with it, to put it into practice, to make it ours. For example, when we adopt a country, we agree to integrate and respect its laws, to speak its language. When we adopt a plan or a project, we ensure we carry out and complete work that is progress.

⊕ An altruistic act of love, devotion, assistance, commitment and conscience. A deep sense of responsibility. A capacity to become totally involved through conviction. A global vision of life. Awareness of a planetary, universal family. Knowledge of Cosmic Laws and their application in daily life.

⊖ Superficial commitment with the aim of gaining some sort of benefit. Commitment taken lightly, without conscience. Irresponsibility. Egotism; selfishness. A lack of altruism. Inconstancy and a lack of transparency when making decisions. A tendency to change our mind. False parent.

ADVERTISING, ADVERTISEMENT(S)

Advertising represents our capacity to broadcast, to diffuse, to publicize information on a large scale, on the collective level. It may be used to educate, to raise awareness, to inspire, to introduce and help us discover ideas, sentiments, values, projects, and objects. An advertisement that attracts our attention in concrete reality, or that is seen in a dream, always represents a multiplication dynamic in our conscience. It indicates that certain parts of us are seeking to amplify and highlight behavior; or, a desire for it to be acknowledged and validated by our conscience. It may be a positive or negative aspect that is in the process of manifesting within us, becoming an inspiration, a way of life, or creating in us consumer and materialization dynamics of whatever the advertisement represents. Large-scale, widespread success of an advertisement reveals behavior, tendencies, states of soul, spirit, mind and conscience on the collective level. Hence, knowledge of symbolic language allows us in-depth understanding of what is hidden in the collective unconscious of a country, a nation, a society, a culture, a company, etc.

The aim of advertising is to reach a maximum number of parts of our being to convince them of something, to incite them to adopt certain behavior, or to buy a certain product or service. Advertisements use images, colors, words, sounds, subliminal messages, music to create a range of dynamics that are symbolically very meaningful, very revealing. A symbolic interpretation of an advertisement follows exactly the same procedure as dream and sign interpretation: we analyze the positive and negative aspects of each of the elements used in the advertisement; this allows us to perceive the energy and subtle messages conveyed by the product featured in it. Simultaneously, these elements offer a great deal of information of the conscious and unconscious intentions and values represented by the manufacturer; or, government concerns and desire for improvement for its citizens in the case of social educational, preventive advertising. Our reaction to advertising messages allows us to evaluate what kinds of energy, dynamics, behavior and values we promote in our conscience and wish to materialize in our life.

⊕ A capacity to make our ideas, values and/or projects known on a large scale, or to inspire us to buy something useful and beneficial, to find an answer to our needs. Efficient tool to inform, raise awareness, and educate. Broadcasting, diffusing and sharing information, knowledge, know-how, new discoveries and inventions on local, regional, national, international or planetary levels. Opens people's conscious and unconscious levels to new ideas. Capacity to discern, feel, sense, perceive what is authentic and truthful, or not. Right balance between material, human and spiritual values. Exerts a healthy influence on society, contributes to its evolution, to the development of beautiful qualities and deep, true values. Divine-inspired creativity. Originality in advertising. Advertisements that create positive atmospheres and ambiances.

⊖ Difficulty making our ideas, values and/or projects known, difficulty commercializing them; or, a naive, too easily influenced person who lets himself be impressed and influenced by advertisements; or, advertisements created intentionally to manipulate the consumer, to convince him at all costs, to impose a need for a product or service. Inducing exaggerated, artificial, useless needs. Nourishing worldly desires. Difficulty creating and propagating interest in a new field. Lack of creativity, inspiration, originality. Over-materialistic interests. Media manipulation. Abusive, fraudulent behavior that pushes people to consume. Diffusion of unhealthy, incorrect thoughts, emotions, products, or services. Harmful, ill-intentioned, destructive advertising that uses negative states of mind and soul, such as frustration, melancholy, sadness, rebellion, existential fear, etc. to incite purchase. Seeking to control on the ideological level, to shock, to provoke unscrupulously, without any respect. Creation of conflicts. Diffusing lies, trickery, calumny. Lacking honesty, authenticity, truth. Need for acknowledgement, success and glory. May indicate a lack of resources to diffuse an idea, product, or service. Fear of asserting ourselves. Lack of confidence to express ourselves in public. Democratic dynamics that legalize the expression of our basic instincts. Disrespect or rejection of Divine Values and Principles. Decadence, political and social disorder.

AFRICA

Africa is thought to be where human beings originated. The African continent, its countries and peoples represent our most ancient memories related to the beginning of human experimentation, as well as to our soul's new learning potential. Africa represents Earth's *young child*. Many new souls are born there to begin their apprenticeship and evolution in matter. Today this cradle of human life is neglected like a motherless child. Its history, which includes some of the most ancient civilizations such as Egypt, as well as some of the most atrocious political, ethnic, economic and environmental abuse, shows how far humanity has forgotten its original birthplace on Earth.

Today, this magnificent continent, rich in all sorts of minerals, where the memory of the first experience on Earth has been recorded, is still a collective symbol representing our first chakras, our instincts, our capacity to survive, our vital energy and human warmth. Despite the extreme ordeals the African people are experiencing today – the highest rates of birth and mortality, the lowest life expectancy (32-41 years old), malnutrition, famine, drought, epidemics, including AIDS, as the principal cause of mortality, corruption, abuse, exploitation, violence, genocide – they continue to smile like children and be joyful, warm and welcoming, ready to trust again and to renew themselves. Africa is like an eternal child experimenting the intensity of life.

⊕ Activation or development of African qualities: eternal youth, *joie de vivre* and intensity. Apprenticeship. Natural optimism. Capacity to live in the present moment, a warm, welcoming state of mind and attitude. Great vital energy. Pleasure of the senses. Capacity to create beautiful atmospheres and ambiances, a sense of ritual, hospitality and sharing. Respect for hierarchy. Mastery and transcendence of basic instincts, respect for the Earth, simple, natural life, mutual family and social aid. The most ancient human memories.

⊖ Abuse, exploitation, fraud, corruption, power struggle. Slavery, racism, war, lack of humanitarianism and global vision. Irresponsible behavior on the relationship and sexual levels. Naivety, lack of knowledge and discernment. Difficulty in social organization.

Indolence, laziness. Waste, poor management of resources, poverty, famine, general misery.

AGGRESSION

An aggressive action is an act of violence, a form of attack through which we exteriorize energies of frustration and deep dissatisfaction that have accumulated over a long period of time, even over several lives. To be attacked in a dream or in concrete reality means that within ourselves, we have memories of aggressive acts committed against others in this life or in a past life to satisfy a thirst for vengeance, or because of a lack of understanding that violence engenders violence. It is important to know that every time we are aggressive toward others on the physical, emotional or mental level, we activate a process that automatically places us under the effect of the Law of karma, or the Law of return: sooner or later, the aggressive energy we emitted comes back to us. Consequently, the aggression, assaults, attacks we experience in dreams or in concrete reality indicate the presence of memories of aggressiveness. As long as we haven't cleansed and transformed these memories, we continue to attract aggressive situations and people. They serve to help us become aware of our inner conflicts and encourage us to settle them.

Aggression or an assault experienced in a dream isn't necessarily related to an assault we may have committed in concrete reality. It may also represent a warning that a certain amount of violence is dormant within us, and that without inner work and behavioral changes, it could culminate in a physical aggressive act. However, an assault in concrete reality is always directly related to an act of violence we really did commit in the past. The Law of Divine Justice is absolute on both the metaphysical as well as the physical plane: we always reap what we sow. The vicious circle of negative karma begins with our experimenting the role of the aggressor before experimenting the role of victim; this means that whenever we find ourselves as the victim, it's because we have accumulated memories and behavior of an aggressor within us that must be cleansed and transformed.

⊕ Transcendence of memories of aggression. Understanding the Cosmic Laws of karma, resonance and Divine Justice. Compassion and a non-violent attitude toward an aggressor. Awareness that violence leads to violence. A conscious choice to no longer nourish evil, wrong-doing, hurt.

⊖ Use of aggression and violence to get what we want. Seeking to control through intimidation and threats. Ignorance of the Cosmic Laws. An accumulation of karmas related to violence. Aggression committed through gestures, words, thoughts, and emotions. Presence of unsatisfied, instinctual needs which engender frustration and aggressiveness. Incomprehension of the dynamics that link aggressor and victim.

AIR

Air belongs to the four elements: fire, air, water and earth. Through its light, invisible nature, air is directly related to the world of thoughts. Our thoughts constantly travel in and around us without our seeing them. They are similar to radio waves, which circulate in the air all the time. All symbols related to air (birds, insects, airplanes, helicopters, winds, etc.) represent dynamics on the level of our thoughts, intellect and mind. For example: a draft (a current of air in an enclosed space) represents thoughts that come and go rapidly or continually.

⊕ Pure air, which circulates freely and harmoniously, symbolizes positive, kind, well-intentioned, altruistic, luminous thoughts that allow us to elevate our conscience and commune with the Divine, with God.

⊖ Problems due to negative, egotistical, malicious, malevolent, impure thoughts.

Polluted Air: Negative, malevolent, unhealthy thoughts that darken our conscience.

Short of air; lack of air: Stifling, smothering, choking, suffocation. Difficulty thinking, limitations on the mental, intellectual level. Incapacity to exist.

AIRPLANE

An airplane is related to the air element and therefore to the mental world, the world of thoughts and the intellect. As a plane is heavier than air, it needs a powerful engine to take off and fly, which translates symbolically as great willpower to raise ourselves up, to seek elevation in the world of thoughts.

Symbolically, traveling by plane consists in leaving a concrete situation, going into our thoughts and heading toward a new region of our conscience. From a metaphysical point of view, the whole Earth is part of us and an airplane allows us to go from one country to another, or, from one state of conscience to another.

Seeing a scene in a dream that takes place in an airplane means that, consciously or unconsciously, we are mentally heading toward a project. An airplane symbolizes a powerful, concentrated thought-form. For example, if an airplane is seen to land in a dream, it means that the dreamer's thoughts are getting ready to materialize, that the dreamer is preparing to act. A plane crashing indicates that we nourish very destructive thoughts, which if left untransformed, will end up materializing in a destructive event in concrete reality.

⊕ A capacity and facility to go from one egregore[1], one state of conscience to another, and to discover new ones. A faculty and motivation for rising up, seeking elevation on the mental level in order to think and then come back down to materialize well. Seeks an elevated point of view, a more global vision. Stability and mastery on the thought level. Power related to a capacity to materialize thoughts, projects.

⊖ Difficulties related to motivation and a capacity to rise up, to seek elevation on the mental level and to travel with our thoughts or to re-descend into matter to experiment, express our thoughts and

---

1. An egregore refers to a reservoir of collective memory, a collective mindset, collective group-thought; it is the vibration that results from the thoughts, emotions, desires, ideals, intentions, and behavior of a group of people, everything in all of the past and present lives of a country, population, or group of people that produces a particular mentality, atmosphere, character, and/or feeling we associate with them. Usually as soon as we cross the border into a different country, we become aware of its different egregore, but a team, a choir, a school, etc., also have their own egregore.

materialize our projects. Flight, escapism, seeking artificial paradises, a superficial life. Instability, hyperactivity, and a scattered mind that prevent us from materializing ideas. Destructive thoughts, lack of mastery. Arrogant attitude, superiority and inferiority complexes. A lack of spirituality and a lack of an overall, global vision of people and things.

AIRPORT

An airport symbolizes an organizational state of conscience offering multiple possibilities of change on the thought and action levels. It represents a place of transition allowing us an elevation of our thoughts and state of conscience on take-off and landing when we soar above or return into the world of materialization. An airport is also a place where there is air traffic control, hence the way we manage our thoughts on both the individual and collective levels.

⊕ An organizational structure allowing us to travel on both the mental and concrete levels. A place of departure, destination, and transition to visit different countries, cultures, egregores (*cf.* this term) or states of conscience. Whenever we are happy to be at an airport: a desire to travel toward new horizons, to discover new mentalities, unknown parts of ourselves, unexplored ways of thinking and behaving, to change our lifestyle. Well-ordered, well-oriented, well-directed thoughts. A soul-state of abundance, a variety of possibilities, a change of destiny.

⊖ Disorganization and difficulty traveling through different egregores or group identities, countries of our conscience and the multi-dimensions of life. The wrong direction, the wrong choice on both the thought and action levels. Nostalgia, a desire to flee, to change our life in order to escape our destiny, as well as to escape ordeals, hardships and difficulties in daily life. Envy, jealousy, appearances, an arrogant, haughty attitude, feelings of superiority and inferiority. Whenever being at an airport awakens anxiety in us: fear of change, of the unknown, of the unexpected, fear of elevation on the thought and action levels. Difficulty organizing, managing and mastering our mind, our thoughts and our needs.

ALARM

An alarm is a signal emitted in order to create a state of alertness. Generally speaking, an alarm warns us of danger, but it can also be used to wake us from sleep, as in the case of an alarm-clock. It is usually a piece of sonorous information that is emitted to signal a necessity to be vigilant, attentive, or the need to protect ourselves. Alarm signals indicate the presence of concrete danger or a malfunction, hence a fault in the way we ourselves function. It is important to analyze in depth the daily situations or messages received in dreams wherein alarm signals appear, because they are always a call to order or a warning that allows us to avoid serious consequences. We should never take such signals lightly.

Alarm signals do not only exist on the physical level in the form of sirens or sharp, strident sounds. They can also manifest on the metaphysical level, within ourselves, in the form of an intuition, a negative premonition, a hunch, or feeling of uneasiness; or, on the outside, in the form of a difficulty, the initial symptoms of an illness, a comment or warning emitted by another person. An alarm may manifest on all levels of our being: spiritual (intuition), intellectual (thought), emotional (emotions, feelings), and physical (action). An alarm allows us to react in time and lets us know there is a choice to be made so as to better live in accordance with our life-plan, with our evolution-program.

⊕ Warning of danger. Call to order. Raises awareness of incorrect attitudes, thoughts, emotions, and acts that need to be rectified.

⊖ An ordeal has been set in motion. Overprotective behavior. Feelings of fear, states of panic; or, unfounded feelings of fear and states of panic.

ALCOHOL (to drink)

As a liquid, alcohol is symbolically related to the emotional level. Taken in moderation, it has no notable negative effects for most people. On the metaphysical level, alcohol acts on our emotions, and stimulates or calms the intensity of our spirit. Sensitive people who have difficulty managing their emotions may have a tendency, in dreams as well as in concrete reality, to consume more alcohol so as to feel loved and acknowledged on the social level, or to relax; or, to flee reality, which is the case of many people who drink alcohol.

Abuse of alcohol has damaging effects on the mind, spirit and body, to such a degree that it is one of the most dangerous drugs that exists, as much for the consumer as for his entourage. A great number of alcohol consumers are dependent on this emotional drug. Alcohol acts as a depressant on the central nervous system and it affects vital energy and how the mind and spirit work. It de-activates our capacity to discern and perceive concrete reality lucidly. The openings of conscience it induces put the consumer in contact with aspects of his personality he doesn't reveal in his normal state. He can manifest surprising personality changes. For example, a usually shy, embarrassed, introverted person can become an expressive extrovert; another person can become violent or very introverted. As mentioned above, excessive consumption of alcohol can indicate a desire to flee the reality and responsibilities of everyday life.

The inflammability of drinks containing a concentration of over 40% alcohol allows us to understand that the abuse of alcohol symbolically inflames our spirit and creates major malfunctions. In the long-term, alcohol causes the following health problems: headaches, weight gain, damage to the heart, liver, stomach, kidneys and brain, memory loss and certain types of cancer.

On the psychological level, short-term, alcohol induces a feeling of euphoric lightheartedness, partial loss of embarrassment and a capacity to better express our thoughts, emotions and soul-states. Medium-term, these effects continue but are accompanied by a gradual loss of judgment and short-term memory. Long-term, certain emotional difficulties appear which can lead to a more and more seriously depressed state. An excessive drinker develops a dependency and feels a frequent need to drink in order to flee everyday reality. A state of intoxication helps him avoid having to face reality. It can also cause him to react violently toward his entourage.

Whether we ourselves have a problem with alcohol, or whether we find ourselves in a context of alcoholism in dreams or concrete life, e.g. with our parents, spouse, brothers, sisters, or people close to us, this indicates that we have a life-program that incites us to work on our sensitivity and on the transformation of our memories of alcoholism and emotional dependency.

⊕ Induces a state of euphoria, feelings of elevation, exaltation and liberty. Favors relaxation. Helps create convivial social atmosphere, ambiance. Feelings of joy and celebration. Facilitates communication and sharing with others. Liberates and activates unknown aspects, ideas, emotions and potential that we have within us.

⊖ Emotional dependency problems. Accumulations of sorrow, heavy, burdensome emotions, difficulties and problems that we try to drown and anesthetize with alcohol. Coarse, unstable, incoherent behavior with a risk of violence. Loss of discernment and memory, deteriorating health. Rebellious attitude caused by lack of love and a need to please and succeed. Great difficulty managing and going through ordeals. Irresponsibility, dropping out, fleeing, despair. Seeking outer means to free us from our inhibitions. A tendency to exaggerate alcohol consumption on festive occasions reveals repression, frustration and inner ill-being. In the long term, seeking artificial paradises only engenders misery, grief and desolation. Important work to be done on emotions and emotional dependencies.

ALLERGY

According to conventional medicine, an allergy is an abnormal, exaggerated reaction or hypersensitivity of our organism when in contact with certain allergens which provokes a reaction in some people's immune system. Harmless substances are often wrongly identified as dangerous antigens, which incite the immune system to produce antibodies and sensitive white blood cells.

Allergies manifest in hypersensitive people whose unconscious is very open and who cannot manage everything they sense, feel or perceive on the individual and collective levels. Allergic reactions represent an incapacity to transform resonance and negative memories related to past behavior in this life or in other lives.

To understand the allergen symbolically, we need to analyze the state of conscience it represents. For instance, if we are allergic to cats, we analyze the positive and negative characteristics of this animal and we draw an analogy with ourselves, asking ourselves how strongly we resonate with its qualities and distortions. An allergy to cats signifies that we are sometimes too independent and sometimes not independent enough. It also indicates an imbalance between emissivity and receptivity, giving and receiving, i.e. certain parts of us display too great a need for independence while others suffer from dependency problems. Consequently both aspects – independence and dependency, sensitivity and insensitivity, emissivity and receptivity – must always be taken into consideration. It is the behavioral instability related to what cats represent that creates the allergic reaction. By identifying it on the symbolic level, we understand the cause. The same goes for all allergies. By working on our unconscious memories with understanding and love, we can purify them and transform the negative that the immune system seeks to combat. We should always remember that all levels are interconnected, just as we are to our entourage and to everything that exists.

⊕ The physical limitations experienced by those who suffer from allergies incite them to interiorize and reflect deeply on certain aspects of their life, of themselves, so as to understand the cause of their difficulties and their hypersensitivity. Hence an allergy, like all forms of illness and ill-being, represents an opportunity to look after ourselves and get to know ourselves better. In order to completely transcend it, it is necessary to understand the symbolic meaning of the allergy as well as the message our body is sending us. Once the allergy has been transcended, we rediscover the following qualities: mastery of sensitivity, tolerance, equilibrium, harmony, a capacity to transform negativity, discernment and understanding of the environment and other people.

⊖ An excessive accumulation of memories that resonate with the allergy experienced in a dream or in concrete reality. Physical imbalance caused by great sensitivity and/or excessive social activities. A need to go within, to interiorize and reflect in order to understand how life works. Whatever bothers and imbalances a person to the point of making them physically unwell or ill always indicates the presence of surplus on the one hand and lack on the other.

ALLIANCE

Depending on the context in which it is used, the term alliance indicates a union contracted mutually on a personal, collective, judicial, or political level. It may also designate a spiritual commitment, as in an alliance with the Divine, or a philosophical one, or on the relationship level, between lovers (as clearly indicated by the French word for a wedding ring: *une alliance*). Generally speaking, the creation of an alliance indicates shared values and goals. Simultaneously it also signifies expanded possibilities and shared responsibilities. It is therefore important to know what kind of energies, values, intentions, motivations, and goals we are preparing to fuse with.

⊕ An alliance with people who share the same values, visions and goals increases our power of materialization and expansion as well as the probabilities of success and prosperity. Seeing himself conclude an alliance in a dream announces the beginning of a new stage in the dreamer's life during which he will receive favorable support and help for the realization of his projects, either on the inside or on the outside, depending on the context. An alliance with Up Above, Heaven, God or the Celestial Hierarchy implies a commitment to act in accordance with Divine Law and Order and to serve true values and high ideals.

⊖ May announce the end of an alliance, or a lack of longevity in an alliance. An alliance agreed upon with ill will, bad intentions, or negative forces symbolically indicates that parts of us choose to associate with what is not right. Such an alliance will, of course, lead to problems, which we should not take lightly and dismiss as unimportant. When we fuse with evil, with wrong-doing, with what hurts, we reap evil, wrong-doing and hurt. We should remain vigilant and not be entrapped by the illusion of fast, easily gained success or expansion. Behind this kind of attitude unconscious dependencies and needs are also hidden. Agreement of an alliance or pact with demonic forces indicates the presence of memories related to black magic, witchery, distorted spirituality and an abuse of spiritual powers.

AMBULANCE

An ambulance is a vehicle that is specially adapted for the transportation of the sick, the injured, or pregnant women, who urgently need to get to a hospital or medical clinic. Symbolically an ambulance reveals a capacity to gain rapid access to emergency care so as to heal a serious imbalance that could be fatal or engender grave consequences. This symbol indicates that we are activating the necessary resources to help heal a serious, negative state. Calling an ambulance when the problem is not serious or urgent symbolizes memories that tend to dramatize situations.

⊕ A great capacity to help ourselves, or others, in moments of great distress and when all sorts of problems arise. Ability to act in emergencies.

⊖ Difficulty receiving help in emergencies; or, assisting others in situations where there is an urgent need for help. Problems obtaining or offering help to heal suffering. A lack of dynamic energy and courage in an emergency. Tendency to dramatize situations.

ANGEL

In numerous traditions, and particularly in the three Abrahamic religions (Judaism, Christianity, Islam) an Angel is messenger for God, i.e. an intermediary between God and man. Sometimes He transmits a Divine message, sometimes He carries out actions in accordance with Divine Will. Initiatic science has always used the metaphor of winged, Celestial creatures to express our human capacity to travel in mind and dream into the multi-dimensions of conscience, and to experiment what happens when we reactivate in ourselves the Divine Powers we bear within us; the Knowledge, Peace, Liberty, and Love that we then experience gives us wings. Our human mission is to rediscover our Divine nature by reprogramming our thoughts, feelings, and actions in accordance with the Qualities, Virtues and Powers symbolized by the Angels.

The age-old teaching of *The Traditional Study of Angels* (*Traditional Angelology*), originating in the ancestral Kabbalah, reveals the 72 original Names of the Angelic Fields of conscience, which are the 72 Names of God, representing His Qualities, Virtues, and Powers in their purest form. Moreover, it explains how, through work on ourselves, we can develop and integrate the potentialities of the Angels in our daily life. Indeed, the activation of Angelic Essences allows us to transform our distortions, which correspond to the faults and weaknesses we have developed throughout our numerous incarnations by acting in disharmony and contradiction with our Divine nature and Cosmic Laws.

Through the symbol of the Tree of Life, this very advanced, initiatic, philosophical teaching also illustrates the structure of the Universe, the Celestial Hierarchy, the function of the Angels and Archangels, as well as the development of Conscience on the macrocosmic (universal conscience) and microscopic (human conscience) levels. In addition to this, it leads to a better understanding of the correlations that exist between our inner world and the outer world, between the reality we perceive thanks to our physical senses and the invisible, metaphysical dimensions we can only consciously experience if we develop our subtle senses and spiritual capacities.

The practical work with Angelic Essences consists in invoking an Angel, with the right intention and a sense of the sacred, by repeating His Name like a mantra several times a day. This *Angel Mantra Practice,* or *Angel Recitation*, that we do for at least five days with the same Angel, allows us to focus our conscience on the Angelic Field of Conscience invoked. Thus, through the creative power of sound and name, we activate within ourselves the vibration frequency it represents. This sets off powerful dreams and signs thanks to which we can observe how the Angel manifests in our life. According to the contents of the conscious and unconscious memories situated in the *department* referred to, the Angel will either manifest His pure aspects through beautiful dreams and signs, or reveal our distortions to us through nightmares and warning signs, or, a dream or dream sequence may include both positive and negative aspects that need to be equated together and analyzed. In our dreams and in the situations of our daily life, we will encounter the precise characteristics of the Angel invoked. This work, which is easily accessible to everyone, is explained in detail in the various publications of Universe/City Mikaël (UCM) (*cf.* List of publications at the end of this book). It is the product of thousands of years of rigorous research on dreams, signs and symbols. With great wisdom and efficiency, it applies the Cosmic Laws, symbolic language, and authentic spirituality in everyday life, thereby allowing us to experiment and experience the marriage of spirit and matter, and to lead an Angelic life on Earth.

⊕ Develops awareness that we are bearers of Qualities, Virtues and Divine Powers, and that conscious work with the Angelic States of Conscience allows us to manifest our angelic nature in our daily life. Develops the willpower to work on ourselves so as to transform our distortions, to rectify our faults and transcend our weaknesses. Cleanses and purifies the unconscious and liberates karma thanks to Angel Recitation. Study of the Cosmic Laws and symbolic language in order to better understand the messages and signs that God, or Cosmic Intelligence, sends us *via* Angels, dreams and symbols.

Seeing an Angel in a dream: A profoundly mystical experience that leads to a very powerful opening of conscience and spiritual transformation. Can contribute to a total reorientation of a person's life, for instance, helping an atheist rediscover faith, a sense of the sacred, reconnection with the Source of Life, belief in a Superior Intelligence, a Supreme Being. The appearance of an Angelic presence in a dream can also occur when a person is going through an extremely difficult phase or who has to endure extreme, survival living conditions; such a dream experience will provide him with the necessary courage, energy, strength, hope and determination to remain steadfast or to find a solution.

⊖ A naive, erroneous vision of what an Angel is. A lack of true spiritual knowledge which allows us to understand that if Angels are realities on the superior levels of creation, they are also realities in our inner world, that they represent man's Divine nature. A person who wants Angels to help and take charge of his life without wanting to make any effort himself to transform his distortions and negative aspects. Great discrepancies between a person's material and spiritual life. Spiritual pride. Fraud, trickery. Abusive use of psychic capacities. Spiritual manipulation of others for selfish, materialistic purposes. The transmission of false, erroneous spiritual knowledge. Illusion, ignorance. A pact with demonic energies, the distorted versions of Angelic Energies.

ANIMAL

The word animal, from the Latin *animalis* (animate, living) and *anima* (breath, air) defines an animate, living, breathing creature capable of movement and perception. However in everyday usage, this word is used to differentiate animals from humans, although humans carry the animal kingdom within them in terms of conscience. The aspect of animals that exist on Earth, as well as their organization, their characteristics and living habits are of varied complexity, from the relatively amorphous colony of sea sponges to the very complex organization of insects and vertebrates. Symbolically, terrestrial animals, whatever they are, represent parts of us. They are one of the aspects of the living world that dwells in us, and in particular the part related to the expression of our needs and instincts. It is partially thanks to our inner animals that we activate our needs and can develop the source of basic energy needed to act, move, think and feel.

To understand the symbolism of an animal, it is important to study its behavior and character when it is alone, with a mate, and in a group. Take dogs, for example. This animal generally has a playful, joyful, expressive, affectionate nature when it is inhabited by positive energy, but it can also be aggressive, even mean, if it is neglected or mistreated, subjected to cruelty and violence. These character traits make dogs a symbol of emotional, affective dependency, the corollaries of which are anger and deep frustration. Hence, by examining the general aspect or the most characteristic features of a dog's character and behavior, we can deduce its symbolic meaning. We can proceed likewise with every animal that exists on Earth.

In order for an animal to represent a positive symbol, it must be in good health, unaggressive and in the right place, i.e. in its natural environment. A spider in a bedroom, even if it is not aggressive, indicates a problem related to intimacy (symbolized by the bedroom). The incoherencies found in dreams as well as in everyday life are very significant, and it is essential to stop and consider them if we wish to correctly interpret a dream or a concrete situation.

If, in a dream, an animal appears in a negative aspect – sick, aggressive, or out of its natural environment – the dream shows us that the instinctive forces and aspects symbolized by the animal in question are out of phase or distorted in our inner world. Such a dream invites us to transform them so as to transcend them.

Although a human being's conscience and intelligence is superior to an animal's, we human-beings are still animated by instincts and needs stemming from our inferior animal nature. We are not pure spirits, and in order to elevate our instinctual vital energy to higher levels, it is important to work on our inner animals so as to integrate their powers and qualities, and to transcend their weaknesses and distortions. The animal forces that dwell in us are located in the first two chakras, wherein dwells our potential to materialize, to procreate, to feel physical, sexual pleasure and to satisfy our basic needs. Their associated colors are red and orange. For the energy of these chakras to radiate positively, it is necessary for the human conscience to evolve from animal conscience to spiritual conscience, represented by the superior chakras. Hence the animal energy present in everyone rises and fuses with more spiritual energies.

⊕ Great force and vital energy. Work on ourselves to integrate animal forces and qualities and transcend their negative aspects (purely instinctual behavior, prey and predator dynamics, a lack of reflection, understanding, global vision and altruism). Mastery and transcendence of emotional needs and instinctual impulses. Respect and protection of the animal world. Awareness of the sacred aspect of our existence as well as the role it plays in the evolution of life and conscience.

⊖ Enslaved by instinctual, primary needs. Incapacity to think deeply about what is right. Acting in the grip of fear. Submitting to *the law of the jungle,* i.e. survival of the fittest. Using aggression to obtain our goals. Extreme egotism, jealousy and vanity. Rigidity, extremist behavior, repressed basic needs and instincts. Indifference, disrespect and abuse of the animal world. A feeling of superiority. Destruction of animal life by global pollution, unnecessary hunting, experimental medicine, and a meat-based diet. A tendency to keep animals at a distance, symbolizes memories that resonate with the negative aspects of these animals.

ANOREXIA *(cf. also **Bulimia**)*

Reducing or giving up food through loss of appetite or a refusal to feed ourselves. Anorexia indicates a great opening of the unconscious, which connects the person to memories that are difficult to digest, often accumulated over several lives. These memories contain the following aspects: existential unhappiness, rejection, feeling of being stigmatized, undervalued, loss of self-esteem, self-mutilation and self-punishment engendered by behavior, deeds, and all sorts of abuse, possibly committed in previous lives. Unconsciously the person tries to suppress, control, and dominate parts of his being that suffer the influence of these abusive forces. Desperately wanting to prevent them from taking over, and not knowing how to transform the related memories in a loving, healthy, non-violent way, the person tries to starve these parts of himself to death. As his anorexic behavior simultaneously deprives other parts of his being of all physical and emotional nourishment, he very gradually finds himself absorbed in a vicious circle of self-destruction and depression that can lead him to the point of suicide and may actually push him over the edge to his physical death. Anorexia, bulimia, depression, and suicidal tendencies are related, and function like the ripple effect. An anorexic person needs to understand that he cannot solve any problem, nor erase any memory by committing suicide, but that he needs to work on his resonances and unconscious memories. Otherwise, they will remain part of his karmic *luggage* (*cf.* this term), and he will still have to confront them in another life, or lives, until he learns to transform and heal them through self-forgiveness, gentleness, clemency and self-love.

⊕ Awareness of the presence of memories, and abusive, destructive forces, and learning to transform them without harming ourselves, without undervaluing ourselves, and without self-inflicted punishment. Becoming aware that it is neither useful nor necessary to be hard on ourselves to rectify negative memories. A capacity to regain, to rediscover self-esteem and accept our weaknesses and faults, knowing that nobody is perfect, that everyone also has beautiful parts, and that each of us evolves over time, over lives. Understanding that it is important to nourish ourselves on all levels: physical, emotional, mental and spiritual. The end of self-punishment, and the beginning of a new stage in life.

⊖ Symbolically, a refusal to nourish ourselves indicates a rejection of life while under the influence of memories dominated by a need to please, to be loved and to succeed socially. A *horizontal* conscience, over-focused on material values and appearances. Conforming to criteria of outer beauty and identifying with our physical body. Non-respect for our vital needs, an extremist, radical attitude, self-punishment, self-destruction. A distorted way of seeking attention. Excessive self-control due to a distorted sense of pride, or fear of losing control. Misled asceticism. In order to heal forces present in the unconscious, it is essential to inscribe true – i.e. spiritual – values in ourselves, and to understand that a human being is never only his faults, but rather a soul experimenting in order to get to know itself better, and to learn what Life is. It is important not to undervalue ourselves, and to meditate on the fact that: *True beauty is Inner beauty.*

ANTIQUE (object)

The term antique, which mainly refers to works of art and furniture, designates the characteristic of something very old, ancient, which allows us to know and study the customs, trends, and lifestyles of former peoples and civilizations. By studying the symbolism of old or ancient objects that attract us, we learn a lot about ourselves. Antiques represent memories of former behavior that dwell in our unconscious. They testify to fashions, customs and lifestyles of our past lives.

⊕ Discovery of former forces that reveal aspects of our past lives. Reactivation of former behavior and values, positive memories and inspiring experiences.

⊖ A tendency to live in the past. Attachment, sometimes obsessional, to old things, old structures. Refusal to evolve and live in the present. A tendency to allow ourselves be blinded by power, privileges and wealth. Nostalgia for former lifestyles. Conservation of useless memories. Overvaluation of old, ancient objects that we treat like priceless treasures.

APARTMENT

A place of dwelling, of structure, related to our personal and/or family intimacy, with a certain number of rooms, which occupies only part of a building generally inhabited by several people who share certain collective goods and services.

⊕ Represents intimacy and a certain lifestyle, a way of living on the personal and family levels. A capacity to live peacefully in close proximity to others. The different rooms of an apartment represent different parts and aspects of the tenant or owner on the intimate level.

A clean, bright, spacious apartment: Represents a neat, orderly, bright, harmonious, peaceful inner life as well as a respectful, pleasant collective life.

Discovery of new rooms in the apartment: Discovery of new spaces in our inner life. A feeling of expansion on the inner level related to sharing and a capacity to live peacefully in close proximity to others.

⊖ Difficulties related to intimacy and lifestyle, way of living on the personal and family levels. Problematic memories regarding peaceful, harmonious co-habitation.

A dirty apartment: Indicates a necessity to cleanse and tidy up our intimacy and lifestyle.

A dark apartment: Pessimism, heaviness, a lack of understanding on the intimate level as well as of life in close proximity to others. A muddled inner situation.

An apartment that is too small: A feeling of limitation on the intimate level as well as in life lived in close proximity to others.

An apartment that is too big: a complex of superiority on the intimate level.

APOCALYPSE

Apocalypse means revelation. It is generally associated with catastrophic events and the end of the world. On the spiritual and symbolic levels, an apocalypse represents a very important initiatic period, during which great openings of the unconscious are experienced, which set off major changes in an *ordinary, horizontal* conscience on the level of its characteristic beliefs, structures and behavioral patterns. Seeing apocalyptic events in a dream announces profound changes in the dreamer's life, the end of his individual world as he knows it, the end of a life lived in an ordinary, horizontal conscience, virtually entirely focused on matter. Henceforth, he will be led to develop a universal conscience and to discover the true meaning of Life.

It is important not to dramatize or project the contents of such a dream onto the outer world and imagine the end of life on earth.

⊕ An intense, rigorous, initiatic period that guides our soul toward the discovery of destructive forces within ourselves that seem to destroy our life, our way of being and living. A phase of great physical and psychological tensions that we need to learn to manage. It is also a time to reinforce ourselves through meditation and prayer, faith in God, or Cosmic Intelligence. Awareness that the development of the highest levels of conscience require Knowledge of good and evil, and an understanding of the educational role of evil, wrong-doing, and what hurts. An apocalypse experienced in a dream announces the emergence of a New Earth and a new world in the dreamer's conscience. Emergence of new knowledge that reveals the Hidden Wisdom of Cosmic Intelligence, of God, which is beyond good and evil. Incites us to work on existential fears and false beliefs, and to develop spirituality based on the knowledge of Cosmic Laws, and on the understanding of the correlations that exist between the workings of the Universe as a macrocosm, and of a human being as a microcosm. We gradually come to understand that everything changes in the universe, and that the end of the world does not exist in terms of conscience, nor does it exist on the ever-evolving spirit and soul levels. It is important to analyze the apocalyptic images and visions in the light of symbolic language and the Law of resonance and not to take them literally. It is also useful to know that the apparition of apocalyptic symbolism in our dreams means that we are called to discover the highest levels of Knowledge through great initiations.

⊖ Erroneous beliefs and false understanding of the term *apocalypse*, which nourish existential fear and an expectancy of the end of the world. An extreme religious, fatalistic vision. A period of great ordeals and inner de-structuring. Visiting somber, pessimistic memories that have a destructive tendency, which activates soul states of deep despair, a vision of the end of the world possibly leading to individual and collective suicide. It is important to understand that apocalyptic dreams and feelings *reveal* first and foremost inner states engendered by accumulations of extremely negative memories, dating from former lives. Instead of projecting onto the outside world what we are experiencing on the inside, it is important to learn to accept that it is an encounter with the negativity that dwells within us. Whenever openings of the unconscious reveal to us the action of destructive forces annihilating our inner world, it is vital to work intensely on the transformation of the memories that maintain these forces, so as to be able to rediscover inner peace and harmony.

APPOINTMENT BOOK *cf.* ***Diary***

ARAB (in general)

The Arab world comprises several different ethnic groups, which are characterized in particular by linguistic and cultural links, and not necessarily religious ones, because even though the majority of Arabs are Muslim, others identify with other religions and ways of thinking. Generally speaking, the symbolism of the Arab world is related to deep sensitivity and a great opening of the physical senses. This particularity leads to great intensity in action and considerable power of manifestation and materialization as the person is well-rooted. Whenever an Arab has developed a humanist, altruistic, spiritual conscience that is right and well-balanced, he then emanates a radiant, luminous energy that he is capable of embodying and manifesting in all areas of his daily life. Such a person has tremendous charisma; he expresses beautiful, heartfelt qualities and has a strong sense of commitment, duty, and of the sacred.

⊕ Intensity and total commitment in everything we do. Beautiful vital energy. Spiritual power in action. Acting in accordance with our convictions, principles, and moral values. A capacity to manifest and materialize. A sense of right, fair trade. A sense of ritual in action. An opening on the level of all five senses. Awakening of vital energy, the kundalini. Absolute fidelity and sexuality that is well lived. A family spirit. A sense of sharing, hospitality, and generosity. Ready to make great sacrifices to evolve and help our neighbor or others. Favors mutual help. Nobility of soul. Incarnated spiritual riches. A well-developed heart dimension. A poetic, universal spirit. Faithful servant. A capacity to devote ourselves to a mission.

⊖ Extremist and fanatical. Deceiving, abusing spirit. Dishonesty and slyness in relationships and exchanges with others. Impulsive, excessive, hot-tempered. Dangerous spirituality. Ideological, religious terrorism. A sectarian spirit, closed to other cultures. Seeking to convince and impose. Rigidly imposing authority and power. Excess and avidity on the material level. Poor use of resources and material goods. Excessive materialization. Following rituals based on old patterns and ancient traditions to the letter. Going from one extreme to the other. Distorted sexuality, polygamy. A dominating spirit that represses the feminine side. Non-respect for femininity, receptivity. Imposing emissivity. Retention and repression of instincts; or, on the contrary, a tendency to exaggeration and lust. Seeking to develop on the material level only, neglecting the evolution of our conscience.

ARCHITECT

An architect is a construction professional whose job is to conceive and direct the realization of all sorts of building projects. He can manifest his vision of society and his era in his creations. The architect profession is a symbol of the way we construct ourselves on the personal and collective levels, the way we work to expand our conscience and vision of the world. God is often referred to as *The Great Architect* to show the High Intelligence used to create Life and the various levels of existence, including the world we live in. An architect is a beautiful symbol of a designer and director of structure, style, mentality, as well as social and private life. He creates, converts and develops places, spaces, and atmospheres so as to materialize harmony and well-being. He is also a symbol of precision, organization, knowledge of mathematics and the universal laws.

⊕ Planning, organization and construction of a new stage in life or a project. Knowledge acquired for the elaboration and creation of projects. Expansion and realization of great ideas. A structured, precise, thorough, visionary mind or spirit. Love of beauty and harmony. Thoroughness and awareness of the importance of structure and planning during the various stages of materialization. Responsible, reliable, trustworthy.

⊖ Problems related to the elaboration of ideas, planning, structure, conception, design, and organization of a project or life situation. Lack of vision, preparation, precision, exactitude, practicality and common sense. Collapse of structures due to poor conception, bad design. Disrespect for laws. Irresponsibility. Over-rapid materialization. Failure.

ARM (body part)

Our arms represent a force of manifestation, work, mutual help, consolation, tenderness and protection. Through exemplary submission, arms help the hands to work, shape, and give form. Through their elongated form, their great mobility, and their muscular strength, arms are a symbol of emissivity, flexibility and force of action. Situated on both sides of the trunk, they also symbolize the two complementary principles: masculine on the right side and feminine on the left. Since they connect in the region of the heart and hands, they are related to motivation, support, and a capacity to give and to receive. As they end in the hands, they are also associated with the capacity to create, construct and produce.

⊕ Potential for manifestation, work, strength, mutual help, tenderness and protection. Easy execution of difficult work. A capacity to use both polarities (masculine and feminine) in action, in a well-balanced, harmonious way. Fairness and balance when giving and receiving, in emissivity as well as receptivity. Flexibility and adaptability. A capacity to obey and submit to instructions and orders. Capable of courage and bravery. Gracefulness.

⊖ Imbalanced, unjust, unfair, or abusive use of strength, mutual help, tenderness, involvement, manifestation and protection. Negligence and indifference when carrying out work or an order; or, refusal to do so. Laziness, carelessness, a lack of motivation for work, for materialization and manifestation. Unfairness in giving and receiving. A lack of will to help, comfort or console. Emotional coldness, incapacity to show tenderness. A coarse, boorish, apish person who lacks intelligence. Clumsiness.

ARMS (weapon) *cf.* ***Gun***

ARMY

The first mission of the armed forces is to ensure State security, the defense and protection of its people and territories in the case of inner or outer threat. In an international context, armed forces may also receive peacekeeping and humanitarian aid missions. Consequently, in terms of conscience, an army symbolizes a capacity for protection, maintenance of order and justice, intervention in conflicts or struggles, and right, just settlement of them, either in concrete reality, or in our inner world, It also serves to develop great qualities, such as discipline, order, a sense of duty and honor, respect for laws, rules and regulations, right, altruistic exercise of power and force, as well as humanitarian aid and social devotion.

Whenever an army appears as a symbol in a dream, its behavior determines whether its symbolic meaning is positive or negative. An aggressive, bellicose army indicates distortions, whereas a protective army reveals beautiful qualities. It may manifest symbolically when we have accumulated a great number of memories marked with aggression, badly exercised control and power, needs for conquest and domination.

A spiritual person with a utopian vision of a perfect world may believe that there is no need for an army here on Earth, but the more we work with dreams, the more we realize that the guides of the parallel worlds are Warriors of Light, and that, like any army, they work to maintain Order, Justice, and Peace in the whole Universe. We can draw an analogy between their role helping us, which may include activating an ordeal for the good of our evolution, and the work carried out by armies here on Earth. Even if armies here on Earth are far from perfect, they are used and supervised by Cosmic Intelligence in accordance with the evolution, apprenticeship, and experimentation programs of the peoples and nations that live on Earth. Just as the guides from the parallel worlds do not use their powers for personal ends, neither does an army (if right), nor even a single, individual soldier, commit acts that have no function or role to play on a vaster, more global level.

It is important to know that beyond, above the protection represented by the army or police on the earth level, there is Divine Protection, and, even though, from an *earthly* point of view, military forces sometimes commit unjust acts, Divine Justice is absolute. Abusive use of military power engenders negative karmas that, one day, will have to be repaired. Hence, if individual or collective abuse is not sanctioned by internal military justice, at another point in time, in other circumstances, or in another life, those responsible for creating such karmas may find themselves reincarnated in a country that will be subjected to military aggression by another nation. Cosmic Intelligence has unimaginable possibilities at its disposal to help us discover Divine Justice in all dimensions of Creation. (*cf. also* **Soldier**)

⊕ A state of conscience of protection, strength, force, and power on the collective level. Skill in settling conflicts and maintaining peace. Respect for authority, law and order. A person capable of withstanding high tensions. A capacity to train ourselves and progress in difficult zones. Ready to make sacrifices. A sense of leadership. Exemplary behavior. A structured, disciplined person. Obedience to what is right. A calm, well-balanced person on all levels (physical, emotional, intellectual, and spiritual); someone who masters his powers. An elevated sense of duty, service, and honor. A sense of altruism and devotion. Feelings of kindness, consideration, and compassion. Knowledge of Divine Justice and the Laws. Respect for the Heavenly Hierarchy. Understanding that good and evil are educational concepts. Initiated into the secrets of the Universe, to the highest levels of good and evil. An ability to confer a sense of sacredness and sacred meaning to our acts and decisions.

⊖ Unfair, unjust, abusive, aggressive, violent behavior. The use of military force and power to conquer, to impose our point of view, our ideology, to obtain privileges, or to manipulate others. Repression on the individual and collective levels. Hatred and a total lack of altruism and compassion. War crimes, crimes against humanity. Non-respect for international treaties, or for whatever has to do with civilians and their goods, destruction of civilian targets, pillage, rape, etc. A lack of authority, rigor, order. A rigid, excessively authoritarian, ill-intentioned, vengeful, megalomaniac mind and spirit. A feeling of superiority or an inferiority complex. Believing ourselves to be indispensible. Seeking acknowledgement. Cold appreciation. Extremist, criminal ideas. Brute strength. Corrupt government. Conspiracy. Never-ending war. Existential combat.

ARTHRITIS

As an acute, chronic inflammatory condition that affects the joints, arthritis essentially concerns suppleness, flexibility, mobility, the capacity of adaptation and freedom of movement. A symbolic analysis of the parts of the body that are affected helps us understand what type of distorted memories we need to work on. Generally speaking it concerns memories marked by laziness, a lack of motivation and suppleness in action, an accumulation of tension which puts the brakes on advancing and manifestation, an overly conformist attitude, the presence of rigid, fixed concepts, which prevent flexibility and adaptability on the physical level. As it affects bones and tendons, it also indicates a deep problem concerning the structure of the way we function. For example, arthritis that manifests in the knees reveals a difficulty or a resistance to submitting, to subordinating to what is right. Such an attitude damages our inner structure as well as our capacity to advance lightheartedly and easily, and it manifests on the outside through joint pains in our knees.

⊕ Awareness that we need to activate our willpower, motivation, flexibility and adaptability for what we love as well as for what bothers us. Work on ourselves to heal forces that simultaneously desire intensely and yet withdraw, and to transform memories of ways of acting caused by rigidity and pressure.

⊖ An accumulation of memories of rigidity and a lack of flexibility and adaptability. Duality and discrepancy caused by excessive pressure on the one hand and a lack of willpower to act, advance and manifest, on the other. Blockages, retention of life forces and impulses through fear. Difficulty with change, with what is new. Limitations due to the presence of memories of abuse and excess on the body level. Deep insecurity regarding action, a tendency to be miserly. An incapacity to transform the negative.

ARTIST

An artist represents a great potential related to self-expression, inspiration and creativity. It is someone who is capable of fully awakening his senses, elevating them, and letting them express themselves through art. No matter the medium chosen, an artist has the technical skill to communicate and materialize his emotions, feelings, ideas and vision. His artistic works can then inspire all sorts of emotions and feelings in others, and give rise to reflection and thought. To do this, an artist has to have developed great sensitivity and have an open mind, as well as a well-developed faculty of perception. An artist also manifests talent regarding the creation of atmosphere, ambiance and esthetics. One aspect that is frequently associated with the life of an artist is acknowledgement, recognition, which can come from family, friends, a larger public, and even extend beyond borders. However it is not easy to come by and this can cause some artists multiple expectations and frustrations, or lead to unhealthy ambition and a permanent thirst for acknowledgement and recognition.

⊕ A capacity to inspire beautiful emotions, to give rise to deep reflection, to awaken innovative, luminous ideas through a creative, elevating, spiritual force. A capacity to create works and projects imprinted with great sensitivity that favor evolution. A source of inspiration and change on the collective level. Positive experimentation of fame and celebrity. An exemplary person, becoming a model to follow through his inspiring lifestyle, which is free and well-balanced on all levels. Abundant, fertile imagination.

⊖ An eccentric, egotistical, immoderate, excessive person. Creative obsession: thinks and lives only for his art. Disturbed, exacerbated sensitivity. A more or less pronounced fear of contact with reality. May also indicate a person who does not believe in his talent, or who is not able to master it. A tendency to let ourselves be influenced or submerged by negative emotions. Sadness. Depression. Retreating into the imaginary. Fleeing reality. Creator of illusionary atmospheres and ambiance. Emotional dependencies. A need for social recognition. Seeking personal success and glory. Structureless experimentations. Thinking we are above the law, above everything. Feeling of superiority or an inferiority complex. Bi-polar personality. May sink into drugs and alcohol. Great need to seduce. An unbridled sexual life. Dark, obscure, destructive art. Seeking to shock, to provoke so as to be recognized at all costs. Difficulty materializing our potential because of a lack of discernment and resources. Not assuming our responsibilities or fleeing them. A bohemian spirit. Only wanting to have fun and take advantage of a worldly, social life. Energetic vampirism, feeding on the admiration, esteem and regard of others. A superficial, materialistic mind that lacks authenticity and depth.

ASIA

Asia represents the largest, most populated area of the world. Today Asia is associated with economic power and expansion as well as a tremendous capacity to multiply and materialize. In Asia, ancient spiritual wisdom and the traditions of age-old civilizations co-exist alongside the positive and negative aspects of the modern world. Asia's economic role continues to grow, although political, social, ethnic and climatic zones of instability persist. In terms of conscience, this continent represents a large part of our inner world, of our collective unconscious, which symbolically bears the same characteristics as the Asia that exists in the outer world. It is a continent of geographic, climatic, demographic, economic, social, technological, scientific and philosophical intensity, and sometimes extremes.

⊕ Great faculties of development, multiplication, growth and expansion. Great mental strength and intelligence. Numerous discoveries. Spiritual elevation. Social, cultural, and intellectual riches. Integration of ancestral wisdom and spirituality in the rituals of daily life. Ideological and organizational intensity. A capacity to break old patterns. The will to be independent. Rigor and discipline.

⊖ Development dynamics that over-focus on matter. A continent of extreme dangers. Noticeable, numerous social and environmental challenges because of excessive population growth and over-rapid, unequal development. Multiple problems and ethnic conflicts. Loss of ancestral wisdom and spirituality. Emotionally cold. Mental rigidity. Intelligence used in an unhealthy way, without principles or moral values, that is content to copy and not innovate. Problems of organization and administration. Corruption, and above all, seeking the satisfaction of basic, primary needs, attachment to matter, success, avidity, abuse of power, and feelings of superiority and inferiority. Social inequality, extreme, inhumane living conditions, woman and child exploitation, poverty, misery. Lack of love and humanity, false liberty, important discrepancies between men and women. Discrimination, extremism, fanaticism.

ASSAULT

An assault is an act of violence, a form of attack through which a person exteriorizes energies of deep frustration and dissatisfaction that have been accumulated over a long period of time, even over several lives. Being assaulted in a dream or concrete reality indicates that we bear within ourselves memories of aggressive acts toward others in this life, or in a previous life, caused by a thirst for violence or a lack of understanding that violence breeds violence. It is important to know that every time we assault others on the physical, emotional, or thought levels, we activate a process that automatically places us under the effect of the Law of karma, or the Law of return: sooner or later, the aggressive energy we emanated will come back to us. As long as we have not cleansed and transformed these memories of aggression within us, we will continue to attract aggressive situations and people. These serve to make us aware of our inner conflicts and incite us to settle them.

An assault experienced in a dream is not necessarily related to an assault we may have committed in concrete reality. It may simply be a warning that a certain amount of violence lies dormant within us and that, without inner work and a change in behavior, this could end up being expressed in an aggressive act on the physical level. On the other hand, the experience of an assault in concrete reality is always directly related to an act of violence we really and truly committed in the past. The Law of Divine Justice is absolute, on both the metaphysical and physical levels: we always reap what we sow. The vicious circle of negative karma begins by experimenting the role of the assailant, the aggressor. This means that every victim has accumulated the memories and behavior of an assailant that he has to cleanse and transform. However, certain great beings who may be subjected to aggression, remain compassionate and deeply understanding, because they have transcended violence and aggression within themselves; in such cases, they serve as inspiring models to raise, elevate, and help mankind.

⊕ Transcendence of memories of aggression. Understanding the Cosmic Laws of karma, resonance and Divine Justice. Compassion and a non-violent attitude toward the assailant. Awareness that violence breeds violence. A conscious choice to no longer nourish evil, wrong-doing, hurt.

⊖ Using aggression and violence to obtain what we want. Seeking to control through intimidation and threats. Ignorance of the Cosmic Laws. An accumulation of karmas involving violence. Aggression, assault through gestures, words, thoughts, and emotions. The presence of unsatisfied instinctive needs which engender frustration and aggression. A lack of understanding of the dynamics that link the assailant, the aggressor, and the victim.

ASTHMA

The word asthma comes from the Greek *ásthma* (difficult breathing). It refers to a respiratory difficulty on the exhale, as well as a non-contagious, inflammatory lung infection that manifests through spasms and hyper-bronchial secretions, and may result in acute respiratory insufficiency. This pathology evolves in attacks of varying duration, which may worsen depending on the psychological reaction of the sufferer (panic, fear, anxiety, etc.). Metaphysically, asthma is related to retention of intellectual and emotional memories that the sufferer becomes aware of and has difficulty transforming. It affects very receptive, hypersensitive people in particular, who, through shyness, embarrassment, lack of emissivity or self-confidence, retain their thoughts and emotions because they dare not express themselves spontaneously. In order to transcend the emotional and intellectual blockages that impede breathing, the asthmatic needs to acquire an understanding of the causes and mechanisms that trigger his asthma attacks. He needs to learn to manage his perceptions and feelings so as not to absorb everything like a sponge.

⊕ Allows the sufferer – and his entourage (especially when the sufferer is a child) – to become aware of the discrepancies that exist between his thoughts and his emotions. The will and motivation to make the effort to acquire the necessary knowledge and understanding to be able to heal. Development of better self-knowledge, of the way he thinks and feels, which helps the person express himself correctly and more freely. Liberation from anxiety attacks thanks to deeper understanding. Acceptance of hypersensitivity, which the person learns to transform into a great force of wisdom and compassion regarding other people's behavior. Conscious cleansing work on resonance and old memories as well as hyperactive tendencies and states.

⊖ A person who suffocates because of an accumulation of unexpressed, retained thoughts and emotions. A tendency to get bogged down and to feed on all sorts of discrepancies. Fear of change and limitations. An incapacity to manage and to transform hypersensitivity. A tendency to overdramatize our condition and to wish to fight it. A lack of understanding that all forms of discomfort, ill-being, and illness are educational.

ASTRONAUT

An astronaut represents states of conscience related to a capacity to discover and explore parallel worlds and universes, to develop metaphysical understanding and a global vision of time, space, matter, conscience, and what we call reality. In dreams, we can see ourselves fly or travel in space and in other worlds without needing a rocket, special equipment, or a spacesuit. To correctly interpret such a dream, we need to take into account all the elements present, including the general atmosphere and the emotions experienced. This allows us to understand how we react on discovering our inner space and the multidimensionality of our being.

⊕ Careful expansion and exploration of our conscience and inner space. Development of global vision and discovery of metaphysical reality and spiritual powers. Integration of the state of conscience of universal citizenship. A feeling of humility faced with the vastness of existence.

⊖ A person who seeks to conquer using his knowledge and intellectual and/or spiritual capacities; or, who seeks to flee the responsibilities of daily life in the name of great ideals. Seeking grandeur as well as a feeling of superiority. Fear and perceptual discrepancy between earthly life and life in the multidimensions of our conscience. It is important to reflect on what it is we seek to flee, or what bothers us so much we wish to escape from life on Earth. There is a reason for Earthly existence; it is an integral stage in our evolution.

ASYLUM

1- Refuge, shelter, political asylum; 2- Psychiatric hospital, mental asylum

Originally, the term *asylum* designated an inviolable place where a pursued person could seek refuge. Generally speaking, it is a place of shelter, safe from danger, and is therefore considered a refuge. It is also associated with calm, silence, peace and a person's reconstruction. Hence its usage today for a psychiatric hospital or asylum for the mentally disturbed. On the symbolic level, an asylum represents a state of conscience that provides us with a capacity to welcome parts of ourselves in difficulty so as to protect them from all danger and to take care of them. It represents a capacity to treat different types of behavior without rejecting, discriminating or suppressing them. In the case of an asylum for the mentally disturbed, it indicates a capacity to take care of ill parts of ourselves on the mental and behavioral levels.

⊕

1- *Refuge, shelter, political asylum*: The beginning of a new departure, a change in life. Receiving assistance in very difficult moments of our life; or, showing great tolerance, generosity, welcome and compassion to those going through trying times and who need a refuge, on the outside in concrete reality and on the inside, to parts of ourselves. Seeking to heal, self-questioning, re-orientation of our life. Kind hospitality and protection for those in need.

2- *Psychiatric hospital*: Seeking to heal parts of ourselves that are mentally ill and to re-discover the meaning of our life. Temporary inner refuge, far from the responsibilities of everyday life. A period of reconstruction, of re-education, after powerful trials and tribulations on the thought, emotional and soul-state levels.

⊖

1- *Refuge*: Isolation, seclusion, internment, limitation, an unfavorable period as we've lost our bearings. An abusive, mean person who gets rid of others by interning them in an asylum. Presence of memories of extreme possessiveness, domination and abuse of power. Belittling and abasing others, preventing them from blossoming and developing their potential. Prisoner of our conscience and emotions. Lacking compassion and humanity. Extreme prejudice.

2- *Psychiatric hospital*: A person in great mental difficulty, on the level of his thought patterns and associations, perception and understanding. Prisoner of past memories. Rebellion, aggression, anger toward everything that exists. Frustration, envy, jealousy. Deep soul suffering. Incapacity to manage the openings and emergences of the unconscious. A limited, lost mind and spirit that battles and rebels against authority and those who'd like to help him. A person who closes in on himself and refuses help through pride.

Internment. Serious discrepancies between the mind, spirit, soul and body, hallucinations, mystical, egotistical delirium, multiple personalities. Needs spiritual knowledge so as to heal.

ATHLETE

A person in very good physical condition who trains regularly, whose goal is to excel in one or more sporting disciplines. An athlete is a model of inspiration representing great qualities necessary for materialization, such as self-discipline, perseverance, physical and moral endurance, the will and capacity to surpass ourselves, to attain our objectives, achieve our potential, as well as a healthy life on all levels. Society highly values its athletes because they motivate young and old.

From a negative point of view, athletes symbolize people who force destiny and who are ready and willing to do absolutely anything to succeed and to impress others. They thirst for renown and very often, they can shatter their own life. They train for years in difficult, even extreme conditions, which often causes injuries and physical pain that can handicap them for the rest of their life. Generally speaking, we hear a lot more about athletes who succeed than those who fail. Today, however, more and more, extreme competition is bringing out the negative aspects of sport through increasingly frequent doping scandals. We can see therein a social tendency to be prepared to seek success and fame irrespective of the price to pay.

⊕ The will to surpass ourselves. A capacity to withstand high physical and psychological tensions. Seeking mastery and right willpower. Use of maximum physical capacities to acquire strength, courage, and thereby give the best of ourselves. Developing discipline, perseverance, endurance, determination and concentration in order to achieve an objective. Capacity for self-sacrifice for a great cause. A social role-model. Heroic spirit. A person who deserves celebrity and acknowledgement and who uses his renown for noble aims.

⊖ Excessive willpower which forces and endures high tensions on all levels because of a need for social acknowledgement; or, a lack of dynamism, motivation and discipline to achieve our objectives and goals. Rivalry, competitive spirit, wanting to win at all costs. Cult of the body and the ego, pride, vanity, narcissism. Desire for earthly glory, sometimes even seeking victory through illegal means, corruption. Imbalanced life, over-focused and founded on the body and matter. Feelings of superiority and inferiority. A person who neglects his physical condition, who doesn't do enough exercise, who doesn't move enough, who leads an over-sedentary lifestyle, preferring to watch others do sport rather than do any himself, *couch potato* phenomenon.

ATTACK

An action triggered by an accumulation of negative forces and memories that pushes us to act aggressively and offensively toward someone or something with the aim of hurting, wounding, dominating, or destroying. A physical or violent verbal attack is often the exteriorization of a great intensity of anger, rage, hatred, thirst for revenge or conquest.

⊕ Awareness that violence only engenders violence. Understanding the interaction between causes and consequences as well as Divine Justice, which is carried out without vengeance, aggression or anger. End of disputes, fights.

⊖ Expression of violence and brutality. Destructive impulsiveness caused by a conscious or unconscious accumulation of aggressive memories and states of intense anger. Danger and de-stabilization on the relationship level. Lack of mastery and self-command of the negative within us. Incomprehension of the Law of return, causes and consequences: when we are attacked and/or assaulted, it's because we too attacked others in this life or another. We always encounter ourselves on the karmic level. Incomprehension of the fact that evil, wrong-doing, what hurts, is educational. (*cf. also* **Assault**)

ATTIC

In concrete reality, an attic is the highest part of the house and it is also a discreet place, sometimes hidden or forgotten, where we store memorabilia and old objects we no longer wish to use for time being. Hence it represents part of our intimacy where we may have stored old concepts, outmoded, obsolete behavioral patterns, and outdated thoughts, which haven't been cleansed or recycled. What is in the attic may also represent valuable treasure and beautiful resources set aside because not immediately needed; however, generally speaking, it is more often an accumulation of memories due to insecurity and an incapacity to renew, transform or purify ourselves in depth. An attic can also serve as storage space for seasonal objects. Consequently it symbolizes a capacity to tidy away and store well, to concentrate on what is essential, and store ideas and thoughts that are not useful at present, but which are available when required.

⊕ Discovery of hidden or stored potential. A capacity to concentrate on the essential by tidying away and storing memorabilia, memories, ideas, capacities, experiences, behavior and attitudes that are still useful, but only serve occasionally or when required. Understanding the importance of sorting through stored resources and memories and disposing of whatever is no longer necessary. Good knowledge of available resources. A well-ordered life. Feeling at peace with our past.

⊖ An accumulation of old concepts, preservation of old habits. Attachment to the past, nostalgia. Difficulty sorting, transforming and purifying accumulated memories. Resistance to letting go of what has become outmoded, valueless, and useless. Insecurity and fear linked to past experiences of privation and lack of resources. Greed, possessiveness. A heavy, overburdened person who always broods on the same thoughts and maintains old thought patterns. A life confused by past experiences that prevent clear vision and understanding.

ATTORNEY *cf.* ***Lawyer, attorney***

AURICULAR (little finger)

The auricular is the fifth finger on our hand – it's our little finger. The term *auricular* comes from Latin, meaning that which is related to the ear; indeed we usually use our little finger to scratch our ear. While English speakers say *A little birdie told me*, French speakers say

My little finger told me, thereby relating the sense of hearing to this finger. This expression is used to indicate that the speaker knows the truth but doesn't say how he came by it; his discerning intelligence has led him to it. It is called our *little finger* as it is the smallest of our five fingers. It is symbolically related to the planet Mercury, hence to its associated characteristics: practical intelligence, the faculty of analysis, the science of analogies and the capacities of the human intellect to discern right from wrong, true from false.

⊕ When giving and receiving, a capacity to manifest sensitively and precisely the following qualities and strengths: practical intelligence, a logical spirit and a privileged mind. A rich, fertile intellect. Facility for learning. Ability to analyze, capacity to listen to ourselves and others with the wisdom of our heart. Capacity to discern good from evil, true from false. Facility in finding the causes of a problem. Understanding our life plan. Capacity to know the unknown through what is known.

⊖ Difficulties related to learning, understanding, knowledge, listening and precision. Narrow-mindedness or an overly analytical spirit. Excessive rationality, a tendency to think too much before acting. Lack of discernment. Use of knowledge solely for material ends. Pretentious wisdom, false reasoning, self-appropriation of Knowledge. Negation of the Divine. Lack of common sense and global vision. Deformation of reality, misinformation. Confusion, mental opacity. An arrogant, critical spirit.

AUTISM

The term autism was created in 1911 by the Swiss psychiatrist, Eugene Bleuler. Autism manifests to varying degrees (mild, moderate, severe) and is now diagnosed as ASD, i.e. Autism Spectrum Disorder. It affects three to four times more boys than girls. People suffering from autism are hypersensitive people who resist full incarnation into physical reality. Generally speaking, it's a question of their being very old souls who transgressed Divine Laws over many lives, thereby accumulating a great quantity of memories related to distorted behavior that they try to flee in their present life by shutting themselves into a kind of bubble, instead of using their intelligence to rectify, cleanse, and transform them.

Manifestation of autism indicates that the person affected bears within himself parts that express or manifest extreme personality traits, which incite him to withdraw into himself because he finds it difficult to communicate and interact with the outside world. Hence, the person experiences deep discrepancies between his mind, his emotions and his physical body.

Autism may be considered a form of unconscious suicide, refusal, resistance to taking responsibility for our life program, to becoming involved in transforming accumulated karma and continuing to evolve. Instead of working on himself to cleanse his unconscious and asserting himself when confronted with forces that crush him, an autistic person simply endures. He tends to take refuge in his bubble and, through his inertia, he limits and excludes himself, and gradually loses all contact with concrete life. When faced with the sensorial floods coming from the outside world, he prefers to cut himself off from the world, to become a *conscience hermit/recluse*. In severe cases, repetitive, stereotypical behavior accompanied by self-mutilation and aggression can be observed. The fact that an autist is more comfortable in a predictable environment highlights his great fear of change, of experimenting and evolving. He can be fascinated, even obsessed by simple things in life, which allow him to avoid reality and more complex involvement. An autist represents a lack of understanding of good and evil, great intelligence lost in the labyrinth, the maze of the soul.

⊕ A person who very gradually reeducates himself and becomes sociable thanks to the cleansing of his unconscious and the transformation of his memories and negative resonance. Liberation and transcendence of withdrawal, self-isolation, introversion, fears, phobias and repressed anger. A study of hypersensitivity. Integration of the Law of karma and the effect of resonance. Acceptance of the fact that other people reflect parts of ourselves and that the different contexts and situations in life reveal our learning program. Understanding that the different levels of existence are related, that life in the physical world is a dream just as dreams are reality in the subtle, metaphysical worlds, and that the goal of existence is to develop qualities and virtues.

⊖ Great accumulation of negative memories that have engendered deep discrepancy in the coherent, harmonious workings of the mind, soul and body as a whole, as a unity. A lack of understanding of the meaning of evolution, and of the Cosmic Laws of karma, of resonance and the mirror-effect. An extremely complicated person with a lot of complexes. Isolation, fleeing reality and ourselves. Repressed, untransformed aggression. Elocution difficulties. Resisting new currents. Going round in circles brooding over the same thoughts. A person with compulsive, obsessive tendencies. A lack of love for ourselves and others. Excessive egotism. Complexes of superiority and inferiority. A rebellious, stubborn, obstinate spirit. Discrepancy between thoughts and emotions. Difficulty taking action, improvising and expressing ourselves. Excessive search for attention.

AUTOMOBILE, CAR

The etymology of this word comes from the Latin word *mobilis* (which moves) and the Greek word *auto* (oneself) which, implicitly, refers to the fact that an automobile symbolizes an extension, a prolongation of ourselves, allowing us to advance toward others more easily, enabling us to get to work, go shopping or advance toward all other social activities more rapidly than if we were on foot; it also allows us to cover greater distances.

An automobile (or car) represents the way we advance in society, the way we behave on the social level. Symbolically, the kind of car we have, its size, color, etc., favors better knowledge of ourselves concerning the way we advance and behave socially. For example, a sports car indicates that its owner likes to go very fast, and a luxurious car denotes an attraction to material resources or a need to impress others.

Whether seen in a dream or related to an event experienced in our daily life, cars reveal a lot about their owners and drivers. For example, whenever we have a problem with our car, a symbolic analysis of the faulty part, of the general state of the car, as well as our attitude in the situation will inform us how we advance in life.

Seeing ourselves as the victim or cause of an accident in a dream doesn't necessarily mean that we will have an accident in concrete reality. However such a dream should incite us to be vigilant and careful of our behavior so as to avoid creating accidents on the mental or emotional levels. An accident that we are to experience on the physical level can be announced in symbolic language but, first of all, everything must be interpreted in terms of conscience. Accidents are engendered by an accumulation of memories. Inner experimentations on the thought and emotional levels first create accidents of conscience on the causal level before they materialize as physical accidents on the level of consequences.

⊕ Facility, ease in advancing toward others. Good social attitude, pleasant behavior, kindness, thoughtfulness. Prudence, foresight. Positive actions and approach. Respect for the rules of conduct in society. Good use of energy. Evolution. Power of manifestation. Global vision when we advance which allows us to anticipate and avoid dangers thanks to our intuition and our sixth sense.

⊖ Limitation on the social level, difficulty advancing toward others, distorted behavior, blockages. Haste. Temerity. Disrespect. Accidents. Advancing without conscience. Focus on personal needs. Lack of respect and consideration for others. Thoughtlessness. Negative actions. Poor use of energy. Imprudence, foolhardiness, recklessness. Lack of foresight. Ill-will, spitefulness. Insolence, impertinence.

AUTUMN / THE FALL

Autumn, with spring, summer and winter, is one of the 4 seasons in temperate zones. It corresponds to the months of September, October and November in the Northern hemisphere, and March, April and May in the Southern hemisphere. In the country, particularly in the farming sector, it is the season of harvesting, and traditional festivities (e.g. Thanksgiving) destined to thank Heaven and the earth for the abundance we dispose of after the efforts made in spring to plough and cultivate the soil, and the summer period of growth, flourishing and ripening.

Autumn/the Fall is also the period when nature offers us a magnificent display of multi-colored leaves and vegetation in general, which go from the characteristic green shades and tones of spring and summer to the warmer colors associated with the 1st chakras and the earth element, i.e. varying yellows, oranges, reds, and browns. At this time of the year, when the odors found in nature intensify, we can also observe the gathering and departure of migrating birds, while for others it is the hunting season.

For schoolchildren and students, the arrival of autumn indicates the end of the long summer vacation and back to school to continue their learning and studies. For adults too, autumn/ the fall is a season when they return to work after summer vacation, and they often sign up for various courses, attend workshops, lectures, seminars and set in motion diverse projects that correspond to autumn and winter dynamics, i.e. work or study that is related to intellectual, creative, art and craft, cultural or health aspects (training programs, language courses, painting, singing, meditation, yoga, tai chi, etc.).

On the symbolic level and in terms of states of conscience, autumn essentially represents the end of one cycle of activity and movement in the outer world and transition toward a phase of interiorization, rest, replenishment and introspection when our attention is more focused on preparatory dynamics and what is going on within ourselves.

Figuratively speaking, when we refer to *the autumn of life*, we are referring to maturity, retirement, the approach of old age, when a person gradually decreases his intensity in physical work and actions, and feels more of a need to share and communicate his life experiences and the wisdom he has acquired on the way. When this stage is not well experienced and a person fears the onset of old age, declining health, loss of vitality, dynamism, physical and mental autonomy, he often maintains soul-states (moods) of sadness, melancholy, nostalgia, regret and fear of death.

Like Spring when we do great inner and outer cleansing so as to liberate accumulated energies that have often become stagnant over winter, Autumn invites us to clean, tidy and check things in view of the forthcoming colder winter climate: preparation of the house, garden, and vehicles, stocking up on various resources depending on the lifestyle and environment we live in.

⊕ Ability to consciously and responsibly complete a cycle, a season of activity, and reap and gratefully acknowledge the fruit, the abundance of our efforts. A period when, after the long summer vacation, we reactivate, re-start the dynamics of professional, school, or student life, as the case may be, as well as take the initiative to seek new knowledge in order to continue individual and/or collective learning and developing on different levels. Capacity to make a harmonious, well synchronized transition from the summer season with its active, extrovert dynamics toward the winter season and its more meditative, introverted dynamics. Ability to allow ourselves well deserved rest, as well as time for necessary interiorization, introspection and replenishment. Period when we take stock of what we have sown in our life in terms of creativity and multiple actions. A time of serenity, peace, wisdom, moderation, meditation, and referral back to ourselves. Inner work favoring maturity. Understanding and respect for the natural cycles on the physical and metaphysical levels.

⊖ Soul-states (moods) of sadness, moroseness, melancholy, nostalgia, boredom, pessimism, dismay, solitude, anxiety, decline and/or difficulty adapting to the transitional dynamics of autumn; or, an incapacity to reduce our pace of life to interiorize, rest, take stock of our life. Faded, withered appearance, depressing atmosphere, cold emotions. A period of slowing down, stagnation, lethargy; lack of vitality, dynamism, enthusiasm, a feeling of paralysis, of death. Tendency to disconnect, lose our aim(s), objective(s), goal(s) and meaning of life. May announce a difficult transition period, visiting memories related to cold zones, loss of vital energy. Poor or bad harvest(s). A period of despair, lack, fear, anxiety. Feeling of being locked in the same patterns, not finishing a cycle favorably.

AVARICE *(cf. also **Miserliness**)*

Avarice, which goes hand in hand with miserliness, corresponds to an excessive desire to have, to accumulate goods because of a need to possess. At the root of this distorted behavior are memories of considerable loss, lack and deep existential insecurity. A miser hoards so as to feel safe and sometimes he deprives himself of essential things in life through fear of wanting. However, miserliness is not limited to the material level. It is also encountered on the emotional level; we can be miserly with our love and feelings. And on the intellectual and spiritual level, we can accumulate great quantities of knowledge, skills and capacities and refuse to share, to let others benefit from them. Avarice and its companion, miserliness, is one of the seven distortions, or major vices, along with anger, vanity, pride, laziness, greed and lust.

⊕ Work on healing memories of lack, loss and insecurity that have accumulated over several lives. Awareness that true wealth and security come from within, that there is no guarantee nor outer means that can ensure the preservation of accumulated possessions, but nothing or no one can take away the qualities, virtues, wisdom and knowledge that we have developed, acquired and integrated within us. Understanding that money and matter have temporal, educational functions.

⊖ A compulsive desire to accumulate and possess. Artificial, illusory prosperity. Excessive egotism and materialism. Insecurity, inner lack and emptiness. Absence of spiritual values and principles. Existential struggle, a vision of life based on false principles. Abuse of and importance given to earthly power. Possessiveness and an incapacity to be detached from matter and to share. Blockages, indifference, coldness, poverty on all levels. Poor use of resources. Diabolic power oriented toward satisfaction of personal needs and material interests. Lack of wisdom, love, compassion, absence of human warmth, an incapacity to express our feelings. A proud, insatiable, mean, wicked attitude; opposes altruistic materializations.

B

BABY

A baby represents the future, our potential being, a part of ourselves in the process of becoming, the most beautiful part of us that will learn and develop. It is also a symbol of a beginning, a start, the birth of a project, of a situation. It is the accomplishment, the materialization of a work that was thought up, reflected upon, and conceived with love and wisdom. It reveals the Force of Life incarnate; the fulfillment of a new, fresh, loving, spontaneous emergence of the force or strength to exist and evolve. It is also a source of renewal of love and a stimulation of *joie de vivre* – joy in life and living.

⊕ A new way of being. A new stage in our evolution and development. Materialization of a project formed with love and wisdom. Wonderment, spontaneity, *joie de vivre.* Purity and unconditional love. Innocence, candor, freshness and renewal. May announce that a child is about to be born or to come into our life. A delicate project requiring continual attention to ensure and strengthen its growth and potential.

⊖ Difficulty related to a new way of being, a new stage in life. A person with a childish, fragile, capricious temperament who refuses to learn and evolve. Lack of love and wisdom in the creation of new projects. Failure in materialization. May announce a difficulty in the arrival of a child or of a birth.

BACK *(cf. also **Spine**)*

As its name clearly indicates, the back is situated in the rear or posterior part of the human body, and as such symbolizes the past, memories that have been inscribed within us since the beginning of our human existence. It also represents the structural basis that serves as support when it is time to act. In both dreams and concrete reality, everything that occurs behind us is related to past memories. Whenever we suffer from backache, we can conclude that past memories are hurting.

⊕ It is important to make the connection between the state of our back and the situation experienced, either in our dream or our concrete reality, because this allows us to become aware of and transform the related memories. A supple, healthy back indicates the following states: flexibility of mind and spirit, adaptability thanks to understanding and acceptance of the past, liberation, well-being, strength to act and advance harmoniously and peacefully toward the future.

Note: While working on cleansing memories, backaches can occur. It is also possible that existing backache can intensify, hence the importance of not dramatizing and of persevering so as to rediscover balance, well-being, and inner peace.

⊖ Having back problems, concretely or in dreams, indicates an accumulation of blockages, tensions, and distortions stored up over lives. They may also indicate an overload for someone who takes on too much, who takes on a surplus of responsibilities; or, who is haunted by his past. A very tense back reveals an accumulation of stress, overload, behavior that forces; and/or, a person who withdraws into himself, who has been damaged by life. Withdrawal into ourselves for fear of being hurt, in fear of advancing. Nostalgia, attachment to the past. Unawareness of the fact that the past guarantees the future; we need to transcend it by transforming our memories to be able to move forward.

BACK, BACKGROUND, REAR (behind)

Everything that is located in the rear, in the background, or behind refers to the past, regarding this life or previous lives. It is important to become aware of the fact that the past guarantees our future. Everything that has not been settled will come back one day, in one form or another, and often more powerfully than in the past.

⊕ Work on awareness, transformation and transcendence of what is behind us. End of a phase, step or stage; end of a difficult period.

Healing of and liberation from the past. Re-activation of positive forces and aspects related to the past.

⊖ Difficulty or incapacity to leave the past behind us. Blockage related to past events. Attachment to the past, which prevents a person from evolving. A past heavy with hurt, wounds, and negative, difficult memories. Advancing hindered because things from the past need to be resolved and settled, a review of the past is necessary.

BACKBONE *cf. Spine*

BAG

A bag is a container, and hence mainly related to potential receptivity. Each type of bag, and the way we carry it, allows a more precise definition of the symbol. For example, *a schoolbag* represents receptivity regarding learning; forgetting our school bag denotes a lack of receptivity in this regard; it reveals that other ideas or occupations are more important than learning at that particular moment in our life. *A grocery bag* is related to a capacity to receive resources on the physical level, to nourish and replenish ourselves on the physical level, so as to be able to continue to advance and experiment in matter. Hence, its contents of good, healthy, or poor-quality foodstuffs reveal the type of nutrition and nourishment we are receptive to. *A handbag* may contain our pocketbook, purse or wallet, money, credit cards, identity papers, keys, and other personal belongings. It symbolizes aspects of our receptivity regarding our identity, intimacy (house keys), capacity to advance (car keys), access to different places (work keys and others), and our resources for exchanges with others (money, credit cards).

The aspect, shape, color, solidity, refinement of the bag, as well as the material it is made of, etc., all reveal aspects of the quality of our receptivity.

In recent years, there has been an increasing tendency for the commercial use of environmentally-friendly, biodegradable bags, or washable, long-lasting cloth-bags, or recycled plastic bags. This reflects the evolution of the individual and collective human consciousness, which inspires a more respectful attitude for the environment and the use of resources. Man is gradually integrating the fact that the quality of his receptivity to resources improves his choices, and increases his responsible involvement in all areas of life. Even if some people don't yet think deeply enough about what they put into their shopping bag in terms of quality, recourse to re-usable bags is an important step. Choosing the bag (the container) will be followed by conscious choice of its contents, which will increasingly be purchased in harmony with nature, bearing in mind the health of our body, mind, and soul. Then, in terms of quality and conscience, both container and contents will be matched.

⊕ A capacity to be receptive and welcoming toward resources available on the physical and metaphysical levels, to choose and treat them with conscience, respect, acknowledgement, gratitude, discretion, and humility. Behavior that is respectful of other people's identity and intimacy. A person who is practical and well-organized.

⊖ A lack of receptivity regarding resources available on different levels: on the concrete level (material goods), the intellectual level (educational material), etc. Negligence, indifference, laxity, waste, and non-respect of physical and metaphysical resources. A lack of conscience and motivation to take care of our bags, to make right and multiple use of them, recycling them adequately with respect for the environment. A tendency to uselessly accumulate things, or a large number and variety of bags so as to be in fashion, and to nourish appearances. Someone who is over-attached to his bag(s), to appearances, to matter. Constant fear of losing our bag, or having it stolen, indicating the presence of memories of lack, miserliness, deep insecurity, as well as negative karmas: having stolen in other lives; the person unconsciously fears the Law of return, because in his soul, he knows that sooner or later, we reap what we have sown. Secret behavior, a tendency to hide our choices, our intentions, refusal to share. A need to make up for deficiencies. A person who is not well-organized and not sufficiently practical. Problems of bulimia and/or anorexia on the physical and/or metaphysical (emotional, intellectual, spiritual) levels.

A bag with a hole in it: reveals a tendency to disperse, waste, or lose our resources, our capacity to receive and exchange through negligence, inadvertence, or indifference.

A dirty, stained bag: indicates a lax, disconnected, '*don't care*', ill-intentioned attitude.

BALCONY, VERANDA

A balcony, and/or a veranda, allows us contact with the outside world and lets us observe life in the neighborhood while remaining in the intimacy of our home. Hence it symbolizes a capacity to exteriorize prudently, or partially, to participate in the social life around us, contemplate nature, and, to a certain extent, to link inner life and outer life. As a balcony is usually higher than ground level, depending on its height, it may also represent a capacity to raise ourselves up, to have an overall view, to attain global vision and a more causal understanding of the situations and events observed.

⊕ A state of conscience related to social observation and participation, contemplation, reflection, rest, renewal, interiorization and receptivity. Seeking understanding. Prudent or partial exteriorization. A link between certain aspects of our intimate life with the outside world and social life. A feeling of elevation and protection although outside. Global vision.

⊖ Distorted attitudes related to the manifestation of our intimacy, which can be either too social or not social enough. Unhealthy curiosity. Gossip, ill-will, jealousy, voyeurism. Feelings of superiority and/or inferiority. A person who feels lonely, who doesn't feel well in his intimacy and who lacks social life, which pushes him to nourish himself energetically on other people's lives by observing them from his balcony or veranda. Difficulty interiorizing, contemplating with detachment. An incapacity to elevate our conscience, to have an overall view, to attain global vision, causal understanding of our life and exterior events.

BANK

Ensuring the deposit, safeguard, exchange, loan, and fructification of the energy of action that money represents, a bank is a symbol of resource management, and of a great capacity to help others to accomplish and materialize projects on the physical level (*cf. also* **Credit, Money**).

⊕ Capacities to manage resources well, to receive the necessary financial support for the accomplishment of projects, and also giving and receiving rightly and fairly. Capacity to materialize and expand.

⊖ Materialistic attitude and behavior. Deep insecurity and trials related to money. Poor management of resources. An incapacity to accomplish projects. Problems giving and receiving. Support and financing for unfair projects that are not right. Abusive use of monetary power. A tendency to waste and be subjected to loss due to lack of planning. Financial difficulties, bankruptcy, theft, ruin. Survival of the fittest. Selfishness, miserliness, and greed. Superficial, worldly life.

BANKRUPTCY

Bankruptcy evokes a state of conscience of failure, ruin, loss, and a feeling of incompetence and incapacity to succeed. At some time in life, for various reasons (financial difficulties, loss of a contract, stock market crash, divorce, illness, a swindle), a person, anyone at all, may find himself unable to pay off his debts or to honor his financial commitments, with no hope whatsoever of sorting out his situation. In order to help such people rebuild a viable economic situation, some countries have established social procedures called *bankruptcy* or *social recovery*, which are always accompanied by financial supervision. They allow those concerned to start afresh if there is no way they can reimburse their debts. It is important to understand that through bankruptcy, Cosmic Intelligence leads us to question our behavior in exchanges and management. Bankruptcy sets off a new life program and triggers important re-structuring of our behavior. It is either the consequence of a lack of knowledge and wisdom in the management and use of resources, or a life experience triggered by karmic causes created during lives of abuse, excessive ambition, poor use of resources, and dishonest behavior in exchanges with others.

⊕ A lesson to learn how to manage resources better, to use them correctly, to become detached from matter, while remaining responsible. A period of reconstruction. Study of cause and consequence. Questioning and deep reflection on what prevents success. Reorganization and return to what is essential. A change in mentality and lifestyle. Development of humility and simplicity. Intensive work on ourselves allowing us to recognize certain aspects, attitudes, and behavior that need to be modified so we can start afresh on healthy, solid foundations. Awareness that bankruptcy represents a second chance.

⊖ A period of failure, loss, limitation of resources. Collapse of structures and ego-based behavior. A feeling of despair caused by attachment to matter. An over-materialistic vision. Deep existential insecurity. Poor management and organization. Karmic problems stemming from this life and other lives. Experience of poverty as a karmic consequence planned for the lives of those concerned. Refusal to call ourselves into question, to assess our life. Projects that are not right, which do not serve the good of the collectivity or evolution. An imbalanced life due to excessive focus on work, ambition, and the social level. Neglect of our private, intimate life. Feeling indispensable. Memories of negligence and irresponsibility. A lack of know-how. Abuse of help received, and continuing to make the same mistakes.

BAPTISM

The term baptism, which comes from the Greek *baptizein* meaning to plunge or immerse, designates a sacred ritual, a sacrament, destined to purify the person who receives it. Over time it has become synonymous with a blessing and naming ritual, and is not only used in relation to human beings, but also to objects such as a ship, for example. On the symbolic level, it indicates a consecration to a spiritual dimension of life, or the consecration of a project, a building, or a vehicle to sacred usage, usage that is in accordance with what is right, just and good.

Being baptized or baptizing someone else represents a deep spiritual commitment, a feeling of belonging to God, and of wanting to be just and upright.

⊕ The beginning of a new spiritual stage. Consecration, a state of conscience related to deep spiritual commitment on a personal and social level.

⊖ Baptism received with an ordinary, superficial conscience, without true faith or serious commitment to a spiritual path. A ritual submitted to out of customary habit, or to satisfy the demands and expectations of family and friends. A tendency to follow social conventions in order to please. Religious indoctrination, a rigid, sectarian attitude. A rebellious spirit that refuses to consecrate himself to the Divine. A lack of understanding of the sacred dimension of the ritual of baptism.

BAR

Whether we go alone or accompanied, a bar is a very popular social place, where mostly alcoholic drinks are consumed (symbolically, drinks represent the emotional level (*cf. also* **Alcohol**, **Drink**(s)). The study of our behavior and needs when we are in a bar informs us of the way we link our social and emotional lives. Hence, aspects of our emotional and social lives are revealed to us depending on the type of drink we choose to consume (alcohol, water, fruit-juice, soda, coffee, tea, etc.); depending on the reasons that made us go into a bar (relaxation in a convivial place, exchange of ideas and opinions, all sorts of discussions, fun, enjoyment with games or music; or, escaping or fleeing from solitude, seeking contact, fleeting love affairs, etc.); depending on the reigning atmosphere and ambiance (friendly, welcoming, relaxed; or, gloomy, dark, convenient for drug trafficking, prostitution, etc.); and/or, depending on our position (standing at the counter or sitting at a table, alone or in a group). A symbolic study of all these details allows us to lift the veil on our emotional and relational needs: a desire for pleasant, serene, interesting exchanges; or, a need for stimulation, affective, emotional dependencies, etc. It reveals to us, in both the **+** and the **–**, the resonance we have with this place, the people there and the events that occur therein.

⊕ A capacity to emotionally renew ourselves in a positive, social, convivial context. A place for exchanges, for sharing ideas, for pleasant social encounters. Conviviality, fraternal spirit. A capacity for beautiful, emotional communication. Relaxed, harmonious, calm, serene, inspiring social behavior. An ability to transcend emotional dependencies and social intensity. Knowledge of good and evil. A capacity to consume alcohol in moderation, responsibly, mindfully, vigilantly.

⊖ Difficulty remaining emotionally stable in a social context. Harmful influences and ambiances that encourage the satisfaction of primary, coarse, boorish instincts; games of seduction and power. An incapacity or a lack of willpower to transcend enticing, negative, emotional forces. Fleeing reality, difficulties, stress, solitude, ill-being. Distorted seeking of comfort, consolation, support, affection, someone to listen to us. Bad company, harmful, endangering associations, an unhealthy, shady, illegal meeting place. Superficial encounters, seeking shallow, fleeting relationships just to take our mind off things or to satisfy our instinctual needs. Subtle or concrete infidelity. Worldly pleasures, a need to please, to impress, importance given to appearances. Excessive confidence, vanity, competition. Immoral behavior, perversity. Someone who leads others or lets himself be led into illegal activities or dangerous situations. False friends. A tendency to trivialize our distorted behavior, not to trust our intuition, but rather to adhere to other people's ideas without discernment. Acting against Divine Laws.

BASEMENT (cellar)

A basement refers to what is subconscious or unconscious; what is veiled or hidden. It is a symbol related to our capacity to descend into our memories, into the positive and negative resources that we have tidied away, stored, and/or forgotten. In a dream, whenever we go down into the basement, it indicates that we are going to encounter our past; or, that seeds of our conscience have begun to germinate and emerge, either positively or negatively, depending on the contents of our former, ancient, memories of this life, or previous lives.

The contents of a basement/cellar, and the use we make of them, symbolically represent the way we use what is stored in our subconscious, the first zone of our unconscious that is accessible to us. Just below ground level, a basement allows the unconscious forces it harbors to continually exert a positive or negative influence on what is above it. A basement concerns our personal, subconscious memories, which are easily accessible to our conscience when we begin to reflect deeply. In a basement, we can discover, or rediscover, treasures, well-organized stability; or, a jumble of old, repressed, or emerging ghosts.

To better understand the symbolic meaning of a basement in a dream, it is important to define the place where it is located: is it the basement of our house, and hence of our intimacy? Or is it the basement of a public building, a school, a police station, a court of law, our workplace, etc.?

⊕ Visiting the structures of our foundation, memories and forces of our subconscious, but that are close to our conscience. Access to what has been hidden, veiled, buried, or forgotten. Allows us to visit and understand unconscious mechanisms. A place of interiorization, of refuge, a family or personal intimate space. A place, or space, related to a capacity for preservation, tidying away, protection, and conservation. An ability to have access to blocks of memories that give us information about ourselves, and help us to get to know ourselves better, to understand ourselves in depth. Allows us to receive revelations, to discover (or rediscover) a treasure within us related to the place where we are, and its corresponding memories.

⊖ Problems regarding the structure of our foundation, regarding veiled, hidden, or forgotten memories, but which are close to our conscience. Fears, anxiety engendered by subconscious and unconscious memories. The discovery of dark, somber parts of ourselves that stem from our depths. Someone who does not want to walk a spiritual path, undertake a spiritual journey, who resists contact with the contents of his unconscious, who resists looking behind the veil, and becoming aware of deep, repressed, buried memories of this life, or previous lives. A place representing difficult, memories, old ghosts, painful family memories, personal or collective dramas. In a dream, visiting a basement in a negative, somber, threatening context may be an announcement that an ordeal, or trying, testing event, is about to emerge in our life from the unconscious memories we have accumulated in this life or others.

BATH

Having a bath is a way to purify ourselves, to decompress and relax. It is related to the physical and emotional levels.

⊕ Purification. Cleansing our aura, our sensitivity, our personal and social energy. A soul-state (or mood) of receptivity, relaxation, rest and calm after effort.

⊖ Difficulty purifying ourselves, cleansing our aura, our sensitivity, our personal and social energy. A feeling of being defiled, sullied, stained, dirtied, muddied and/or bogged down. A problem of emotional instability. Difficulty relaxing; or, a tendency to lounge around, laziness. An exaggerated need to purify, due to memories full of experimentations that were not right. Puritanism. Lack of receptivity, accumulation of tensions.

BATHROOM

A bathroom is a place devoted to personal, corporal hygiene such as taking a bath or shower, washing our hands or face, shaving, etc. It represents a field of conscience related to cleansing moods, soul-states, attitudes, behavior or interactions with the outer world. It preserves the occupants' intimacy, while helping them evacuate their tensions, states of stress, overload and overflow, etc. Whenever we wash ourselves, we don't only purify our body but also all of our senses, all of our sensitivity and metaphysical antennae, which we use constantly, every day without realizing. Our hair, and all the pores of our skin, receive and continually transmit physical and metaphysical information to us. To ensure the renewal of our cells and personal, corporal hygiene, as well as the refinement of our senses toward the perception of multi-levels and the liberation of metaphysical tensions, daily hygiene is necessary. A bathroom is a place where purification can be carried out, where we can relax with beautiful, warm, reassuring emotions (bath, shower), where we can renew and refresh ourselves intimately so as to better manifest with renewed energy.

⊕ Cleansing moods, soul-states, experimentations and interactions with the outer world. Purification and transformation of negative energies; liberation from stress, tension and worries. Renewal of our intimacy, relaxation, soothing, return to calm, stimulation of self-esteem and self-love. Beautiful reward, satisfaction after intense effort in the world of action. A moment of reflection, interiorization, and self-questioning. Someone who takes good care of himself, who takes time for himself. Renewal, a preparatory phase for new actions.

⊖ A lack of cleansing of moods, soul-states, experimentations and interactions with the outer world. Incapacity or difficulty renewing ourselves, freeing ourselves from stress and accumulated tensions. Someone who doesn't take enough time for himself, who lacks self-esteem and self-love; or, on the contrary, who spends too much time in the bathroom, who is too focused on his physical body, on his appearance; self-centeredness, a need to please and be admired. An accumulation of negative energies and actions, self-neglect, letting ourselves go, laxity, a lack of willpower; or, extremism in the way we purify ourselves and becoming obsessive about being clean. A lack of personal hygiene on all levels of life. Difficulty adapting, *recycling* ourselves.

BATTERY

Represents the capacity to generate, accumulate, and concentrate the energy and energy potential that we have, as well as our capacity to seek within ourselves the required strength and energy to advance and act in our concrete life. The quality, capacity, power and workings of a battery in a dream context indicate the energy potential available to manifest ourselves in matter. A low or flat battery symbolizes a lack of energy: the person will feel exhausted, incapable of finding within himself the necessary resources to regain his strength, vigor and vitality. Each type of battery indicates more specifically which areas are affected. For example, car batteries are related to energy for advancing in life; microphone batteries are related to the energy for communicating collectively; batteries of any object used to listen to music are related to the energy for creating atmospherics and ambiances, etc.; razor batteries are related to the energy for removing unwanted hair from the face or body, i.e. putting our instinctual needs, our emissivity in order.

Note the commonly used expression: *to recharge our batteries,* which means finding new resources on all levels; renewing ourselves. It usually refers to our doing something (e.g. physical activity, sport, vacation, resting, painting, yoga, meditation, etc.) to regain, to renew energy that has been depleted after considerable effort.

⊕ A reserve of inner energy offering the possibility to be active, to advance, to materialize. Energy power, a capacity to store, to stock energy, a capacity for self-regeneration.

⊖ A state of exhaustion, deep fatigue, lack of dynamism and resources; or, an excess of energy, poor usage, dispersal and waste of energy in useless things. A lack or excess of motivation. Negative energy.

BEACH

As a place where land and sea (or other waters) meet – i.e. where the earth (sand, rock) and water (sea, ocean, lake, river) elements join – a beach symbolically links the physical and emotional levels. Hence, time spent at the beach consciously and unconsciously favors the awakening of our emotional memories *via* contact with the water, and our material memories *via* contact with the sand and rock formations.

The great attraction people of all ages feel for the beach comes from the fact that we intuitively associate it with an idyllic, paradisiacal, simple, contemplative life in harmony with nature. In our modern life, the beach is closely linked to the idea of vacations, walks, games, sport, relaxation, rest and renewal, contact with the sand, water, sun, wind, pure air and blue skies.

As the calming, soothing ambiance of a beach makes us more receptive, we tune into and assimilate more easily the subtle vibrations emanated by the sand, rocks, and water. Favoring contact with our personal and collective emotional unconscious, the beach inspires us to deeply reflect on our active and emotional life, on our values, choices, and deeds, on what we have dreamed of becoming and what we have become.

Since water is very easily magnetized, it is also imprinted with these memories, so that when we bathe in sea, lake, river, or other water, we simultaneously soak in an ocean of collective memories that affect us according to our resonance with them.

The positive or negative effect of a beach depends on its general aspect and the atmosphere and ambiance it engenders. Is it clean or polluted, large or small, private or public, isolated or exposed, empty, only a few people or overcrowded? What climate, flora, fauna do we find there? What sort of human activities take place there?

Hence, beaches marked by excessive tourist activities, denoting a search for vacations tainted by hyperactivity, futile leisure, and superficial renewal, indicate a lifestyle and conscience dominated by seduction, matter and physical action. Some beaches also bear the imprint of a lot of violence or other distortions. This is the case when they provided invaders, conquerors with a way into the country; also when they witnessed battles, slaughter, slave trading, weapon and drug dealing, debarkation of the boat people, etc. Such beaches inspire deep reflection on our collective or personal history, accordingly.

However, beaches that have kept their natural aspects intact, that are tranquil and clean, with pure, limpid water allowing us to observe aquatic flora and fauna, reveal that we seek on the inside whatever resonates with the beauty, peace and purity that we see on the outside.

In a symbolic analysis of a beach we visit concretely or in a dream, we need to remember that all of the elements found or observed there – objects, vegetation, animals, people, installations, amenities, etc. – represent facets of ourselves.

⊕ Oasis of renewal, relaxation, rest, contemplation, and meditation in contact with nature. Facilitates interiorization, introspection, self-questioning, taking a step back to better reflect on our life, our destiny. Favors work on our memories, inner cleansing, de-pollution of our life. Lightheartedness, *joie de vivre,* feelings of liberty, expansion, happiness, serenity and harmony. Helps us contact, connect with and encourage the manifestation, expression, and fulfillment our inner child. Discovery of the natural beauty and simplicity of our inner beaches that rejoice and gladden our soul, and open our heart and spirit. New departure, fresh start with an expanded conscience, wider horizons, more positive, better-balanced dynamics.

⊖ Superficial vacations and leisure, seeking idleness, luxury, futile amusement, *dolce far niente* (carefree idleness), and laziness. Flight from responsibilities, frustrations and dissatisfaction felt in our daily life. Attitudes and behavior that nourish a need to please, emphasis on appearances, games of seduction and power, passion, jealousy, envy, superficial friendships and love-relationships, licentiousness, as well as different forms of dependency (affective, emotional, sexual, alcohol, gambling, drugs, and others). Difficulty connecting with our inner child, being joyful, spontaneous, simple and natural whenever we find ourselves in a suitable environment for this. Incapacity to renew ourselves, to rest, re-harmonize with nature, rejoice in its beauty and purity. Difficulty adapting to a simple, healthy, natural pace of life. Incapacity to cleanse and transform negative memories that resonate with what a particular beach may represent for us on the personal or collective level: solitude, isolation, abandon, rejection, sadness, pessimism, escapism. Lack of an ecological conscience, thoughts and emotions that pollute and are destructive for the environment, fauna, flora, air, water, as well as for mankind, and hence for ourselves.

BEARD

A beard represents a state of conscience related to an assertion of masculinity and mastery of our instincts. It is a symbol of authority, wisdom, virility; it inspires respect, a sense of responsibility and hierarchy.

⊕ Assertion of the masculine polarity on the personal and social levels. Right expression of authority, wisdom, maturity, and virility. Respect. Right hierarchy. Mastery of instincts. Protective attitude and behavior.

⊖ Excessive or deficient assertion of masculinity. A lack of maturity, wisdom, virility. Neglected appearance. Giving in to our instincts. Disorderly mind or spirit. Disorganization on the personal and social levels. Confusion. Drop out. Irresponsible behavior. A wild, anti-social tendency, fleeing reality.

BEAUTY

Symbolically, beauty represents Divine Qualities and Virtues: the purity, harmony, order and justice of the spiritual world is reflected in the material world in the form of beauty. It is esthetics, the perception of beauty in nature and art. True beauty touches the senses, mind, spirit, and soul; it represents excellence. It is a source of inspiration and elevation, capable of arousing feelings such as joy, love, bliss, and serenity, and it engenders meditational, contemplative states. It reveals what is ideal and touches people's hearts.

⊕ An elevated state of conscience that nourishes the soul and inspires people to evolve, to improve spiritually. The manifestation of Divine Qualities and Virtues in the material world.

⊖ Superficial beauty that focuses on appearances, the outer façade, and is used to seduce and manipulate to obtain personal privileges. A person whose outer beauty tempts him to believe he is superior to others and can do as he pleases. Capricious, haughty, roguish behavior that engenders serious karmas. Inferiority and superiority complexes. Illusion, temptation, erroneous perception. A lack of understanding of true beauty.

BED

A bed is a symbol of personal intimacy, a place where we rest, where we interiorize, renew ourselves, and sleep. In a dream, a bed concerns the dreamer's personal intimacy or the couple's intimacy, as the case may be. In an in-depth interpretation of its symbolism, the general context of the dream, the people present in the bed, their attitudes and behavior, as well as the color of the sheets and the quality of comfort, of the atmosphere and the environment should be all taken into consideration.

⊕ A capacity to rest, relax, go within, renew ourselves, be at ease in our personal intimacy or in the couple's intimacy. A healthy, pure, well-balanced, happy life. A comfortable, clean, well-made bed indicates well-balanced, well-ordered, right, true intimacy. A natural, healthy, harmoniously colored, restful atmosphere. Favors states of reflection, meditation.

⊖ Difficulty resting, relaxing, going within, renewing ourselves. Intimacy problems. May be related to an unhealthy, impure, unbridled intimate life. Imbalance between our inner and our outer life. A disorderly, unclean bed indicates an intimacy where disorder and distorted behavior and emotions reign. A synthetic, superficial atmosphere. Use of a bed as a place for seduction and emotional power games or sexual abuse. Not reflecting on our life, not meditating. Stressful, imbalanced life. Too many people in a bed symbolizes a lack of intimacy and needs to fuse with others.

BEDROOM

A bedroom is related to personal or marital intimacy, renewal, replenishment, interiority and tranquility. It represents a place of discreet, intimate well-being that we do not show to everyone. Its aspect, decor, furnishings and fittings, tidiness or untidiness, as well as its ambiance, reveal how we live in our personal private life, and how we fuse our two polarities, masculine and feminine, on the level of our inner and/or outer couple.

⊕ Reflects harmonious, healthy, well-balanced personal or marital intimacy. A beautiful, bright, peaceful, restful ambiance. A period of interiorization, calm, renewal, replenishment, meditation, and well-being.

⊖ Difficulty sleeping, resting, renewing and replenishing ourselves, being comfortable and at ease when tranquilly alone, or with our spouse. Problems related to personal or marital intimacy. Heavy, disharmonious, cold decor and ambiance. Untidy, lacking warmth and affection, inner emptiness. No respect for the intimate, private space that a bedroom represents. A tendency to isolate ourselves there, and to sleep excessively in order to flee family and social life or, through laziness. Discrepancy between inner and outer life. A lack of comfort, or a person who over focuses on his personal comfort.

BEE (honeybee)

The symbol of the honeybee is related to the animal world as well as the air and earth elements, so it is related to instincts, thoughts and a capacity to materialize. The honeybee represents a great work force on the level of thought, social organization, and capacity to materialize collectively. It lives in a faultless economic dynamic, which structures each step toward production very precisely. In a dream, this social insect can symbolize totalitarian, extreme attitudes to work and materialization because worker bees are entirely devoted to the community and they all die on the job. During the course of their short life, they carry out various tasks including feeding the bee colony and its queen. The queen bee is the only fertile bee because worker bees are sterile and cannot lay eggs. The negative aspects related to bees are very surprising as they define a tyrannical society, revealing one of the worst social scenarios possible. The males exist only for potential reproduction, which will occur for only one of them, chosen by the queen. The chosen male dies during mating; all the other males die during the winter because the females forbid them access to the hive. Unproductive bees are also eliminated. This aspect of their social behavior allows us to understand the extremely materialistic dynamics a bee can represent in the context of a negative dream, even though it produces very nutritive food (honey).

⊕ An extraordinary potential for work, organization, productivity and accomplishment on the collective level. Materializing sweetness.

⊖ An extremist, radical, social attitude, which focuses only on work, results and matter. Difficulty organizing ourselves socially, being productive and materializing. A lack of organization, discipline, rigor, leadership and efficiency at work. Rigidity with ourselves and others.

BELLY *cf. **Stomach***

BENEFACTOR, PHILANTHROPIST

A benefactor is a philanthropist who looks beyond his personal needs and offers others help, support and protection. He acts with an altruistic state of conscience, which allows him to do beautiful deeds, to do good around him, to selflessly improve the lot of his fellowmen through many means. Altruism, benevolence, generosity and kindness are elevating qualities that beautify and nourish the soul and what is most beautiful and great within us. (*cf. also* **Voluntary work**)

⊕ Indicates that we receive, or are offered, help and support free of any self-interest. Favorable contacts for the realization of projects. A kind, generous person.

⊖ A person who helps out of self-interest; or someone who seeks the easy way, and wishes to receive help without having to make any effort. Needing acknowledgement and recognition for help offered. Granting support to useless or unjust causes. Poor use of providential resources. An overly materialistic conscience, lacking a sense of sacredness in our exchanges.

BICYCLE

A bicycle represents a means of transport and physical activity, which specifically uses vital energy to advance individually, or to keep fit, to do an outdoor activity, and hence renew and replenish ourselves and our energies. It favors the development of willpower, determination, and dynamism, and symbolizes the desire to go ahead and advance with personal projects and plans.

⊕ A capacity to make an effort, to strive to advance in life. Increased tenacity in order to reach our goals. Relaxation and renewal, maintaining physical fitness. Dynamism. Simplicity. Conscious progress. Seeking well-being. Consideration for the environment, environmental awareness. Evolution at our own pace, without competition. A desire to live in a well-balanced, healthy way.

⊖ Limitation in our capacity to advance individually; or, excessive willpower to go ahead, to advance. Laziness or hyperactivity. Competitive spirit. Difficulty making efforts to advance in life, or to enjoy life when we advance.

BILL

A bill is related to a balance between giving and receiving. It corresponds to a state of conscience of payment, settlement of what is due. A bill reveals the efforts invested and the price to pay to obtain, to materialize something. It is a transfer of energy to the other person, or organization, that will help them, their families, to continue to manifest themselves in matter and experiment life. Paying our bills is a gesture of respect, acknowledgement and gratitude, a gesture of altruism. In honoring our bills and debts, we acknowledge the importance of the continual circulation of the forms of energy represented by money (*cf. also* this term), various resources, and services rendered. In metaphysical terms, paying bills also indicates settling karmic debts. A symbolic analysis of the amounts inscribed on the bills may also be very revealing.

⊕ Honesty, fairness and respect in exchanges with others. A capacity to pay with a spirit of helping, participating in the growth of the other person. Awareness of the importance of balance between giving and receiving. Capacity for materializing harmoniously and fairly. Respecting commitments. A clear situation. Good management of resources. Settlement of karmic debts.

⊖ Problems giving, receiving and exchanging fairly. Difficulty materializing projects, managing resources. A deep feeling of insecurity when faced with bills to pay. Abuse of other people's trust. Selfish attitude, not wanting to pay our debts through meanness. Living above our means. Not knowing how to assert our rights, to claim what is due to us. A tendency to allow ourselves to be dominated or swindled. A rebellious spirit who believes himself to be above the law, who does not respect his commitments. Behavior that creates and adds up karmic debts. A lack of generosity. Imbalance in exchanges. Waste, useless expenditure. A tendency to take everything for granted. Lack of altruism, difficulty sharing, helping others.

BIRD

As birds belong to the animal kingdom, they represent aspects of our vital energy related to instincts. The fact that they have wings and can fly means they also belong to the world of air, which symbolizes the world of thoughts. For a detailed symbolic analysis, the type of bird, its characteristics and living environment need to be studied. We ask ourselves: is it a big, small, or medium-sized bird? Is it diurnal or nocturnal? Does it mainly live up high, on the ground, or in water? Is it a pet, a common and garden bird, a bird of prey, a vulture or carrion eater? Does it live in a flock, a couple, a family, or alone? Hence certain characteristics are brought to light. Then the way we perceive the particular bird(s), e.g. as attractive, fascinating, intimidating, or repulsive, etc., reveals facets of ourselves related to our way of thinking, which often concerns reflexes, agility, rapidity, power, perseverance, endurance, determination, vision, grace, joy, light-heartedness, etc., depending on the bird(s). Generally speaking, birds indicate instinctual thought dynamics, which are not based on the intelligence and capacity for discernment and reason that human-beings have at their disposal, but which are essentially the result of the innate functioning every species possesses and conveys through its primary vital energy, thereby ensuring its survival, its adaptation to its environment, and its natural evolution. Therefore, it is important to understand that symbolically, birds do not represent thoughts themselves, but rather instinctual forces that influence our capacity to think, as well as our way of thinking.

To understand the symbolic message or sign represented by a bird featured in a dream or that crosses our path and attracts our attention in concrete reality, we need to link it with what we were thinking about, saying, or doing either the moment it manifested, or also sometimes what we were going through during that period in general. For instance, if a bird collides against our vehicle as we are driving, or is hurt banging into a window of our house, the symbolism is negative. It indicates that whatever we are thinking about or doing at that precise moment may become the source of an accident and risk hurting or destroying part of our vital energy and potential that it allows us to materialize. On the other hand, if we notice a beautiful bird flying in the air, or singing joyfully, that is a sign that our thoughts are light-hearted, elevated and happy at that moment in time.

We should also link all of the elements of a situation or dream if we wish to obtain a detailed symbolic interpretation of the bird in question. An aquatic bird is more related to the emotional level, whereas birds that mostly move and live on the ground, such as hens, partridges, pheasants, peacocks, cranes etc., denote aspects related to the earth element and matter. A nocturnal bird is symbolically related to the night and darkness; e.g. an owl.

It is possible to refine our understanding of the positive or negative symbolism of a bird by analyzing its behavior. E.g. a very aggressive eagle swooping toward the ground to attack its prey would be a negative sign, revealing thoughts related to subjects concerning power, domination, conquest, and aggression; whereas seeing an eagle soar peacefully in a harmonious landscape, over the mountains, in a beautiful blue sky, would be positive, and could represent a person's mental power, his capacity to elevate his thoughts and attain global vision, allowing him to use his power and force with wisdom and discernment.

⊕ Allows us to become aware of certain aspects of our instinctual vital energy and the dynamics we use on the mental level to elevate ourselves (birds that fly); how our thoughts create and maintain our feelings and emotions (aquatic birds); and how we use our thoughts to act in matter (ground birds). Depending on the bird in question, revelation of characteristics we resonate with, or that we wish to develop, such as well-being and ease in our living environment, agility, vivacity, rapidity, grace, elegance, endurance, power, a feeling of vastness and freedom, global vision, elevation of conscience, etc. An ability to manifest beautiful thoughts on the concrete level.

⊖ Problems resulting from poor use of instinctual vital energy on the thought level. Attitudes and behavior manifesting unhealthy needs, and depending on the behavior of the bird, engendering states of fatigue, injuries, accidents, or illnesses on the thought level. Instinctual thoughts of fear, panic, fragility, vulnerability, dispersal, agitation, nervousness, inconstancy, aggression. A lack of stability, adaptability, endurance, resistance on the vital energy and mental levels. Scatterbrained. Incapacity to raise ourselves up. Heaviness, inertia, weak reflexes. May indicate a person who is too absorbed in matter, in too down-to-earth thoughts that prevent him from *spreading his wings*, raising his conscience, and acquiring a more detached, more global vision; or, on the contrary, may indicate a person with his head in the clouds, who mainly functions on the mental level, closed off from the emotional level, and lacking anchorage, not rooted in the physical world.

BIRTH, GIVING BIRTH

On the physical level, giving birth is the natural process by which a woman brings a child into the world. On the symbolic level, we can give birth to a project, work, situation, new stage in life.

If a pregnant woman dreams of the labor and birth, her dream shows her what she is experiencing on the inside, her inner feelings, regarding the pregnancy and the child's arrival; the dream can also be premonitory and indicate what will actually happen both for the mother and child.

In dreams, if we see a man giving birth to a child, it symbolizes a depolarization and indicates that the dreamer puts too much emphasis on material aspects when he creates projects. It is also related to a person who tends to be self-sufficient, who relies only on himself.

We can receive dreams wherein we see ourselves giving birth to an animal or object. In such cases, the birth represents a major distortion because it is unnatural for human beings to do this. If we give birth to a fish, for example, we need to consider the characteristics of this animal and link them with the situation we are going through in concrete reality. As an animal that can only live in water, a fish represents our instinctual needs, emotional dependency and incapacity to express ourselves, since a fish cannot speak. This could indicate that we are about to plunge into an emotionally dependent relationship that could even become obsessive (because a fish is an animal and animals are solely concentrated on their needs). In order for the birth to represent a positive element, it must concern a child, who symbolizes our power to procreate, our future self, our potential, or work that symbolizes our creative power.

⊕ A period of healthy, flourishing materializations, achievements. A new stage or project that will bring great happiness. Undergoing a major personality transformation. A new cycle of life that will engender new apprenticeships, new learning experiences. Important, beneficial changes on the personal level. May sometimes announce that the person will actually become pregnant in concrete reality.

For pregnant women: Seeing yourself give birth easily, without any problems in a dream, is an announcement that all will go well. A capacity to experience a happy, serene pregnancy as a state of grace, divine materialization; labor and birth will then be joyful and complication free. Awareness of the importance of the quality of a mother's thoughts and emotions, and of her capacity to communicate with the child's soul. Spiritual elevation through prayer, meditation, and consecration of the child to Heaven, to God, is beneficial for the mother and child on all levels of evolution.

⊖ Problems giving birth indicate difficulties achieving and materializing our projects, exteriorizing the potential we bear within us, starting off new projects, a new stage in life. Memories of failure and loss.

For pregnant women: Experiencing a difficult, complicated birth in a dream can indicate two things:

1) The presence of fears and anxieties regarding giving birth and visiting memories marked by lack of love, devotion, confidence in God and our life plan.

2) A premonitory announcement of a difficult birth in concrete reality, with severe complications that could lead to losing the baby.

In both cases, it is important to work on ourselves spiritually, to meditate and pray so as to transform the unconscious memories and negative forces that obstruct our capacity to give life harmoniously. It is essential to remain hopeful and maintain a state of receptivity and abandonment to Divine Grace and Will. Hence we can change our destiny, improve it, experience it positively. Should we have to go through a voluntary or involuntary abortion (*cf. also* **Miscarriage**) for health or other reasons, it is of the utmost importance to accept the ordeal without rebelling and to consider it in the light of the Law of resonance and from a karmic perspective. There's no need to worry about the baby's soul. It will come back in more appropriate circumstances, or be directed toward a different destiny if this child isn't part of the couple's present life plan.

BLACK

Black represents an absence of light, obscurity, darkness. An object is black whenever it absorbs all the light rays that manifest in the form of colors. (It is white when it reflects all of them.) Black is usually associated with the night, interiorization, rest, death, mourning, pessimism, negation, rebellion, chaos, the void, the nether world, evil, the Forces of Darkness.

However, black is not necessarily a negative symbol. Just like white, it has an important mystical meaning. On a spiritual path, black symbolizes the alchemical, invisible transformation that occurs within a person, as well as initiatic deaths that precede rebirth on a superior level of conscience. It veils the Knowledge and Truth of the Spirit that can only be revealed to great initiates: those who have taken and followed the Initiation path in quest of meaning, understanding, perfection, and evolution. After delving into the depths of their unconscious, where they faced the nether world and darkness of their own being, by working on themselves with great intensity and pure intention so as to transform and enlighten themselves, they end up achieving Enlightenment. Hence, black symbolizes the hidden Mysteries that are only revealed to those who are ready to receive them. It also represents the unknown, the invisible, the intangible, everything that has not yet manifested, materialized, or that is still misunderstood, elusive. This is why it is often the color chosen by people who have a great capacity for concentration, creation, materialization; by teenagers in search of identity; or to manifest soul-states governed by depression, indecision, anger, and rebellion.

The word *black* is to be found in several idiomatic expressions, illustrating some of these states of being: to be *in a black mood* (very angry, likely to become aggressive), *the black sheep of the family* (the thought-to-be difficult, troublesome, rebellious child), *a black mark* against your name (a misaction* that will be remembered and may spoil an otherwise good reputation), *a black day* (a day that will be remembered for a very bad, or sad event). Black is also associated with illegal, clandestine, undeclared activities such as *the black market* and *black economy.* However, it is also used positively in expressions such as to be *in the black* (not having any debts), or to have something *in black and white* (clearly and officially). (**cf.* this term)

⊕ Represents the hidden aspects of things, the mysteries of the Universe, the occult, creative Power, veiled Wisdom and Knowledge, discretion, the unconscious, the unknown, the invisible, which is in a latent, preparatory, immaterial, non-manifested state, waiting to be discovered, unveiled, recognized and acknowledged. Facilitates interiorization, introspection, meditation, development of inner vision, subtle perception, and contact with the parallel worlds.

⊖ Negativism, pessimism, fatalism. Profound ill-being, overwhelming sadness, despair, a feeling of inner emptiness, the dark night of the soul. An incapacity to understand the meaning of ordeals, limitations. Confusion, blurred vision, a feeling of being lost in the dark, floating in a void. An aimless person, who is incapable of grasping the meaning of his life, who considers existence absurd. Absence of Light, Knowledge, clarity, understanding. A lack of spiritual conscience, a dark spirit obscured and blinded by matter. Existential fear and anguish, gloomy thoughts, suicidal tendencies. Absence of reference points, a loss of direction, difficulty finding our bearings, advancing, manifesting. Someone who wears black clothes to hide his feelings, faults and weaknesses, his true identity, his clandestine activities, his erroneous, illegal misactions. Abusive, distorted use of occult powers. Dark, demonic forces that nourish destruction and devastation.

BLIND

The word *blind* generally designates an incapacity to see with our physical eyes. It may be present from birth, or occur after an accident, illness, or gradually develop in the course of a lifetime. On the metaphysical and symbolic levels, blindness corresponds to a state of conscience related to attitudes and behavior in this life or in past lives, where a person didn't make good use of his sight, his capacity to observe and see himself and others in an authentic way. It also reveals a tendency to withdraw from the outside world to mainly live in our head, i.e. on the mental level. To do so, a person cuts himself off from the emotional, affective level and refuses to observe deeply so as to see all aspects of existence. A person who loses his sight has no other choice but to learn to feel, to listen, to touch differently, in depth, with his heart. A handicap lived with a spiritual conscience can become an accelerator for the evolution of the soul, because it allows the person to develop previously lacking abilities and strengths, and hence rediscover new balance and equilibrium. Loss of sight usually affects old souls who have gradually damaged their visual potential throughout the course of several incarnations; or, who prevented others from seeing and having access to the light of knowledge and understanding.

⊕ Healing of memories marked by an incapacity to observe and see in depth. Opening of the heart and conscious activation of sensing, feeling, touching and listening. Interiorization, introspection, meditation. Development of clairvoyance, inner vision, and discovery of clairaudience and clairsentience. No longer influenced by the outer aspect of people and things.

⊖ An overly materialistic person, who is too focused on his vision of life. Superficial, critical, judgmental observation. Excessive logic, dry, withering analytical mind. Loss of discernment, lack of lucidity, mental opacity. Confused, obscure life. Incapacity to see and perceive in depth. Tendency to self-delusion. Obstinacy, stubbornness. Possessive, controlling behavior. Badly used intelligence. An old soul paying a karmic debt, who needs to learn to go within, to interiorize, as well as to face reality.

BLOND

The word *blond*, generally associated with hair, symbolically represents the solar aspect, the idea of radiance and light on the thought level. Hence, Angels are often presented with blond hair. The Roman gods were depicted with blond hair in order to express divine power. In our era, Hollywood culture and the image of blond actresses sometimes gives rise to a pejorative connotation of blondness, which then symbolizes superficiality, an easy, shallow life.

⊕ A blond-haired person, featured in a dream or encountered in a particular concrete situation, depicts a person's radiance, manifestation, creativity and accomplishment. It is associated with the sun, a symbol of enlightening, spiritual thoughts and divine materialization.

⊖ Negative blond hair reveals a search for artificial radiance. Superficiality, a need to please, a shallow life, worldly pleasures. Naivety, deficient intelligence; or, a superiority complex.

BLOOD

Blood, a red liquid that circulates in the organism, ensures several vital functions including the irrigation of tissues, to which it supplies nutrients and oxygen, and from which it collects waste. It vitalizes the body and allows it to function. Symbolically, blood represents vital energy and the world of vital emotions. Its color, red, is the color of the 1st chakra, which represents materialization, concrete action on the physical level. The pathways it uses to circulate (arteries, veins, capillaries) are comparable to the various pathways traffic uses (streets, roads, highways). (*cf. also* **Circulation**)

Blood links all of our cells together and behaves as a messenger/transporter when something happens to the body (hormones, platelets, immune defenses, etc.). It is made up of red and white blood cells, platelets, and plasma composed of 91.5% water, which allows blood to circulate in our blood vessels. Symbolically, harmonious blood flow indicates beautiful management of vital energy, thoughts and emotions; whereas, circulation problems, such as hemorrhages or blockages, reveal the fact that negative states of conscience engendered such difficulties.

Red blood cells ensure the transportation of oxygen to our cells and the evacuation of carbon dioxide. Oxygen is related to the air element, which symbolizes the world of thoughts. When thoughts are healthy, they favor good health, whereas unhealthy thoughts, like harmful gases, engender ill-being and illnesses.

White blood cells constitute the body's immune defense. Any illness related to this defense system indicates an accumulation of memories on the spiritual level (white) in the form of distorted thoughts, emotions, or behavior, which cause a loss of a person's white blood cells, i.e. his natural, innate capacity for protection. White blood cells are symbolically related to Divine Protection, which we all benefit from as long as we behave in accordance with Cosmic Law and Order, thereby ensuring the maintenance of harmony and balance on all levels.

As for platelets, they preserve the body by allowing hemostasis, whereby clotting stops hemorrhaging; clots block the flow of blood on the outside or inside of the body. They play a vital role in the maintenance of blood balance. On the symbolic level, platelets symbolize protection against loss of vital energy.

Whenever the level of platelets falls, hemorrhaging is frequent and dangerous; anyone who is subject to this has recorded memories of abuse and waste of energy, excessive willpower, and exaggeration; he didn't know how to protect his vital energy, which he dilapidated through carelessness. This manifests in all sorts of excess, from hyperactivity, emotional problems (anger, jealousy, passion, etc.), or inner tensions. The body signals a lack of active energy and in-depth understanding of life, of vital energy, thanks to which we can materialize on Earth.

⊕ An abundance of vital energy and force of action on all levels: physical, emotional, mental, and spiritual. Great vitality and force of life. Strong willpower and dynamism to take action. Healthy circulation of vital energy, stability, equilibrium. A capacity to materialize, create, and multiply life. Health and vitality. *Motor of life*, motivation. Protection. Foresight. Understanding the importance of vital energy and its function on the physical and metaphysical levels.

⊖ Difficulties on all levels regarding vital energy. Loss or waste of energy, overwork, hyperactivity, excess, exaggeration. A lack of willpower, motivation and strength to take action, to live. Someone who doesn't understand the importance of maintaining well-balanced vital energy. A lifestyle that causes a loss of vitality. Difficulty becoming involved, manifesting. Fear, deep insecurity. Someone who has his energy stolen or *vampirized*; or who steals or *vampirizes* other people's energy. Excess or lack of emissivity, too much or too little action. Blocked energy. Circulation of negative energies. May announce illness or someone's death, or the end of a situation. Carelessness, lack of foresight regarding the consequences of our acts. A lack of respect for life.

BLUE

Blue is the color of the throat chakra, whose main function is communication and verbal expression. This energy center represents intellectual expression, inner listening, inspiration and creativity, which are exteriorized through words, speech, eloquence, song, music, gestures, and the arts in general. For the precise symbolic meaning of blue in a given context, we need to take its particular shade into account (dark blue, light blue, turquoise, etc.), as well as its luminosity (shiny or dull, etc.), the object it characterizes (clothes, sheet, vehicle, pencil, flower, etc.), and the place where it is seen, etc.

The result of a mixture of blue (communication) and white (spirituality), light blue, sky blue, or cyan generally represents a communicative aspect related to the spiritual level, man's divine nature, his capacity to communicate spirituality, to diffuse it, to be able to travel through his conscience in the Heavenly spheres, the Superior Worlds, and the other dimensions of the Universe. Dark blue or midnight blue, which is almost black, symbolizes communication related to the mystical aspect of things, to matter, to the hidden aspect of knowledge, wisdom, the unknown. If this color is somber and dull, or appears in a negative atmosphere, it then represents communication in its negative aspects, i.e. incomprehensible, inexistent, complicated, difficult, aggressive, vulgar, etc. communication. It may also indicate the closure of a passageway toward the unconscious, or vice versa. Navy blue is close to midnight blue, although more radiant. Owing to its connection with the navy, maritime forces, and the sea, emotional communication in general, as well as communication related to instinctual, emotional forces are added to this symbolism. Furthermore, just like the sea, there are also the aspects of renewal, regeneration, and purification. Turquoise is a mixture of blue and green, hence this color combines communication, love, and the world of vegetation, as well as the throat and heart chakras. It refers to communication regarding Universal Love, and through its association with vegetation, to well-established, growing emotions and feelings, to tenderness, gentleness, affection, beauty, receptivity, devotion, compassion, mutual help, interest, friendship, to beautiful, true bonds that may be woven between people, between a person and himself, between ourselves and nature, between ourselves and the Divine, between ourselves and God.

Blue is also associated with boys, hence the masculine polarity, emissivity, and wisdom expressed in action that is just and good; while pink tends to be attributed to girls, to the feminine polarity, love, gentleness, softness, and receptivity.

⊕ A state of conscience allowing for easy, sincere, eloquent communication. Precision and clarity in the expression of our thoughts. Depending on the shade of blue, communication related to beautiful emotions, stable, serious feelings and sentiments, mastery of instinctual emotional forces, purification, renewal, spirituality, etc.

⊖ Numerous problems related to communication and the expression of our thoughts and emotions. Difficulty expressing ourselves; or, vulgar, coarse language. Negative words, verbal aggression. Eloquence and communication used for solely selfish purposes; a slick, wheedling attitude. Forms of communication expressing violence, destruction, negativity, ugliness, etc. A person who, under the influence of unconscious, distorted forces and memories, is blocked, closed on the communication level. Misleading, deceptive, manipulating spirit. Dull, somber blues relate to distorted aspects of communication regarding negative emotions and sentiments, subjection to over instinctual emotional forces, fear of the unconscious, of the unknown, of hidden things.

BOAT

A boat, and any vehicle capable of working on or in the water, represents our emotional, affective capacity, and the way we advance and behave on the emotional level. The craft's or vessel's condition, size, capacity, shape, means of advancing, mobility, what it is used for, etc. are all factors that need to be analyzed to determine the state of conscience, and level of emotional stability of those people who use it, either individually or collectively.

⊕ A capacity to advance and behave right on the emotional level. Stability, relaxation, renewal and replenishment of our emotional energy, a contemplative, well-balanced, harmonious spirit in affective, emotional relationships, protection and safety in the way we advance emotionally (marine forces, army, coastguards).

⊖ Problems regarding our way of advancing and behaving emotionally. Emotional, affective instability, tumultuous, overflowing emotions, inner capsizing and sinking. Memories of emotional accidents.

BODYWORK (vehicle)

The bodywork of a vehicle shelters and protects the inner parts of the vehicle, thereby symbolizing protection of the energy and mechanisms that allow people to advance on the personal and collective levels. It concerns relationships and the social levels because it is the visible part that we see on the outside and that is in contact with our entourage. Its shape, color and general state reveal our self-image and the image we project onto the outer world while moving around in society. Its condition – whether it is well looked after or neglected by its owner – shows the owner's interest in and care of his appearance, as well as how he moves from one place to another. We can compare its purpose to that of the skin for the physical body, and the aura for the spiritual body. Bodywork also ensures protection against bad weather: wind, rain, snow, cold; and, to a certain degree, physical aggressions. Hence it symbolizes a capacity to protect ourselves on several levels such as thoughts, emotions and actions when we advance in our social life.

⊕ Bodywork that is in good condition and well looked after indicates protective solidity and a beautiful way of manifesting and advancing. Protection against life's collisions and *bad weather,* selfish advancement, and conflictual situations. Reflects an authentic image of a person, the features of his personality, such as his way of advancing on the social level and his way of going to meet others. Transcendence of appearances.

⊖ Difficulty related to our way of advancing and conducting our life. Rusted, dented, damaged bodywork indicates negligence, a tendency to let things go, a lack of prudence and protection, a tendency to create clashes and *collisions,* bumps and shocks, accidents on the physical and metaphysical levels when we advance toward others. In the case of a person granting exaggerated attention to the appearance of the bodywork, this denotes a superficial personality that is obsessed with appearances as well as the need to attract attention, to impress his entourage and be acknowledged and recognized on the social advancement level.

BOHEMIAN

Bohemian represents a state of conscience which manifests itself through a lifestyle and behavior on the fringe of society where a person sets himself free from old patterns, from a lifestyle and environment that no longer suit him; or, because he refuses responsibility on all levels in the name of so-called freedom. A bohemian life represents a carefree state of voluntary poverty and flight from material and social responsibilities. A bohemian is an eternal adolescent who is entirely self-centered, who refuses to grow up and participate in society, in the collectivity. This life on the fringe generally goes hand in hand with a temperament that is rebellious against the outer world, and tends toward anarchy on the structural levels as well as within his inner self. Bohemian life is often idealized by people who are overly absorbed in material cares and responsibilities. Some of these people may feel like going from one extreme to the other, abandoning their active life and daily living from one day to the next. Such a lifestyle, which in itself is not ideal, may correspond to a transition period which allows a person to follow an inner quest, reflect on the meaning of life, on the direction he'd like to give his life, to prepare to be reborn to a new stage in his evolution that will be lived in a truer, more correct way, on both the personal and social levels.

⊕ A transition period in life where a person detaches and frees himself from old patterns, from a lifestyle and environment that no longer suits him. A period of reflection on the meaning of life, the values advocated by society, each person's role within the community. Frequent moves, a nomadic rhythm of life, experimentation of non-attachment on the material, personal, social or professional levels. Cleansing memories marked by excessive responsibilities and materiality. Preparation for a new stage, a new life program. Seeking freedom, a simple, modest life.

⊖ A period of no longer being responsible, as well as personal and social instability. A life of wandering which leads to great discrepancy between our inner life and our function in the outer world. A rebellious, uncommitted, unfaithful spirit. Refusal to recognize and respect social laws and society's moral values. Committing illegal acts that have serious consequences. Difficulty making decisions, setting goals, following right, well-balanced principles. Nourishing a false image of freedom.

BOMB *(cf. also* ***Explosion)***

The word *bomb* usually designates a projectile filled with explosives, and generally speaking, all explosive equipment or devices that a shock, an automatic trigger mechanism, or exposure to a source of intense heat, sets off and causes to explode. Symbolically, a bomb indicates an accumulation of memories, thoughts, and emotions that exert great pressure, and engender extremely destructive forces and tensions. It is usually a question of a reservoir of memories full of anger, rancor, bitterness, frustration, hatred, and violence buried deep in the unconscious. Such memories represent dangerous potential that may be activated by resonance as soon as appropriate circumstances occur, and are then expressed with explosive impulsivity and aggression.

It is very important to manage, and above all, to work in our inner world, in the metaphysical dimension of our being, and transform the forces of destruction and sabotage contained in our memories, thoughts, and emotions so as not to be subjected to serious consequences in our daily life.

⊕ A capacity to defuse and master explosive soul states. An ability to identify, isolate, and transform memories that make us act impulsively and aggressively, in anger. Willpower to transform the mental and emotional forces, as well as the destructive attitudes and behavior we bear within ourselves. Dissolving aggression and violence. A capacity to bear high tensions without exploding.

⊖ An impulsive, explosive character that indicates a great accumulation of aggressive, angry energy on the soul level as well as in the unconscious. Behavior that engenders fear, terror, danger. An incapacity to master or neutralize violent forces, over-emissive, rebellious, conflicting energies, within us, which risk causing considerable destruction and serious damage in our life and in the lives of those around us.

BONE

Bones, which are hard, solid elements that constitute man's skeleton and structure, symbolize the fundamental concepts on which we build our life, our relationships, and our materializations on the physical, emotional, mental, and spiritual levels. Even though they are solid, bones are naturally flexible, especially at the beginning of life, which reveals basic, fundamental flexibility, a capacity to trust, to let ourselves be guided, without wanting to control everything. Bones also protect our inner organs (e.g. the rib cage/lungs and heart; the skull/the brain), and they are the place of muscle fixation, which allows movement, and symbolizes the willpower to act, materialize, and create.

Bones also play an essential role in the formation of blood cells and the storage of minerals, which represent man's vital energy potential for creation, manufacture, and capacity to store fundamental resources to build his life. Given their composition, bones concern the mineral kingdom, which represents a very deep part of our unconscious, related to old memories recorded in either this life, or previous lives. Bones are white, the color of spirituality and Wisdom.

If we suffer from an illness related to our bone structure, we can find its source in symbolic language. Osteoporosis, for instance, denotes distortions in the person's structure, on the level of the foundations (concepts and values) on which he has built his lives, or distortions in his materializations, permeated by wrong, negative intentions, through which he has engendered an imbalance, firstly on the metaphysical level, which then eventually ends up expressed in his physical body in the form of decalcification of his bones, which become fragile and brittle, breaking very easily. This illness symbolizes the collapse of a person's structure on all levels.

⊕ A healthy, solid, inner structural frame and foundations in good condition. Flexibility, suppleness, an excellent capacity for adaptation and manifestation. An ability to store resources, to protect life. An understanding of the deep layers of our unconscious. Allows us to study the past, and old, former ways of functioning. May announce healing and renewal on the physical level.

⊖ Problems related to a person's structure, his solidity. Difficulty manifesting. Unstable, fragile, or old, destructured, unreliable foundations. Rigidity, stiffness, excessive harshness, crystallization, a lack of flexibility, suppleness, an incapacity to adapt. May announce the death of a person, project, the end of a structure, lifestyle, way of functioning.

BOOK

A book is a great symbol of knowledge. Ever since the existence of writing, human beings have sought to preserve their knowledge, discoveries, and experiences so as to be able to transmit them to the following generations as well as to have recourse to them as needs be. To write a book, man had to invent written language, and find the appropriate support and tools to be able to keep a long-lasting record of his writings. From his first steps in this field, he has gradually evolved through more and more sophisticated inventions: from the initial discovery of ink and papyrus, to the later invention of paper and various pens and pencils, followed by the invention of the typewriter, and more recently, the computer. The journey through all these evolutionary stages allows man today to diffuse and broadcast his knowledge on a global scale. Before the development of the Internet, books were the fastest, most direct source of access to knowledge and culture. To this day, they remain an essential source of information; a major, diversified learning and study support. In spite of the great usefulness of the Internet, the information found there is sometimes superficial and its sources unreliable, therefore, the researcher is obliged to carry out supplementary investigations from various printed works. For a correct, in-depth interpretation of the symbolism of a book (printed or electronic version), the following should be taken into consideration: the subject dealt with, accuracy of contents, quality of expression, presentation, size, shape, the colors used, as well as the energy and conscience emanated by the author(s) and the publishing company that publishes it.

⊕ An important source of knowledge and sharing of experiences, discoveries, cultural riches, and literary creativity. Preservation and transmission of original Knowledge and ancestral Wisdom. A tool for learning, studying, teaching, exploring new horizons, broadening the mind and conscience. Favors the development of intellectual and emotional capacities, the imagination, concentration, perseverance, patience, a taste for learning, knowledge, discovery, and evolution.

⊖ Diffusion of false, erroneous knowledge, information, beliefs or concepts, which hinder progress and evolution. Manipulation of readers by ill-intentioned authors. Bad inspiration, influence. Expression that is heavy, clumsy, imprecise, over-intellectual or over-technical; a style that is over-analytical and dry, sometimes obtuse, making it difficult to understand and integrate the subject matter. Using the writing and publication of books to feed the ego, express a haughty, arrogant, moralizing, critical attitude, or feeling of superiority. An author who doesn't practice what he transmits through his works. Old, fusty books may indicate a need to update the knowledge and concepts we have acquired. A difficulty or refusal to read books may reveal a person's tendency to think they already know everything; to doubt or mistrust what other people think and say; or, their non-desire to learn. Problems of intellectual concentration, understanding and assimilation.

BOOKSTORE

Through the different medias and the multitude of books found therein, a bookstore is a symbol of diffusion, broadcasting, access to information and knowledge, and of sharing real-life experiences, as well as literary creativity. It is a place we go to find knowledge, to learn, to be informed, to evolve. The symbolic meaning of a bookstore also relates to that of writing, publication, printing, reading, and business.

⊕ Access to a great abundance of knowledge and information. A place of discovery that encourages writing and reading, the diffusion and sharing of ideas, experience, research, imagination, and literary talent. Respect for different tastes, points of view, opinions, understanding, tendencies, and vision of things. Awakening discernment. Favors awareness and renewal on the level of ideas, knowledge, and discoveries. Inspires us to invest in knowledge in order to evolve on all levels. A bright, spacious, well-structured, well-organized bookstore that emanates a beautiful ambiance, offers a warm welcome, useful, competent advice, and favors open-mindedness.

⊖ A lack of interest in reading, knowledge, and literature. Difficulty sharing our experiences, and knowledge through writing, and diffusing our works. Lack of discernment in our choice of reading. Tendency to be interested in futile subjects, which nourish illusion, appearances, dependencies, superficiality and false knowledge. Refusal to invest in knowledge, to contribute consciously and responsibly toward information and evolution on the individual and collective levels through the quality of books on offer and bought. Only interested in profit and the quantity of sales. Diffusion of writings that propagate erroneous understandings, negative, unhealthy, destructive ideas and visions, which favor mis-information, distortions, and attachment to old structures. Unhappy writings. Sharing useless memories. Using intelligence to serve obscure powers. Over-consumption on the intellectual, mental level; a tendency to live too much in our head, and not apply the knowledge we have acquired to daily life. A badly organized bookstore, in a restricted, overcrowded space, which emanates a heavy, dark, cold, haughty, over-intellectual atmosphere and ambiance, without a warm welcome or competent service.

BORDER, FRONTIER

The term border or frontier has a military, protective origin. It is etymologically linked to the word *front* meaning a fortified, protected limit. A territorial frontier, now usually referred to as a border, is considered as a defined line marking the separation between two territories or countries with different jurisdictions. It represents protection and authorized passage between two States, each with its own mentality, culture, and way of functioning. On the symbolic level, it indicates the dividing line between two states of conscience as well as energic, metaphysical protection. Crossing a border in a dream, or in concrete reality, may scare us, present obstacles, or even be dangerous. Such difficulties are related to memories of limitation, oppression, imprisonment, or slavery that dwell in our unconscious. In order to free ourselves of such memories, we need to analyze what the two countries separated by their respective borders represent for us. If the border is crossed legally, if the passage is easy and favorable, then this indicates that the person is becoming, or has become, more and more universal in terms of conscience, that he is integrating, or has integrated, the qualities of both countries.

⊕ Symbol of justice, of a mind and conscience that are at ease, and protection against crime, abuse, ill will, malevolence, conflicts, and all sorts of danger. An aptitude for discovering and integrating the qualities of the countries connected by the border in question. Ease in exchanges with others, and in passing from one egregore (*cf.* this term), one state of collective conscience, to another. A capacity to travel and understand the mentalities and lifestyles of different peoples and nations. Inspires us to develop a universal spirit. A taste for adventure, a desire to go beyond the frontiers of the known to discover new countries, new cultures, and ways of thinking, different mindsets, new states of soul and conscience.

⊖ Problems related to justice, protection, respect for rules and regulations. May indicate that the person is subjected to restrictions. Presence of obstructing forces. A state of conscience that indicates excessive surveillance and control. Over protectionism. Fear of welcoming others, exchanging, discovering, exploring. Attitudes and behavior that block universality, altruism, openness of mind, spirit, soul, and conscience. Division. Separation. Limitation.

Isolationism. Fear of losing our liberty, of being arrested, halted, stopped. Infringement of rules and laws. Tendency to rebel against all forms of limitation; or, to flee, to go into exile. Totalitarian regime. Abuse of power. Sequestration.

BOSS *(C.E.O, managing director, manager, head of department, foreman, etc.)*

A boss has the role of authority, leader and director in the decision-making and organizational hierarchy of the workplace, as well as on the economic level, since he also has power over remuneration, and improvement and expansion of the company or organization. His role, his strategic position, his skills, intentions, vision and level of conscience are essential in the planning and materializing of objectives, aims and goals, in seeking solutions, in productivity and the well-being of his employees as they determine the success or failure of the company/organization on all levels. His close collaborators, as well as the dynamics and atmosphere at work, symbolically represent aspects of the boss.

Whether a company/organization's image and politics are positive or negative, the head of the company/organization always resonates with all of the elements that it comprises. That is why, when a company/organization has problems, the first person to be blamed is usually the president, the boss, or managing director, head of department, foreman, etc. as the case may be. When the boss is changed, the structure, workings, and even the very nature of the company/organization changes. A good boss who is able to work as a part of a team, and to listen to his co-workers, creates a healthy, harmonious, stable, well-balanced structure and work climate more easily and sustainably than an authoritarian, tyrannical, arrogant boss who is entirely focused on the task to be completed, the goal to be achieved, who doesn't respect his employees, nor acknowledge or recognize their competence, skills, values and contribution to the company/organization. A true, authentic boss knows how to surround himself with the right people, to bring out the best in them, to attribute positions, and delegate tasks in accordance with their potential, to sum up a situation, and ideally, to anticipate it, to protect his company/organization and see to the correct, right usage of resources and fair distribution of its benefits. He may also fulfill the role of trainer and educator for his employees while simultaneously motivating them and acting as a mentor, sometimes becoming like a parent figure to them.

This symbol of authority in the workplace may appear in our dreams to reveal to us the dynamic(s) engendered by our emissivity and receptivity at work or in our decision-making. It also reveals to us our behavior, our sense of responsibility, our capacity to manage, lead, motivate and be a good example for everyone. A boss should always be an inspiring role-model. Having difficulties with our inner and/or outer boss, indicates that we have negative resonance regarding the exercise of power and authority in general. A poor boss may be filled with insecurities, be afraid of failing, lack confidence, or display a complex of superiority or inferiority; he may abuse his power; or, have difficulties making decisions that benefit everyone. Open-mindedness, global vision, a high level of conscience, kindness, compassion, and altruism are some of the qualities needed to be a good boss, a good director, a good manager. The radiance such qualities confer quite naturally ensure loyalty, respect for rules, and acceptance of the rigor he may have to manifest in certain situations. For the majority of bosses on any level (president, managing director, head of department, foreman, etc.), the application of the Values and Principles of Divine Justice and Protection in their actions is still utopian because, due to a lack of spirituality, they give priority to matter and continually seek personal, selfish privileges that cloud and dilute their authority.

⊕ Capacity to apply right, fair authority. Sense of justice, responsibility and duty. Intelligence and global vision, visionary. Capacity to make decisions that favor equity on the economic level, to ensure that projects are right and protected, and respect the environment. Skill and justice in the management of conflicts. Important qualities of mediation, conciliation, arbitration. Attentive listening, receptivity. Ability to organize, administer, and communicate diplomatically, to elaborate inspiring initiatives and evolutive creations on the collective and individual levels. Open-mindedness regarding new ideas and situations. Great adaptability. Someone who gives priority to Values, Laws and Divine Principles, who understands that true power is not of a material, monetary nature. Understanding the temporal, educational role of matter. Love and respect for our neighbor. Caring about the welfare of the individual, the collectivity, and the planet. Educator, trainer. Capacity to delegate with discernment and fairness, as well as to trust.

⊖ A person who abuses the power and authority conferred to him by his position. Superiority complex. Arrogance. Vanity. Egocentricity. Unfair, incorrect, abusive, megalomaniac behavior. Seeking privileges, luxury, control, domination. A need to be admired, loved, to impress others, to exert power over them through fear, threats, seduction, corruption. Sexual harassment. A lack of openness, listening, receptivity; or a lack of emissivity, leadership, confidence, self-esteem. Feelings of impotency and inferiority. Incapacity to make decisions and assert ourselves. Disrespect for the law, for rules, regulations, and others. Tendency to force the materialization of projects through insecurity, fear of failure; or solely for profit. An extreme perfectionist, who overworks to the point of becoming dependent on work due to a need for acknowledgement; or, greed, avidity for power. A very materialistic conscience, with no opening regarding spiritual values. Meanness, spite, and indifference regarding working conditions; participating in the creation or maintenance of slave conditions on the subtle or concrete levels. Someone who only thinks of himself and the success of his company/organization, even forgetting his family and friends. Giving the go-ahead to projects that may be potentially dangerous or that don't respect the environment.

BOUTIQUE, *cf.* ***Store***

BRAKE

A system to slow down and inhibit the motion of moving parts of a machine or a moving vehicle. On the symbolic level, brakes represent an important security device; or, a state of conscience that brakes (slows down) advancing, through fear or desire. We can be slowed down and halted by a memory, thought, emotion, or exterior element. A brake also allows us to regulate the speed of inner movement. With a good inner capacity to brake, we are capable of mastering our impulses, and of correctly dosing our thoughts, emotions, and actions. Finally, brakes also include an aspect of adjustment: often the act of braking is a preventive reaction, an adjustment to something, either on the inside or on the outside.

⊕ Allows us to stop or slow down an impulse, to have self-control and self-command or mastery, and hence a capacity to respect synchronicity.

⊖ A person who slows down or halts, who *puts the brakes on* his evolution and experimentations through fears stemming from old, painful memories. An incapacity to correctly evaluate distances, stages, and the necessary appropriate speed to cover them. Excessive emissivity that makes us advance too fast in life. Danger of an accident, a collision with others.

BREAD

For thousands of years, bread has been a symbol of staple food on the physical level. It provides us mainly with slow carbohydrates, which are consumed gradually, thereby allowing a balanced, steady, stable distribution of energy in the body to nourish our active vital energy. It also represents an abundance of resources and development of fundamental knowledge of the process of self-nourishment since it requires transformation work; it is the product of a mixture and fusion of the 4 elements: various types of cereal (earth) with water (water), it has to be kneaded and left to rise (air), then it is baked in an oven at the correct temperature, so it is exposed to heat (fire).

⊕ Healthy, staple food allowing stable, balanced action. A symbol of abundance, of materialization of vital resources and of work to earn a living, to feed ourselves, as in the expression: *to put bread on the table.*

⊖ Problems related to basic food resources, to work and earning a living. Poverty, lack of abundance or a person who nourishes himself in an unhealthy, superficial way. Creates a weakening of our active, vital energy.

BREAK (1- to break; 2- pause, intermission)

1- The act of breaking is related to memories containing forces of separation, break ups, breakages, discord, conflicts and this is true even when the breakage is accidentally caused by a momentary distraction or excessive use of physical strength. It can also be the result of an intentional, willful gesture in a conflict. We never break anything by coincidence. A break on the outside always reflects a break on the inside.

2- The word *break* is also used to refer to a pause, interval, intermission between two sequences of a lecture, concert or meeting, between classes, etc.

⊕

1- A capacity to repair damage we have caused. Acknowledgement of our mistakes. Sincerity, honesty, humility. A capacity to break old structures, old patterns, vicious circles of dependencies and bad habits so as to start afresh, on new foundations.

2- Symbolically, a break means the capacity to pause and have a rest, time to interiorize before starting up or resuming an activity, to have an intermission in terms of conscience.

⊖

1- An obstacle to repairing. Damage caused by anger, aggression, impatience, revenge. Ignorance of our responsibility for the breakages we cause and refusal to repair the damage. Broken relations, separations, divisions. Poor use of strength, of power. A feeling of injustice, a lack of understanding of the Law of resonance in difficult karmic situations.

2- Memories that prevent us from taking breaks, from having a rest, triggered by memories of insecurities, ambition, a need to be acknowledged or loved. The other extreme may also be applicable; i.e. being overtired or lazy and only wanting to take breaks, no longer able to take up our activities once again, to become active.

BREAKDOWN

A breakdown is a malfunction in a mechanic, electric, hydraulic, or computer system evoking a complete, partial, definitive or temporary, sudden or gradual, halt of an action, activity or function. Its role is to announce an error, blockage or dysfunction in our inner mechanism, or to indicate the need to rectify certain behavior or attitudes in our outer action dynamics. For example, a car breaking down indicates that our manner of advancing in our personal, social or professional life, depending on the context in which the breakdown occurs, no longer works and must be changed. A computer breaking down indicates that our soul, our memories, our intelligence, and our capacity to communicate multi-dimensionally have been impaired; consequently we will find it difficult to connect with our inner computer, with our Divine potential, and the collection of conscious and unconscious memories we've inscribed during the course of our multiple lives, which represent the foundation of our capacity to act. Of course a detailed analysis of the malfunction will be based on the function and role of the defective part or system in concrete reality and its corresponding symbolism.

During the day following a dream about a breakdown, it is normal to feel tired, heavy, or lacking in any desire to manifest socially, or be physically active, because our soul-state and spirit will have been affected by the dynamics of the dream and what a breakdown implies: limitation, a flaw, a lack, an emotional or energy dysfunction, a loss of potential or certain capacities. Such a dream invites the dreamer to rectify the attitude that originally caused the breakdown so as to be able to move on to another stage in his evolution and avoid the materialization of this breakdown, in one form or another, in his concrete life.

⊕ Announces the presence of a difficulty, a limitation of our potential, or a problem on a certain level, as well as the need to repair, rectify and redress. Awareness of what isn't working, of erroneous attitudes and behavior that have led to the breakdown. Capacity to recognize our errors, to call ourselves into question, and seek the cause of the problem. Capacity for discernment, which allows us to discover the original cause of the breakdown. Intelligence to solve enigmas with serenity, patience and harmony. Interiorization and deep reflection on the mechanisms of our inner functioning, and our positive and negative resonance. Capacity to renew, reform, re-educate ourselves, and repair, while understanding that our principal objective is not the result, but the path toward it, which is formative and essential. Understanding and detachment when faced with negative situations, submission to the Divine Plan. A humble, calm, confident attitude, which allows us to find practical, wise, simple solutions.

⊖ Presence of blockages, dysfunctions, or discrepancies, which hinder our capacity to advance and manifest, thereby slowing down actions and projects in progress. A complicated person who dramatizes and panics when confronted with a problem that affects his manner of advancing, rendering him incapable of repairing with discernment. May also indicate a lack of knowledge, understanding, or motivation to change, evolve, or seek answers to the enigmas of life. A lack of understanding of the educational, evolutive role of breakdowns and problems in general. Difficulty activating our potential to fix and repair. A person who does not refer back to himself, who does not know the effect of resonance and karma. Impatience and resistance to understanding that breakdowns are the logical consequence of our own erroneous behavior, that the manifestation of evil in one form or another should incite us to rectify within ourselves whatever diverted us from good.

BREASTFEED

Human beings and certain animals can breastfeed. Breastfeeding represents an essential aspect of motherhood: it is considered to be an extension of pregnancy, and the continuity of the formation of body and mind on the physical and metaphysical levels. There are numerous advantages to breastfeeding, such as reinforcing the immune system, improving the baby's psychomotor development, decreasing the risk of allergies, etc. A breastfed baby does not need any other food for several months as breast milk is complete in itself. In symbiosis with its mother, the breastfed baby is simultaneously nourished by maternal love, an essential, vital element for life. The intimate bond established between mother and child during breastfeeding creates a wonderful relationship of love that is essential for the healthy, well-balanced development of the child. Furthermore, this experience helps the child incarnate and manifest altruistic values in their purest form. On the symbolic level, breastfeeding indicates that the person nourishes the emotional and spiritual dimensions of her being as well as her works and projects in progress, which represent her inner children. However, if a man sees himself breastfeeding in a dream, it will mean that he is depolarized, and has difficulties being a man due to having too much feminine energy; or, because of his excessive desire to take care of and to feed, to nourish others.

Beyond the physical nutritional qualities of breast milk, science has not yet fully recognized the metaphysical virtues of this divine liquid. As well as providing a baby with magnificent physical, magical nourishment, breastfeeding also transmits a whole set of multi-dimensional attributes. It symbolizes the gift of ourselves, an offering of love and pure spiritual feelings. We offer a new part of ourselves, a new project, our future its first food. Breastfeeding also means accompanying the other person and giving our best to favor their healthy, serene and happy growth.

⊕ A capacity to nourish our child, our future, and our projects with love, tenderness and devotion. Transmission of beneficial, necessary, spiritual and physical nutrients as well as moral support for the healthy development of a project or work. Unconditional love. Gift of ourselves. Kindness. Generosity. Altruism. Protection. Immunization. Ready to receive or offer the best of ourselves at a new stage in life. Elevation through devoted service. Sensitive to the purity and fragility of new life. A capacity for self-sacrifice to provide a child or an important project with its essential needs. Satiety on all levels. Revitalization. Feelings of security, peace and plenitude. Nobility of soul. Purity. Gentleness. Goodness. An opportunity to radiate spiritual values.

⊖ Difficulty or refusal to feed our child, our future, our projects. Nourishing the child with negative thoughts and emotions. Abandoning our projects, not providing the necessary resources for their achievement, or only in a very mediocre way. A selfish attitude that puts personal needs and desires first. Emotional deficiency. Possessiveness. Excessive mothering. Over-protection due to a deep sense of insecurity. Infantilization. Fear of losing or letting our child grow up. Believing ourselves to be indispensable. Creating dependency in the child and arousing fears of lack through games of manipulation. Abuse of power. Domination. Control. Feelings of attraction and repulsion.

BRICK

A brick is a symbol of solid, long-lasting construction. Generally speaking it allows us to build walls and to consolidate buildings. In terms of conscience, it represents the reinforcement and consolidation of the structures of our lives.

⊕ Construction, edification of life. Reinforcement of inner structures. A capacity to build on long-lasting foundations and to structure our projects solidly.

⊖ Difficulty or incapacity to build solid structures. A life based on rigidity, coldness and heaviness. A lack of lightness in the way we *construct* and edify ourselves.

BRONCHITIS

Bronchitis is a respiratory ailment resulting from an inflammation of the bronchial tubes. As the bronchial tubes ensure the transportation of air from the trachea and bronchi into the lungs, they are symbolically related to the world of thoughts. Given their position in the lungs, they are also close to the heart, the seat of our emotions. Since an inflammation is a part of the body that becomes reddened, swollen or hot, it is also related to the fire element, i.e. the spirit and vital energy that are negative or destructive. The onset of bronchitis indicates the presence of factors hindering a harmonious, well-balanced renewal of thoughts and emotions and vital energy. Bronchitis may be caused by a viral or bacterial infection, atmospheric pollution, or tobacco consumption, which plays an important role in the manifestation of this illness. However, inner causes correspond to these outer trigger elements: disturbing, negative memories, thoughts, emotions and vital energy which infect, inflame, pollute, obstruct and upset our balance and harmony. Accumulated over shorter or longer periods, they end up crystallizing on the physical level in the form of acute or chronic bronchitis, or other malfunctions or diseases of the respiratory system. This indicates that cleansing and correction of discrepancies on the mental, emotional, and vital energy levels are recommended since the body can no longer regenerate itself.

⊕ Allows us to become aware of the thoughts and emotions that need to be rectified and transcended, to understand that we must not ignore, repress, or maintain them. Reveals that it is important to learn to communicate well with ourselves and others, to keep a check on the quality of our thoughts, emotions, and vital energy, and to manage our moods, our soul-states well. Invites us to analyze our feelings so as to better manage our sensitivity.

⊖ Indicates an accumulation of negativity, a tendency to repress, or be overwhelmed, by emotions and thoughts that pollute our inner world, and hinder the renewal of our being. A lack of mental, emotional and vital energy mastery. Deep insecurity. Imprisoned in old concepts. Disharmony and discrepancy in both inner and outer communication, between what we think and feel and what we feel and express. A problem of hyper-sensitivity.

BROOM *cf. **Sweeping brush***

BROTHER

Given his proximity in our personal life, a brother – whether a biological brother, a half- or step-brother, a brother-in-law, or male person with whom we have a deep friendship – symbolizes an important part of us; he is a mirror of our masculine polarity, of our emissivity, and our concrete actions. He represents help, support, consolation, and the capacity to act at important moments. A brother is also the complement of our father, our protector, the person we can count on in the good and bad times of our life. When family bonds are right and constructive, they are sources of altruism, and very evolved, unconditional help. On the symbolic level, a brother indicates behavioral dynamics related to our memories of past lives. To better understand the symbolism related to the presence of a brother in a dream, we need to ask ourselves what he represents for us in terms of qualities and strengths, when he is shown in a positive context, and in terms of distortions, flaws and weaknesses, when shown in a negative context.

In various circumstances, when we wish to recognize, establish and/or encourage qualitative brotherliness – e.g. in the context of friendships, religious/spiritual communities, extended family relationships – terms such as brotherhood, soul-brother, etc., tend to be used. In official contexts, potential brother bonds are acknowledged by terms such as brother-in-law, half-or step-brother. Whenever these bonds grow into deep, true, brotherly relationships, then the people concerned usually prefer to use the term brother, thereby indicating the existence of a good, qualitative relationship that goes deeper than any official status.

⊕ A symbol of protection, helpfulness, support, availability, unconditional help, altruism, inspiration, sharing and exchange in both good and difficult moments in our life. May replace or represent the father, may be an advisor, a confidant.

⊖ Depending on the context, he may represent competition, comparison, jealousy, envy, selfishness, self-centeredness, or abuse of power. Family problems.

Half- or step-brother: Using the term half- or step-brother is never really positive because it denotes dynamics of repulsion, setting aside, relational and emotional problems regarding the family, an attitude of separation, a lack of brotherhood, fraternity, fusion, trust in the other person, and/or non-acceptance of the remarriage of a parent or loved one, difficulty renewing, starting our life afresh, and making deep, sincere friends. It indicates a tendency to exclude the other person due to very old, deep, unhealed affective wounds. It is a term that nourishes conflict, comparison, lack of love, acknowledgement, support and attention, and its use may create flagrant injustices. Whenever we love the other person deeply, even though biologically speaking he is only partially our brother, we don't use these terms because we always consider him as our soul-brother.

Use of the term brother to manifest or underline belonging to a gang or criminal organization: A person who is ready and willing to become an outlaw and eventually commit grave acts in order to be acknowledged and appreciated; or, whose need to belong and search for identity cause him to trust and fuse with the wrong people. False, dangerous friendships. Someone who is easily influenced and manipulated, who, seeking to flee and escape from his family problems, takes refuge in unhealthy relationships. Memories marked by a lack of love, and/or violence, presence, support, or extreme selfishness. Rebellion, disconnection, dropping out, aggression.

Use of the term brother to underline belonging to a minority group or marginalized population: A person who nourishes feelings of exclusion, inferiority, poverty, rebellion, revenge, bitterness, frustration, injustice, and anger. Need to strengthen ourselves when confronted with unaccepted or misunderstood difficulties. Lack of understanding and acceptance of the fact that we always reap what we have sown in this life or in a previous life or lives.

BROWN

Brown is associated with the element earth and it represents earthly action, materiality, the concrete level.

⊕ Correct, right materialization, accomplishment, action and attitude toward a project. A capacity to plan and construct on the material level. An understanding of the educational, temporal sense of matter.

⊖ Attention exaggeratedly focused on matter, and a lack of understanding of its educational, temporal nature. Flight from, difficulty with, or fear of concrete materialization.

BUCKET, PAIL

A bucket or pail is a cylindrical, flat-bottomed recipient with a foldable handle for transport. Sometimes it also has a lid, and it usually serves to contain, preserve, or transport liquid or solid substances. In everyday life, it is very frequently used in household tasks, such as when washing the floor, cleaning windows, etc.

Through its form, a bucket is related to the feminine principle and receptivity because it allows us to receive, welcome, and preserve a certain quantity of resources, provisions, and all sorts of matter, to be used as needs be. When used for washing and cleaning, a bucket is a symbol of purification; in the context of renovation work (such as a bucket of cement or paint), it symbolizes inner and outer construction; when used by children playing (e.g. on the beach, with water, in the garden, etc.), it is a symbol of apprenticeship, learning, and creativity. Given its multi-usage versatility, its symbolic meaning depends on its contents, the context in which it is used, the material it is made of, its color, size, where it is found, and its general state (clean, dirty, open, closed, full, empty, damaged, spilled, etc.). Its contents reveal a more accurate indication of what we are receptive to: if it contains water or another liquid, its symbolism concerns the emotional level; if it contains food, it is related to our capacity to receive resources, to receive nourishing energies that allow us to be active on the individual or collective level, as the case may be.

⊕ A good capacity to receive, contain, transport, and distribute resources. Abundance, generosity, sharing, altruism. Depending on the type of bucket: a capacity to cleanse, to work, to build, or do maintenance work in both our inner world as well as in our concrete life. A capacity to contain and master the emotional level (liquid contents), or the action level (solid resources). A capacity to play, to create, to shape and form and give free rein to our imagination (e.g. recreational games on the beach, in the garden).

⊖ Problems related to receptivity, the feminine principle, and a capacity to work, carry, help. Difficulty receiving, containing, preserving, transporting, or distributing available resources. Someone who wastes resources, makes poor use of them, or doesn't appreciate them. May also be related to heavy, burdensome memories that create muddle, confusion, quagmire or a feeling of being bogged down in matter

An oversized bucket may symbolize exaggerated needs, revealing considerable unfulfilled lacks regarding a capacity to cleanse or prepare resources.

An undersized bucket may indicate a limitation, a lack of receptivity regarding resources, resistance to receiving, or cleansing, maintaining, preparing, or making them available.

An empty bucket (in a negative atmosphere, ambiance, context) indicates an absence of resources, a feeling of inner emptiness, a lack of concrete motivation; or an incapacity to cleanse, to clean up our life.

A bucket whose liquid contents have been spilled is a sign of emotional overflow, a lack of vigilance, benevolence, loving kindness and consideration, regarding a capacity to cleanse or prepare resources on the collective level.

BUILDING, APARTMENT-, OFFICE-, *or other*

Buildings can have many floors and many different sections. In our dreams, they represent aspects of our inner space on the collective, social levels. They reflect the way we manifest, live, or work in society. They are also a symbolic representation of our capacity to expand and multiply on the material level.

⊕ Symbolize the way we structure activity on the social level (our outer world), or our relationship between our intimacy (our inner world) and the collective life when it is an apartment building. Represents social organization. A capacity to build, construct, edify great things. Feeling of expansion and achievement.

⊖ State of conscience that only seeks grandeur, prestige, expansion, and power on the material, social, and intimate levels. Problems related to the way we materialize, organize, and work with others. Ambition. Feeling invaded by other people's energy, a lack of privacy. Materialistic spirit. Excessively seeking power and materialization, without conscience. An unfavorable period for putting together great ideas or building projects. A megalomaniac attitude.

BULIMIA

Bulimia is an eating disorder related to man's animal, instinctive, unconscious nature. Like obesity, bulimia is characteristic of a person whose state of conscience is inhabited by a feeling of lack. Hence to fill his lacks, needs, material, emotional or intellectual insecurities, the person eats excessively and compulsively beyond all feelings of real hunger. The dysfunctional behavior of a person suffering from bulimia is dictated by memories of deep insecurity experienced in this life or inherited from other lives. In a more or less distant past, the person lacked resources and did not take sufficient care of himself, his intimacy, his vital energy. This is one of the reasons why his brain makes an association and thinks of food as a reward, comfort, or compensation for what he did not have, or why he considers food as an element of happiness or exaltation. By eating more, the person seeks security and self-protection, and tries to compensate for his memories of lack. Furthermore, he unconsciously seeks to stock up on reserves in case he should encounter a situation of lack or find himself incapable of satisfying his needs.

The memories of survival that dwell in a person suffering from bulimia provoke and accentuate the dysfunction of vital, instinctual forces. A person suffering from this disease has difficulty managing his needs; he oscillates between states of excessive control and states of completely letting himself go, which are typical of loss of self-control and mastery. Sometimes the person controls his needs in a disproportionate, excessively rigid way, and at other times, he lets his needs dictate his behavior. A bulimia sufferer ingurgitates more food, more energy than he needs or is capable of absorbing. This *force-feeding* usually occurs on the physical level, but it can also occur on the emotional, thought, or even spiritual level.

⊕ A person who becomes aware of the true causes of his bulimia problem and undertakes intense work on himself to heal himself of this disorder by cleansing and transforming memories of all sorts of excesses, lacks, and insecurities. End of a period focused on disordered, malfunctioning needs. New dynamics of balance regarding nourishment on all levels.

⊖ A person who is enslaved by his instinctual needs and memories of lack. The presence of deep insecurities stemming from his present life and other lives. Extreme behavior, which manifests alternately through excessive control or complete laxism. Difficulty nourishing ourselves in a healthy way on all levels. Lack of self-control and mastery. Inner imbalances and discrepancies. An unmastered animal, instinctual force. Excessive, compulsive, punitive behavior.

BURN-OUT *cf.* *Overwork*

BURN, TO

The verb to burn is associated with the fire* element (**cf. also* this term), which represents the spirit, creative fire and the vital energy that animates the body. The action of burning generally indicates transformation, changing one substance into another through the effects of fire. This transformation can be positive or negative, depending on the context. When negative, this symbol is used to show that our spirit maintains very destructive forces that are harmful for ourselves and others.

⊕ A symbol of transformation, alchemy, of a positive, recycling force. A capacity to *extinguish* or put a stop to a dangerous situation, energy, or ambiance. Sublimation, purification. The end of a cycle, a stage in our life. The spirit dies to old or false concepts so as to be reborn to new understanding, a new, larger, more global vision.

⊖ Symbolizes a destructive, extreme, puritanical force. A person who flares up, becomes easily inflamed, and whose negative, impulsive behavior *burns* others. Energy that creates friction and conflict. An uncontrollable temper. A spirit that *fans the flames* and aggravates a situation, seeking to hide the truth, or to make it disappear. Burn-out (*cf. also* **Overwork**), a person who has completely used up his inner resources.

BUS

A bus is a vehicle destined for communal, public transport. Symbolically it represents the way we advance toward and with others, a state of conscience related to the social, collective dimension.

School bus: Symbolizes collective advancing in our apprenticeship related to ourselves and others.

City bus: Symbolizes collective advancing in social life, in the world of actions and matter, related to ourselves and others.

Coach or tour bus: Represents a way of advancing collectively with the aim of visiting and discovering countries, cultural sites, historic places, etc. that we resonate with.

⊕ Represents the way we advance on the social and collective levels. A capacity to share and learn through exchanges with others. Appreciation and appraisal of ambiances; possibility of studying people's attitudes and behavior. Knowing how to approach people easily by manifesting in a right, harmonious, polite, well-mannered, warm and friendly manner. A beautiful social and environmental conscience. A capacity to visit other regions of ourselves in terms of conscience.

⊖ Difficulty, refusal, or incapacity to advance toward and with others. Poor conduct or badly behaved in society, an antisocial, unsociable, or extremely shy, conflicting, capricious, and complicated person. Egotistical, lacking humility, simplicity. Too many needs to advance collectively and socially.

BUTCHER (occupation)

A butcher's job represents the expression of an accumulation of memories related to aggressive forces. As this job is socially accepted, these forces appear to be positive, because they serve to help nourish the collectivity. However, even if this job is one of the oldest in the world, it brings us back to the most primary, brute energy that exists, that of killing for food. Symbolically it indicates that the person is not aware of the way he nourishes himself on all levels – physically, emotionally, intellectually, and spiritually; he is also related to sharp, coarse, brute forces and boorish instincts. Moreover, this job refers to a lack of global awareness on the environmental level. Most of the time, people who eat meat feel a certain apprehension and reticence about killing animals; the majority of them would not be capable of doing this job. To understand the influence that this job exerts on the metaphysical, energy levels, we need only imagine being in daily contact with death, with animal carcasses and limbs. Figuratively speaking, the term *butcher* refers to a cruel, bloodthirsty man. The more we evolve spiritually, the more we naturally tend toward vegetarianism so as not to nourish ourselves on the instinctual forces of the animal eaten (among other reasons).

⊕ An opening of conscience and understanding of the fact that an evolved person does not need to kill for nourishment, and that this archaic attitude is no longer necessary today in our modern, civilized, evolved world. Cleansing distorted memories related to the way we nourish ourselves.

⊖ A person who, without realizing (through ignorance, or under the particular influence of an ancient culture, or way of doing things, etc.), nourishes aggressive forces and shows cruelty when killing for food on the personal and collective levels. A person who lives according to old, ancient rules and customs, who finds it difficult to evolve healthily. Non-respect for life. Fierce traditionalist. Resistance to change. In extreme cases, may indicate a person who harbors very burdensome memories of violence, destructive forces, and insecurity, and who is ready to do anything to have food. A bloodthirsty, executioner spirit. Behavior that adds considerable karmic content to personal and collective karmas. A lack of conscience, wisdom, and love.

BUTTERFLY

As an insect, a butterfly belongs to the animal kingdom. Since it flies, it represents instinctual vital energy related to thoughts. Its growth and development cycle, from caterpillar to chrysalis to butterfly, symbolizes a potential for transformation, transmutation, metamorphosis, death, and rebirth. The short life of a butterfly, from a few days to a few weeks, indicates a capacity for rapid transformation and evolution. As a symbol, a butterfly represents the state of conscience of change, the powerful alchemy of metamorphosis. During the course of our evolution, we go through a great number of cycles comparable to those of a butterfly. Through the multiple situations and events life exposes us to, as much on the inside as on the outside, we can experience the stage of the fragile, vulnerable, clumsy, greedy caterpillar, still far, far from the ethereal beauty of the final product. Then, during our initiatic trials and ordeals, we find ourselves in the chrysalis stage, where great transformations take place on the subtle levels of our being. And finally, once our metamorphosis has been completed, we reveal ourselves in our true splendor, just like the butterfly.

Seeing a butterfly in a dream may indicate that the dreamer is going through a process of inner transformation; or, depending on the context, it may announce a change on the outer level.

It is also interesting to think about the figurative use of the word butterfly to describe a person who keeps changing, flitting from one activity or person to another, never staying long with any of them, never taking time to do anything in depth. Also, *to have butterflies in our stomach*: to feel very nervous or excited about something that we have to do, especially something important, and finding it very difficult, virtually impossible, to remain calm, stable, and serene.

⊕ Potential for change, transformation, metamorphosis from a dense, material, very down-to-earth state of conscience to a more subtle, lighter, airy state that is detached from matter. Rapid evolution. Lightheartedness. Awareness of the ephemeral fragility and beauty of the physical forms through which life manifests itself in the dimension of condensed matter. Understanding and respect for the evolutionary cycles of death and rebirth on all of the different levels.

⊖ Difficulty changing, transforming our thoughts and behavior, metamorphosing, evolving, dying on one level of conscience to be reborn on another. A tendency to flit from one activity or person to another, to live superficially or, to function mainly on the level of thoughts so as to flee the heaviness of dense matter. A lack of understanding of the importance of each evolutive stage. A tendency to reject, or wish to skip the caterpillar and chrysalis stages, i.e. the learning and transforming stages, as well as the initiatic trials and ordeals related to the process of materialization, in order to manifest directly in our final form. Fragility, vulnerability. Inconstancy.

C

CAMERA (video, TV or movie camera)

A TV or video camera is a tool used for creation, information and large-scale, even worldwide, diffusion. It is a powerful means of communication that combines image and sound, engendering atmospheres, ambiances, and transmitting emotions, values, life experiences. At the same time, it allows us to discover, to awaken our mind and conscience by showing us new ways of seeing, doing, living; or, of re-watching old recordings so as to remind ourselves of, to remember all sorts of memories. The positive and negative aspects of a TV or video camera are determined by the context and intention of their usage. It is also a symbol of receptivity because it allows us to perceive and record everyday life scenes, special events, or fictional scenarios. Like all recording apparatus, it is a tool that symbolically records our thoughts, emotions, and actions in forms of states of conscience in our memory. Viewing what has been recorded also allows us to get to know ourselves better by observing, studying and validating our personal and social attitudes. Moreover, using a TV or video camera helps us remember, review the past, recognize both right actions as well as errors we committed, and thus learn lessons from the past instead of remaining imprisoned in karmic cycles. In metaphysical terms, there is always an invisible camera within ourselves, recording our gestures, feelings, and thoughts on our soul. This is what constitutes our karmic and dharmic *luggage*. (*cf. also* **Photography** for personal camera and/or photographs)

⊕ Develops a sense of observation of ourselves and others. Facilitates the apprenticeship and study of attitudes, behavior, situations and events. Leads us to travel in our conscience. Capacity to memorize atmospheres, ambiances, moods, soul-states, to call on memories from which to deduce lessons and teachings. Diffusion of positive messages. Sharing recordings to educate, reflect on and inspire the creation of a new future. Right use of our potential for imagination and innovation on both the personal and collective levels. Deepening our powers of observation and analysis of situations thanks to different angles and points of view. A surveillance tool that records and serves as proof to reveal the truth. Encourages and favors opening onto the world, helps us study and get to know different cultures and traditions. A creator of atmosphere and ambiance; an educator of conscience.

⊖ A need to be acknowledged. Problems of observation, analysis, and discernment regarding atmospheres, ambiances, behavior, situations, and events; or, may indicate someone who is too curious, who, on the energy level, nourishes himself on other people's lives, who isn't in his place, or who lacks concentration on the present moment, on here and now. Reinforces egocentricity, someone who is over-focused on his own personality. A feeling of all-powerfulness, a megalomaniac attitude. Too concrete or too indiscreet vision that ignores the symbolic, multi-dimensional meaning that is to be found in everything. Difficulty traveling in our conscience, entering the metaphysical worlds, seeing and understanding in depth. Incapacity to memorize new data, new events, due to an unconscious that is overburdened with negative memories. Accumulation of useless information. Blockage in the diffusion of messages. Difficulty or resistance to learning from our experiences. An over rational intellect that doesn't allow the development of the imagination. A sleepy, limited, closed-minded spirit. Poor use of the camera giving rise to media manipulation, the diffusion of erroneous information, indiscretion, negative, destructive criticism, etc. Illusion of possessing someone because we possess his memories. A manipulative, possessive, jealous mind and spirit. Violation of a person's intimacy, or being *vampirized* because of a need for recognition and acknowledgement.

CANADA

Canada is a country and an egregore (*cf.* this term) that represents a state of conscience associated with the idea of vastness, freedom, purity, beauty, the grandeur of nature and great open spaces, which favor an opening of heart and spirit, fusion with the elements and the environment, and the rediscovery of what is essential. This *New World* country, which is comparatively young in terms of social development, is also characterized by a great capacity for welcome and expansion on all levels. As its collective memory is less burdened with historic events and heavy karmas – unlike many European countries – it inspires the exploration of new states of conscience, which are less saddled with old concepts and ancient traditions. Generally speaking, the people who live on the North-American continent are noted to be less complicated than the inhabitants of continents with an older history; they also communicate and express their emotions and feelings more easily. This country, whose motto is *from one ocean to another,* tolerantly encompasses the vast array of different cultures that co-exist on its immense territory. Given its original First Nations' name *kanata,* which means *village,* Canada is also a symbol of hospitality without borders, simple, modest, humble hospitality that welcomes others like brothers or sisters, like members of our planetary family.

Canada is also a symbol of prosperity and wealth of natural resources, justice, peace, social equality, religious and spiritual respect and liberty. It is one of the best countries in the world to live in. Its great open spaces, innumerable lakes and rivers, as well as the diversity of its fauna and flora, reveal and reflect great emotional and instinctual power. Several animals symbolize this country, such as: the loon, the beaver, the moose, the caribou (wild reindeer), the bison (buffalo), and the bear. These reveal great vital energy and power on the level of instinctual needs. Canadians are reputed to be courageous, persevering, uncomplaining workers. They are ingenious, creative, communicative, peaceful, well balanced, and very adaptable. The one-leafed Canadian flag is red with a white square in the center featuring a red maple leaf. Red indicates great willpower and materialization energy. White calls to mind the spiritual aspect and open-mindedness, and the red maple leaf symbolizes the importance of the natural and emotional resources of this country on the material, concrete level. A tree is a great symbol of divine materialization, and moreover, the fact that it is a maple tree, which provides us with its world famous maple syrup, illustrates the sweet, gentle generosity and warm-heartedness of the inhabitants of this country.

⊕ Loving energy. Humanism. Warm welcome. Soul-states related to the great open spaces, freedom, exploration of the unknown, discovery of the potential that we bear within us, as well as intense contact with nature and solitude, experienced as an encounter between ourselves and the environment. A lifestyle in harmony with nature. Great personal and collective potential. Great vital energy. Important emotional and instinctual power. A considerable capacity for work. Adaptability. Flexibility. Tolerance. Conciliatory spirit. Open to others and the world. Ability to renew ourselves. Prosperity. Generosity. A place of divine grace where it is possible to start afresh as well as being a good country to live in.

⊖ A feeling of inferiority regarding other countries, especially the United States. Immense leadership potential on the individual and collective levels that is blocked by a lack of self-confidence and difficulty asserting ourselves. Absence of refinement on the personal and collective levels. Boorish, coarse behavior. Lack or excess of confidence. Excessive materialism. Needing renown and expansion. Abuse, waste and poor management of resources. Refusal to share. Insufficient or over-abundant structure. Poor use of space. Stubborn, headstrong attitude regarding ideas and ideals and taking a stance. Difficulty getting respect and finding our identity. A tendency to be imposed upon, impressed. Need to please. Separatist, individualistic spirit. Extreme conservatism.

CANCER

Illnesses that come under the heading of cancer are characterized by an incessant proliferation of anarchic, uncontrolled cells that form a tumor, which begins by developing in one organ, from which it then grafts onto other organs *via* the lymph or blood system. These secondary tumors, which reproduce the structure of the original tumor, are called metastases. The particularity of this more or less widespread illness is the multiplication of rebellious cells that seem to wish to oppose natural, harmonious growth. By invading different regions of the body, cancerous cells colonize and kill healthy cells, and this gradually upsets and disrupts organ function.

Symbolically, this illness reveals an accumulation of memories and energies related to dysfunctional behavior regarding the way we nourish ourselves on all levels; an accumulation of frustration, resignation, things left unsaid, repressed anger, rage, retained rebellion and revolt. It mainly manifests in people who do not express their discontent, who generally find it difficult to share their feelings. The number of people affected is indeed considerable as our modern civilization greatly contributes to engendering multiple discrepancies through a more and more artificial lifestyle and the daily glorification of materialistic values. However, we are living at a time when great openings of the unconscious are occurring, which means that, on both the individual and collective levels, we are facing the awakening and activation of a multitude of negative, hitherto repressed, dormant forces and memories. Due to a lack of appropriate knowledge and global understanding, most people are subjected to the influence of these energies in their subtle bodies without realizing how they affect them. For example, the simple fact of choosing food on the concrete level that has no nutritional value, or that is harmful for our health, is a rebellious act that nourishes and favors the development of anarchic cells, and simultaneously reflects how the person chooses his energy nutrition on the subtle levels. Moreover, on the conscious level, the effort and aspiration of many people to become exemplary citizens in accordance with socially recognized values, incites them to keep quiet and not manifest their inner feelings. All these negative energies, retained within, accumulate on the metaphysical level of their being, then gradually condense, and end up materializing in the physical body, where they sow disharmony, disorder, chaos, and anarchy on the level of cell growth, gradually causing the dysfunction of different systems of the body.

A symbolic analysis of a diagnosed cancer must take into consideration not only the region of the body and the organ affected, but also the patient's general living conditions, his family, professional, social, and cultural context, as well as his emotional, mental and spiritual world, his level of conscience, his soul states, his open-mindedness regarding the causal level, the power of self-healing, his desire and willpower to take himself in hand regarding his way of nourishing himself on all levels, and working on himself to participate in his recovery.

It is important to know that dreaming of an illness indicates that certain parts of the dreamer function according to dynamics that favor the development of this illness on the metaphysical level, and that if the person doesn't change the attitudes and behavior that maintain such dynamics, then sooner or later the illness will appear in his physical body.

⊕ Healing in process and/or awareness of the affected person that he harbors a lot of old, former memories of repressed emotions, anger, and rebellion. Acceptance of his state, of the deep spiritual journey undertaken (or to be undertaken) *via* this experience. Calling our life into question, a period of interiorization. Serving as a model and example of wisdom for others, sharing our life experience to help teach others not to reproduce the same patterns. Learning to express our emotions and feelings without repression. Transcendence of anger, frustration, aggression, and behavior that is contrary to our health on all levels.

⊖ Difficulties related to an accumulation of negative memories, and unexpressed multiple tensions, repression, things left unsaid, dissatisfaction, and anger. A lack of understanding of the meaning of illness, of the fact that evil is educational. Role of victim, wanting others to feel sorry for us, letting go, giving up. Pessimism. Discouragement. Pride. A lack of spirituality, depth, and involvement in the healing process. Someone who nourishes himself badly on all levels, who continues to accumulate anger and aggression, and to nourish rebellion on the inside. Dreaming of cancer (without a concrete diagnosis) may indicate that, on a certain level, the dreamer maintains functioning dynamics that are favorable to the creation of this illness; or, it may announce that the illness is on the point of materializing in his physical body.

CANDY (or sweets)

Contrary to what we may believe, candy/sweets are not necessarily unhealthy, because all sorts of candy, made of natural sugar and other natural ingredients, without artificial coloring or flavors, exist. Wisely consumed in moderation, quality candy represents a beautiful symbol of reward, festivity, and sweet kindness for both children and adults. However, chemical, poor quality candy, and excessive consumption of sweets symbolize needs, lacks, and deficiencies of sweetness, kindness and affection.

⊕ Qualitative reward used with wisdom and moderation. Capacity to offer sweet kindness and consolation at the right moment, in an appropriate way.

⊖ Excessive consumption of candy to compensate for affective lacks; or, a person who doesn't grant himself enough sweetness or gentleness. Illusory search for sweet kindness and reward, nourishing affective dependencies. Poor physical and emotional nutrition. Affective manipulation, tendency to want to *buy* love for ourselves, and to bribe children to obey with candy; or, not keeping an eye on the quantity and quality of candy and sweets our children, or ourselves, eat. Lack of wisdom toward children, young and old. Lack of understanding of the importance of taking care of our health and adopting a responsible attitude regarding others' health on all levels.

CAR *cf.* ***Automobile***

CARNIVORE

A carnivore represents part of a person that nourishes itself on animal energy, i.e. primary instincts and needs. Animal energy, both positive and negative, is linked to the first two chakras. It is a very dense action energy that provides great force on the physical level, but which simultaneously nourishes aggression and feelings of dominance and power. When an animal attacks another for food, it experiences an extremely violent energy when it eats the other animal. A carnivore lives according to the law of the jungle: every man for himself and survival of the fittest, where might is right. It is important to become aware, to become fully conscious of the fact that consuming meat automatically involves aggression toward another living creature.

To dream of a carnivorous animal in the throes of killing and eating flesh, indicates that the dreamer's way of nourishing himself is tinged with aggression and an intense thirst to appease his instincts or the primary needs of his inner animals.

⊕ Transcendence of aggressive instincts. Understanding the law of nature and of animals. Understanding that the use of violence to feed ourselves, or eating animals killed by others, nourishes violence. Developing awareness of the way we nourish ourselves on all levels. Developing the will to transcend our animal nature so as to be able to recognize our Divine nature. Integration of the fact that not only do we become what we think, but we also become what we eat.

⊖ A person who nourishes his conscious and unconscious forces of aggression, abuse of power and domination. Very emissive behavior motivated by the will to satisfy instinctive, primitive needs, and a desire to rival and dominate. A lack of knowledge of how to eat healthily on all levels. Primitive, rudimentary conscience.

CASTLE

A castle represents a state of conscience where power, authority and wealth are concentrated in the hands of one or a few people. In the history of mankind, a castle is particularly associated with abuse of power, waste of resources, self-centeredness, megalomania, multiple intrigues and conflict often leading to war, hypocrisy and a superficial lifestyle focused on worldly pleasures, appearances, seduction and all sorts of excesses. In spite of the predominance of these negative aspects, a castle may also symbolize material abundance devoted to the service of others. Furthermore, through its architecturally solid structure, it may also symbolize protection on the collective level, in the event of conflicts or threats from the outside. Used as a public building or museum, it represents a positive, renewed (recycled) energy, which serves educational purposes.

When a castle features in a dream, symbolically it indicates a part of the dreamer that is marked by memories of power, authority, wealth and protection. Independently of its positive or negative aspect, it always reveals attitudes, behavior, and states of soul and mind, in a context of earthly power and riches. It highlights the dreamer's deep intentions and shows him how he behaved when he had a lot of power and important resources.

⊕ Transformation and transcendence of old memories related to badly used power, wealth and authority. Rectification of erroneous attitudes and behavior, and fair, equitable use of resources. Awareness of a sense of social responsibility and of Divine Justice. Modesty, humility. Kindness, generosity. Great protective force. Honesty in exchanges with others. Understanding the fact that altruism and abundance are universal principles and states of conscience that are accessible to everyone, not only a small number of privileged people. Access to Knowledge allowing us to materialize abundance and prosperity on the earthly level, and to use them for the good of the collectivity and the evolution of mankind.

⊖ Selfishness, self-centeredness. Megalomania. Abuse of power. Conquering spirit. Will to control, dominate and exploit others to feed personal, selfish, materialistic desires and ambition. A feeling of superiority. Arrogance. Pride. Vanity. Wasting resources. Indifference to the fate and vital needs of others. Ignorance of the Law of karma and the fact that Divine Justice is absolute.

CAT

Like all animals, a cat represents certain aspects of our vital energy and instinctual needs. Cats are animals that are very independent, reserved, territorial, silent, supple, agile, and gifted with an extraordinary sense of balance. They are clever, patient predators that usually hunt at night and sleep during the day. Although generally very gentle, affectionate, and playful, they tend to be solitary, and can be capricious and sneaky, devious, or cunning. They are very receptive to subtle energies and, to a certain degree, they are able to transform the negative emotions emanated by people (sadness, sorrow, illness), by plants, stones, or places (telluric knots, electromagnetic fields, etc.). They are very sensitive to touch, noise, and strong vibrations. Their hearing is particularly sensitive to high frequencies. Cats perceive ultrasounds up to 50 000 Hz while the human ear is limited to 20 000 Hz. Their sight is also highly developed and they have a larger field of vision than humans. Their acute perception of high frequencies leads them to choose low frequency places when they need to rest or sleep. Hence, by going toward their complementary opposite, they achieve balance;

this is why they are capable of transforming certain negative energy. Due to their receptivity, sensitivity, subtle perception, gentleness, and grace, cats are often associated with the feminine polarity, with the moon aspects. Generally speaking, a cat is a symbol of the capacity to transform the negative while remaining gentle, calm, well-focused and well-balanced.

It is interesting to note that whenever a person has difficulties with independence, while maintaining the powerful intensity of a cat toward his need(s), consciously or unconsciously, he may swing toward behavioral and relational dynamics of extreme dependency.

⊕ Right independence, autonomy, and individualism. Capacity to transform the negative. Flexibility, grace, balance, patience. A highly developed sense of sight, hearing, touch and subtle perception. Calm, restful, relaxing energy that is conducive to interiorization, going within. Correct balance between action and rest. A capacity to play and have fun without being excessive. Gentle and affectionate.

⊖ Excessive independence and individualism, keeping others at a distance; or, extreme dependencies. A tendency to nourish our basic instincts; to act in the grip of our instinctual, unpredictable, devious, hypocritical impulses and needs. A lack of listening, receptivity. Obstinacy. Surprising aggressiveness and impulsivity. Untamed, feral energy that catches and then repulses, seeks to control and possess, likes to play at being a predator, has fun with, teases, and plays with its prey. Negative, demonic energy, associated with witchery, black magic, and superstition.

CAVE, CAVERN, GROTTO

Symbolically a cave represents unconscious memories related to our intimacy and our actions. The contents of these memories take us back to our prehistory, to the beginning of our experimentations in matter. We can draw an analogy with the womb, which brings us back to the essence and offers us the possibility of a new life with a new program. What happens in the cave is very important: it may refer to a fresh start; or, it may reveal a problem related to very old memories that have to be transformed if we want to continue evolving in the situation presented. Visiting a cave can also indicate the beginning of inner awakening if the spiritual symbols therein are positive. As a cave relates to the mineral kingdom, the earth element, it can also indicate a new birth on the action level, signaling to the visitor that a new way of life has been set off in his deepest being.

⊕ Visiting very deep unconscious memories related to action and intimacy; awareness of which memory is important, which memory we must work on. The beginning of a new evolution program. Meditation and reflection on the origin, on ancient memories. A positive feeling of solitude, of protective refuge. Facility to go down into our depths to detect the cause of our difficulties, problems, sufferings, and ill-being. Discovery of hidden potential.

⊖ Memories of difficulties and of very old behavior concerning action and intimacy. Regression. Isolation. Attachment to old memories. Discrepancy between the modern world and old life styles. Fear of visiting the depths of our unconscious and entering initiation. An oafish, rough, instinctual, rudimentary temperament.

CAVITY, DENTAL *cf. Tooth decay*

CEILING

The ceiling is the highest structure of a room. Hence it represents the thought level related to the room it is in. Since a kitchen is related to the preparation of resources and a capacity for transformation, a kitchen ceiling is related to the way we prepare our projects, our life, etc., on the mental, intellectual level.

As a ceiling is generally a solid, reliable structure that we can build upon, and under which we feel protected and safe, it also has a protective role, and may serve as the foundation support for other floors in a house or apartment building. Consequently, it symbolizes a capacity to superimpose different ways of thinking and being depending on which floor is concerned, and the perspective or point of view it allows.

Whenever the state of a ceiling is problematic, it denotes the presence of structural problems on the thought level. It may also indicate emotional outbursts or overflow, for example, if there are leaks at ceiling level; a collapsed ceiling represents de-structuring of ideas, or a major structural problem on this level.

⊕ Reliable, stable structure on the thought, idea, and concept level. Solidity. Protection, shelter, refuge. Intellectual elevation. A capacity to have a more global, more causal point of view, thanks to a good capacity for discernment.

⊖ A ceiling in bad condition indicates difficulties on the thought, idea, and concept level. A lack of structure, discernment, global, causal vision. A period of de-structuring, indicating a need for adjustment on the mental, conceptual level. A haughty, or fleeing attitude, autistic tendencies. Unhealthy, unjust thoughts that are not right, or overly curious, over-emotional thoughts. An absence of objectivity, thoughts that are either too down-to-earth or too flighty, not rooted in concrete reality. An incapacity to feel sheltered, protected; deep insecurity on the conceptual, structural level.

CELLAR *cf. Basement*

CEMETERY

A cemetery, a burial ground, symbolizes an inner space where dead parts that have become memories of past experimentations repose. Hence it concerns continual transformation, the cycle of death and rebirth that evolution entails. Whenever we consciously walk a spiritual path, we learn to recognize aspects of ourselves – attitudes, behavior, ways of thinking, feelings, doing – that have to die because a cycle of evolution has come to an end; or, because we have understood that they are distorted. We learn to accept their death and to accompany them in the process, knowing that their demise will allow us to manifest in a more correct, right, authentic, just, good way. The deceased represent parts of our history, our journey on the path of evolution. And as a cemetery also has a public dimension, it contains both individual as well as collective memories.

In an ordinary conscience, we may tend to remain attached to the deceased person and manifest an inability to let him go. Such an attitude is due to not knowing that the person continues to exist as a soul and spirit, that he has only left his physical body that served as his vehicle in this one life among many others. It is also identification of life with form, of people with their body, that incites such a large number of people to reserve and pay for a cemetery plot for themselves and their family, sometimes for generations to come. As limited, erroneous understanding of life and death is replaced by correct, broader spiritual knowledge, conscience and awareness, the habit of burying the dead will disappear. Cremation will then be the most appropriate option, more in line with the new understanding of the cycles of life and the evolution of the soul and spirit. Instead of remaining attached to an inanimate body, we will let the deceased's soul pursue its path, and, through a sacred act of dispersing his ashes in nature, we will symbolically participate in his liberation from the earthly, terrestrial level. A cemetery is also a place where a sacred atmosphere reigns that favors contemplation, interiorization, reflection on the meaning of life and death, and communion with the Divine.

⊕ Visiting old memories, revelations regarding former behavior. A period of contemplation, interiorization, and acceptance. Announces the study of our past. Reflection and meditation on our memories and the phases and stages of life. Development of a sense of sacredness, respect for personal and collective experiences and memories. Preparation for a new stage in life. Understanding reincarnation, rebirth, and karma. Developing awareness, emotional liberation. Conclusion of a phase or stage of life.

⊖ Resistance to change. Fear of death. Difficulty moving on to another stage. Incapacity to let outdated concepts and behavioral patterns die, hanging on to the past, to old memories. Fear of karma, memories, past actions and deeds. Burying our positive potential; depression and suicidal tendencies. Emergence of destructive forces. Negative change. Difficulty accepting the process of transformation that is inherent to life. Non-respect for the past and the sacred. Lack of faith, of spirituality. Believing ourselves to be above everything. Superstition. Grief. Unconscious death. Fear of losing the other. Not believing in a Superior Power.

C.E.O *cf. Boss*

CHAIR

A chair represents a state of conscience related to receptivity, listening, and rest. When the body finds itself in a seated position, we re-assemble and re-center our energies, which naturally intensifies receptivity; we listen more easily to what dwells within us, to what surrounds us, and to what others share with us.

An office chair: receptivity related to work;

A rocking chair: receptivity related to relaxation, comfort and consolation, going within, contemplation, renewal and replenishment of our energies, memories of the past;

A child's chair: listening and receptivity regarding our inner child;

A wheelchair: represents a necessary healing period related to our way of advancing; or, temporary or permanent assistance and support, stemming from memories related to problems created by a lack of receptivity and listening, and excessive, destructive willpower in our way of advancing.

⊕ A state that is favorable to receptivity, rest, sharing, listening to ourselves, and others.

⊖ Problems of receptivity and listening to ourselves, and others. Laziness, disconnection, a lack of motivation to become active; or, a tendency to be overactive, and not take time to rest, nourish ourselves, listen to, share, and exchange with others.

CHAUFFEUR *cf. Driver*

CHECK (GB: Cheque)

A check is a means of payment *via* the banking circuit. It is generally used for money transits from one bank account to another. Like money, it represents condensed energy. As it allows exchanges and energy transfers to materialize projects, it concerns giving and receiving. A check represents power of realization, accomplishment, a force of action, acknowledgement of assets, credit, and an opening regarding the possibilities of the material world. It is also a certificate of trust between the people who exchange a check. Synonymous of stability and good management of our resources, because to obtain a check-book, we need to fulfill certain criteria such as solvability, reliability and integrity.

⊕ Capacity to pay our financial commitments easily (bills, salaries, rent, etc.). Obtaining resources, materials, services or money to accomplish our projects. A symbol of trust between the parties that use a check as a means of payment for their business transactions or in exchange for services rendered.

⊖ Poor management of resources, a person who spends more than he has, negligence, waste and lack of resources, loss of energy and power to materialize. Profound insecurities linked to money, to our accessible resources. Avarice, miserliness. Checks used dishonestly reveal a fraudulent attitude. Refusal to grant or accept checks indicates a period of limitation synchronized by Cosmic Intelligence so that the person concerned will rectify the way he manages and uses resources. He needs to work on his credibility, reliability, solvability and integrity so as to regain other people's trust in him on the level of exchanges.

CHICKEN *cf.* ***Hen***

CHINA

After remaining closed in on itself for a long time, since its opening to the world, China has known unprecedented economic growth, thanks to a great expansion of its production capacities on the material level. The most densely populated country in the world, China has become one of the most important world powers, and its egregore (*cf.* this term) represents a considerable force of materialization and a great influence on the level of global exchanges. Furthermore, Chinese civilization is ancient and its history has been marked by several discoveries and innovations in many fields such as science, medicine, the arts, and spirituality. Hence, although China concentrates its force in matter today, its evolutionary acceleration is so important that, sooner or later, the problems arising in various areas of life in this country, will require it to find fair, equitable, altruistic solutions. When this time comes, China will naturally draw on its ancestral wisdom and activate its great spiritual potential.

⊕ A great potential for materialization, production and expansion. A period of openness and accelerated economic development. A rich, varied culture. An extraordinary spiritual and medical heritage. Ancestral wisdom. Capacity to use its multiplication potential positively and altruistically. An apprenticeship in the management of matter and large-scale growth. A force for work and social involvement. A sense of duty. Respect and subordination.

⊖ Imbalance created by unbounded, excessive expansion. Abusive use of the power of materialization. Ancestral memory marked by deep insecurity and a lack of resources, a lack of food. Spirit and mentality conditioned by efforts to survive. Extremely materialistic attitude. Granting matter more importance than human life. Valuing quantity rather than quality. A lack of spirituality, wisdom, love and compassion. Emotional coldness. Hypocrisy. Underhanded, sly. Problems with organization, order and structure. Feelings of inferiority and superiority. The law of the jungle, survival of the fittest and might is right. Poor management of resources. Environmental, social and health problems as a result of materialization without conscience. Imposed ideology. Totalitarian regime. Corrupt government. Only thinking about getting rich. Selfishness, self-centeredness. Abuse of power and material wealth. Ready to do anything to succeed, to attain our objective(s), our goal(s). Megalomaniac behavior, believing oursleves to be the center of the world. Great dependency on others on the level of resources. Abortions and extermination of the feminine principle so as to favor the expansion of the masculine principle.

CHRISTMAS

Christmas is one of the 4 feast days related to the passage of the Sun through the 4 cardinal points: the Spring equinox/Easter; the Summer solstice/Midsummer and the feast of St. John (a national holiday in Quebec, Canada); the Autumn (Fall) equinox/the feast of St. Michael or Michaelmas Day; and finally, the Winter solstice/ Christmas. These 4 feast days correspond to cosmic phenomena and precise periods of the year when a great influx of energy movements occur in Nature and influence the Earth and all of its inhabitants. It is no coincidence that these feast days and major ceremonies of various religious traditions coincide with the occurrence of natural, cosmic phenomena. This is because the deep meaning and major aim of religion is to *link* man to Up Above, to Heaven, to the Universe; to keep alive in his conscience the memory of his origin and his belonging to the Great Whole; to remind him that he himself and the Earth do not exist or evolve in an isolated fashion in the Universe, but are influenced by and subjected to Cosmic Cycles and the Laws and Principles that govern them.

In the Christian religion, the feast of Christmas is associated with the birth of the Infant Jesus, who symbolizes the birth, the beginning of the awakening of the Christic Principle of Universal, Divine Wisdom and Love in the heart of man. This birth represents the birth of the spiritual body, which cannot occur without preparatory work in our heart, mind, spirit and conscience. Unlike our birth into a physical body, which takes place through the intermediary of our biological mother, the birth of our spiritual body must be undertaken by ourselves. And like the birth of our physical body, the process is preceded by a period of gestation. For our spiritual body, this takes place on the level of our heart chakra. Indeed, it is only when this energy center is awake and fully active that we can incarnate and manifest Universal, Divine Love and the Wisdom it confers.

For Christians, the feast of Christmas is an important period in the year as much on the personal as on the family level. It reminds us of the importance of love and protection within the family to ensure an appropriate structure and welcome for the manifestation of the Divine in matter. It is a period when everyone and every family carries out both inner and outer preparation to celebrate the event.

Inner preparation is also favored by the fact that this celebration traditionally takes place in winter, a season that naturally invites interiorization, introspection, inner listening and receptivity. Moreover the cold exterior climate in the Northern hemisphere incites us to activate our inner fire, to deploy human warmth and the qualities of the heart. Hence, Christmas has become an important feast day to reunite as a family, to devote some time to get-togethers, love, peace, forgiveness, generosity, sharing abundance, exchanging good wishes, and both material and immaterial gifts with everyone, young and old. It is also symbolically related to Father Christmas (Santa Claus), who traditionally brings and distributes presents to all those who were good, just, and did their best to improve throughout the year. It is a unique feast day and festive season, which revives an elevated sense of family because its altruistic, magical, universal spirit succeeds in joyfully reuniting, appeasing and consoling believers and non-believers, not only within our biological family, but also within the whole human family.

Since Christmas touches people's hearts so deeply, it also particularly affects those who live in solitude, isolation, sadness, distress, and material, emotional or spiritual poverty. In our society of over-production and consumerism, the feast of Christmas has become so commercialized and focused on decorations, food and material presents, that it is very easy to lose sight of the true values and the sacred sense of its existence.

⊕ A symbol of the birth of Divine Love, the Christic Principle in people's hearts and conscience. An example of the spirit of life we should follow so as to incarnate this dimension of ourselves on the earthly, terrestrial level every moment of our daily life and not only at Christmastime. The realization of divine potential in every man, woman, and child. Awareness of the sacred meaning of the Holy Family, of the Trinity. An altruistic, universal family. Development of a capacity to give and receive unconditionally. Awareness that Providential gifts are for everyone. Consecration of wealth and prosperity on all levels. Encourages the gift of ourselves, devotion, altruistic service. Exchanges and sharing of abundance on the family, social, and humanitarian levels. Generosity. Goodness. Loving kindness, thoughtfulness and consideration. Mutual help. Solidarity. Human warmth. Inner and outer joy, happiness, serenity, harmony and peace.

⊖ A state of mind, spirit and conscience focused only on matter. A person who has no sense of the sacred, of family and tradition. A lack of love and human warmth. Ignorance of and disrespect for true values, for the heart dimension, for the spiritual, divine nature of human beings and life in general. Difficulty being generous, sharing abundance, giving and receiving. A closed heart. Selfishness. Egotism. Greed, avidity, avarice, miserliness. Envy. Jealousy. Solitude. Isolation. Deep sorrow. Melancholy. Nostalgia. Inner emptiness. Ignorance of what family spirit is, no experience of a feeling of belonging. Feeling excluded, rejected. Lacking faith, beliefs, spirituality.

CHRISTMAS: FATHER CHRISTMAS (SANTA CLAUS)

Father Christmas is a legendary, mythical character related to the feast of Christmas. This tradition originated in Northern Europe, became popular in the United States in the 19th century, and at the beginning of the 20th century in France. No matter what name he is given in different languages, Father Christmas symbolizes generosity, reward for good behavior and attitudes, altruistic sharing of universal abundance, gifts from Providence. His white beard refers to Divine Wisdom, unconditional Love, his resemblance to God. His red suit (red is associated with matter), with its white edging (white is related to spirituality) indicates that the material aspects, the capacity and will to materialize projects, to make dreams come true, the creative potential of children, young and old, takes place within a framework of spiritual values. Father Christmas represents an altruistic, universal state of conscience that dwells in the individual and collective conscience of everyone who likes to believe in his magic.

Many parents wonder if it is right to teach this belief to their young children. If we present Father Christmas as a state of conscience, a magical energy that exists in each of us, that gives us the strength and willpower to be generous, good and compassionate, to help the poor, the weak, and the sick, to reward good actions, then it is right to encourage our children to believe in Father Christmas and to transmit the values and qualities of Father Christmas all their lives.

⊕ Generosity. Kindness. Unconditional, altruistic Love. Nobility of soul, great-heartedness. Universal spirit. Represents God's infinite Goodness, providential gifts. Reward for good actions. Help and encouragement for those in need. Sharing and distribution of universal abundance. Donations. Disinterested actions. Joy. Happiness. Magic.

⊖ A lack of generosity, kindness, love and altruism. A very materialistic, selfish, self-centered, mean, miserly spirit that holds back, retains and refuses to give, share or help his neighbor. Exchanging presents out of habit or a sense of obligation. An incapacity to receive or offer a present unconditionally, without any expectations. Greed. Jealousy. Envy. A lack of understanding of the sacred, symbolic meaning of a gift, merit and reward. Giving in order to be loved, recognized and acknowledged; or, to stop feeling guilty. Choice of present made without conscience, without reflecting on the usefulness of it or the consequences, the effect and influence it will have on the life and evolution of the person who receives it. Clannish, tribal spirit, only thinking of our immediate family. A lack of understanding of the sacred, spiritual, universal dimension of the feast of Christmas. A lack of faith in Providence, in the magic of life, in the existence of God.

CHURCH

The term *Church* with a capital *c* refers to the ecclesiastical state, the clergy, as well as all the practicing Christians united in a particular faith. As a building, a church designates a place dedicated to Christian religious worship. On the symbolic level, it represents a place of prayer, a moment of interiorization, of going within ourselves, a place of teaching and spiritual renewal and replenishment. As an institution, the Church provides a structure, a physical framework for a religious life. When people go to Church services, they take part in a ritual that enables them to incarnate, experiment, and share their beliefs with others. Today, many Christians are no longer practicing Christians but they continue to go along to the most important ceremonies offered by the Church. Such people associate the Church with symbolic stages in life, such as: baptism, first communion, confirmation, weddings, funerals, etc. In this respect, the Church represents a certain solemnity through which a spiritual meaning is attributed to life.

⊕ Period of prayer, meditation, reflection. Needing Heavenly consolation, support, and encouragement. Seeking inner peace. Walking an intense spiritual path so as to acquire Knowledge and to expand our conscience. Spiritual communication and communion. Community spirit and altruistic support for those who need consolation. A capacity to unify, to assist others, to help the poor.

⊖ Because of the various excesses of the Christian religion throughout the course of history, the Church is sometimes associated with puritanism, dogmatism, abuse of power, the Inquisition, rigidity, religious extremism, and an attachment to old structures. It can also represent a lack of knowledge and autonomy on the spiritual level.

CIGARETTE

Cigarettes are related to the vegetable kingdom (tobacco), hence, symbolically, to the emotional world. They also relate to the air element and the world of thoughts since to smoke, we inhale. Furthermore, because we raise the cigarette to our mouth, it also relates to the way we nourish ourselves and communicate. Cigarette smoke symbolizes mental confusion caused by dependence on erroneous thought systems. A smoker aspires to expansion on the intellectual level but, given the emotional limits imposed by some of his false concepts, he adheres to one theory after another, with no guideline, hence creating obfuscation, muddle, confusion on the mental level. In other words, a cigarette smoker maintains thoughts that cut him off from Knowledge and deep, global understanding.

The elongated form of a cigarette relates it to emissivity. Indeed, consciously or unconsciously, a smoker emits an emissive energy in order to appear more powerful, rebellious, or provocative, showing that he does what he likes and that he rejects the concepts and rules of a healthy life. People often begin to smoke during adolescence, i.e. at a time in life when we seek values and valid concepts to edify our personality. In the absence of these, teenagers resort to cigarettes to imitate certain adults who try to escape from, to flee reality behind a cloud of smoke; or, to superficially elevate themselves by giving a false impression of self-assurance.

A lot of smokers light up a cigarette when they feel stressed, nervous, anxious, destabilized. Unconsciously, they are seeking focus in order to master a state of dispersal, or a disturbing situation. In actual fact, smokers are very sensitive people who use cigarettes to create a calm, relaxed atmosphere, and try to appease and soothe their inner tensions, to bring about a sort of mental vacuity. They turn to cigarettes and become dependent on them because they don't know how to transform the inner forces and memories that pollute their mental world and push them to protect and separate themselves from others by means of a cloud of smoke. Cigarette smoke doesn't only pollute the body and physical surroundings, but also the mind, spirit and metaphysical environment.

In a social context, whenever a person smokes to be like others and feel accepted, in answer to real or presumed expectations of other people, or to indicate his belonging to the group, a cigarette then represents a search for identity, conviviality, a need to conform, to be acknowledged and loved; all of this hides a lack of self-confidence and difficulty asserting personal values, taking our place while respecting who we truly are. These deficiencies engender behavioral, social dependency corresponding to the reflexes induced by the desire to smoke in certain precise circumstances (when having a coffee, with friends, etc.).

Smokers should question themselves as to the needs, impulses, and memories that dwell in them, which engender these feelings of lack or inner emptiness. They try to manage their stress, their ill-being, anguish or anxiety, and their unconscious fears through outer rather than inner means, such as cigarettes, nowadays held to be a soft drug. When smoking, people begin by feeling strong pleasure or temporary relief from their problems. Then, they try to renew the experience more and more often, since the pleasure wears off and disappears, or the problem reappears as soon as the drug no longer has any effect. Thus smokers move from pleasure to a more and more urgent, imperious need to smoke to alleviate their suffering. This is followed by the *management of lack* phase, which co-exists with pleasure or relief. The dependency process has now been set in motion.

In the collective unconscious, a cigarette is a symbol of virility, self-assertion, relaxation on the personal and social levels, as well as a means of seduction favoring affective encounters and sexuality. On the symbolic level, the negative, confused thoughts with which a smoker nourishes his mental body multiply in an anarchic way, reducing his vital energy and destroying his health, causing death sometimes.

Because of the ever-increasing costs smoking causes the public health care system, numerous countries have understood the urgent need to devalue, to depreciate cigarette consumption. Hence, in a growing number of countries, laws have been created forbidding smoking in public places; the price of tobacco has been and continues to be increased; and every packet of cigarettes includes one or more of the following: alarming photographs as well as the obligatory mention of the average percentage of tar and nicotine, and various messages such as: *Smoking kills*; *Smoking causes mouth and throat cancer; Smoking can cause a slow and painful death*; all of which aim to discourage anyone tempted to take up smoking.

The fact of having to withdraw from others and go outside to smoke causes smokers to feel set aside, excluded, judged, and rejected by non-smokers, while at the same time, it sometimes creates a sense of camaraderie among smokers when they are together outside (perverse effect, discrepancy). It is important to know that the negative effects of smoking do not only manifest in this life. If a smoker doesn't manage to solve his dependency in this life, he transposes his problems into a future life, where he may be reborn in an unhealthy, smoky environment on the physical level (passive smoking) and on the metaphysical level (mental confusion). Then, he himself, and the members of his close family, may experience major health problems as a consequence of smoking (the Law of resonance).

We can also be a non-smoker in concrete reality but receive dreams wherein we see ourselves with smokers and/or smoking ourselves. Such dreams indicate that we have resonance with this type of dependency, that we still harbor rebellious aspects, erroneous concepts, and memories of escapism that need to be rectified.

⊕ Understanding the fact that smoking is bad for our health on all levels and that this harmful habit does not induce true well-being or true relaxation. The willpower to heal ourselves of this form of dependency by working on ourselves to cleanse, rectify, and transform confused, affective memories, as well as the feeling of not knowing how to manage tension and confused, rebellious, polluting thoughts that are at the root of the desire to smoke. Development of a capacity to assert ourselves in the right way on the personal and social levels, to reinforce our willpower to live a healthy life on all levels. May be a temporary support for a person who needs to release major stress that could cause violence, anxiety, suicide, irresponsibility, discouragement, despair, violence, aggression, abuse of power, etc.

⊖ Someone who seeks to escape, to relax, or to change his state of conscience in a superficial way, *via* external means. A tendency to flee, to take refuge in a cloud of smoke. Difficulty managing stress, actions, emotions, and thoughts. Lack of self-confidence. An artifice used to dissimulate anxieties, fears; an accessory for seduction. Lack of transparency, the projection of a false self-image, machismo behavior. A limited, polluting, destructive mind and spirit; a blocked mind. An impulsive desire for independence, a rebellious attitude, rebellious behavior; or someone who is hyper-tense and/or dependent. An illusion of strength, power, personal autonomy. A lure or delusion when trying to settle inner problems. A false feeling of assurance and ephemeral joy. An easily-influenced person who smokes to be like others, to be accepted, to feel important and a member of the group.

CINEMA, MOVIE THEATRE

The term cinema simultaneously refers to the art of film/movie-making, the cinema industry, the process of recording and projection, and the actual place where projection rooms exist, also referred to as a movie theatre. The cinema is very present in our modern world. This is due to the fact that the plot and scenario of a film/movie explores and reflects – just as dreams do – our soul-states, hopes, ideals, nightmares, fears and anxieties, our strengths and weaknesses, our qualities and distortions; in short, all that we have accumulated in the form of memories in our unconscious throughout our many lives. Whenever films/movies deeply move us, the characters and plot show us what we have already been, what we presently are, and what we may become. The art of the cinema (films/movies) associated with the Law of resonance and symbolic language is an excellent means for studying ourselves and learning to know ourselves better through the characters and plot. They help us travel to the heart of our unconscious memories and reveal to us hidden aspects of our personality or undeveloped potential. The cinema inspires, educates, reveals, enlightens and transforms when considered and studied with an awakened mind or conscience. However, in the case of excessive viewing, without discernment and in an ordinary conscience, it may also become the source of the following manifestations: dependency, illusion, artificial paradises, manipulation, exploitation, dull-wittedness, superficial values and principles, multiples personalities, ego problems, etc. The actors (*cf. also* this term), actresses, plots and types of film that appeal to us best reflect our states of mind, our moods, our soul-states, our level of conscience and the way we influence and create our life-program.

⊕ Observation, study and analysis of our attitudes and behavior. Discovery of new potential. Inspiration of beautiful qualities, noble, right behavior. Revelations, apprenticeships, education. Development of the faculties of seeing, perceiving and understanding deeply. Self-acknowledgement. Allows us to understand that illusion is educational, and that everything is symbolic.

⊖ Identification with and imitation of negative characters; ingestion and assimilation of bad influences. Seeking renown, celebrity, fame. Idolatry. Activation of wrong behavior. Easily-influenced, lacking discernment and right, true values and principles. Superficial mentality, lacks authenticity. Hiding behind roles. Fleeing reality, living in illusion. Seeking mundane pleasures. Needing to be loved, multiple dependencies. Discrepancy between what we are and do and what we would like to be and do.

CIRCLE

Generally speaking, geometrical shapes relate to the beginning, the initial stage of a new structure. A circle represents a state of conscience that unites, merges or fuses, and concentrates energy.

It connects the different levels of Creation, the world of causes and the world of consequences. It is also associated with the cycles of life, from the wheel of rebirth and reincarnation, to the universal principle of receptivity and continuity. The letter O, a circular shape, is often used to indicate zero; whereas a vertical line represents number 1, which is a symbol of emissivity.

The circle with a point in the center represents the union of the masculine and the feminine, the marriage of spirit and matter, the correlation that exists between the world of causes and the world of consequences. It also represents the Eye of God, of the Divine, that sees and records everything, as well as the 3rd eye, and the maternal breast that provides our first nourishment

⊕ May announce the setting up of a new structure related to receptivity, a capacity to unite, concentrate, and merge or fuse. Understanding the continuity and interdependence of the cycles of life, of perpetual change, renewal and beginning again.

⊖ A tendency to go round in circles, repeating the same patterns, the same negative experimentations without learning any lessons from them. The beginning of a new, difficult, karmic circle. Structural problems related to a lack, or excess, of receptivity. Difficulty concentrating, finding our center, our sacred space. An incapacity to harmoniously unite the different aspects of ourselves, a situation, an object. A lack of understanding of the cycles of learning and evolution. A tendency to accumulate negativity, to focus on evil. Someone who is too egocentric. A lack of a Divine, Universal dimension. A mind and spirit that is too down-to-earth.

CIRCULATION, TRAFFIC

Circulation is the term used to designate the movement of different fluids such as blood, lymph, vital energy, sap, etc. in humans, animals, or vegetables. In French this very same word also designates traffic, by road, rail, air and sea. Symbolically it represents the capacity of our spirit to move and travel in the different worlds and states of conscience. According to the context and faculty of perception, circulation (whatever its type) can be free-flowing, fluid, dense, difficult, blocked, stagnant, physical, metaphysical, visible, invisible and multidimensional.

⊕ A capacity to follow the right, just, good, natural movement and to create a balanced life and synchronicity with the Divine Plan. Flowing, harmonious, responsible progress. The circulation of information and positive energies. Well-balanced exchanges.

⊖ Difficulty advancing and manifesting. Poor circulation leading to serious consequences. Blockage, restriction, obstacle, stagnation. An accumulation of memories containing forces that push toward hasty manifestation; or, which impede movement, progress, evolution. Loss of synchronicity.

CIRCUS

The Western concept of a circus was inspired by Ancient Roman games as well as the street performers and troubadours of the Middle Ages. The circus represents a desire to publicly show off our skills, inspiration, powers of the imagination, capacity to create magic and extravaganza, soul-states, and extraordinary atmospheres. It can be intelligent entertainment, or futile and ridiculous, particularly when, in a search for fame, glory and wealth, people risk their lives by performing extreme feats. It is also associated with an unstable life and a lifestyle where people constantly play superficial roles, which nourish the need to please and impress others.

⊕ Public demonstration of a capacity to surpass ourselves and acquire certain skills through discipline, endurance, perseverance and patience. An aptitude to de-dramatize life, to make people laugh and amuse the crowd. Inspires and delights the child in us. Awakens unconscious forces and memories. Mastery of our instincts. Experimentation of states of conscience related to magic. Relaxation. Seeking freedom, a desire to travel, and the discovery of new horizons.

⊖ Seeking fame and strong sensations, wanting to impress. A superficial lifestyle. Emphasis on the body and appearances. A lack of authenticity and depth, living hidden behind masks. Nourishing illusion, futility. Power games. A lack of evolutive objectives. Excessive behavior, a bohemian life, fleeing reality, irresponsibility, all sorts of dependencies. A lack of values and principles. Nostalgia, sadness, feeling of rootlessness. Exploitation of animals and abusive use of vital energy. Multiple desires, licentiousness.

CITY, TOWN

A city or town is a relatively important agglomeration, characterized by a concentration of people and activities in one and the same place. The activities in a city or town are mostly commercial, political and cultural, compared with a village where they are more agricultural or related to craftwork. The density of a city's population and activities facilitates the exchange of goods, services and resources. Since a city or town's revenue is greater than that of a village, it allows its inhabitants to conceptualize and realize projects on a larger scale, with a greater collective and social dimension than a village. For all these reasons, a town or city symbolically represents expansion in matter, an abundance of personal and collective activities, as well as the orchestration of all the movement involved therein. It is also very interesting to make a comparison between a city and the heart and/or brain of the human body in terms of multiple activities and feelings, both positively and negatively.

Of course, a city or town doesn't only have positive aspects. It may disturb, cause stress, incite hyperactivity, harbor nonchalance, indifference, lack of love, mutual help, and fraternity on the social level. If anyone feels these disturbances, it's because he resonates with the negative aspects of a town or city: he harbors within himself parts of all of these distortions, which prevent his access to the positive potential a town or city offers.

Another negative symbolic aspect of a city or town is excessive materialization: too busy in matter, we may lack spirituality, seek material power and make poor use of the abundance offered to us. Likewise, a city or town may symbolize pollution on all levels: muddled, confused thoughts and emotions, a selfish, self-centered, demanding, complicated lifestyle, a frenetic pace of life, over-consumerism, waste of resources, a vindictive attitude, competition, criminality, etc.

⊕ Manifestation of creative, multiplying power; ability to feel at ease in the heart of great material, structural density. Abundance and success in commercial and social exchanges. Capacity to remain centered and stable in large-scale concrete action. A symbol of the multiplicity of choices and possibilities. Right, just, good management that cares about its citizens' well-being. Mutual help, shared goods, exchanged services. Accessible, efficient community organizations. Racial diversity, cultural and religious open-mindedness. Access to different ways of thinking and living. Well-orchestrated, fluid, safe road, rail and air traffic management, which symbolically reflects good management of relationships and human exchanges.

⊖ Difficulties related to hyperactivity, a proliferation of activities, management of the intensity of life, large-scale materialization, high demographic, social and commercial density, multiplicational economics, traffic, as well as intensive pollution of both the physical and metaphysical environment (thoughts, emotions). A superficial, over-materialistic place. A lifestyle that nourishes the ego. A desire and quest for power and renown. A culture focused on ambition. A complicated, overwhelming environment that lacks true human warmth, contact and mutual, fraternal assistance. Isolation. Problems helping others and sharing goods, services and resources in a well-balanced, fair way. Very high cost of living, social inequalities. Exploitation, social injustice. Social disharmony, survival of the fittest. Multiplied social problems. Racial, cultural, and religious tensions and/or segregation. In extreme cases, poverty, shantytowns, slums, extremely underprivileged, poor areas neighboring opulence, skyscrapers, expensive housing and luxurious residences. Ethnic ghettoes. Criminality. Poor management of resources, waste, corruption of town or city councilors and adminstrators. Poor management of road, rail and air traffic causing congestion, accidents, etc., on both the physical and metaphysical levels.

CLAIRAUDIENCE

Clairaudience is a paranormal hearing capacity, which allows us to hear beyond perceptible sounds on the physical level. We often experience clairaudience without even realizing, for instance, when, beyond a person's words, we perceive his true intention, the subtle atmosphere, the multi-dimensional aspects of a situation.

Clairaudience allows us to listen in depth, to tune into and perceive what the other person is expressing on different levels of his being.

Other expressions of clairaudience consist in receiving the answer to a question or reflection through words pronounced by a third party, a phrase picked up from the radio or television, a few notes of a tune, a song, or a voice which suddenly resonates in our mind, etc. Cosmic Intelligence or God always answers our questions, but most of the time, we are not receptive enough to hear the messages, which do not necessarily reach us through the usual, customary means when we function in an ordinary conscience.

Clairaudience also includes a capacity to perceive other people's thoughts and soul-states beyond the limitations of space and time. Hence, we can hear what a person thousands of miles away is thinking, or even messages coming from a soul that has passed away. The more our conscience evolves, the more we integrate the multi-dimensionality of existence, the more normal phenomena that are considered paranormal today become.

In the meantime, when we have the faculty of clairaudience, it is wise to remain discreet so as to allow others to evolve in the discovery of psychic powers at their own pace. We must not reveal what we perceive to impress others or to show off extra-sensorial faculties. In this field, it is also essential to apply the Law of resonance and refer back to ourselves, because everything we perceive or hear always reveals aspects of ourselves at the same time.

Children are true magicians in the field of multi-dimensional perception. They often make remarks that adults consider incoherent, but if we analyze these remarks deeply, symbolically, we discover that they contain revelations about themselves, others and what is going on beyond appearances.

When the gift of clairaudience starts to manifest itself, it is important to always call it into question, to practice discernment, because the voices that we begin to hear may also come from unconscious forces lodged in the depths of our being, forces that are not always positive. Clairaudience may open a door onto the expression of negative forces that we bear within ourselves, and in certain cases, it may be confused with schizophrenia. Schizophrenics' unconscious is very open, but through lack of knowledge and understanding of the clairaudient phenomena they experience, the gift of clairaudience leads to great suffering. That is why psychic powers are not available to everyone. Within the framework of right, just, qualitative development however, these gifts of spiritual powers become active very gradually, or when we are ready.

⊕ Truly great receptivity and sensitivity, in-depth listening and understanding. Revelationary perception through the sense of hearing. Capacity to guess intentions, to perceive atmospheres and ambiances, to symbolically analyze resonance. Access to multi-dimensions. Listening to music and ambiances coming from the Highest Spheres.

⊖ Difficulty being receptive, listening and understanding in depth. An incapacity to perceive intentions, the true meaning of words, ambiances and situations. Confusion between physical and metaphysical reality. Unhealthy curiosity that falsifies perception. Poor, conscience-less use of spiritual powers, manipulation, mediumnity or psychic powers. Hearing problems caused by an overloaded unconscious. Mental illnesses, schizophrenia. Refusal to hear messages coming from superior levels. Over rational.

CLAIRSENTIENCE

Clairsentience is a psychic faculty, a subtle power that allows us to perceive what exists beyond the physical level, in the metaphysical dimensions through our senses. A clairsentient person has the capacity to sense the different facets of other people, their emotions, intentions, memories, learning programs. He can anticipate reactions, deeds, events, and obtain all sorts of information. Clairsentience allows us access to a person's conscience and unconscious. It can be developed gradually through intense work on ourselves; or, it may be activated all of a sudden in certain circumstances. It is also related to the sense of smell, which becomes more subtle and renders us capable of perceiving odors on the metaphysical levels.

⊕ A high level of sensory feeling, receptivity and sensitivity. Multi-dimensional perception. Deep understanding of people, situations and events, which allows us to intervene and help appropriately, with discernment and wisdom. Revelations engendered by premonitory, sensory feelings. Access to Knowledge and Memory. Discovery of hidden information. Integration of the Law of resonance. Understanding that clairsentience is a divine power that needs to be mastered and used only while respecting the Divine Laws and each person's life-program. A capacity to smell odors and perfumes on the subtle levels.

⊖ A lack of receptivity, an incapacity to feel, to sense deeply; or, false perception. Wishing for clairsentience and sensing the multidimensions for selfish, personal purposes, out of curiosity, ambition, or a desire for power. Ignorance of the dangers and karmic consequences brought about by misuse of psychic powers. A lack of discernment, love, wisdom, and compassion for what we perceive and feel or sense. Judgment, criticism, coldness, disrespect, contempt, and pride. Use of clairsentience to manipulate, dominate or hurt others. Feelings of superiority and inferiority. A mentally unbalanced psychic or medium. A tendency to isolate ourselves in order to protect ourselves from the negative energies that we perceive. A lack of understanding of the Law of resonance and the necessity to work on ourselves to transform memories that resonate with what we perceive in the subtle levels. A feeling of being put out, bothered, or disturbed by resonance between the negative odors we perceive in the subtle levels and the memories that dwell within us.

CLAIRVOYANCE

Clairvoyance represents a subtle form of perception, the faculty to *see clearly*, which does not occur through our customary physical sight, which is why it is also referred to as extra-sensorial perception.

It is a metaphysical phenomenon that occurs in a higher than usual state of receptivity and conscience. It is one of the mediumnic capacities and psychic powers that allows us to perceive information on the parallel levels, in the multi-dimensions. When it manifests itself, it is a sign that we are in the process of developing our subtle senses, which open us up to understanding and sight or vision beyond the physical level. It is related to the functions of the 3rd eye and the medulla oblongata, and it gives us access to the multi-dimensionality of our being.

When the unconscious opens and our receptivity increases, we become capable of piercing the veil and seeing clearly into our depths and other realities. Clairvoyance may manifest itself through images and visions that appear as we talk to another person, look at an object or place, or when we meditate on a precise subject. The vision can give information about a person's hidden, unconscious intentions or memories linked to a place, object or event. It may manifest suddenly, unexpectedly, or be activated as needs be by a person who has developed this faculty. He will then see images that surpass his ordinary visual capacities and help him make his choices and decisions with deeper understanding and a more global vision. This higher power, which corresponds to latent potential that exists in everyone, develops after long work on ourselves through meditation, visualization techniques, and the transformation of negative memories.

Wishing to activate clairvoyance to acquire Knowledge, to satisfy our ego's needs and thirst for power, without purifying our unconscious may turn out to be very dangerous, and we could end up in a psychiatric hospital. When the opening of the unconscious produces effects that are too powerful to be managed on our own, it is essential not to panic, but to try and talk about this to someone who has a spiritual conscience and who is able to understand the metaphysical dimension of this phenomenon; for example a meditation teacher, an evolved therapist, psychologist or psychiatrist, or a friend who is on a spiritual path. It is important to know that, sooner or later, spiritual work activates psychic powers naturally and safely. Young children are often clairvoyant because their 3rd eye is still open, and they can keep this faculty if their parents are able to understand them and guide them wisely in the correct interpretation and right, just use of this gift.

⊕ Capacity to see deeply through images, symbols and visions. Perception of the multi-dimensions. Access to information in the subtle, metaphysical levels. Deepened understanding of people, events and life in general. Great receptivity, increased sensitivity, global vision.

⊖ Dangerous clairvoyance serving the ambitions of the ego and negative forces. A tendency to isolate ourselves in order to protect ourselves from the negative energies we perceive. A lack of understanding or ignorance of the Law of resonance and the educational function of evil, wrong-doing and what hurts, as well as the necessity to work on ourselves in order to transform unconscious memories that resonate with what we tune into and perceive. False visual perception of people and events, or an incapacity to see deeply because of a lack of receptivity. Thirst for power, blinded by our ego, unbalanced psychic powers, manipulation. A superiority complex, a haughty, arrogant attitude, judgment, criticism, and contempt of others. Coldness, a lack of wisdom and love.

CLASSROOM, CLASS

A classroom is a symbol of apprenticeship, learning, teaching, and personal development related to the collectivity. It represents an inner space where we encounter different parts of ourselves, symbolized by the students and teachers. On the one hand, they reflect a capacity to learn and the attitude we adopt when learning, during an apprenticeship, and, on the other hand, a capacity to receive teaching or to teach, educate, transmit knowledge, and be a model. A class of students and a classroom are also symbols of structure and organization, because students have to respect certain rules and regulations, and the learning activities that take place therein usually follow a precise timetable.

⊕ A teaching, learning space, which includes sharing, creativity, games, joy, and self-discovery. A capacity to structure ourselves and be organized so as to facilitate teaching, the transmission of knowledge, and an awakening of the potential we bear within, as well as intellectual and emotional efforts, and the integration of the lessons learned. A place allowing us to develop new skills, to acquire new experience and understanding, to learn respect, tolerance, discipline, concentration, perseverance, kindness, friendship, and social relationships, etc.

⊖ Difficulty related to learning and self-development, or problems concerning the capacity to transmit knowledge. Ignorance, refusal to learn, study, evolve. Turbulent energy. Distraction. Lack of discipline. Lack of concentration. Competitive spirit. Feeling of superiority, thinking we know it all, a haughty, arrogant attitude. Over rational behavior. Lack of warmth, compassionate listening, encouragement, right, just motivation. A lack of understanding of the fact that we are all continually both student and teacher. Problems adapting and integrating. Limitations, blockages. Discouragement, withdrawal through shyness, timidity, insecurity and a lack of self-confidence. Ambition. Rivalry. Comparison. Severity. Rigidity. Ignorance of the Law of resonance which explains that everything we go through, everything we experience and experiment on the outside, reveals apprenticeships and teachings taking place on the inside, within ourselves.

CLEANSE, CLEAN UP

Cleansing is to render something or someone clean; it is to clean up (do the housework) both on the inside and on the outside, to free ourselves of accumulated dirt, impurities, tension, blockages, stress and problems. Cleansing is probably one of the most important concepts in human life, on the physical as well as the metaphysical levels. The cleansing process is also essential when we wish to renew and rebuild ourselves, to evolve, to prepare a new stage, begin a new cycle. It allows us to establish order and cleanliness, essential, primordial states for well-being, serenity, peace and harmony within and around us. Conscious, gradual cleansing and purification of all the levels of our being, and all the domains of our life, allow us to rediscover our original purity, Divine Purity.

Just as a person, who neglects bodily hygiene, and lives in a physically dirty environment, risks infection, illness and all sorts of malfunctioning, so too is his life on the metaphysical level defined by difficulties, obstacles, dependencies to be overcome, numerous karma to be settled, conscious and unconscious memories to be purified and transformed. (*cf. also* **Wash; Bath**)

Similarly, just as we or our environment can be dirtied, polluted by various matter, liquids, gases, etc., so too can a person be affected, dirtied, polluted by distorted, unhealthy thoughts, emotions, and attitudes engendered by himself or others. Even when leading a healthy, spiritual life, with right, just, the most correct behavior possible, one way or another, we are continually in contact with polluting energies emitted by the mental, emotional, and physical activities of all the people we come in contact with. Whenever we feel negatively affected by someone's presence, it is important to call to mind the Law of resonance and the mirror effect, which tell us that others reflect parts of ourselves, that they mirror our own thoughts, emotions and behavior, both on the conscious and unconscious levels. We are constantly in the present of contaminating factors, just like in a hospital; and just like in a hospital, we have to carefully wash and/or disinfect ourselves regularly so as not to catch an infection or illness. Body and soul hygiene and cleanliness are important elements for those who work on themselves to improve, progress, advance and evolve. It is through the alchemical process of multi-dimensional cleansing and purification work that a person is deeply transformed and renewed.

Soul cleansing is carried out in exactly the same way as the environment is cleansed, exactly as we clean our living and working conditions, since they are the outer representation of our inner being. A good, simple way to begin inner cleansing is to cast an evaluating look at our surroundings, both in concrete reality and in situations experienced in our dreams. If our house, our outer home, is dirty and uncared for, this indicates that our inner world needs a good clean-up. Whenever windows are covered in dirt and grime, this means that our vision of both the outside and the inside is blocked, that our judgment and sense of discernment is deformed, erroneous. Whenever a bathroom needs to be scrubbed clean, it is a sign that we need to work on the way we purify ourselves. Tidying up and cleaning the sitting-room symbolizes the cleansing of memories related to our social life, what we emit and emanate in the presence of others. A dirty, untidy kitchen reveals negative, unhealthy, harmful energy with which we nourish ourselves and others. The presence or absence of cleanliness and order at our workplace, our desk, in our workshop, garage, etc., reveals the way we use our creative potential, our capacity for materialization, maintenance, and care. The general atmosphere and aspect of the company where we work, as well as the attitude and behavior of our colleagues, employers and employees, regarding order and cleanliness reflect facets of ourselves in this respect on the collective and social levels. The same goes for all the other domains of our life: places of apprenticeship and teaching, care and healing, means of transport, recreation areas, parks, our neighborhood, streets, the countryside, and so on. The state of cleanliness or dirt and pollution, order or disorder, as well as our active participation one way or the other, reveals the resonance we have with cleansing, and the conscious and unconscious memories we have to transform in regard to this.

Everyday life situations, as well as those experienced in our dreams, through symbolic language, show us more precisely what it is we need to or are in the process of cleansing, purifying and/or transforming. A single image can indicate all sorts of distorted behavior. By establishing a correlation between the situations experienced or observed on the one hand, with the thoughts, emotions, states of mind, spirit, and soul that we had at that particular time, we discover what needs to be cleansed in us. We proceed step by step, analyzing each and every detail of the dream or concrete situation, using each clue that is provided. Another way to discover what we need to cleanse is to be receptive to resonance, dependencies, interferences, limitations, or obstacles encountered in our daily life. If we feel bothered, put out or upset by anything or anyone's attitude, behavior or lifestyle, it is certain that we have memories of the same ilk within ourselves that resonate with whatever reproaches or criticisms we may have.

However, we mustn't confuse *cleansing* with *getting rid of* what bothers us, because everything we set aside, sooner or later, in one form or another, everything we flee or circumvent comes back to us to be cleansed, until finally the day comes when we have no more distortions; our soul has regained its original purity thanks to all the cleansing, purification work we carried out on all levels of our being. Everything can be cleansed, transformed, transcended. If we don't do this little by little, difficulties arise, because the misactions (*cf.* this term) disorder, pollution, and all of the distortions we engender are inscribed in our soul, take root in our memories, weigh and prey on our inner world, tarnishing and darkening it, just as layer by layer, everything that is neglected and abandoned in the outer world is covered in grime.

⊕ A period of intense inner and outer cleansing. Seeking cleanliness, clarity, limpidity, purity, order, transparency, and harmony on all levels. Understanding the importance of consciously cleaning up both in the inside and on the outside, consciously doing our inner and outer housework, so to speak. Feelings of accomplishment, liberation, and success when the cleaning up has been done, favoring the setting up of new projects, the realization of new ideas. A wise, vigilant person who is receptive to the signs and messages he receives in his dreams, who aspires to original purity, who knows how to recognize his resonances, and who works on himself to adjust, transform, and continually improve himself. Allows us to evolve on the level of our soul and conscience by rectifying erroneous, wrong, unfair behavior and attitudes, by transforming tensions, heaviness, congestion, clutter, obstacles, and misactions that have been engendered and accumulated in our unconscious throughout our many lives. Cleansing and reprogramming of negative memories. Transmutation and transcendence of faults and weaknesses and the whole of our karmas. In-depth purification, which leads to renewal, inaugurates a new stage. Training for order, discipline, rigor. Development of a sense of responsibility, ritual, sacredness, duty, purpose and accomplishment. Facilitates communication, harmony in exchanges and sharing. Reinforces intuition. Favors the reactivation of the subtle senses. A sense of beauty, esthetics. Sober, well-structured order, inspiring a state of peace, harmony and serenity, a *zen* atmosphere favorable to re-centering, realignment, refocus, elevation of our conscience and the awakening of creativity on all levels. Healthy evolution on all levels.

⊖ Difficulties, resistance, and blockages related to cleansing and purification. An unclean, neglected, lazy person, who revels in disorder, dirt, clutter, mediocrity, or even decadence; or, who only cleans superficially and occasionally, whenever he wants to impress or gain something from someone. A lack of willpower and motivation to transform our faults and weaknesses, to settle and free ourselves from our karmas. A tendency to flee our responsibilities, to procrastinate and constantly put off our obligations and duties till later. Refusal to change, to evolve. A lack of organization, rigor, discipline; or, a puritanical, hyper-perfectionist, exaggerated, obsessive, maniacal desire for cleanliness and order. An extremist, destructive mind and spirit, ready to kill, to exterminate, in order to impose his vision of moral, racial, ethnic, ideological purity; genocide. The presence of polluting forces that foul and clog up a person's inner and outer worlds, as well as those of others, through a lack of conscience, though ignorance, or indifference. An unhealthy, impure intimate and social life that could engender health problems, illnesses and serious infections. A cause of contagion. A difficult life due to a constant accumulation of tension, conflict, and ordeals. Incapacity or resistance to recognize and acknowledge our resonance, our distortions. A soul that is a prisoner of memories that sustain malfunctioning on several levels. Continual return to erroneous behavior.

CLINIC *(cf. also **Hospital**)*

A clinic symbolizes an inner space where we can find the resources and services to take care of and guide us on the path to healing on all levels. The parts of us that need to be taken care of, treated, and healed can be examined and diagnosed there, and we can take the time to understand in depth the origin of our ill-being or an illness. This understanding will shed a light on the attitude or behavior that needs to be rectified, which will lead to true healing, i.e. healing as much on the physical level of the body as healing of the soul and spirit, thus allowing the person to improve his capacity to manifest and evolve.

⊕ Access to resources and services allowing us to be taken care of and accompanied when a health problem arises. Good use of inner resources to heal ourselves. Contributes to awareness of distorted thoughts, emotions and behavior that create blockages, malfunctioning, states of ill-being and illnesses, and to rectify them. Correct analysis of the metaphysical causes related to every illness and all ill-being that affects us. Strengthens faith in our healing potential on all levels. Capacity to take care of people and guide them toward healing, with love, compassion, devotion and wisdom.

⊖ Difficulty finding resources and services to care for us and provide treatment. A lack of resources within ourselves to take care of us and provide treatment; or, an incapacity to use such resources. Putting ourselves in other people's hands only in order to be rapidly healed without taking any interest in the deep-rooted cause of the health problem. Seeking healing focused exclusively on the physical body. A lack of understanding that every illness starts in the metaphysical dimension of the person, on the level of his thoughts and emotions. Incapacity to find the metaphysical causes related to ill-being or an illness; lack of depth in healing. Medicine mainly oriented toward financial profit. Malevolent, prejudicial, wrongful motivations and intentions. A person who uses his knowledge, skills, influence and power to abuse others rather than help them regain health and well-being on all levels. An irresponsible, corrupt doctor, nurse or caregiver who has no morals, conscience or humanity.

CLOCK, WATCH

A clock or watch helps us to manage time, and our various occupations and activities, with precision and accuracy. It gives a rhythm and structure to our day, our family and professional lives, meals, meetings and appointments, leisure activities, meditation, etc. A clock or watch is also related to concepts of punctuality, performance, competitiveness, reliability, patience and impatience, a sense of commitment, duty and responsibility. As a reference tool allowing us to follow a schedule and situate ourselves in time, it helps us discipline ourselves and be organized. As a watch is generally worn on our person, it is more related to our individual aspect, compared with a clock, which has a more collective impact.

⊕ Good management of time. A well-organized, well-structured schedule. Punctuality. Respect for commitments, stages and cycles. Love of precision and accuracy. Understanding the concept of time. Aware that everything happens at the right time. A sense of patience. A capacity to trust in synchronicity, to recognize it when it manifests; or, to know how to wait for it when it is absent. An ability to live the present moment well. Flexibility and adaptation to time. Good use of waiting periods. Makes the time factor clear in the concrete world, brings us back to the essential. Allows us to measure and establish correct balance regarding our various commitments and involvement, so as to live a well-balanced life with ourselves, and others.

⊖ Rigidity. A tendency to impose an inflexible schedule on ourselves, obsessed with time, granting it too much importance, constantly feeling we haven't enough time to do everything. Stress. Impatience. Restlessness, nervous tension. Fear of being late, of not having enough time. Great insecurity. A too down-to-earth way of functioning, over absorbed in matter. Hyperactivity. Competitiveness. Ceaselessly pushing ourselves to perform. Absence of global vision. A lack of understanding of time. A person who chases after time; or, who rushes his actions. Non-respect for rules and time limits leading to disorder and disorganization on the individual and social levels. A lack of structure, organization, and discipline. Laxity. Wasting time. A tendency to be overactive, too much in action, and not giving ourselves time to go within and interiorize.

Affected, stressed by the ticking of a watch or clock: Great insecurity. Fleeing the inner world. Not allowing ourselves enough time to rest. Stimulation of the mind and spirit to continually go toward matter, to remain in action.

A stopped watch: May indicate that a person is inactive, that he wastes his time, that he lacks structure and organization, and doesn't take time to materialize his projects, that he is de-synchronized.

A flat watch battery: A lack of energy to structure ourselves, to be organized, to fulfill our responsibilities.

A watch that is late or fast: Indicates that there are forces within us that make us late, that halt our evolution; or, make us act too hastily. Presence of discrepancies on several levels, along with fear that we are going to miss something.

CLOSET *cf. Cupboard*

CLOTHES

Clothes mainly symbolize our aura. They reveal our intentions, what kinds of energy we emanate, what qualities and virtues we radiate. They also represent our activities, our social status, our personality, character, moods, states of mind and soul. They may also play a protective role.

A sad person won't easily wear lively, joyful, colorful clothes because they won't attract him. He quite naturally won't feel any resonance with such clothing. Hence, in the morning, we partly choose our clothes for the day consciously, but most of the time, we choose unconsciously in accordance with our inner feelings and the activity we are going to do. A melancholic, morose person who is discontented with his life will be more inspired to wear dark, mismatching clothes, whereas a happy, joyful, serene person will wear bright, lively, joyful colors and emanate an organized, healthy, happy attitude. It is important to always relate a person's soul-state (mood), behavior, facial expression with the clothes he wears because dark, or black clothes may be positive if, for instance, they denote a serious, well-structured person, who doesn't show off his knowledge, but remains discreet, even secretive, in a positive way. Dark clothing is not systematically negative. Likewise, very bright, luminous clothing may be worn by a radiant, joyful person, but also by an over-confident person, who is forcefully positive.

Once we know how to sense an atmosphere or ambiance deeply, how to interpret a facial expression and symbolically analyze a person's choice of clothing, we obtain a vision or very accurate, precise estimate of the deep meaning of a situation experienced in a dream or in concrete reality.

⊕ Reveals our personality, and conscious or unconscious mood, our character, our aura, our social status, the intentions and energies we emanate, the type of activity we do, the qualities, virtues, and soul-states we radiate. In some cases, clothing symbolizes protection from cold ambiances, or from the sun, from excessive radiance, from extremism. Comfort, consolation, and warmth. Reflection of inner qualities, mirror of the soul, and revelation of our soul-states, or of who we are, depending on the colors, shapes, styles and patterns.

Clean clothes associated with a lovely attitude: indicate that the person feels good in himself, is efficient, happy, and organized. Radiates qualities, respect, a sense of responsibility, well-balanced fair-mindedness.

Dirty clothes in a positive context: May indicate that the person has been, or is, working intensely, that he is very busy, conscientious, humble, feels good in himself, relaxed, lives his experiences to the full; or, they may indicate an experimental, play context, where we get dirty like a child playing, discovering, experimenting.

⊖ Represent the distortions of our personality, our bad mood or ill-being, our discontent, frustrations, the unsaid, our hidden, veiled soul-states. Erroneous behavior, a person who has harmful radiance, who exerts a negative influence on his entourage. A lack of protection and warmth when confronted with cold emotions, or with someone who is wearing clothes that are too warm, because of memories marked by fear of lacking warmth, love, kindness, and consideration. Unhappy soul-states, indifference regarding what clothes we wear, neglect of our physical aspect, not granting enough importance to having neat, cared for clothing; or granting too much importance to clothes, a superficial, vain, over proud person who is too focused on his appearance, his wardrobe, his clothes.

Clothes that are too big: reveal a superiority complex, an over-confident attitude, an ego problem and excessive emissivity, a lack of receptivity, a need for attention as well as needing to feel above everything, to feel bigger and better than others and capable of dominating every situation.

Clothes that are too small: indicate an inferiority complex, a lack of self-esteem, deficient self-confidence, a need to be taken care of, supported, *piggybacked,* and acknowledged in spite of our lacks and weaknesses. May indicate a tendency to demean ourselves, to allow ourselves be impressed by superficiality, power, wealth and glory.

Dirty clothes associated with a neglectful, careless attitude: reveal behavioral neglect, rebellious dynamics; or, laxity, nonchalance, a lack of responsibility to ourselves and others. An unclean person, who emanates a state of heaviness, discrepancy, laziness, coarseness, and who has an uncouth, boorish, disorganized lifestyle.

Clothes with holes: denote negligence, shame, social wear and tear, and in some cases, rebellious, provocative behavior.

CLOUD

A cloud is mass of steam, condensed into very fine water droplets, suspended in the atmosphere. Clouds are formed thanks to the evaporation of water from seas, oceans, lakes, rivers, streams, etc. Cloud formation and displacement are natural climate processes. As they ensure the distribution of water on Earth, they are essential for the correct functioning of the ecosystems. On the symbolic level, they represent a state of conscience that is related to the world of emotions through the water element, and to the world of thoughts through the air element, the wind and the atmosphere. Hence, clouds symbolize man's capacity to circulate his emotions, to elevate them, and transform them through the power of his thoughts and spirit. The positive and negative aspects of cloud symbolism is determined by the color, shape, and density of the cloud, as well as the ambiance and context of its presence and movements (calm and tranquil, or fast and threatening).

⊕ *Regarding climate*: Beautiful, white fluffy clouds drifting gently in the sky symbolize beautiful emotions and inspiring, elevating, spiritual thoughts, circulating harmoniously, activating those parts of us in need of emotions. A capacity to elevate our feelings and thoughts to the causal level, to attain global vision and understanding. Fertile life in both the inner and outer worlds. Conscious participation in the creation of abundance by providing the right resources at the right time, in the right place, in order to concretize fertile ideas and materialize altruistic, humanitarian projects, in a right, just, wise, qualitative way.

Rain cloud: Symbolically positive whenever it occasionally provides the quantity of water the earth, flora, fauna, and people need to live and flourish.

Cloud of sand, sand storm: Work on ourselves to learn mastery of our thoughts related to matter. Transformation of memories marked by a great number of tiny, little distorted actions, a multitude of misactions (*cf.* this term), the accumulation of which ends up engendering a destructive force.

Cloud of insects: Awareness of the difficulties resulting from a strong concentration of instinctual needs on the thought level, which scatter and disperse a person's vital energy, distracting, flustering, maddening him, and eventually, possibly destroying his resources and his life.

⊖ *Regarding climate*: Great, big, heavy, threatening clouds, accumulating rapidly and racing across the sky, indicate an accumulation of emotions and thoughts, heavy with tension, anger, and malevolent, destructive forces. An incapacity to let our emotional and mental energies circulate in a harmonious, well-balanced way, thereby causing aridity, infertility, poverty, and a lack of resources on all levels of our being. Emotional and intellectual instability. Disharmony. Sadness, sorrow. Affective, sentimental, emotional overflow. An unbalanced life, lacking equilibrium. A lack of inspiration and creativity. Emotional and intellectual instability. Blocked, limited mind and spirit. Negative emotions and thoughts, which trouble our serenity, obscure our soul and create states of heaviness and despair. An incapacity to activate the light and heat of our inner sun, the fire of our spirit within us. A lack of spirituality. A dark, somber, confused period, without principles or values.

Cloud of sand, sand storm: Intense disturbance and perturbation on the thought level owing to a great number of material needs, or memories of distorted, hyperactive actions. A lack of self-command, control, mastery. Unstable, agitated, overly materialistic thoughts. Frustration. Confusion. Dispersal, scattering, and dissipation on the material level.

Cloud of insects: Multitude of small, invasive instinctual needs, which attack on the thought level. Destruction of resources and creative potential by the concentrated power and force that comes from an accumulation of little, untransformed, instinctual needs on the thought level.

Cloud of dust: Triggering of thoughts related to old, former actions that haven't been cleansed, which prevent us from seeing clearly, and hinder our capacity to advance.

Cloud of smoke: Usually associated with the presence of an intense, raging, destructive fire (e.g. a forest fire, or one caused by heavy, industrial pollution), a cloud of smoke is a symbol indicating a negative, uncontrolled, abusive, irresponsible, and destructive use of the force of our spirit, of our vital energy. It signals intense, devastating tension.

Head in the clouds: Denotes the state of a person who is too absorbed in his emotional thoughts, which creates a discrepancy on the level of his physical functioning; he tends to lack concentration and presence of mind when doing physical tasks, as well as being unrealistic and incapable of concretizing his ideas.

COFFEE

As a beverage, coffee, like all liquids, refers to the emotional level. Coffee is the seed of a coffee plant, a shrub, hence a vegetable element which symbolizes the world of feelings and emotions. The dark brown color of roasted coffee seeds is related to the earth element and so to the world of action and matter, whereas the black color of liquid coffee evokes the symbolism of what is hidden, occulted, dormant, buried potential that we try to awaken and activate through this stimulating drink. In actual fact, coffee is a psychoactive drug that acts on our mood, behavior, and intellect. It is part of a daily ritual for many people, especially in the field of work where non-stop action and performance is sought. It is mainly used as a stimulant for intellectual and physical activities. Studies have demonstrated that coffee makes rats more intelligent and alert. Drinking coffee may indicate a person's desire to be more efficient, dynamic and alert. Drinking coffee may help when we feel very tired, lacking in energy, and in the case of depression, where it temporarily, gently, sets us free from the inhibitions characteristic of such moods, such soul-states. Unfortunately many people drink too much coffee and are dependent on it. In such cases, the symbol becomes negative and nourishes certain aspects that confine people's conscience to an overly rational, concrete understanding of situations and events. This engenders hyperactive behavior, survival dynamics, as well as an attitude of competition and rivalry with ourselves and/or others solely in the name of material or honorary success.

In people with memory problems, and in the elderly, coffee taken in moderation may create beneficial memory stimulation and favor a capacity to remember as well as to work on themselves, rather than prepare the way for progressive memory loss (Alzheimer) by taking refuge in systematic forgetfulness of negative, unpleasant events. In the case of migraine or chronic headaches, coffee also exerts a stimulating effect, just as it helps regulate intestinal transit in the case of constipation. However, it is important not to rely on coffee only for its beneficial physical effects, but also to do some deep self-questioning. In the case of migraines and headaches in general, we need to keep an eye out for contradictory thoughts that create tension and obstruct our evolution. In the case of constipation, we need to become aware of attitudes and behavior that prevent us from transforming and evacuating the negative energies and waste that we have accumulated during our actions in matter. Excessive coffee consumption also encourages the manifestation of different types of cancer. Moreover, the caffeine contained in coffee is not recommended for people suffering from asthma and high blood pressure. It may also have a negative influence on the quality of our sleep because it decreases the secretion of melatonin, the sleep hormone.

⊕ Someone who drinks coffee with discernment to temporarily fulfill an important need for energy, or to remain awake in the case of an emergency or necessity. May support a second chance in problematic situations by liberating the necessary energy to purify emotional and physical negativity, and understand the true cause of the problems encountered. Development of a capacity to stimulate, to motivate ourselves, and to remain active. Work on ourselves to transform and transcend the feeling of stress and the need to surpass ourselves in order to feel good, as well as to attract attention and admiration. Apprenticeship of moderation and the right middle path. Understanding hyperactivity, which is the result of our granting too much importance to action and success in matter. Someone who listens to and respects his body, his need for healthy balance between action and rest, between doing and being, between emissivity and receptivity.

⊖ A stressed, anxious, hyperactive person, who constantly stimulates himself emotionally so as to maintain his level of energy and performance. Non-respect of our physical and mental need to rest. A very materialistic state of mind, focused on competition, acknowledgement, and success in the outside world. An unhealthy lifestyle that drains our vital energy, and stimulates and maintains survival dynamics. Physical and professional exhaustion. Superficial values. Lack of depth, interiorization, inner listening, rest, calm. Seeking to prove our worth and to please by projecting the image of a tireless person, someone who never stops, who is continually efficient. Excessive perfectionism.

COFFIN

A coffin symbolizes the end of a cycle and the beginning of a new stage. It represents a capacity to die to certain ways of thinking, feeling, being, and/or doing, to phases and stages that have come to an end. It may also announce death on the physical level.

⊕ Understanding death, and cycles that begin and end. Capacity to die to old concepts and behavioral patterns in order to be reborn into a new state of conscience, a new way of living. Ability to be detached, to let go of a situation we are experiencing. Introspection, contemplation, and intense reflection on life and the changes that occur. May announce someone's death. Integration of the fact that life is eternal, that it continues beyond the death of our physical body.

⊖ A lack of understanding of death and an incapacity to simply accept it as the end of a cycle, the completion of a stage that prepares a new birth. Difficulty letting go, being detached, accepting the deep changes that accompany the completion of a stage. Nostalgia that pushes us to hang on to old patterns, to want to preserve them, to live in the past. Refusal to die to old concepts and erroneous or outdated ways of life. Resistance to change, to renewal, to rebirth. Existential fear. Deep sorrow, pessimism, inner emptiness. Feelings of loss, of failure. Bearer of death, a destructive attitude. Lack of spirituality, ignorance and a lack of understanding of the multi-dimensions of life.

COLD (climate, temperature)

The cold (as a climate factor, as a reference to temperature) represents a vivifying soul-state or mood; it stimulates, makes us active and warm because it activates our inner warmth. From a negative point of view, it indicates a state that emanates indifference, harshness, emotional coldness, rigidity, lack of love, absence of kindness, good will, and human warmth. It is also representative of relationship problems, and an over-reserved, coarse, combative attitude.

⊕ Vivifies and stimulates human warmth, support, consolation, kindness and goodwill. Helps us go within and interiorize. In some cases, the cold may be a symbol of preservation and pleasant freshness.

⊖ An absence of warm feelings. Emotional coldness. Rigidity. Harshness. Relationship difficulties. Presence of memories marked by a lack of love and kindness. An over-reserved, anti-social, introverted mind and spirit. A coarse, harsh, combative attitude.

COMA

A coma is defined as a partial or total alteration of our state of conscience. According to the extent of the affliction and malfunction, there are several types of coma of greatly variable duration (from a few days to several months, even years). Different outer causes can trigger a coma: a serious accident, brain damage, asphyxiation, an epileptic fit, medical or alcohol poisoning, drug overdose, as well as different illnesses. On the metaphysical level, a comatose state represents withdrawal into ourselves, unconscious fleeing from the demands and difficulties of daily life.

⊕ Coming out of a coma announces healing, or a return to concrete life with a much vaster conscience, greater awareness, allowing the person a fresh start, a new departure, and correction of the discrepancies between body, soul and spirit. Transformation of memories that limit our conscience and our capacity to manifest. A period of profound self-questioning, of work on our inner *luggage*, the *storage-trunks* or reservoirs of memories accumulated in our unconscious, work on the difficulties that incite a person to withdraw into himself and wish to flee the outer world.

⊖ Loss of all capacity to react and manifest following a traumatic situation. A period of inertia, a vegetative state, a state of dropping out or disconnection, profound discrepancy. Flight reaction, escapism, in response to an important shock that engenders an incapacity to face life. Loss of motivation to actively and consciously participate in life. Existential fear. Unconscious death.

COMPASS

A compass is an instrument that serves to indicate a direction; it is made up of a face with a mobile, magnetized needle that points toward the magnetic North. Hence it is a symbol of orientation, a reference point, enabling us to situate ourselves and choose a direction.

⊕ A capacity to orient ourselves, to know where we are and where we have to go. Facility heading toward our objectives, or finding our way again. An ability to feel or sense our inner compass and trust it, to recognize which way we must go, to follow the path of Destiny, remain in alignment with our life plan.

⊖ Disorientation, dispersion. Loss of our sense of direction. An incapacity to find our way, our destination, to recognize our destiny, our life plan. A period of confusion, loss of our aims and objectives. Discrepancy. An incapacity to determine our orientation, to know which direction to follow.

COMPUTER

A computer is an electronic device that works through the sequential reading of a collection of pre-defined instructions, called programs, allowing the execution of determined operations whose data processing is based on numbers. A tool for work, research, learning, and leisure that is used globally today, and which, *via* the Internet, also allows access to, and management of very important personal and social databanks. Symbolically, God or Cosmic Intelligence can be compared to an immense, multi-dimensional, Living Computer, and a person to a personal computer integrated into this Cosmic

Computer, whose software, i.e. data and memories of personal experimentation, is managed by Divine Programs.

The parallel between God, people and a computer, helps us understand how both Cosmic Conscience and human conscience work, as well as the correlations between the macrocosm and the microcosm. It gives us a glimpse of the beauty and complexity represented by God, the Universe, human-beings, matter, and the constant interaction among all levels of Creation.

A computer works on the basis of programs, software, and files, and it needs electricity to function. If we look at the symbolic parallel with man, we see that human beings have their vital energy, similar to electricity, to activate their body and experiment matter. Our evolution is made possible through inner programs that are linked to the Divine Program, which sets the goals to be attained, the qualities to be developed and integrated during the course of our experimentations in our multiple lives. These programs are accessible through the symbolic study of dreams and daily situations; they engender happy events and/or ordeals to help people evolve by gradually transforming their distortions so as to one day attain perfection. However, the human dimension is much more powerful that a physical computer, and the multiple possibilities this tool offers only provide us with a brief insight into the capacities and powers we human-beings possess and are led to develop.

Another parallel that can be established between a computer and a human-being is the link between the internet and access to Knowledge, to the Parallel Worlds and the multiple dimensions, which is possible in dreams, meditation, through our intuition, subtle perception, psychic powers, as well as signs received in concrete reality.

In a way, a computer symbolizes our soul, wherein the positive and negative memory and memories of our different lives have been recorded and stored. It represents our capacity to memorize, to use and deal with memory, to connect with the Divine, to activate our learning, our apprenticeship programs, to study ourselves on the inside, and to discover the various *files* of our unconscious, the multiple potentiality that we are, as well as all that we need to realize and do to improve ourselves and develop Qualities, Virtues, and Pure Powers.

⊕ A great capacity to memorize, work, communicate, organize, deal with and provide access to large quantities of recorded data and information. Helps us understand the way our conscience and unconscious work. The ability to recognize the kind of program that is underway in our inner computer and, if necessary, to consciously change it so as to evolve and transform ourselves positively. Allows us to establish a connection with other souls, to visit them, to understand their program and our affinities with them. Visiting the parallel worlds, other dimensions. Infinite possibilities for expansion, connection with the Universe and its infinite secrets. An intellect that is fast, skillful, multi-disciplinary, multiparous, and multi-operational. Intelligent, patient analysis, well-structured organization, and pertinent use of data. Interest in the computing world, how it works, as well as the multi-dimensional, efficient, fast communication that it allows both the individual and the collectivity. A period of inner analysis and understanding in the light of Knowledge. Helps us understand the way our conscience and unconscious work. The ability to recognize the kind of program that is underway in our inner computer and, if necessary, to consciously change it so as to evolve and transform ourselves positively. Seeking and maintaining a connection between our personal computer and the Divine, Cosmic Computer. Awareness of the fact that working with computers in the outer world, symbolically corresponds to the same work on the inner level, both individually and collectively. Responsible, wise use of computers and the possibilities of work, study, research, learning, broadcasting, communication, and materialization offered by them. Awareness of the fact that through computers we are constantly in contact with very great quantities of memories and parts of ourselves, and at the same time, with the soul, spirit, mind, and conscious and unconscious memories of the other users.

⊖ Problems with our soul, our memories, our access to the multi-dimensions, our capacity to concretely communicate with the Divine, the Universe, and other souls. Problems related to the management of information; or, the transmission of personal and/or collective data. Inadequate use of information and existing potential. Accumulation of useless data. Blocked data revealing a lack of cleansing. Refusal to acknowledge the need to update, install, and activate new programs. Absence of capacities regarding transformation, adaptation, and accounting of data, thereby limiting the integration and correct functioning of new programs. An incapacity to renew ourselves, to regenerate on the soul, mind and spirit level. Conserving distorted memories. Memory overloaded with negative information thereby leading to inner malfunctioning, or the destruction of memory by viruses. An over-analytical, arid, megalomaniac mind and spirit. Dependency. A self-centered person, fleeing from reality. Discrepancies between mental, emotional and action plans. Inner combat, seeking conquests, extremism.

CONSTIPATION *cf.* ***Excrement, feces***

COOK, TO

An action which consists in transforming and creating changes, mutations, through heat and fire. Symbolically speaking, heat represents love, and the fire that produces heat represents the power of the spirit and vital energy. Hence cooking symbolizes a capacity to transform resources, composing elements, emotions, thoughts, and situations in life thanks to love and the power of our spirit. Cooking also allows the evaporation of surplus water, symbolically representing emotions. It is also a process of alchemical transformation, purification, and transcendence.

⊕ An active force or power on the energy level allowing transformation, change, alchemy and transmutation in a right, well-balanced way. Capacity to nourish others with love, service and devotion. Provides warmth and consolation. Purification, transcendence. Conscious evolution through the power of love and the strength and force of our spirit.

⊖ Inner blockages that prevent us from nourishing ourselves and others with love and a right, qualitative attitude. Problems related to excessive, insufficient, or inactive vital energy, lack of warmth and intensity, of capacity to transform. Difficulty using the power of spirit and love to transform ourselves and evolve. Fear of change. Distorted mutations and transformations. A way of loving and using our spirit that causes burns and destruction. An alchemical force used with malevolent, even demonic intention. Over- intensity in the use of vital energy.

Over-cooking symbolically indicates the presence of forces that tend to burn and destroy the benefits of nourishing others, as well as the possibility of nourishing ourselves on all levels.

Refusal to eat cooked food: May indicate someone whose desire to eat healthily has led to his becoming extremist in his values and principles; who lacks love and human warmth, as well as adaptability and flexibility in his choices; or, who has anorexic tendencies.

COOKER *cf. Stove*

CORPSE

The word corpse generally refers to a dead human body. A corpse also symbolizes a suspicious, violent or disrespectful death. Seeing a corpse in a dream means we are discovering parts of ourselves, memories related to unresolved karmic behavior and attitudes. Everything that doesn't die a peaceful, natural death is linked to unsettled karma. Our karmic *luggage* (*cf.* this term) is governed by what is called The Law of karma, which can be summed up as our always reaping what we sow.

Following an intense quarrel or conflict on the concrete level, without there having been any fatal physical violence leading to someone's death, we may receive dreams in which we see corpses. In terms of conscience, *corpse* symbolism shows us that the anger and aggression experienced killed aspects of our being, our confidence, our *joie de vivre*, our creativity, etc. Our dreams can show us that whenever we have negative behavior and attitudes, parts of us become criminals, murderers. Unless a very high level of evolution has been attained, everyone has a potential for aggression and violence in their karmic luggage. In certain circumstances, this can push us to commit a criminal, even murderous act, on the physical level. That is why we should never ignore dreams where we see ourselves acting violently, criminally. Such dreams should be considered as serious warnings inciting us to transform our potential for violence before it materializes in concrete reality.

⊕ Awakens compassion for the deceased and for those who go through great ordeals marked by violence. Helps us work on transforming and transcending memories related to violent death. Incites us to think about The Laws of karma and reincarnation, as well as the consequences of our behavior, as seen both in dreams and in concrete reality.

⊖ Memories related to an accumulation of violence and aggression. Vengeful spirit. Destructive force. Lack of understanding of the Laws of karma and reincarnation. Fear of death through ignorance of the true, sacred meaning of life. People haunted by their past, either of this life or other lives (often the case of people having witnessed, assisted or survived massacres, executions, genocides, catastrophes, etc.). Existential fear, constant anxiety that the negativity experienced will come back to life.

COSMETICS

The term cosmetics comes from the ancient Greek word *kosmetikè,* which signifies 'the art of dress and ornament' as well as 'the art of beautifying.' Also used as a synonym for make-up*, it is more an indication of the whole range of beauty* products and physical appearance in general, including care, maintenance, and embellishment of the body. Cosmetics symbolize the search for beauty, well-being, health and harmony. They are related to a wish to improve our appearance, self-esteem, and capacity to manifest while emanating beautiful energies. (**cf. also* these terms)

⊕ Helps to exteriorize inner beauty, to manifest it concretely. A capacity to take care of ourselves. Protection and reinforcement against polluting elements. Effects of purification, gentleness, softness, regeneration, rejuvenation, refreshment, vivification. Supports natural beauty. Embellishment, refinement. Well-being.

⊖ Artificial beauty. Behavior based on appearances, superficiality. Use of cosmetics to please, seduce, create illusions and hide faults, lacks, fears and insecurity. Worldly pleasures. Arrogant, haughty attitude, feelings of superiority and inferiority. Exaggerated make-up to compensate inner feelings of ugliness in terms of conscience.

COUCH, SOFA

A couch or sofa represents a state of conscience of receptivity, rest and well-being on the intimate or social level. It also symbolizes the way we relax and use comfort.

⊕ Capacity to allow ourselves relax and rest. Receptivity on the intimate or social level. Communication, sharing and renewal in an atmosphere of conviviality and well-being.

⊖ A state of laziness in our personal or social life. Lack of willpower to act. Inertia. Disinterest. Inhibition of the necessary motivation to be involved and committed on the physical level, in everyday life. Superficial listening. Communication without any depth, shallow exchanges. Desire to lounge or laze. Difficulty relaxing, resting, being receptive.

COUNTRY (Nation)

All of the countries that exist on Earth represent, on the subtle levels, collective *egregores* (*cf.* this term) or reservoirs of memories, which can be considered as living entities, consisting of the emotional, mental and spiritual energies of the people who live there. Symbolically speaking, in terms of states of conscience, it can be said that everyone bears within himself all of the countries and populations that exist, and have existed on Earth. This is explained by the fact that during the course of its numerous terrestrial lives, throughout the history of humanity, our soul has incarnated in different countries, among different nationalities, races, etc. Each human being harbors in his unconscious the entire collection of the memories he has accumulated throughout his many, varied lives. This also explains why a person can feel an attraction or aversion, in differing degrees of intensity, for a particular country, historical era, mentality, culture, etc.

Each country represents a state of conscience, a mentality, a temperament, and certain specific characteristics, which have been developed throughout the course of its history. A country's collective, conscious or unconscious, memories creates an egregore of thought-forms, an intelligent energy that inspires, influences, permeates, and is imprinted on the inhabitants of this country. And even though we may leave one country and go and live in another, we remain energetically connected and conditioned by everything our country of origin represents, while simultaneously experiencing and experimenting the influence of the new country.

Whenever we visit a country in concrete reality, in our imagination, or in a dream, on the metaphysical level, in our inner world, we visit aspects of ourselves that resonate with that country. We can then experiment the qualities and virtues attributed to the country as well as its distortions. As our conscience gradually evolves, we are called upon to surpass and transcend the constraints, limits, flaws and weaknesses of various countries that prevent us from developing our potential to be universal. This is also the ultimate aim aspired to by international organizations, such as the United Nations or the European Union. To nourish feelings of fraternity and belonging to a planetary family, to evolve in a universal conscience, not only must each person develop in himself the qualities and strengths of every country and nation, but he must also transcend their faults and weaknesses. This work can be achieved through the study and symbolic analysis of the particularities of the different countries on Earth, their origin, history, culture, development, and their future. In general, the affinity or aversion we feel for a country gives us quite clear indications of the positive and/or negative resonance we have with it, as well as the karmic *luggage* (*cf.* this term) we have collected and registered within ourselves during the course of our numerous lives in such a country or ethnic egregore. Our being born in a particular country is never a coincidence, just as changing country at a particular time in our life is never a coincidence either. It is inscribed in our destiny, written in our Life-Plan, pre-ordained by our Evolution Program. (*cf. also* **Emigrate; Immigrate**)

Work on our inner countries allows us to better understand what our personal, family and collective unconscious is comprised of, as well as how the forces and memories we have accumulated over our innumerable lives on Earth work. In our inner world, in terms of conscience, there are rich and poor countries, some are more evolved, others are developing, emerging, or going through all sorts of difficulties and ordeals. According to the various activities of our mind and spirit, our conscience travels and visits our inner countries and the memories related to them. These travels are sometimes very rapid, which can cause major fluctuations in our soul-states (moods), emotions and our way of functioning.

The fact that the Earth is divided into countries separated from one another by borders in the physical world, is a reflection of the numerous divisions and separations terrestrial humanity experiences on the metaphysical level, on the levels of our conscience, thoughts, feelings and sentiments. Existing borders have their place because the present level of man's evolution still requires limits and specific structures, which allow us to perfect the development of qualities and the transformation of distortions within a more restricted framework. It is important to know that each country has its own learning and evolution program, which is right for the level of conscience and the collective karma of its inhabitants.

⊕ Incites us to reflect on the affinities and aversions we feel toward certain countries and become aware of the resonance we have with them, with the qualities and distortions they represent on the collective level. Understanding the influence egregores (*cf.* this term) have on the subtle levels. Work on ourselves, on our conscious and unconscious memories, in order to develop the qualities, forces and strong points of each country, and transcend within ourselves, the distortions and weaknesses that characterize it. Development of compassion, tolerance, non-judgment, an ability to altruistically and unconditionally love all countries as beings experimenting on the path of evolution. A better understanding of the correlations and interactions among different peoples, and different life-plans and learning programs that connect them on the individual and collective levels. A great opening onto the world. Respect for the customs, mentalities, values, levels of conscience and rhythms of evolution in all countries. Ease in exchanges and communication on the international level, worldwide. A capacity to integrate very powerful states of conscience and to continually function with global vision. Acquisition of a planetary, universal conscience and a capacity to consider ourselves not only as citizens of a particular country, but to feel like a citizen of the Universe. A planetary ambassador who radiates Divine Wisdom and Love, and works in accordance with the Universal Laws.

⊖ Problems related to the characteristics of one or several countries, their mentalities, cultures, administrative, social, political, judicial, etc. systems. Ignorance of the Law of resonance, which explains not only the attractions and affinities we may feel for a country, but also the aversion, perturbation and disturbance we may feel. Difficulty fitting in and becoming integrated into other mentalities, lifestyles, ways of thinking, etc. A lack of opening, adaptation, tolerance on the social and humanitarian levels. Seeking to preserve our previously acquired benefits, knowledge, habits and customs by isolating ourselves, and by living in ethnic groups, through *ghetto-ization.* Sentiments of isolation, exclusion, discrimination, inferiority, impotence, or a feeling of superiority, imposing haughty, arrogant behavior, which seeks to control, which erects barriers, borders, restrictions. A critical, complicated, rebellious mentality that refuses to become integrated, that treats others with contempt and disrespect. Separatism. Nationalism. Extreme patriotism. Chauvinism, jingoism, flag-waving. Racism. Religious, ideological, cultural fanatism. A very materialistic, selfish, egotistical spirit that only seeks wealth, power and expansion on the material level, that hogs all the resources and refuses to share them equitably, to use them altruistically to serve the good of the collectivity.

COUNTRY, COUNTRYSIDE

The country and the countryside is a symbol of peaceful tranquility and calm, of communion and harmony with nature, wide-open spaces, vastness and expanded horizons, as well as rest, retreat, regeneration and renewal, a return to natural simplicity, to a lifestyle that respects the cycles of life. It is also where man cultivates the earth and raises animals to provide food. Hence it is related to the emotional level through the vegetable world and to instinctive instincts through the animal world.

⊕ An understanding of the cycles and laws of nature, of the fact that we always reap what we sow. Rest, calm, serenity, regeneration and renewal, peacefulness, a soothing balm for mind and soul, a place that is conducive to reflection, introspection, solitude, return to our inner selves. Simplicity, a healthy life, return to what is essential in life. Helps us rediscover our origins, our roots. Fertility, fecundity. Gratitude for the abundance of resources. Respect for the environment, flora and fauna, a love of nature. Pleasure working the earth, fusing with the elements. Purification, transformation.

⊖ Visiting infertile inner spaces. A lack of resources, an incapacity to slow down, calm down, renew ourselves and re-establish harmony in our lifestyle. Seeking refuge in the country so as to flee the frenzied hyperactivity in town. De-connection from a social, cultural life. Poor harvests on the inner and outer levels; lack of understanding that we always reap what we sow. A period of inactivity, laziness, dropping out. A feeling of being far away from everything, isolation; a tendency to behave like a hermit. A lack of global vision, a limited spirit due to a lack of education, rough, uncouth behavior directed toward instinctual needs. A lack of understanding of the cycles of Nature, disrespect for the environment, for animal and vegetable life. Fear of expansion, of industrialization; or, abusive exploitation and destruction of nature for material profits, to make money.

COURT OF LAW *(cf. also **Justice**)*

The Court (law court or tribunal) is jurisdiction that includes all of the magistrates and judges charged with administering justice. It is also the place where magistrates and judges exert their profession. It is where people in conflict come to seek justice, and where those who did not respect the law are judged. Symbolically, a court of law represents our structure for justice, our capacity to recognize behavior that strays from those same Laws, and to take appropriate measures to rectify them.

Seeing ourselves in court in a dream reveals a situation or behavior that needs to be rectified. It is a sign that we are not on the right path, that there will be consequences, no matter the context or circumstances. It may also indicate a situation regarding corruption, injustice, and manipulation of the judicial system. It is essential to remind ourselves that, both in a dream and concrete reality, the court and those present (judge, lawyer, prosecutor, the accused, the witnesses, the members of the jury, policemen, etc.), all represent often unconscious parts of ourselves. By studying the behavior of all the actors of justice, we become aware of the way in which we apply human laws, how we behave regarding transgression, and what sort of programs we set up to rectify the distortions that lead us to court.

If, for example, we receive a dream wherein we are justly condemned by the court, this indicates that a program is being activated where we could encounter problems with justice if we do not work on rectifying our memories and needs that cause us to break the law, in physical or metaphysical reality. It is important to always relate the contents of our dreams to what we are going through in our physical reality. If we receive a dream concerning justice, wherein we feel we are unfairly condemned and receive what we consider to be a disproportionate sentence, and at that time we have nothing to reproach ourselves with in concrete reality, where we respect the Law, this indicates that on an inner level, we tend to judge in a disproportionate, authoritarian, or corrupt way.

The role of the Court is to shed light on a case, to ensure that truth emerges, and that justice is rendered fairly, equitably. It is a symbol that represents the integrity of the Law and that truth must always be given priority. While earthly, terrestrial laws are conceived by human beings according to their level of conscience to govern life on Earth, Divine or Cosmic Laws take priority over human laws and guarantee Divine Justice on our planet and in the parallel worlds. Furthermore, no matter what strengths or weaknesses we humans may have, each of us has a court or tribunal of conscience within us, where certain parts of ourselves are judges, magistrates or lawyers, others are witnesses, and others are the accused and/or criminals, etc. This law court of conscience allows us to identify our inner delinquents and lawbreakers so as to re-educate them and set them back on the right path.

In situations where the court sentence seems unfair, even inhumane, it is vital to remind ourselves that Divine Justice and the Law of karma are also constantly in application through terrestrial laws, and that all judicial systems that judge a person or group of people are also governed by the Law of resonance, whereby we always attract what we are on both the conscious and unconscious levels of our being. It is important to understand that true Justice operates over the course of several lives, not only over one life, and it is governed by the Divine Program which is fair and equitable for everyone, which ensures that we always reap what we have sown.

⊕ Capacity to understand the multi-dimensional function of a court of law. Capacity to accept any judgment with serenity and dignity; or, to appeal and provide further elements of favorable proof without any anger, bitterness, or vengeance. Ability to submit to what is right, to repent, to overcome an ordeal, or admit a mistake no matter how serious. Capacity to render rigorous judgment whenever it is right and necessary for the evolution of the person in question. A fair, honest, upright, calm, fearless person who knows that the foundations of his inner justice are stable, who is at peace with himself and serene before his inner tribunal, regarding his own conscience. Capacity to accept whatever judgment is pronounced, whatever sentence is given, to recognize in them the application of Divine Justice, even through the weaknesses and flaws of human justice. Respect for and integration of the Divine, Cosmic Laws. Development of the capacity to study and interpret the work of human courts in the light of the Law of resonance and symbolic language. Great capacity to humbly admit our mistakes, to accept responsibility for the ensuing consequences, to call ourselves to order, or accept being called to order by any authority, court, tribunal, without protesting, without rebelling. Evolution of our soul *via* understanding of Divine Justice, which operates over the course of one or several lives. Behavior rectification thanks to a symbolic study of signs and dreams. Seeking the truth above all, while remaining loyal to Divine Principles. Perfect judgment, free of any criticism. Rigor. Integrity. Incorruptibility. Rectification work by referring back to ourselves and through understanding. Discernment. Love of Justice, liking to apply the Laws and knowing how to do so with clemency, compassion, and deep understanding. Capacity to recognize and acknowledge the importance of Justice on all levels. Will to re-educate, re-program, and repair our negative karmas. Capacity to face both earthly justice and Divine Justice with dignity, courage, and submission. Understanding the Wisdom hidden behind a judgment and sentence. Testimonial of some of the highest levels of conscience a human being may attain on Earth. Deep understanding of the Law of resonance, which enables us to remain committed and to forgive at all times, in all circumstances.

⊖ Problems with justice. Someone who is badly judged; or, who judges other people's actions, emotions, thoughts, or energies unfairly, rigidly, extremely harshly or severely. Attitude of rebellion, insubordination, refusal to accept the court's sentence, lack of understanding of the innumerable ways in which Divine Justice may be manifested on Earth. Ignorance of the Cosmic Laws, and especially of the Laws of karma and resonance. Lack of understanding that we always reap what we sow, and that we always attract what we ourselves are, on both the conscious and unconscious levels of our being. Refusal to appear before the inner tribunal of our own conscience, to acknowledge our errors and misactions (*cf.* this term), to repent and ask for forgiveness, to rectify and repair our misdeeds. Poor judgment, critical, complicated mind and spirit. De-structured, disorganized human justice. A judicial system that has lost all meaning, all logic, all ethnics. A corrupt court that has become a place of combat to satisfy personal ambitions, or to be involved in power games and scheming. Numerous difficulties related to justice, truth, sincerity, and integrity. Lies, dishonesty, adversity, confusion, revenge, puritanism, extremism, guilt, or lack of discernment and justice. Judicial corruption, manipulation of power, accumulation of serious karmic debts. Lack of Knowledge and multi-dimensional understanding.

CRAMP

A cramp is a violent, fleeting, painful contraction of a muscle or group of muscles. It represents forces that have become bogged down, as well as wounded memories, which hold back and refuse to manifest because they are suffering from hyperactivity, from too much action; or, because they are tired, exhausted, anxious, and/or have become lazy and passive through a lack of love, motivation, and wisdom. A cramp may also indicate the presence of unconscious fears related to trauma or an ordeal experienced in the past.

⊕ Incitement to work on memories marked by fear, anxiety, worry, stress, hyperactivity, fatigue, an over- or under-active lifestyle. Awareness that we need to re-evaluate the way we function in matter so as to allow for the physical re-balancing and re-harmonization of body, soul, mind, and spirit.

⊖ Expresses a muddled, bogged down state, as a result of hyperactive behavior, or a lack of activity, or anxiety that creates multiple tensions; or, it may indicate the presence of repressed feelings, sentiments, fears, stress, pressure, and doubts, all of which prepare the way for illnesses. Obstinacy, anger, rebellion, poor, wrong, distorted way of advancing, which causes pain, blockages, paralysis. Difficulty slowing down and decreasing our activities in the world of matter in spite of obvious symptoms of overwork. Overmotivation, excessive willpower and physical action, an incapacity to let go; or, a lack of motivation and will to move our body, a lax attitude. Nutritional and affective, emotional deficiencies, and also possible bulimic or anorexic tendencies. Lack of energy, structure, and organization, all of which prevent us from advancing; or, an unconscious refusal to materialize. Tendency to ignore physical body signals and to seek an outer medical solution rather than calling our values and lifestyle into question.

CREDIT

Credit, from the Latin words *creditum* (trust) and *credere* (believe), is a loan that a person, a business, or a bank, agrees to grant a private individual, a company, an organization, or a state. It includes various forms of monetary loans or payment delays granted to customers by suppliers. A symbol of help, trust, and support regarding resources, credit is closely related to the capacity to materialize. It may allow a form of expansion, and it may also provide a second chance when there are financial difficulties.

⊕ When a request for credit, for a loan, is granted, this indicates that the credit or loan is in accordance with the person/company/organization/state's program of apprenticeship and evolution; Cosmic Intelligence orchestrates and synchronizes circumstances so that the person/company/organization/state receives the necessary resources, providential help, an opportunity or new chance to create, materialize, manifest their potential, realize a project, experiment expansion. Credit contributes to the development of a sense of responsibility, trust, and mutual respect, motivation to work and make efforts. It may indicate a new *departure*, new beginnings, restoring a person's self-esteem and hope in the future. It opens access onto considerable reserves of energy, resources, services, possibilities to materialize, to concretize ideas, visions, projects. Periods of experimentation, evolution, expansion, abundance and prosperity thanks to the credit(s) granted. Gratitude, acknowledgement, deep appreciation. Good management of resources, ensuring reimbursement of the credit within the required time limits.

⊖ Poor use or management of credit received which leads to serious difficulties on different levels. Fear of requesting or accepting credit due to memories of abuse, waste, and bad experiences on the financial level. Fear of lacking, financial insecurities, material dependencies, which engender numerous blockages. A superficial lifestyle, based on buying things on credit to nourish artificial needs, expensive tastes, desires for luxury and excessive consumerism, superfluous spending. Breach and loss of trust. Excessive debt leading to bankruptcy (*cf. also* this term) and ruin.

Credit request denied indicates that Up Above refuses to back our project; or, that other measures must be undertaken to achieve our objectives.

CRIME

The word crime, from the Latin word *crimen* (accusation, fault, blot, stain, blemish), designates serious acts of moral or legal infractions. If there are crimes that present-day earthly, terrestrial justice and the law leave unpunished, these criminal acts as well as the conscience of those who commit them, do not escape Divine Law and Justice; they accumulate heavy karma that they will have to face one day. On the metaphysical and symbolic levels, the term crime comprises all of the distorted thoughts, emotions, and intentions – e.g. thoughts of murder, anger, revenge, abuse of power, theft, etc.– through which a person nourishes malevolent forces, that one day, will push him to commit criminal acts in concrete reality. It also represents the memories of crime accumulated in our unconscious throughout the course of our many lives, that, sooner or later, we have to cleanse and repair in accordance with the Laws of karma, resonance, and Divine Justice. These memories represent a collection of dangerous forces that are parts of ourselves, prepared to do anything to achieve and justify their aims.

If, in a dream, we see a crime committed by ourselves or another person, we need to be very vigilant because such a dream is a warning that we harbor very aggressive forces within ourselves that may suddenly manifest and risk devastating or destroying our life. Crime is an extreme manifestation of a great accumulation of anger, envy, jealousy, avidity, greed, rancor, bitterness, hatred and revenge, under the influence of which a person becomes capable of harmful, devastating acts, destroying his and/or other people's lives, thereby creating karma with serious consequences for this life or his future lives.

⊕ In a dream, crime serves as a warning to incite us to work on ourselves to transform our extreme, violent parts, to reflect on our unjust thoughts, behavior and deeds that have a criminal tendency, and the consequences they engender. A warning signal attracting our attention to aspects of ourselves, that need to be rectified and healed so as to avoid their manifesting one day, pushing us to concretely commit a crime or destroy ourselves. Awareness of malevolent, ill-intentioned, aggressive, destructive forces inscribed in our unconscious, the awakening of which, through resonance, may lead us into situations where we risk committing a crime, or being the victim of one. Development of compassion and deep, global understanding of people involved in criminal acts. Integration and understanding of the Law of karma and the principle of Divine Justice, by which we always reap what we sow. Cleansing, liberation, and transcendence of karmic memories marked by all sorts of crime. Integration of the fact that evil is educational, and that all wrong-doing, every unjust act can be repaired if we renounce evil, set off on the right path once again, and accept to forgive ourselves and others.

⊖ An outburst, an explosion of long repressed, negative, destructive forces and emotions: rancor, jealousy, anger, hatred, spite, intolerance, discrimination, fanaticism, a feeling of superiority, racism, etc. Materialization of long nourished criminal thoughts. Conscious or unconscious violation of the law, and/or other people's rights. An incapacity to distinguish between good and evil, or to voluntarily choose not to do evil. A lifestyle that nourishes negative forces, and stimulates malevolent, unjust behavior, as well as extreme destructive impulses, that push a person to commit criminal acts. A lack of understanding of the effect memories and criminal thoughts exert on us, on both the individual and collective levels. Someone who wants to force Destiny, who is prepared to do all it takes to get what he wants, or to take revenge. An outlaw, a rebel. Believing we have to take the law into our own hands and make our own law and justice. Crime victims experiencing the Law of return, who reap the fruit of their own criminal acts committed in this life or in previous lives. A lack of understanding of the fact that evil, wrong-doing, what hurts always engenders evil, wrong-doing and hurt. Ignorance of the Laws of karma and resonance. Someone who, through crime, creates very heavy karma and very difficult future lives for himself. A lack of understanding that Divine Justice is absolute and present even in cases or situations that seem unfair, unjust in the eyes of earthly, human laws.

CROCODILE

The crocodile is one of the most ancient animals on Earth. Since it is semi-aquatic, it is related to both the earth and water elements, i.e. symbolically speaking, to the physical and emotional worlds. It lives in slow-moving rivers and is carnivorous; it feeds on a large variety of dead or live mammals and fish. Its appearance, and ways of moving and hunting make it a symbol of primitive, aggressive, ancient instincts that push it to do everything possible to satisfy needs for physical and emotional nourishment. Like the lion and the shark, the crocodile can act with great rapidity and agility, and its strength allows it to attack very powerful animals. These characteristics symbolize powerful instinctual, rapid, agile forces that dwell within us and can be mobilized to attack, defend, procure nourishment, and satisfy our needs with violence. Living mainly in water, the crocodile can also be active on land, which symbolically indicates the presence of powerful emotional needs that can emerge at any moment and push us to manifest on the concrete level, in the world of action, with great force and intensity, even aggression and violence.

⊕ Great instinctual force that can be activated with agility and rapidity. Powerful emotional potential. Mastery and transcendence of primary instincts of aggression and violence regarding emotions and needs. Someone who is working on very old, ancient emotional memories.

⊖ Great instinctual force and powerful emotional energy, which are activated aggressively, violently, destructively. Incapacity to master our needs, to keep our instincts under control. An impulsive, explosive, devastating temperament. Emotional coldness. Powerful, surprising, threatening energy. A dark force lodged in our unconscious. Very old, ancient memories related to aggressive, untamed, unpredictable emotions.

CROSS, CRUCIFIX

A cross (crucifix), which is a great spiritual symbol, is made up of two lines, two movements, one vertical, the other horizontal, thereby symbolizing the encounter of the celestial, heavenly world and the earthly, terrestrial world. Moreover, the point of intersection between them reveals that true access to and application of Knowledge stems from the heart, from motivation that gives rise to beautiful, right feelings and sentiments, as well as from the transcendence of negative, selfish, egotistical emotions.

The crucifixion of Jesus in the history of the Christian religion refers to the cross as a symbol of death on the human level leading to resurrection, re-birth, on the Divine level, to the manifestation of non-vengeful love, love that does not judge, love that forgives all faults, love that has the capacity to transcend a destiny inflicted by people living in a limited conscience, incapable of understanding true values, and the model or example of life offered by Jesus. Hence, *surpassing the cross* symbolizes elevation toward very high levels of Conscience and Divine Love.

For a large number of people brought up in the Christian tradition, the cross is associated with martyrdom and the belief that we have to endure life, bear our cross, like Christ's Calvary.

The cross may announce a person's imminent death, or the death of certain aspects of himself, or indicate having to go through a great ordeal on the spiritual level. It is also used to commemorate a deceased person, on a tomb, funeral monument, or at a burial place. In such a case, it symbolizes homage to a past life, remembrance, and the passageway into the next world.

⊕ The encounter of celestial and terrestrial levels, of Heaven and Earth, of Spirit and matter. A high level of transcendence. The opening of our heart, awakened by love and wisdom, or by great difficulties, major ordeals. A symbol of faith, of work on ourselves on the spiritual level, and communion with the Divine. A capacity to transcend suffering, calumny, scorn, meanness, spiritual attacks. An understanding of death, rebirth, and the meaning of life after life, eternal life. An ability to accede to Knowledge and to develop the highest levels of conscience. May be an announcement of a person's physical death, or the end of a situation, of a project.

⊖ Spiritual extremism, or rejection of the Divine. May be related to a person who imposes his faith, who wishes to convert others to his religion, to his beliefs, proselytism. Fear of death, difficulty mourning and accepting bereavement. A complaining, whining person; behaving like a victim. Suffering related to religion, a feeling of injustice, abandonment, disconnection from God. Fear of being subjected to calumny, injustice, and persecution because of our spirituality. Mystical delirium.

CROSSROADS, INTERSECTION (junction)

Usually, a crossroads is an intersection of several roads. Consequently it offers a choice of directions. Symbolically, the possibilities offered by a crossroads or intersection apply to all levels of our being: physical, emotional, intellectual, and spiritual. Finding ourselves at a crossroads in our life is a decisive, even crucial moment in our life, and this situation may require deep reflection as to which direction to take. Hence, a crossroads, an intersection, obliges us to slow down, and sometimes even stop, to evaluate the options offered before making our choice. Arriving at a crossroads may also symbolize a passage toward a new stage, during which we allow ourselves time to stop and reflect and refer back to ourselves, to our life; it is a good time to look back on our life, and take stock of our experimentations and apprenticeships, before taking a new direction, before continuing our spiritual journey along a different path.

⊕ An opening of conscience, allowing us to catch a glimpse of new possibilities. A capacity to explore new avenues. Discernment, a capacity to make the right decision, to set out on a new path, to advance and commit ourselves to it with confidence, determination, and courage. A good sense of direction. An ability to intuitively choose the right path, to follow the stages of our life program, to let ourselves be guided by signs, dreams, and synchronicity. Attention and respect for others. Flexibility and fluidity in the way we advance; and when the intersection is in the form of a roundabout, an easy possibility to retrace our steps, to return to our past.

⊖ Difficulty making choices, orienting ourselves, choosing which direction to follow. A period of confusion because confronted with multiple possibilities. Feelings of insecurity, doubt, hesitation; feeling of being in an impasse. Fear of committing ourselves to a new path, of starting a new apprenticeship, of beginning a new stage in our learning program, in our life-plan. Inertia, stagnation, being bogged down. A tendency to go round in circles. A lack of courage to try out new paths, to explore the unknown. Difficulty yielding or taking our place.

CROWN

Through its round shape and the fact that it is worn on our head, a crown is a symbol of Divine Power and receptivity to what comes from Above. It represents consecration, royalty, a noble state of mind and conscience, loyalty to Divine values, principles, authority and power, power to make decisions, and a capacity to materialize our ideas, objectives, aims, goals, convictions, ideals. It is also used as a sign of distinction, reward, merit; or, as a decoration to highlight certain atmospheres, ambiances and occasions such as weddings.

⊕ A royal conscience, nobility of mind and spirit, fidelity to high principles and values. Power to make decisions and wealth devoted to serve the Divine, to serve God, and the good of the collectivity. Capacity to exercise authority and power in the right, just way, in accordance with Divine Laws.

⊖ Megalomaniac behavior. Abuse of power, avid for glory and material riches. Egoism, domination, meanness. A major superiority or inferiority complex, which makes it difficult to recognize and acknowledge our true worth, to develop our authority and power of materialization, concretization. A person who is easily influenced, who needs to be admired, adored, glorified by people he puts on a pedestal, without any discernment, without questioning the quality of the values and principles they truly represent.

CRUTCH

A crutch represents an outer support that a person with a serious leg injury leans on to be able to move around. It symbolizes the fact that the person needs help and support to manifest, to advance, or to face a difficult situation experienced either within himself or in outer reality. Metaphorically, the term crutch designates all forms of physical, social, psychological, medical, therapeutic, etc. help and support to which we may have temporary recourse in order to re-balance our state of health or a situation in our life.

⊕ Support during a difficult period. Acceptance of limitations and difficulties regarding mobility and advancing. A capacity to recognize our limitations as an opportunity to rest, to re-balance our life, to regain strength and heal our wounds. A period of self-questioning, reflection and inner listening so as to understand which part of us needs to be helped, re-harmonized and healed. Awareness of the causes, attitudes and behavior that need to be rectified so as to no longer need crutches and to rediscover our autonomy on all levels. Re-alignment and reconstruction of our life with new consciousness.

⊖ A period of difficulties and limitations on the action level. A complaining attitude, resignation, behaving as a victim subjected to his state. A person who continues to force in order to advance without changing his behavior or attitude. A lack of willpower to call ourselves into question and reflect on thought patterns and habits that are at the origin of our state of being. Pride, refusal to ask for or accept help from other people. An incapacity to understand and admit to a need for crutches on the outside reveals a need for support, help and healing on the inside.

CRY, TO

Crying allows us to attenuate or relieve soul-states and free ourselves from certain intense, negative feelings and emotions, such as physical pain, psychological, emotional suffering, sadness, disappointment, despair, or fear. However we also cry for positive reasons such as deep joy, or a powerful feeling of exaltation, ecstasy, happiness, bliss, when deeply moved by the beauty of a landscape, the purity of a child, an altruistic gesture, or when we fuse with the Divine. An important revelation received in a dream, vision, or meditation that allows us to know our destiny, our mission in life, or the meaning of existence, can also make us cry.

Whenever what we are experiencing (on the soul level, in our subtle bodies, in our conscience, and in our mind and spirit) cannot be contained or integrated in our physical body, crying serves to re-establish balance *via* the element of water (we are constituted of approx. 70% water), symbolically *via* the emotional level. Showing our emotions by crying also indicates that we don't try to reject or repress them, hence indicating a need for authenticity, sincerity, and transparency.

Crying bears witness to the fact that we are deeply moved by a situation, a gesture, an event, or by memories that resonate in the depth of our heart. Crying requires a certain amount of humility, especially for men, who often receive an education that inculcates the idea that crying is a sign of weakness. However, when we develop our sensitivity, when we awaken to the more subtle dimensions of life, it is natural to free ourselves of this kind of old thought pattern and concept, and show more honesty and nobility of soul by crying.

Crying and tears may also indicate letting go, releasing the need to always be in control, to feel superior, or to be superficial.

However, crying does not always involve right, sincere emotions, because multiple dependencies, and conscious or unconscious intentions, such as a desire to manipulate others may motivate hypocritical, forced tears. Similarly, tears of joy and positive emotion become negative when excessive.

A tendency to cry at the slightest opportunity indicates excessive sensitivity and an incapacity to manage it; or an emotional surfeit that overflows for the slightest reason. On the other hand, an incapacity to cry indicates a high degree of insensitivity and emotional coldness that the person has cultivated for a long time so as not to be affected on the sentimental level; it may be related to serious, unhealed emotional wounds, dating from this present life or previous lives, which have incited the person to close his heart, become insensitive, sometimes even to the point of losing his humanity, so as not to risk going through the pain and suffering caused by such wounds again.

⊕ A capacity to express our emotions and soul-states. An ability to let go, stop wanting to control our feelings at all costs. Someone who is capable of acknowledging his great sensitivity with humility and acceptance, who is not ashamed of being moved to tears by beauty, purity, truth. Someone who knows how to face deeply moving emotions and who can manage the emotions created by deep, intense experiences. A source of liberation, cleansing, purification. Feelings of relief, liberation, light-heartedness, renewal. Helps recycle life experiences on all levels. Liberating, transforming tears that announce a new stage. An expression of authenticity, sincerity, transparency, happiness, joy, and gratitude. Favors the manifestation of compassion, clemency, kindness, forgiveness, love, and wisdom. Tears of exaltation, and happiness revealing a person's experience of communion and fusion with the Divine.

⊖ Crying and tears associated with lamentation, complaining, whining, angry or hysterical outbursts, capricious, hypocritical behavior, testifying to behavioral patterns based on dependency, manipulation, emotional blackmail, victim dynamics, a tendency to make others feel guilty, a desire and will to persuade, control, and dominate others; or, to maintain the status quo through fear of change. Fear of crying in front of others for fear of showing our vulnerability; memories of emotional coldness and repression. Crying that expresses emotional overflow, outbursts, or negative states that a person is incapable of overcoming and transforming because he lacks the awareness and knowledge that would enable him to understand the evolutive meaning – which may be both karmic and initiatic – of emotions, feelings, and sentiments such as disappointment, mourning, sorrow, suffering, depression, despair, dismay, solitude, rejection, abandonment, etc. Crying bouts, accompanying violent rows or quarrels where frustration, tension, and long accumulated things left unsaid due to an incapacity to communicate peacefully, respectfully, while truly listening to the other person, are exteriorized. Crying provoked by exaggeration, a tendency to dramatize situations and problems. A stubborn, obstinate person, who finds it difficult to call himself into question, preferring to judge and accuse others, reproaching them for his own faults and difficulties. A tendency to become hardened and to crystallize to the point of being unable to cry. False belief that crying and tears are automatically related to suffering and authentic emotions.

CUPBOARD, CLOSET, WARDROBE

A cupboard represents a state of conscience related to the structure, order and organization of our inner world. In the form of a wardrobe, it allows us to tidy away, preserve or keep what helps us manifest or emanate a beautiful aura through our choice of clothes. It can also shelter practical objects or those with sentimental value. Moreover, it symbolically shelters our usual soul-states (or moods) as well as our intimacy, since our cupboards/closets/wardrobes are not left open for everyone's eyes.

⊕ Symbolizes a capacity to organize and create order in our intimate life, and in our inner world in general. Protection and preservation of aspects of both practical and sentimental value.

⊖ Lack of structure, disorder, disorganization, or rigidity in our manner of tidying and arranging things, and taking care of our inner space. Accumulation of useless, superfluous things; or, a lack of resources on the personal, intimate level.

CUSTOMS (public administration)

Customs are a public administration set up to establish laws and collect taxes on goods on leaving or entering a country. Customs officers also check the right of passage and entry of people on their arrival in a country. When fair and equitable, its role is to protect a country so as to ensure a healthy, well-balanced development of the collectivity. In an ordinary conscience, we may believe that customs and borders should not exist. However as long as people from all over the world don't live in accordance with values of justice, wisdom and divine love, this concept is utopian. The European Union represents the beginning of a universal concept. At the present time, although it is mainly a common, shared economic space, with no real power as a united organization, with numerous problems to solve, it is a constructive, positive example of gradual evolution of the human conscience toward a universal conscience.

In the parallel worlds, and in the dynamics of our conscience, customs also exist. Like all human beings on the earthly dimension, the inhabitants of other dimensions cannot enter, leave or go wherever they like if they haven't got the necessary *passport,* i.e authorization to do so. On the metaphysical, spiritual level, the Universe can be considered as a fortress of Light that protects everyone's destiny and evolution, where borders can appear and disappear instantaneously. Heaven's *Customs Officers* are continually at work for Cosmic Intelligence Security.

⊕ Procures a feeling of respect for others and what we may rightfully have. Seeing ourselves go through customs in a dream indicates access to new states of conscience, new understanding and knowledge. Being able to go through customs without any difficulty signifies a capacity to travel freely in different countries on Earth and to feel at ease with the mentalities they represent. Evolution and transition between two stages. Understanding Divine Justice, which protects and regulates passages in and between the different worlds for the good of all souls. Integration of new egregores (*cf.* this term) or collective memories and levels of conscience. An elevated sense of justice. Obedience and respect for the laws governing the Universe. Honesty. Integrity. Citizen of the Universe. Global vision and universal spirit. Knowing that areas of our conscience and of the Universe are protected by Cosmic Intelligence is reassuring.

⊖ Whenever we have problems going through customs either in concrete reality or in a dream, this indicates that we need to face and accept restrictions, that we have difficulties with authority, honesty and integrity as well as a limited or erroneous understanding of the protective role of customs. Fear of customs indicates that, consciously or unconsciously, we have something to hide. Difficulty gaining access to expansion, discovering new resources in new areas. Lack of certain qualities required for travelling, visiting and exploring new cultures, forms of life and states of conscience. Forcing a passageway or Destiny. Limitations, confronting the authorities. Lack of honesty and integrity. A rebellious spirit that thinks he's entitled to everything. A person who isn't ready to move on to another mentality, another vision or way of looking at something, to another level of conscience.

CUT, TO

The action of cutting symbolizes a capacity to wisely divide, slice, section or separate links or connections. It is a decisional dynamic of power, a symbolic action necessitating a lot of discernment, tact, and finesse to ensure that it is done well, that it is right, just, and good. It is important to learn to cut with pure intention and motivation, without any negative emotions, on both the concrete and subtle level. The act of cutting and cuts carried out and inflicted in a bitter, begrudging, angry, vengeful state, with a desire to hurt, engender karmas that will have to be paid for one day, because we always reap what we sow.

⊕ A capacity to divide, to separate and section precisely, accurately and wisely. A capacity to discern good and evil. Dynamics of power, decision, emissivity and authority.

⊖ A sharp, cutting, peremptory, extreme attitude in the application of justice. Unfair, wrong cut; a cutting remark that inflicts hurt. An incapacity to assert ourselves for fear of reprisals. An over-emissive spirit that imposes its choices. Difficulty discerning good and evil. A lack of love and wisdom in manifestation. Abuse of power. Harshness, vulgarity, violence, brutality, bloodthirsty behavior. Thirst for revenge. A sectarian mind and spirit that creates division and disunity.

D

DAM, ROAD BLOCK

The words *dam* and *road block* indicate a river, terrain, or even region that has been blocked, dammed, to retain water, as in the case of a hdyro-electric dam; or a path, road, or highway that has been barred to prevent access. The positive or negative symbolism of roadblocks or dams depend on their use and the intention with which they were installed. Thus, a roadblock set up to ensure safety at the scene of an accident, disaster, or crime is essentially positive as it serves to protect people. However, a symbolic analysis must take into account the attitude we adopt when faced with a roadblock, as well as the thoughts and emotions it arouses: understanding, acceptance, patience, awe, gratitude; or, impatience, annoyance, irritation, insecurity, fear, criticism, ingratitude, etc.

When it concerns a hydro-electric dam, its symbolism concerns more global dynamics of the collective, physical, and emotional levels, since a great force of action has to be deployed to build it to retain a considerable quantity of water, usually a river that flows through an inhabited or uninhabited region. Given the fact that it serves to produce electricity, it is also related to the fire element, hence willpower, as well as the power of our mind and spirit, a search for light, heat, and a force of action in matter. It represents the will to create and use powerful collective energy, thanks to the control and mastery of emotions on the personal and social levels. It may also symbolize a person's emotional state when he over-represses his emotions, virtually *damming* them up, forcing, *bullying* them to remain hidden, though fear of overflowing, flooding, and destroying others; or, through fear of revealing himself. As the installation of such a dam doesn't only affect the inhabitants of the region, but also its flora and fauna, its importance and meaning are also related to our environmental conscience. The construction of a dam in an inhabited region creates all sorts of detrimental damage and problems on the individual and social levels. The economic benefits of a dam (river transport, fishing, tourism, etc.) reflects our benefitting from the increase and diversification of our inner, personal, or collective forces. As for re-settlement, in many cases, it represents forced opening onto new horizons, also obligatory detachment, and often, the death of an established lifestyle, along with its customary activities and traditions, etc.

In regions where beavers have built a water dam, which may cause problems for the human beings sharing the same territory, such as flooding their houses or farmland, the symbolic meaning in this case relates to the instinctual level, the way those affected manage their instinctual, emotional energy when they build and organize their habitation to shelter and nourish their families.

If we find ourselves on a road blocked by one or several trees that have fallen or been blown down in a storm – symbolically related to the air element, the world of thoughts – we need to reflect on the intention and motivation with which we advance, as well as the way we use our mental powers, our knowledge and intellectual capacities when we head toward an aim, objective, goal, destination, or relationship.

⊕ A capacity to create protective structures on both the inside and the outside, thereby allowing us to safely and soundly manage a whole set of actions, with foresight and good planning. Regulation work on instinctual, affective relationship potential, so as to concentrate our energy on materializing projects. Engendering energy for action, and right, altruistic motivation. Respect for the environment.

Water or electric dam: Allows us to adequately channel the force of our intentions and emotions on the personal and collective levels. An ability to contain and master great emotional power. An increase in collective, emotional resources.

⊖ Attitudes, behavior, and actions that engender blockages, obstacles, dangers. Someone who has difficulty interacting with others. Problems resulting from a lack of energy on the physical, emotional, and spiritual levels, to become involved on the social, collective level; or, the presence of an overflow of energy and excessive willpower, engendering exaggerated, negative, dangerous, even fatal dynamics and action force.

Water or electric dam: A lack of control and mastery on the emotional level. Unhealthy emotional retention and repression, which, one day, ends up overflowing, causing major damage: flooding, drowning, devastation, re-settlement, destruction. An incapacity to contain and transform our instinctual, emotional energies. Rebellion, harmful repercussions for the flora and fauna. Non-respect for the environment.

DANCE

In certain populations, tradition attributes a religious origin to dance, and in others, it is a social ritual. Dance is a corporal art, which celebrates movement, and it is a way for human beings to communicate their soul-states through pleasure and fun and in a recreational state of mind. It constitutes a series of well-ordered gestures made to the rhythm of the music. It expresses a person's way of being. It is associated with joy, zest, liveliness, pleasure, emotion, and festivity. It sometimes represents an idea or a story. It favors the liberation of physical and emotional tensions, and may also create trances, induce out-of-body experiences, astral voyages, or allow the dancer a spiritual experience. As the body has the capacity to execute multiple gestures such as: turning, bending, stretching, jumping, etc., their combination, in various dynamics, allows the invention of an infinity of steps, figures, and postures which compose a dance, through which is expressed the quality of the soul, its depth, beauty, intentions, etc.

As well as offering the dancer an opportunity to express his emotions and soul-states, dance is an art that cultivates discipline and mastery of the body. Depending on the populations and eras, dance has been, and still is, practiced in different ways, for various motivations, in accordance with personal and social lifestyles. This art form generates contacts, openings, and encounters with others. We dance in groups, in a couple, alone; or, we may watch a dance show performed in public.

⊕ Healthy expression of soul-states, ideas, or emotions. A sense of rhythm and synchronization. Favors physical health, as well as encounters, exchanges, and contact on the emotional level. Joy, vivacity, expression of vital energy, pleasure, festivity, celebration. Development of qualities such as: poise, suppleness, strength, fluidity in action, mastery of the physical body and soul-states. Elevation of the senses, exaltation, optimism. A means to induce out-of-body experiences, visions, trances, sacred, spiritual communication, and to activate psychic faculties, depending on the context and the dancer's inner preparation.

⊖ Difficulty physically expressing our emotions, ideas, and soul-states. Retention, rigidity, shyness, embarrassment; or, resorting to dance out of a need to impress, please, be acknowledged and recognized, to seduce, attract attention; or, to provoke. Imbalance between the masculine and the feminine. A lack of self-esteem.

DARKNESS *cf.* ***Obscurity*** *and also* ***Night***

DEATH, DYING

Death is a stage all human beings and all organic organisms go through at the end of their life, at the end of a cycle. The irreversible halt of vital functions marks the retreat, the release of the spirit, or breath of life, from the physical form it animated through the intermediary of the soul. After its detachment from its earthly envelope, the spirit, clothed in more subtle bodies, woven of emotional, mental, and spiritual matter, continues its evolution in other worlds, in other dimensions of existence. The choice of these worlds, these dimensions, is determined by Cosmic Intelligence, and depends on the level of conscience the person has attained, as well as the apprenticeships, the learning experiences, he needs to go through in order to move on to the following stage. Hence, the phenomenon called death, in actual fact, is only a passageway announcing the end of one experimentation and the beginning of another.

Nothing is lost in the Universe; everything is continually transformed and recycled, and it is the same for human beings. The fact of considering death as a dramatic event, defining it as the absence of life, accompanying it with grief, desolation, and despair, stems from lack of Knowledge on the spiritual level. Death and dying are omnipresent in life, as are birth and rebirth. We are born; we die, and are perpetually reborn. Every day, every second, parts of us die and are transformed to manifest in a different form, revealing other aspects of the creative potential contained in our being.

We experience and feel the process of death more intensely whenever we go through an ordeal, such as the end of a love relationship, a separation, burn-out, bankruptcy, depression, etc. The feeling of dying on the inside, or the feeling of wanting to let ourselves die, that assails us in certain circumstances are clear signs that certain parts of us are dying and other parts are preparing for birth, for emergence. This is what awareness reveals: each time we become aware of something, a new door opens for and in us, thereby offering us the opportunity of a new path, new experimentation, deeper understanding; at the same time, like worn clothes that have become too tight for us, we leave behind what we have moved on from, what we have grown out of: a way of thinking, an emotion, attitude, behavior, or even a lifestyle. Often, this stage is accompanied by a feeling of expansion, of being reborn.

Death can also be experienced in dreams. Whether we see ourselves or another person, or people, die in a dream, it is important not to take this literally, but to understand that first of all the dying person (or people) represents parts of ourselves. By applying the Law of resonance we can distinguish which aspects of ourselves are dying and what the dying person reflects on the symbolic level. In our dreams, it is also possible to visit or encounter people who are deceased, or about to die. Such encounters are always very spiritually evolutive for those who experience them, because they lead to revelations and a deeper understanding of life, or serve as inspiration and guidance, as the case may be.

Death symbolizes metamorphosis, which may be positive or negative, depending on the context. Whenever we receive recurring dreams about death, we must not take them lightly, because they are warnings. For example, if we repeatedly see ourselves die in a car accident, the dream is warning us about our behavior and way of advancing, which is too fast, reckless, thoughtless, irresponsible, unsafe, etc., and which leads to the destruction of our manifestation potential on the individual and social levels. In the case of recurrent dreams about drowning, we are being shown destructive forces at work on the emotional level. If we have frequent dreams of violent death caused by our being assaulted, it is a sign that our unconscious harbors a large quantity of extremely aggressive forces, which, not only devastate and destroy parts of us on the metaphysical levels, but risk plunging us into fatal situations in concrete reality, if we don't transform them.

The process of dying and the experience of death on any level is always highly initiatic. Thus, it is crucial never to try and fight death, or resist the process of dying, but rather to welcome it with confidence and serenity, knowing how to let go and abandon ourselves to Divine Will, Grace, and Justice. Very few people have attained a sufficiently high level of spiritual development to know what time and in what manner they will leave their physical body. Hence we should be humble and accept the circumstances and time Cosmic Intelligence orchestrates for us in accordance with Cosmic Laws, which perfectly integrate the global concept of Creation.

⊕ A capacity to accept death when it comes, no matter the circumstances, form, or aspects it may take. May announce a period of revelations regarding the process of death and rebirth. Understanding that death represents a passage, a stage of evolution, the manifestation of the end of a cycle, liberation, an expansion of conscience, transition toward birth on another level. A person who is not afraid of physical death, or initiatic deaths, deep transformations, extreme changes. An ability to be detached, to let go, adapt, and integrate new concepts leading to wider understanding and allowing us to attain a higher level of conscience. Reflection and meditation on life after death, or rather life after life, the Life that exists behind the veil of life, the multi-dimensions of existence. Study and integration of Cosmic Laws. Conscious preparation for death and rebirth. Development of the ability to accompany dying parts of ourselves, as well as the dying, those people in their terminal phase, in the outer world, while remaining conscious that they always represent aspects of ourselves.

Note: In a dream, a positive death is always announced by luminous symbols as well as *via* deceased people who love us.

⊖ Fear of death and the dying. Fear of metamorphoses and deep transformations; or, the manifestation of Divine Justice through great upheavals or natural catastrophes. A lack of right, spiritual knowledge, allowing us to understand what needs to be rectified, transformed, or recycled; or, on the contrary, dying or causing the death of what should live. A lack of understanding of the fact that even death caused by evil, by wrong-doing, is educational, and eventually leads to good. Erroneous vision of death, considering it as a tragic, dramatic end, a transfer into nothingness. Death and dying experienced in despair, grief, non-acceptance, rebellion, and anger against God. Loss of faith. Religious beliefs that give and maintain false ideas and erroneous understanding of death and the hereafter, fear of purgatory, hell, eternal damnation, etc. Superstition, fatalistic, apocalyptic spirituality. Fear of deep transformation and inevitable change. Thoughts, emotions, and behavior that bear death on the individual and/or collective level. A person who obstinately refuses to change and evolve, doggedly, relentlessly hanging on to old thought, emotional, and behavioral patterns, old habits and established privileges, as well as to acquired material goods and possessions. Fierce traditionalist. A lack of understanding or non-acceptance of the fact that life on Earth, including human birth and death, occurs in a series of cycles, and these cycles, in their turn, belong to greater cycles on the Cosmic level. Ignorance of Cosmic Laws. An incapacity or refusal to believe in reincarnation, karma, multiple lives, the multi-dimensions of Creation, and the eternal, immortal nature of our spirit. A somber, dark, heavy, burdened conscience, imprisoned in matter, that imposes a very limited vision of existence. Great resistance to letting go and accepting renewal, rebirth. Possessiveness, selfishness, egotism. Complaining, accusing, critical, over-rational behavior. A suicidal mind and spirit, or unconscious death. (*cf. also* **Suicide**)

Symbolic representation of death, of being killed by a somber, negative, aggressive, destructive person: Announcement of a difficult destiny, a karmic consequence, the person reaps what he has sown; on the one hand, Justice Divine has him experience ordeals to enable him to settle his karmic debts, and, on the other hand, to allow him to learn the lesson(s) provided by his erroneous actions committed in this life or in previous lives, before being able to move on to a new stage.

Feeling ill-at-ease and at a loss when confronted with a person who suffers and dies: Reveals our ill-being, impotency, attachment, dependencies, incapacity to let go, to act adequately in difficult situations, our resistance to move on to another stage, our incapacity to accompany our own dying parts, which are symbolized by the person or people dying in the outer world.

DEBT

On the concrete level, a debt is a sum of money that a person owes to another person, or to a bank, organization, etc. Figuratively speaking, this term is also used to indicate a moral obligation that a person may have actually contracted toward another, or simply feel he owes something to another person. On the level of the universe, it refers to karmic debts that we create and accumulate over our various lives by acting against Universal Laws and Principles.

When debt is the subject of a dream, it is important to analyze the contents of the dream in depth to discover what kind of obligation it refers to, because it indicates to the dreamer that his soul is linked to a person, situation, event or object. When we dream we have a debt, we absolutely must pay it back, in this life or another. We cannot rid ourselves of our obligations; they are carried forward from one life to the next and always end up materializing in concrete situations that correspond to their nature. Paying back a karmic debt is not necessarily carried out directly to the person we are indebted to. There are situations where this is not possible; however, it is always a similar program. When a person's intentions are unkind and selfish, or when he consciously refuses to pay his debts, they increase, as do their consequences, thereby creating numerous problems for such a person that will manifest sooner or later.

On both the concrete and dream level, a debt is not always negative. It is also an aid, a constructive support, a loan granted that will be reimbursed according to the terms agreed upon in good faith, according to the capacities of the borrower and what has been programmed for the Life plan of those involved. It is even very common to have debts, to owe someone or an institution something. It is important not to panic when faced with debts. All we have to do is simply to structure and manage the situation with a view to reimbursement to the best our abilities. Wisdom is required in order to avoid borrowing more than necessary, and to use the obtained resources correctly, for the good of our evolution and that of others. Debt is then an investment, useful, altruistic assistance, as well as an opportunity to practice giving and receiving.

However, debt becomes an apprenticeship *via* the negative when a serious imbalance is created between its contraction and its reimbursement, such as witnessed on the level of individual and collective, private and public debt worldwide. The present planetary situation manifests the degree of man's capacity to manage resources correctly, fairly and altruistically. We need to recognize, without panicking, that this situation is the result of negative experimentation. This result requires the correction of unfavorable attitudes and behavior, wise use of resources and altruistic management for the good of all. It is right to stop waste, to practice moderation, and to honor our commitments without seeking an easy way out.

⊕ A capacity to make good use of aid received. Healthy management of this aid supports re-construction, development, and expansion. An apprenticeship in giving and receiving. Mutual aid, altruism, and an understanding of inter-relationships between people. A second chance to succeed in life, to carry out beneficial projects.

⊖ Excessive debt. Difficulty paying back our debts. Management problems. Poor use of resources. Waste. Over-confidence. Ambition. Avidity, greed. Imbalance between giving and receiving. The presence of memories marked by great material insecurity, bankruptcy, ruin and existential fear. Inability to plan and organize our life in a well-balanced way, according to available resources. A risk of shortages and poverty if the person does not rectify his attitudes and behavior; if he does not transform his negative memories related to the use of resources.

DECEASED

Seeing a deceased person in a dream can indicate two things: on the one hand, it symbolically reveals parts of ourselves, aspects, attitudes, behavior that resonate with whatever this person represents for us.

On the other hand, it may mean that we have been in touch with that person in the subtle dimensions, that we have visited his soul, or that the deceased person visited us in our dream. In this case, it is also essential to refer back to ourselves and to ask ourselves what this deceased person represents for us, because his presence as a symbol serves to help us become aware of certain aspects of ourselves.

To be able to confirm whether it is an actual encounter in the subtle dimensions, we must validate the following points: first of all, the person in question must not have died a long time ago; 4 or 5 years can be considered a good reference point, although a fixed point in time cannot be stipulated. If we see the person in a dream only a few hours, days or weeks after his death, and there is verbal, telepathic or physical communication, it is indeed a soul to soul contact. For example, the person may console us, tell us everything is fine for him, that we needn't worry, or give us clear proof of his identity so as to awaken our faith, our understanding of there being life after this life.

It is important to know that, generally speaking, a long deceased person has either already reincarnated on Earth or in another world, or has gone on to a different spiritual dimension. Gradually, deceased people free themselves from their former earthly life and assimilate the fact that life continues according to the program planned for each person, for them in their new existence as well as for those still incarnated on Earth. Integrating this fact allows them to move on to a new stage in their evolution.

We also need to know that physical death does not transform a person into a saint. Consequently, the energy of souls visiting us in the parallel worlds can be beautiful, well-intentioned and positive; or, it can also be sinister, malevolent, and negative.

No matter what their degree of evolution, the deceased are not lost in darkness or emptiness. They live in worlds as real as this one and therein continue their apprenticeships and experimentations.

The best way to understand what being dead means on the physical level is to draw an analogy with dreams. At the moment of death, the person leaves his physical body and travels in parallel worlds toward another level of existence, in exactly the same way as what happens at night when we dream, except, in the case of death, the person doesn't return to his earthly envelope, but continues his life in other dimensions. The passage is easy if the person doesn't resist and isn't afraid.

To help the deceased continue his path in peaceful serenity, his beloved family and friends that are still alive on the earthly level must go through the grieving process as naturally as possible, without dramatizing or considering the departure to be a tragedy. By remaining emotionally attached to the deceased, they create very painful feelings of remorse in him, because the deceased are able to feel their loved ones' suffering beyond earthly time and distance. The suffering resulting from the separation that accompanies the mourning period is what is most difficult to transcend, both for the departed as for those who remain on Earth. In these difficult moments it is a great consolation to remind ourselves that the deceased find themselves in the dimension and *department* or country that corresponds to them, and that they are not alone there. At the moment of earthly death, the deceased is welcomed by guides from the parallel worlds that help him understand the world he has arrived in and how to find his way. We should never forget that we reap what we sow. If during our lives on Earth, we cultivate qualities, virtues and true values, then, after our departure, we'll arrive in a place where these same values reign. However, if we devote our lives to experimenting and nourishing our faults, weaknesses and vices, we'll be guided toward places of apprenticeship and learning that resonate with what we cultivated on Earth.

As aforementioned, a deceased person that we know and see in a dream, may also simply represent parts of ourselves, like all the other elements in the dream. For example: in our dream if we see our deceased sister cleaning up the kitchen, but in the reality of our dream, we don't remember she's dead, then her presence in the dream is purely symbolic and represents part of ourselves. To understand the message of the dream, we need to ask ourselves what our sister represents for us. The first thing that springs to mind when we think about her is the principal symbolism of our sister for us. The people we see in our dreams represent very personal, characteristic aspects of ourselves and their symbolic meaning is determined by our perception of them. In the example of the deceased sister, if the first thing that springs to mind is that she is a calm, discreet person, then these are the aspects of ourselves that she symbolizes. She represents a part of us that is usually calm and discreet, and that is presently cleansing the way we prepare the resources and physical energy we need to live (symbolic meaning of a kitchen).

One way or another, when a deceased person visits us in a dream, there is always a multidimensional lesson for us. It's no coincidence when a deceased person appears in our dreams. He corresponds to a deep symbol and message for our evolution.

⊕ *In the case where the deceased person simply represents parts of the dreamer:* His presence should incite the dreamer to become aware of the resonance he has with the deceased. By reflecting on what the deceased person represents for him, the dreamer will discover aspects and parts of himself, qualities he didn't know he had, or faults and weaknesses he needs to work on.

In the case where the deceased person visits us: We receive proof that death as an end to life doesn't exist, that life continues beyond the earthly dimension. We also analyze the symbolism of the context of his apparition in the dream: his clothing, the general decor of the place, what the deceased says and does. Each detail means something. Contact with a deceased person in a dream often brings us great solace, consolation and a certain serenity, which helps us mourn, get over the death and let go. Such a dream is an experience that can transform the life of the person who receives it forever.

It is also possible that *a deceased person in a dream announces our own death, or the death of someone close to us.* In both cases, we mustn't panic. The message should be considered a gift, divine grace. Indeed, it offers us the opportunity to prepare ourselves both on the inside and on the outside, to work on our conception and understanding of life and death. It incites us to go within and meditate so as to accompany the dying person with love, compassion and serenity.

And if it concerns our own physical death: we are forewarned and so we can leave in the best conditions possible.

⊖ *In the case where the deceased person represents distorted parts of the dreamer*: His presence in a dream then indicates attitudes, behavior and character traits the dreamer needs to rectify and transform.

The appearance of a deceased person in our dreams can also symbolize fear of death, fear of evolving, discouragement, lack of vital energy, depression, despair, resistance to change. However, we must remember that change is the only constant in life and that all forms of life evolve following cycles of birth, growth, decline, death and rebirth.

In the case where a negative deceased person visits us in a dream: In this case too, we must apply the Law of resonance and know that we always attract what we are. This is valid for both the physical and metaphysical levels.

It may be a *karmic encounter*. For example, someone who is responsible for the death of another or of a large number of people can be haunted in his dreams by his victims. Energy of death and existential fears.

In the case where the dreamer is followed or chased by *ghosts, dark, obscure, tenebrous, demonic entities,* symbolically these represent old, former, ancient memories marked by very negative actions. This kind of dream can be extremely difficult and we need to call on the Light of Knowledge and invoke Spiritual Protection to transform the memories and forces that engender these dreams.

DECOR

Decor (interior style, decoration and furnishings) is an excellent symbol to reflect our personality, our soul-states and the various ambiances of our inner world. Consciously or unconsciously, the decors we create and the decorations and furnishings therein reveal our deep memories; they reveal who we are. Our qualities and virtues as well as our weaknesses and distortions are exhibited on the walls and in the furnishings and decoration of our home, our work place, and also in all the places we see, visit or inhabit in our dreams. Close observation and a detailed analysis of the decor and decoration of the places we frequent informs us of the ambiances and energies that we transmit and also what we are experiencing, learning and experimenting.

⊕ Beautiful, bright, pleasant, harmonious, peaceful, light-filled decor reveals wonderful states of soul, conscience and inner ambiances. A serene, tidy, well-structured living space inspires well-being, peace and harmony. Beauty, refinement and a warm, welcoming ambiance are conducive to inspiration and the elevation of the mind, spirit and soul.

⊖ Decor that is dark, heavy, excessive, cluttered, untidy, neglected, disharmonious, imposing, luxurious, etc. also reflects the person who created it or who inhabits it, because the Law of resonance always applies. An expression of soul poverty and impoverishment, as well as difficulties. Superficiality, overly concerned with appearances, artificial appearance, lack of taste, refinement and sense of beauty. A place filled with old memories; or, a place that is empty, that has no life in it, that engenders melancholy, sadness and despair.

DEMON, DEMONIC *cf.* ***Devil***

DENTAL CAVITY *cf.* ***Tooth decay***

DENTIST *(or* ***dental surgeon****)*

A dentist or dental surgeon is a doctor specialized in treating acquired and/or congenital pathologies related to the mouth, teeth, gums, jaws and their adjoining tissues. Symbolically, therefore, he helps take care of and heal our structure on the level of primary needs, as well as encouraging, promoting wisdom (symbolized by the white color of teeth) in the way we nourish ourselves and express our needs. This profession is also related to self-esteem and nutritive, nourishing intimacy.

Given its composition, a tooth (*cf. also* this term) also belongs to the mineral kingdom, which represents old, former structural memories of the human-being. Through his work on teeth, which are also related to our combative, instinctual forces as well as to our survival, a dentist may activate, both in himself and in his patients, very intense, unconscious forces and memories related to the manifestation of needs. That is why a visit to the dentist's very often arouses fear and deep discomfort. When we consult a dentist, consciously or unconsciously, we discover the way we nourish ourselves on all levels.

Through the work they accomplish on the fundamental needs of their patients, dentists are continually exposed to vibrations of conscious or unconscious fear, anxiety and trauma. On the energy level, the dentist and his assistants, mostly unwittingly, are constantly immersed in the vibratory jumble of their patients' thoughts, emotions, tensions and projections. As a rectifier of the structure of our primary needs, a dentist has to face, on the metaphysical level, instinctive, untamed forces related to numerous memories of survival. Even if he masters his work well on the physical level, and it is carried out in a calm, pleasant atmosphere, on the subtle level, a dentist is incessantly called upon to transform and transcend the energies of fear, tension, discomfort and pain emanated by his patients. However, most of the time, dentists are not aware of these phenomena that occur in the subtle levels, because they don't know they exist or how they work. Statistics reveal that dentists have a shorter life span and a higher rate of depression, ill-being and suicides than other professions.

⊕ Capacity to treat, cleanse and repair the deep structure of our primary needs, and to rectify the way we nourish ourselves on all levels. Helps prevent problems related to needs, lacks, deficiencies. Re-education of combative dynamics related to instinctual needs. Offers new chances on the structural level. An ability to repair, rectify and re-structure ill-will, deficiencies, and difficulties created by erroneous nutritional and structural behavior. Facilitates access to healthy nourishment. Embellishment work to favor a person's radiance and simultaneously improve his well-being and self-esteem. Good psychologist. Capacity to metaphysically help transform primary needs and forces. Awareness that each patient represents part of ourselves and that the work carried out to help others also reflects inner work on ourselves.

⊖ Difficulty treating, cleansing and repairing the deep structure of primary needs and instincts, as well as the way we nourish ourselves on all levels. Reflects fear of pain and/or fear of change, fear of activating old memories, of calling into question our fundamental level and to rectify the way we nourish ourselves or our instinctual combativeness on either the behavioral or energy level. Medicine without conscience, without humanity. Someone who chooses to exert this profession only to become wealthy and/or for prestige. An incapacity to transform other people's projections, to see the connection between dentistry work and patients' fundamentals needs, and to understand that our patients represent parts of ourselves. De-structuring. Collapse of structures related to needs. An incapacity or difficulty nourishing ourselves correctly, healthily.

DEPRESSION (ill-being)

Depression corresponds to a great opening of the unconscious, which leads to the emergence into our conscience of a hodge-podge of long-accumulated negative memories. It indicates that the person's inner computer is no longer able to manage and deal with the quantity of reactivated memories. His soul is telling him that he is under too much pressure, that he cannot take it anymore. A change in behavior is called for; cleansing memories has become indispensable. As the word itself indicates, depression reveals an accumulation of pressure that wants, that needs to be released. Long-repressed memories emerge very powerfully from the unconscious, like a volcano that suddenly becomes active and threatens to destroy everything around it. It envelops the person in a cloud of negative energy engendered by thought patterns and erroneous behavior that need to be transformed, recycled. Depression sets in when a person can no longer function according to socially recognized and imposed values and criteria; in the depth of his heart he knows they are wrong, superficial, ridiculous. Contrary to general belief, depression is not an illness, but rather a sign indicating that a process of awareness has been set off, leading to discrepancies that will oblige the person to change his behavior and lifestyle in order to regain his health and balance.

⊕ Awareness, revelations, initiations and opening onto a new dimension of ourselves. A study and understanding of anxieties, anguish, and ill-being. Liberation of a large number of repressed memories. Deliverance from and cleansing of former negative, erroneous behavior. The beginning of a true spiritual path. A capacity to heal and transform ourselves, to change our life. Readjustment to Divine Norms. A period of inner alchemy that transforms evil, what hurts, into good. Regeneration, vivification, re-established harmony. Rebirth, re-engenders the seeds of a new beginning, a new life. Understanding that depression is not an illness but a state of ill-being that incites us to work on ourselves, to transform memories that emerge from our unconscious.

⊖ A tendency to swim against the tide, to force ourselves to continue to function without any change of lifestyle whatsoever. Refusal to evolve, to call ourselves into question, to work on ourselves and to cleanse our negative memories. Ignorance of the Laws of resonance and reincarnation, a lack of understanding of the multidimensions of life. A complaining, self-pitying attitude, putting the blame on others. Negative thoughts, tension, confusion, blockages, retention. Difficulty expressing our feelings, state of mind, mood and soul-states. Insecurity, anxiety, anguish and existential fears. Visiting burdensome memories marked by a lack of joy, confidence, wisdom and love for ourselves and others. Going from one experience to another without understanding. Seeking solutions on the outside only. Sadness, dejection, despondency, turmoil, discouragement, ill-being, a lack of faith and spirituality, isolation, collapse, ruin. Rebellious spirit, dwells on and broods over the same ideas, inner struggle, demonic forces, feeling distraught, going astray, erratic behavior, mental illness.

DESERT

The desert designates a region characterized by an absence of water and vegetation, infertile soil, mostly composed of sand dunes whose form and height are subjected to continual change due to wind and sand storms. Heat that is hostile to life reigns during the day and intense cold at night. Desert regions are sparsely populated. Human life, as well as flora and fauna, tends to be concentrated around the rare sources of water found in the oases. Life in the desert demands a very great capacity of adaptation to extreme living conditions as well as knowledge of and respect for the laws of nature. Constantly aware of the fragility of life, the people of the desert have developed a great sense of hospitality. Furthermore, those who live in the desert must not fear solitude or death.

Figuratively speaking, the desert is a great symbol of trials and initiation, as illustrated by the 40 days Jesus spent in the desert. Generally speaking, from a positive point of view, the desert symbolizes a state of conscience of interiorization, contemplation, and intense reflection on the meaning of life. It is also a living context that favors the development of receptivity as its extreme conditions are unfavorable to all unnecessary activity, all excessive emissivity. The silence and monotony of the outer landscape, the absence of continual sound and visual stimulation and distraction are conducive to the development of mental imagery and visiting unconscious memories. Thus, the person turns inward, which leads him to do some soul-searching and to reflect upon the advantages of abundance on all levels as well as on how he himself welcomes, appreciates and uses abundance in his own life. The absence of water and vegetation symbolically represents a considerable lack on the affective level, and great shortages, drought, hostility and coldness on the emotional level.

Seen in a dream or experienced as a soul state, the desert may also represent a tendency to isolate ourselves, the encounter of desert regions in our inner world, or a journey through great initiatic ordeals. It may also reveal a destructive dynamic, total rejection of the world; or, it may indicate an important awareness of both the sacred dimension of life and the fragility of the material forms through which it manifests.

⊕ Incites us to introspection, meditation, turning our attention within ourselves, soul-searching, reflection on the meaning of life and the right use of resources and abundance on all levels. A great capacity of adaptation to extreme living conditions, atmospheres, ambiances, and climates. Its vastness, its sober beauty, calm, silence, intense daytime light and starry night sky soothes our soul and facilitates the opening of our spirit, and fusion with the immensity of the universe. Beneficial for spiritual quests, initiations and the exaltation of our conscience.

⊖ A period of great trials and ordeals. Solitude, inner emptiness, isolation, discouragement, despair. Destructive inner fire, emotional drought, aridity of soul, lack of love and resources on all levels. An incapacity to understand the initiatic, evolutive reason for trials and ordeals, for a journey through the wilderness. May reveal the presence of memories of destruction and extremism, which have created desert regions in our inner world. An attitude of rejection and dropping out of society and life in general. A tendency to go from one extreme to the other. A state of sterility, of infertility.

DEVIL

In the Judeo-Christian tradition, the devil, Satan or Lucifer, is the supreme representation of evil (*cf. also* this term), which manifests in the form of demons, also referred to as Satanic, demonic, Luciferian forces and powers that the Devil rules over. The devil symbolizes spiritual powers used against Divine Laws and Order, which manifest in both men and women, through human flaws, faults, weaknesses, and vices, through a person's corrupt materializations, dark, somber conscience, blindness to true values, turning away from Beauty, Harmony, and Original Light, Knowledge and Truth. The devil is a collection of all the distortions produced by ill-used spiritual, mental, and emotional energies, as well as negative, malevolent, prejudicial, destructive behavior and deeds, which blur our vision, veil our conscience, and prevent us from recognizing and acknowledging our Divine nature.

In terms of conscience and memories, the devil represents huge blocks of concentrated dark, negative memories that a human being bears within, like a reservoir of forces whose vibration connects him to all other reservoirs of similar energy. Simultaneously, on the subtle levels, these reservoirs constitute an egregore (*cf.* this term), which, through resonance, exerts an individual and collective influence on all those connected. This means that the devil also represents a state of conscience that can act through a person who has strong resonance with the devil. This is what is meant when we describe a person as *the Devil incarnate*; we believe such a person is capable of acting like the devil; we instinctively sense that he is the bearer of forces that resonate with what the devil represents.

It is very important to take these forces seriously because they act with great intelligence and multi-dimensionally. Associating with egregores of energy directed by the devil through invocation, requests, or specific rituals, encloses a person in a vicious, satanic, demonic circle, which he can only get out of through an understanding of the educational role of evil, the Laws of karma and resonance, as well as the Principle of Divine Justice.

Indeed, when we refer to *the temptation of the devil*, we refer to the free will everyone has at his disposal, which allows him to choose to evolve and experiment his existence within the framework of Divine Laws and Order; or, to transgress these Laws. The latter option leads him to experience *the fall;* this enchains him to the karmic consequences resulting from his choice, until the day he voluntarily decides, not only to renounce doing evil or wrong himself, but also to consciously choose good, and act in a manner that is right, just and good when faced with evil, with wrong-doing, with what hurts. This new choice will give his life a new direction, help him transform the resonance he has with demonic forces, and free him from their hold over him. The person will then also understand that evil (universally identified under different names), and the entities that different religions and faiths associate with it, do not have a separate existence, but play a well-determined role in the heart of Creation. They are used by Cosmic Intelligence to help people who have fallen by the wayside to rediscover the pathway back to good, and to understand that God, the original Creating Principle, exists beyond good and evil.

To dream of the devil: indicates to the dreamer that he is to experience a very powerful initiation. *Having a nightmare where the devil or demonic beings appear* indicates that the dreamer is subjected to extremely negative forces he has resonance with. On awakening from such a dream, the person may feel very aggressive, angry, destructive, and animated by compulsions motivated by excessive instinctual needs. It is vital not to remain in this energy, or in the states of mind and soul that accompany it, but rather to meditate, pray, and intensely invoke Divine help – from the Angels, Archangels, spiritual Guides, according to our faith and beliefs – to purify and alchemically transform within ourselves the negative memories and forces that resonate with the devil.

If the dreamer is not afraid, if he remains calm, serene, and full of faith and trust in the Divine, and if he doesn't do anything negative in the dream, then the presence of the devil indicates that the dreamer is going through an initiatic stage that is very important for his evolution; that he is working on huge blocks of negative karma accumulated during the course of his numerous lives; that he is strengthening and reinforcing himself and his capacities; and learning to transform and transcend his negative karma through the highest levels of Divine Wisdom and Love. Such a dream indicates that the dreamer's positive forces are more powerful than his negative aspects.

In dreams, the devil may use all sorts of strategy to tempt us, to incite us to do wrong. Hence he leads us to discover our darkest facets and memories that exist deep down in our depths. Depending on our character, our qualities, strong points, and virtues, or our faults, weaknesses, and vices, the devil's presence in our dreams can strengthen or weaken our deep desire to live in accordance with Divine Laws by trying and testing us, without our losing our determination; or, by making us fall when we succumb to his temptation, or give in to the fear he inspires in us. The devil interacts with us according to the resonance we have with the negative aspects he represents. If the devil often manifests with hideous, repulsive features, he may also take on seductive forms and don superficial beauty, which symbolizes the way we camouflage, excuse, and justify selfish, egotistical ambitions, bad intentions, pernicious motivations, perverse desires, or dangerous, malignant, destructive forces latent in our unconscious.

An encounter with the devil and demonic forces is an integral part of great spiritual initiations, during which a person learns to heal his dark forces in the right way: i.e. by declining demonic temptations and provocations, and refusing to respond to negativity with negativity. That's where ultimate transcendence lies: using our free will and the Light to rid ourselves of evil. The initiatic trials and ordeals that manifest on our path represent evolutive stages that lead to Enlightenment.

⊕ Understanding the fact that God is above good and evil, that the devil's presence is never fortuitous, but part of the life-program of people who have very heavy karmas to settle, because even the devil obeys Cosmic Laws and Divine Justice. A capacity to understand what the devil represents on the esoteric and exoteric levels, that in everyone's experimentation the devil has the role of an educator of conscience *via* evil, wrong-doing and hurt: he leads people who have sowed evil in this life, or in past lives, to experience the same ordeals with the aim of helping them develop better, deeper understanding of what they put others through. Integration of the fact that the function of the devil is to redirect people toward good, to incite them to seek the path of Qualities, Virtues, and Pure Powers, that his work is supervised by Cosmic Intelligence and hidden Wisdom.

An initiatic test period to reinforce and strengthen good in us, to become aware that God exists beyond good and evil, and that by asking for His help, and activating Divine Power within ourselves, we can dissolve and transcend demonic forces and energies. A great capacity to transform evil, first of all in ourselves by working on our faults and weaknesses, and then the negative memories residing in our personal and collective unconscious. Warrior of the Light.

⊖ A tendency to yield to major harmful temptations, to fall into the worst possible excesses that engender very difficult karmas the person will have to face in this life, or in his future lives. A lack of knowledge of the fact that the devil and demons are always present when there is doubt, duality, a lack of faith, anger and rebellion against God, pride, vanity, seduction, passion, lust, sexual abuse, aggression, violence, carelessness as to the consequences of misactions (*cf.* this term), a lack of confidence in ourselves and in life, dissatisfaction, frustration, irritability, a desire to control, to conquer, and seeking glory, celebrity, earthly wealth and powers, a lack of spiritual conscience and true Knowledge. Someone who is confronted with huge blocks of very negative memories on the personal and collective levels, who experiences the effects of this as a victim because of false beliefs, or an erroneous understanding of evil, under whatever name we choose to give it; or, someone, who, when faced with negative forces, relentlessly rages and fights out of fear, anger, and vengeance, believing himself capable of destroying evil with evil. A tendency to believe we can fight the devil, ignoring the fact that by doing so, we engender those very same negative forces that feed and increase his power. An incapacity to transform, transmute, and transcend demonic forces on all levels through a lack of faith and Knowledge. Ignorance of the fact that through the abusive, amoral use of the gifts, talents, and resources bestowed on us, entrusted to our care, the devil and demons represent the inverted, distorted manifestation of Qualities, Virtues, and Divine Powers. A person who experiences the Law of return without understanding it, who reaps what he has sown, after having dabbled in black magic and experimenting the dark forces, in his recent or distant past. Ignorance of what the devil represents on a person's inner level, in terms of conscience and memories, and of what he corresponds to on the outside: a negative spiritual energy, subordinate to Cosmic Intelligence, employed by it to fulfill, through evil, an educational role in our apprenticeship.

Satanic pacts and black magic rituals undertaken to invoke the devil and to become his ally. Superstition and religious indoctrination that use fear of the devil and demonic forces to exert an abusive spiritual power over believers. When these extremely negative forces end up manifesting not only in a person's dream reality – on his subtle levels – but also succeed in entering his physical body, this is referred to as *possession.* Knowledge of the Cosmic Laws of karma and resonance help us understand why the people concerned – the person who goes through the experience as well as his entourage – are exposed to such ordeals, to this kind of very difficult, traumatizing experiences. However to face such a situation in a right, appropriate way, to succeed in transforming the forces at work, it is indispensable to call on Divine Power, through prayer, invocation, faith, a request for help on the spiritual and physical levels. In the case of possession, for example, we may call on a person who is experienced and competent in exorcism. In the case of a person who sees the devil in nightmares, sharing with people who have been initiated into symbolic language, who know about the effects of resonance and the Divine Laws, who may even have been through similar experiences themselves and successfully healed, could help him, just as the acquisition of high-level spiritual knowledge.

DIABETES

The word diabetes comes from the Ancient Greek *dia-baïno,* which means passing through or siphoning. Greeks doctors, like their Egyptian counterparts, noticed that certain patients had to urinate as soon as they'd had something to drink; it was as though water, liquids, simply passed through them, were siphoned off, without their being able to retain them. Symbolically, the difficulties of diabetes manifest in old souls who overindulged in pleasures and sweetness in other lives. An accumulation of memories of excess and overindulgence leads to the diabetic problems that accompany various illnesses. Diabetes may also manifest in people who need to purify former, excessive emotional behavior.

Difficulties related to diabetes experienced in a dream, or in concrete reality, inform us that we need to develop our receptivity in order to overcome the malfunctioning caused by excessive emissivity that pushes us to be overactive.

⊕ A period of purification and healing of past excesses. An opportunity to learn how to manage stress, develop receptivity, find the right balance between giving and receiving, and teach ourselves how to nourish ourselves healthily on all levels. Inner work to find true gentleness and sweetness in terms of states of conscience.

⊖ Memories of excess, overindulgence, and emotional problems. A difficult Life Program that obliges us to purify ourselves and change our behavior. Excessive emissivity, an unhealthy lifestyle that focuses on pleasures and the satisfaction of desires and needs. Indulgence in sweet food to compensate for a lack of inner softness and loving sentiments. Refusal to acknowledge the consequences of our choices on our health. Ignorance of the necessity to undertake work on ourselves so as to cleanse memories and reconstruct a healthy life on all levels.

DIAMOND

A diamond is a sculpted piece of quartz crystal and therefore representative of the mineral kingdom, which symbolizes the most ancient memories deeply lodged in our unconscious. It is the shiniest of all precious stones and the hardest of all known natural materials. Symbolically it represents successful purification, alchemy and spiritual transcendence of a person's ancient memories, initiatic accomplishment, enlightenment. It is also a great symbol of perfected structure, since before attaining its perfect shining transparency, it has to go through many transformations from crude, dark, black coal to luminous white, bright, shining quartz crystal. These transformations, which take place in the high temperatures and strong pressure of the depths of the earth's mantle, symbolically indicate a person who, throughout numerous lives, has worked in the depths of his unconscious to perfect himself and evolve spiritually, *via* exposure to the intense pressure and alchemical fire of initiations. A diamond is the mineral symbol *par excellence* of an initiate who, after purifying and transforming all the memories of his unconscious, has achieved a solid, enduring spiritual conscience as well as a capacity for divine spiritual materialization on Earth.

⊕ A person who has the capacity to materialize with a high level of principles and values. Symbol of the soul's greatest achievement of evolution. The highest level of divine materialization, of the capacity to create divine projects on Earth. Purification and transformation of ancient memories that result in a solid, pure structure. A very high level of initiation and spiritual evolution in material and concrete achievement. Great capacity to transform raw materials, crude substances into perfectly structured, transparent, luminous substances. Exploration and understanding of the history and evolution of the unconscious. Great inner prosperity and the possibility to materialize Knowledge and profound understanding of the cycle required to attain perfection, to reach high levels of manifestation and realization. Discovery of the philosopher's stone, of ancestral wisdom. Solid, stable spiritual values and principles. Transparency and purity of conscience. A highly evolved soul.

⊖ Diamonds become a negative symbol when worn or owned by a person in an ordinary, very materialistic, ambitious conscience, by someone who is greedy for power, wealth and luxury. In such cases, diamonds reflect false, illusory beauty and purity, a desire to shine and/or outshine others, to show off our wealth, a feeling of superiority, a lack of spiritual conscience, incomprehension of right materialization, and a capacity to do anything whatsoever to succeed, to reach a material objective or goal. When a person is willing to be corrupt, to exploit others, to provoke political, economic and social tensions, and is ready to kill in order to deal in and possess diamonds, this indicates the presence of great blocks of very old memories heavy with karmas, which will have serious, far-reaching consequences on the individual and collective levels. Ignorance of Cosmic Laws.

DIARRHEA *cf.* ***Excrement, feces***

DIARRY (appointment book)

A diary is a tool that helps us manage our time and plan our schedule efficiently by noting in it the activities, appointments, and tasks that we want or have to do. Its symbolic meaning is therefore related to organization and time management. The use of a diary facilitates the structuring and planning of life in general because it allows us to free our thoughts from multiple information.

⊕ An ability to organize and plan our time well, to have a well-balanced life. Inner potential allowing us to manage our actions efficiently so as to grant time to each activity. A global vision of things to be done, making it easier to plan our time and determine our priorities. Respecting commitments. A capacity and the will to re-adapt a planned program depending on events that occur, flexibility in our organization.

⊖ A lack of organization. Problems resulting from poor time management. Dispersal, difficulties structuring ourselves, planning efficiently, respecting our commitments; or, a tendency to always want to plan, to foresee, calculate and program everything. Over rigid planning, a lack of flexibility and adaptability when anything unforeseen arises.

DICTATOR

The word dictator dates back to Ancient Rome and referred to a magistrate appointed in critical situations and given unlimited power. A dictator dictates what is to be done. He introduces laws and decides what measures are to be taken in a crisis or in an extremely threatening situation so as to avoid collective panic and general chaos. The history of mankind bears witness to the fact that dictators usually emerge in countries where survival has become the primary concern, for example because of wars, catastrophes, epidemics, etc. Although their initial intention may be to use rigor and determination to maintain a certain order to allow solutions for the general good to be found, once dictators have usurped total and absolute power, they yield to the temptation to abuse their power and consequently become tyrants or despots. As long as a person harbors unconscious memories of thirst and greed for earthly power, glory and success, the latent forces contained in these memories can awaken and manifest at the slightest opportunity, even though his conscious intentions are right, just and good.

It is important to know that we do not need to be a head of state to have dictator memories to work on. Such an attitude may also exist in a company or family unit. A person is a dictator as soon as he thinks he is always right and does not consult others often enough or not at all, taking unilateral, arbitrary decisions that he imposes forcefully and threateningly.

⊕ Purification and transcendence of memories of excessive, abusive power and megalomania, despotism and tyranny.

⊖ Abuse of power and extreme manipulation of others in order to satisfy personal ambitions and needs. Badly exercised power. Thirst for control, domination, wealth and glory. A tendency to impose our point of view and to want to decide everything without consulting others. Refusal to listen when it comes to making decisions. Excessive emissivity when communicating ideas and achieving goals. Problems of authoritarianism, aggression, and excessive behavior. A feeling of superiority. Memories of megalomania, despotism and tyranny.

DICTIONARY

A reference book offering a collection of words, expressions and terms of a language, presented in a set order, giving definitions and information about them. On the metaphysical level, a dictionary represents a quest for understanding and knowledge, allowing people to communicate and manifest precisely and correctly. It indicates a pursuit of structure, exactitude, precision, accuracy, a capacity to think deeply, to grasp what is essential, tune into and perceive the essence of things and reach syntheses, as well as a wish to continually improve and learn.

⊕ Enjoying consulting, reading, browsing through dictionaries, or having a job that necessitates frequent consultation, reveals a love of knowledge and study, a quest for understanding, a wish to deepen and refine our knowledge. A period of study, apprenticeship, structuring, and acquisition of new knowledge, concepts, and understanding of people, things, and phenomena of life.

⊖ An over-rational, strict mind and spirit, which tends to take information literally. Rigidity in learning, which prevents the mind from opening to true knowledge and attaining deep, global understanding. A state of confusion and difficulty in studying, learning, and integrating knowledge. Limitation on the level of the development of our conscience. A person who is content in ignorance; or, who seeks to impress others with his knowledge.

DIET

Although the word diet generally refers to the food we eat, it is most commonly used to refer to a particular nutritional program, which either limits or excludes certain foodstuffs. It may also refer to a nutritionally enriched food-program. A diet may be undertaken for health reasons, when there have been nutritional excesses leading to the malfunction of certain organs, and the body functions need to be re-harmonized, re-balanced. However, for a diet to be truly effective, it should not only concern the physical body, but also our conscience and the way we nourish our other bodies: our emotional, mental, intellectual and spiritual bodies. Whenever we feel the need to go on a diet, it is not only our body, but also our soul that indicates it is time to detoxify, to purify ourselves, to end abuses, to liberate ourselves from the superfluous, to undertake deep-cleansing of our unconscious, otherwise physical and psychological consequences (illnesses and ill-being) will manifest, if this is not already the case.

To be on a diet, or to be prescribed a diet, in either a dream or in concrete reality, should incite us to take time to reflect and evaluate our general consumption habits. It is often a message, a sign, telling us that we need to avoid excesses and to regulate our instinctual needs, the voracious, unbridled appetite of our inner animals. It may also indicate an imbalance on the emotional and relationship levels, a tendency to nourish emotional dependency, a lack of love, the need to be loved and acknowledged, etc. It is always the accumulation of heavy, burdensome memories that incite us to go on a diet. Excessive recourse to dieting may, in extreme cases, lead to anorexia.

⊕ A period of detoxing, cleansing, and purification of both the physical and subtle bodies, as well as unconscious memories. Liberation of behavior and attitudes that create abuse and excesses. Re-harmonization of vital energy and awareness of the need to adopt a healthy, well-balanced diet, and to educate instinctual needs and inner animals.

⊖ The presence of memories and behavior marked by the need to please and be loved. Someone who puts too much emphasis on physical appearances, who is ready to mistreat his body and ruin his health so as to correspond to criteria of fashion and outer beauty. A tendency to compare ourselves with others, an inferiority complex, a lack of self-esteem. Nutritional problems on various levels. Discrepancy between the body, soul, spirit and mind. Malnutrition combined with the need to continually diet indicates a troubled conscience, ill-being, a feeling of guilt, being mired in negative memories. Compulsive eating habits through which a person seeks to compensate for a lack of *joie-de-vivre* and gentleness. A feeling of heaviness, a lack of energy, poor health. Anorexic, bulimic tendencies. (*cf. also* **Anorexia; Bulimia**)

DINOSAUR

As it belongs to the animal kingdom, a dinosaur represents aspects of our instinctual vital energy, powerful primary needs related to ancient memories lodged in our unconscious. Seeing a dinosaur in a dream reveals serious discrepancies. It indicates that intense, excessive, disproportionate, coarse, rough, prehistoric needs and behavior are being or have been activated in us. In such dreams, we find ourselves in contact with a primary conscience and an inner world of survival dominated by the law of the jungle, survival of the fittest.

A dinosaur is a symbol that often appears in children's dreams, because their prehistoric needs, dating from ancient, former lives, become their first mode of expression. Children manifest the duality they feel on the inside by projecting it onto the outside in quarrels and rows with their parents, brothers and sisters, and other people close to them, which reflects their sometimes very intense needs. It is the same for children who are attracted by dinosaur toys, stories, and films.

⊕ Reactivation of very powerful, ancient forces related to instinctual vital energy and primary needs. Work on ourselves to transcend these forces. Visiting memories related to the beginning of our existence and our experimentations on Earth. The necessary strength to incarnate, to begin a cycle.

⊖ Seeking domination through violence with the aim of satisfying our instincts and primary needs; or, a tendency to let ourselves be dominated by violence. Brusk, impulsive behavior when manifesting our demands, our expectations. Bestial, primitive, savage, insatiable brute force. Imposing our presence with great intensity in order to get what we want. Resisting evolving, an involutive, very down-to-earth conscience. Aggression and anger stemming from ancient memories. A lack of human feeling and sentiment. An incapacity to reason. Difficulty listening and understanding. Coarse, rough, insensitive, unrefined behavior. Attachment to old structures and behavior.

DIPLOMA

A diploma is a printed document, usually issued by an official organization, conferring or attesting to a right, a title, an honor or a grade. On the metaphysical and symbolic level, receiving a diploma, in positive concrete reality or in a dream, certifies that Cosmic Intelligence acknowledges the acquisition of certain qualities, virtues, knowledge and competence, either *via* study and successful examinations, or the way we succeed in our projects, or deal with ordeals in our life, with life's initiations. Obtaining a diploma automatically sets off a new cycle of experimentations in our life, a new stage with more important responsibilities. To find out what new potential these new responsibilities will develop, we need to analyze the symbolic meaning of the field of activity for which we receive the diploma, the characteristics and ambiance of where we receive it, and the people we meet there.

⊕ Receiving a diploma confirms that we have successfully completed an important stage, that our work on ourselves and the efforts we made have been recognized and acknowledged. The knowledge, qualities and faculties acquired are now an integral part of us and open the door to new life experiences.

⊖ The sometimes obsessive need to have or accumulate diploma after diploma reveals an inferiority complex, a lack of inner acknowledgement and feelings of insecurity that we try to compensate for by striving for outer acknowledgement on the professional and social levels. Diplomas serving the ego, feeding our pride, ambition, personal, professional or social glory, a feeling of superiority and unfair privileges, or diplomas dishonestly acquired through the power of money or the intervention of extremely influential people, are creators of illusions and serious karmic consequences. Sooner or later, the person will be called to order and will have to do his classes all over again, recommence his apprenticeship with humility, perseverance, honesty, integrity and courage.

DIRT (dirty)

Dirt, in all forms, is a manifestation of distorted aspects of different levels of our being: attitudes, behavior, thoughts, and/or emotions that need to be purified, corrected, rectified, put in order. The idea of dirt is closely linked to pollution (*cf. also* this term), which is more of an indication of the collective consequence of dirt created and maintained by all of us.

Generally speaking, the lack of cleanliness, dirt, and pollution we encounter in the outside world is a reflection of what we engender in our inner world: in our conscience, mind, spirit, thoughts, and emotions, which are at the origin of what we do, what we manifest and materialize on the physical level. When there is laxity, laziness, indifference, negligence, disorder, hyperactivity, a '*who cares?*' or an '*I couldn't care less*' attitude in our inner life, we needn't be surprised that we don't feel like cleaning and maintaining order and hygiene in our outer world environment: the different rooms in our house or apartment, our workplace, office or study, our car, and, of course, our body, clothes and food.

A person who lives with a multi-dimensional conscience knows that cleaning is synonymous with well-being, change, transformation, transcendence, alchemy, and evolution. Indeed, every time we clean and tidy a space or object on the outside, we simultaneously carry out purification and re-organizing, re-ordering work on the subtle levels of our being, in those aspects of ourselves that resonate with whatever the place or object in question represents for us. For example, if dirty dishes pile up in the sink, on the workbench and kitchen table, it is a sign that we need to purify and rectify the way we nourish ourselves concretely and energetically, as well as the manner in which we share nutritional resources with our entourage (spouse, children, parents, room-mate(s), etc.). If our bathroom hygiene leaves a lot to be desired, the problem is more related to our capacity to purify ourselves on the emotional level, since a lot of water is used when cleaning bathrooms. Whenever disorder and a lack of cleanliness manifests in the bedroom, it reveals a lack of purity and harmony in our personal intimacy, as well as on the level of our inner and outer couple.

Some people excuse dirt and disorder saying they have no time to tidy up and do housework, but a closer analysis of their situation reveals that in a majority of cases, their attention, interests, activities, values, and efforts are essentially directed toward the outside, thereby leaving them no more energy or time to devote to their private, intimate, inner life. A great number of people experience problems which are the outer manifestation of a serious imbalance between emissivity and receptivity, exteriorization and interiorization, activity and rest, dispersal and concentration, being scattered and being well-centered or focused. When we live in constant discrepancy and out of tune with ourselves, there necessarily comes a time when exhaustion, discouragement and resignation regarding the dirt accumulated around and in us sets in, completely polluting our universe, on all levels. It is then essential to apply the Law of resonance and refer back to ourselves. Of course, we may have recourse to outer help to do our housework, especially when we are going through a period of great fatigue, a serious illness, or burn-out, but as soon as we feel better, it is up to us to re-educate those parts of our being that are overactive, that overwork, and are scattered and dispersed on the outside, that refuse to clean up and maintain order on the inside. Whenever we have a busy job with major responsibilities, we may employ a housekeeper or cleaning-woman, but at the same time, it is important to remember that the person who cleans our house is a symbolic representation of a part of ourselves, and that we must always have great respect for anyone whose services help support our projects and work; also the plus and the minus sides of this person need to be analyzed, just like in a dream.

Some people become so terribly annoyed by the slightest speck of dirt they see, they can't stop themselves from tidying or dusting even when in other people's homes. Having accumulated too many impurities and dirt in their inner world, in this life or previous lives, they unconsciously feel a constant need to get rid of them, to free themselves from this inner dirt, these inner impurities. Not knowing how to cleanse within themselves, on the level of their dirt-laden unconscious memories, they develop excessive cleaning behavior on the outside, possibly going so far as the development of a compulsive disorder, known as ODC (obsessive compulsive disorder).

Furthermore, we may be very clean and tidy ourselves, and yet attract into our life untidy, negligent people on the hygiene level, who are insensitive to dirt. In such cases, we need to know that being clean and tidy on the outside does not mean that we are clean and tidy on all of the levels that exist within us. The unclean, untidy people that Cosmic Intelligence puts on our path, brings into our life, serve as mirrors: they show us hidden, unconscious aspects of ourselves that still need to be transformed, and help us work on the qualities of patience, tolerance, and humility, while teaching us to assert ourselves by asking them to do their share of the work. By wisely and gently inviting our spouse, family members, or room-mate(s), to maintain hygiene and order, we re-educate the corresponding parts of ourselves that have become or became used to negligence in this life or another. When we deal with dirt, cleaning and tidying up with a spiritual conscience, knowing that each time we tidy and clean up dirt created by others, we re-educate that part of ourselves that the person symbolizes, then dirt management becomes a truly initiatic, evolutive experience. This principle applies to all of the cleaning professions.

When dirt appears in a dream, depending on the context, it may indicate that it is time to purify and transform certain aspects of ourselves; or, to re-organize, renovate, or restructure certain areas in our environment to make them pleasant, functional, and/or convivial once again. Analyzing the place, object or person that is dirty in our dream will help us better understand what it is that needs cleansing in ourselves.

⊕ A period in life necessitating deep cleansing within and around us. An alarm signal telling us it is time to take care of our inner and/or outer worlds. An ability to make a connection between misactions (*cf.* this term), hyperactivity, negligence, and laxity on the one hand, and outer and inner dirt on the other. Understanding the fact that outer cleaning helps inner cleansing, and *vice versa*, that dirt is a multi-dimensional manifestation that engenders and reflects all sorts of malfunctioning and discrepancies among the various levels of our being. Life situations that confront us with our karma, obliging us to undertake the cleansing, purification, and transcendence of it. Someone who consciously cleanses the dirt he causes, who doesn't mind cleaning up other people's dirt, knowing how to devote his whole heart to this and applying discernment, right intention and motivation. An ability to call ourselves into question, to reflect on our lifestyle, and to apply the Law of resonance, each time a dirt context manifests. Someone who has the wisdom to consider cleaning up dirt as an opportunity for a new departure, a new beginning, a fresh start. Awareness of the importance of cleanliness and hygiene, of their educational, transformational, evolutive role on both the inner and outer levels. Inner feelings of joy, liberation and well-being during and after doing housework, re-establishing order and cleanliness. Understanding that it is normal to dirty things when working, preparing food or other things, and that cleaning up is the natural follow-up stage. A person who has a sense of ritual, organization, and planning.

⊖ An unclean, untidy person, who lacks refinement and is indifferent and insensitive to the dirt he himself creates, and to that created by others. A lack of hygiene in our inner and/or outer life. Laxity, negligence, laziness, disconnection, dropping out, an '*I couldn't care less*' attitude. Dirt resulting from hyperactivity, dispersal, disorganization; or, a person who is a maniac about housework and cleaning, unable to bear the slightest speck of dirt, with an extremist, radical, intolerant attitude toward those who cause the dirt; obsessive disorder compulsion (ODC). Discrepancies and malfunctioning indicating a lack of structure, discipline, motivation and willpower to call ourselves into question. Resignation, despair, lack of self-esteem. Ignorance of the Laws of karma and resonance. A lack of understanding of the fact that Purity and Order are Cosmic Principles that need to be respected on all levels of Creation in order to ensure coherent, harmonious, well-balanced evolution, health and well-being in human life.

DISABILITY *cf. Handicap*

DISEASE *cf. Illness*

DISGUISE (dressing up)

Disguising ourselves, dressing up, is a conscious choice to wear clothing that will make us unrecognizable so as to be able to go under a different identity than our usual one. Whether it's disguise or dressing up in concrete reality, at Halloween or during Carnival for example, or whether shown in a dream, on the symbolic level, it may represent facets of ourselves that we wish to camouflage or hide in order to be able to avoid or fool others; or, roles that we play to be loved, to attract attention or to manipulate; or, aspects and qualities we'd like to have. The disguise we choose – consciously or unconsciously – always reveals parts of ourselves.

For a disguise or costume shown in a dream to be a positive symbol, it is important that it is beautiful, bright, and represents harmonious, inspiring aspects. Otherwise, it indicates that we prefer to bask in illusion and that we play roles in order to manipulate and to be loved.

⊕ To represent a positive symbol, a disguise must be beautiful, harmonious, bright, luminous, and evoke beautiful, inspiring qualities. Allows us to experiment unconscious facets of ourselves. Creates atmospherics, ambiances and a celebratory, festive, joyful, party atmosphere. Allows us to express our wish for transformation, renewal, our soul's need to exteriorize its potential, hence children's attraction to the game of dressing-up.

⊖ Donned in order to play a role. Tendency to hide our true nature, to flee reality. Need for recognition and acknowledgment at all costs. Lack of confidence and self-esteem inciting people to choose a costume that gives an impression of superiority or domination. Hiding behind illusions. A deceitful, manipulative mind. Lacking authenticity. Serves to camouflage embarrassment and shyness. Double life and problems of multiple personalities. Inferiority and superiority complexes.

DISHES, CROCKERY, CUTLERY

Generally speaking, crockery and cutlery represent receptivity related to nourishing resources, as these terms refer to all the dishes and utensils used to eat, prepare, store, and present food. Hence they symbolize the capacity to welcome and offer others, and ourselves, nourishing energy. Some utensils, and in particular, knives and forks, have a more emissive aspect. The use made of crockery and cutlery also represents a more evolved, less instinctual, acquired way of nourishing ourselves. Among other things, this distinguishes us from animals when we eat and helps us remain civilized, receptive to other people's needs. Moreover, we can sometimes perceive a greedy, instinctual, animal energy when people only use their fingers or hands to eat in a rough, uncouth, boorish manner. However, it can also be positive and practical to eat with our fingers or hands. On such occasions, we can see a greater symbiosis with the food, relaxing, letting go of an often rigid code of good manners. When a child eats with his fingers, it indicates an unfinished apprenticeship, blunt, unhoned energy, and a conscience that is focused only on the need to eat without taking into account the environment or the unconsciously created mess and dirt, provided, of course, that such energy is present in a dream or in a child's behavior.

However, the use of crockery and cutlery may also be extreme, i.e. it may show excessive attachment to material values and certain rigid, exaggerated traditions when laying a table with a large number of serving dishes, plates, glasses and cutlery; or, by collecting and displaying cups, plates, dinner services, etc. in a cabinet as though they were museum pieces or a national heritage, thereby reflecting excessive, disproportionate pride. This may also denote a haughty, arrogant attitude, a worldly mind and spirit; or, indicate the presence of memories of deep insecurity following the experience of lacking food.

Doing the washing-up is also a daily household task that can engender and develop qualities and educational concepts in children and adults alike. Indeed, it is by doing the washing-up that we can learn to make an effort, to adopt a certain discipline and regularity in purification work and personal and collective cleansing.

⊕ A symbol of receptivity to resources and of the structure of physical renewal, gestures to nourish ourselves, and to prepare and/or serve food. Allows us to give and to receive. Refinement on the level of needs, behavior, and hygiene. A capacity to prepare ourselves well to offer or receive food. Tools to bring people closer, conviviality, sharing. Allows us to receive and deal with nourishing energy in a harmonious, evolved way. A person who nourishes himself well and healthily. A capacity to divide well and share nourishing resources fairly.

⊖ A lack of receptivity or respect regarding nourishing resources. Difficulty giving and receiving, nourishing ourselves and/or others. Problems related to the way of preparing food, nourishing and physically renewing ourselves. A rough, uncouth, boorish person; or, a person who is too refined, too sophisticated, a snob, who associates food and the way it is served with power games that control how and what is given or not. A lack of refinement, hygiene, and civilized manners. A tendency to pay too much attention to the material form and not enough to the energy with which we nourish ourselves; excessive refinement and worldliness, a haughty attitude. Someone who nourishes himself in an unhealthy way; or, who bears within memories of insecurity and lack regarding food and vital resources.

DISMISSAL

Dismissal represents an experience that manifests in a person's life when change in his learning and evolution program becomes necessary. It may also correspond to a wake-up call by Up Above to make us aware that we need to rectify the way we work or cooperate with others; or, that we need to re-orient our field of activity and our efforts to earn our living, to support ourselves and our family. It may also be an act of Divine Justice through which a person experiences the Law of return (the Law of karma), after having deprived other people of their work or caused their unemployment, in a recent or distant past.

Dismissal may also serve to reveal material insecurities and fear of lacks that dwell within us; or, help us understand just how much our self-esteem depends on our job. Generally speaking, dismissal symbolizes the end of a stage, and indicates the need to undergo deep self-questioning so as to undertake the necessary steps to re-orient our life and begin something new, start afresh.

⊕ A capacity to consider dismissal as a sign inciting reflection on the values and priorities in our life, our understanding and vision of work, the importance we grant it, the way we execute it, the possibilities of self-fulfillment and achievement it offers us. Understanding that dismissal indicates the end of a cycle. It invites self-questioning, a new job direction, a new departure, a new stage in our evolution. Motivation, willpower, courage, determination and confidence to re-adjust, re-train, and begin a new work dynamic. Awareness that, independent of outer circumstances, dismissal always has a deep *raison-d'être* that serves our evolution, including those cases where it serves to settle a karmic debt. Awareness that the work we do in the outer world corresponds to a learning program that allows us to develop certain qualities, virtues, and capacities on the inside, that dismissal may sometimes prove necessary when we are to move on to a new stage but find it difficult to let go of the comforts, material security, and privileges we have acquired. An indication that it is time to acquire new knowledge, to go toward new experiences that our soul needs to perfect its evolution.

⊖ Discouragement, depression, pessimism, despair. A feeling of failure, an inferiority complex, and loss of self-esteem. An incapacity to consider dismissal through a causal vision, not to judge it solely in terms of material consequences, losses, inconvenience, and disadvantages. Rebellion, refusal to call ourselves into question, to accept the situation and consider it as an opportunity to evolve. A period of deep insecurity that awakens fear of lacks, existential anguish, which tests our confidence and faith in life, in others, and in ourselves. Fear of change, anxiety about the future. A lack of motivation to re-orient our life, to take the necessary steps to find another job, to acquire new knowledge and professional skills. A tendency to accuse and blame others, the job market, society.

DISPUTE (quarrel, row)

A dispute is a state of conscience that represents an opposition of ideas and interests. It indicates ambivalence, an inner contradiction that separates and divides us. Dreams wherein we quarrel with other people indicate the presence of conflicting memories, which, if we don't transform, will end up materializing in the form of real life conflicts. Disputes, rows and quarrelsome situations show us the resonance we have with the people and subjects concerned. By studying the symbolism of the elements involved, we can become aware of the corresponding contradictory aspects within ourselves.

⊕ A dispute is an alarm signal revealing our inner conflicts and contradictions. It is important not to ignore disputes, but rather to apply the Law of resonance and to take time to reflect, question, and reassess ourselves. The ensuing understanding will lead to true, enduring reconciliation on both the inside and the outside. Quarrels and disputes offer great teachings to all parties involved, even when one of them is in the wrong. They are always a reflection of ourselves; they mirror attitudes and behavior we have already had in other lives.

⊖ Disputes we do not learn a lesson from indicate a refusal to reassess ourselves, to refer back to ourselves when we are bothered, put out, disturbed, upset, as well as a lack of wisdom, self-command and openness to others. We need to know that a tendency to be stubborn, to blame others, to impose our point of view aggressively, or to seek revenge creates tension and supplementary karmas.

DIVIDE, DIVISION

To divide is an action where we fragment, fraction, separate an element or a collection of elements into several parts so as to distribute and use them separately. The act of division represents a state of conscience of sharing resources. Fair division creates a state of balance, equity, trust and peace. On the universal and symbolic levels, division is the act whereby the Creator manifests Himself in the multiplicity of His Creation. Originally, the division of One in order to create the Whole is a gift of self through Love and Wisdom. Altruistic division generates harmony because each fragment of the whole is used for the good of all.

⊕ In a dream or concrete reality, when a division is fair and equitable, it represents an act of great wisdom and true love as well as a sense of responsibility, organization and right use of resources. Sharing is essential for balance, for equilibrium on all levels.

⊖ Unfair, dishonest or arbitrary division indicates forces and memories that engender separations, quarrels, break-ups, dissension and isolationism. A dualistic, conflicting, dictator spirit that divides to better dominate. Difficulty sharing with others. Egotism. Solitude. Problems with justice and the law. Lack of global, long-term vision.

DOCTOR, MEDICAL

A medical doctor is a university qualified health professional, who has acquired scientific, anatomical knowledge allowing him to find remedies for different health problems. His work – his vocation or life mission – consists in diagnosing, deciding, and proposing the necessary care to prevent, relieve, or cure his patients' illnesses, pathologies, wounds and pains, either as a general practitioner or as a specialist in a particular field. Through medication, surgery, and a variety of therapeutic means, a doctor tries to help the ill person re-establish the correct functioning of his body, and regain his physical and psychological health. A doctor can also diagnose, study, analyze, and understand illnesses, malfunctions, physical and psychological disorders, depending on his specialization. A person with knowledge of the human body and how it works, as well as of the medical field and certain prevention strategies, is able to intervene more efficiently on the health level if he is also able to understand the metaphysical and symbolic meaning. For example, a person suffering from cardiac problems can analyze the symbolism of his emotional, affective, sentimental world, his capacity to give and receive love, and to show his feelings.

Generally speaking, globally, a doctor symbolically represents a capacity to heal ourselves, and to help heal others. This capacity stems from the fact that every human being bears the Divine Creator's signature in his mind, spirit, and soul, as well as in each and every single cell of his physical body. The saying *A doctor anoints and bandages a wound, God heals it* is a good expression of the fact that outer medical care is not enough to obtain integral, holistic healing, which aims to heal not only the physical body, but also a person's spirit and soul. Indeed, to enjoy complete rehabilitation and to fully benefit from the second chances offered by Cosmic Intelligence, God, or whatever name this Pure, Superior, Creative Power is known by, the ill person has to have the willpower to participate in his healing. He does so by recognizing and acknowledging the omniscience and all-powerfulness of the Divine Force that animates his being, and by learning to direct this Force by means of his conscious intention toward healing his physical and psychological wounds, while respecting the Laws of Creation.

For some time now, the accelerated evolution of conscience in more and more people has also led to a new perception of medicine, and modified the general image of doctors. A change in attitude can be noted, especially in the Western world, where people used to idealize doctors, put them on a pedestal, and blindly put their whole faith and trust in them. This evolution, among others, manifests in a growing disenchantment with the unsatisfactory results offered by medicine that only acts on the symptom level, with a health service where doctors no longer take time to listen to and consider their patients as whole human beings, but only as medical cases, problems to be solved, and hence limit their time and treatment as though each patient was simply a file or number on their *to-be-dealt-with* list. The tendency to unquestioningly put our whole faith and trust in our doctor perfectly suited the attitude of exoteric science, which seeks answers and solutions solely from an exterior point of view, i.e. based on the manifestations of ills and not their meaning.

Today, however, the spiritual awakening of an ever-increasing number of people is helping toward the rapid growth of esoteric, initiatic science, leading to the development of natural, holistic medicine, to a reminder of our self-healing power, and the appearance of a new category of doctors who, rather than think of themselves as gods, learn to cooperate with Superior, Divine Intelligence and Power, with God. They are more humane, humble, and altruistic, and work with a new conscience that offers them global vision and multi-dimensional understanding of life. These new doctors also understand the importance of knowing and respecting Cosmic Laws, and analyzing illnesses and their symptoms using symbolic language in order to detect their true, metaphysical causes.

Consulting a doctor in either concrete reality or a dream indicates that an imbalance or malfunction has manifested on a certain level and requires healing, rectifying. Depending on the context, it may also be a sign that the person is activating his will to get better, to regain good health, to be guided toward healing, to learn how to heal himself, or what preventive measures he should take in order to respond to the needs of his organism. Today health professionals agree that a person who actively participates in his well-being, who strives to find balance in his personal, family, social, and professional life, increases the probabilities of enjoying good health. Even those of us who have no medical knowledge know that physical exercise, a healthy diet, restorative sleep, relaxation, rest, silence, meditation, prayer, introspection, and inner listening have positive effects on our health on many levels; that harmonious relationships, a stimulating, creative, inspiring job, or a positive, grateful attitude toward whatever work we do, as well as social activities that offer the opportunity for fulfillment on the humanitarian, altruistic level, greatly contribute to our general, global state of health.

Sooner or later, through deep work on ourselves, seeking to find the cause of our health problems, we understand that our outer state (the symptom-consequence level) is the reflection of our inner state (the causal level). Becoming aware of this is the key to change that we need to bring to our way of thinking and behavior, not only to find a suitable doctor on the outside, but also to activate our own inner doctor each time a health problem arises. Then we will also know and understand that the doctor we consult on the outside is the mirror reflection of our inner doctor. Interestingly, the expression most commonly used for recovery, for healing, is *to get better*; when we manage to go beyond the outer symptoms to find the distortion at the root of our health problem, we do indeed get better on deeper, quality levels, and we become a better soul.

⊕ Great healing potential, an active healing force allowing second chances and rehabilitation on all levels. A capacity to find or be guided toward competent, understanding doctors when the need arises. Activation of the power of self-healing, and the potential of the multi-dimensional, universal doctor we all have within ourselves. An initiated sage with extensive knowledge of the body, soul, and spirit. A capacity to analyze, study, and understand not only the symptoms, but also the deep causes of illnesses and general health problems. Helping and supporting the ill. A compassionate person who seeks solutions on the health level. Social renown, a model of altruism, a trustworthy person, a missionary, a humanitarian mind and spirit. Awareness that leads a person to carry out the necessary changes in order to heal or prevent illness. Accountability, empowerment, developing a sense of self-responsibility. Work on ourselves – whether as a doctor or patient – to develop our intuition, receptivity, inner listening, and subtle perception so as not to consider only the physical body, but also the subtle, emotional, mental, and spiritual bodies. Reconnection with the omniscient, all-powerful Divine Force, Energy, or Power that ensures coherency, order and harmony in all of the systems of Creation, including the human body. Seeking original Knowledge. Study of Cosmic Laws, symbolic language, as well as remedies and traditional, holistic healing methods. Development of a spiritual, universal conscience. Understanding the karmic aspect and the influence of unconscious memories in the manifestation of an illness, as well as in the healing process. Acknowledgement and gratitude for Divine Grace and all of the second chances we receive.

⊖ Problems related to our capacity to heal, to look after and treat ourselves and others, to understand illnesses, to find competent, understanding doctors, as well as appropriate health resources. An excess or lack of willpower to heal ourselves, or help others in their need for healing. Lack of discernment when choosing a doctor. A tendency to blindly trust anyone entitled doctor. Ignorance of the symbolic meaning of symptoms and illnesses, which hinders a person's access to the causal level and an understanding of the origin of ills. A doctor who only takes into consideration the physical body and symptoms, who lacks openness regarding new, complementary, alternative, holistic medicine which takes into account the spirit-soul-body triad. An excessively logical, rational, scientific approach. Atheism, practicing medicine without faith, without believing in a superior power, energy, or force. A completely closed, even hostile, mind regarding the metaphysical, spiritual realities of life. A limited, unilateral vision. A cold, purely intellectual evaluation. A haughty attitude. Arrogance. A feeling of superiority. Seeking social recognition and acknowledgement, renown, glory and personal prestige. An unscrupulous doctor with no conscience, who doesn't hesitate to abuse and misuse his influence and power to get rich and obtain personal advantages.

DOCUMENT

A document is the materialization, the physical medium of a collection of data, knowledge and information on ourselves, others or a particular subject. Documents are a symbolic representation of communication and an exchange of information and knowledge.

⊕ A symbol of communication, organization and sharing knowledge, ideas. A state of conscience that transmits useful ideas that are favorable for the evolution of a situation or project.

Expansion made possible thanks to knowledge and know-how. An information medium that contributes to working on and accomplishing projects. A symbol of work and sharing.

⊖ Problems of communication and organization. Difficulty giving or receiving information; for example, mislaying, losing or not being able to find important documents. Poor use of knowledge, for instance for self-serving, egotistical, purely materialistic ends. Badly drafted or incomplete documents indicate a lack of rigor, structure and precision. Sharing and spreading false information, or mis-information. Problems expanding.

DOG

As a protective pet and devoted, obedient companion to man, a dog represents aspects of our instinctual energy that tend to be docile, easy to train and master, if we take time to look after them.

A dog also symbolizes affection, joy, spontaneity, vivacity, sociability, fidelity, fun and games, pleasure and enjoyment. Its emotional world is strong and intense, hence it represents great emotional intensity, which needs to be channeled with rigor and authority so it doesn't overflow, get out of control, and become threatening. With its highly developed sense of smell, it explores, identifies, and communicates with its environment and entourage, mostly through smells. Symbolically, this represents a capacity to perceive and know the people around us through instinctive clairsentience. Moreover, a dog is able to hear ultrasounds, which makes it a symbol of clairaudience on the instinctual level. Through its very good sense of direction, it also symbolizes ease and great agility to situate ourselves in space, and to navigate in all sorts of environment.

The kind of dog we have, and its character, always reveals aspects of ourselves. If a person chooses a dangerous dog that has a tendency to bite, this indicates that he harbors aggressive forces within that are threatening for others and for himself; or, that the person feels a need to protect himself by scaring others and keeping them at a distance with threats and aggression.

⊕ Abundance of vital energy and emotions, joy, spontaneity, vivacity, fun, sociability, fidelity, obedience, devotion, protection, instinctive clairsentience and clairaudience, a sense of direction.

⊖ Emotional dependency, affective insecurity, overflowing emotions, a compulsive need to please and be loved, fear of solitude, problems obeying, unpredictable behavior, aggression.

A disobedient dog and a dog that runs away as soon as it has the opportunity indicates that we need to work on educating, training, and mastering our repressed, impulsive, intense needs on the emotional, personal and social levels.

DOLL

Dolls are toys (*cf. also* this term), or sometimes ornaments, symbolically representing human beings of various aspects, size, color and age. Although as a toy, they quite naturally attract little girls more than boys, it is wise and correct to allow and encourage little boys to include them in their games from time to time so as to develop their parental, protective sense for the fragility of the young child and his affective and physical needs, and thus incite them to accept and assume their feminine polarity from earliest childhood.

Through playing with dolls, children experiment and develop a sense of psychology along with maternal and paternal qualities. In their doll games, they usually have the dolls live and experience what they themselves are going through in their inner world. These projections allow parents to know their child better and to become aware of how he/she functions as well as his/her inner learning and evolution programs. If the parents know symbolic language, they can interpret the symbolic messages their child's soul exteriorizes through the various staging and storylines of his/her games with dolls, and in this case, guide and help their child to rectify distorted thoughts and/or behavior.

A doll is a very important pedagogical, educational tool to teach children to become responsible, attentive, gentle, patient, tolerant and compassionate, and to develop love, respect, and right, well-balanced authority in different family and social contexts. It is interesting to note that for children, playing has the same symbolism as work for adults: the way children act and behave in the external world reveals the learning dynamics and challenges or trials and ordeals their soul needs in order to evolve.

⊕ An important pedagogical, educational instrument, which favors the development of masculine and feminine polarities and qualities, as well as an apprenticeship regarding parental and relational roles in love and wisdom. A means of expression and experimentation, which helps a child develop and expand both on the inside and in concrete reality. Apprenticeship and integration on a small scale of what adult, parental, family and social life is. Allows the development of a sense of duty and responsibility, the gift of self, qualities, virtues and unconditional, altruistic love. Gradually prepares a child to realize, concretize his thoughts and consciously participate in the materialization of more complex situations, especially regarding maternity, paternity and the family. Helps a child discover the sacred, Divine meaning of life, to understand the role of our Heavenly Father and Mother, to feel a sense of belonging to the planetary, universal family, to acquire confidence, trust, and a feeling of protection and security on the physical and metaphysical levels.

⊖ Play dynamics that indicate difficulties related to the capacity of being a parent, of being patient, gentle, loving, understanding, receptive and able to listen. A lack of noble sentiments, such as the gift of self, unconditional love, and altruism. Excessive emissivity. A child or adult who withdraws into his own imaginary world and fantasies because of a lack of love, attention, creativity, wonder and awe in his concrete life: the doll becomes his mirror. Loss of innocence, natural freshness and enthusiasm, loss of confidence and trust in the adult world, as well as the spontaneous, intuitive expression of *joie de vivre*: the child refuses to grow up; the adult remains a child. An incapacity to be attentive and receptive to a child's physical and psychological needs, to the messages, requests, and appeals of his soul. Difficulty realizing and concretizing ideas, going from the imaginary play world to concrete reality. An incapacity to integrate into daily behavior what is learned while playing, to let an idea or project evolve in a healthy, right way. Playful activities revealing ill-treatment, child abuse, violence, domination and abuse of parental authority, loss of confidence and trust, and all sorts of fears. Selfish, self-centered, arrogant, haughty, sly, insidious, angry, destructive behavior. Revelation of serious wounds and discrepancies on the level of our inner child. Memories of domination, aggression, brutality, and abuse on the intimate level. Problems with the feminine and/or masculine polarity, with the maternal and/or paternal instinct. A need to please, to be noticed, to convince, to always be right. A tendency toward manipulation, lies, hypocrisy, superficiality. An over-naïve, over-servile attitude. Feelings of indifference, rejection, abandon, inferiority.

DOLPHIN

Since a dolphin is a marine mammal, it is a symbol that relates to our needs regarding instinctual vital energy and the world of emotions. A dolphin symbolizes *joie de vivre*, kindness, gentleness, mutual help, cooperation, a capacity to communicate by telepathy, an ability to make our way rapidly and easily in the world of emotions. It is very peaceful and generally lives in a group, and manifests a great disposition to help others; hence it has a very altruistic social dimension. It is also gifted with great intelligence, which makes it a symbol of the capacity to transpose our intellectual powers onto the instinctual and emotional levels to help our neighbor.

⊕ Mutual help, cooperation, pacifism, and altruism on the emotional and instinctual levels. Kindness, gentleness, *joie de vivre*, vivacity, at ease in emotions, rapidity in action, A capacity to communicate intuitively as well as by telepathy. Power of protection.

⊖ A lack of mutual help, cooperation, altruism on the emotional and instinctual levels. Absence of courage and involvement to help, to protect. Difficulty advancing on the emotional level due to a lack of generosity and altruism. Sadness, heaviness, moroseness, isolation, captivity. Difficult social life. Egoism. An incapacity to communicate our feelings either intuitively or by telepathy.

DOOR

A door is an element that ensures a passage from one enclosed space to another, access to and from a building or delimited grounds, e.g. a courtyard, garden, enclosure. It facilitates protection of a place, as in the case of a door that can be locked and/or barred. It also preserves intimacy when we need to be alone somewhere to interiorize, meditate, work or renew our energies, without being disturbed.

Symbolically, depending on the context, a door may represent a passageway between different soul-states, ambiances, mentalities, or levels of conscience, respectively represented by the rooms and spaces it connects. It is a sign of openness, hospitality and welcome for the entering energies when it is open, and a halt, blockage, or protection, when it is closed and/or locked. In either a dream, or concrete reality, if we find ourselves in front of a door that won't open, it indicates that for the moment, we do not have access to whatever there is on the other side of that door. When we force a door open in a dream or concrete reality, it reveals the presence of forces within us that seek to impose. Forcing may relate to unconscious memories where abuse of power, or intense, unfulfilled needs have been recorded, which push us to invade others and monopolize them socially.

⊕ A beautiful, harmonious, welcoming door, that is neither too wide nor too narrow, neither too high nor too low, represents a capacity to move in a right, pleasant manner from one state of conscience, spirit, mind, or soul to another; or, a capacity to discover a state of conscience, ambiance, access to resources. An ability to open up to others and to welcome them with confidence and hospitality; and, also, to retreat into our intimacy, or protect ourselves, as needs be. A capacity to maintain a harmonious balance between interiorization and exteriorization, between our private, intimate, inner life and our social, professional life in the outside world. An attitude of respect and discretion before a closed door. Someone who opens and closes doors gently, without making any noise, without banging them, who is capable of thinking of and having respect for others. A partial or entire glass door (e.g. a patio door), with clean panes, that is kept clear so we can see what is happening both on the outside and on the inside, is a sign of transparency and openness toward others, the world, and life in general.

⊖ A dark, heavy, constantly locked or barred door indicates a state of closure to others, the world, and life, an intense need to protect ourselves, to remain alone, barricaded in, through fear of being disturbed, robbed, burgled, or assaulted. On the contrary, a door that is always open and unlocked may indicate excessive availability, undiscerning welcome to all sorts of energy, a tendency to allow ourselves and our sacred space, our intimacy, to be invaded, and to behave likewise with others. Imbalance between moments of interiorization and exteriorization, either an overly introvert or an overly extravert personality. A separatist mind and spirit, that divides and sets aside.

A habit of opening and closing doors noisily, or of banging them indicates an over-emissive, over-intense, hasty, impatient, hyperactive, bad-tempered, aggressive, inconsiderate character.

A tendency to insistently knock on a door, or to force it indicates a lack of respect, discretion, and sensitivity toward others; a selfish, egotistical, monopolizing character that unashamedly imposes his will on other people's lives and intimacy.

A glass door will have a negative connotation if, for instance, the panes are dirty, or if it has imposing, dirty, or torn curtains, indicating an overly reserved, negligent, or rough attitude; or, if it allows us to look outside, but prevents anyone from looking inside, it thereby denotes a lack of transparency, as well as simultaneous excessive curiosity regarding the outer world, along with a refusal to unveil our own inner world.

Cupboard doors left open inadvertently, or as the result of a bad habit, indicates a lack of attention, vigilance, presence of mind, a tendency to be too open, too exposed, scattered, dispersed, insufficiently incarnated, over-focused on the mental level, on ideas, projects, and thoughts spinning in our head, thereby weakening the protective effect of a cupboard; or, excessive desire for rapid access indicating lacks on the level(s) corresponding to the contents therein.

DRAGON

A dragon represents a state of conscience of power and a tremendous need for personal achievement and fulfillment. Through its incomparable power, this animal symbolizes a very great instinctual force that dwells within us. Depending on the use we make of it, this force, this powerful energy, can express itself either positively or negatively. Capable of using the four elements: fire (the spirit), air (thoughts), water (emotions) and earth (action) to nourish itself, as well as to manifest or satisfy needs, the dragon is also a symbol of the forces of nature. In Chinese Tradition, it is associated with the emperor's power. Symbolically, this legendary, mystical animal reflects the needs and primary forces man must learn to master and transcend before being able to make right, just, good use of his vital energy, and have access to the power he has within himself in all circumstances and on all levels. Whenever we see a dragon in a dream, we must consider it cautiously, because the forces and memories it represents can manifest with extreme intensity on the level of primary needs related to power. In a dream with a negative tendency, it may indicate the awakening of forces, which in their quest to satisfy personal needs, can act very destructively for both ourselves and others.

⊕ Transcendence of instincts related to needs of power, domination, and personal achievement and fulfillment. Very great vital force. Powerful charisma and capacity to manifest. Great capacity to use power, to be an extraordinary leader. Work on memories that engender fear. Mastery of needs and right, well-balanced use of the four elements within ourselves, and the power they represent.

⊖ Megalomania; or, a profound lack of self-esteem in leadership, of our capacity to use power and be a good leader. Domination, excessive control. Abuse of power for personal ends; or, submission and a tendency to let ourselves be crushed by domineering people, by energies of unhealthy power. Violence, aggression in the satisfaction of personal needs. A person with powerful charisma that he uses negatively and destructively on the social level. Authoritarian, inflexible force.

DRAWER

A drawer serves to tidy away, order, and organize personal, and/or family belongings. Metaphysically, a drawer is related to organization, a love of tidiness and cleanliness; it is also related to discretion and intimacy. The various states of conscience that are being *tidied*, or need to be organized, are determined by analyzing the type of drawer (or chest of drawers), the room it is in (kitchen, bathroom, bedroom, sitting-room, etc.), and the belongings concerned. Opening a drawer also evokes a sense of discovery, or re-discovery, of forgotten, lost, or un-used objects. Symbolically, we rediscover potential that had become unconscious in order to use it with new knowledge.

⊕ Indicates a sense of organization, order, cleanliness, discretion, and structure on the level of resources. A practical mind and spirit. An ability to take care of our inner and outer resources. A responsible, farsighted attitude toward the abundance we have at our disposal. Discovery of hidden treasures and potential.

⊖ Difficulty being organized, tidy, and practical on the inside and/or on the outside. A necessity to clean and tidy up our inner memories. Difficulty finding resources due to a lack of order; a complicated, disorganized person. A lack of discretion, structure, organization or tidiness; or, excessive tidiness and order on the outside in order to compensate for inner disorder. A tendency to want to hide what we possess through shyness; or, to dissimulate our weaknesses; or, on the contrary, to enjoy displaying our possessions to impress others and to attract attention. Perfectionism through obsessive order.

DRINK, A

A drink is a liquid which, depending on its composition and the desired effect, is drunk to quench our thirst, hydrate our body, nourish, relax, purify and warm us up or to celebrate. The most natural drink is water. Water is also the fundamental substance of most drinks. Like all liquids, drinks symbolize feelings and emotions. The quality of the drinks we consume reveals the quality of the emotional, affective nourishment we absorb ourselves and offer to others.

⊕ Healthy, natural, nutritional drinks that are good for our general health and well-being indicate a capacity to renew ourselves and nourish ourselves positively on the physical and emotional levels.

⊖ Consumption of drinks that are harmful for our health and well-being reveal problems of affective malnutrition and emotional dependencies.

DRINK, TO

To drink is an action whereby we swallow liquids to hydrate or nourish ourselves. The drinks we absorb represent the way we nourish ourselves on the emotional level. A symbolic analysis of the liquids we drink and the context in which we drink them is very revealing, because it allows us to become aware of the quality of our feelings and our emotional state.

⊕ The absorption of pure water and healthy, nourishing drinks favoring the renewal of our emotional and physical body through rehydration, inner purification and energetic balance, indicates a beautiful conscience and harmony on the emotional level. Discernment and autonomy in the choice of the feelings we nourish. Healthy, inspiring emotional, affective relationships that are good for our evolution.

⊖ Drinking liquids that are harmful to our health (unnatural, highly sweetened, stimulating drinks containing artificial coloring and all sorts of chemical additives) reflects poor nutritional habits on the emotional level, emotional dependencies and lacks, difficulty nourishing ourselves with pure feelings and healthy emotions. Resistance, lack of willpower, or refusal to opt for drinks that are good for our health reveals a lack of understanding of the concept that not only do we become what we think and eat, but also what we drink. Ignorance of the links and correlations that exist between the physical, emotional and intellectual, mental bodies, as well as the necessity to nourish ourselves in a healthy, well-balanced way.

DRIVER (Chauffeur)

The driver or chauffeur of a vehicle is the person who directs the moving, mobile energy, the progression, of a movement or activity.

He reveals the state of conscience that guides and directs us, that drives, leads, or conducts our life. The job of professional driver or chauffeur also represents a need to learn to drive, organize and manage responsibilities safely, respecting the law, respecting rules and regulations, as well as the power of our vital energy when we set ourselves in motion, when we set out to do something; or, when we help others reach their goals, their objective(s) of evolution.

⊕ Work on the mastery of our driving force, our force of action. Development of prudence, vigilance, a sense of responsibility, respect for the law, and for other drivers. Confidence, help, support and protection when advancing.

⊖ A tendency to let ourselves be led, guided by negative, malevolent, incompetent, inexperienced forces. Hyperactivity, hurried, speedy, irresponsible, reckless driving. A lack of vigilance and prudence, risk of accidents. A way of driving that causes problems and blockages; or, a tendency to give our decisional power to others, due to a lack of confidence in our capacity to drive. Complex of superiority or inferiority.

DROUGHT

Drought is a state characterized by a major shortage, or total absence of humidity, of water, hence, symbolically speaking, by a serious emotional, affective deficiency. In the outside world, drought manifests periodically or permanently in countries with a hot, dry climate, which engenders arid, desert regions. However, it may also exceptionally occur locally, for example during very hot summers, or during a change in climate.

An experience of drought reminds us of the vital importance of water, without which life would be impossible for human beings, as well as the flora and fauna. On the symbolic, metaphysical levels, this means that an absence of emotions and feelings dries up our soul and our heart, our vital, driving force, as well as our motivation, enthusiasm and vitality.

Generally speaking, a lack of water always indicates an emotional, affective deficiency, a lack of emotions, feelings, and sentiments.

On the personal level, drought indicates a lack of love, kindness, compassion, a tendency to be very harsh and *dry* or arid, lacking in love toward ourselves and our entourage. Such an attitude automatically creates a difficult, sterile evolution climate. Often, such a person will go so far as to forbid himself to quench his emotional thirst, even when life offers him the wherewithal to satisfy his thirst. Of course, such behavior destroys *joie de vivre,* vitality, the capacity to regenerate and renew ourselves, thereby engendering inner harshness, aridity, rigidity, and emptiness. On the level of the physical body, it may manifest through dry skin, intense, almost constant thirst, and a tendency to drink greedily; or, through the manifestation of symptoms and illnesses that reflect what the person is going through on the inside.

Dry-hearted people in an emotionally arid world are not creative, constructive entrepreneurs, because they don't have the necessary energy to manifest and realize their full potential. They may have a very intense mental, and even spiritual life, but they don't succeed in incarnating it right and harmoniously in the physical world, because their emotional level, the driving force behind setting projects in action, has run dry. Just like a spring running dry, and a lack of water gradually leading to the disappearance of life and the desertification of the surrounding earth, so too does a *dried-up*, desiccated, arid heart and an absence of life-nourishing emotions – love, gentleness, tenderness, joy, kindness, compassion, etc.– induce drought in the inner territories of an insensitive person, along with the loss of his fertility and creative power, symbolized by the abilities, gifts, and talents each of us has come to incarnate on Earth.

To compensate for this lack, an amplification of the mental level and cerebral capacities may be observed, which, if excessive and poorly channeled, may lead the person to experience serious distortions: intellectual overwork (burn-out), mental illnesses and disorders, ideas of *grandeur*, a feeling of superiority, megalomania, racism, erroneous scientific research, abusive use of power and knowledge, criticism, chronic dissatisfaction, etc.

Whenever a whole collectivity is concerned, the result is an ethnic or national egregore (*cf.* this term) that is rather cold, reserved, insensitive, distant, introverted, unable to express feelings, and disconnected from the values of the heart.

Furthermore, a dry, arid mentality may also be found on the spiritual level; e.g. in the form of extreme puritanism, or a stiff, rigid religious life, based on illusory, forced transcendence of the emotions and instincts, on imposed celibacy and religious indoctrination with wrong, censored, or false spiritual beliefs and values. Religious fanaticism and everything related to it is an example of this kind of drought.

Emotional drought is revealed on the physical level through dry, wrinkled, crevassed skin, dry, brittle hair, hard or brittle nails, and a fragile bone system that breaks easily. Moreover, the correspondence between the psychological, emotional climate on the one hand, and the physical level on the other, has long been observed in ancient oriental medicine (Chinese, Indian, Tibetan, etc.). Such medicine uses the same terminology for organ malfunctions as for outer climates: hence, an organ may have too much water, or lack water and be dry, another may be too cold, have too much wind, etc.

⊕ A great capacity to resist harsh, extreme, climates that are hostile to life. A capacity to nourish beautiful emotions (love, compassion, kindness, generosity, clemency, gentleness, joy, etc.), despite an austere atmosphere or hostile climate. Awareness of aspects we need to transcend in order for affective, emotional energy to start flowing again, so we can rediscover an abundance of beautiful, positive, healthy, exalting emotions and feelings, that elevate the soul, spirit, and conscience. Working on ourselves with perseverance and determination so as to transcend negative, desiccating, destructive emotions. Cleansing distorted emotions and negative karma that we have engendered throughout the course of our lives by neglecting our emotions. Re-connection with the Divine, and understanding that Love is the Essence of existence and all Creation.

⊖ A lack of heart- and soul-nourishing emotions and feelings. Someone who is harsh, rigid, brittle, and insensitive toward himself and others. An arid, desiccating mentality caused by an excessively intense, extremist character, an overactive spirit and an over-powerful, controlling mind that forbids the expression and demonstration of feelings, affection and emotions. A tendency to repress our feelings, which leads to their drying up and an underdeveloped emotional level; affective, emotional, sentimental malnutrition. Waste, exhaustion, and poor use of emotional resources. Infertility, sterility on the physical and metaphysical levels because the person is no longer capable of being receptive to receive, integrate, and benefit from positive, beneficial emotional energies. Difficult memories related to love. Suicidal tendencies, despair, extreme fatigue, exhaustion, lassitude, depression, existential emptiness, A lack of vitality, creativity, motivation, enthusiasm, which leads to all sorts of dependencies, because, instinctively and unconsciously, the person seeks circumstances and people on the outside to take responsibility for his unfulfilled emotional, affective needs. Antisocial behavior; or, on the contrary, too sociable, invasive, seeking love at all costs, draining others of their energy. May also be related to extremist, fanatical, puritanical religious zeal. Violent negative emotions, full of aggression and possessiveness, which burn and consume vital energy, drying up a person's potential and Divine nature: anger, rage, hatred, feelings of revenge, devouring passion, fanaticism, extremism, radicalism. Someone who no longer feels a link uniting him to the Divine, to God, who finds it difficult to renew, to regenerate his energies, to let his vital energy flow and circulate within him, to feel emotional well-being.

DROWN, TO

Drowning symbolizes the state of someone who is absorbed and submerged on the affective, sentimental level, and incapable of managing his emotions. It also indicates a tendency to live *over-emotionally*, i.e. to create an unhealthy overload and overflow of emotional energy, which destroys the person's individuality, as well as his capacity to manifest freely. Drowning may also correspond to a great opening of the unconscious, revealing the presence of huge blocks of memoires of affective dependencies, sometimes accumulated over several lives, causing tension, imbalance, and discrepancy between the inner and outer worlds.

⊕ Awareness of excessive, negative emotions that threaten our emotional stability and security. Understanding the necessity to work on ourselves to cleanse and transform affective dependency memories and behavior, to set ourselves free from tumultuous, distorted, unhealthy emotional relationships. Rebirth of new feelings and sentiments that reflect a more correct, right, well-balanced way of thinking and feeling.

⊖ Submerged by emotional problems and affective, sentimental dependencies. Emotional overflow; or, on the contrary, a tendency to repress emotions. Profound affective instability. A fatalist attitude, discouragement, despair, and/or depression owing to a lack of love and attention. An excessive need to be liked and acknowledged by others. Inner storms leading to emotional shipwreck, with the risk of experiencing shipwreck on the physical level, in concrete reality, if the person makes no effort, does no work on himself to prevent the materialization of the distorted emotional energy that he has accumulated in this life and others. Imbalance, discrepancy between thoughts and feelings. Tumultuous emotions, anger, aggression.

DRUGS, RECREATIONAL (for prescription drugs *cf.* ***Medication***)

Drugs such as alcohol, tobacco, cannabis, heroine, cocaine, etc., are psychoactive substances that act on the brain: they modify mental activity, sensations and behavior. They expose users to health risks and dangers, and may lead to consequences in everyday life; moreover they may engender dependency. Drugs induce somatic and psychic effects depending on their properties, effects and toxicity.

On the symbolic level, drugs are mainly related to the mind, spirit and vital energy. They are usually taken by people who either have a tendency toward laxity and carelessness, or, quite the contrary, ultra-performers and rebels who seek escape from their difficulties, responsibilities, emotions and negative states *via* drugs. Not understanding the reason for trials and ordeals, nor the spiritual meaning of life, not having the appropriate knowledge to extract themselves from their difficulties, they use artificial means to seek feelings of well-being and expansion similar to those felt during meditation, or in work on ourselves to improve our life by transforming our negative thoughts, emotions and behavior. However, by taking drugs, they unwittingly release memories of rebellious forces that have been recorded in the unconscious.

Without knowing it, they are actually in search of the transformational, spiritual dimension of their being, their angelic potential, the awakening and access to universal conscience, to enlightenment.

Drugs that are inhaled such as cigarettes and cannabis, symbolize an attitude of flight, an attempt to manage daily stress by seeking well-being on the level of thoughts and concepts. Liquid drugs such as alcohol, are related to emotions, and the strongest, such as heroine and cocaine, relate to the world of the spirit and vital energy.

⊕ Understanding that drugs are a form of escape, flight from and repression of problems, as well as a distorted form of seeking spirituality, an illusory, superficial quest for well-being, happiness and meaning. May lead to a weaning period and work to free ourselves from a circle of dependencies. Conscious, selective use of a recreational drug in a medical context for pain relief.

⊖ Seeking artificial paradises. Dependency. Rebellion. An easily-influenced person, enslaved by his needs, his passions. Pain, distress, deep suffering. Lack of love, wisdom, understanding. Discouragement. Dropping out. Flight, escapism *via* illusions. Absence of spirituality and trust in the Divine. Tumultuous emotions. A waste of our potential and life. An impulsive, destructive spirit. Extremist. Collusion with the forces of the abyss.

DUMBNESS, MUTISM (deaf mute); *impaired hearing inducing difficulty or an incapacity to speak*

The fact of being deaf, of suffering from impaired hearing that induces serious difficulty or an incapacity to speak due to lesions in the phonation organs or centers, results in a person being unable to use verbal language easily, or sometimes not at all. To fully understand this state, it is essential to consider the global context of the deaf, or hearing-impaired person's life, and the resonance he has with his family and general entourage. This gives indications as to the hidden, karmic causes of his state, as well as to the unconscious memories, often dating from previous lives, when the person made poor use of the gift of speech and of the creative power of language. For example, he may have radically and abusively imposed silence on others, prevented them from expressing themselves freely by threatening them, oppressing them, or, in extreme cases, by actually cutting out their tongue.

It is essential to understand the following principle: we are never a victim without first being an aggressor, oppressor, torturer, executioner, or dominator. This is how the Law of karma, the principle of Divine Justice, and the other Cosmic Laws work.

Sometimes, depending on the negative memories recorded in a person's soul, several lives may go by before Cosmic Intelligence sets up a life program that includes conditions and situations for learning and evolution that allow the person to rediscover right balance, correct equilibrium, while simultaneously settling his karmic debts. When abuses from previous lives concern communication, language, and self-expression, a life program featuring impaired hearing or deafness, speech difficulties and impediments may help repair the accumulated karmas. Hence, after numerous incarnations where a person displayed superior airs and dominating behavior, which belittled and crushed others, the person has to experience one or more lives where he, in his turn, feels inferior, limited, belittled. Such a life program helps him understand what he made others go through in the past, while simultaneously offering him an opportunity to consciously choose to no longer do evil, to consciously renounce evil, wrong-doing, hurt.

Whenever the phonation organs are not affected, the hearing impaired sometimes develop mutism, i.e. refusing to speak, brooding, being silently but obstinately rebellious; or, psychologically unable to speak. Mutism may be selective and manifest in particular, specific situations; in such cases, it is associated with extreme shyness, extreme emotional dependency, or social anxiety. Gaining such a person's confidence and trust, and certain surprise effects, such as those induced by humor, for example, can help toward unblocking voluntary or temporary mutism.

The fact of not being able to say what we think and feel, or having difficulty expressing ourselves through verbal language, always indicates a major problem related to communication. It expresses inhibition of self-expression, of who and what we are, deep discrepancy between our soul states and inner ambiance, and the conditions of our life on the outside. An incapacity to speak easily engenders a tendency to repress our thoughts and emotions, and to develop a shy, timid personality. Someone with speech impairment, problems, or blockages has difficulty asserting himself, and prefers self-effacement, or flees contact with others and the outside world, thereby increasingly shutting himself up in his inner world, feeling misunderstood, rejected, ignored.

Generally speaking, handicaps and limitations concerning the senses (hearing, speech, and sight impairment) always indicate that there was abuse in previous lives. In the process of re-balancing, rediscovering right, correct equilibrium, both on the inside and on the outside, too much always engenders too little, and *vice versa*. For example, a person who talks too much might end up losing his voice so as to temporarily put a stop to his excessive verbal emissivity, his exaggerated need to be listened to and/or acknowledged, thereby obliging him to listen not only to others, but also to himself, to his soul, to his inner voice. A person who nourishes unhealthy curiosity, who focuses his mind and spirit solely on the outer world, may either lose his sight, gradually over time, or, abruptly, in an accident, for instance, thus finding himself obliged to develop his inner vision and his clairvoyance.

The Laws that ensure balance and harmony on the macrocosmic level also govern the microcosmic level. Hence, some people may find themselves experiencing difficult, limiting life conditions over several incarnations, if they have accumulated a large number of distorted memories of having harassed, wounded, and/or destroyed other people's lives through their thoughts, words, and actions. Cosmic Intelligence offers their soul multiple opportunities to repair their abusive experiences, cleanse their memories, re-educate their attitudes and inner forces, re-learn how to speak, how to communicate and behave in a right, correct manner, understanding, on the inside, what they made others suffer.

If such a person does not work on himself to understand the deep cause of his state so as to be able to transform on the inside, deep within himself, the memories, attitudes, and behavior they have engendered, he will feel that destiny has treated him unfairly; he will feel like a victim. He will then project his frustrations, anger, rebellion, sadness, discouragement, and despair on the outer world.

We may receive dreams wherein we are dumb, mute, suffering from serious speech difficulties, impediments (or deaf, or blind). We should never take such dreams lightly because they are warnings that we maintain attitudes that render us dumb, mute, unable to express ourselves verbally, deaf, or blind, in certain situations, when confronted with certain people. They may be a warning that dumbness, mutism or a speech impediment is being prepared on the metaphysical levels, and risks materializing on the physical body level if we don't rectify our behavior.

After experiencing the loss of speech in a dream, or its temporary loss in concrete reality, when we regain the use of speech, we feel relieved, liberated, full of joy and gratitude. Simultaneously, after such an experience, we become fully aware that from now on, we must pay attention to how we speak, how we communicate, and we take time to choose our words before expressing ourselves, because we now know from experience what it is like to no longer have the sacred gift of speech and the creative power of words at our disposal.

On the other hand, a person suffering from speech incapacity may receive dreams wherein he can speak. Through such dreams, Cosmic Intelligence may be showing him that healing is taking place on the subtle levels, that it will manifest when the time is right, in his present life, or in his next incarnation. Such dreams also indicate that the person is being called to develop his capacity to communicate subtly, to convey his intentions, thoughts, and emotions through other means of expression.

⊕ A person who is unable to speak (dumb, mute, speech impediment) who accepts his state as a karmic consequence without rebelling or being resigned, who strives to learn other forms of language so as to be able to communicate. Awareness of the multi-dimensional, symbolic, and karmic meaning of dumbness, mutism, and speech impediments, thereby inciting the person to work on himself to improve his capacity to express himself, communicate, and use language in a right, just, good, well-balanced, healthy manner. Understanding of the importance of consciously choosing our words, and using beautiful, clear, positive, well-intentioned, kind, considerate, inspiring language. Avoiding repressing our thoughts and emotions, so as not to engender memories of things left unsaid. Creating beautiful atmospheres and ambiances, as well as understanding and common ground that is favorable to mutual trust and respect, and the expression of truth and authenticity, through the way we communicate. Developing our capacity to listen to ourselves and others, as well as discretion, receptivity, introspection. The will to understand the true origin and causes of dumbness, mutism, impaired speech, so as to be able to help those affected. The study and analysis of our resonance with dumbness and mutism, and work on ourselves to transform and liberate its corresponding negative memories.

⊖ Non-respect for the sacred gift of speech and the creative power of words, which leads to karmic consequences that may materialize in the form of dumbness, mutism, speech impediments in a future life. A lack of understanding of the fact that dumbness, mutism, and speech impairment are the result of abusive, erroneous attitudes and behavior – sometimes over several lives – regarding the way we use language, the gift of oratory, and the power of words, the power of speech, to slander, belittle, oppress, dominate, seduce, or convince others to divulge secrets, spread lies, or harm others through a lack of discretion and diplomacy. Ignorance of the Law of karma, according to which we always reap what we sow. Someone who finds it difficult to accept his inability to speak (his dumbness, mutism, or speech impediment), who feels he has been unfairly treated by destiny, and who adopts the attitude of a victim, nourishing a feeling of anger and rebellion against God; or, who lets himself sink into resignation and despair. This non-acceptance may also render a person morbidly shy, withdrawn, making him feel isolated, ashamed, rejected, abandoned, or guilty. The presence of great blocks of negative memories that inhibit verbal expression, paralyzing our capacity to speak. A tendency to sulk, to be obstinate. Adopting an attitude to provoke our entourage. Complexes of inferiority and superiority.

DUTY

Duty is a responsibility; it is an obligation or a particular dynamic defined by a system of values, laws and socially accepted moral conventions. On the metaphysical and symbolic levels, doing our duty as regards ourselves and/or others goes hand in hand with an awareness of responsibility toward our life plan and what we need to do to evolve and be *right*, i.e. just and good on all levels (physical, intellectual, emotional, and spiritual) in accordance with Divine Laws and Principles. The more we evolve, the more we are inhabited by a sense of duty that inspires us to become totally involved in and fully committed to the projects we undertake and participate in.

⊕ Sense of responsibility, values, right principles. Total commitment to the accomplishment of what we consider to be our duty. Capacity to recognize priorities. A person of his word who respects his commitments. Ability to receive and take on great responsibilities. A disciplined, organized, stalwart, dedicated person.

⊖ Carelessness, negligence, irresponsibility; or, overly rigid in our understanding of duty on the personal, family and social levels. A poor attitude and false understanding of duty can have a disorganizing effect on others and create conflict. Difficult period caused by a lack of rigor or by excessive authority. An over-literal understanding of duty.

E

EAR

The ear is the organ that allows us to capture and hear sounds. It represents a capacity to be receptive to all of the vibrations that surround us, whether in the form of words, music, or natural sounds. Hence, the ear concerns our capacity to listen, to be attentive, to concentrate on, and to be sensitive to what is going on around and within us. *Outer* listening is when we listen to others, to signs, atmospheres and ambiances in our general environment; *inner* listening is when we are attentive to our emotions, feelings, senses, our inner voice, our intuition, messages received in dreams, as well as when we are in contemplative, meditative states, or in communion with the Divine.

The symbolic meaning of the ear also relates to clairaudience (*cf. also* this term), a capacity that develops in those who know how to open up to the multi-dimensions of sounds. A person can then hear beyond words, tune into and become aware of the subtle energies they convey, perceive people's conscious and unconscious memories, emotions, motivations, and intentions; this capacity also confers an ability to understand in depth, and to communicate intimately with the other person's soul.

The ear also plays an important role in balance. Indeed, the semi-circular canals of our inner ear allow us to find our physical balance, and position ourselves appropriately in space.

Symbolically, the ear symbolizes a capacity to find healthy inner balance or equilibrium, to adopt a right, just, well-balanced position when we visit memories harbored in our unconscious, and to have solid bearings to help us remain well-centered, well-focused, and stable while going through initiatic difficulties and ordeals.

On the metaphysical level, the ear is associated with the 5th chakra, the energy center of communication, situated on the throat level. It is through this chakra that we hear our inner voice.

⊕ Receptivity; in-depth listening to ourselves, others, and our environment. A capacity to hear our inner voice, as well as the deep meaning of words and languages. Discovery and understanding of conscious or unconscious, hidden intentions. A capacity for deep, authentic communication. Development of clairaudience. Good inner and outer balance. An ability to feel stable, well-centered, and to know how to position ourselves right (in a just, good manner seeking to develop Qualities and Virtues) thanks to healthy, true, inner bearings. Sensitivity to ambiances.

⊖ A lack of receptivity and listening to ourselves, others, and life in general. Scattered, dispersed, excessively active on the level of our senses and inner needs. Difficulty hearing the messages of our inner voice, our intuition, or our dreams. Refusal to understand or accept signs. Someone who is too self-centered and too focused on himself and his multiple selfish needs; or, who tends to repress his opinion and emotions, who doesn't listen, and who finds it difficult to communicate. Tinnitus. A lack of balance and stability on both the inner and outer levels. An absence of reference points, bearings, feeling lost. Excessive or deficient emissivity. Unhealthy curiosity, a tendency to want to hear everything, to know everything, through insecurity, lack of confidence; or, through a need to be and/or remain in control. Selfish, megalomaniac behavior, displaying a desire for and seeking power and domination.

EARTH (element)

Along with fire, air, and water, earth is one of the 4 elements. It represents materiality and the world of action in matter. It evokes our creative potential, our capacity to create, sow and reap. It is also directly related to our behavior, the way we act and manifest concretely; it represents grounds for experimentation to learn how to marry spirit and matter. The mineral kingdom, an integral part of earth, symbolizes different layers of our subconscious and unconscious, which represent memories of the way we acted in the near or distant past of this life, or our former lives. When we enter our inner earth, when we dig deep down and explore it like archeologists seeking ancient civilizations, we visit our old, former actions, our former ways of being, which are the root cause of everything that happens in our present life. Thus the element earth contains all the seeds of our future, of our life program, and it is up to us to ensure that our actions, our reactions to what happens to us, are right, just and pure so as not to create new karmas, which will form the seeds of our future lives.

⊕ Represents matter, the world of concrete creation and action, as well as the world of condensed matter. Helps and inspires us to be fully incarnated, to want to experiment matter. Refers to memories related to the world of action in present time (those which we create by our actions here and now), in the past (those which are the consequences of our past actions), or in the future (those which predict our future). Apprenticeship of patience, cycles of materialization, of the fact that we always reap what we sow. A capacity to fructify, produce and create resources. An environmental, ecological conscience.

⊖ Difficulties related to the world of concrete action and creation in general. An incapacity or difficulty to experiment in matter, to work, to manifest. Someone who isn't sufficiently incarnated, or who flees the world of action; or, a selfish, materialistic person who is too busy in matter, in his active life. Someone who is too down-to-earth; or, rejection and flight from matter, from responsibilities, from our life plan. Difficulty fulfilling ourselves on the concrete level. Problems related to density, tangibility. Visiting negative memories related to the world of action, to our way of behaving in concrete reality. Fear of the unconscious, of the discovery of memories of our past.

EARTH (the planet)

The Earth is our habitat, our home, our laboratory for experimenting and experiencing life as human beings. In our solar system, it is the only known planet to offer us the essential conditions for survival, such as breathable air and sunlight rendering existence possible through its contribution of thermal energy and light. Hence the Earth represents the world of materiality, grounds for learning, for our apprenticeship to experiment life and action in matter. The different layers that compose it also represent the different layers of our conscience and of our unconscious. Everything that is to be found underground, or near the center of the Earth, is associated with our unconscious world given its capacity to create, its force of action and power of materialization, because, as archeological discoveries have proved, it preserves the memories and relics of our past experimentations. The Earth is also a collective symbol *par excellence*, because all humanity lives on it. No matter our origin, color, religion, or job, the Earth is our common home, the vital space of all Mankind, territory where we all have to learn to live together in peace and harmony and share resources for everyone's benefit.

When we see it from outer space, we realize both its immensity and its tininess on the Universal scale. It leads us to understand that we have all of the countries on Earth within us in terms of conscience and that our goal is to become universal, to integrate the qualities of all countries, of all cultures, of all mentalities. This concept of integrating all countries within ourselves helps us take a step back, gain some distance, put things in perspective and de-dramatize, see our concrete, material experimentations as a tiny part of who we are, as an infinite representation of our potential. In a way, the Earth is our planetary mother, given its welcoming, verdant aspect and its nourishing capacities, as well as being an emotional cradle with its oceans, seas, rivers and lakes, which cover 70% of its surface, which is why it is referred to as the Blue Planet. Remarkably, this percentage is exactly the same percentage of water contained in our body. The Earth is also a wonderful living laboratory, capable of producing, transforming and renewing different vital energy resources. It is our Mother Earth, which helps and supports us, offering us indispensable resources to live and experiment.

⊕ Symbolizes the world of materiality, the incarnation of spirit in matter, the capacity to materialize, to concretize the creative potential inherent in the human mind and spirit, to experiment life and action on the physical, terrestrial level. Understanding that the Earth is a School, experimental grounds for the spirit. A person who is well-incarnated, well-rooted on Earth, without having lost his connection with Up Above and the other dimensions of life. An environmental, ecological conscience. Good use of resources. Altruistically minded, apprenticeship of sharing and equity of resources. Conscious participation in the evolution of life on Earth.

A force of transformation, work, multiplication, materialization and realization *par excellence*. Capacity to produce and create on both the personal and collective levels. Ability to fructify resources and to manage harvests on all levels in a right, fair, altruistic manner. Capacity to visit and transform within ourselves the forces and conscious and unconscious memories engendered by Humanity since the beginning of our existence. Understanding the fact that all of the aspects of the Earth (the different kingdoms, climates, landscapes, countries, and everything that characterizes them) exist in us in terms of states of conscience, and our evolutionary goal is to integrate their qualities, transform and transcend their distortions, so as to learn to marry spirit and matter while simultaneously becoming a universal citizen, with an open mind regarding the multi-dimensions, and capable of understanding the infinitely big as well as the infinitely small.

⊖ Problems regarding our capacity to experiment in matter. May represent someone who is too busy in matter; or, on the contrary, someone who is too *airy*, i.e. whose head is in the clouds and who finds it difficult to keep his feet on the ground, who isn't sufficiently incarnated. Lack of respect for resources, the environment and ecology. A wasteful person; or, someone who is always afraid of lacking resources. Large-scale materializations that are not right; a selfish person who has no sense of duty to the collectivity. Someone who feels apart, who doesn't feel he belongs on Earth, who feels disconnected and who would like to be elsewhere; conscious or unconscious suicidal tendencies. Rejecting or fleeing matter, daily, terrestrial responsibilities, our Life plan. Earthquakes related to openings of the unconscious, to the re-surfacing, the re-emergence of memories of former negative actions. A lack of understanding that all of the aspects of the Earth exist within us in terms of conscience. A stubborn, limited, too down-to-earth, or megalomaniac mind and spirit.

EARTHQUAKE

The word earthquake defines a sudden movement of part of the earth's crust, occurring at a certain depth. An earthquake (or seism) usually occurs whenever the tensions accumulated deep down in the earth's rocks are liberated, thereby creating energy that shakes the earth, provoking more or less powerful vibrations and seismic waves (earthquakes). This phenomenon is a regular occurrence; approximately 100,000 earthquakes are detected in the world each year; however, they are not all felt by man.

As an earthquake originates underground, it is symbolically related to thoughts, beliefs, emotions, and behavior recorded in the different layers of our unconscious, in the depths of our inner being, our inner *earth.* Hence it concerns a process of liberation of long accumulated, unconscious tensions relating to a way of acting, behaving, being, that concretely destabilizes our life. Symbolically, an earthquake is the consequence of resurfacing old, former, repressed negative actions.

Metaphysically, an earthquake (seism) concerns the world of action, because it is related to the earth, which is suddenly and abruptly shaken; this upheaval symbolizes a mutation, a need to change and re-adapt to a new way of manifesting and acting, behaving, on the physical level.

Experiencing an earthquake in a dream favors awareness of memories recorded in the unconscious, and allows us to carry out important cleansing, because an earthquake always provokes great upheaval in a person's life. His entire way of life may be completely de-structured and disturbed for a certain length of time. This kind of initiatic dream is very difficult and de-stabilizing. However, it is normal to receive such dreams when our lifestyle is not right, just, or stable, or when it is too fast and excessive. People affected by an earthquake have a shared collective program, wherein they all have something to understand regarding this phenomenon.

⊕ Allows a person to become aware of and cleanse the unconscious tensions that dwell in him, memories related to past gestures that engendered accidents and karma regarding materialization and the concrete world. A good time for right, just, quality-oriented, solid, stable, steadfast reconstruction, when a person can rebuild himself and his life. Announcement of the end of a cycle and the beginning of a new one. Awareness regarding former erroneous behavior, distorted ways of acting in matter. A period of re-structuring. Preparation for rebirth, a new way of living. May be a warning that inner work needs to be done, otherwise a catastrophe may materialize. An indication of a wrong, incorrect way of behaving, of memories and intentions that need to be rectified.

⊖ A period of de-structuring, the collapse of erroneous values and false principles; a period of ordeals and great upheaval on the concrete level. Limitations. Poor foundations, ruins. Great difficulty related to what we have actually, concretely constructed on the physical level. An excessive, angry, hot-tempered, destructive person, who resists new currents and renewal, who is attached to former structures. Announcement that a person's program may become complicated if he doesn't change his way of behaving, acting, doing.

EAST

East is one of the four cardinal points that define space. As opposed to the West and the setting sun, the East represents the rising sun, the morning, the birth of a new day, the beginning of a new cycle, a new stage, the rebirth of nature, a desire to move, to undertake and act on the physical level.

⊕ Point of departure for a new stage, a new cycle of life, of evolution, orientation, materialization, and action.

⊖ Difficulty renewing ourselves, starting afresh, entering a new learning stage. A lack of understanding of the meaning of evolution, the cycles of death and rebirth. A prisoner of old, former ways of evolving, behaving, materializing. Confusion regarding our orientation.

EAT, TO

The verb *to eat* designates the action by which a human being ingests food to nourish his physical body so as to have enough energy to grow, develop and act on the material level. For a correct, deep interpretation, the quality of the food we eat, the attitude and state of mind, spirit and soul we nourish ourselves with, as well as the general context and reigning ambiance of the meal should all be taken into consideration. It is important to know that when we eat, not only do we ingest solids and liquids, but also the states of conscience they represent, and the concrete manner in which we eat is a reflection of our manner of eating on other levels. Furthermore, in a dream, we can see ourselves eat things other than physical food. For example, we could see ourselves eat a book, which would indicate an excessive hunger for knowledge; or a crocodile (or other animal), which would show us that we feed and nourish ourselves on aggressive, instinctual energies on the physical and emotional levels, which would lead to aggressive, voracious behavior similar to the animal in question.

It is also interesting to reflect on the symbolic expressions containing the verb *to eat,* such as *to eat out of someone's hand* (to be manipulated, dominated and very willing to follow, obey or agree with them), *to eat into our capital* (dilapidate our financial resources), *to eat our words* (admit that what we said was wrong), *he won't eat you* (he isn't as severe as he seems), *to eat up the miles* (to rapidly cover a distance), *What's eating you?* (What's wrong? What's bothering or worrying you?) *to be eaten up with jealousy* (to be consumed by jealousy), etc.

⊕ A person who receives resources allowing him to act, to become active. Ingestion of healthy food so as to renew ourselves, to provide us with new energy resources enabling us to activate our physical forces, to act and manifest in our life, or in a particular situation presented in a dream. Awareness of the importance of a balanced diet and eating well in a pleasant, calm, harmonious atmosphere so as to ensure good digestion and favor the assimilation of all the nutritional elements. Awareness that eating represents a sacred act through which human beings maintain the physical body, the home of our mind and spirit and soul. Gratitude and acknowledgement for the nutritional resources we have at our disposal. Understanding that we become what we eat, that we don't only ingest physical nutrients, but also the subtle energy that they themselves convey, along with that of the people who participate in their production, harvest, transport, marketing, and their final transformation into food on our table, into a meal for us.

⊖ A habit of eating without conscience or awareness, eating quickly, in an atmosphere of stress and agitation, while working, in front of the TV or computer, or standing up. A tendency to eat unhealthy, artificial, negatively modified food. A person who lacks resources, who is going through great difficulties and states of inner and/or outer poverty. A lifestyle that is characterized by overeating, malnutrition and junk food. Food habits dictated by instinctive, coarse, boorish needs. A rebellious spirit that lacks the good sense, wisdom, discipline and willpower to call into question his manner of eating and nourishment, on all levels. Ignorance of the multi-dimensional aspect of the act of eating, not knowing that we become what we eat. A lack of gratitude and respect for the food we have at our disposal and for the work involved by so many people, near and far, to bring it to our table.

EDUCATION *(cf.also **School**)*

Beyond its didactic, pedagogical role in training and developing intellectual faculties, social manners and moral values, education also needs to serve on the metaphysical level in the global training of our soul, spirit, and conscience. Without education, there cannot be any evolution. Even if we are not always aware of the fact, day and night, we continually receive our educational program, the learning experiences and apprenticeships we need to go through, which will gradually lead us to manifest our true being. Beyond the transmission of purely intellectual, material knowledge, the real, true function of education is to help us develop qualities, virtues and divine powers and to consciously marry spirit and matter, the metaphysical and the physical.

⊕ Capacity to organize learning. Educational projects and apprenticeships that favor evolution. A true teacher is conscious of being an eternal student himself.

⊖ Difficulty organizing learning and dispensing knowledge appropriately. Problems related to the capacity to evolve.

EGREGORE

An egregore refers to a reservoir of collective memory, a collective mindset, collective group-thought; it is the vibration that results from the thoughts, emotions, desires, ideals, intentions, and behavior of a group of people, everything in all of the past and present lives of a country, population, or group of people that produces a particular mentality, atmosphere, character, and/or feeling we associate with them. Usually as soon as we cross the border into a different country, we become aware of its different egregore, but a team, a choir, a school, etc., also have their own egregore.

EJACULATION

Ejaculation symbolically represents an expression of love, a capacity to create life, a child. It is an intense emotional discharge through which a man's creative power manifests, as well as the magnificent joy, exaltation, and euphoria of souls that bond and fuse on all levels. It can also be related to the materialization of a new project thanks to the inner fusion of a person's masculine and feminine principles, and if applicable, to the outer couple too.

⊕ A state of conscience that allows us to create life, or materialize a project, with love and wisdom. An exalted expression of creative power. Unfurling of creative potential. Fecundity. Enjoyment, well-being and divine pleasures. Soul-bonding and fusion. Transcendence of sexuality.

⊖ Waste of vital energy. Perverse emotions. Sexual abuse. An incapacity to create life with love and wisdom. Impotency. Loss of connection with our creative power, with intimacy on the relationship level. Creativity without conscience. Seeking brief pleasure to satisfy instinctual needs. A lack of responsibility in the creation of projects. A materialistic spirit. Rushing to act and making decisions thoughtlessly. Seeking artificial paradises. Creation of projects with negative, problematic consequences for ourselves and others. Giving our instincts and animal impulses free rein without thinking about the consequences. Selfishness. A need to please, to impress others to be loved. Premature ejaculation indicates that the person gets excited too quickly and cannot master his creative force, his impulses and desires, desires; this resonates with a woman who may be too emissive. A lack of composure, moderation, and wisdom.

ELDER

An elder can play a similar role to that of a big brother or sister, or even a parent or grandparent. As such, an elder represents a part of ourselves that has experimented more and so has more experience; he may have attained a certain wisdom, and generally speaking, through his rank as first-born, or elderly member of the community, through his acquired knowledge, he naturally inspires respect. Today, most elders have lost their patriarchal or matriarchal role, because they were not sufficiently altruistic or inspired by the desire to help their family or their neighbor. Normally, an elder should be a wise sage in the family or community, who helps and advises, and whom we can completely trust. An overly materialistic, individualistic life diminishes the natural role an elder should represent. To be a good, right, wise elder, we need to have the wisdom to help others unconditionally, with goodwill and kindness, just like the guides in the parallel worlds. By analyzing our elders, we can understand parts, aspects, of our origins and memories. Hence an elder has a whole potential to raise great awareness in his younger siblings or descendants. We can have an elder's state of conscience within ourselves at any age, even if we are the youngest in the family.

⊕ Unconditional help and support. Transmission of ancestral knowledge, wisdom and know-how. Understanding life's lessons and sharing experience. Participation in the evolution of others. May compensate for absentee parents or for certain lacks engendered by such absence.

⊖ In its distortion, an elder may represent an overly materialistic, self-centered person, attached to old concepts, which prevent him from helping others unconditionally. He is also related to complexes of superiority and inferiority, to an accumulation of memories of fear, insecurity, unrealized dreams, frustration, heaviness, rigidity, authoritarianism, lack of wisdom; or, in other cases, dropping out, feeling useless, lonely, unacknowledged, lax regarding family and social authority. A tendency to self-appropriate, or even usurp parental authority.

ELECTRICITY

Electricity is an omnipresent energy in nature. We find it in the nerve influx of human beings as well as in storm lightning. On the symbolic level, it represents Divine Essence and defines the two complementary principles: the masculine and the feminine, which manifest on the level of the vital energy that animates us. This intelligent energy allows us to exist, to think, feel, and act on both the physical and metaphysical levels. It is the very Essence of the existence of God.

⊕ Creative force and power. Vital, bi-polar energy that is inherent in every living thing. A creative phenomenon of life and materialization. Heat. Light. Enlightenment. Understanding that Cosmic Intelligence is an Energy that can take on any form, that everything in the Universe is energy.

⊖ Either an excess or lack of energy, of vitality. Difficulty materializing. Thoughtless consumption and excessive energy. A lack of balance. Immoderation and waste. Hyperactivity. Destructive spirit. Dangerous energy charge. Risk of catastrophe. Over-excitement. High tension. A rebellious spirit that forces too much. Perilous intensity. Destructive behavior. A lack of knowledge, conscience, and wisdom in the use of the positive and negative polarities of vital energy. A tense atmosphere that could cause damage and fatal accidents.

ELEPHANT

This animal represents superior instinctual intelligence and a great capacity for memorization and remembering events, atmospheres and ambiances, people and things in very precise detail. Elephants like and seek water, hence, symbolically speaking, beautiful emotions. They have great vital power and strength as well as impressive stature and presence. Their vegetarian diet provides them with a calm, peaceable temperament. Their long, supple trunk ensures a highly developed sense of smell that compensates for their weak eyesight, and is used not only to sniff and smell, but also to communicate, collect and transport.

Elephant live in a matriarchal clan where females are the decision-makers. This functional structure explains the presence of characteristics that are typical of the feminine polarity in this animal; i.e. great capacity for interiorization, great powers of concentration and receptivity. These aspects are also at the root of elephants' memory and intelligence. The negative aspect of these characteristics manifests in the fact that male elephants are sometimes chased away, evicted from the group. Symbolically, this represents soul-states that are focused on the inner level, and that avoid becoming active and setting things in motion on the outer level. Another symbolically interesting feature is the fact that during migration, elephants move in single file. This indicates their capacity to submit and follow rules. Their tusks, which are deeply implanted in their skulls, serve for defense and also to dig the ground in search of food. Symbolically, tusks represent a powerful structure that links the thought level to needs for protection and nourishment.

⊕ Prodigious memory capacity. Well-rooted, well-grounded. Powerful presence in manifestation. Capacity to unite our sense of smell and touch with the capacity to act. Longevity. Sensitivity. Harmonious force. Great receptivity and capacity for interiorization and concretization. Instinctual intelligence. Peaceful vital force. Powerful stature.

⊖ Problems regarding memory and the capacity to remember, resentful attitude, tendency to hang onto negative memories and refuse to forgive; or, heavy, very down-to-earth person, who finds it difficult to advance. May be related to problems of weight and heaviness. Lack of flexibility, suppleness. Difficulties with our sense of smell and touch on the physical and metaphysical levels. Affective, emotional problems between the masculine and feminine polarity. An overly interiorized person who is focused on his memories. Distorted feminine polarity, that seeks to control everything. Lack of vision and discernment; forging ahead regardless. In women, memories related to seduction and dominating instincts; in men, combative attitudes. Law of the jungle, i.e. survival of the fittest. Attachment to old structures, old behavioral patterns. Tendency to dominate and crush through an imposing presence and stature.

ELEVATOR

An elevator offers the possibility of easily ascending or descending the different floors of a private or public building. On the symbolic level, it represents individual and collective potential to raise our conscience and go toward an action, place or project. In an elevator, we find ourselves in transition between two places, two situations, and we are usually thinking about where we are headed, what we are about to do. An ascending elevator can also represent access to the causal level, which allows observation of situations and events from a global point of view so as to acquire correct, deep understanding. An elevator also allows us rapid descent into matter and concrete action; it also allows us to visit memories lodged in different layers of the unconscious. Whenever we take an elevator to go down to the basement, it indicates that we are heading toward memories that are to be found in the subconscious, i.e. the underground floor nearest to awakened, everyday conscience. The lower the elevator descends into the depths of the earth, the more it symbolizes a visit to memories contained in the depths of the unconscious, and the more it leads us to discover unknown parts of ourselves.

⊕ Easy, rapid elevation of conscience on the individual and social levels that leads toward an action, or better, more correct, more global understanding of a situation; or, rapid descent to enter action, or to visit deep memories. Ease and rapidity in the realization of objectives. A great capacity for adaptation, mobility, elevation of our point of view. Possibility of incarnating understanding and getting down to action rapidly and efficiently. Easy access to resources.

⊖ Difficulty raising ourselves up, elevating our mind and spirit; or, getting down to action in matter. Escapism, discrepancy, instability. Fear of being closed in. Claustrophobia caused by negative memories related to ascending or descending. Complexes of superiority or inferiority. Seeking to rise above others; or, a tendency to belittle ourselves. In the case of an elevator being stuck on upper levels, unable to come down, it may symbolize escapism, or fleeing concrete reality, and a tendency toward autism.

EMAIL *cf. Letter, email*

EMBASSY

An embassy is a permanent presence of a representation of one State in another State whose function is to favor dialogue and exchanges between the two countries involved. To understand the symbolism of an embassy in either a dream or in concrete reality, we need to analyze the characteristic features of both the country it represents and the country where it is situated, as well as the events that occur in or around the embassy in question. An embassy also symbolizes a capacity to peacefully and diplomatically settle controversial, conflicting situations arising from a difference of ideas, opinion, behavior and mentality. It is also there to protect its citizens in case of difficulties.

⊕ Symbol of international diplomacy, capacity to deal with other countries and people in a sensitive, effective way, even if they have different mentalities, or ways of living, of being. A great capacity to dialogue and communicate on the collective, social level in order to reach favorable agreements and accomplish fruitful projects. Help to protect its citizens in case of difficulties or emergencies. A faculty to express ourselves in ambiguous situations. A highly protected person, supported in his initiatives. A possibility to accomplish projects and materialize ideas on a social, international, and collective scale. An altruistic spirit, a sense of commitment to social causes of major importance.

⊖ Difficulty dealing with other countries and with other mentalities. Great difficulties on the social and collective structure or levels due to a lack of openness, diplomacy and dialogue. Manipulating others and seeking personal privileges, ego problems, abuse of power and authority. Befuddled, complicated destiny.

EMBRACE (kiss, hug)

Embracing (kissing, hugging) is an intimate gesture that expresses love, affection, and tenderness. Whenever we embrace someone, there is an exchange of emotions, which makes us vibrate and feel happy, which allows us to reveal and materialize feelings and energy of the heart. Embracing is also a symbol of appreciation and affection in family, friendly, and social exchanges.

⊕ Expression of love, intimacy, fusion, happiness, appreciation, commitment, and respect. Sharing, exchanges. Reconciliation. Harmony. Union. Fusional state. Capacity to nourish ourselves and others with love.

⊖ Lack of love and tenderness; or, difficulty expressing our affection, our feelings. Problems on the intimate, relational level. Affective deficiencies. Obsessive desires. Coarse, instinctual emotional needs. Devouring passion. Possessiveness. Infidelity. Betrayal. Violation of a person's intimacy. Emotional aggression. Perverted tendencies. Someone who vampirizes the other person's energy, who nourishes himself on seduction, manipulation, and affective dependencies. Superficial or instinctual expression of love and emotions.

EMIGRATE, EMIGRATION (*cf. also* ***Immigration***)

The act of emigrating is the fact of leaving our country of origin to go and live in another country. In doing so, not only does the emigrant leave his lifestyle, but also the mentality and state of conscience represented by his country of origin, to discover new ones in his host country and thus, symbolically speaking, to get to know new facets of himself. Emigration always indicates a new apprenticeship and program of expansion and evolution.

To understand well the meaning of a dream regarding emigration, or indeed a concrete experience of emigration, it is important to analyze both the characteristics of the country of origin, and the reasons why we are leaving it, as well as those of the host country, and the reasons why we chose this particular country. Such an analysis allows us to become aware of the qualities and distortions, strengths and weaknesses that we will need to work on during this evolutive stage. To avoid developing discrepancies and a feeling of isolation, it is vital that the emigrant learns the language and integrates the culture of his new country, while maintaining the heritage of his country of origin. Generally speaking, no matter what the circumstances of emigration (or immigration) are, it is important to remember that man is essentially a universal citizen, and as such, he is called on to develop within himself all the strengths and qualities of all the countries on Planet Earth where man experiments incarnation in matter, and to transcend all the distortions of all countries.

⊕ A new departure. A path of new experimentation. An apprenticeship to learn a new way of functioning, communicating, and living. The integration of a new mentality and culture. A change of lifestyle. A capacity to easily adapt, communicate, share and exchange with our new environment. An improvement of our personal and family life, as the case may be. An experience of change lived gratefully, as divine grace. Expansion of conscience, apprenticeship of a new language. Tolerance. Fraternal spirit. Exploration. Discoveries. Expansion. Evolution. Development of a state of conscience of a universal citizen.

⊖ Feelings of having been uprooted, nostalgia, flight, discrepancy regarding others; or, exclusion, being judged, set aside, rejected, abandoned. Adopting the role of victim. Ingratitude, a tendency for the person to think that everything is his due, that he is entitled to everything. Refusal to adapt to others, to learn and integrate new ways of functioning, of living. Rebellion, insubordination to the laws and customs of the host country. Forcing destiny. Memories of deep injustice stemming from previous lives. Refusal to accept our life-plan and the karmic ordeals it may contain. Incomprehension of the evolutionary process. Ignorance of the Law of karma, which explains that we reap what we've sown in this life and in others. Emigration with the aim of getting rich, satisfying our materialistic ambitions and aspirations. Abandoning our family and former life without finishing things off properly, without *closing the circle*, so to speak. Inner conflict. Poverty, lack of resources. Abuse of the host country's system and laws.

EMPTY, EMPTINESS

Empty, a term that is defined as containing nothing, designates potential for receptivity, the state of being able to receive, to be filled, with different interpretations for different levels. On the physical level, empty refers to the state of a recipient with no visible material contents; on the emotional level, it refers to an absence of feelings; on the intellectual level, an absence of thoughts; on the spiritual level, an absence of receptivity, serenity, beatitude, inner calm and peace; or, a lack of Knowledge. Emptiness represents a state of soul and mind where our previously known bearings no longer exist to allow us to evaluate a situation, to make choices, or to reassure us as to our abilities or to the rightness of our acts. A negative feeling of inner emptiness often occurs following a shock (a death and subsequent mourning, a break-up, an accident, a natural catastrophe, etc.), causing deep disorientation, destructuring, resulting in our no longer knowing what to do, nor what we are going to become. This state may also occur when we are very tired, when we have exhausted our batteries, depleted our vital energy. Furthermore, emptiness may designate an idea of height, discrepancy regarding the ground, where we lose our sense of the concrete, our capacity to keep both feet on the ground, to know what direction we should take. (*cf. also* **Abyss**)

Emptiness may also mean isolation, solitude, and is sometimes referred to as a void. It may also refer to a meditative state where we empty ourselves of all sorts of idle mental chatter to be better able to meditate.

⊕ Calling ourselves into question and seeking to find our true selves, new bearings, or a new (or renewed) state of peace, well-being, bliss, calm, and plentitude. A period of intense initiation, the trigger element of a spiritual path. A feeling of spiritual elevation, of material detachment. A state of mind and soul that is favorable to questioning and seeking to find out what we should do for our evolution. A capacity to find answers during meditation, in solitude. A learning period where we validate what we have learned without any specific framework or mentoring, without our usual bearings or reference points.

⊖ Extreme ill-being of the soul, a state of lack and intense insecurity on several levels, existential fear. An overly materialistic mind and spirit, vision that is limited to a solely horizontal perspective level of life. Hyperactivity, compulsivity, a frenetic lifestyle so as to avoid finding ourselves alone with ourselves; or, an incapacity to act, a lifeless, passive person who has a feeling of being paralyzed. Inertia, lethargy, total absence of stimuli, of motivation, enthusiasm or heart to undertake anything whatsoever. Someone who feels lost regarding his life goals, who is incapable of formulating projects for the future, who doesn't believe in any future. A feeling of failure, disorientation, and not knowing which direction to take. Fear of solitude. Being out of touch with our emotions and inner life, which makes it difficult to communicate our feelings. Ignorance of the fact that a feeling of emptiness is an indicator that we are in initiation, visiting distorted memories in our unconscious. The state of someone who is disconnected from the Divine, from God, who doesn't believe in a Superior Power, absence of spirituality, atheism.

ENEMY

An enemy is the symbolic representation of a concentration of negative memories within us. He reveals to us attitudes and hidden, ignored, or repressed faults and flaws. His manifestation teaches us, and gives us a mirror reflection of what we need to change in ourselves in order to evolve. The Law of resonance allows us to understand that through others, we always encounter ourselves. The transformation of negative resonance that we may have with one person, or a group of people, gradually erases the word enemy from our vocabulary. Henceforth, people previously considered enemies, represent people who are experimenting, although not always correctly, i.e. not always with respect for the Divine Laws, whose behavior and deeds don't always seek or reflect qualities, virtues, and spiritual, altruistic values.

⊕ Awareness that an enemy represents part(s) of ourselves. A capacity to accept the mirror effect, apply the Law of resonance, and stop projecting disturbing aspects onto the world and people on the outside. The beginning of work on inner conflict and enemies. Acquisition of better knowledge of ourselves. Development of understanding, tolerance, compassion, and a peaceful attitude toward former enemies and the world in general. The will to forgive and live in peace.

⊖ A person who ignores or denies those parts of himself that he doesn't like, and those parts with which he is in conflict. A tormented state of conscience, full of aggression when confronted with what bothers, annoys, or upsets us. Rebellion toward ourselves and others. Discord, conflict, and betrayal that lead to violence. Envy, jealousy, duality, inner war. A tendency to impose our point of view and lifestyle. Lack of love, tolerance, understanding, and compassion.

ENERGY

The word energy comes from the Greek word *energeia* meaning force in action. It designates the capacity of a system to produce movement, light, or heat. This word also defines physical vitality, dynamism, force of action, and in the absolute, the original Creative Energy that dwells in everyone and everything. On the symbolic and metaphysical levels, energy represents the force at the root of all creation, without which nothing would exist. Ultimately, everything is energy. What we consider as reality, as well as our dreams, is in actual fact the perception we have, according to our level of conscience, of Divine Energy. Ultimately, energy is the essence of life, the nature of God, Creative Fire, the beginning of everything.

⊕ Understanding that all forms of energy come from the same origin, the same Source; that Cosmic Energy is omnipresent, intelligent, and inherent in all that exists. Symbolizes the creative force, power in action, dynamism, vitality. Has the capacity to take on color, to be imbued with a person's intention, who then uses it and finds himself transformed. Obeys the Laws that govern the different levels of existence. Used as a synonym for: Divine Essence, Life Principle, vital energy, *prâna*, *chi*, *ki*, etc. Respect and consecration of Divine Energy.

⊖ Dispersion or negative use of vital energy and force of action, causing loss of vitality, exhaustion, illness, destruction, collapse, annihilation. Ignorance of the Laws that govern all forms of energy on all the different levels. Not understanding the fact that all forms of energy come from the same Source. Difficulty managing and proportioning energy. A person who manipulates energy unconsciously through ignorance; or, irresponsibly, with an evil intention. Visiting difficult memories, or intense initiations that may lead to a serious lack of energy; or, to an awakening of unconscious forces that push us to become dispersed, to waste, or make poor use of our physical, emotional, mental, or spiritual energy. In a dream, activation of blocks of memories containing excessively negative or evil energy, indicating that the dreamer has resonance with demonic forces.

ENGINE (or motor)

The term engine or motor generally applies to any device that allows us to transform any sort of energy into mechanical energy. This term is also used to designate a motive, an acting cause, a force, which induces movement. On the symbolic level, it represents activated energy that creates movement, and helps us, parts of us, or aspects in our life, advance. Metaphysically, an engine can be associated with the stimulation of vital energy, thanks to which we can manifest and experiment matter in the world of action. It also symbolizes spiritual willpower, emotional power, and the intensity of an intention that motivates us, giving us a surge of enthusiasm, fervor, vigor, and zest. An engine/motor is therefore an important symbol that reveals the way we use our energy in action, when we set in motion our potential, inspiration we've received, as well as the knowledge and talents acquired to help us advance our projects and evolve on all levels.

⊕ An engine/motor that is in good condition and functions well symbolizes a capacity to motivate ourselves and activate our resources to evolve, to advance on our spiritual path, and to set ourselves in motion in the world of action. A feeling of strength and power. An abundance of energy. Commitment. Enthusiasm, vigor, zest, fervor, and perseverance to carry out and complete our projects. Hope. A great capacity to materialize, accomplish, and advance projects and situations. A multiplying force. Reliability and solidity in advancing. Missionary spirit. Vivifying, stimulating spiritual dynamics.

⊖ *An engine or motor that forces too much, or that is too powerful for the envisaged action* may indicate: excessive willpower and emissivity; a tendency to hyperactivity in our actions; too great a desire to create projects, materialize, to be in motion; a tendency to always want more, to force destiny, to forge ahead without respect for our entourage, regardless of others; impulsive, instinctive, rash, thoughtless, opportunist, unscrupulously ambitious behavior; useless energy expenditure; a need to impose our energy on others; a way of covering up our incompetence.

An engine or motor that breaks down, or is not powerful enough for the envisaged action indicates: a lack of energy, willpower, and motivation to advance; difficulty setting ourselves objectives and achieving them; a tendency to inertia, apathy; a feeling of heaviness, an accumulation of fatigue or a tendency to overwork, to overtax ourselves; lack of hope, enthusiasm and optimism.

ENGLISH (language)

English is the most widely spoken language (*cf.* this term) in the world. Originally from England, it belongs to the family of Germanic languages. As an international language spoken and used all over the world in political, economic, and cultural relationships, as well as in the fields of science, technology, computing, and humanitarian work, it has become a symbol of worldwide communication and expansion.

⊕ International communication. Material expansion. A capacity for worldwide travel, exchanges, and work. Universality. Large-scale, world-wide broadcasting. An easy language to learn, simple structure. Practical logic, synthesis. Direct, efficient communication. An energy of confidence, concrete presence.

⊖ Overly materialistic communication focused on seeking renown, expansion, and domination. Difficulties regarding materialization, expansion, synthesis, and capacity to communicate simply, directly and efficiently. Over-confidence and a superiority complex; or, a lack of confidence and an inferiority complex.

ENTRANCE

An entrance is a symbol of a passageway, a transition between the outer world and the inner world. It represents a state of conscience that allows entrance into our personal intimacy (house, apartment, lodgings), or into a collective space (public places, offices, etc.). It also represents the beginning, the start of something.

⊕ Easy transition between the inside and the outside. A warm, welcoming person and atmosphere. A passageway toward beautiful states of conscience. An action of interiorization or exteriorization. The beginning of something positive.

⊖ Difficult transition between the inside and the outside. A lack of welcome, kindness, warmth. Blockage with others. A wild, hermit spirit; or, an overly sociable person who lacks interiority. Discrepancy between social life and intimacy. A lack of receptivity. Difficulty beginning; or, a tendency to push and force to begin.

EPIDEMIC

When a disease or other phenomenon suddenly and rapidly affects a large number of people in a particular region, it is called an epidemic. Symbolically, it represents the manifestation of a collection of related, collective, negative memories, and their emergence creates major agitation, fear, and tension, which can lead to widespread disorganization and chaos. It is important to study the epidemic disease or difficulty to better understand what it is we need to heal within ourselves.

Dreams or concrete situations representing threats of an epidemic nature, greatly affect a person's social involvement, because they weaken his medium or long-term potential to manifest. They indicate that because of an accumulation of negative memories that resonate with the nature of the epidemic in question, the person has made his collective strength ill. The epidemic symbolizes a distortion, fault, or flaw that has gathered a lot of strength and expansion until it materializes in the form of a disease or illness. Dreams with the symbol of an epidemic may be sent to initiates and lead them to experience powerful initiations. Such dreams reveal to them that, on the one hand, they have resonance with the epidemic phenomenon shown, and consequently they need to work on the corresponding memories lodged in their unconscious; on the other hand, they serve as training for them to learn to transform and transcend important doses of negative energies on the collective level. Confrontation with an epidemic on the metaphysical level, or in concrete reality, indicates that deep-cleansing is necessary; that it is time to become aware of thoughts, attitudes, and behavior that engenders the manifestation of epidemic forces and phenomena.

⊕ Study, understanding, and transformation of large doses of negativity recorded in our unconscious. An initiatic ordeal destined to strengthen us and help us learn to transcend negative forces on the collective level. Development of global vision and understanding of social problems. Expansion of conscience. Integration of the fact that evil, wrong-doing, what hurts is educational, both on the individual, as well as on the collective level. Awareness of the original causes and rectification of the attitudes that created disorder and disharmony on the collective level.

⊖ An immense expansion of negativity related to the multiplication of erroneous personal behavior recorded on the unconscious over several lives. Massive limitation. Multiple blockages. Disorder. Disorganization. Despair. Loss of vital energy, preventing us from manifesting. Fear. Serious problems on both personal and social levels. An incapacity to become involved socially. Bogged down. Lack of resources, famine.

EPILEPSY

Contrary to what might be believed, epilepsy is not a mental illness, but rather the manifestation of a profound discrepancy between the spirit and matter. It may also be considered as the manifestation of cerebral hyperactivity that occurs when a huge quantity of memories regarding instinctual, negative experiences suddenly resurfaces in our conscience, thereby leading to a loss of physical and mental control, and sometimes hallucinations and fainting. Several symptoms of epilepsy incite us to make a link with out-of-body experiences that may occur during profound mystical, spiritual experiences; or, while sleep-walking, a state where the person functions under the influence of profound or obsessive thoughts, primary, instinctual, very old memories that he doesn't usually remember when he returns to his normal state.

As the physical reactions and body movements during an epileptic fit can be very impressive, in the past, epileptics were believed to have been possessed. They were judged, rejected, scorned and harshly treated. In a way, during intense fits, they are actually possessed, but by their own memories, not by any exterior elements. That's why an epileptic fit should really be called *a memory fit*. The person subject to this ailment is no longer capable of controlling the *pressure valve* of his unconscious and so retained memories manage to escape.

Similar symptoms may be experienced during deep relaxation; or, when we maintain certain yoga postures for a long time. Our body suddenly begins to tremble and shake and we may experiment out-of-body experiences and astral journeys. When this happens, it is important not to panic, but to remain calm and become an observer so as to be able to get over these moments of inner discrepancy and resistance. With time, we learn to live with out-of-body experiences quite naturally, without any shaking, trembling or body jerks and jolts.

⊕ Incitement to work on ourselves to heal the discrepancies and imbalance caused by primary, obsessive or unconscious memories. Awareness of the impact and power that forces contained in our memories exert on all levels of our being. Development of the will to adjust and harmonize the desires and forces we bear within us. Integration of the knowledge of good and evil. Acceptance of our life program. Liberation, release from, transmutation and alchemy of dark, destructive, inner forces.

⊖ Impotency when confronted with unconscious discrepancies and imbalance stemming from impulses or obsessive forces and needs as well as dark, archaic memories. Emergence of primary, instinctive forces that dwell in our unconscious. Aggression, inner violence. Possession by extremely negative forces that the person himself engendered throughout the course of his lives, which he harbors in his unconscious. Shame, rejection, judgment, isolation. Lack of knowledge to understand the phenomena and experiences that occur during an epileptic fit.

ERASE

The action of making something disappear. On the physical level, it is relatively easy to erase proof, evidence, clues, to make negative, distorted materializations disappear, and to believe we can simply start all over again with a clean sheet. But on the metaphysical level, the possibility of erasing is quite a different matter because Cosmic Memory, in which we live, and which lives in us, records everything. It stores the data as long as we haven't completed our apprenticeship, rectified our errors and integrated the Law of karma. It is also possible to receive positive dreams wherein we see ourselves cleanse and erase memories. Such dreams indicate that we have succeeded in transforming the negative contents in these memories on the metaphysical level so they can no longer manifest through difficult situations, ordeals, or trying events in physical reality.

⊕ A transformation state of conscience that seeks to repair what is not right, just, good, focused on the development of qualities and virtues. Wanting to erase distortions, cleanse memories, repair karmas, forgive, start afresh, create second chances. Throughout our evolution, it is important to give ourselves, and others, new chances so we can improve and continue to advance while making other choices. This allows us to understand our errors and to repair them. In doing so, we also learn to forgive others as well as ourselves. Erasing can also be a symbol of hidden wisdom, not everything needs to be said. When it is not possible to communicate with the other person on the physical level, or if a person is not able to understand, with our thoughts, we have the power to sincerely ask for forgiveness on the metaphysical level and thus consciously repair karmas.

⊖ Tendency to camouflage errors, to want to hide our mistakes, faults, weaknesses. Manipulation of the truth. Making the existing karma heavier and worse. The Law of return exists: *we always reap what we sow*; sooner or later, what we seek to hide and camouflage will resurface.

ERROR

An error or mistake is an involuntary misaction (*cf.* this term), because by its very nature, it is unconscious. When a misaction is committed consciously and intentionally, it is negligence, carelessness, irresponsibility or a lie. Symbolically, an error represents lack of knowledge or haste, which can create confusion and hamper, hinder and hold up or even block our materializations. Errors are teachings that show us incorrect attitudes and behavior that need to be improved or rectified. It is important not to be hard on ourselves or others, to learn to recognize the errors we make and to correct them naturally, without anger or resentment. Ideally, we should see ourselves as children who learn by experimenting. When we always do our best, the idea of errors disappears from our conscience and other people's misactions don't bother or upset us any more because we know that everything is experimentation. Sometimes, what seems to be an error or a misaction can in fact be help to settle a problem; e.g. a person knocks on the wrong door and it is actually an important encounter of destiny.

⊕ Allows us to become aware of what we need to rectify in our way of thinking, loving, behaving. Teaches us that everything is experimentation. Allows us to discover new ways, methods and concepts. Improves our knowledge of ourselves. Helps us find a right way to evolve. Helps us evolve in a more correct way by rectifying our misactions. Incites us to constructive self-questioning, soul-searching. Offers beneficial teachings for our evolution. Leads to an understanding of karma and teaches us humility.

⊖ Tendency to be negligent, lack rigor and organization. The unconscious becomes burdened with erroneous patterns, which limit the realization of the potential available. Lack of synchronicity. Difficult destiny. Pride. Difficulty recognizing our errors and calling ourselves into question. Confusion which creates similar blockages over and over again. Misleading, deceptive, deceitful mind. Lacking structure, vigilance and prudence. Lacking humility and having difficulty learning.

ETHNIC GROUP *cf. Race*

EVIL, WRONG-DOING, WHAT HURTS

Evil, wrong-doing, what hurts represents a distortion of Divine Energy that is created when a person acts individually, and collectively, beyond the wise limits set for our good by Divine Law and Order. Evil encloses us in a vicious circle from which we can only free ourselves by deciding not to do it anymore. In this way, evil is an educational force, a path that leads us to become aware of the fact that negative thoughts, emotions, behavior and deeds necessarily engender cycles of trials, ordeals, and reparation. From this perspective, difficulties, limitations, and suffering are apprenticeships, learning situations for our soul. An evolved soul is a soul that consciously renounces evil, refusing to do evil or wrong, because he knows that evil engenders evil.

Evil may affect each level of our being: physical, emotional, intellectual and spiritual, and it can manifest in various ways: illness, physical pain, psychological suffering, fear, anxiety, aggression, ordeals, nightmares, accidents, natural catastrophes, war, etc. Just like good, evil is to be found within us, in our conscious and unconscious memories, as well as around us, in the circumstances of our life, people, events, difficulties, and ordeals that we attract, and which, through resonance, reflect or mirror back all that dwells within us, and all that we engender.

In the transcendence and transformation work on evil, the fact that it is not *dramatic* must also be noted and applied; i.e. we must never dramatize evil, wrong, hurt. Evil is used by Cosmic Intelligence in accordance with the Law of karma and Divine Justice, to help us understand that we always reap what we sow. From one life to another, we experiment evil without always being aware of it. Our negative experiences and our nightmares correspond to an accumulation of tension, frustration, negative emotions, malevolent thoughts, ill-will, and all sorts of misactions (*cf.* this term), first experienced on a small scale, then intensified over the years, or even lives, until the negative energies thus created and condensed engender difficult consequences. Such consequences manifest themselves in concrete reality in various forms of evil, wrong-doing, and suffering. It is important to know that when we nourish negativity, we condition ourselves to work against the flow: we force, lose our balance and harmony, become exhausted, destroy ourselves and/or others, our environment, our planet, instead of following the natural paths which guarantee happiness, harmony, good health, plenitude, and prosperity.

When Cosmic Intelligence puts us in touch with the wrong, the evil, the hurt we ourselves created in the past, it teaches us the Principle of Divine Justice, and leads us to become aware of the consequences that result from an incorrect, erroneous, hurtful way of thinking, loving, and behaving. The negative aspect of things, on no matter what level(s), only exists to incite us to think, reflect, and call ourselves into question, to change, evolve, and better understand what conforms with Divine Principles, and what does not.

It is also important to know that if the existing evil on the emotional and intellectual levels is not transformed, one day it will materialize in the form of an ordeal, suffering, illness, pain, or difficulty on the physical level. And in its more condensed form, the work required to transcend it will be more demanding. Hence the importance of being very vigilant regarding our thoughts, emotions, and intentions, and studying our nightmares in order to transform evil in the metaphysical dimensions, rather than encounter it in physical reality.

⊕ Understanding karmic consequences and the educational role of evil. A capacity not to dramatize difficult situations or soul-states (moods), but to remain calm, confident, well-centered, focused, and connected to the Divine. Awareness of the initiatic, evolutive value of ordeals. Receptivity and openness to new perceptions and ways of living. A capacity to recognize and acknowledge our own negative forces, and accept those same forces in others, with understanding and compassion. Conscious work to transcend evil and develop Qualities, Virtues and Divine Powers. An altruistic attitude of mutual aid, solidarity, generous contribution to help others, whether on the individual or collective level, when in need, in difficulty, in catastrophes, etc. Awareness that every weakness is a distorted form of a strength, that the good we do helps transform the bad; that cleansing our resonance with negativity and the forms of evil around us that annoy and bother us, means that evil cannot affect us. Discovery of the highest levels of the Knowledge of good and evil, and understanding that the Divine exists beyond these concepts, which will result in our experiencing Enlightenment in all of our cells and on every level of our being.

⊖ Erroneous understanding of evil, of karma, and Divine Justice. A feeling of injustice, as well as feeling a victim of the ordeals, misfortunes, and sufferings we experience. Dramatization of evil; or, a tendency to adopt a *bury our head in the sand* attitude, and not face up to the situation, event, or emotion. Disconnection from good, and from the Divine within ourselves, as well as an incapacity to recognize this in others. An angry, rebellious attitude toward trying, testing situations. Ignorance of the fact that the dramatization of evil helps amplify it; that Divine Justice is absolute; that the real remedy consists in not fighting evil on the outside, but educating and transforming it, both on the inside and on the outside, by applying the Law of resonance each and every time we are put out and feel annoyed, bothered, upset.

EXCREMENT, FECES

As excrement, or feces, are the residual matter evacuated after digestion, symbolically, they represent purification of conscience related to material aspects, concrete experiences; or, a liberation of memories accumulated in this life or in previous lives. They may also symbolize a situation, events, or undigested elements; or, resistance to assimilation and acceptance. The elimination of excrement in the form of diarrhea symbolically denotes inner hypersensitivity and hyperactivity, difficulty managing negativity, which prevents us from digesting well and transforming concrete and emotional difficulties we have encountered. Constipation, on the other hand, indicates resistance to letting go, a tendency to hold back, to repress, and hence accumulate waste on the physical and metaphysical levels of our being. After evacuating excrement, we usually feel a sense of liberation, well-being, renewed readiness to experience and experiment life. In medicine, an analysis of excrement can reveal information about our state of health, and help establish a diagnosis.

Depending on the context, excrement may indicate poor hygiene, that a place is insalubrious, and hence suggest the need for purification in our intimacy, for example, if the place is our house; or in our social, collective life, if it is a public building, a school, hospital, hotel, or means of transport, etc.

In a dream, when a person is sullied by his own excrement, or if a person dirties a place or other people by defecating, it may be a sign of degradation, degeneration, a form of regression of his personality. The person is then in the process of visiting memories of situations where he felt dirty, sullied, judged, insignificant, worthless, diminished, humiliated, undesired. These denigrating dynamics are to be found in expressions such as: *to feel like shit;* being told that what we've just said is *a load of crap;* or a place being described as *a shithole.*

⊕ Purification, cleansing experiences and memories related to the material level and concrete action. A natural, healthy capacity to free ourselves from negativity, superfluity, the useless, which would otherwise get in the way of our health on all levels. A feeling of liberation, well-being, and renewal after the elimination of tensions. A healthy person on all levels, who digests his material and concrete experiences with awareness, and who regularly and easily eliminates negative aspects, accumulated waste.

⊖ Difficulty purifying ourselves, eliminating distorted aspects of actual experiences we've had on the material, physical level. A person who retains the negative within himself, who can't digest, evacuate, or let it go in order to overcome ordeals, difficult situations. Blockages, retention, shame, fear of bothering others, unease and ill-being regarding relationships and/or concrete experiences. A lack of emissivity, of ability to assert ourselves; or, excessive receptivity. Too severe self-criticism of our deeds accompanied by excessive emotionalism. Problems related to our way of dealing with, of managing matter. May announce the beginning of an illness, a precarious state of health; or indicate degradation, even decadence, a lack of cleanliness and hygiene, laxity, letting things go, insalubrity, regression, subservience to matter. Deep, unhealthy insecurities. An overdose of purification regarding matter when we dream of someone sullied by his own excrement.

Frequent diarrhea: Problems of hyperactivity and hypersensitivity as a result of survival dynamics, of an overly fast ejection of disagreeable experiences that haven't been understood. Difficulty or incapacity to manage negativity. Stress, fear, deep anxiety.

EXECUTIONER

In human history, the term executioner is mainly used to designate a person who inflicts the physical sentences ordered by a court of law, and in particular, the death penalty. By extension, depending on the context, it is also associated with the following meanings: a murderer, a cruel, inhumane person who mistreats, torments, tortures other people physically or morally, making life very difficult for them. A *lady-killer* designates a seducer, a Don Juan type of man who is successful with women but who makes them suffer. Generally speaking, an executioner represents a state of conscience that is characterized by cruelty, a rigid, intransigent, uncompromising sense of justice, an identification with the law of might is right, and ignorance of the Divine, Cosmic Laws and the spiritual, metaphysical dimension of life.

⊕ An understanding of the importance of work on ourselves to transform our memories of cruelty, violence, lack of compassion and humanity so as to liberate ourselves from the karmic consequences they entail. An understanding that there is no legal violence to reply to violence. Awareness of the effect the job, role or behavior of an executioner has on the soul. Cleansing and transcendence of the forces and aspects that characterize an executioner.

⊖ Rigorous, inflexible, intransigent, uncompromising application of earthly justice. Conscience limited to the law of might is right, without humanist, spiritual values and principles. Cruel, bloodthirsty behavior in the name of justice, which nourishes hatred, violence and a thirst for vengeance. Abuse of power, wickedness, malevolence, meanness, rejoicing in the misfortune and suffering of others. Ignorance of the Cosmic Laws. A lack of understanding of Divine Justice, karma and reincarnation. A period of great ordeals and suffering, which corresponds to the settlement of negative karmas contracted by breaking Divine Laws in this life or in previous lives. Memories of violence and cruelty. Erroneous, abusive application of justice. A corrupt legal system. A lack of love, compassion, kindness and humanity.

EXHAUSTION *cf. **Fatigue; Overwork***

EXPLOSION (bomb)

Represents a state of conscience which manifests in sudden, extreme violence. In a dream, an explosion relates to an accumulation of anger, of things left unsaid, and inner tensions. It may also represent a powerful outburst of forces capable of displacing matter, of creating an opening and new forms.

⊕ A powerful force that helps start off a new stage, which recycles, creates, and reforms old structures so as to build new ones.

⊖ A very destructive force that represents a sudden outburst of violence and tension that has been repressed in the unconscious for years, or even lives. When we are committed to a spiritual path, it is normal to receive dreams and nightmares with explosions. They reveal the dangerous, destructive forces that, unknown to us, dwell within us, and are an expression of our lack of understanding that evolution takes place *via* good and evil. The explosion may be related to intense needs that express themselves through meanness. When we receive such dreams, it is important to be careful and vigilant in our exchanges with others, as an explosive temperament may manifest in the way we behave and communicate. It is essential to transform the memories that maintain these destructive forces.

EYE(S)

Since they perceive and receive light, concretely, our eyes allow us to see, to orient ourselves in space, to distinguish shapes, colors, brightness and darkness on the physical level. Simultaneously, through their expression, they also express our moods, our soul-states. Windows onto the unconscious, they give access to the hidden depths of our being. Looking into someone's eyes, we can perceive his deep nature, his intentions, and we can detect the truth or a lie. We can only see through our own eyes, and at the same time, through the look in our eye, through the expression our eyes emanate, we – consciously or unconsciously – manifest our thoughts, feelings, desires, and beliefs. Eyes also symbolize deep, spiritual understanding of life.

In a fanatic's or extremist's eyes we sometimes notice an overly intense or glassy look, a look that is domineering, controlling, haughty, cold, pitiless, even inhuman. Likewise, for blood-thirsty warriors or terrorists in action, we can observe eyes full of anger, misted over with destructive feelings, such as hatred, desires of annihilation, denial of life, and abuse of power. The more evolved a person is, the brighter, the more luminous and benevolent the look in his eyes, revealing purity, joy, a spiritual dimension, awakening, awareness, alertness, intelligence, nobility, goodness, honesty, love, and deep respect for others. An evolved person gradually becomes clairvoyant; i.e. capable of perceiving beyond the form, of very compassionate understanding of the level of conscience of the people close to him and/or encountered daily. He is also capable of having access to the memory of the Universe, of Cosmic Intelligence. It is important to analyze well the expression in the eyes of the people we mix with as well as those who visit us in dreams. If, for example, an apparently spiritual person appears in our dream but he does not have beautiful, luminous eyes, or if his eyes are shifty, then he represents a negative, hidden, veiled part of our unconscious, dishonest or malevolent, ill-willed aspects of our personality, which reveal that we only desire the satisfaction of selfish, egotistical needs.

Eyes are not only the mirrors of the soul, they are also an emissive organ of materialization through which our spirituality, our spirit translates its decisions and its willpower to act concretely. Through a look, we can transmit to another our empathy, love, or the energy that dwells in us. If we are receptive, when we look into the eyes of a great initiate, we can gain access to Knowledge, receive and integrate it more easily and reach understandings that help us evolve, or which can even heal us energetically.

Physically, the pupil and the iris form the image of a circle with a point thereby evoking one of the most ancient symbols that represents the marriage of spirit and matter, of the masculine and feminine principles.

Physical eyes have their metaphysical counterpart in the frontal chakra, also called the 3rd eye, which is situated in the middle of our forehead, just above our eyebrows. Whenever this energy center is active and functioning correctly and fully, it allows the perception of subtle realities and the multi-dimensions. The person is then receptive to new concepts, new mentalities which help break old structures, the circle of dependencies, and subjection to matter. He then stops acting and behaving only to satisfy the expectations and needs of others, or out of fear.

⊕ Right, global vision of the path to be followed in order to evolve. Mirror of the soul, allowing the discovery of deep intentions. Beautiful, bright, radiant eyes reveal purity, joy, an alert, lively, intelligent, awakened spirit, spiritual conscience, global vision, a capacity to transmit the Light of Knowledge and Truth. Ability to see on the material level (physical eyes) and also to perceive the multidimensions on the metaphysical level (3rd eye). Opening of the 3rd eye, activation of the gift of clairvoyance, access to the parallel worlds. Clear vision, a deep, authentic look, the power of discernment, the reflection of an evolved spirit. A capacity to look within ourselves, to see ourselves as we truly are. A capacity to examine our negative memories with fear, and to work on ourselves to purify them.

Blue eyes indicate a relationship with Up Above, Knowledge, hence a spiritual vision which allows good communication.

Brown eyes relate to the earth element, terrestrial action. They correspond to a capacity to manifest the material world in a right way, inspired by Heaven.

Black eyes reveal magnetic, mystical vision, discretion, hidden Wisdom, the hidden spirit in matter.

Green eyes refer to the heart chakra, to love, beautiful feelings and sentiments, affections, to a pacifist, ecological spirit.

Odd-colored eyes (each eye is a different color) convey the positive aspects of both colors.

A wink is used to give confidence, to indicate approval in a veiled, discreet way, to indicate sympathy, or to de-dramatize a situation that may seem to be serious or dangerous, but which deep down is not.

Blindness leads a person to interiorize, to develop his other senses: touch, hearing, smell, and taste, and hence learn to *see*, to perceive in depth.

⊖ Difficulty seeing and understanding reality as it is. A lack of global vision and capacity to understand in depth. Confused vision of situations, lack of discernment, authenticity, depth in our perceptions, absence of receptivity, of clairvoyance. Indiscretion, judgment, criticism, haughtiness; or, a meaningless look, with no values or principles. Emotional coldness preventing us from seeing deeply. Eyes may also convey seduction, thoughts and desires of hidden infidelity, and a perverted nature. Mistrustful eyes are more closed, more interiorized and dark; overly piercing, insistent eyes emanate an overly emissive, willful energy, a dominating or controlling expression. Problems resulting in a difficulty or incapacity to see ourselves as we are. Refusal of inner perceptions, a lack of spiritual goals. A pessimistic vision of life, depression, seeing evil everywhere. Not recognizing love and not expressing love ourselves. A person who can be hurt or frightened by what he sees, who closes his eyes on truth, who doesn't say or do anything to change a situation. Use of Knowledge, of what is seen and perceived, for selfish, egotistical or manipulative purposes, to satisfy personal needs. A tendency to hide behind false truth. A confused, somber, obscure life. Obstinacy, an over emissive force or blindness caused by instinctual, personal desires.

Blue eyes indicate a superficial spirit, empty of deep meaning, which only lives in the world of consequences. They may reveal a complex of superiority, false spirituality, a non-authentic means of communication with the aim of gaining selfish, egotistical, material profit.

Brown eyes reveal a person who is too down-to-earth, only interested in the material world; or, on the contrary, who finds it very difficult to realize his vision in matter.

Black-colored eyes indicate an excessively secretive, intense, concentrated, introverted spirit, an overly discreet or malevolent attitude; or someone who is blinded by matter, as well as a refusal to see things in depth, and a secret desire to remain unconscious. They can also refer to a multitude of hidden memories, buried in the unconscious; or, denote the willful desire to dissimulate the person's destructive tendencies, his spiritual powers used for corrupt purposes.

Green eyes denote problems of affective, emotional dependencies and manipulation, a considerable lack of love; or, they may indicate the closing of the heart, a refusal of love. They may also convey the state of mind and spirit of someone who maintains a dynamic of conflict, war, hatred, a lack of respect for the environment, who manifests a selfish, self-centered attitude, who thinks and acts only in accordance with his personal needs.

Odd-colored eyes (each eye is a different color) convey the negative aspects of each color.

Red, irritated, bloodshot eyes express states of intense or extreme fatigue, when a person has had to make extreme efforts; destructive fire, badly channeled energy, willpower that is excessively concentrated on matter, a lot of needs or dangerous, even evil, demonic intentions. In a dream, a red-eyed person or animal indicates that the dreamer's vision is limited to the level of matter and action; he isn't aware of the other dimensions.

Short-sighted (difficulty seeing afar) denotes a person who is too self-centered, who lacks global vision, and who has a simplistic vision of things, and, not grasping their global dimension, is always overconfident and sure that he is right, hyper-positive, does not want to see the future that sometimes holds negative situations, and therefore does not understand that evil or negative situations are always educational.

Long-sighted (difficulty seeing up close) indicates someone who is too sociable, who doesn't take enough care of himself, of his intimacy, of his near and dear ones, who lacks inner connection; or, who has accumulated memories of criticism regarding hyper-focusing on detail, difficulty making a link between causes and consequences, perceiving the interconnections and global nature of things. Long-sightedness is frequent among people growing old; they have become too used to, and too concentrated on living on the outside, living for others, or projecting their annoyances onto others, and not sufficiently calling themselves into question. Metaphysically, one of the extreme consequences of long-sightedness may be Alzheimer's disease.

Astigmatism (lack of convergence, clarity in vision) may indicate uncertain, inconsistent discernment, a lack of detailed precision; or, an unjustified meticulousness, a deformed, distorted, superficial vision of things, and a general lack of depth.

Shifty eyes reflect either a lack of self-confidence, authenticity, or honesty; or, vague, shaky, false principles that lack solidity, steadfastness, and consistence.

Cross-eyed (eyes that squint) evoke someone who has too many needs, who lacks focus, and who is under the influence of memories and forces of dispersal and scattering.

Tired eyes indicate a need for renewal, rest, interiorization.

A wink may denote a desire to attract the other person's attention with an intent to flirt, seduce, and hence includes a tendency to infidelity. It is part of our non-verbal language, and is induced by memories of conscious or unconscious seduction. A wink stimulates the other person on the intimate level and engenders needs to be closer. A wink may also serve to trivialize negative behavior; or, seek to gain forgiveness for misconduct, a misdemeanor, or an objectionable misaction (*cf.* this term).

Hiding our eyes behind tinted glasses (sunglasses) indicates a tendency to want to hide our moods or soul states, our intentions, our deep nature; or, someone who wishes to remain incognito, or who plays a game, who wants to seem important, wants to impress, intimidate, or frighten.

To gouge someone's eyes out in a dream symbolically indicates that we either refuse other people's point of view or part of ourselves, that we seek to kill, to repress truth that really bothers us. Visiting memories of excessive control, megalomania, mental cruelty with the aim of proving our point at all costs. An excessively mean person who doesn't want to be evaluated, judged, discovered.

Tearful, watery eyes indicate deep sadness related to a situation that hasn't been understood; or, may relate to affective, emotional dependency, and fear of lacking on one or several levels. Whenever there are lacks within us, we tend to manifest excessive emotionalism.

F

FACE

Part of our body that serves to identify us through our anthropomorphic features, the face offers a multitude of expressions, which generally allow us to know a person's mood or soul-state, to know what state of conscience he is experiencing (joy, sadness, worry, etc.), thereby providing a keen observer with deep understanding on the personal and/or relational level.

Like all parts of the body, the shape of a face, its particular signs or features are not the result of coincidence. Our spirit creates a vehicle for experimentation in its likeness; it represents what we are, what we have been in previous lives, our strengths and weaknesses, all of which are reflected in and animate our face and body.

In a dream or concrete reality, it is important to analyze facial features and/or expressions from the positive and negative points of view; or, the symbolism of any feature that seems particular or deformed (heavy brow, overlapping jaw, pointy nose, scars, etc.) so as to be able to trace the cause through the memories such physiological signs refer to, and, where necessary, transform them. Likewise, resorting to cosmetic surgery to modify an outer aspect of our face, without any inner transformation work, (except in the case of accidents, or illness requiring medical intervention), indicates that the root cause related to this aspect remains unchanged on the metaphysical levels of our being, on the level of our soul and memories, and often denotes a superficial character; or, a need to hide our true nature because we don't feel good since our appearance doesn't correspond to ideal beauty. This is a concept of the body serving as a screen, where the visible physical aspect considered a deformity actually hides a serious psychological problem; this is called dysmorphophobia in psychiatry. It is all the more vital then to carry out changes first and foremost within ourselves, in order to regain well-being; thereafter true, rediscovered, inner beauty is reflected on the outside.

Similarly, a face that is heavily or excessively made up indicates a need to mask certain aspects of ourselves, to flee authenticity, to hide memories marked by seduction, suffering, a lack of self-esteem, and a need to be loved.

⊕ Mirror of a person's soul, his conscious and his unconscious. Attracts through its inner beauty, lights up or illuminates with its inner light. Allows us to express our moods, our soul-states; emanation of beautiful qualities. Authenticity, reveals who we are. Inspires trust and confidence. Facilitates deep understanding of others, of what the other person is experiencing on the inside.

⊖ An expressionless, lifeless, mask-like face. A tendency to repress, to hold back and not show our feelings; or, to portray false emotions, a lack of authenticity, depth, truthfulness, and sincerity. Multiple personalities that manifest and are revealed through facial expressions; or someone whose face reveals difficult soul-states, deep suffering regarding conscious or unconscious memories. May express concrete or subtle seduction; or, soul-states imprinted with fear, frustration, worry, envy, jealousy, etc.

FALL, The *cf.* ***Autumn***

FALL, TO

Falling, i.e. moving from a higher to a lower level, indicates a problem of stability related to a lack of confidence; or, a life lesson caused by excessive confidence; complexes of superiority or inferiority. A fall may be the result of hyperactive dynamics, a tendency to scatter and disperse our energy, to lack centering and focus. It is an action that takes us by surprise, happens quickly, and, in some cases, engenders pain. This word is rarely used positively since it is not something we wish for. It is therefore an unmastered, de-stabilizing act.

Symbolically speaking, falling raises an essential evolutive dynamic of human existence and life: knowing how to fall and how to pick ourselves up and get back on our feet. When we fall, we learn, and we always develop various qualities: humility, self-questioning, acknowledgement of our errors, self-acceptance, determination to pick ourselves up and get back on our feet, the willpower to surpass ourselves, to transcend certain blockages, perseverance, and courage. The use of the verb *to fall* in the expression *to fall in love* indicates a fear of falling and being hurt if we open up to love. The use of this expression indicates the presence of memories, recorded in this life or in past lives, related to difficulties in relationships and being in love.

⊕ Awareness of the difficulties that led to the fall. Willpower and determination to activate our courage, to pick ourselves up and get back on our feet after an ordeal, to persevere in our efforts to advance and overcome obstacles. Work on complexes of superiority and inferiority, on hyperactivity, and on lack of attention to ourselves, to what and how we do things. Ability to become aware of our errors, to question the cause of the misaction (*cf.* this term) without feeling guilty or ashamed. A fall invites us to call ourselves into question, to get to know ourselves better, to improve and become a better person. Helps develop humility, patience, clemency toward ourselves and others, non-judgment, tolerance, mutual aid. An opportunity to practice referring back to ourselves and applying the Law of resonance. Understanding that there's no such thing as chance or coincidence, that everything that happens has an educational purpose. Revealing awareness.

⊖ A period of limitation, blockage, halt. Indicates a complex of superiority or inferiority, or a period of *falls*: loss of prestige, employment, or other losses. Difficulty understanding what causes us to fall, which holds up our development because of over-limited vision and too down-to-earth analysis. Highlights hyperactivity, or discouragement (a fatalistic spirit), a lack of motivation and courage to face up to life's ordeals. A haughty attitude. Someone who has difficulty acknowledging his errors, who takes himself too seriously. A tendency to fall easily, to suffer consequences through a lack, or refusal, to call ourselves into question. Nonchalance, irresponsibility, repetition of the same errors without wanting or seeking to understand the reason, the cause. A tendency to renounce, to give up easily when confronted with an obstacle. Pride. A person who wants to be perfect immediately, without going through all the necessary stages of an apprenticeship. Difficulty accepting the meaning of an ordeal. A rigid person, who wants to control everything, who tries to force destiny.

FAMILY

A family is a group of people united by bonds of kinship. It is an institution of the utmost importance because it represents the first place of a person's emotional development and socialization, and constitutes the basic, fundamental social unit. A family is also the principle place of upbringing, education, solidarity and mutual assistance. With its transmission mode from parent to child, it is the place *par excellence* for the transmission of heritage (affective, emotional, social, cultural, financial), and hence the reproduction of social, cultural groups. Symbolically, a family represents important parts of ourselves, our personality traits as well as psychological aspects of ourselves. It also personifies the positive and negative aspects that we have inherited from our past actions, behavior in this life, and in our previous lives.

Before our birth on Earth, a country, a region and a family are attributed to us, all of which correspond to evolution goals that we are to attain, as well as memories we need to work on to become a better soul. Each individual is related to the other members of his biological or adopted family through positive and negative resonance. It is in the dynamic of a family that our earthly life plan begins. Family members may appear as symbols in our dreams: they reveal to us either the qualities and strengths they represent that we should cultivate, or their flaws and weaknesses that we need to transform. We cannot maintain bonds of true, unconditional love with our family unless we have transcended the negative aspects its various members can manifest, because they always reflect conscious or unconscious parts of ourselves.

⊕ Development and apprenticeship of love and human relationships. A place of intimate, private life and evolution for the body, soul and spirit. Comfort and consolation, mutual help, support and solidarity on all levels. A feeling of belonging. Happiness, harmony, equilibrium. Protection, security, supervisory framework, structure. Heritage, harmonious relations, powerful affective, emotional bonds. Well-being, altruism. Transmission of ancestral wisdom. Seeking what is essential, family unity, a feeling of completeness.

⊖ Memories and difficult experiences related to family ties. Development and learning problems within the family. Malfunctioning family relationships. Problems with a sense of belonging, feelings of rejection, solitude, suffering, deep insecurity. A lack of love, consolation, wisdom, presence and support. An energy of discord, disharmony, rivalry, betrayal, division and separation. Possessiveness and clannish attitudes. Abuse of power and authority, verbal and physical violence. Loss of identity. Difficult inheritance. A lack of understanding of the sacred sense of family, of the happiness a united, well-balanced family represents. A selfish person, who chooses to become isolated and cuts himself off, becomes estranged from his family.

FARMER

A farmer is a person who cultivates the land in order to grow useful, vegetable products, particularly for food. He may also raise animals. Hence, in both dream and concrete reality, a farmer represents the way we sow and cultivate our inner lands, our thoughts, emotions and actions. He is a symbol of great wisdom, which reminds us of our origins and teaches us that we always reap what we sow. Whenever we see a farmer with animals, he reveals the way we raise and treat our inner animals, the attitude we have regarding our instincts, the way we take care of our instinctual vital energy, of our basic needs.

⊕ A person who works on his inner lands and uses quality seeds to materialize his resources well so as to obtain a good harvest. A symbol of physical strength, vitality, patience, and respect for nature and the cosmic cycles in the realization of his projects. A return to our roots. Awareness of the essential values of work.

⊖ A lack of patience and perseverance in work and in achieving projects. Forcing nature and destiny to achieve personal ambitions. A way of functioning that is based on feelings of insecurity and a lack of confidence in the Divine Plan. A person who is overly instinctive in satisfying his own needs. A wild, anti-social, very down-to-earth spirit.

FAT *cf.* ***Weight gain*** *and/or* ***Obesity***

FATHER

A father is a symbol of manifestation, emissivity, and action in the outer world, i.e. in concrete reality. He also represents authority, wisdom, respect, and justice in a person's choices and commitments. Seeing our father in a dream refers to concrete reality. As a positive symbol, his presence may announce the setting in motion of a project or the development of a situation. As we are his child (no matter our age), he also becomes a symbol that presents us with a current learning situation, or one that is about to begin, that we have to go through and integrate.

A person who has been through particularly negative experiences with his father – violence, injustice, abuse of power – may receive dream scenarios symbolically reflecting his relationship with his father, the image he has of his father, the way he has been marked by his father's attitudes, behavior, and actions.

We can also received dreams where another person plays the role of father; e.g. an uncle, grandfather, brother, boss, colleague, a known or unknown character, whose features, character and personality traits reveal the dreamer's own, personal father-dynamics.

Someone who has had a difficult experience with the father figure in his life, whether his biological father, or whoever had the role of father in his life – adoptive father, step-father, foster father, older brother, etc. – who works on himself to heal his wounds and father/son; father/daughter relationship, will one day receive dreams wherein his father or father figure has been transformed. He will display more positive, right, just, good, even luminous behavior. This doesn't necessarily mean that his father (or father figure) has actually changed or is going to change in concrete reality. It mainly indicates that the dreamer has transformed, within himself, the distorted memories and negative resonance regarding his father. The same dynamics apply to our relationship with our mother or mother figure, or indeed, anyone close to us, by consciously working on ourselves to positively transform our relationships, to heal our wounds, and to cleanse all of our difficult, conscious and unconscious memories regarding them.

⊕ Capacity for action, leadership, manifestation, self-fulfillment, and learning on the physical level. A symbol of protection, respect, authority and emissivity that are right, just and good, as well as wisdom in action. Power of materialization, accomplishment of projects in concrete reality. Ability to assert ourselves and make decisions. Paternal love and fatherly behavior that encourages, motivates, inspires and educates by example as well as right, just, fair authority. A father who is present, attentive to the needs of his family, who participates in his children's upbringing. Responsible, loyal, faithful, exemplary behavior; a right, just, good model regarding rigor, courage, perseverance, justice, and efforts made to provide for his family.

⊖ Distorted paternal attitudes and behavior: overly authoritarian, tyrannical, dominating, crushing, castrating, abusive; or, irresponsible, proud, vain, selfish, and immature. Incapacity to accept and take on this role because of a lack of love, wisdom, altruism, and the will to become involved; or, difficulty making decisions, absence of dynamism, motivation, and force of action. Lack of goodwill, care and consideration for our family, only interested in matter, in projects we want to accomplish. Tendency to devote ourselves entirely to work, only thinking of our role as provider, being a hyperactive but absent father, who doesn't take part in family life, in the upbringing and education of his children. Aggression, physical and verbal violence. Difficulty asserting ourselves in action due to a lack of authority, leadership, and self-confidence. Incapacity to manifest our potential, to materialize. Over-protective attitude; or, incapacity to protect our family. Lack of determination and discernment on the structural, decisional levels. May indicate affective, emotional problems, an incapacity to express our emotions, to truly love.

FATIGUE (tiredness, exhaustion)

Fatigue, or tiredness, represents a state of being that is characterized by total or partial incapacity to accomplish a physical, emotional, or mental effort. Physiologically, it occurs after an activity, or an intense, prolonged period of being in demand. However it may also have pathological origins. In some cases, no apparent outer reason explains the deep fatigue we may feel. Such fatigue is due to an awakening of numerous memories, accumulated over the course of multiple lives, marked by physical and mental exhaustion, weakening, becoming fragile and vulnerable, lethargy, despondency, dejection, and disheartenment. It is important to know that fatigue is first and foremost an inner state. It is easy to realize this when something interesting and unexpected happens, although we are feeling tired, there is a sudden renewal of energy and our tiredness magically disappears. The manifestation of fatigue often goes hand in hand with a lack of interest and inner motivation. It may also indicate over-involvement and over-activity in matter, which prevents us from resting, relaxing, renewing and replenishing our energy and resources correctly. Fatigue may also result from an intense spiritual path where phases of intense or chronic fatigue are experienced when deep memories are being visited.

⊕ A healthy, natural feeling of fatigue accompanied by a state of general well-being and satisfaction at having fulfilled our duty, our work and responsibilities. A capacity to recognize when fatigue represents an alarm signal indicating a need for rest, restoration, interiorization, renewal and replenishment on all levels. Awareness of behavior and lifestyle or ways of being that need to be modified to enable us to preserve a body/mind balance that is right and healthy.

⊖ Overwork and exhaustion due to excessive motivation, and physical or mental activity. Feelings of fatigue, lethargy, and apathy engendered by deep demotivation, despair, and an absence of goals. A decrease in the threshold of tolerance on all levels, which automatically leads to a lack of endurance and motivation. Fatigue may also be engendered by feelings of anger, frustration, discouragement; or, discriminatory, unequal, unfair treatment. Stagnation, inertia, idleness, slackness, laziness. A tendency to use tiredness or fatigue as a way out, as an excuse to flee our responsibilities, our duties. A waste of vital energy due to constantly pushing ourselves to perform in spite of a clear need for rest. A feeling of guilt for no longer being as efficient and productive as before. May indicate the beginning of an illness or pathological state. (*for burn-out, cf.* **Overwork**)

FAULT *cf. Flaw*

FECES *cf. Excrement*

FEEL, SENSE, TO

The capacity to feel or sense is related to the sense of smell, but also to the capacity to perceive through touch, and to feel sentiments and emotions. Feeling and sensing allow us to perceive odors, atmospheres and ambiances, moods, states of mind and soul, true intentions behind words, gestures, and appearances. Such capacities require great receptivity, and, like all the other senses, these capacities evolve thanks to the development of sensitivity, receptivity, in-depth listening, subtle, metaphysical perception, which manifest in the spiritual power of clairsentience (*cf. also* this term). Our sensorial perception becomes gradually more and more refined and leads us to discover that behind a physical odor, a state of conscience is emanated; a metaphysical odor exists which expresses the atmosphere and ambiance that reigns in a place, the way a person thinks, feels, behaves, etc. It is the analysis of what our physical and metaphysical senses perceive that continually gives us access to multi-dimensional information. An evolved person is guided in life thanks to the messages, signs, and information he receives and constantly evaluates in order to make the right decisions and accomplish the right actions at the right time.

In dreams, just like in concrete reality, what we feel, what we sense when we are with someone or in a particular situation, always reveals the positive or negative resonance we have with that person or situation.

Many people don't smell any odors on the physical level. In actual fact, their capacity for clairsentience is limited. They still function for the most part with an instinctual, animal conscience that is focused on survival and the satisfaction of their primary needs. However, as we gradually develop our receptivity and sensitivity, we become capable of discerning a person's state of conscience, or the deep meaning of a situation, through one single odor. Hence, not only does the smell of burned food, for instance, tell us that the dish has been overcooked, but also that the person responsible has too much fire, too much intensity, which causes him to be dispersed, to lack presence, and not to pay enough attention to what he is doing. He loses his vigilance, prudence, and foresight because of his inner fire, which is too intense, and even destructive sometimes.

To help such a person develop his capacity to think and reflect, first Cosmic Intelligence programs a weakening of his sense of smell so as to avoid his mainly seeking the uncontrolled, animal-like satisfaction of his primary needs. Since smells are perceived and very quickly processed by the brain, and since they have great power of attraction or repulsion, it is important for us to be protected from their influence and hold over us so our sense of smell is limited until we are capable of making good, well-balanced, right use of this powerful sense of ours. As we gradually evolve spiritually, our capacity to *smell,* to feel and sense multi-dimensionally is led to develop in the right way; i.e. it remains more and more under the control of our divine nature, hence focused on the development of Qualities, Virtues, and Powers in their purest state. We then choose to activate it to guide us only when a real need for it arises. For example, we could smell a very strong, unpleasant odor when approached by an ill-intentioned person; it's as if the smell were amplified. Before having cleansed their distorted memories and learned to master their needs, people with a very developed sense of smell have a most uncomfortable experience of daily life. They are subjected to the continual, very intense stimulation of their 1st chakras and their associated needs, which they must choose to either transcend, satisfy or repress.

⊕ Great sensitivity and receptivity regarding a person or situation. Capacity to perceive odors, atmospheres and ambiances, moods, states of mind and soul, as well as true intentions. Conscious, harmonious development of metaphysical, spiritual perception through intuitive feeling, through sensing, so as to understand in depth, discern correctly, and make the right decisions. Awareness that every smell reveals a state of conscience, a way of being, living, behaving. Ability to tune into multi-dimensional information conveyed by smells, to decode a warning, danger. Great capacity of foresight, anticipation, and healthy, right activation of clairsentience. Knowledge through the senses. A great capacity to feel, to sense what is right and what is not. Discernment that leads to empathy, compassion, protection. Hidden wisdom, someone who makes right, just, good, wise use of what he feels, senses, perceives, and discovers. Discretion, subtle delicacy, tact, a sense of diplomacy. Respect for other people's intimacy.

⊖ An incapacity to intuitively feel or sense authentically, deeply, and transparently due to a lack of receptivity, sensitivity, discretion, tact, subtlety, diplomacy. May denote a person who is disturbed by his great capacity to sense things, to feel subtle energies, due to negative resonance. Someone who isn't sufficiently incarnated, who represses his vital needs, and is too abstract, too intellectual; or, on the contrary, who is too incarnated, too instinctual, who continually lives under the influence of his needs. A very critical, complicated, affected person. Indiscretion, using his capacity to intuitively feel, sense, perceive on the subtle levels in order to judge others; or, to enter their intimacy. Someone living in an ordinary, horizontal conscience, limited to what his physical senses perceive, incapable of feeling or sensing atmospheres and ambiances, situations, intentions, subtle, metaphysical odors. A tendency to isolate ourselves so as not to feel, introversion, anti-social behavior; or, relationship dynamics that are too social, too extrovert. Refusal to feel or sense deeply out of fear of our feelings, of discovering certain things about ourselves or others, of calling ourselves into question, or of having to assert ourselves. A lack of opening and receptivity.

FENCE

A fence is a symbol of limitation and protection. Usually installed to delimit property and to indicate ownership, as well as protect the animals in a field. It may represent positive or negative aspects depending on the context, its appearance, constitution, shape, color, etc. It also allows us to create a private space, an intimate atmosphere and ambiance, to protect children's play areas, school courtyards and playgrounds, parks, natural sites, swimming-pools, etc.; or, forbid access to potentially dangerous areas.

⊕ A capacity to delimit and protect our life space, our intimacy, to set limits and respect those of others. Protection against negative, harmful forces and influences coming from the outside.

⊖ An incapacity to define our limits, our vital space, our intimacy, and have them respected; or, on the contrary, a tendency to over-protect ourselves, to isolate ourselves from the outside world, to barricade ourselves behind fences through insecurity, fear of being invaded or assaulted, attacked; or, because we have something to hide.

FINE, A

A fine is a pecuniary sentence imposed in civil, penal, or fiscal matters following a breach or violation of the law or a ruling. To understand what behavior needs rectifying, we need to analyze if it is a case of:

Civil violation: indicating problems on the social level;

Violation of the Highway Code: indicating problems related to the way we advance toward others, or materialize our projects;

Violation concerning another person: a sanction relating to inter-personal relationship problems;

Violation committed by taking goods that do not belong to us: a sanction relating to selfishness, the law of the jungle (i.e. survival of the fittest), lacks, profound feelings of insecurity, and excessive needs.

⊕ Awareness of the meaning and necessity of applying the law to everyone, and understanding that its application serves to maintain the balance of social organization in our life. Encourages people to rectify erroneous behavior, to regain the right path. Experimentation and apprenticeship of the science of Justice and good behavior. It is important to analyze the reason for, and the symbolism of a fine, because as well as being a sanction of earthly justice, it is also a clear, strong warning from Up Above. In the case of a fine that is unjust and unfair: the person visits or experiments forces (or memories) of injustice caused by abuse of power or authority in his past, whose aim is to bring to light an abusive person, and hence set in motion acts of rectification and reparation. The amount to be paid is also something to be analyzed in the light of the symbolism of numbers.

⊖ Violation of earthly law and reprimand by Divine Justice. Ignorance of the Law of cause and consequence engendering numerous problems, because we always reap what we sow. Hence the importance of not taking fines lightly, nor downplaying them, dismissing them as unimportant, because they reveal areas in our life where our behavior needs to be rectified. Selfishness. Law of the jungle; survival of the fittest. A rebellious attitude. Thief. Lack of belief in God, in the Law of karma, in Divine Justice.

FINGER

Fingers represent precision when manifesting, creating and helping; harmony in our work and involvement. They also represent sensitivity and refinement of touch, a capacity to give and receive delicately. The fingers on the left hand are related to receptivity and the feminine polarity of our being, while those on the right are related to emissivity and the masculine polarity. Each finger has a different symbolic meaning:

- The positive symbolism of the *thumb* (*cf. also* this term) is altruism and a capacity to get involved in helping others; it is also related to Divine Power. In a negative context, it represents distortions related to power and difficulties or blockages that prevent altruistic involvement

- The *index* gives direction; it also symbolizes authority, a capacity for organization and achievement as well as abundance, power and autonomy; it is also a symbol of warning and a request for discretion or silence. From the negative point of view, it indicates the wrong direction, problems with authority and imposed discretion or silence. It also indicates disorganization, difficulty accomplishing things; or, excessive will to achieve and accomplish things as well as problems related to abundance and power.

- From a positive point of view, the *middle finger* symbolizes structure, strength and concentration; it is also related to respect for the Law. In its negative aspect, it represents a lack of structure, strength and concentration, and a rebellious, egotistical spirit that refuses to conform to the Law. It may also indicate rigidity.

- The *ring finger* symbolizes union, bonding, fusion or marriage. In a negative context, it represents problems with union or a tendency to bond and fuse without discernment, without thinking about the consequences.

- The *auricular* (*cf. also* this term), or little finger, symbolizes knowledge, intuition, wisdom, listening, delicacy and prudence. From a negative point of view, it symbolizes a lack or absence of these qualities.

Positive Aspects (of fingers in general): A capacity to manifest and create precisely and accurately. Attention to detail. Dexterity. Delicacy of touch. Refined motor skills. Creativity. Ability to touch, take, fashion, shape, transform and build with conscience. Strength for work, materialization, development and expansion.

Negative Aspects (of fingers in general): Difficulty creating and materializing through a lack of precision, skill, dexterity, refinement. Limitation of the potential for action, construction, work and expansion following injury to the fingers. A capricious attitude, and a tendency to only work with our fingertips for fear of getting dirty. A lack of willpower to get fully involved in the process of materialization.

FIRE (element)

Fire is one of the 4 elements (fire, air, water, and earth), and part of the fundamental basis of symbolic language regarding all kingdoms (mineral, vegetable, animal, human, and divine). Symbolically it represents a state of conscience expressing willpower, the energy of life that animates everyone and everything. Hence, its direct relationship with the Spirit, Divine Energy, the Breath of God. On the symbolic level, it is also related to our mind and spirit, our vital energy, to the force of energy that activates our will, our capacity to manifest, to animate our creative power.

In either a concrete situation or a dream, fire bears witness to vivacity, motivation, power of manifestation, radiance, and the active, luminous source behind everyone and everything, every action, every event. Depending on the context, it may appear positively, as a symbol of energy, or purification, transmutation, sublimation and transcendence; negatively, as a destructive power, force, energy or attitude due to indifference or hyperactive behavior, a lack of prudence and vigilance; or, it may express anger, hatred, and extremism. On the negative level, it is associated with the forces of hell.

In both the physical and metaphysical worlds, fire also represents heat, warmth, and all of the associated emotions. A hearth fire, for example, warms and brightens places and hearts, and suggests the inner world, intimacy, human warmth and gentleness; it often represents the end of the day and evening tranquility. In accordance with the context (individual, couple, or group), as well as expressing safety, warmth and love, a camp fire may also evoke contemplation, interiorization, as well as joy, singing, games, the outer world. It may also serve as protection from wild animals, and thus, symbolically, protection from brutish, harmful, little or poorly nourished instincts.

⊕ Represents the Prime Energy of Creation, the Fire of the Divine Spirit, Willpower and Light (Knowledge). A source of life, vital energy, motivation, inspiration, creative power animating everyone and everything. Abundant energy, charisma, intensity, dynamism, force of action, vivifying force. Someone who radiates and diffuses light, warmth, *joie de vivre,* and hope via his bright, luminous aura, his state of mind, spirit and conscience. A capacity to bring people closer. Mastery of passion, impulses and ardent emotions. An understanding of the power of the human mind and spirit, of its constructive or destructive force, and of the inherent responsibilities of this power.

⊖ Hyperactive, destructive or extremist vital energy and power. A fiery spirit, devouring passion, impulsivity, excessive willpower; or, on the contrary, a lack of vital energy, dynamism, willpower, capacity to manifest, lethargy. Either a limiting mind and spirit; or, one that is overly expansive, aggressive, dangerous, hyper-critical, and sharp, that uses its power and charisma badly. Imprudent or ill-intentioned use of vital energy. A vengeful, destructive use of vital energy. A force that transforms the positive into the negative. A vengeful, destructive spirit that when extreme, invokes demonic forces, the devil, and wishes to trigger hell on Earth.

FIRE, A

The word fire may also designate a conflagration, a blaze, violent, unmastered combustion, which spreads through a house, a building, a forest, etc. A conflagration, or fire, is a particularly destructive element for human activities and nature; for housing, workplaces, storage depots, vehicles, crops, forests, historic monuments, etc. Moreover, modern materials, notably those containing chlorine, release toxins on burning.

On the symbolic level, fire represents the spirit that animates us, our vital energy; and setting fire to something, causing a fire, reveals that the person uses his inner fire, his inner energy in an imprudent, ill-intentioned, destructive manner. A raging, devastating fire may also indicate the presence of memories of anger, rage, devouring, unmastered passions, an explosive accumulation of energies of intense frustration, discontent, and tension. A fire always manifests a need for deep de-structuring, followed by reconstruction on new foundations. To better understand the origin of the state of mind that engenders destructive fire, the symbolism of what was destroyed in the fire also needs to be studied.

⊕ Allows us to become aware of destructive forces that exist within us; or, a period of major transformation, purification, elimination, recycling of our life, our environment. Regulation and transformation of the intensity of our spirit's willpower and fire. Re-education of our needs. Mastery of passion, impulses, and ardent emotions. Understanding the power of vital energy, and a person's responsibility regarding his use of it. Conscious work on impulsivity, hyperactivity, and on the desperate, very intense desire for a particular result. Integration of the Divine principle that evil, wrong-doing, what hurts is educational.

⊖ Spirit of revenge. Aggression. Intolerance. Great accumulations of frustration, negative energies. Behavior that inflames conflict. An explosive temperament, which incites a person to cause havoc, to burn everything in his pathway. Excessive willpower. Impulsivity. Hyperactivity. Blazing, devouring, destructive passion. Anger. Rage. Lack of mastery. Lack of understanding of the correlations that exist – as much on the individual, personal level, as on the collective level – between fires that are set off and materialize in the outer world and the forces of the spirit that engender them initially on the subtle levels of willpower, thoughts, and emotions. Excessive motivation, a tendency to push ourselves and others to succeed, to strive persistently for results.

FISH

As an animal, a fish represents our needs and certain aspects of our instinctual vital energy; and as it lives in water, it symbolizes our instinctual emotional needs. Symbolically speaking, its capacity to breathe in water thanks to its gills indicates a capacity to live in a very emotionally intense environment, often regarding very old memories as fish generally live in deep waters (seas, oceans, lakes, rivers). For a detailed symbolic analysis of the meaning of a fish/fishes in a dream or concrete reality, the characteristics of the fish need to be taken into consideration: size, shape, role in the marine ecosystem, predator, etc., habitat (sea, river, etc.), habits/lifestyle. This ensures a more detailed, in-depth analysis, which better helps the dreamer/the person in his personal evolution. A fish is also a cold-blooded animal. As such, it indicates a need to reflect on emotional coldness. Given the fact that it cannot emit sound, it refers to an incapacity to express ourselves audibly; an incapacity to verbally communicate our thoughts and emotions. Note too that in the case of a flying fish, the element air is added to the analysis, hence the mental domain, more specifically instinctual thoughts.

⊕ Stability and transcendence of instinctual, affective, emotional needs. Capacity to remain inwardly stable when faced with emotional needs. Feeling of being emotionally nourished and renewed. Ability to renew ourselves on the emotional level, to swim happily and freely, in the waters of life, following the natural current, going with the flow, while maintaining our connection with the Source. Excellent capacity to live, adapt and evolve in collective emotional ambiances along with their related unconscious affective, emotional memories *(to take to something like a fish to water).*

⊖ Difficulty facing our memories and instinctual, affective, emotional needs; difficulty expressing, managing and transcending them. Affective, emotional deficiencies and dependencies. Emotional coldness. Predator/prey dynamics; aggressive, dominant, devouring attitude; or, vulnerable, fragile, fearful, anxious, victim attitude(s) on the emotional level. May indicate a lethargic person who lacks vitality, enthusiasm, vivacity, stimulation, objectives and goals.

FLAW, FAULT

The word *flaw* refers to a physical or moral imperfection, a fault, an anomaly, an insufficiency or a weakness in a work, an object, an activity, etc., that diminishes the quality of the whole. On the spiritual level, a flaw represents a distortion of a quality or virtue. The flaws that are revealed to us in our dreams show us what we need to correct and improve to favor our evolution. Acknowledging our flaws teaches us humility and allows us to transform the weaknesses and distortions that create negativity in our lives. It is important not to make light of and consider little flaws trivial and insignificant, believing that only big ones are really harmful. Each flaw indicates a goal for improvement, a rung to climb, a step on the path of our evolution. However, we must not be hard on ourselves and intransigent when we work on our flaws; we must not become obsessive perfectionists. It is important to understand that experimentation is the basis of qualities as well as flaws and faults. Hence, to rediscover the quality of patience, we need to work on our impatience, which represents the distorted, deformed, warped form of an originally positive energy. In the Universe, nothing is lost, everything is transformed.

⊕ Transcendence of our flaws serves our evolution. Development of discernment and common sense. Working on our flaws constitutes beneficial periods of introspection, evaluation and improvement. Understanding how evolution works, the role of good and evil (*cf. also* this term). Allows us to integrate the fact that evil, wrong, what hurts, etc. is always educational.

⊖ By ignoring our faults and flaws, we favor the multiplication of distorted attitudes and behavior that end up materializing in our lives in the form of ordeals, trials, hardships and difficult situations. Lack of vigilance, self-discipline and discernment. Straying from and deforming reality due to a lack of commonsense. Tendency to accumulate negative aspects by making light of flaws, for example, by saying *nobody's perfect*, or by considering a flaw as a little luxury we allow ourselves to better enjoy life. Encouraging flaws hampers the accomplishment of our projects and our potential.

FLOOD, FLOODING

A flood is an overspill of water, hence, symbolically speaking, it represents an overflow of emotions. A situation, accident, illness or shock can provoke a strong emotional reaction that we cannot always control or master. Feelings of sadness, anxiety, fear and insecurity sometimes create an emotional charge that we cannot retain and this state can manifest in dreams through flood scenes. It is normal to experience this kind of phenomenon from time to time in the world of dreams. However, it is important to know that not only do floods cause a lot of damage when they occur in outer reality, they also cause a lot of damage within, in our inner world. That is why it is important to go to the source of the problem and understand what causes emotional overflow.

⊕ Intense cleansing and purification on the emotional level. Liberation of powerful retained or repressed emotional forces that re-surface so we can become aware of them. Submersion in emotional memories followed by a period of reconstruction on new foundations. Understanding causes and consequences thanks to work on ourselves. An opportunity to put mutual aid, solidarity and altruism into practice. Integration of life lessons offered by emotional ordeals, and rectification of the attitudes and behavior that caused them. Willpower and determination to work on developing emotional mastery.

⊖ Presence of very destructive emotional forces. A lack of emotional mastery. Loss of control over accumulated, repressed emotions that begin to overflow and submerge us. Deep sadness and dismay. A *ship-wrecked*, despairing, tumultuous soul-state. Disorganization on the personal and social levels.

FLOOR

A floor designates the surface on which we walk, place furniture and other objects of daily usage inside rooms or a building. It is symbolically related to the basic structure with which we build and edify our personal, family, and professional life. It relates to stability and balance in the way we advance and move in action to materialize our intentions, our projects, our potential. A more precise, concrete and symbolic meaning of a floor depends on where it is and the state it is in. Symbolically, a ground-floor floor may be considered as the veil that hides or separates the conscious level of our being from the subconscious; a cellar or basement floor represents the passage toward the different layers of our unconscious. Upper-storey floors represent structures separating our different levels of elevation. Floor problems indicate a lack of stability and balance on the action level and in physical manifestations.

When symbolically analyzing a floor, its general condition needs to be taken into account: is it clean or dirty, clear or cluttered, level and intact or sloping, cracked, and damaged? What color and texture is it? Is the material it is made of and covered in natural, healthy, smooth, pleasant to touch; or, unpleasant, hard, rough, synthetic, toxic, badly insulated, too cold, etc.?

⊕ A stable, solid, level structure serving to support us in our movement, our advancing, and the edification of our life. A fundamental element in the way we construct ourselves; important support that ensures equilibrium and security in our actions and manifestations. A beautiful, straight, clean, clear, smooth, shiny floor that is pleasant to see and touch relates to a stable, well-balanced, reliable, steady, constant, upright personality. A floor that is being renovated may indicate that stabilization or fundamental re-structuring work is in process.

⊖ A lack of foundation, structure, equilibrium, as well as solid, stable, reassuring support to materialize with reliability and constancy. Instability, imbalance in advancing and movement that serve to manifest ourselves. A floor that is in poor condition indicates a lack of inner solidity and security. A period of de-structuring, difficulty on the concrete manifestation level.

FLOWER

A flower is the colored, fragrant end part of certain plants. It rests in a protective receptacle and includes reproductive organs. As it belongs to the vegetable kingdom, it symbolizes the manifestation of feelings and emotions. It also concerns femininity, sensitivity, beauty, love, and receptivity on the love and reproductive levels. It also reminds us of our fragility, gentleness, and purity. A sweet, gentle person is sometimes compared to a flower to express the state of conscience of beauty and harmony emanated by calm, regenerative, beneficial, nurturing behavior. It is interesting to note that most plants are hermaphrodite; i.e. they are both male and female: they have both stamen and pistil. Such flowers combine emissive and receptive characteristics regarding the demonstration of affection, affectionate gestures and expression of sentiments, and may indicate perfectly balanced polarities of the person who offers flowers. Whenever we have fully incarnated the positive state of conscience represented by a flower, we no longer feel the need to be surrounded by physical plants and flowers in our home because they exist within us in terms of qualities and states of conscience.

Just like the vegetable kingdom, from a positive point of view, a flower represents stability, emotional and affective harmony. From a negative point of view, it may express seduction, sentimental manipulation with a view to obtaining tenderness and affection; or, vulnerability, a lack of love, gentleness, purity, and noble sentiments and feelings. Flowers have always inspired artists, poets, sculptors, and decorators. We also use them to express our feelings to those we love and appreciate. It is important to know that the color of the flower defines the type of feeling or sentiment that is manifested. For example, a yellow flower corresponds to beautiful feelings of confidence; a red flower, true or passionate love, a desire to materialize our love; a white flower corresponds to the spiritual level; and a blue one to sentimental communication, etc. Generally speaking, flowers symbolically represent our feelings and to ensure they blossom, we need to look after them, take care of them, water them so they bloom and create fragrant, colorful, gentle, harmonious, authentic, and inspiring atmospheres and ambiances.

In a dream, as in reality, the person who offers them, as well as the occasion on which they are offered, the place or room where they are displayed, all add to the symbolic interpretation of the type of feeling expressed. For instance, the symbolic meaning of a floral decoration for a wedding is different from a wreath for a funeral service. Likewise, an overabundance of flowers in a room reflects an invasive personality; or, someone who lacks flourishing emotions, who is avid for lively, happy feelings.

⊕ Expression of beautiful, noble feelings and sentiments and feelings of sweet gentleness, tenderness, sensitivity, receptivity, appreciation and acknowledgement, as well as right, just submission. Abundance and flourishing on the emotional level, opening of the heart. Inspirational, communicative joy. A living anti-depressant, comfort and consolation. A capacity to create beautiful atmospheres and ambiances. A symbol of beauty, well-being, emotional, affective stability, a happy, harmonious sentimental life, well-balanced masculine and feminine polarities. A capacity to reproduce, create and communicate happy feelings.

⊖ An incapacity or difficulty expressing our feelings. Problems related to someone who has either too much or not enough gentleness, or who lacks sensitivity, delicacy, and appreciation. A tendency to offer flowers to manipulate others, to nourish affective, emotional dependency, to erase feelings of guilt, to make amends after misactions (*cf.* this term); or, to surround ourselves excessively with flowers to compensate for lacks, or to camouflage feelings of solitude, sadness, moroseness, and despair. Emotional fragility and instability. Happiness in love that lacks sincerity, that is based on pretense. A lack of authentic docility or receptivity; or, an overly docile, submissive, hypersensitive, fragile, vulnerable person. A vegetative state of mind or spirit, someone who lacks assertion, who accepts everything without saying anything, who lets himself be dominated, subjugated, and enslaved. A lack of sentimental vitality, of loving expression. An absence of human warmth, compassion, gentleness, of emotional, affective atmosphere and ambiance. A coarse, insensitive person who lacks delicacy. Infidelity, betrayal. Emotional, affective abuse, rape. Loss of virginity. A superficial spirit, focused solely on exterior beauty and appearances.

FOG

Fog is a natural phenomenon produced by the suspension of very fine water droplets (emotions) in the air (thoughts), which limits visibility. Consequently, it represents thoughts that are overburdened with emotions, which prevent us from seeing clearly, from being able to discern correctly, on both the concrete, physical and metaphysical, symbolic levels. It creates disorientation through a lack of visibility. Fog also denotes a state of conscience where dark, somber, errant thoughts prevent clear vision of the future: it is confusion, disorientation, insecurity, straying off the right path due to blurred vision that gives rise to doubt, fear, anguish, anxiety, and despair. In a positive context, fog symbolizes a state of interiorization, reflection, calm, and mystery.

⊕ A period of interiorization, concentration, deep reflection, solitude, renewal and replenishment, return to our inner self, intense, inner, spiritual journeying. A capacity to transform and transcend confused, muddled mind, spirit, and soul states, to dissipate confusion and doubt. A capacity to remain calm, to orient ourselves well, to be discerning and clear-sighted even in difficult, emotionally charged situations.

⊖ A muddled, confused person, who lacks vision, orientation or direction, and discernment. Loss of bearings. Heaviness. Straying off the right path, feeling lost. Emotional and mental coldness. A feeling of discrepancy. Sadness. Withdrawal, isolation. Distance from loved ones. A tendency to flee others, to flee society. Inner and outer paralysis. A lack of understanding, courage, and willpower to dissipate our inner fog, to work on our muddled, confused, *foggy* emotions and thoughts.

FOOD, NUTRIENTS, NOURISHMENT

Food or nutrients represent nourishment that is consumed for energy or nutritional purposes. Food provides us with energy that allows us to act on the physical level. To correctly interpret the symbolism of food seen in a dream, we analyze its nutritional quality, shape, color, origin, liquid or solid form, and its taste. This also applies if we wish to analyze the symbolism of food we eat in concrete reality.

⊕ Whenever we eat good quality (fresh, organic) food in a dream, the following day we will feel physically and energetically re-energized, a new lease of life and vitality to act or undertake new projects.

⊖ A tendency to eat badly, to eat anything at all, without caring about the quantity or quality, indicates a horizontal conscience oriented toward the satisfaction of instinctual needs, desires, and animal forces within us. Poor regeneration of vital energy. An unhealthy diet may also indicate a lack of resources. Eating negatively in a dream, or in concrete reality, constructs illness.

FOOT

In a human being, the foot is the inferior part of the leg, thanks to which he can stand up and walk in a vertical position. It is through our feet that we are in contact with the ground and perceive the earth's nourishing energies. A foot's relatively complex bone structure ensures balance, shock absorption, and propulsion into different types of leg movement. Feet are essential elements in all forms of movement and corporal expression involving the concrete world and action: standing up, walking, advancing, reversing, dancing, running, climbing, cycling, skiing, and most other sports and physical activities. Like a point of anchorage, or roots, they ensure our stability on the physical level while allowing us straight, upright posture, which symbolizes a vertical conscience that maintains its connection with Heaven, Up Above, the Divine. The importance of always taking care to link spiritual practice to concrete action is well illustrated by the African proverb: *When you pray, move your feet.*

There are many idiomatic expressions that refer to the concrete and symbolic meaning of feet. Here are a few of them: *to put our best foot forward* (do our best); *land on our feet* (be successful or lucky after difficulties); *to put our feet in it* (to offend, upset, or embarrass someone), *to keep or lose our footing* (keep or lose our physical or emotional balance, control, decisional power); *to find our feet* (grow in knowledge and confidence in a new domain); *to be swept off our feet* (to be astonished, amazed, de-stabilized by someone's unexpected behavior); to put our foot down (to exert our authority, refuse to accept, and put a stop to or prevent distorted behavior); *to get off on the right/wrong foot* (start a relationship well or badly).

The importance of the foot in the concepts of incarnation, in being grounded, as well as in physical action and concrete experience, is clearly conveyed by the fact that the average length of a foot (12 inches) was long used as a means of measurement. The following idiom refers to the foot as a unity of measurement: *I wish I were six feet under* wishing to be under the ground (dead and buried) indicates a tendency to hide shameful aspects of ourselves under the veil of the unconscious; preferring to remain unconscious of distortions, rather than having to face the necessary work of cleansing, purification, and transcendence). Foot is also used to designate the base of a wall, hill or mountain, hence the starting point of our structure, or quest for elevation; or, return from elevated states of conscience to materialize in concrete reality.

Generally speaking, the state of our feet, and the way we treat, take care of and use them reveal the way we put down roots, as well as our physical, psychological, and mental stability, agility, and flexibility in the way we advance and act on the personal, professional, and social levels, as well as our power of adaptation, and our capacity to journey in the right direction. In the case of foot injuries, accidents, or health problems, it should be taken into account that the *left foot* reveals the receptivity and dynamics with which we move in our inner world, whereas the *right foot* is more related to emissivity and action dynamics in the outside world. Congenital or other malformations, such as a club-foot, flat feet, high arches, etc., need to be analyzed according to the malformation. Flat feet, for example, are due to muscle deficiency in the foot, causing the weakening of the arches; hence, laxity on the level of strength, motivation, and willpower in our advancing. Furthermore, as in flat feet the arches come wholly into contact with the ground, this denotes relative difficulty regarding the person's spiritual elevation because of a too down-to-earth vision.

⊕ Solid, well-balanced contact with the concrete, action level thanks to healthy feet. A capacity for orientation, direction, force of advancing. A good ability to stand up, walk, be active on the horizontal, physical level, while keeping a vertical conscience linking us to Up Above, our universal dwelling place. Well rooted, well grounded in the world of earthly materiality, and receptivity to nourishing, telluric energies. A person who takes good care of his feet, who is conscious that they are an essential incarnation element, necessary for the manifestation of his potential, the expression of his capacity to find his way, his direction, as well as to move around in order to realize his intentions, achieve his aims, objectives and goals.

⊖ Difficulty standing up and walking because of feet in poor condition. An incapacity to find our way, our direction, and to manifest our intentions in action. Movements and displacements revealing an excess of motivation, willpower, hyperactivity; or, an unaware, overly instinctual, rough, boorish, clumsy way of walking, such as walking heavily, noisily, dragging our feet, frequently stumbling, etc. A way of walking and advancing that indicates indecision, a lack of willpower, motivation, and determination to move, change places, or act, which denotes a refusal to fully incarnate; or, difficulty concretely manifesting our potential due to memories and unconscious forces that delay, demotivate, destabilize us. A too down-to-earth person, lacking in spirituality, who only believes in what is tangible. A lifestyle limited to the acquisition of material wealth, goods, and powers that weigh us down, chaining us to the earthly, terrestrial level, shackling our wings, cutting us off from our angelic nature, our capacity for elevation and evolution. Problems of balance and stability that reflect a state of imbalance and insecurity on the inner levels.

FOREHEAD

This part of the face, situated between the hairline and eyebrows, is related to our capacity to think, reflect, concentrate and use our intellectual potential. The frontal chakra or 3rd eye, which is situated between the two eyebrows, represents clairvoyance, i.e. a capacity to perceive beyond appearances, the ability to detect other dimensions.

⊕ Mental strength, intellectual potential. Emissivity and receptivity on the idea level. Open-mindedness and psychic perceptions.

⊖ A person who is dynamic, forceful and stubborn on the idea level. Functioning solely on the basis of the mind, the intellect. Over-rational dynamics leaving no room for the heart dimension, for what we sense, for listening to feelings and emotions. An exaggerated spirit of analysis. False or mistaken psychic perceptions that may be used for negative purposes.

FOREMAN *cf.* ***Boss***

FREEZER

A freezer allows us to preserve products, usually food, for a long, or even undetermined, period of time, by freezing them. It is a symbol of storage, reserves, preservation, foresight, organization, and management of resources, nutritional or otherwise, depending on the life- or work-place where it is located. It differs from a refrigerator, which can preserve products and keep them fresh and chilled for a limited time only.

⊕ A capacity to create reserves and preserve different kinds of resources over long periods of time, thanks to a process of freezing. Farsighted, long-term management of accumulated reserves. Helps to face times of shortage, insecurity, great difficulty. Allows us to economize and manage family and collective resources well. In order for the symbolism of a freezer to be positive, the products it contains must serve an aim that is beneficial from all points of view.

⊖ A tendency to accumulate reserves out of fear of lacking, deep insecurity, or greed; or, on the contrary, a tendency to manage resources too rigidly, without showing any flexibility, generosity, or humanity when a need arises. May indicate the presence of memories of extreme coldness, carelessness, and/or a lack of foresight. Problems planning and preserving resources. Poor management of reserves and waste through negligence and irresponsibility. A tendency to nourish ourselves badly, eating only prepared frozen meals out of laziness or hyperactivity. A power failure or freezer breakdown leading to the loss of its contents may reveal surplus heat or passion, which prevents the preservation and protection of reserves, thereby causing a considerable decrease in vital energy. Difficulty managing an abundance of resources.

FRIDGE *cf.* ***Refrigerator***

FRIENDSHIP

Friendship is a relationship of affinity between two or more people. It also implies shared moral values, which create reciprocal inspiration. A relationship founded on friendship may take different forms: mutual help, availability, listening, exchange of advice, support, sharing, leisure activities, cooperation in shared projects, etc. To know what our friends represent in concrete reality or in a dream situation, we analyze what it is about them that inspires or bothers us, because the positive or negative resonance we have with them reveals facets of ourselves.

⊕ A symbol of support, mutual aid, availability and sharing. Positive influences and affinities that exist between different parts of our being. Awareness of the quality and symbolism of the friendship we offer others and that which we receive.

⊖ Poor or bad relationships and associations, problems with others. Aspects and behavior of our friends that bother us indicate the presence of similar, conscious or unconscious memories that dwell within us and influence us. A lack of moral and spiritual values in our friendship(s). A tendency to confide in the wrong people and to indiscriminately consider everyone to be a friend. Limiting, karmic relationships based on personal needs and material interest.

Feeling lonely, having no friends: A state of solitude and sadness due to excessive introversion and a lack of openness to others. Emotional, affective, relationship problems. Communication difficulty. A lack of spontaneity. Lonely, solitary heart.

FRONT (in front of, ahead)

What is in front or ahead of us symbolizes what we are heading toward, our conscious or unconscious aim, objective and/or goal. It also symbolizes what may have an influence on us. Whenever something is in front of us, we pay particular attention to it; hence the importance of analyzing well what we are advancing toward so as to better understand our future. We always resonate with what is in front of us, whether it is a person, an object, a building, a view, a problem, a difficulty, a challenge, etc., because whatever or whoever it may be is never there merely coincidentally.

⊕ A capacity to foresee and plan where we are heading. Awareness of the resonance we have with what we find in front of us. Ability to detect what influences us either consciously or unconsciously. Good discernment to find the right path for our evolution. Analysis of choices related to what direction to take. Studying and seeking synchronicity. Favorable future.

Feeling at ease, confident, reassured before a group of people, a situation: Indicates good leadership potential, a capacity to orient, inspire and guide others well.

⊖ Difficulty or fear of being in front, taking the lead, anticipating; or, leaving a situation or a state of conscience behind. Tendency to follow whoever is in front, without question or reflection. Lack of discernment, which may cause paralysis, stagnation; or, engender an over-impulsive force of advancing, which lacks awareness and conscience. Absence of synchronicity. Fear of the future. Difficult destiny. Problems resulting from a lack of foresight and planning.

Wanting to be in front at all costs: Indicates a great need for power and acknowledgement.

FRUIT

As a fruit is the result of a natural process of growth and development, and since it bears within itself a potential for multiplication, in the form of seeds, stones or kernels, it is a great symbol of materialization, reproduction, renewal, and abundance of resources. Not only is fruit a very varied, nutritional element of food, that is essential for a healthy, well-balanced diet, it is also a natural remedy that may help prevent illness, reinforce the immune system, regularize weight, hydrate and mineralize the body, etc. Hence, to better understand the symbolic meaning of any particular fruit, its nutritional and therapeutic value, its shape, color, composition (percentage of water, flesh, fiber), where it comes from, and its quality (organic, chemically treated, genetically modified), all need to be taken into consideration. Furthermore, expressions such as *the fruit of our labor*, or, *the fruit of our womb* illustrate the aspect of accomplishment, completion, and success, after having come through different cycles, or after accomplishing different stages of inner and/or outer work.

⊕ A symbol of accomplishment, completion, materialization, success, abundance, creative, multiplying potential, healthy, well-balanced natural nourishment. A capacity to renew ourselves and our resources, to help them come to fruition. A symbol of vitality, vigor, health.

⊖ Problems regarding abundance. Difficulty realizing our potential, growing, and naturally blossoming, flourishing, and maturing; difficulty renewing ourselves, multiplying, and helping our gifts and talents fructify. Waste or indifference regarding essential health resources. May indicate an infertility or sterility problem caused by the presence of unconscious forces and memories that sabotage the stages of materialization and the process of multiplication, hindering, preventing the end result, the fruition, of the investment of great effort. The production, sale, purchase, and consumption of devitalized, chemically treated, non-organic, genetically modified, and hence unhealthy, harmful fruit. A lack of conscience on the nutritional and environmental levels. Someone who doesn't eat fruit, whose diet is imbalanced and unhealthy, who doesn't worry about the consequences for his physical health.

FURNITURE

Furniture represents all of the furniture used in a house, an office, or any other place inhabited by human beings. Some furniture serves our comfort, such as a chair, armchair, sofa, and bed, whereas other furniture is used for storage, such as a cupboard, wardrobe, chest of drawers, or bookshelf. On the symbolic level, furniture represents a sense of order and structure, a capacity to be practically and efficiently organized. Furniture also emanates influences and creates ambiances. The period, style, origin, and color of the furniture, whether it is old or new, natural or synthetic, disproportionate, arranged harmoniously, etc., not only reveals the personality of those who use it, but also what dwells within them, what they harbor in their unconscious. Furniture gives us an indication of a person's structure and mode of functioning regarding comfort and order; his way of renewing his inner resources, and taking care of himself and others, as well as his way of tidying up and creating order in his life.

Furniture also reflects a person's taste, his sense of esthetics, his need for luxury, pomp, splendor, and show. It reveals how a person functions on the level of purification (bathroom furniture), of his aura (wardrobes), his way of nourishing himself (kitchen furniture), his personal intimacy (bed and bedroom furniture), his social dynamics (sitting-room), his capacity to exchange and share, be receptive and listen (table, chair, armchair, sofa).

⊕ Well-being. A sense of comfort and renewal of ourselves, and our inner resources. Well-structured storage. Order. Esthetics. Simple, sober, zen elegance that reflects a pleasant, harmonious, well-balanced inner radiance. A capacity to create soft, gentle, warm, welcoming, healthy ambiances. Good, well-thought-out manifestation of abundance.

⊖ Problems regarding a sense of comfort and renewal of ourselves and our inner resources; or, exaggerated comfort and a need for luxury, show, and superficial abundance. Feelings of poverty, and inner emptiness, which are reflected on the outside in a lack of furniture, or the presence of old, damaged furniture. Reflection of old structures. Heavy, old-fashioned, bygone energies. Clutter. Disorganization. A tendency to live in the memory of times gone by. Nostalgia. Attachment. Emphasis on outer decor only, as well as on the monetary or historical value of things, because it feeds memories of grandeur or distorted power. Artificial ambiance. A lack of love, harmony, light-heartedness and *joie de vivre.* Problems regarding intimacy.

G

GAME *cf.* *Play*

GARAGE (1- house; 2- reparation)

1- The garage of a house is mainly used as a place to park and protect a vehicle, which represents a capacity to advance and move around individually on the personal, professional and social levels. Whenever the vehicle is in the garage, it represents a halt in advancing in order to devote ourselves to other activities, to renew and replenish ourselves; or that it has broken down and requires maintenance or repair work.

2- As for an automobile/car repair garage, it represents a capacity to check and repair vehicles in order to ensure they are safe to drive. Whenever our car requires the professional services of a garage, it reveals that we need to repair, examine, correct and adjust aspects of our force and manner of advancing individually on the personal, social or professional level depending on the type of vehicle.

⊕

1- Capacity to protect our way of advancing, to carry out little repairs or maintenance work so as to maintain our mobility and force of action on the personal, professional and social levels.

2- Capacity to check, correct and repair personal or collective capacities of advancing and moving around safely. Helps renew active forces on the individual and collective levels. Re-discovered, reactivated and repaired potential to advance.

⊖

1- Difficulty protecting, maintaining or making minor repairs to ensure our mobility and force to advance; or, refusal to advance, to move around through insecurity, fear, inertia or laziness. A period of stagnation, blockages on the personal, social or professional levels. May also indicate an incapacity or difficulty to maintain the upkeep of our home, our renewal structure on the personal, intimate level. Needing to overprotect a vehicle because the person is too perfectionist and grants too much importance to external aspects.

2- Difficulty checking, maintaining, rectifying and repairing our capacity to advance, move around and be active in our personal or collective life. Negligence, imprudence and indifference that can transform into sources of danger and accidents.

GARBAGE BIN/CAN (trashcan, rubbish-bin)

A garbage bin/can or waste container is a recipient of varied size, usually equipped with a lid, into which we throw the waste products (garbage, trash, rubbish) generated in our everyday life and living, such as used and damaged objects that have become useless. The use of waste containers such as garbage bins, trashcans, dumpsters, etc., allows us to concentrate garbage in a container specially designed for this purpose instead of leaving it lying around to pollute the environment. The fact that we usually feel good when we throw something into a trashcan indicates that this gesture corresponds to a human being's innate need to live in cleanliness and order, freeing himself from everything that has become superfluous, dated, and burdensome. When we clear our vital space in the physical world, we also liberate it on the metaphysical level. Therefore a garbage bin represents the capacity and will to cleanse and purify our environment and living space on both the inner and outer levels; our capacity and will to keep them clean, healthy, tidy, beautiful, and pleasant. Whenever we consciously put an object in the trashcan, it means that we are consciously freeing ourselves from behavioral patterns, concepts and ways of being, thinking, and acting that the object in question represents. When we do a thorough clean-up (or spring-clean) that may fill several garbage cans, or even a dumpster or two, as is sometimes the case when we move, rearrange and reorganize, or renovate a house, the feelings of liberation and expansion we experience reveal that we have just completed a cycle and created space to welcome something new.

However, a dirty, foul-smelling, overflowing garbage/ trash can indicates behavior and a state of conscience that are characterized by lack of hygiene, a lack of interest, care and concern, indifference, laxity, wastage, excessive, thoughtless consumerism. Full garbage cans that are left open may become a source of illness and disease. Such a garbage-can represents potential dangers due to the process of decomposition and rotting that occurs therein, added to the fact that it attracts mice, rats, insects, and, in certain regions, wild animals, such as raccoons, skunks, bears, foxes, etc. Moreover, garbage bins left open and/or overflowing reveal a lack of ecological, environmental awareness, responsibility and motivation to play our part in ensuring the recycling of the waste matter that we all produce every day on both the individual and collective levels, which dangerously disturbs the Earth's natural balance.

⊕ Understanding the necessity of keeping the environment and our living space healthily clean and tidy. Lifestyle and consumerism that consciously reduces the amount of garbage to a strict minimum. Responsible behavior that aims to protect the environment and restore its natural balance. Voluntary participation in personal and collective efforts to recycle our refuse, our garbage (trash, rubbish). Capacity to use our discernment to be detached from useless things, to cleanse and purify our vital living space, in a right, just, good, wise way, without any extremism. Cleanliness, order and balance on the inside and on the outside. Feelings of lightness and expansion. Liberation, release from the past, from completed stages, from bygone experiences. The will to move on to something else, to be detached from matter, superfluity, over-consumerism, and waste; to begin afresh. Capacity to accept necessary changes and transformations, to transit toward a new learning cycle, a new apprenticeship, to live with a higher, more elevated conscience.

⊖ Problems regarding hygiene, cleansing, purification, recycling and transformation of physical and metaphysical waste products (garbage). Pollution of ourselves and others, of our living environment and nature in general, through laziness, indifference, insouciance, selfishness, a lack of awareness, a lack of conscience, and good manners. A soul that is overloaded and burdened by the garbage that blocks up his inner world and his unconscious. Incapacity and multiple blockages to transform and help our life evolve. Lack of hygiene on the level of our conscience, thoughts, emotions, acts and deeds. Accumulation of experiences and old memories without understanding them, without integrating their lesson, without sorting and recycling them. Over-consumerism, waste. Excessive attachment to matter, to old, former structures. Tendency to retain, to get bogged down and remain stuck. Resistance and fear of change, fear of death, which is the introduction to a new stage.

GARBAGE, RUBBISH, WASTE PRODUCTS

Generally speaking, garbage designates refuse, leftovers of no intrinsic or material value, unusable debris or waste products of materials we are working with. Sometimes, however, garbage comes from waste caused by people making poor use of the resources at their disposal, purchasing more goods than they need and throwing away the surplus. Some waste products are biodegradable or compostable, others recyclable, and others, which are toxic, are buried in the ground or thrown into the oceans, causing serious, irreversible damage to the eco-system. Symbolically, garbage represents residual parts, behavior and attitudes that are considered useless, and which have been engendered by materialization, misactions (*cf.* this term), and the sometimes right and sometimes wrong use of our resources on all levels. As they accumulate, they weigh, prey on, and burden our memories, which, if left uncleansed, may obstruct our evolution and even prove dangerous for us, on all levels, by polluting and contaminating our inner world. Like all concrete waste products, certain memories can be naturally transformed or recycled into something positive, thereby leading us to renewed, *renovated* states of conscience.

It is therefore essential that the waste produced by our experimentations and apprenticeship in matter should be recycled, purified, and transformed into re-usable resources. The principle, according to which nothing is ever lost in the Universe, that everything is continually transformed, applies not only on the cosmic, metaphysical level, but also on the physical, material level. The transmutation of waste is a responsibility of conscience. Man is destined to use all of the material and immaterial resources that Up Above, God, the Source of all things, puts at our disposal in a respectful, altruistic, well-balanced way. The role of matter is educational and temporal. Above all, for all humanity, it constitutes grounds for learning which offer us the opportunity to experiment and put into practice our creative capacities, and materialize with respect for the Divine Laws. We need to spiritualize matter and consecrate our works to the Divine and not become attached to them by cultivating a possessive, grasping, egotistic mentality.

⊕ Responsible attitude and behavior regarding the use of resources and matter in general. Conscious, well-balanced, right, equitable consumption and consumerism. Active, intelligent, right participation in the renewal of resources. Awareness of mistakes committed, and an understanding of the importance of recycling, cleansing, purifying and transforming waste products, pollution, and imbalance caused by past experimentations. A source of renewable energies. Creative, practical mind and spirit. A capacity to rectify and repair our karmas. Respect for the environment; ecological conscience and activities. Love for nature and the different cohabiting kingdoms on Earth. Leading to conclusion, helping finish what we have begun. Global, altruistic, evolutive vision.

⊖ Outdated attitudes and behavior that need to be purified and recycled because they obstruct both the evolution of an individual person as well as humanity in general. Accumulation of burdensome memories, harmful ideas, and misactions that weigh on our conscience and pollute the environment. Irresponsibility. Excess. Poor use of resources. Abuse of and desire for material possessions. Aggravation of personal and social, collective karma. Materialist philosophy. Lifestyle dominated by the over-exploitation of resources, over-production, over-consumerism, and waste. A lack of wisdom. Negligence. Poor hygiene, lack of cleanliness. A polluted, destructive mind and spirit, criminal behavior. Ignorance of the fact that we always reap what we sow. Going from one experience to another without understanding. Violation of the natural order. Infertile, unusable works and materializations. An anti-life attitude.

GARDEN

A garden is a great symbol related to the nourishing, creative force of the feminine principle, to the development of wisdom, a capacity to cultivate life and bring projects, life to fruition, and understand that we always reap what we sow. The plants, flowers, fruit, and vegetables that we grow therein represent great potential for food resources on the physical level, as well as emotional resources on the affective level. A garden is also associated with the gift of ourselves, and with the kind, considerate, generous, nourishing energy of Mother Earth. It also represents a capacity to adapt to the seasons, to the climate, as well as to respect the various stages and cycles necessary for evolution. An analysis of the symbolic meaning of a garden seen in a dream, or existing in concrete reality, should not only take into consideration the general state of the garden and its context, but also the vegetation – flowers, trees, vegetables – it contains. (Garden of Eden: *cf.* **Paradise**)

⊕ Teaching and development of patience, love of work and effort, a sense of responsibility, respect for cycles, natural rhythm, harmonious fusion with life and the environment. A capacity to cultivate a beautiful garden within ourselves, developing beautiful qualities, beautiful feelings and sentiments; and also a capacity to materialize our inner garden on the outside through abundant harvests, nourishing forces, and useful, altruistic projects. Gift of ourselves, an altruistic conscience.

⊖ A neglected, abandoned garden, or one that is overgrown with weeds, or with dense vegetation growing all over the place, giving an impression of disorganization, lack of structure and maintenance, indicates difficulty cultivating our inner soil, *growing* beautiful qualities and feelings, materializing our projects. It may also represent a tendency to force in order to obtain particular results, a lack of patience, love, wisdom, perseverance, longevity, and non-respect for the cycles of growth, development, and expansion, for the basic life cycle from seed, to growth, to leaf and fruit, etc. that exists for all things, on all levels. A tendency to sow and grow bad seeds within ourselves, to forget what we have sown, and not take care of our seeds, shoots, or saplings, and then be surprised by the poor harvests, the difficulties, and ordeals that materialize. A lack of understanding of the Law of karma and resonance. A lack of resources and energy deficiencies on the physical and emotional levels.

GAS (US), **PETROL** (GB), (fuel)

Symbolically, gas (US), or petrol (GB), represents a state of conscience related to emotional energies (since it is a liquid) allowing us to advance and manifest on the social level. Given the fact that it is highly inflammable, and has large-scale polluting effects, gas (petrol) also symbolizes the multiplication and concentration of dangerous, possibly explosive emotions that affect the environment, as well as the quality and security of life in general. It is also associated with notions of dependency and political manipulation as a very high percentage of the world population, traffic, and economy depends on gas (petrol) to ensure travel, services, exchanges, and business in all walks of life.

⊕ Understanding that gas (petrol) is an energy resource that facilitates advancing, but which, sooner or later, must be replaced by a healthier form of energy that is more environmentally friendly, safer, equitable and sustainable.

⊖ Lack of gas (petrol) indicates a lack of energy or motivation to advance on the personal and social levels. Presence of polluting emotions on the individual and collective levels. Explosive emotionalism. A lack of planetary conscience and respect for the environment. A tendency to negatively multiply ways of advancing. Bribery and political pressure through the abusive manipulation of the price of gas (petrol), of a resource that allows us to advance on the collective level.

GAS STATION (GB: FILLING/PETROL STATION)

A gas station is an infrastructure built next to a road or highway to provide motorists with fuel. Fully equipped gas stations offer several useful services for automobile vehicles: gas pumps, a store with automobile accessories, tire-inflation, minor mechanic and breakdown services. Hence, a gas station symbolizes access to the necessary resources to advance rapidly and efficiently toward others, and to manifest easily while achieving our objectives.

A gas station is also a place where we can stop for a break, and stretch, relax, go to the toilet, hence purify, on the physical and metaphysical levels, the emotions, feelings, and experiences that traveling and advancing have caused us to experience, both on the inside and on the outside. It is also a place to get solid and liquid food provisions; symbolically, dense, emotional energies, favoring harmonious driving on the highways and byways of life, safe, steady, well-focused advancing toward our destination.

⊕ A capacity to have access to resources, allowing us to advance and attain social objectives faster and more efficiently. Action energy, the will to act on the social level. A halt, an *intermission*, to renew and replenish personal energies, as well as to carry out physical and emotional purification.

⊖ Difficulties and blockages preventing access to the necessary resources for advancing, acting, becoming involved on the individual or collective level. An incapacity to advance and achieve our objectives through a lack of resources, enthusiasm, *drive*, motivation; or, an overflow, dispersal, or waste of resources due to a hyperactive lifestyle. A tendency to move around unnecessarily, to have excessive will to move, to undertake superficial, futile projects. An incapacity to evaluate priorities in our advancing. Haste and imprudence in our way of materializing, refusal to take breaks, to allow ourselves an *intermission*, and take time to purify ourselves, relax, and replenish our energy resources, which leads to unnecessary states of stress and tension. A poor way to replenish on the personal and physical health level. Boorish, uncouth attitudes and behavior. May be connected to a person that creates environmental or relationship problems with his negative emotional forces and motivations to advance in life.

GAS

Gas, liquid and solid are the three states in which we perceive the material world with our physical senses. The gaseous state is light, airy and abstract in comparison with the other two. It is symbolically associated with the world of thoughts and our intellectual, mental faculties. As it spreads throughout whatever space is at its disposal, gas symbolizes a very great capacity of our thoughts to disperse, spread and expand. For a complete, correct interpretation of the symbolism of gas in a given context, we need to take into account the type of gas concerned, whether it is natural gas or artificially produced, and what we use it for. Natural gas dispensed from a simple stovetop can generate heat, making it a powerful domestic cooking and heating fuel. In much of the developed world it is supplied to homes *via* pipes, where it is used for many purposes including natural gas-powered ranges and ovens, natural gas-heated clothes dryers, heating/cooling systems, and central heating. Heating in homes or other buildings may include boilers, furnaces, and water heaters. So symbolically, gas also represents energy in our thoughts that can warm, refresh, transform, etc., both individually and collectively.

⊕ A positive, fair, well-balanced, altruistic use of gaseous energy resources, of the creative force of thoughts as well as intellectual, mental faculties that are recycled from our past life and former behavior. A capacity to transform, sublimate and transcend polluting, harmful, dangerous, fatal thoughts. Awareness that the pollution of our environment with harmful, life-endangering gases represents the materialization of their corresponding thought-forms engendered on the metaphysical level, in the mental world. An ecological conscience, respect for the environment and general health.

⊖ Polluting forces and thoughts that are harmful and dangerous for our health, or explosives that could lead to death and destruction on a small or large scale, which come from our past life and former behavior. Suffocation, death caused by carelessness, accidentally or intentionally. Irresponsible use of resources. Destabilization and destruction of the Earth's atmosphere, which is vital for our life and survival. Use of synthetic, devastating, annihilating gases in war situations. Ignorance and a lack of understanding of the correlations that exist between the production of gas in the outer world and the use of our mental powers on the inside.

A gas leak reveals a lack of control on our thought level related to our past life or our past behavior, which can cause the destruction of lives and material goods.

GERMANY

To discover the symbolism of a country or nation, we proceed in the same way as for a person or character. As a country, Germany is a major economic power with great capacity to materialize. Its main qualities are: great practical intelligence, reliability, strong willpower, a sense of organization and planning, rigor, structure, intense capacity for work, perseverance, order and discipline. These qualities represent important assets on both the individual and collective levels. The two world wars, and especially the atrocities committed under the Nazi regime, have profoundly marked the collective conscience of the German people. Whenever this country appears in a dream associated with its negative aspects, it is an indication that we are visiting distorted memories related to excessive discipline, rigor, work and control; or, abuse of power, authority and ideological indoctrination.

⊕ Visiting collective memories related to structure, rigor, order, discipline, respect for law and authority. A great capacity for work, a powerful force of expansion. A symbol of quality, precision, solidity and durability. A capacity to pick ourselves up, get back on our feet and reconstruct ourselves after tremendous ordeals.

⊖ Powerful memories related to problems with authority, rigidity and harshness. Excessive discipline, repressed vital needs, cold logic, lacking humanity and compassion. Visiting repressed memories related to aggression, brutality, domination, authoritarianism. Forced expansion and work. Incapacity to work and materialize with love and wisdom. Excessive instructions, a tendency to want to control everything.

GHOST

The word ghost usually designates a supernatural apparition of either a deceased person, character, object that haunts our memory, or an imaginary being. Depending on the context, the terms phantom, specter, spirit, or entity are also used.

A ghost is not only the apparition of a deceased person, a phantom returned from the next world seeking vengeance or wishing to help his loved ones, or condemned to eternally wander on Earth as punishment for bad past actions. It also reveals facets, attitudes, and characteristics of the person who perceives it in a dream or waking state. This perception is possible because the person resonates with what the ghost represents for him; it reflects unconscious parts of him, forces that need to die to be reborn to Qualities and Virtues.

Ghosts, phantoms, specters, or entities constitute forms and forces of subtle energies through which spirits of the parallel worlds may enter into contact and communicate with the physical level. Their mere presence is an important message, even if there is no verbal or telepathic exchange. If, for example, we feel aggressed or disturbed by the energy presented, we analyze this intrusion, the context in which it occurred, and its characteristic aspects. Referral back to ourselves, symbolic analysis, and resonance allow us to understand what the apparition reveals about ourselves. If the apparition is negative, it means we are afraid of becoming what it represents, of integrating it in ourselves. In the case of a positive force, it may lead us to experience great openings of conscience and to integrate new dynamics of evolution within ourselves.

⊕ Opening of conscience onto the subtle worlds and parallel, spiritual dimensions; revelation of hidden, unconscious aspects to transform. Contact with deceased beings. Mystical experience bearing an important message favoring evolution, or offering good-willed guidance, support, and consolation. Activation of happy memories. Communication with the Divine, with God.

⊖ Visiting large blocks of distorted memories that, through resonance, attract negative, ill-willed apparitions. Entering into contact with dark, somber zones of our unconscious. Confrontation, on the subtle, metaphysical levels, with our misactions (*cf.* this term), our negative karmas. Fear, anxiety, panic when faced with deceased beings and the parallel worlds. Imbalanced, perturbed psyche, haunted by aspects of the past that the person thought he had settled. A mind that is possessed, bewitched by his own unconscious, negative forces. Lack of understanding of evil, wrong, hurt. Ignorance of the Laws of resonance and karma, which explain that we always reap what we sow; that we always attract situations and people or beings that reflect what we bear within ourselves, what we are, both consciously and unconsciously. Ill-willed forces that manifest with the one and only aim of realizing their desire for revenge. May also correspond to old, former negative memories regarding a person or a situation that we thought was over or dead, but which was only repressed, and it comes back to remind us that work for change has to be done. Black magic, satanic pacts.

GIFT, PRESENT

A gift is a present that is offered unconditionally, either in material form, or as a service, which is destined to please. It is a gesture of generosity to testify to our love, friendship, respect, gratitude, and/or acknowledgement. A gift always has a symbolic meaning. Furthermore, it may represent a sign, a reward from Heaven.

⊕ Dynamics of generosity, sharing, acknowledgement. Capacity to give and receive unconditionally. A moment of joy, happiness and gratitude. Appreciation, love. A capacity to understand the symbolic, multi-dimensional message conveyed through the gift received. Development of a capacity to choose and offer gifts which serve the other person's evolution, the awakening of his conscience.

⊖ Difficulty with generosity and sharing. Incapacity to give and to receive. Gifts offered out of a sense of duty and obligation, out of habit, or with an unkind, selfish intention, whose aim is to manipulate or ensnare the other person. A person who gives under certain terms and conditions, with certain expectations. Ingratitude and dissatisfaction with the gift received. A lack of understanding of the signs and messages that gifts convey.

GIRAFFE

Since it belongs to the animal kingdom, the giraffe represents certain aspects of our needs related to instinctual, vital energy, and these are: a calm, peaceful, steady, poised attitude, as well as non-violent behavior, because giraffes are herbivorous. Thanks to its long neck, it also symbolizes foresight, capacity to see into the distance, to raise and elevate our perception to be able to observe and anticipate potential danger. Given its color and structure of its coat, which looks like plots of land (brown patches) and multiple borders/frontiers (beige-yellow lines), a giraffe may also be related to organizational, structuring, or divisional dynamics on the level of material action.

⊕ Peaceful vital energy and behavior. Global vision, contemplation, foresight and anticipation of potential situations and dangers. Confidence on the action level given its main colors: beige or creamy yellow and brown. A well-organized, structured person. Ability to find resources and energy for action through elevation, since a giraffe is able to graze on the topmost growing leaves and twigs.

⊖ A haughty attitude, a feeling of superiority, excessive confidence, pride, vanity, seeking acknowledgement, recognition, and possessions. Exaggerated curiosity about what is going on on the outside. Discrepancy between our thoughts and deeds/actions. Tendency to flee danger. May indicate an attitude of separation, division, segregation; tendency to create frontiers between ourselves and others.

GIVE, TO

To give means to unconditionally transfer something to another person. Although a gift implies an unconditional transfer, very often the giver has expectations, which are not necessarily conscious, or which are material. For example, he may expect to be considered generous, or he may expect certain favors in exchange, or that his gift be used according to his criteria. It is important to be detached from what we give and let the other person use it as he so wishes. Giving requires discernment, wisdom and good measure. Generally speaking, it is a good idea to ask ourselves if the gift is beneficial for the other person's evolution.

⊕ Helps develop generosity, thoughtfulness, consideration, solidarity, sharing, altruism, a feeling of global interconnection and an awareness of universal abundance. Giving leads us to understand that on the spiritual level, the gift of ourselves is the foundation of every creative act. It is essential to observe the true intention that motivates our act as well as our state of mind or spirit when we give.

⊖ Fear of giving indicates a problem of insecurity as well as fear of lacking something. A tendency to give exaggeratedly, even compulsively, reveals a great need for love, attention and acknowledgement. A gift is also distorted when it is given out of self-interest, to attract attention or praise, or with the aim of controlling, possessing, or manipulating the other person.

GLASS (material)

Glass is a material that is simultaneously solid, fragile, translucent, or transparent, imperishable (rot-proof), and noninflammable. Because we can see others through it, and others can see us (e.g. through window panes, glass doors, etc.), it represents an aspect of transparency and integrity. Through its fragility, it symbolizes the delicate aspect of a structure related to authenticity. However, it also denotes great power of resistance against negative thoughts (strong winds), harmful energies (fire), problems and illnesses (bacteria). When it breaks because of a shock(s), it shatters into pieces, and usually cannot be invisibly mended. Its multiple uses (food-processing, optics, construction, chemistry, etc.) make it a multi-dimensional symbol to which can be added the metaphysical aspects of the objects made out of it, including the symbolic meaning of their shape, color, thickness, etc. For instance, in a dream, seeing a blue, glass, horse-shaped ornament break may express a problem of communication (blue), that the person is very fragile, or lacks authenticity, regarding the expression of instinctual thoughts and emotions related to the symbolism of a horse; i.e. physical strength engendered by vital energy in his communication, endurance, motivation to speak out, speed, freedom to advance, to manifest on the levels of communication, etc.

⊕ A symbol of authenticity, transparency, honesty, integrity, and purity; or, a person who knows how to measure well what he lets emerge in his words and gestures, who is wise, and who does not unveil what should not be unveiled. Structure allowing us to see through it, that lets the light through, thereby symbolizing receptivity to understanding and knowledge. Protection and insulation, while maintaining the possibility of seeing, hence of analyzing and understanding. In the case of tinted glass, understanding that sometimes hidden Wisdom is necessary and useful.

⊖ Someone who lacks authenticity, transparency, honesty, integrity, delicacy, finesse, openness. A fragile, delicate, brittle personality; or, someone who is too transparent, who wants to show too much of himself, who reveals too much, who lacks intimacy, and doesn't know the importance and usefulness of hidden wisdom. Difficulty letting what we have on the inside be seen. Veiled, controlled attitude. A lack of flexibility, a rigid mind and spirit; a person who hides, veils the truth. A confused, muddled situation. A lack of protection and insulation. Difficulty analyzing and understanding what is going on around us. An incapacity to receive information; a person who sets up a wall between himself and others, and thinks that it cannot be seen, that it's invisible. Someone who takes refuge in his bubble, who is disconnected from others; or, a very selfish, self-centered attitude, mindset.

GLASSES (eye glasses, spectacles)

Glasses serve to correct our eyesight, to improve our vision when there are flaws and weaknesses. Glasses are an exterior means that allow us to correct our capacity to see on the physical level. However, having recourse to glasses does not correct or heal the various eye problems in depth, i.e. on the level of the true causes and origin of the problems, which are metaphysical. Hence glasses are a sort of crutch, which help the affected person function, while inciting him to reflect on the reasons for the discrepancies he is experiencing in his capacity to see, perceive, and discern.

In certain circumstances, glasses also take on a role of protection, especially in the context of work where eyes can be physically damaged (e.g. welding goggles), or sunglasses that prevent us from being dazzled by the sun, which could lead to eye problems due to ultraviolet rays, cause all sorts of accidents, or snow blindness in winter. In these cases, wearing glasses is a sign of prudence, precaution, and foresight.

⊕ A capacity for external correction of deficient vision, distorted perception, and way(s) of looking. Allows the affected person to be functional, to rediscover clearer vision. Awareness that having recourse to glasses does not settle the fundamental problem. Acceptance of the need to work on ourselves to understand the cause(s) of the discrepancies and distortions in our inner and outer vision. May also be a symbol of protection, prudence, and foresight in a particular situation.

⊖ Rigid, limited vision whose focus is too unilateral. A tendency to look, observe, and analyze in an exaggerated way, to nitpick and quibble due to a concern for perfection. Incapacity to disregard and look beyond details. Difficulty seeing more globally, having an overall view, in-depth perception, or clear, accurate discernment. A handicap on the perception level. A tendency to get lost in abstraction, and not be able to harmonize our physical, concrete vision with our metaphysical perception. An incapacity to see the multiple realities, the multi-dimensions of life. Vision limited to the narrow conception that we have of ourselves and our environment. Confused, muddled inner and outer perception.

A negative aspect of sunglasses is when, for example, they are worn to hide our eyes so as to veil our emotions, our inner fragility and vulnerability, our intentions, to create an aura of mystery, and/or to hide our identity, to prevent us from being recognized. They are often used by certain types of people belonging to the criminal underworld, gang-land, etc., to intimidate, frighten, and hide the truth; or, by haughty, arrogant people who wish to give themselves an air of superiority, and who nourish themselves on games of power and seduction, or don a machismo air.

Protective glasses, in their negative aspect, symbolize over-protection; or, on the contrary, a lack of protection, as well as a difficulty to distinguish real danger from imaginary danger because of the presence of memories of fear and accidents recorded in our unconscious.

A person who doesn't want to wear glasses even though he needs them: indicates that the person places importance on appearances, that he doesn't want to see his own, or other people's flaws, that he prefers to maintain a vague, hazy vision, to remain in illusion and not see the truth.

GLOVE

A glove serves to protect our hands – hence our capacity to give and receive, to create and manifest – against the cold and extreme heat or against dangers related to certain jobs, professions, sports, etc. In the case of protection against the cold, a glove symbolizes protection against emotional coldness, and whenever it is a protection against fire or excessive heat, it represents protection against ebullient energies and emotions. As a fashion accessory or decorative, traditional element in official ceremonies, it symbolizes superficiality, inequality between the wearer and others, a kind of hidden domination, a superiority complex, or a purist attitude. To correctly interpret its symbolic meaning, we must also take into account the other elements related to the context in which it appears in a dream or everyday situation (oven glove, sports glove, fashion glove, etc.).

⊕ A capacity to protect and reinforce our ability to give, to receive, create, make, and manufacture when required. Helps avoid injuries or contamination in difficult or dangerous situations. In certain contexts, a symbol of authentic, natural elegance and nobility.

⊖ Difficulty protecting our capacity to manifest, create, give and receive. A lack of authenticity when sharing. Behavior based on appearances, seduction. A person wearing gloves to give himself an air of nobility, or a purist attitude. Hypocritical, arrogant, puritanical attitude. A superiority complex. Sectarianism. Megalomania. May also indicate over-protection and a tendency to hypochondria.

GOLD

Gold is a precious metal, most often shining yellow in color, which is malleable, dense, unalterable, and stainless. For millions of years, it has been greatly sought after because of its beautiful, esthetic, permanently luminous aspect, as well as for its resistance and dependability on the concrete material level, since it is solid, well-structured and smooth. Moreover, it doesn't become oxidized on contact with either air (thoughts) or water (emotions). Its yellow color reinforces its symbolic link with the sun (the fire element, light), hence with the spirit, while its origin being deep in the ground (the earth element) makes it a symbol of Divine materialization. The fact that it is a metal connects it to the mineral world, which symbolically represents resources and a potential for action and materialization. Furthermore, given the pre-existence of the mineral world to the vegetable and animal kingdoms, gold also symbolizes the most ancient memories of materialization that a person may have, as well as a capacity to recycle them, to transform them and begin new concrete experimentations once again.

In the history of mankind, gold has been a monetary reference in commercial and economic exchanges for a very long time. As such it is a symbol of power, wealth, abundance, success, celebrity and renown. Simultaneously, this all-time attraction for gold has been the cause of numerous distorted experimentations, such as the gold rush, when many crimes were committed in the name of the attraction exerted by gold; or continued prospecting for gold by international companies that pillage the resources of the countries prospected and exploit the local work force, etc.

Gold is also symbolically associated with the 8th chakra, the chakra of Divine materialization. This means that in its purest aspect, this chakra allows a person to work on materialization of the Divine Plan in the Universe. The person who has reached this level can help others, guide them in their destiny, receive precise information in both dreams and on the concrete level *via* signs, in order to create projects that favor the evolution of humanity.

⊕ A symbol of abundance, wealth, power, success, celebrity, renown, and solar force and power. Exchange value on worldwide, global, economic and commercial levels. Represents the 8th chakra, the power of Divine materialization, unification and fusion of the spirit (light) and matter (earth).

⊖ An overly materialistic spirit, a need for luxury. A desire to be admired and socially recognized. A feeling of superiority on the level of resources, earnings, what we have achieved; or, a complex of inferiority, deep material insecurity owing to a lack of resources for materialization. Only seeking material enrichment on the personal level. Greed, avidity for wealth, power, celebrity, renown. Egoism, an insatiable person. Displaying, showing off our wealth, our opulence. A superficial person, a megalomaniac.

GOLF

Golf is a sport that helps us develop concentration, precision, mental strength, calm and perseverance in attaining goals, as well as a symbiosis of mind and body. It is played by people who like to think, plan, organize, materialize and create in a right, just, good, correct manner. Golf represents the stages and cycles that we find in the world of work, in a company, as well as in a family, and between a man and a woman.

It is interesting to make the link between golf and the masculine and feminine principles, the two complementary, creative forces that unite in order to engender life. On the symbolic level, the golf club represents the masculine principle, and the hole, the feminine aspect. The little white ball, which attains its goal when it is played into the hole in the ground like a seed that will grow and yield fruit, symbolizes a sperm cell. We can also draw a parallel with the vagina, the sacred, feminine zone where the forces of creation meet to fuse and engender human life. Furthermore, golfers walk on the grass; the specific area where they have to sink the ball in the hole is called the green; the fees for playing are called green fees; green is a color that is associated with love.

When we analyze sports symbolically, we discover that the masculine and feminine principles of emissivity and receptivity are to be found in all of them.

⊕ Allows us to develop the following qualities: concentration, precision, exactitude, mental discipline, perseverance, good coordination of our movements, good capacity to plan, patience, self-esteem, camaraderie, gentleness. The player learns to go within and focus, to think calmly, and to remain focused on achieving a precise aim or goal. Hence he develops a great capacity to materialize and a feeling of having achieved fulfillment through his projects. Symbiosis of mind and body in movement.

⊖ Lack of concentration, precision and perseverance to attain our goals. Mental strength and action forces directed toward satisfying ambitions and personal needs or desires. Worldly pleasures. Determined to control our destiny. Egoism, selfishness. Mind and spirit focused exclusively on succeeding. Impatience, anger, pride, comparison, competition.

GOODS (material things)

Goods are material things, resources, objects, or property that belong to us, that we may have had or desire to have. The very name *goods* designates something positive that contributes to our well-being, security, or a certain comfort. Hence, in their positive essence, goods represent abundance related to matter, as well as a capacity to use, manage and fructify them. On the metaphysical level, goods can also represent our gifts and talents, our qualities and virtues, our energy potential, and our God-given power of action.

⊕ A symbol of available, acquired, or project for acquiring, favorable abundance and resources. Favors an apprenticeship of responsibility. Confers a feeling of security. Beneficial, useful resources and a capacity to manage and fructify them positively and altruistically. Allows us to invest in projects and experiment matter. A sense of responsibility and commitment. A confident, prudent, foresighted, stable, conscious person who is detached from matter. An understanding of the fact that matter is illusory, and plays a temporal, educational role in the evolution of people's souls and consciences.

⊖ An overly materialistic person, who never has enough, or who lacks resources and confidence because of memories of poor management and planning that led to bankruptcy and poverty. Jealousy, envy, fear and anxiety regarding the future. A person without an altruistic conscience, who doesn't share; greed and miserliness; or, a difficult destiny on the material level, caused by erroneous, distorted attitudes and behavior in this life, or in former lives. A selfish person with a tendency to manipulate others and take advantage of his status and power, who is ready to do anything to obtain what he wants, what he covets. Unjust, wrong intentions, nourished by a thirst for renown, acknowledgement, and glory. Abusive or fraudulent use of goods. A tendency to waste. Use of goods without any spiritual conscience.

GPS or **SATNAV**

A *GPS,* the acronym for ***G**lobal **P**ositioning **S**ystem,* or *SatNav,* ***Sat**ellite **Nav**igation,* is a system of geo-spatial positioning with global coverage *via* satellite, indicating, for a particular area or territory, all or some of the roads and landmarks existing on the earthly level. It allows us to plan itineraries, to find out the distance and duration of journeys, and other useful details. It offers an overall view, global vision, and facilitates journeys, trips, advancing, orientation, and efficient travel planning. Symbolically, a GPS represents a human-being's spiritual capacity to locate, situate, and rediscover himself at any time, in any place, when he is in action in matter on the earthly level, thanks to his subtle, metaphysical senses.

⊕ A faculty of orientation and multi-dimensional guidance. Easier, efficient, well-planned advancing and manifestation. Allows us to find our location, avoid accidents, to travel more calmly and get to our destination more easily. Revealing perception. Intuition. Foresight. A capacity to use our subtle senses, our psychic powers. Enlarged intelligence. Vaster knowledge and understanding. Global vision. Conscious use of supernormal guidance faculties on the concrete level. Great receptivity and confidence in guidance from Heaven and others.

⊖ Difficulty going forward, advancing. Wrong road and erroneous orientation or direction due to a limited, too down-to-earth vision. Dependency on seeking guidance to the detriment of common sense, intuition and a natural sense of direction. Using the faculty of subtle perception solely for personal, selfish purposes; or, to impress others and be acknowledged. A need to know and plan everything in advance. A lack of confidence in our own and others' intuition. Fear of the unknown, of the unpredictable. Harmful, detrimental memories and guidance powers. Either an excess or lack of logic and common sense when advancing. Fear of decision-making, going ahead, taking responsibilities. Advancing guided and motivated solely by material needs. An out-dated GPS symbolizes delays and discrepancies between orienting ourselves, finding our direction and being guided by an old way of advancing.

GRANDFATHER

A grandfather concerns the masculine polarity, emissivity and the concrete world. He symbolizes protection in action, wisdom, support in the materialization of projects. In a healthy, harmonious relationship with a grandfather, he may also represent an experienced advisor, a generous patriarch who comforts and consoles and sees to it that everything goes well in the works he has helped to create. He also symbolizes the collection of influences or specific behavioral patterns coming from ancient memories lodged in our family unconscious, which fashion and mould the way we act and manifest our emissivity on the concrete level.

⊕ A symbol of protection, wisdom and support in action and materialization. Represents a patriarch, a sage who provides security, comfort and consolation, judicious advice, love, fair, right authority and global understanding of the world of action. A symbol of generosity, sharing, kindness and goodwill.

⊖ Difficulty related to protection in action due to a lack of wisdom, love and support. Inheritance of old behavioral patterns and concepts with a negative connotation, which can lead to great difficulties on the manifestation and materialization levels. Abuse or lack of authority. Authoritarian, sharp, cutting opinion. A rigid person who adheres too strictly to principles and has an exaggerated, destructive spirit. Carelessness regarding family responsibilities. An accumulation of memories of wounds and frustrations, which engenders closed, negative or stubborn behavior. Pride. A person who thinks he is indispensable. Someone who thinks he knows everything; always wanting to be right.

GRANDMOTHER

A grandmother concerns the feminine polarity, receptivity and the inner world. In particular, she represents inner protection, support, comfort and consolation, an example to follow, generosity and unconditional love. She also symbolizes the collection of influences, specific behavioral patterns – both positive and negative – and the qualities and distortions that stem from ancient memories lodged in our family unconscious.

⊕ Inner protection bringing comfort and consolation, a feeling of support, security, kindness, goodwill and confidence. Inner inheritance favoring the evolution of the soul through a legacy of beautiful qualities related to the feminine polarity such as love, receptivity, gentleness, listening and generosity.

⊖ A lack of inner protection, support, responsibility and involvement on the affective, emotional level. A feeling of abandonment. Deep insecurity. Repressed emotions. Rigidity. Refusal to evolve. Fear of change. An attitude of flight, escapism. Inheritance of old behavioral patterns and concepts with a negative connotation, which can lead to great difficulties in affective relationships, self-expression and our inner senses. Nostalgia, a tendency to live in the past. Impressed by matter. Dispersal, dissipation in superficial activities. Wasting time, energy and resources. Old, former, accumulated wounds that create heaviness and are harmful to inner transformation. Nourishing ourselves on old, ancient, former concepts. Inner emptiness. A boring, monotonous, limited life. Difficulty indulging ourselves, asserting ourselves. An autistic, rebellious attitude. Hearing only what we want to hear. Resisting or refusing to make an effort. Senility. Forgetfulness. Loss of memory.

GRASS *cf. **Lawn***

GREEN

Green designates the color from the visible light spectrum situated between blue and yellow. It is a color that is related to love, to the affective, emotional, sentimental aspect, to relaxation, which reflects the positive emotions nature generally helps us feel. It inspires unconditional love, gentleness, sensitivity, consolation, and it soothes the senses.

A beautiful green awakens a desire to give, to be altruistic, humane, and to love. Its negative symbolism relates to the opposite of love, i.e. war, hatred, conflicts, etc. This helps us better understand the symbolism of the camouflage soldiers wear during simulations or acts of warfare.

Green has numerous other symbolic meanings, which come from its analogy with nature. Here are a few, non-exhaustive examples:

To have green fingers refers to a person who is gifted at gardening, maintaining plants, everything that grows, and hence a capacity to cultivate beautiful feelings.

A green party in politics represents an ecological, environmentally friendly movement that works in favor of the protection of nature and the environment, and therefore listens to the surrounding world, and tries to preserve and understand the different cycles of life.

A green product is a resource cultivated with respect for the environment, and where food products are concerned, without the use of pesticides, GMOs, etc., so as to protect both the land and consumers. The person nourishes himself on beautiful energy that ensures vitality and good health.

⊕ Symbolizes unconditional love, transformational, regenerating emotional energy, vitality, ecological conscience, a humanist, a sense of altruism, sensitivity, gentleness, consolation, bliss, and soothes the senses.

⊖ Symbolizes feelings of rejection, conditional love, affective dependencies, emotional lacks, as well as affective insecurity. Invasive, over intense, dominating, tumultuous emotions. Discord, hatred, conflict, war. Rigidity, coldness, emotional indifference.

GREY

The color grey is a mixture of white and black, hence spirituality (white), hidden wisdom or mystery (black). A bright, luminous grey symbolizes the beginning of wisdom, entry into maturity, material and spiritual knowledge. A dull grey indicates duality between good and evil, a grey zone that creates confusion and also the dark side of people and things.

⊕ Birth of wisdom, maturity and knowledge on the material and spiritual levels. Seeking to understand good and evil.

⊖ Difficulty marrying spirit and matter. Lack of wisdom. Misty, foggy, confused dynamics. Duality in choices. Dull, sad, lifeless spirit. An impasse, torment, incomprehension, pessimism, moroseness. Lack of purity in the way we materialize. Difficulty seeing clearly, remaining lucid during initiations.

GROCERY BAG/SACK *cf.* ***Bag***

GUN (a shotgun, rifle, revolver, etc.)

Like all weapons, a gun has an emissive potential that can be activated for defense, when it is used to protect us against a danger or a threat; or, for offence, when it is used to aggress or attack others with an intention to steal, take revenge, dominate or kill whatever bothers or scares us. It is important to understand that the act of killing, in a dream or in concrete reality, through aggressiveness, anger, revenge, meanness or evil, is inscribed within us as a karmic debt that we have to settle one day, because violence always engenders violence.

⊕ Symbol of power, of authority to protect when confronted with negative, threatening forces. A means of protection and dissuasion. An emissive potential used for positive ends so as to master instinctual energies when they represent a danger. In certain circumstances, allows us to control and dissolve aggression and threats. Awareness that evil is educational.

⊖ Abuse of power and authority. Abusive use of an emissive potential to wipe out and destroy what bothers us or to kill in order to nourish instinctual needs. A thirst for violence or revenge. Destructive emissivity. Creation of karma with serious consequences. Ignorance of the Law of return and the rigor of Divine Justice. Complex of superiority or inferiority. Engendering fear.

H

HAIR (body)

Body hair is a filiform production of the epidermis covering the skin of certain animals and the human body. Its main role is to protect the organism; e.g. the hair on our head protects our scalp from sunrays, our eyebrows and eyelashes protect our eyes, the hairs in our nostrils and ears prevent the penetration of outer irritating agents. Body hair also serves as thermal insulation, sensory detection, and camouflage.

Body hair links us to our animal dimension, indicating states of conscience related to our instinctual needs. It is more representative of the masculine, emissive polarity. A very hairy torso, back, arms and legs reveals a primary, coarse mentality that tends to focus a lot on our most basic needs, recalling the era of prehistoric man, of the *human animal.* Symbolically, ugly, disproportionate body hair indicates states such as coarseness, a lack of education and evolution, a boorish, uncouth, rudimentary, lazy, careless attitude, negligence, a lack of hygiene, and laxity. However, if the body hair is harmonious, it symbolizes antenna that can pick up information from the environment, and, in some cases, extra-sensorial, psychic perception.

⊕ Transcendence of our primary, instinctual, rudimentary needs. Refinement. Protection. Warmth, intimacy, softness, closeness, comfort, a reassuring, protective spirit, virility, good emissivity, and/or sensitivity, warm femininity. Helps our perception, sensitivity, and psychic powers or mediumnity. Development of self-assertion, vital energy. Inner harmony. Mastery of emotions. Healthy relationships with others.

Animal hair: Characteristic of warmth, softness, discretion (camouflage) and instinctual sensitivity, qualities associated with our instinctual, vital energy.

⊖ An overly instinctual, animal nature. An unrefined, rudimentary, coarse state of conscience. Excessive emissivity or a sign of negligence. Not enough hair on a man may symbolize a lack of emissivity, of assertion of his masculinity, a refusal to manifest; or, an extremist, radical attitude. A tendency to self-punishment, weak self-esteem, fragile vitality, or rejection of his instinctual nature. Difficulties related to perception and sensitivity. Vulnerability, hyper-sensitivity. A tendency to over-protection; or, a lack of protection.

Animal hair: Difficulty regarding our vital energy, related to what the animal in question represents. Precarity, health problems, or illness on the level of our vital energy, our force of action. A lack of warmth, comfort and consolation. A lack of discretion. Difficulties related to perception and sensitivity.

HAIR (head)

Hair that grows on our head, mostly symbolizes thoughts and the intellect. Each hair is a veritable antenna that picks up personal and collective thoughts and ambiances, and can easily absorb air pollutants and other harmful agents stemming from both our outer environment and our inner organism. Our hair also reflects our personal hygiene and is a barometer of our morale, our inner equilibrium, and the multiple tensions that nourish our thoughts. Stress, fatigue, a violent emotional shock can make our hair more fragile, dull, dry, and brittle, or even lead to sudden, major hair loss.

Our hair also protects our skull from physical or thermal shocks, and participates in the thermo-regulation of our body by helping evaporate sweat. Symbolically, it provides covering, extra protection for our thoughts, and also helps regulate, pacify, and stabilize mental energies and activities by allowing the evacuation of toxic, distorted, cognitive emotions.

Since time immemorial, people have always given great symbolic importance to hair: receptivity and emissivity of thoughts, intimacy, seduction, strength and virility, or femininity – sometimes shown, sometimes veiled. Our hairstyle also expresses a social (fashion, culture, provocation, rebellion, etc.), or religious (veil, tonsure, turban, etc.) message.

Over time, hair has given rise to many symbolic expressions:

Hairsplitting: over-caring about details, making too fine distinctions. *Hair-raising*: making us shudder, inspiring terror. Similarly, *Make our hair stand on end*: causing us to be very frightened. *Turn our hair white*: to make us worry. *Tearing our hair out*: feeling very anxious and stressed about something. *Don't harm a hair of his head*: don't harm him in any way whatsoever. *Having a bad hair day*: feeling annoyed, tetchy, in a bad mood, because of negative thoughts. *Let our hair down*: ⊕ relax; ⊖ over-relax and give in to our instincts; or, negligence, indifference, laxity.

⊕ Harmonious, clear, well-structured, orderly, polarized thoughts. A well-balanced, serene person whose hair reflects his well-being, self-esteem, self-confidence, beautiful, shining receptivity and emissivity. A positive reflection of femininity, gentleness, and natural elegance; or, virility and strength, as applicable. An abundance of thoughts, great potential and lucidity on the intellectual level.

Short hair (man): Active, well-organized thoughts; practical-minded, right rigor, discipline, tranquil strength, a good worker.

Short hair (woman): Active, practical thoughts, a lively, dynamic, independent person who is at ease in action and work. It may also indicate a responsible person who doesn't spend too much time on her appearance.

Bald-headed (man): Brilliant, clear, intelligent thoughts reflecting wisdom and knowledge; a scientific, wise or spiritual mind. Shaving hair to complete baldness (buzz cut) may reveal practical mindedness and detachment when confronted with major hair loss.

Long hair (man): Symbol of freedom, of creativity, of virility that is easy-going, relaxed, combined with gentleness, and wisdom.

Long hair (woman): Symbol of sensuality, youth, beauty and acceptance of her femininity.

Blonde hair: Sunny, radiant thoughts; divine manifestation.

Brown hair: Inspired thoughts turned toward action and practicality.

Black hair: Concentrated, discreet, mystical thoughts full of wisdom in matter. Opening onto the understanding of unconscious forces, mysterious aspects that manifest on the metaphysical level or that are perceived in dreams.

Red (ginger) hair: Thoughts manifesting very active, powerful vital energy. Intense mental power, an expression of dynamic willpower.

White hair: Thoughts related to spirituality, wisdom, purity, Divine Power.

Dyed hair (using natural products that are not harmful for the environment): A person who needs a change, who needs to reconstruct his self-image and self-esteem. Need for renewal, to feel good about himself. Reflection of a new stage in life.

Straight, silky hair: Fluid, light, simple, determined, upright, loyal, sincere thoughts.

Curly, wavy hair: Supple, flexible, adaptable, soft, warm, enfolding thoughts.

Tightly curled, frizzy hair: Thoughts related to concentrated vital energy, an intensity of life on the thought level, a simple, natural, optimistic side, well-rooted in the energy of the Earth.

Rasta hairstyle: Innovative thoughts, open to experimentation, a sense of diversity, mystical thoughts. A free, artistic mind and spirit. Transcendence of the negative side.

⊖ Confused, muddled, easily influenced, distorted, dirty thoughts. Difficulties regarding femininity or virility. An aspect of hair that reveals a state of ill-being, negligence, dispersal, a lack of confidence and self-esteem; or, a seductive attitude, over-confidence, a need to please, to be admired. Seductive energies for personal, selfish ends; or, personality problems. Disharmony and inner disorder.

Short hair (man): Conformist, overly materialistic, overly rigorous, strict or austere thoughts. Shaved hair (crew-cut or skinhead) also symbolizes extreme submission, extremism, constraint; or, machismo.

Short hair (woman): Overly emissive, intransigent, radical thoughts. Overly masculine behavior, too focused on concrete action. Problem of de-polarization, problematic relationships with men, rebellious attitude.

Bald-headed (man): Rejection or repression of thoughts, an inferiority complex, with a lack of self-assertion; or, a superiority complex. A mentality that wants to control too much. Materialistic thoughts that are self-centered, overly monastic, and extreme. Inner emptiness. A lack of discernment and knowledge, conformity to a fashion trend without any personal reflection.

Hair loss: Too strong, stressful, over-intellectual thoughts. In a dream, may announce an illness.

Long hair (man): Rebellious or superficial thoughts, laxity on the social and intellectual levels, refusal to shoulder responsibilities, rejection of today's business world (the hippie movement, an overly bohemian, carefree lifestyle); or, someone focused on appearances and seduction. De-polarized or overly feminine thoughts. Behavior that is over focused on matter and pleasure.

Long hair (woman): Superficial, complicated thoughts, focused on appearances and seduction. An illusory, artificial lifestyle. A haughty, capricious attitude. A fragile personality.

Blonde hair: Superficial attitudes and behavior, seeking luxury, radiance, attention, and renown. A materialistic mind and spirit. Difficulty asserting ideas and luminous concepts. A lack of authenticity, falsity, a complex either of superiority or inferiority.

Brown hair: Too down-to-earth thoughts, over focused on matter.

Black hair: Hidden, solely materialistic thoughts with no opening on the spiritual level; or, a dark, somber, pessimistic, dangerous attitude in either spiritual or material thoughts. Destructive, even malevolent thoughts. A person who lacks light, radiance.

Red (ginger) hair: Excessive, overly intense, headstrong, passionate, burning, perverted thoughts; in the extreme: a satanic attitude.

White hair: Aging, lifeless, aimless thoughts, lacking wisdom. The expression of extreme stress due to an incapacity or refusal to accept the ordeals, the dramatic, sometimes tragic events, which are part of our life path. Spiritual power used only for personal, selfish ends.

Dyed hair: Need to please, attract attention, seduce. Lack of authenticity. Refusal to grow old. Expression of an overly strong desire for change. An unstable person, who doesn't feel good in himself, who manifests *flight* behavior (escapism), multiple personalities, or schizophrenic tendencies. Camouflage, mask, a non-authentic, confused, disturbed person.

Straight hair: Rigid, arid, severe thoughts; a person who is too direct, brittle, cold, who lacks empathy, who doesn't feel good in himself, who seeks to please and be appreciated.

Curly, wavy hair: Thoughts that are too supple, too flexible, superficial, focused on appearances, seduction, and manipulation; or, devious, tormented, convoluted, tortuous thoughts.

Tightly curled, frizzy hair: Imprisoned in our own thoughts. Discrimination, exploitation, slavery, racism, poverty, famine, violence, a disorganized social life, general misery, laziness, corruption. Very powerful, unmastered instinctual force, which combined with a lack of knowledge and education may lead to distorted sexual activity. Submission to instincts, irresponsibility, a lack of long-term vision.

Rasta hairstyle: Laziness, irresponsible thoughts, focused on laxity and appearances. Rebellious, egocentric (narcissistic, self-centered) behavior. An attitude of dropping out, a neglected, unclean appearance.

Dirty hair: Unpurified, muddled, bogged down, rebellious, coarse, boorish thoughts. Lack of self-esteem, laxity, dropping out.

Untidy, unbrushed hair: A lack of organization on the thought level. A dispersed, scatterbrained, disturbed, rebellious person. Head in the clouds, too airy, paying no attention to the physical aspect.

Exaggeratedly styled hair (or, too much hair gel, hairspray, perfume, etc.): Superficial, artificial thoughts, need for recognition and acknowledgement, as well as a need to please, seductive behavior; or, a tendency to mental, intellectual stiffness and rigidity.

Having animal hair instead of human hair (in a dream): Thoughts solely focused on instinctual impulses that push us to quench and satisfy our primary, animal needs at all costs, regardless of those around us. Extreme egocentricity. Demonic energy, someone who is prepared to do absolutely anything to satisfy his primary needs. Announces danger, great disturbance of our personality, which could lead to a crime.

HAIRDRESSER

Hairdressing concerns our hair and our head, and hence, is directly related to the intellectual level. Symbolically this profession represents a capacity to cleanse and purify, tidy, adjust, shape, and modify thoughts. The hairstyle we choose reveals the image we have of ourselves, as well as our self-esteem and self-confidence. It may also reflect the image we wish to project, whether it be positive or negative, conscious or unconscious. Among other things, it may denote dynamics of superficiality focused on appearances, outer beauty, a need to attract attention or impress others. Since the Law of resonance always applies, our hairdresser also represents aspects of ourselves.

⊕ Capacity to cleanse, tidy, look after and maintain thoughts, and to structure ideas. Conscious work on our self-esteem, self-confidence, self-image, as well as our way of manifesting. May indicate renewal; or, a need to refocus, to re-center, re-organize our way of thinking, our conception of life. Great capacity to listen, to inspire and to advise. Psychological skills and talents. Helps activate a sense of beauty in the world of thoughts and ideas.

⊖ Difficulty taking care of our thoughts, of tidying and organizing our ideas, of recycling an outdated self-image; or, problems with self-esteem, a lack of self-confidence. A state of conscience that is interested in, keen on, even *hooked* on seduction, appearances, and superficiality. Someone who is too worldly, who gossips, spreads rumors, and feeds on renown, wealth, and a need for celebrity.

HAND

Generally speaking, hands represent a capacity to give, receive, touch, shape, form and make. They also symbolize the power of creation and materialization. Since the left-hand-side of our body represents our inner being, and the right-hand-side, our outer world, our left hand symbolizes manifestation and the power of creation in our inner world, as well receptivity; and our right hand, manifestation and the power of creation in the outer world, and emissivity. Through the multiple functions it can accomplish, our hands are one of the characteristics that differentiate us from animals. Thanks to hands, man can carry out a great variety of daily activities (wash, dress, feed himself, write, work, make things, build, drive vehicles, handle all sorts of devices, etc.). Hands are also an important means of expression that reinforce, or sometimes, replace speech. It is thanks to our hands that we can manipulate and shape matter. Hands also serve to manifest our feelings, concretize our ideas, and materialize our projects.

⊕ Finds it easy to give, receive, take and hold in a fair, right, loving manner. Generosity. Capacity to manifest tenderness, gentleness, kindness through touch. Tactile communication imprinted with love and compassion (e.g. holding out our hand to someone, caressing, consoling, massaging him). Capacity to work, produce, make, materialize in accordance with Divine Laws. Empowered to create useful, inspiring works. Capacity to carry out precise, complex tasks that are favorable to evolution. Discernment in the way we give, receive, and generally use our hands.

⊖ Difficulty giving (through a lack of generosity, altruism, or gentleness), difficulty receiving (through a lack of receptivity and self-love); or, a tendency to over give so as to be acknowledged and loved. A closed hand represents a lack of openness, or a refusal to act. A fist may also represent anger and violence; or, a lack of inner stability, love, and peace. Delicate, limp, weak hands, without any strength may indicate passiveness, laziness, and limpness, difficulty manifesting, and a lack of willpower and energy to act. Difficulty touching, coming into contact with people and things. A one-armed, or armless person, or someone who has lost one or both hands, has lost his capacity for self-fulfillment on the physical level; such a limitation indicates a considerable accumulation of distorted memories related to giving and receiving, and unjust, wrong, abusive use of the capacities our hands offer.

HANDBAG *cf. Bag*

HANDICAP, DISABILITY

A handicap or disability represents a limitation of a physical, sensorial or mental nature; it may also be an invaliding health problem. Generally, to different degrees, a handicap restrains a person's capacity to function autonomously and prevents him from fully participating in social life. Such a situation is always the result of a consequence engendered in this present life or in past lives. When a person has accumulated too many distorted memories, these may one day materialize in the form of a handicap. The type of handicap and the context in which it manifests itself provides clues enabling us to understand what kind of memories and erroneous behavior are concerned. Experience of a handicap in a dream must be taken seriously because it represents a warning to change certain attitudes, habits, ways of doing things, ways of thinking, otherwise, sooner or later, a limitation could manifest itself concretely in the dreamer's physical body, or in his life.

A deficiency in a person's life informs him that in the past he exaggerated, was excessive, that he acted badly toward himself and others. For example, if a person can no longer walk either in his dream or in his daily life, it means he has accumulated memories where he forced too much to advance; or, he imposed and intervened in other people's advancing; or, he lost all motivation to go ahead, to advance. A person who has a handicap on the leg level that prevents him from walking, develops the desire and willpower to walk again, if he's lost them, or to walk in the right way, without forcing or imposing his will on others.

To understand the meaning of a handicap concerning the eyes, e.g. blindness, we interpret the symbolic meaning of eyesight. Our eyesight allows us to see, to appreciate the beauty of our environment, to choose a direction, to discern what is good and what is bad in our choices, to communicate our soul-states through the expression in our eyes. Partial or total loss of eyesight in a dream or in concrete reality, indicates that the person abused this attribute, this gift, in this present life or in previous lives. He used this sense negatively by looking at others with a lack of love and kindness, by judging people's appearances, by overriding people's privacy out of unhealthy curiosity, by abusing his charisma through a look, or by generally manifesting disregard for the beauty of life.

Having to experience and live with a handicap, a limitation on a certain, level has an educational effect which incites the disabled person to rectify his erroneous, conscious or unconscious, attitudes. Simultaneously, it allows him to repair several karmas. It is very important to understand the cause of a handicap by identifying and analyzing the related signs and symbols.

⊕ Inspires ourselves and others to discover what a person's real beauty is, the importance of a soul journey through many lives. Helps us to believe in reincarnation, that one life represents a fraction of time in terms of evolution. Understanding that having a handicap is always a blessing; that sooner or later, acceptance of it, understanding it, triggers extraordinary evolution for the soul. Intense work on ourselves on all levels. Capacity to understand the meaning of an ordeal. Integration of the fact that memories materialize if we do not transform them. Understanding the importance of cleansing our unconscious and rectifying the behavior and attitudes that are the root cause of our difficulties. Development of other compensatory faculties. Great capacity for adaptation, acceptance. Appreciation and gratitude for the help and assistance we receive from others. Contributes to developing humility, to rediscovering the meaning of what is sacred, to fully appreciating our health and the gift of life. Incites us to go within, to interiorize and take time for introspection, meditation, prayer and work on ourselves with the aim of becoming a better person.

⊖ Difficulty accepting handicaps and limitations that we experience ourselves; or, behavior that manifests judgment, disdain, disgust and rejection when confronted with handicaps, disabilities, limitations in others. Lack of understanding of the fact that we always reap what we sow. A disabled person who lacks kindness toward those who help him, who tends to take everything for granted, to believe everything is his due because of his limited condition. A very negative attitude toward our handicap: withdrawal, anger, aggression, incomprehension, revolt, rebellion, rage against God. Incapacity to understand the meaning of an ordeal and an inability to put ourselves into a position of evolutive dynamics. A tendency to manipulate, dominate and control others by completely and wholly identifying with the victim role, seeing ourselves as a victim only. Fear of a handicap, or being ill-at-ease in the presence of disabled people, may indicate that the person unconsciously fears the activation of his own negative karma, which could manifest in the form of a limitation.

HEAD OF DEPARTMENT *cf.* ***Boss***

HEAD (part of the body)

The head is the most elevated part of the human body and it contains the brain (*head office* of our conscious and unconscious decisions); hence it represents the essential *headquarters* of our capacity to think, reflect, and make decisions. It is the home of our integrated personal computer, through which we are continually connected to the Divine, to all that exists in the Universe. It allows us to receive and transmit information, to engender action, the manifestation of our being. The sense organs situated on the head level (eyes, ears, nose, mouth) ensure sensorial receptivity; when these senses expand, extra-sensorial perception can manifest (clairvoyance, clairsentience and clairaudience). Through words and non-verbal communication, we can enter into contact with others and transmit our soul-states to them (facial and eye expression, voice intonation, deep, intense concentration, etc.). The head, the headquarters from which all commands are issued, concerns all levels of our being.

⊕ Headquarters, head office of our intellect, reason, capacity for thought and logic, concentration, decision-making, governing our life. Lucidity. Antenna of reception and transmission. HQ for perception, for coordinating physical and subtle senses. Harmony between thoughts and emotions, which manifests in a clear, rested, lightheartedness, as well as in easy, precise, well-structured communication.

⊖ Problems related to our capacity for thought, reflection, and decision-making, for being in charge of our life. An overly intellectual person, who lacks human warmth, who only lives in his thoughts, on the mental level; or, who finds it difficult to materialize his ideas, aims, and inspirations; or, on the contrary, who is not intellectual enough, who neglects the development of his intellect and mental capacities. Capacity for receptivity and emissivity that has become muddled and confused by selfish desires and needs that obstruct our global vision and prevent us from making right, just, good decisions. Egocentricity. Tendency to want to manage and control other people's lives. Reasoning power and intellectual capacity subjected to instinctual impulses and needs; or, hampered by an accumulation of distorted memories that engender health problems or malfunctioning on the mental level: intellectual, mental hyperactivity, dispersal, lack of concentration and discernment, a complicated, over-rational mind, fixed ideas, obsession, neurosis, psychosis, schizophrenia, depression. Flight/escapism into virtual realities, destructive games that engender anarchic behavior. A feeling of superiority, a haughty, arrogant, domineering attitude, megalomania. Someone who is cut off from Divine Thought.

HEADACHE

Headache (cephalgia) is a self-defining, subjective symptom of sometimes unilateral or generalized pains felt on the cranial level. They manifest through burning, prickling, stabbing, oppressing pains or heaviness. They are an extremely frequent occurrence and may reveal numerous illnesses. However, in the majority of cases, headaches are not serious, although some (e.g. chronic migraine, or exceptionally shooting, piercing, or constant pain) may require the attention of a doctor. On the whole, tension and cluster headaches, plus migraines, are the most common.

Metaphysically, a headache represents a state of conscience that engenders difficulties on the level of concepts, ideas, and the field of management in general, because the head represents the physical place where we deal with, manage, organize, and structure information and knowledge. Symbolically, since everything starts with a thought that materializes from the head down, a headache indicates that we are no longer able to manage the information, the impulses that reach us. This untreated, misunderstood data accumulates within us, encumbering us, and leading to an experience of pressure, which prevents harmonious functioning of our mental level, of our capacity to think with clarity, light-heartedness, precision and accuracy. For a deeper understanding of the headache manifested, we need to outline and define those thoughts that *hurt* us, that aren't right, etc.

Prickly headaches: instinctual, agitating thoughts.

Oppressive headaches: thoughts that oppress and crush us.

Stabbing headaches: discrepant, agitating thoughts.

Burning headaches: thoughts dominated by our being too strong-willed, by a too lively mind and spirit, whose overly intense fire burns and consumes us.

Thoughts that hurt us may be related to what we are going through in the present, but, most of the time, they concern accumulations of tension and distorted thoughts in our past, thoughts and memories that were not right. Moreover, they always set off various negative emotions, such as fear, sadness, anger, frustration, etc.; or, are engendered by these very emotions, which creates a vicious circle that it is difficult to get out of as long as we function with an ordinary, horizontal conscience.

The message a headache sends us serves to incite us to renew our thoughts, our mental structures, by working on our old ways of thinking, so as to liberate ourselves from the accumulations of information and data that weigh us down, encumber us, put pressure on us, while also transforming their related negative emotions.

If we dream of having a headache, it doesn't necessarily mean we will have a headache in concrete reality, but it is absolutely sure that if we don't do anything to transform the stress caused by tension and distorted, wrong thoughts, one day, we will indeed suffer from real headaches. Even a person who works intensely on himself can have a headache in concrete reality. This indicates that the block of negative thoughts he needs to transform is a major block, so he needs to intensify his transformation work.

Whether experienced in a dream or concrete reality, a headache represents an accumulation of pressure on the intellectual level due to excessive will, rigidity, or criticism, a desire to control; or, it may result from an accumulation of frustrations, of repeatedly feeling diminished, put down, a recurrent feeling of helplessness or fear of losing control of our life. A headache indicates a state of disconnection, or a hindrance or hampering of the free circulation of vital energy on the intellectual and other levels (emotional, physical, and spiritual). This discrepancy sets in when we always cast aside, ignore and/or reject our emotions and give priority to logic, reason, and the intellect; when we repress our physical needs, our personal desires, our sexual life; when we ignore our instincts and intuition, when we don't listen to our heart, don't express love; or refuse love in our life so as to remain focused on results, success, control and the abstract.

A headache is also related to an inability to let go, a tendency to take things either over seriously or to keep them constantly in our mind. Lack of spontaneity, flexibility, as well as difficulty adapting, a tendency to always want to impose our ideas and vision that is too restrained, too concentrated on details instead of being global and multi-dimensional.

Whenever we suffer from a severe headache, we also become hypersensitive to light and noise, and we are often obliged to retire to our bedroom, draw the curtains and sleep so as to put a stop to the hyperactive thoughts that imprison us. Pain and the other symptoms associated with our headache oblige us to withdraw from the outer world to go within, interiorize and question ourselves. Such an intense headache concerns realities that we cannot or do not wish to confront, an incapacity to truly listen to ourselves and others, so as to reach deep understanding of our situation.

A headache on the left side of the head is more related to our inner world, the feminine polarity and receptivity; while a headache on the right side is more particularly related to the way we use our masculine polarity and our emissive potential to act in the concrete world, in matter. Occipital pain, i.e. pain at the lower back of the head, or at the nape of our neck level, speaks of our distorted memories concerning intellectual blockages and/or limitations. Frontal pain refers to our fears and anxieties about our future, as well as regarding our social identity, the way in which we show our personality in the collectivity.

⊕ Incites us to go within and question our way of thinking, of using our mental powers in general. Open-mindedness and search for the deep, true causes of headaches rather than simply being satisfied with an external remedy that erases the symptoms through medication. Willpower to work on ourselves, on negative thoughts, on our old, erroneous, outdated concepts, and to deal with surplus information that has accumulated over time. Invites us to learn to manage and pace our mental work in a healthy way, to also spend time and look after other aspects of life: emotions, relationships, leisure activities, and spirituality. Development of the capacity to delegate work and responsibilities, to trust others and the help we receive from the Universe if we ask for it. Awareness allowing us to re-harmonize the different levels of our being in order to live a better-balanced life.

⊖ Negative, burdensome, encumbering, accumulated, unhealthy thoughts that put pressure on us and upset the proper functioning of the mental level in harmony with the other levels. Excessive willpower, an overly intense, disorganizing, burning, consuming, fiery mind and spirit. A need to organize, manage, and control everything. Unceasing mental activity, a tendency to intellectualize everything. Arid thoughts, a stubborn mind that goes around in circles brooding over the same ideas. Thoughts that have been accumulated and retained for too long, without our taking time to deal with them, to sort, analyze and transform them. A tendency to ask ourselves too many questions; or, not to want to think, reflect, analyze. Resistance to making efforts on the intellectual level, mental inertia or laziness, which, in all likelihood are caused by memories of former lives where we abused our intellectual potential, thereby engendering unconscious fear of repeating the same mistake. Intense inner conflict between an intellect overloaded with information, a body whose vital needs are neglected, a heart that lacks consideration and love, a soul, mind and spirit that lack spirituality. Dark, somber, negative ideas that tighten their vice-like grip on our mind.

HEART ATTACK

A heart attack is defined as the death of cells of part of the heart muscle. It occurs when one or several coronary arteries are blocked, resulting in a lack of oxygen, and the malfunctioning of the affected area. This provokes pain and triggers a heart attack, which can lead to death. On the symbolic level, it is a warning signal, which indicates the presence of problems related to thoughts, feelings, and emotions: an over accumulation of tension, fear, stress, emotional difficulties, an over intense desire to do things well, over strong willpower and excessive motivation, which overtax the heart and perturb its healthy, well-balanced function. Weakening of the heart may also result from the fact that we do not use the potential it represents; for example, by forbidding ourselves to love and receive love, through fear of being hurt; or, refusing to truly, deeply love out of selfishness. Emotional coldness may also cause the heart to die by gradually extinguishing its fire, vitality and driving or life force.

⊕ Becoming aware of the seriousness of the heart's malfunctioning and imbalance created by thoughts and emotions. Calling into question our values, priorities and lifestyle. Introducing and applying the necessary changes on the personal, professional, and social levels, in order to re-harmonize our life. Intensive work on ourselves to rediscover balance and health. Understanding the fact that not only must the physical body, but also the emotional, mental and spiritual bodies, be nourished in a well-balanced, healthy manner. Modification of nutrition on all levels. Apprenticeship of stress and tension management. Reflection on the deep, sacred meaning of life. A capacity to accept the learning programs Cosmic Intelligence orchestrates for each person to help him evolve. Becoming aware that we cannot control everything. A new look, a new vision of life.

⊖ A dangerous state caused by extreme imbalance between the active, emissive, exteriorization phases and those of renewal, replenishment, receptivity, and interiorization. Great accumulation of tension, stress, harshness, fear, fragility, vulnerability, and emotional, sentimental, affective lacks. Refusal to call ourselves into question. An overly materialistic life-direction based on performance, efficiency, and productivity or output. A general neglect of love, of the wisdom and values of the heart. A lack of spirituality, an overly materialistic mind and spirit. Excessive motivation, involvement and stimulation. A workaholic. A need to control everything. Abuse of power. A megalomaniac attitude. Fear of delegating. A tendency to believe ourselves to be indispensable, and to over-dramatize when things do not go as we'd like. A lack of confidence in other people's competence and potential, as well as in Cosmic Intelligence that synchronizes and watches over the evolution of the infinitely big as well as the infinitely small. Neglecting our vital needs and not paying attention to the body's warning signals. Excessive intensity in the way we function. Waste of vital energy. Too much emphasis on the pleasure of the senses. A state of survival.

HEART

The heart is a very important symbol because it is at the center, the core, the heart of our being; it is the seat of the love that animates us and feelings that motivate us and help us advance. As a physical organ, the heart is red and the color red associated with the root chakra, symbolizes vital energy, the force of action, incarnation and rooting in matter, on the earth level. It is the pump, the motor that activates our willpower and our force of life, which help circulate vital energy in our whole being. Thanks to love and feelings activated by the heart we are capable of compassion, forgiveness and altruism.

⊕ A capacity to love, be motivated, to give and receive unconditionally, to circulate vital energy, the force of life within us. Magnanimity. Generosity. Noble, pure feelings. Altruistic love. *Joie de vivre*. Inner peace. Compassion. The gift of pardon, forgiveness. Serenity. Felicity.

⊖ Difficulty in loving ourselves and others, in circulating the life force and vital energy within ourselves. Lack of motivation or, on the contrary, excessive motivation. Stress. Poor circulation of vital energy. Cardiac problems, illnesses or malformations. Conditional love. Selfishness, egotism. Passion. Possessiveness. Jealousy. Envy. Holding a grudge, bitterness. Hatred. Revenge. A lack of *joie de vivre*. Hard-, dry- and cold-hearted.

HEAT, WARMTH

Heat represents a soul-state related to vital energy, our inner fire, the power of mind and spirit capable of creating well-being, comfort, consolation, a capacity to feel and radiate feelings of love and affection, as well as intense emotions, strong sensations, ardor, vitality, and enthusiasm.

⊕ A creative force of atmospherics, ambiance and vitality. An expression of vital energy engendering well-being, comfort and consolation. Willpower to advance, which encourages, kindles emissivity, and fuels the fire of action. Emission, radiance of our inner fire. Love, tenderness, support. Motivation, impetus, ardor, optimism. Favorable for relaxation. An ability to warm up atmospheres and ambiances, emotions and soul-states marked by coldness, discouragement, and lack of motivation.

⊖ Excess or lack of heat, warmth, and intensity. Hyperactive vital energy. Excessive emissivity that stifles, dries up, and burns. Destructive fire of action. Ambition, devouring passion. Anger, blind jealousy. An incapacity to activate and express heartfelt warmth, love, compassion, comfort and consolation, support. May be linked to pessimism and indicate a lack of motivation, ardor, and impetus, or laziness, dropping out.

HEAVEN *cf. Sky*

HEIGHT

Height symbolizes a potential for spiritual elevation, to see and understand life from a global, multi-dimensional point of view. In comparison, being down low represents a capacity to incarnate and enter into action in matter. The contemplative, global vision offered by height facilitates discernment and allows us to put situations into perspective. Height gives us access to serenity, detachment from matter, open-mindedness and an expanded horizon. From a negative point of view, it may boost our ego, lead to a haughty, arrogant attitude and a feeling of superiority. To correctly understand high and low, it is important to integrate the cosmic principle that *what is above is like what is below and what is below is like what is above.* This principle expresses the fact that Qualities, Virtues and Divine Powers are the same throughout the entire Universe.

⊕ A capacity to raise our conscience, to have a global point of view as well as a causal, spiritual understanding of situations and to manifest the right way in matter. An opening of our spirit onto the multi-dimensions of life. Discovery of the vastness of creation. Discernment. Contemplation. A feeling of universality.

⊖ A superiority complex. A haughty attitude. Too much of a *head-in-the-clouds* character, a tendency to be too up in the air; or, to have difficulty elevating ourselves and attaining global vision of people and things. Difficulty incarnating and manifesting in matter; or too grounded if we can't reach a higher point, or if we tend to fall. Fleeing concrete reality. Getting lost in abstraction. Autism.

HELICOPTER

A helicopter is related to the world of air, hence thoughts. It represents the possibility of getting to distant, difficult to access, or dangerous places, through a capacity to elevate our thoughts, often in order to rescue someone. A helicopter also symbolizes mental power that allows us to move powerfully, but also slowly and deliberately, with great agility and adaptability. It also allows us to have global vision, to elevate our point of view to better understand a situation. Moreover, it represents the ability to manifest thoughts on the social and collective levels.

Not only are helicopters used to rescue people and ensure rapid, often life-saving, direct transport to hospital and immediate high level medical care, they are also frequently used by the police and the army and peacekeeping forces for surveillance, protection, rapid intervention and the reduction of criminality. They may also be used by high-level public officials to ensure safe, rapid transport to and from important, often international, meetings concerning affairs of state and worldwide issues. Wealthy businessmen and celebrities may also use helicopters for rapid, safe conduct to various destinations. In mountain areas helicopters are frequently used to bring supplies to mountaintop restaurants and refuges and to take away waste products. They are also used to help transport, deliver and/or remove large objects for mountain construction and forestry work. Aeronautical clubs also offer helicopter flights to the general public. A person's desire to go on a helicopter flight often indicates a wish to elevate his thoughts and achieve a more global vision of his situation. A symbolic analysis of the type, color, size of helicopter and the purpose it is used for, contributes to correct, deep understanding of its meaning.

⊕ Great power to manifest thoughts on the social and collective levels and/or capacity to bring help, to give assistance to and protect parts of ourselves that may be in difficulty. Thoughts containing a force of intervention, action, and protection. Great mobility and agility that lead to flexibility in the way we convey our thoughts. Stability in the world of thoughts. Skill and dexterity facilitating the exploration of different places in our inner world through thought. Global vision of a situation.

⊖ Tendency to intervene in other people's lives, to impose our thoughts because we are convinced that we can help and/or save them; or, an incapacity to raise ourselves up, to elevate ourselves and achieve global vision so as to be able to understand, to have an overview of a situation, or to rescue others. Negative power, misuse, abuse on the thought level that has collective impact. Difficulty directing our mental power toward right, efficient action. Agile, but sly, shifty, unhealthy thoughts. Instability and loss of mastery on the mental level.

HELL

Hell is a state of conscience that truly exists in our human conscience as well as in the parallel worlds. It represents a state of soul, mind and spirit wherein we feel great torment, suffering, and intense confusion, caused by an accumulation of erroneous behavior and very negative actions. It is important to know that the hell we see in a dream (nightmare) shows us aspects of ourselves. It is a condensed manifestation of both personal, negative memories and collective, distorted memories that have amassed in certain spheres of the Universe. Whenever we *go through hell,* i.e. when we experience hellish moments and soul-states, it is important to remind ourselves that the Divine, that God continues to exist in us in the form of positive forces and luminous regions of our conscience. We need to rally and unite with these positive, luminous forces and regions of our conscience through meditation and prayer in order to get safely through the infernal zones and transcend the forces of darkness. It is essential to know that we cannot escape from hell by fighting evil, because fighting and a spirit of opposition, duality and doubt are exactly what engender evil and nourish the dark forces that serve it. Nor is it possible to escape by becoming an ally with evil, which, by definition, is suffering, anger, devastation, despair, and perdition. When negative forces manifest, it is wise to apply the Law of resonance and accept the fact that we ourselves have engendered them through behavior that was contrary to Qualities, Virtues and Divine Laws; or, that we are going through a period of initiation, that we are being tested by Up Above through very trying people or situations so that we may reinforce Good and the Divine Light within ourselves.

⊕ Advanced initiation. Period of transcendence and alchemical transformation of memories engendered by evil and negative forces or powers. Awareness that evil is educational and that God or Cosmic Intelligence is above good and evil. Strengthening, reinforcement of faith. Conscious choice to turn away from darkness, to serve the Light, to live in accordance with the Divine Laws, and form an alliance with the Celestial Hierarchies.

⊖ Encountering dark, tenebrous zones of our conscience. Visiting very condensed, negative memories marked by darkness, obscurity, suffering, violence, duality, destruction, and perdition, recorded over numerous lives. Lifestyle that nourishes inner and outer hell, through films, music, and contexts of violence, horror, and destruction. Lack of awareness and understanding that violence engenders violence, that the devil teaches through evil, wrong-doing and what hurts, and only has power over those who choose to do evil, or who, either consciously or unconsciously, call on him. Believing ourselves to be imprisoned in hell; ignoring the fact that everything can be repaired, that everything can be transformed, through unremitting work on our negative memories and conscious cooperation with the Angels and Spheres of Light. Religious extremism, someone who creates hell while believing he is creating heaven, paradise.

HEN, CHICKEN

A hen is a female chicken that is an omnivorous, domestic animal that is raised for its flesh, eggs, and sometimes for its feathers. Like all animals, depending on the context, it symbolizes, positively or negatively, certain aspects of our instinctual, vital energy and primary needs. As a bird, it also represents the world of thoughts. However, the fact that it isn't able to fly very high or for any great length of time denotes more instinctual, down-to-earth thoughts related to the concrete world and a capacity to materialize, produce, and work intensively in matter. A free-range hen (except when laying) is always busy, running up and down the ground, scratching the earth. Its great capacity to produce eggs – one per day depending on its living conditions – symbolizes the creative power of the feminine principle within us, on the one hand; and, on the other hand, the capacity to make manifest in the outer world that which was engendered and formed on the inside.

A hen also displays great ability to work individually because it doesn't need its mate, the rooster, to produce eggs, to seek food, or to look after its young. As an important food resource for humans, it symbolizes a great capacity to nourish forces that allow us to advance, to manifest daily, and to act in matter.

It is especially during fecundation that a hen reveals its submission to the masculine principle. Its normally gentle, docile nature then proves to be a weakness. For reproduction, it lives in a polygamous environment, where the bigger, more imposing rooster fertilizes the egg without respect, without any affectivity, even with a certain degree of aggression. Generally speaking, the dynamics of the hen/rooster couple display considerable imbalance regarding the two polarities, which do not fuse harmoniously or respectfully.

A laying hen continually looks after its eggs, thereby showing a protective, maternal attitude toward its offspring. However, it doesn't look after chicks that are weak or in difficulty; it doesn't seek to protect, support or take care of them, not even immediately after birth. Such an attitude reveals resonance with the cockerel that behaves in a similar fashion toward the hen. A hen lacks affectivity and instinctive intelligence to take on its maternal role in the right way. Its behavior actually nourishes a force of dispersal, an attitude of unconditional acceptance and submission to the law of the jungle; i.e. to the survival of the fittest and he who acts unscrupulously and inconsiderately toward others. A comparison could be made, for example, with a battered wife and mother, who prefers to ignore the fact that her spouse or companion is abusing one of her children.

A hen also symbolizes a good capacity for communication and peaceful co-habitation. It also lets itself be easily tamed and tricked. The fact that it is rarely alone – there are almost always several hens in a hen house – denotes a very sociable aspect, a capacity to be in society and exchange with others. However, these exchanges are not necessarily positive, constructive, or deep. On the contrary, as well illustrated in the descriptive expression, *cackling like hens in a henhouse,* such exchanges are more often useless, idle, superficial chattering and gossip.

Several idiomatic expressions reveal how present the hen/chicken dynamic is in human life, whether we are aware of it or not. These expressions do not stem from instituted knowledge, but rather from our experience as human beings. Through idiomatic language, we illustrate the states of conscience that dwell in us: fears, anxieties, desires, behavior, associations, etc. Here are a few examples:

To run around like a chicken with its head cut off; or like a hen on a hot griddle; or like a headless chicken: a lack of discernment and overall intelligence, as well as a tendency to let ourselves be abused and dominated by the masculine polarity, excessive emissivity and hyperactivity in matter, continually seeking to act, produce, materialize, concretize, without stopping to think and call ourselves into question. The image of a hen whose head has literally been cut off, that instinctively continues to run around all over the place, is a good illustration of a person's reactive behavior. Having lost his head, his capacity to think, and all his means, he is incapable of acting in a conscious, well-reflected manner.

Chicken-hearted: a fearful person who lacks courage.

To chicken out of something (or on someone): to manage to get out of something, not to respect commitments, usually due to fear or cowardice; hence the adjective *chicken* to mean afraid, cowardly, as in children's taunt: *You're just chicken!*

The hen that lays golden eggs: great material abundance; and *to kill the hen that laid golden eggs* means to destroy a sustainable source of income by yielding to the lure of immediate gain.

Chicken feed: a very small amount of money, especially money paid for doing a job.

Don't count your chickens (before they're hatched): A warning not to make plans based on expected good things; wait till they actually materialize.

Chickens come home to roost: bad or silly things done in the past are now beginning to cause problems and there are consequences to be faced.

If it ain't chickens, it's feathers: there are always problems.

No spring chicken: not to be young anymore.

As scarce as hen's teeth: scarce, seldom found.

The word *hen* is also used familiarly to designate a person of the female sex, as in *a hen night,* which refers to an evening spent exclusively with female company, and *a hen party,* a party exclusively for women, specially organized for a woman who is soon to be married. *Chick* is a pejorative slang term for a woman. Its use reveals that the speaker has *rooster* tendencies, i.e. dominant tendencies, lacking in right, true respect, consideration, and affection for women in concrete reality, and also regarding his own inner feminine polarity. This term implies that the woman is easily influenced, lets herself be dominated, and is too focused on matter and productivity. Similarly a *chick-flick* refers to a romantic, sentimental movie, most likely to be enjoyed by women, and the gentle, loving approach featured in it is denigrated, scorned or rejected by men who use such a term, sometimes because they are afraid to admit their own attraction to such gentleness, etc. As for the expression *mother hen,* it indicates someone who is excessively attached and pays too much attention to his/her children, a tendency to over-mother, to over-protect them, and to project their own weaknesses and insecurities, as well as their own fears of being abused and dominated, onto their children.

⊕ Symbol of prosperity, of a creative, productive capacity on the material, concrete level. Ability to work diligently, intensely, and efficiently on the individual level. A fertile (fecund, prolific) maternal, protective person. Nourishing abundance and stability. Capacity for long-term multiplication of food/nourishment resources and/or projects. Ability to conceive and give birth on all levels, to materialize, and multiply in a way that is right and healthy. Development of the capacity to assert ourselves, to put a stop to domination by our masculine polarity. Mastery of hyperactivity and excessive emissivity. Finding it easy to communicate and live peaceably with others. Well developed social life. Positive, inspiring exchanges; constructive criticism. Transcendence of a tendency to wish to over-protect others, a project, work, or enterprise, to behave like a mother hen toward our children, family, and entourage.

⊖ A person who lets himself be dominated and accepts infidelity due to a feeling of insecurity on the material level, or due to a lack of courage and determination to assert himself and be respected. A hyperactive state of conscience that is over focused on matter, business, and productivity. Absence of principles and values in our instinctual behavior; licentiousness, prostitution, sexual abuse. Someone who accepts just about any behavior from anyone. Tendency to excessive mothering, overprotection and sheltering our children, entourage, and our works. Or, on the contrary, a hen that doesn't lay eggs, or that doesn't care for its offspring, is a sign of poverty, lack of or incapable of productivity, absence of a maternal instinct, incapacity to create, to concretize, to materialize. Too down-to-earth thoughts that prevent us from raising ourselves up, from attaining more elevated states of conscience; or, limit us to a heavy, burdened, narrow-minded way of looking at things, not allowing us an overall view, detached, global vision. Life situations that are difficult to bear: tensions, violence, marital problems or abuse that haven't been solved. Superficial, inefficient and disorderly activity and efforts. Inner and outer disorganization. Incapacity to work efficiently and diligently on the individual level. Superficial, voluble, discordant, aimless communication. Negative exchanges, judgments, destructive criticism.

HERITAGE *cf.* ***Inheritance***

HIGHWAY (freeway, expressway, motorway)

A highway is a collective infrastructure allowing vehicles to circulate rapidly, smoothly, and safely over long distances. If we see a highway in a dream it means that we have access to a great force for advancing, the possibility of reaching a destination quickly. Symbolically a highway represents an easy path, a state of conscience of expansion.

⊕ An easy path, rapid access to our aims, objectives, and goals. Confidence in the achievement of our goals. Safety-minded. A period of expansion.

⊖ Difficulty or incapacity to advance rapidly to reach our aim(s), objective(s), and goal(s). Fear when we advance rapidly. Limited access, a closed horizon. Over-speeding or over-slowness that could cause accidents. Multiplication of distortions in our personal and social way of advancing. Haste. Impatience, frustration, and anger when confronted with delays or an impossibility to advance. Hyperactivity.

HOCKEY

Like many sports, hockey has a collective dimension and is related to a person's expansion, as well as the manifestation of the two principles that underlie all creation: the masculine and the feminine, emissivity and receptivity. The hockey stick represents the masculine aspect; the puck or ball denotes vital energy that heads for the net, a symbol of the feminine principle and a capacity to receive, to create life, a child. Knowing this, we can better understand the powerful, unconscious, individual and collective effect of this sport. It reveals the manner in which several masculine elements (players, outer action) behave and strive to score a goal; symbolically to engender a project with a view to obtaining success, expansion, fortune, celebrity, and happiness. Similar dynamics are found in the business world where teams concentrate and work intensely on projects mostly related to states of conscience regarding success on the material level.

In the case of ice-hockey, played on frozen water that symbolizes emotional coldness, this sport represents a search for human warmth, love, recognition and acknowledgement of the efforts put into obtaining success and reaching our goals on the social level. Moreover, it manifests the will to learn to transform and master frozen emotions, and hence constantly maintain a warm attitude, concentrated on qualities, no matter the situation or relational climate. As for field-hockey, it represents the same general characteristics, but oriented toward a search for more concrete, emotional mastery, symbolized by the earth element, grass, and the color green.

As well as favoring the development of beautiful qualities, sport touches on the essential principles of life that we encounter in one form or another in all daily situations. That is why team sports resemble each other on the symbolic level, and why they inspire so many people all over the planet.

⊕ Force of achievement and materialization of aims, objectives, goals, projects, no matter the situation, atmosphere, ambiance or problem encountered. Unification of numerous parts of ourselves that engender the realization of our projects. Development of beautiful qualities such as: team spirit, strength, accuracy, goal-seeking, concentration, intensity of presence, flexibility, suppleness, willpower, perseverance, self-discipline, endurance, speed, precision in exchanges, respect for rules and regulations. Helps us understand that when we play and act with right (just, good) intention(s) and manifest qualities, even if we lose a match, thanks to the experience we acquire each time we play like this, we always win on the inner level, in the *soul-league*, so to speak, i.e. regarding the evolution of our soul. Awareness that what is important, that the essential aspect required for a project of any sort to succeed is an altruistic, participative attitude and state of mind, spirit and soul.

⊖ Difficulty regarding the achievement and materialization of aims, objectives, goals, projects; or, a lack of strength, willpower, determination to attain our goals; or, a tendency to jostle, force, and fight to win, as well as being too focused on results. A coarse, rough attitude. A cold person, lacking in love, who acts with a competitive, fighting, conquering spirit, ready to do anything to succeed. Acrimonious, incisive, quarrelsome, brutish behavior. Loss of self-control. Lack of team spirit; or, living too much for the team, clannish or tribal spirit. Unjust, wrong intentions and motivation. Lack of respect for rules and regulations in exchanges. Egoism. Hostile, boorish, barbarian climate. Absence of refinement in exchanges with others.

HOLE

A hole represents the notion of an opening in the unconscious, an in-depth search to discover ourselves; or, to rectify, repair, or build something in our life. It may indicate the planting of new seeds, of potential that will manifest; or indicate a dynamic of emptiness, a lack to be fulfilled, being bogged down in matter, and represent a period of depression, material problems, insecurities, deep anxiety or anguish (*black hole).* It is related to the mineral kingdom and the earth element, hence action and materialization.

A hole in our clothes represents a tendency to be de-structured or neglectful in the way we present ourselves on the individual and social levels. It may also indicate excessive openness, which causes a loss of energy on the personal level, e.g. the teenage tendency to buy and wear clothes with holes in them. This tendency is even more negative given the fact that generally speaking, clothes are not meant to be worn with holes, apart from old clothes (cardigan, work trousers, etc.) that end up with holes because they have been worn so frequently and can no longer be darned or patched.

Finally, a hole may also represent sinking into misery, difficulty, or poverty; a place where there seems to be no way out, no exit. This is the case when we casually refer to a poor, dirty, miserable, lifeless places as a *hole*; or, to a very isolated, difficult to get to place with few resources as *a lost hole.*

⊕ May denote a period of preparation, construction, consolidation of a structure, repair works; or, indicate that we are visiting the depths of our unconscious related to our former actions, our past lives. Allows us to enter into contact with normally inaccessible, hidden areas. Discovery of long, deeply repressed parts of ourselves. A capacity to rediscover treasures in our memories. A period of sowing and activating new projects. Work on old, former behavior that manifests in our current life. May serve as protection, shelter, and refuge.

⊖ Collapse of structures. A person who becomes burdened in matter, or who is depressed, completely disturbed by the opening of his unconscious and visit of his memories. Indicates a void, fears and anxieties related to the awakening of old memories, old ghosts, and unsettled situations. A forced opening of consciousness that is difficult to manage; or, someone who doesn't want to dig deeply to see where he is, to visit his memories related to former actions. Excessive willpower and emissivity to penetrate the unconscious. Depths we could get lost in; someone who suffers endless collapses, who gets lost in abysses; or, who resists deep self-knowledge. May also symbolize difficulty opening up to others.

To hole up: To choose to be overly isolated from the rest of the world; difficulty mingling with others, joining the collectivity.

Asshole: Insulting someone in this way means nothing good, nothing worthwhile can come from him. May indicate a tendency to be totally servile, to accept being diminished, humiliated, dominated by others, to let ourselves be psychologically crushed or devastated.

HOME *cf.* ***House***

HOMELESS *cf.* ***Tramp*** *(homeless person, vagrant)*

HORIZONTAL

Horizontal is orientation parallel to the horizon, to the ground, hence the earthly material world, to what is observable by means of our physical senses. Depending on circumstances, it offers close, medium, far, or infinite vision of what surrounds us, events that take place in physical reality, and allows us to envisage actions, establish objectives and goals, to accomplish projects as regards concrete observation. The concept of horizontality may also be associated with vision that is too down-to-earth, too rational, that only takes into account visible, tangible results, with no interest in the causal level, the vertical dimension of conscience, the metaphysical and spiritual worlds.

⊕ Someone who is open-minded and who continually wishes to broaden his horizons, knowledge, and understanding of his life so as to live and materialize in a just, right manner (i.e. giving priority to developing qualities and virtues, striving to evolve and become a better person). Capacity for foresight, organization, materialization, accomplishment, creativity, and multiplication. Ability to go from a unilateral, horizontal vision to a multi-lateral, vertical vision. Understanding that the concrete, physical dimension and the world of consequences are the material representation of metaphysical dimensions and the causal world. Integration of the universal principle according to which *everything that exists above is like what exists below and everything below is like what exists above.*

⊖ Vision and understanding that are limited to the horizontal level, to the world of consequences; or, a limited, obstinate, stubborn, overly rational, overly rigid, or overly materialistic mind and spirit. Excessive rationality, someone who is too down-to-earth. Conscious only of the physical aspect and material dimension of people and things. Lack of understanding of the metaphysical dimension and the causal significance and impact of events. Lack of spiritual knowledge and global vision. Resistance or refusal to detach our conscience from the horizontal level to envisage the multi-dimensions of life.

HORSE

A horse symbolizes instinctual, vital energy, as well as physical strength that allows us to advance with stamina, endurance, and speed toward a goal. It is an intelligent, social, tamable animal that loves and seeks freedom. It is a noble servant, companion, and friend to man, provided it is treated with respect, love, and right, fair authority. A person also needs to have courage and self-confidence to be able to ride and master a horse, because even though tamed, it remains easily excitable, and may buck and gallop off at any moment. One of the characteristics of a horse is its need for very little sleep, and its capacity to sleep while standing. Symbolically, this indicates a great capacity to be always ready to spring into action; or, to flee in case of danger. Due to their physical strength, for a long time, horses were, and in some countries still are, used to carry out farming and transport work. Consequently a horse also symbolizes a great capacity for work, hence the popular saying *to work like a horse*. Given a stallion's very long penis, it is also associated with powerful sexual energy.

⊕ Abundance and correct use of vital energy. Mastery of instincts and physical strength in action. Stamina and endurance, resistance, motivation, willpower, speed. Great capacity for work. Rapid recovery. Right self-confidence, authority and sense of action. Love of freedom and great open spaces. Powerful sexual energy.

⊖ Difficulty in advancing and working with endurance and speed due to lack of strength, vitality, resistance, motivation, willpower, and self-confidence. Excessive will, forcing to advance, using vital energy and physical strength impulsively and excessively. Excitability, agitation, competitive spirit. Authoritarianism. A tendency to flee when we feel attacked. A fiery, rebellious spirit Unbridled or repressed sexuality.

HOSPITAL

A hospital represents a capacity to take care of and heal ourselves and others on all levels, to relieve suffering, to give assistance and act in an emergency. Whenever a hospital appears as a symbol in a dream, it reveals the presence of unwell, ill parts that need treatment. A symbolic analysis of the hospital features, its state, structure, equipment, the quality of treatment and care offered, all give indications as to the ability or inability of the person to take care of himself, to heal a dysfunctional state of his, or of others.

⊕ A capacity to structure and organize ourselves in order to take care and help heal parts of ourselves in need of care and healing. A person in the process of healing who receives a second chance, a new departure, a fresh start, through rectification, consolidation and healing of his dysfunctions. A sign indicating that we need to stop and go within, interiorize, and take care of ourselves, of our healing so as to avoid the manifestation of an infection or serious illness.

⊖ An incapacity to structure and organize our healing; or, difficulty treating ill parts of ourselves, or of others, adequately. A period of illness, suffering, limitation. A lack of understanding of the meaning of ordeals, the educational role of evil, wrong-doing, what hurts, of ill-being, of illnesses, and the fact that they represent the harvest of what we sowed in this life or other past lives. Inadequate treatment and care, a lack of resources or skills to heal. Abuse of the health system. A tendency to have others take responsibility and look after us; or, a refusal to receive treatment and care. Fragility. Medicine without conscience; or, an impatient, ungrateful patient. A lack of resources to heal ourselves or to help heal others.

HOTEL

A hotel is an establishment that offers a service of usually short-term accommodation to travelers passing through a region. It may simultaneously correspond to several criteria and states of conscience: vacations, rest, personal renewal and replenishment, a search for well-being, meetings and reunions of all sorts – business, clubs, associations, etc. –, seminars, workshops, culinary art, sporting, cultural, social activities, therapeutic treatments, etc.

⊕ A period of rest, relaxation, renewal, replenishment and well-being on the personal and social levels. A warm welcome, good will, help and accompaniment in taking care of and looking after ourselves. A return to the freedom and carefree feelings of childhood since there is no need to deal with the usual daily household tasks and responsibilities. A period of transition from one state of conscience to another. A change in our rhythm of life, mentality and habits. A great capacity to adapt and feel at home anywhere in the world.

⊖ Behavior that is too oriented toward personal needs. A tendency to laze around, to let ourselves be served, to live without any responsibilities. Seeking vacations at all costs in order to flee daily reality; or, difficulty allowing ourselves a vacation, rest or well-being in a social context, detaching ourselves from work or our daily routine. Seeking to get away from it all, escapism, worldly pleasures, superficiality, illusion, laziness, idleness. Feelings of superiority and inferiority. A haughty, arrogant, complicated, demanding attitude. Abuse of and excessive prodigality, lavishness, extravagance. A lack of roots and stability, an incapacity to create a personal, private, intimate home for ourselves.

HOUSE, HOME

In its global dimension, the house or apartment we live in represents our intimacy, our inner space, the place where we renew and replenish ourselves. A house contains several rooms and each room reveals a particular symbolic aspect of our private life. (E.g. the aspects of the kitchen will indicate how we prepare resources on the physical level; a dining-room will represent the way we take and share meals; the living-room will not only reveal the way we relax at home, but also how we welcome others into our home, how we live our private and social life; a bedroom will reveal aspects of our intimate life; the bathroom will give indications as to how we cleanse and purify ourselves, etc.) When a house has several floors, each floor has its own symbolic meaning; for instance, the basement is related to our subconscious; the ground floor is related to the concrete level and the way we go from our inner world toward our outer world, and vice versa; the upper floors relate to the causal level and the world of thoughts and concepts.

⊕ A place of intimacy, renewal and replenishment, beautiful, pleasant, luminous, harmonious, orderly, clean, personal and family life, which reflects the global inner structure of the people who live there, what characterizes them on the personal level, as well as their resonance with each other. A capacity to live together in harmony and respect. A private, privileged place to retire to after activities in the outer world, to re-center, refocus, rest, purify, and renew ourselves. A well-balanced life on the personal and family levels. An understanding of the symbolism and resonance revealed by the different rooms, their decor, color(s), furnishings, the ambiance they emanate, as well as the general aspect of the house, its architecture, the materials it is built of, its location, the relationship with neighbors, etc., the conscious choice of the house we wish to live in, buying, having it built, or building it ourselves.

⊖ A disorderly, untidy, neglected, dirty, abandoned, run-down house reveals problems related to the structure, organization, and running of our private, intimate life, as well as difficulty renewing ourselves, resting, creating a personal living environment where we feel at ease and in harmony with ourselves. In a house with negative aspects, details of the kind of problem manifested can be analyzed: for example, a house that has leakage problems, on the symbolic, metaphysical levels, indicates a tendency to be submerged by our emotions; a house with a roof problem indicates difficulties in the structure of our concepts and thoughts; cracks in the inner walls also reveal structural problems, but more regarding our relationships with others, since walls in a house serve to separate the physical space shared with other members of the family, flat-mates or other residents. Not wanting to go out of the house would show a tendency to over-interiorize, to flee, or even reject the social world. And the contrary, when a person is rarely at home, this would indicate a lack of interiorization, an incapacity to feel good with himself or his family, an exaggerated, unhealthy need for social life. A tendency to mislay or lose the keys of the house would indicate an excessive active, social life, and the presence of inner forces that prevent access to our place of rest, renewal and replenishment of our private, intimate life. Resistance to taking care of our house, tidying it, furnishing it pleasantly, and keeping it clean could denote an important discrepancy between our personal, private, intimate life and our social life; or, laziness, indifference, and/or insensitivity to our living environment. An unclean, disorganized house may also indicate inner conflicts if we live on our own; or, on the contrary, difficulty sharing a house, co-habiting pleasantly in peace and harmony, and managing our inner world peacefully in relation to others.

HUG *cf.* ***Embrace***

HUSBAND *cf. Spouse*

HUNGER

Hunger represents a state where we feel the need to eat in order to subsist, to ensure our health, and continue to live. Being hungry in a dream, depending on the context, may indicate a nutritional deficiency on the metaphysical level, on the level of the subtle bodies, hence emotional, intellectual, or spiritual hunger. Healthy hunger felt on the concrete, physical level indicates that it is time to nourish our physical body so as to avoid its becoming weak, to prevent a loss of energy that could result in organic malfunctioning. When we ignore the existence of our subtle bodies and their nutritional needs, we often confuse hunger felt on the levels of these bodies with physical hunger. We then tend to seek to satisfy our hunger by physically over-eating. Hunger may also be the manifestation of great instinctual needs, an ardent desire to fulfill affective, emotional lacks as well as different sorts of deficiencies and dependencies. It may also lead us to all sorts of excesses and abuse.

⊕ A state of receptivity and availability to receive the necessary resources and forms of energy to nourish ourselves healthily on all levels for well-balanced, harmonious growth and evolution.

⊖ Lack of food and nutritional deficiencies inscribed in our memories. Unsatisfied vital needs. Survival state. Nutritional obsessions. Slave to our desires and instincts. Bulimia, anorexia. A feeling of inner emptiness that we try to make up for and fulfill by eating.

HURT, INJURE, WOUND, TO

The verbs to hurt, injure, or wound indicate the state of conscience of a person who painfully affects or offends part of himself or others, through his tactless, clumsy, aggressive, or underhand thoughts, words, attitudes, or deeds. They concern an action which, voluntarily or involuntarily, engenders physical or moral disturbances, pain, hurt. However, it is important to know that even in the case of voluntarily inflicted hurts, injuries, or wounds, they are the unconscious manifestation of a state of discontent, disturbance, or aggression. The part of the body, soul, or mind that is hurt, and the way the injury or wound occurs gives precise indications as to the exact nature of the symbolic interpretation.

⊕ Allows us to become aware of the Law of resonance and the Law of karma, both of which help us understand that it is no coincidence that we have been hurt, injured, or wounded; or, that we have hurt someone else. An opportunity to learn acceptance, clemency, consolation, reparation, forgiveness for ourselves and/or others. An understanding of the subtle mechanisms that incite us to hurt others; or, which attract hurts, injuries, or wounds to ourselves. Work on ourselves to heal and rectify our behavior, and cleanse our conscious and unconscious memories of discontent, anger, frustration, and aggression that push us to hurt, injure or wound. An apprenticeship through consequences, which leads to an understanding of how Divine Justice works.

⊖ A frustrated, discontent, bitter, hot-tempered, mean, or aggressive person, who deliberately hurts, injures or wounds; or, a person who harbors unconscious memories and forces which, through resonance, attract hurt, injury and wounds. Repressed fears and needs. A lack of love. Selfishness. An accumulation of energies of violence, hostility, meanness, which creates accidents and conflicts. A dominating spirit that imposes his will or choices. An impulsive person who seeks to control, and to be right at all costs. Pride, arrogance. Abuse of power. An excess of emissivity. Unmastered instincts. A wrong act or deed, which creates negative karmas.

HYPNOSIS

Named after Hypnos, the Greek god of sleep, hypnosis designates a state between waking and sleep that a hypnotist induces in a person by means of suggestive techniques that are capable of influencing the person's willpower and modifying his state of conscience. Introduced to the world of medicine in the 19th century by an English doctor to anesthetize his patients, hypnosis was later used in psychological treatments where it led to the discovery of the importance of the unconscious and the powerful effect of its contents on the way we function. A hypnotic state offers access to memories lodged in our unconscious as well as the possibility to become aware of and heal them. Hypnosis has contributed toward proving that the known, conscious part of our being is only the tip of the iceberg. The greatest part of ourselves, all that we have accumulated throughout our numerous lives – experiences, knowledge, conditioning, behavioral patterns, positive and negative thoughts, emotions, and soul-states (moods) – is hidden in the depths of our unconscious and influences us without our knowing. Generally speaking, it can be said that all methods of meditation and deep relaxation induce, consciously or unconsciously, a state of self-hypnosis.

⊕ Awareness of the power and impact of unconscious memories. Work on ourselves to know ourselves better and to transcend the influences of the past. Interiorization and induction of a state of conscience that provides access to hidden knowledge and information. Deeper understanding of certain events and experiences. Liberation and/or healing through karmic cleansing, through awareness of our inner *luggage* (*cf.* this term). Experimentation and development of the powers of the mind, of our mental capacities and psychic powers (mediumnity). Apprenticeship of work on ourselves during a state of modified conscience. Facilitates access to the contents of our subconscious and unconscious. Meditation. Deep relaxation. Self-study. Contemplation of our inner worlds. Visions. Deep receptivity.

⊖ Use of hypnosis for selfish, egotistical, dishonest purposes, or to impress others. Forcing an opening onto the unconscious and access to memories, at the risk of creating numerous discrepancies that could activate very negative attitudes and behavior on the conscious level. Seeking power over and domination of other people by manipulating their mind and state of conscience. Creating discrepancies between the mind and body. Interfering with other people's life plans. Seeking to control destiny. Malevolent, ill-willed intentions. Inducing mental and psychological dependencies. Awakening obsessive behavior. Bewitchment. Black magic. Absence of authentic spirituality. Knowledge without conscience. Infringement of Cosmic Laws. Ignorance of the karmic consequences resulting from abusive use of mental and psychic capacities. Lack of autonomy. Tendency to allow ourselves be manipulated; abandoning our own decisional powers. Fear of encountering our unconscious memories, of truly, deeply knowing ourselves.

I

ICE

Ice symbolizes a state of conscience marked by frozen emotions, i.e. a state of being where human warmth and love are absent. This creates a climate of austerity, severity, rigidity and coldness in relationships and exchanges with others. Ice may also indicate a state of freshness, coolness and preservation, as well as a capacity to refresh, cool down and moderate over-hot emotions and overheated minds and spirits.

⊕ A capacity to create and maintain a state of pleasant freshness, coolness, and ensure appropriate preservation. A capacity to welcome and understand ambiances of emotional coldness and not be affected by them. A capacity to cool down and moderate hot or burning emotions and spirits.

⊖ Frozen emotions and feelings. Great difficulty opening up on the affective, emotional level, expressing warm emotions, kindness, gentleness, goodness, compassion, love. A person who emanates a cold, austere, rigid *climate*, or who seeks to forget and hide his emotional difficulties.

ICEBERG

An iceberg represents a great, big reservoir of frozen emotions, most of which are unconscious as the greater part of an iceberg is invisible. A single iceberg is more related to frozen emotions on the individual level, whereas a large number of icebergs refer to the emotional level of the collective unconscious. Melting icebergs symbolize the gradual, conscious and unconscious liberation of either the creative or destructive potential contained in frozen emotions.

⊕ Gradual liberation, transformation, and expansion of emotional potential on the individual and collective levels. An opening of conscience and access to a great reservoir of hidden knowledge, of emotional resources. Gradual change of our inner climate. Reconnection with repressed, frozen, forgotten potential. A capacity to let our inner ice melt, to accept to feel deeply and intensely. Work on the mastery of emotions and feelings. Activation of new potential for warmth, love, gentleness, sensitivity. Intense work on awareness and an emotional journey, which is not always visible on the outside, but which emerges gradually and manifests in stages. Transformation of our conscience, which allows us to remain very calm when faced with inner and outer changes. A capacity to feel good when visiting cold, frozen regions in our personal or collective unconscious.

⊖ Enormous, frozen emotional potential left adrift. Unawareness of the presence of memories of coldness and the destructive force therein on both inner and outer levels. Risk of sudden emotional collapse and gradual flooding in different areas of life. An incapacity to contain and master the devastating power of negative emotions. Coldness, severity, hardheartedness, and indifference when faced with emotional wounds. Ignoring and hiding our feelings has become a habit, a way of life. A closed heart, an incapacity to feel, to love, to open up to others and to life itself.

ILLNESS (ill-being, disease)

Illness (ill-being, disease) manifests and materializes in the physical body after taking root in the metaphysical body and the causal world. It has an educational function. An illness (ill-being or disease), always reveals the presence of memories marked by erroneous experimentations, ways of being and behavior, on one or several of the following levels: spiritual, intellectual, emotional and physical. An accumulation of distorted memories over a long period of time prepares the way for illness. These distortions are maintained and nourished in the subtle bodies for a certain length of time, sometimes even over several lives, before manifesting in concrete reality in the form of the symptoms and dysfunctions that affect the physical body. If they are not rectified and transformed before attaining the degree of densification and crystallization that allows them a physical form, an illness materializes. It appears in order to help a person become aware that it is time for him to change his way of being, thinking, living. The message of an illness varies according to the part of the body that is affected.

Illness also allows us to experience different states of conscience and to learn to heal ourselves, to take care of ourselves, or to ask others for help. It is important to know that an illness is not the fruit of chance or hazard; it always corresponds to a person's karmic *luggage* (*cf.* this term) and Life-plan. It reveals the distortions and blockages buried in the unconscious, which crystallize in the physical body and signal that the time has come to listen to what our soul needs. An illness informs the person of his soul's and inner need for change, purification, transformation, and evolution. Initiatic teaching teaches us that we mustn't rebel against an illness or want to fight it; rather we should welcome it so as to transform and transcend it by correcting and educating it within ourselves, on the levels of our conscience, memories, thoughts, emotions, and behavior that are the root cause of the blockages, and contrary to harmony and natural balance.

⊕ Revelation of which memories, ways of thinking, loving, and behaving need to be rectified. Understanding the evolutive role of illness and integration of the teaching it offers. Reflection on our lifestyle and re-evaluation of our values and priorities. Awareness that an illness does not mean the person is less evolved, but rather that illness represents a transitory stage, a major initiation which, even if it involves the death of the physical body, allows a great cleansing and reprogramming process of the person's memories, which will have a positive effect in his next life. Gratitude, acknowledgement and a new, or renewed, appreciation of the sacred gift of life. Awareness of various aspects allowing deep transformation. Development of qualities and essential capacities such as patience, detachment, letting go, interiorization, introspection, meditation, symbolic analysis, the activation of the self-healing power of the mind and spirit, the will to take care of ourselves or others, the gift of self, mutual help, compassion, and altruism. Discovery of hitherto unsuspected inner resources. Reconnection with the Divine, with God. Development of acceptance, authenticity, humility. Favors renewed closeness among family, friends, and general entourage.

⊖ Impatience, rebellion, anger, non-acceptance, discouragement, dejection, despondency, resignation in the face of illness or great ordeals that shake a person's faith, possibly leading to a rejection of God and an atheistic approach; or, a person who lacks compassion for the sick, who is afraid of illness and contagion. Persistence in considering an illness as injustice or punishment, believing ourselves to be an innocent victim. A plaintive, complaining attitude, depressive, aggressive or disagreeable behavior, which provokes rejection by our entourage. A lack of understanding of the causes as well as refusal to think about them, refusal to consider the illness from its symbolic, resonant aspects, or call into question our lifestyle, values and priorities. Risk or threat of disconnecting, dropping out, fleeing, or, in extreme cases, committing suicide, rather than accepting the suffering, pain, and limitations imposed by an illness. Prejudice against and judgment of the ill. A tendency to interpret illness as a lack of evolution.

ILLUSION

From the Latin *illusio* (illusion, mockery) derived from the verb *illudere* (to play with or mock at), the word illusion indicates a false material or moral appearance which, while making us see things other than they are, seems to play with our senses or our mind. The term is also used as a synonym for chimera, mirage, dream and utopia, and always refers to an erroneous or distorted impression, interpretation, vision or belief, as in an optical illusion, for example.

The definition of illusion is closely linked to that of reality, because what we consider reality is often an illusion, depending on our level of conscience and our capacity to understand the multi-dimensions of existence. Thus illusion is educational and evolutive. As our conscience evolves, as we re-activate Qualities, Virtues and Divine Powers, and recognize and acknowledge our true identity – that we are spiritual beings experimenting matter – we gradually move beyond the various levels and forms of illusion or illusionary realities and learn to live with a more global conscience in a much vaster, multi-dimensional reality. Hence, work on our illusions – our delusions – goes hand in hand with cleansing and transforming the memories we have accumulated during our many incarnations in the world of materiality, which we have ended up considering as the one and only reality there is. Work on our illusions allows us to discover who we really are and helps us free ourselves from the false identities and identifications we have created and maintained in the course of our many different lives. Discovering these, along with their deep influence on the way we behave, constitutes an important step in our evolution.

When we begin to become aware of the illusions in our life, it is important not to judge ourselves harshly, but rather learn to accept the fact that they are the result of our various experimentations and are part of our learning process, our many apprentices, on all levels. The more we evolve, the more our illusions disappear. Knowledge of symbolic language and the Cosmic Laws, the interpretation of dreams as well as the capacity to recognize and de-code signs, coincidences, and synchronicity are indispensible tools if we want to free ourselves from illusions. Analyzing our dreams helps us to make the link between what we consider to be physical, material reality and what we experience on the metaphysical and spiritual levels of our being, in our spirit, soul, mind and feelings. Understanding the correlations that exist between the different dimensions, we are able to make more enlightened choices and lead our lives with a more global, more universal conscience. The process of *dis-illusioning* is a dynamic that takes place in stages, parallel to the awakening of our conscience. Ultimately it leads us to Enlightenment, an illusion-free state of being.

⊕ Awareness that illusion is a temporary state and has an educational role. Conscious use of illusion as a teaching and learning tool. Respect and tolerance when faced with the illusory reality of others who are not ready to change their level of conscience to integrate a universal vision of life, of existence. A capacity to veil access to Knowledge and Truth in order to ensure people's protection and respect their rhythm of evolution. The will to work on ourselves to cleanse our unconscious, to free ourselves of illusions and to live with a more global conscience in a vaster, multi-dimensional reality. Study of symbolic language and the Cosmic Laws, which allows us to decode and understand dreams and signs. A period of revelations, surprising discoveries and mystical experiences. High spiritual studies that re-connect us to Knowledge, lead us to Cosmic

Conscience, and allow us to understand the Divine Plan, which contains everyone's life-plan and learning and evolution program.

⊖ A person who hangs onto his illusions, who refuses to face facts, to *dis-illusion* his conception of life, to open his mind, enlarge his conscience and acknowledge the temporal, educational function of illusion. Fear of looking behind the veil, of encountering memories lodged in our unconscious and recognizing our own distortions, faults and weaknesses that we need to work on and transform. A stubborn attitude. Refusal to admit our ignorance, our lack of knowledge of ourselves, others, and the multiple realities and dimensions of Creation. A tendency to project everything that does not suit us onto others and the exterior world.

IMMIGRATE, IMMIGRATION *(cf. also **Emigration**)*

Immigration represents a change of *egregore* (*cf.* this term), of state of conscience on the collective level. Whenever a person immigrates, he passes from one country's egregore to another to discover therein new parts of himself, a different way of being, of conceiving life, of communicating. It is a complete change on the level of daily routine and habits. Every country has its positive and negative aspects so we have to consider where we are immigrating to, what we are heading toward, and what it represents in its + and its –. Why does a person feel called to leave his native land and immigrate to another country? On the outer level, reasons for immigration may be economic, political, cultural, professional, humanitarian, personal or family reasons. However, on the inner level, the level of our soul and spirit, immigration always corresponds to a new stage of evolution, a new life-program, which leads those concerned to activate new parts of their being, new states of conscience that they wouldn't experience if they stayed in their native land. As a human being evolves, he visits and lives in his inner countries so as to integrate the qualities and virtues of each country, and he gradually becomes a citizen of the Universe who no longer resonates negatively with other cultures and mentalities. Immigration also serves to learn how to adapt, to begin a new life, to become detached from our negative life habits and affective links, and hence re-discover greater liberty.

⊕ A favorable change of life. A new departure. Renewal. An expansion of conscience. A new stage, a new cycle of evolution, which allows us to discover and develop qualities related to a new country. Open-mindedness. Discovery of particular resources and soul-states. Adaptation to a different culture and mentality. Acquisition of global vision and understanding. Development of the conscience of a citizen of the Universe and a capacity to feel good, to feel at home everywhere. Apprenticeship and integration of new cultures, mentalities, and languages, if necessary.

⊖ Adaptation and integration difficulties. Fear of the unknown; afraid to renew our life, to move on, to progress. Nostalgia for the past, difficulty re-building on new foundations. A tendency to take everything for granted, to exploit and abuse the social system of our host country, to let others take charge of us and our responsibilities. Refusal to make any effort to integrate, find our place and shoulder our responsibilities in our new country. A materialistic spirit that immigrates in the hope of becoming materially rich, but who refuses to adapt to the culture and mentality of his new country as well as its language, when necessary. A closed, sectarian, rebellious spirit. Tendency to isolate ourselves. Superiority and inferiority complexes. Resistance to change; or, a tendency to want to force destiny, to insist on immigrating at all costs, even though the signs are unfavorable and there is no synchronicity. According to the context and circumstances, immigration may also indicate the beginning of a difficult evolution program, which will engender a period of hardships, trials and limitations. Dissatisfaction. Dependency. Lacks on the material and affective levels.

IMPRISONMENT *cf. Prison*

INCEST

Incest, from the Latin, *incestus* (impure), is the term used to refer to forbidden sexual relationships between members of the same family. Incest is a violation of the other person's intimacy, extreme lack of love, and abuse of power, which are a response to instinctual impulses and primal needs. Sexual abuse caused by incest is a serious crime because it handicaps, steals, and kills the possibility for the victim to develop love and self-esteem.

Incest is a traumatizing experience, which breaks the seal of purity and trust; those who should have helped, protected, and loved the person betray them and become aggressors instead. It is a crime against the soul and the result of a difficult karma for both the aggressor and the victim. To heal the deep wounds caused by incest, the victim, either concretely or in a dream, must do very intense inner work so as not to rebel. He needs to understand that if a person experiences such a crime, it means that in another life he too committed this very act. To be able to accept and forgive our aggressor, we have to remember the Law of resonance, the Universal principle whereby we reap what we sow, in this life or another.

In a not too distant past, incest was commonplace. Families mostly lived in isolated villages, unable to travel, unable to leave their daily lot and change their lives. Added to a lack of occupation and socializing outside closed, limited perimeters, this proximity led to abuse of power and authority, and activated people's most basic instincts. Children lived in a world where such abuse, despite its destructive, disturbing nature ended up becoming the norm.

However, seeing ourselves abuse or being abused in a dream does not always indicate that we committed such deeds on the concrete level. The dream can bring to light memories related to sexual abuse in other lives that now need to be cleansed and transcended. It can also explain that such forces are under construction within us, and if we do not want to attract incestuous situations sooner or later, it is important to cleanse them. Moreover, the abuse is not necessarily of a sexual nature; every time a person uses his power of authority, his intelligence, or his strength to impose his will on another in order to satisfy his personal, intimate, affective needs, we can speak of abuse. Hence, in a dream, rape or incest may symbolize accumulations of imposing, destructive attitudes and behavior on the affective level. Such a dream would explain that the person has inscribed in his conscience that it is normal to do all in his power to obtain love, attention, tenderness, no matter whether he hurts others or not. Whenever we have been a victim of such abuse, emotionally or sexually, the best way to succeed in accepting the experience is to develop compassion by remembering that one day the abuser will be abused. Always in accordance with the Law of resonance, the aggressor will one day experiment the fact that we cannot get away with mixing, fusing, and confusing the essence of evil and love without causing great suffering.

It happens that victims of sexual abuse feel torn between revolt and guilt, because in some cases, the victims felt pleasure. This pleasure intermingled with fear is extremely perturbing and de-stabilizing. The confusion induced in the victim destroys the mechanism of divine pleasure that is naturally engendered in a healthy love relationship. Thus the karmic cycle is often maintained: in turn the victim abuses a child or another person in order to rediscover this dualistic force of love and violence.

⊕ Cleansing, liberating work on memories of affective, emotional or sexual abuse. Reveals a lack of love, inner wounds, and abuse of power. Awakens discernment, understanding that one day the aggressor will be a victim, that we always reap what we sow, and that at some time or another, in this life or a previous one, the victim was an aggressor. Understanding that Divine Justice is absolute. Forgiveness, clemency, acceptance, and sometimes, activation of human justice to protect ourselves or others.

⊖ Abuse of power, manipulation so as to nourish our basic instincts; or, submission to unhealthy, sexual and affective, emotional needs. Violation of the Principles of Divine Wisdom and Love. Going against the natural order of things. Destroying innocence, candidness, *joie de vivre*, any heartfelt surge of spontaneity, purity, confidence in ourselves and others. *Feeding* on the qualities of a child. Vampirism. Destruction of the most beautiful, learning, developing parts of ourselves or of the other person. Difficulty expressing our desires other than through possession or destruction. A person who remains in the role of victim; a lack of understanding of the Laws of resonance and karma through which Divine Justice manifests Itself. Repressed feelings of guilt, shame, rebellion and anger. Superiority and inferiority complexes. An incapacity to call on the forces of justice and file suit against the aggressor so he can be arrested, tried and sentenced; fear for ourselves; lack of protection and/or protection of others.

INDEX FINGER *cf. Finger*

INDIGO

The color indigo is associated with the frontal chakra, the 3rd eye. It represents spiritual discernment, in-depth understanding, and generally speaking, the activation of the subtle senses and psychic powers (mediumnity), such as clairvoyance, clairaudience, and clairsentience. This color illustrates the power of creative, intuitive thought and its primacy over matter. It is also related to spiritual intelligence, Primary Wisdom and Knowledge, as well as a capacity to discover hidden wisdom. It is composed of blue, the color associated with the throat chakra, communication and the creative power of words, and mauve, the color that symbolizes spirituality. It is also the color chosen to designate new children, *indigo children*, because they often manifest the psychic faculties, intuitive intelligence and spiritual wisdom that characterizes the vibration of indigo and the potential of the 6th chakra.

⊕ Activation of the subtle senses. Awakening of the gifts of clairvoyance, clairaudience and clairsentience. Psychic powers (mediumnity). Ability to perceive, feel, and sense deeply in the invisible levels, to see and understand what has been occulted, hidden. Global, multi-dimensional perception and understanding. Expansive intelligence. Discernment. Powerful, intuitive mind and spirit. Development of a spiritual, universal vision of life. Elevation of conscience. Revelatory meditation.

⊖ A person who uses his psychic powers (mediumnity) with impure intentions, without any spiritual conscience, only so as to be recognized and acknowledged, to impress or dominate others, out of a need for gratitude; or, to attain material goals. Lack of discernment and opening regarding spirituality and mediumnity. An intense desire for material possessions. Hyperactive behavior to hide or flee from problems. Deep blockages on the level of the 3rd eye, the 6th chakra. Badly oriented sensitive, intuitive intelligence. Black magic. An incapacity to raise our conscience, to attain a spiritual, multi-dimensional vision. Atheism. Confusion of the mind and spirit. Mental illness.

INFERIORITY

The state of that which is inferior, of lesser rank, strength, power, value or merit. Whenever there is a feeling or complex of inferiority, the term refers to the difficult, sometimes painful impression of being inferior to the norm, of being of less worth than others, or of not corresponding to a desired ideal, to an idealized image. Feeling inferior indicates that we have a pejorative image of ourselves. This is caused by the presence of conscious or unconscious memories of experiences where we felt rebuffed, debased, where we felt we didn't measure up, we didn't fulfill our own or others' expectations. It also comes from a tendency to compare ourselves to others and to judge ourselves according to criteria and values defined by society, by public opinion. It is important to understand that feelings of inferiority and superiority always go hand in hand, not only on the outside but also on the inside, within ourselves. That is why the Law of resonance is applicable at all times, in all circumstances, and on all levels. Hence, a person who has an inferiority complex, bears within, in his unconscious, memories of past experiences, not necessarily in this life, where he had feelings and attitudes of superiority that incited him to judge, criticize, diminish and ridicule others. Therefore, in accordance with the Law of resonance, one day, an accumulation of memories of this kind will lead the person to experience what he subjected others to; one day he too experiences what it is like to feel inferior. This allows him to rectify his attitude and integrate the lesson learned from his own experience.

Whether an experience is lived in a dream or in concrete reality, it is important to always refer back to ourselves, to consider all of the aspects and elements shown as parts of ourselves. It is important to know and be able to accept that we are never a victim without first being an aggressor, in this life or another. It is by considering what we experience in the light of Cosmic Laws that we can better understand our Life-Program as well as the resonance we may have with people and situations encountered either in our dreams or in our daily life. It doesn't matter if our experiences occur in a dream or concrete reality; what is important is that, from all points of view, they reveal who we really are. It is also useful to know that in the reality of a dream, an inferiority complex can be manifested through symbols that are smaller than usual, or through dwarfism, whereas feelings of superiority are shown when objects or people appear bigger than normal, even gigantic, depending on the degree of the distortion in question.

⊕ Improvement of self-esteem and respect for ourselves and others. Re-discovery of self-confidence. The end of comparison, of underestimating, criticizing, and judging ourselves and others. A capacity to accept difference and appreciate everyone as they are. Awareness of the interdependence of feelings of inferiority and superiority. Conscious work on ourselves to transform the memories, forces, and distorted needs that engender such feelings. A global, integral vision of ourselves and life in general. Acceptance of our Life-Plan with all it comprises, benefits and ordeals, knowing that it was conceived to favor our evolution while getting us to work on our faults and weaknesses, to repair our errors and misactions (*cf.* this term), as well as to settle our karmic debts.

⊖ A tendency to compare ourselves to others and to analyze and evaluate ourselves according to outer criteria. Undermining, diminishing, humiliating criticism and judgment. Self-contempt and scorn. Rejection. Enslavement and submission to what isn't right. Pessimism. Mistrust. Despair. Dropping out, giving up, abandonment. A feeling of uselessness. Jealousy and envy. An incapacity to acknowledge our own and others' true worth and to appreciate life. Ignorance of the Law of resonance that allows us to understand that behind every feeling of inferiority hides a feeling of superiority.

INFIDELITY

Infidelity designates a state of conscience of someone who is not faithful, who does not keep his word, his promise, or fulfill his commitments. Whether in thought or in deed, we can be unfaithful to people, values and principles.

In a dream, it is commonplace to see ourselves in love with a person who is not our spouse. It may be someone we know, such as an ex-spouse, a friend or someone else, or it may be someone we don't know. We can also see ourselves married to someone other than our present spouse or life-partner. To understand whether it really is a question of infidelity, which can be associated with a fantasized desire or reveal a lack, it is important to ask ourselves if, in the dream, we are conscious of betraying our spouse. If our real spouse is not present in the dream in any form, it is not a question of infidelity. In such a case, the dream indicates fusion with another part of ourselves, represented by the dream spouse or partner. In such cases, the dream is an indication and a precious explanation of our soul-states and the kind of positive or negative affective energy, that we are experiencing or developing on the inner, affective level. If, however, we desire another person and our real spouse or partner is present in the dream, it is clear that we are being put in touch with memories and forces of infidelity. This kind of dream does not necessarily mean that these forces have already manifested concretely, but it is a sign that they could be building up in the dreamer's unconscious. If we don't work on these forces of infidelity, which destroy life and happiness, they will continue to develop until they bring forth desires that could lead to infidelity on the physical level.

It is not necessary to be in a conjugal (couple) relationship to bear infidelity within ourselves. This kind of energy can also dwell in a person who is single. This is true, for example, for someone who fantasizes about a person who is already involved in a love relationship. Desiring a man or woman who is not free indicates that, within ourselves, we bear memories of infidelity and betrayal. The origin of such desire is to be found in the multiple needs that cause us, and others, suffering, on either the concrete level or on a more subtle level. Infidelity is a very powerful energy and it is vital not to nourish it, either within ourselves or on the outside. When we feel attracted to someone who is already in a couple, we need to work on ourselves to transform the conscious and unconscious impulses and forces that incite infidelity, and even more so whenever that person has children. It is important to know that when we destroy the life, happiness and stability of a family, we create karmas of infidelity and unhappiness for ourselves that we will have to pay back and transform sooner or later. We too will attract difficult love relationships with unfaithful partners. If our desire leads us to someone in a childless couple, we need to know that, as a general rule, we have no right to break up a union, because it is never a coincidence that those two people are together. It is always a learning-, repairing-, or experimentation- love program, in accordance with the Laws of resonance and karma.

When a person is unfaithful, even in his thoughts, he continues to secretly nourish destructive forces, and therefore diminishes the possibilities of experiencing a stable love relationship and knowing true happiness. When someone acts incorrectly and keeps flirting to nourish himself on seduction and thoughts or emotions of infidelity, he is playing with dangerous fire. In the beginning, it seems harmless, but by continuing to feed this kind of energy, the person becomes obsessed with his desire and is soon incapable of putting a stop to the devouring fire of passion that burns inside him.

The best way to become immune to infidelity is not to envy other people's happiness or lives. Wisdom means building our own happiness, step by step, day by day. And if we are in an unhappy relationship, it is important to ask Up Above for dreams and signs to know if it is right to end it. Otherwise, we risk not finishing the apprenticeship, the learning experience planned as part of our Life Program with our spouse, and, consequently, having to continue it in the future by attracting the same kind of person.

If a dream can reveal to us our infidelity to our spouse, it can also show us our infidelity to Divine Laws and Principles. For instance we could dream about neglecting our family for work. In such a dream we could see ourselves spending more time on our mobile phone with people who are far away rather than being available at home for our spouse and children. Focused on our ambitions and selfish, ego-based desires, we'd forget what is right and gradually destroy the beautiful, loving relationships we have with our loved ones. Thus isolated in our own, personal world, we'd pay more attention to material values and concepts rather than the Qualities and Virtues that go hand and hand with Divine Laws and Principles.

⊕ Awareness and reparation of memories of infidelity. Apprenticeship of fidelity and loyalty to Divine Principles. Understanding that we reap what we sow.

⊖ Problems in a love relationship, lack of sexuality, of intimacy in the couple. Lack of love and affection, emotional dependencies.

Multiple or obsessive desires. Lack of morality. False virtue. Deceiving appearances. Inconstancy. A person who takes love for granted. Problems of infidelity, or memories and forces that engender multiple relationship difficulties. Difficulty to truly commit, to honor our promises and keep our word; or, a person who doesn't care enough about his love relationship, doesn't take good enough care of his spouse or partner. Treachery, jealousy. Two-timing, double-dealing, duplicity. Loss of confidence and trust in the other person.

INHERITANCE, HERITAGE

On the physical level, an inheritance represents the goods and possessions left by a deceased person and transmitted to his successor/s. On the cultural and historical levels, it is the heritage left by civilizations and ancient eras of evolution. On the symbolic level, it designates a state of conscience related to the gift of ourselves, to the wish to transmit the fruits of our efforts, of our work, to one or several people of our choice so as to help them develop and prosper on all levels. It is a privilege, an honor, an act of trust and love.

Receiving an inheritance in a dream announces that the dreamer will receive help/support on the material, human, emotional, conceptual, or spiritual level. We need to analyze all of the elements and ambiances in the dream to understand which level the inheritance is situated on.

We can also receive an inheritance of negative aspects, namely weaknesses, debts, etc. In the medical world, negative inheritance refers to hereditary diseases passed down through generations of people from their ancestors. Symbolically, this means that a person who is affected by this type of disease has memories that resonate on a certain level with the negative behavior that has engendered this disease, which is also why he has incarnated in this family.

⊕ A person who deserves providential aid and support, and who receives resources to continue his evolution. A feeling of gratitude, acknowledgement, respect and Divine grace. Transcendence of negative inheritance through inner work on the memories that have attracted this situation.

⊖ Not receiving an inheritance we expected, or being deprived of it through illicit means, intrigues and scheming indicates that we reap what we sowed in this life or in past lives. It is one way that the evil, wrong, hurt we committed in the past toward one or more people can manifest itself; or, an indication that we have already used resources selfishly and unjustly, without any gratitude or acknowledgement, but just taking them for granted. Use of an inheritance to repeat distorted behavior and acts. Memories to be worked on related to greed, avidity, malevolence, envy, conspiracy, betrayal, theft, energy vampirism, desire for power, domination. Refusal or anger at having received a negative inheritance through a lack of understanding of the Law of resonance.

INSECT

Generally speaking insects belong to the animal world of instinctive vital energy and consequently represent aspects of our most basic, primary needs. They represent the occasional dispersal of our needs; or, a person with multiple, hyperactive energy related to little needs that can become obsessive and compulsive. The behavior and living environment of the insect in question (air/thoughts, water/emotions, earth/action, underground/the subconscious and the unconscious) help us determine more precisely what aspects of our instinctual nature they symbolize. Insects are part of the ecosystem and they contribute to its natural balance. They serve life in many ways by transforming, shaping, working, and recycling various components of the environment. In order for their presence in a dream or in concrete reality to be positive, they mustn't be invasive or threatening, or produce harmful or destructive effects. Their action must correspond to the principle of the harmonious cohabitation of large and small, generating good on all levels.

⊕ Awareness of certain aspects of vital energy related to instincts and primary needs. Mastery of the tendency to dispersal, hyperactivity, and obsession with our little needs. A capacity to activate, transform, and recycle manifestations of life. Participation in the harmony of ecosystems. Transcendence of instincts and of small needs that can become invasive and destructive. Understanding that a tiny threatening force or need can become a danger if we allow it to multiply.

⊖ Scattering, dissipation and dispersal of instinctual vital energy. Insidious, invasive, threatening manifestation of little primary needs. A lack of vigilance which allows a dangerous multiplication of little negative forces. Loss of control and an incapacity to master instinctive needs. Invasion and massive destruction of resources and vital energy. Bearer of illness. A lack of understanding that a tiny little threatening force can become a serious danger.

INSOMNIA

Insomnia is the inability to get enough restorative sleep (*cf. also* this term). It indicates that forces that are too emissive and hyperactive prevent the body and mind from finding rest. It often manifests when a person is hyperactive, over preoccupied with his work; or, when a problem, ordeal or illness triggers a state of shock, fear, anxiety and insecurity. Insomnia reveals the presence of forces and memories that create an imbalance, a dysfunction. It is not enough to take sleeping pills to settle the problem; on the contrary, it is important to discover its true cause and work on it so we can always sleep well, without having to take any forms of medication.

Periods of insomnia may also manifest during a spiritual path while we are working intensely on ourselves; in this case, we should see this time as a period of meditation, of interiorization and reflection on our life. Deep reflection, becoming aware of many aspects, crucial choices, and important decisions to be made can keep us awake at night. In such cases, sleepless nights are often very useful and beneficial, because, in the dark, in the calm of nocturnal inactivity, we are generally more receptive to our inner voice, to intuition, messages and advice from Divine Intelligence, from God, and from the superior Self.

⊕ Reveals the necessity to clean up certain areas of our lives, to work on unconscious memories. Helps to develop intuition, inner listening, intellectual lucidity, discernment and mastery of our mental power. Reinforces our capacity to accept and adapt in difficult situations. An opportunity to come to terms with solitude, darkness, silence and the calm of night, as well as to practice meditation, relaxation, conscious breathing, reflection, deep analysis, prayer and connection with Up Above.

⊖ Excessive emissivity. Hyperactivity in matter, or awakening of negative memories related to past actions. Need to remain in control, profound insecurities. Difficulty letting go. Inability to relax, go within, restore, renew, and take care of ourselves. Extreme fatigue, exhaustion. Great tensions and insecurities due to either an excess or lack of work. Emotional, affective problems, grief, sorrow. Inner agitation. Irritability. Annoyance. Impatience. Bad mood. Anxiety. A lack of spirituality and connection with Up Above, with God. Someone who doesn't meditate, doesn't seek to understand.

INTERNET

The Internet is a worldwide computer network that renders various services accessible to the public using the IP (internet protocol) communication protocol; i.e. in accordance with a specific set of usage rules for a particular type of communication. Its technical architecture, based on a hierarchy of networks, has led to its being called *the network of all networks.* It is linked to computer and information technology, which symbolically represent the programming of our conscience, the memories of our soul (all the data recorded therein over our multiple lives), as well as a capacity to communicate, send and receive messages and information on all levels. The way we use this network in the outer world, both on a professional and personal level, reveals how we deal with the knowledge and data contained in our personal inner computer, in our inner world. In other words, with what state of mind and conscience we seek, activate, analyze, transform, cleanse and share experiences and our potential.

On the physical level, the Internet represents the material, ideological, conceptual aspect of access to the information and knowledge earthly humanity disposes of at the present time. On the metaphysical, symbolic level, we can compare the world of dreams and the parallel worlds to an immense multidimensional Internet, or *Skynet,* in which we can communicate, learn, travel, and live. In this regard, the notions of God, the Creator, or the Original Source, refer to a Superior Intelligence that manages the whole of Creation like an immense Living Computer, in which each element that has been created has its own usefulness, and every living creature has its own evolution program with pre-established perimeters and various stages which are set in motion at opportune moments. Hence, the existence of the Internet and information technology in the physical world can help us better understand how Up Above, Divine, Cosmic Intelligence and Universal Conscience, how God works.

The Internet can also be considered as a *Universal Server*, which offers us its tremendous possibilities so that we can connect our personal computer – symbolically, our memories, our intelligence, our soul, mind, spirit and conscience – to other people's computers in order to have access to information on all levels and in all dimensions. The observation and symbolic interpretation of the Internet in concrete reality, its creation, development, functions, workings and evolution, show us man's capacity to materialize and share his ideas, his potential and his creative powers. Thus, the very complex, vast world of the Internet reflects the complexity and vastness of our inner world. Our inner world is revealed to us through our dreams, which give us access to parallel realities as well as to the Universal Library (Daath). One day, by gradually achieving his full, multidimensional potential, man will surpass everything that he now knows; not only will he be able to travel and *surf* on the Internet, but he will also consciously explore the multi-dimensions on *Skynet*.

⊕ A capacity to communicate and carry out research in concrete reality as well as in the parallel worlds of our conscience. Helps us find the information we need to make the best decisions and to materialize our lives in general. Favors wide-scale, worldwide, personal and collective exchanges. Facilitates large-scale expansion. Introduces us to the function of multi-dimensions. Allows us to reach deep understanding of the dynamics of the action and creative power of the mind and spirit on the individual and collective levels. Good discernment and non-invasion when confronted with an overabundance of information.

⊖ Problems regarding the capacity to communicate and do research both in concrete reality and in the parallel worlds of our conscience. Difficulty connecting with others, and travelling in our conscience. Seeking and using information for personal, selfish ends, in order to satisfy egotistical ambitions and boorish, coarse desires; or, with a view to obtaining a certain prestige, acknowledgement and recognition. The risk of retreating into the illusions of a virtual universe, creating a fictional life and a false image of ourselves and others. Badly used, the Internet can create serious discrepancies between real, concrete life and virtual life online. Escapism, fleeing into the possibilities offered on the Internet to satisfy our needs as well as lacks on the affective, emotional and social levels. Multiple dependencies, erroneous knowledge and false information. Feelings of superiority and inferiority. Manipulation of the masses and abuse of power *via* messages diffused on the Internet. Transmission of erroneous, superficial information, or information from a doubtful source. Information overload. A lack of discernment, wisdom and scruples when using this tool. A limited mind that lacks the will to overcome and surpass its limits.

INTERNSHIP

An internship is a training period of apprenticeship, of work experience, that offers the opportunity to improve, perfect and renew our knowledge. In certain professions, an internship is required to acquire practical knowledge.

In a dream, doing an internship indicates a period of evolution, an apprenticeship, a learning period to know ourselves better and to become a better person. The field of internship indicates the area we need to pay attention to, knowing that training on the physical level always corresponds to a global dynamic on the metaphysical level, whether we are aware of it or not. It is good to bear in mind that improvement, the development of our abilities, gifts and talents in concrete reality, is fundamentally based on the development of Qualities, Virtues and Divine Powers, which are the weaving threads of our existence here on Earth. Also, an apprenticeship that is lacking in love and wisdom leads to destruction rather than construction.

⊕ A period of practical studies, apprenticeship, training, evolution and improvement on all levels. Someone seeking self-improvement. Awareness of the fact that every apprenticeship is founded on the development of Qualities, Virtues and Divine Powers, which we learn to use in the right way. Exploration of a new field of competence. Love of learning. Receptivity, humility. Someone who learns and teaches at the same time, who has a good capacity to receive and transmit Knowledge in different ways.

⊖ Problems related to the capacity to learn, to continue our personal and/or professional evolution, refusal to improve ourselves, to perfect ourselves on all levels. Restraint and blockages regarding learning, a feeling of being obliged, pushed, forced to learn, to renew ourselves, to evolve. A lack of confidence in ourselves, in our capacity to receive and transmit Knowledge. Unhealthy perfectionism, a tendency to take everything literally. An imbalanced lifestyle, over focused on studies with the aim of acquiring notoriety, and eventually becoming rich. A need to boast, a feeling of superiority as regards others.

INTERSECTION *cf. Crossroads*

INTERVIEW

An interview is an encounter agreed upon by two or more people to exchange on a specific subject. It may refer to a journalist interviewing a well-known person (e.g. a writer, artist, athlete, scientist, inventor, politician, mayor, pop star, etc.) with the aim of publishing his replies in the media. It also refers to a job interview between an employer and a potential employee. An interview serves to discover the opinions, points of view, or lifestyle of a public figure; or, the qualities and skills of a candidate for a job.

One of the main, subtle purposes of an interview is to set an example, to share innovative ideas, to introduce new concepts that will act on the collective conscience and help toward opening and preparing a new path. During an interview, the responsibility of those involved is multiplied because they are observed and imitated by a lot of people, who may take their ideas, reflections, attitudes and behavior as an inspiring example that will influence them, mostly without their being aware of it. In a job interview, it is important to make the candidate feel at ease so as to discover whether both the timing (for all concerned) and the candidate are right for the position.

Symbolically, an interview represents a state of conscience that indicates the will to communicate, to know ourselves better, or to deepen a specific aspect of ourselves in a particular field. In negotiation dynamics, or in a context requiring learning and diplomacy, it includes the notion of an exchange of information among several parts of ourselves. Provided we know how to *read* deeply, the information divulged in an interview may contribute toward important awareness. It may help us form an opinion, develop deeper understanding and knowledge of a situation, and help us evolve; or, it may help a person come to a decision as to the suitability of a candidate for a job that will eventually contribute toward changing his destiny, his life.

When we attend or take part in an interview in a dream, it means that we are questioning ourselves on certain aspects related to renown, celebrity, the subject discussed, or work. It is important to analyze the attitude, behavior and general energy emanated by both the interviewer and the interviewee, because both reveal positive and negative facets of ourselves. Interviewing a famous person or public figure indicates that we grant importance to what he represents, so we are influenced by him on the individual and collective levels. Such a dream shows us how we present ourselves in public, the aspects of ourselves that we highlight or display (showcase), how we live our own renown, our own glory. A symbolic analysis of the positive or negative image we have of the people present at the interview allows us to discover ourselves. Hence, by studying the people involved in an interview and its subject matter, we can better understand what is going on or developing within ourselves.

⊕ Great capacity to communicate on the social level, to offer a message of public interest. Source of information and inspiration favoring individual and collective evolution. Positive influence *via* exchanges and sharing personal or collective experiences. Beautiful inner and outer communication. Transparency. Courage and the humility to publicly admit our weaknesses, our errors, which allows us to unblock entangled situations, to rectify misunderstandings. The will to understand life, events, the paths and destinies of people who influence public opinion and who mark the values of an era. Ability to focus on the essential, to ask the right questions, at the right time. Help toward discovering hidden aspects, solving enigmas, finding answers, bringing out the truth. Authenticity. Social conscience. A collective sense of responsibility. Global vision. Perspicacious questions. An analytical mind, capable of synthesis. Discernment. Sense of listening. Balance between receptivity and emissivity. At ease in public. Capacity to remain centered and calm in situations of collective diffusion, or under public pressure. A well-prepared person who knows his subject well and who does not let himself be influenced, confused, or manipulated. Eloquence, the art of speaking without hurting or wounding anyone, harmonious exchanges, ability to assert our values without imposing them, ability to converse with wisdom. Charisma. Natural renown. Strength of character. Manifestation of qualities, exemplary attitudes and behavior. Skilled in questioning or answering questions while remaining completely authentic. Ability of both interviewer and interviewee to perceive the true intentions of the other person, to sense, on all levels, the positive or negative potential of the person or job, and to give appropriate answers, and to make right, wise decisions.

⊖ Communication difficulties on the collective, social level. Hurtful language. Verbal sparring. Useless, endless arguing. Sterile conversion, gossip. Lack of inspiration and discernment. Incapacity to articulate our ideas, ask clear questions, give precise answers. Superficial communication. Shallow, empty messages. Contributing toward manipulating and negatively influencing public opinion. Forcing to be right. Seeking to hide our game, our ill-willed intentions. Diffusion of erroneous messages, inverted principles, negative influences. Tendency to let ourselves be taken in by glory, to encourage harmful, prejudicial values, attitudes and behavior. Difficulty coping with social pressure, with other people's opinions of us, difficulty facing adversity and de-stabilizing questions. Lack of authenticity, transparency. Indiscretion. Meddling in people's personal lives. Intrusive behavior that *feeds* on other people's intimacy. Mockery. Judgment. Criticism. Problems with receptivity and emissivity. Impatience. Lack of understanding in exchanges.

INTIMACY

Intimacy represents a state of conscience related to our inner world, our soul, our deep affective relationship with ourselves, our spouse, child, or any other trusted person close to us. Intimacy also refers to our body, our sexual life, our creative, sacred vital energy that we use and unveil in right, correct circumstances. The way in which we live our intimacy reveals our capacity to restore and renew ourselves, to go within and interiorize, to respect ourselves and others. A well-lived, respected, protected intimacy is essential for our personal, family and social equilibrium.

⊕ Moments of affective presence with ourselves, our spouse, child, or a person we are close to, in healthy, right conditions. A capacity to go within and interiorize, to restore and renew ourselves, to cleanse, purify and take care of ourselves, as well as to help others do likewise. Harmonious sharing of vital, sexual energy with discretion, respect and a sense of the sacred. Mastery of instincts, of excessive sexual impulses, emotional overflow and affective needs. Manifestation of noble feelings and sentiments, authenticity. Experience of divine pleasures in a calm, pleasant atmosphere. Awareness that we ourselves and the other person come from the same Source. A stable, well-balanced person, who radiates a tranquil, reassuring force that inspires confidence, security and protection.

⊖ May indicate a superficial or overly extrovert person, who does not have a private, intimate life, who doesn't know how to go within and interiorize to restore, take care of and renew himself; or, someone who tends to isolate himself, to close himself off from others, to limit and diminish himself. A tendency to lose ourselves in a social life, to become dispersed and scattered in worldly pleasures. Over-consumption of activities and social outings, which contribute to the development of all sorts of dependencies. Excessive fusion with the ambiances and energies emanated by people and places. Energy vampirism. A lack of understanding that intimacy is a natural aspect of life that allows us to relate to and fuse our inner and outer worlds, interiority and exteriority. Affective manipulation through seduction, indifference and inaccessibility. A lack of respect for ourselves and others. Merely physical sexuality without any intimacy. Fear of intimacy with ourselves and another person. May indicate the presence of memories of rape, incest, or other trauma suffered on the affective, intimate levels. A person imprisoned in aggressor-victim dynamics. An intimate life marked by unhealthy, perverse power games.

ISLAND

An island is a symbol of refuge, of retreat from the outer world, a search for solitude, renewal and replenishment. As a piece of land surrounded by a lot of water, from a positive point of view, it represents emotional intensity and regenerating contact with water, i.e. emotions. From a negative point of view, when we retire to an island all alone, it indicates a tendency to flee emotions and action; or, a desire for intense emotions and superficial renewal and replenishment through sensual pleasures, as is often the case when we spend vacations on very popular sland resorts.

⊕ Tranquility. Interiorization. Reflection. Introspection. Self-questioning, soul-searching, analyzing our life. Developing awareness. Work on ourselves. Rest, renewal and replenishment. Refocusing and restoring emotional balance. Well-being, inner harmony and peace. Inspiration. New departure. Refuge for survivors of emotional shipwrecks.

⊖ Isolation. Escapism, fleeing reality. Refusal to face our responsibilities. Emotional wounds. Bitterness. Drowning in our memories and negative emotions. Inertia. Imprisoned in illusion. Locked in a golden cage. Limited conscience and vision. Inability to call our life into question, to detach ourselves from the past, to understand the importance of work on ourselves. A state of discrepancy, of being out of phase with others. A feeling of being lost, shipwrecked. Existential limitation.

J

JEALOUSY

Jealousy represents a state of conscience of envy, dissatisfaction, where personal needs are mixed up with an obsessive attitude and abusive use of power. It is related to memories of lack, loss, deceit, lack of success, vain efforts to succeed. Leading to instability and extreme, tumultuous emotions, jealousy represents great suffering for the soul. It is a distorted force that seeks to control, possess and bind, and it engenders a great number of disputes and conflicting situations that may lead to crime. It is therefore vitally important to consciously work on transforming the forces and memories that trigger discontentment, envy, and jealousy.

⊕ Awareness that jealousy is related to memories of lack in this or other lives; that the key to setting ourselves free from it consists in working on ourselves and trusting God, trusting the Life-Plan Cosmic Intelligence has arranged for our evolution. Development of detachment and unconditional love. Integration of the deep meaning of liberty and Divine Justice. Understanding that we reap what we sow, but also that we can work on our negative memories, transform them, and hence reprogram our unconscious.

⊖ Deep dissatisfaction regarding our life-program, our destiny. A person tortured by possessiveness, multiple desires, an imperative need to succeed, who seeks to control everything. A period of obsessive envy. Multiple fears. Manipulative behavior. An unhealthy, sterile attitude. Mistrust through a lack of understanding of Divine Justice and the Law of karma. An incapacity to let go and advance in life in a healthy way. Refusal to recognize the erroneous behavior and errors made in the past, and to do our best to repair them. Selfish, egotistical attitude. A tendency to want to force destiny. A limited, materialistic mind and attitude, lacking spiritual elevation. Problems stemming from other lives, difficult memories and deceit in relationships. A person who does not refer back to himself, who doesn't apply the Law of resonance when he feels annoyed, perturbed, or upset.

JEWELRY

Object(s) of personal, body adornment, which can be worn for symbolic, decorative or superficial reasons. Jewelry also represents allegiance, membership of a group, a way of thinking and living, on both the conscious and unconscious levels. Knowledge of the symbolic meaning of jewelry in general, and a more detailed analysis of a specific piece of jewelry, allows us to detect the state of conscience, the motivations, deep intentions and hidden aspects of the person who has chosen to wear it.

⊕ Symbol of identification, of wealth, protection, loyalty and fidelity to something or someone that is important to us, allegiance to a cause or noble, elevated, universal principle.

⊖ Symbol displaying attachment to matter, false values and appearances. A need to be seen, to show off and display material wealth, a fixation on outer beauty, avidity. Feelings of superiority, superficiality, waste, prey to the illusion of matter. A person who wears a lot of jewelry at the same time, or who wears very large pieces of jewelry, reveals a materialistic, arrogant and greedy mindset.

JOURNALIST

A journalist is a person who relates facts, transmits the news so as to inform people collectively. His work has a major impact since it influences thoughts, emotions, and actions on a collective scale. Consequently a journalist has great responsibility. He has to be well-documented and informed, do research on the subject presented, understand it in depth, and come to a clear, objective synthesis. He symbolizes that aspect of ourselves that transmits information rigorously and accurately. A good journalist needs to be receptive, listen well, and have good global understanding that goes beyond social prejudice, in order to inform the public as faithfully and truthfully as possible.

⊕ A person who seeks the truth, knowledge, who diffuses and spreads knowledge on a very wide scale, with the intention of serving and helping the collectivity toward an in-depth understanding of the world. Positive influence on people's ways of thinking, as well as on their emotions and actions. Represents a level of conscience regarding concern for humanity, guardian of democracy, the law, and freedom of expression. A protective spirit that loves what is right. At ease with communication, easy eloquence, a synthesizing spirit. A sense of responsibilities, commitment, duty, objectivity, impartiality. A logical, well-organized, open-minded person.

⊖ Someone who exercises the profession of journalism merely for recognition and acknowledgement, notoriety and prestige; or, out of a thirst for sensationalism. A selfish, self-centered, arrogant, extremist attitude. Poor use of information. A lack of depth, seriousness, integrity, honesty, global vision, humanism. Destructive criticism, media manipulation, deliberate misinformation, gossip. Generator of conflict. Abuse of power, calumny, bribery, destruction of a person's reputation, and/or of his, and others' private and professional life, through the widespread diffusion of false, malevolent, superficial information. Exaggeration or minimalization of facts. Prejudice, a lack of objectivity, rigor, structure, and a spirit of synthesis. Exerting a negative influence on collective thoughts and emotions. Serving unjust, wrong, dishonest people or causes. A lack of understanding of the educational nature of evil, wrong-doing, what hurts, and of the necessity to apply Hidden Wisdom in certain cases or situations. Fear of revealing facts, truths; or, a tendency to deform them.

JUICE

As a liquid, juice refers to a person's emotional dynamics. It also possesses nutritional, restorative qualities. Hence, healthy juice(s) represent emotions that bring us energy, nutrients, vitamins, and can help regenerate us. Its taste, generally naturally sweet, confers on it a stimulating, vivifying effect. It is usually made from fruit or vegetables, which directly associate juice with the symbolism of these foods, just as its color reveals data that helps us better understand its deep symbolic meaning. When also used to heal or improve a physical deficiency, problem, or illness, it represents an emotional capacity to heal, console, and regain well-being.

⊕ An energizing, vitalizing, nourishing stimulant on the emotional, sentimental level. A nutritional, vitamin, energy stimulant symbolizing emotional health and well-being. Conscious choice of the juice we drink or offer others, knowing that it reflects the way we nourish ourselves individually and collectively on the emotional, affective, sentimental level. Understanding that quality is more important than quantity, on both the concrete level (juice), and on the metaphysical level (emotions). The willpower to change our food habits and to buy, drink, and produce healthy, natural juices that are good for our health and do not harm the environment.

⊖ Difficulty finding and producing regenerating, revitalizing, nourishing energies on the emotional, sentimental level. Seeking artificial, unhealthy, emotional stimulation to compensate an inner lack. Affective, emotional dependency. Ignorance of the link between the liquids we consume and the emotional, affective, sentimental level; consuming poor quality juice and other drinks indicates that we maintain similar poor quality emotions; or, that we don't allow ourselves good quality juice, because, consciously or unconsciously, we don't believe we deserve better. A mental attitude that cultivates affective, emotional, sentimental, nutritional, and relational poverty. Production and consumption of artificial juice, containing substances that are harmful to our health and environment (e.g. artificial flavoring and coloring, dangerous sweeteners, harmful synthetic vitamins, etc.); or, poor food combinations, which indicate that the person nourishes his emotional health and well-being in a superficial, unhealthy way. An indifferent, negligent attitude regarding the harmful effects that unhealthy juices, with no nutritional value (harmful emotions), have on us, our children, and the collectivity. Conditioned to seek cheap quantity rather than nutritional quality. Lack of information, knowledge, discernment, and wisdom to make wise, informed, well thought out, responsible choices in the way we nourish ourselves emotionally.

JUNCTION *cf. Crossroads*

JUSTICE

Justice is a fundamentally philosophical, judicial and moral virtue whereby people's actions are sanctioned or rewarded according to their merit as regards a legal, moral, or other source of behavioral evaluation. Justice is closely linked to concepts of uprightness, equity, impartiality, and integrity. It rests on the application of a set of laws that ensures respect for everyone's rights and merits. The human concept of justice may differ from one country to another depending on the cultural, political, or religious context.

However, on the cosmic, spiritual levels, the Principle of Justice is absolute and invariably based on Cosmic or Divine Laws, which govern the multiple dimensions of Creation. It is very important to understand how Divine Justice works, because this allows us to accept the different forms of justice on Earth, which reflect the evolution of human conscience.

The manifestation of Divine Justice and the perception of injustice are associated with concepts of grace, karma, forgiveness, and redemption. Hence, an event, incident, act, judgment and/or sentence may seem unfair, unjust, according to human laws, but be right, fair and just in the light of Cosmic Laws, notably the Law of karma and the Law of resonance. Indeed, Divine Justice does not only take into account acts committed in this life, but applies to all of what we have done during the course of our multiple lives.

Consequently, it is always important to consider any given context with global, multi-dimensional vision, even in very serious cases where human justice is corrupt, seems farcical, or illogical, arbitrary, abusive, lacking true founding principles. When confronted with the atrocities that pave the paths of the history of humanity, many people in an ordinary, horizontal conscience have lost faith, turned away from any belief in a Good, Intelligent, Superior, Cosmic Power, turned away from God, considering Him to be unjust, cruel, or inexistent. Needless to say, it is easier to believe in a Good, Just God when we witness an act of Grace, pardon or redemption. However, each time we experience a situation that seems unfair or unjust to us, it is essential to understand the educational role of everything that happens, that manifests in our lives on any level; to remind ourselves that Divine Justice is absolute; to accept that essentially the reason for our going through ordeals is to develop qualities and virtues in their purest form. Sometimes a long journey is required before we learn to consciously apply the Law of resonance in all circumstances, to recognize and acknowledge what we may have subjected others to in this or previous lives, and to decide to no longer act, behave, think in such ways. To integrate the spiritual, multi-dimensional aspect of Justice, we need to understand that when we act unjustly, we exert our free will, but that such a choice automatically leads to negative consequences called karmic debts, which we have to accept responsibility for and settle, either in this life or in a future life, or lives.

Understanding that evil is educational means accepting that we have to reap what we sow. Throughout our spiritual journey, in each life, at every moment, we make choices where positive or negative consequences are inscribed in our memories. If we sow and grow evil, we will reap evil; if we commit an injustice, we will be subjected to injustice; if we abandon the path of balance, equilibrium, equity, and justice, we engender distortions, misactions (*cf.* this term), errors, misfortunes, unhappy situations, whose lesson we need to learn so as to be able to get out of their grasp, out of the vicious circle they enclose us in. This is how the experience of evil, wrongdoing, human injustice, what hurts, serves as educational terrain, as grounds for an apprenticeship, providing us with learning experiences that allow us to settle our karmic debts and rediscover the right path once again. In this sense, when considered with a multi-dimensional conscience, Divine Justice is absolute, and injustice does not exist.

Whenever we receive dreams related to justice (e.g. when we see ourselves appear in court for a crime we have committed; or, acting as a lawyer, procurer, judge, jury member, or bailiff, soldier, police officer, etc.), it is important to remind ourselves that in principle all of the elements in the dream represent parts of ourselves. Such dreams really should be taken seriously, because they reveal our conscious and unconscious sense of justice; they show us how we apply law and order in our inner world, before the court, judge, and jury of our conscience; in other words, how we judge, call to order, or educate certain aspects of our being; or, how we find excuses for our distortions.

They can also warn us that we have thoughts and emotions that lead us astray, that our intentions are dishonest, or that we are subjected to the influence of negative forces that provoke us to commit unjust or criminal acts. A detailed, symbolic analysis of the dream will help us recognize which aspects, tendencies, and behavior we need to rectify and transform so as to avoid the materialization of the dream situation in our concrete life. It is, of course, always easier and more pleasant to carry out rectification work on the subtle levels of our being – in our thoughts, intentions, emotions – rather than see sometimes interminable ordeals and difficult situations come into being through resonance, possibly upsetting not only our own life, but also that of our loved ones and entourage.

⊕ Understanding that Divine Justice is absolute, that it prevails over human justice, and that we always reap what we sow. Understanding that, consciously or unconsciously, we create our ordeals and injustice. Respect for Divine Law and Order. A capacity to accept the ways and means through which Divine Justice manifests, even when they do not correspond to our expectations. Transcendence of the feeling that we have been subjected to injustice. An ability to accept the fact that evil, wrong-doing, and what hurts is educational. Understanding the meaning of ordeals and the necessity of settling our karmic debts. A capacity to evaluate and judge how right a situation or an act is using global, multi-dimensional vision. Someone who can give others a second chance, and if he receives one himself, knows how to use it well. Love of truth. Rigor. Uprightness, integrity, honesty, sincerity, fairness, equity. Discernment. Right, fair, just judgment. Incorruptibility. A sense of morals, ethics. A capacity to show clemency, compassion, magnanimity, and mercy. The gift of forgiveness, pardon. Recognition, acknowledgement, understanding of and gratitude for acts of Divine Grace.

⊖ Ignorance of the Law of resonance, of the fact that evil is educational, and that we always reap what we sow. Projection onto others of what bothers, annoys, or upsets us; criticism and condemnation of others, and of injustices we observe in the world without referring back to ourselves, without taking into consideration the mirror effect. Puritanism, moralism, rigidity. A tendency to either blame others; or, to feel guilty ourselves. Erroneous understanding of human justice and its laws, ignorance of the fact that they are always governed by Cosmic Intelligence in accordance with our life-plan. Refusal or incapacity to recognize and acknowledge the Principle of Divine Justice and the necessity to respect Laws that ensure order, harmony, and balance throughout the Universe. A lack of understanding of the meaning of ordeals and karma. A tendency to consider ourselves as a victim subjected to injustice. Feelings of rancor, bitterness, anger, rebellion, and revenge. Refusal to call ourselves into question and recognize our own errors, dishonest intentions, unjust attitudes, and a tendency toward fraudulent, criminal behavior. A lack of integrity, rigor, uprightness. Deformed, manipulated truth. A corrupt sense of justice and judgment. Refusal to forgive or to ask for forgiveness. A megalomaniac, tyrannical, dictatorial mind and spirit. Abuse of power.

K

KARMA

A Sanskrit term that means *action, deed, function, work.* It is used in several esoteric traditions and world religions to designate the effects of a committed act or deed, the correlation between cause and consequence, the fate set in motion by our actions, the *baggage or luggage* (*cf.* this term) acquired in our past lives. It is the negative and positive sum of what a person has done, is doing, or will do as he experiments in life in order to evolve. Although the term refers to both positive and negative actions, when we say a person is creating karma for himself by acting in such a way, we generally mean that he is in the process of engendering difficult consequences for himself, and that one day, he will have to pay for what he has done. The *Law of karma*, which says that *we reap what we sow,* is a central concept used to define Divine Justice in many philosophies and religions.

⊕ Understanding the Law of karma and Divine Justice. Analysis and awareness of the causes and consequences of human experimentation in this life and in previous lives. Conscious work to settle karma, to rectify our misactions (*cf.* this term) and liberate our unconscious. Discovery of the evolutive power of good and evil. Seeking and applying Divine Knowledge. Respect for Cosmic Laws and submission to Divine Hierarchy.

⊖ A lack of spiritual knowledge, ignorance of the Law of karma, and a lack of understanding of Divine Justice. Irresponsibility regarding our misactions, refusal to see the correlation between cause and consequence, refusal to accept that we always reap what we sow. Feelings of inferiority, defeatism, negativism, fatalism. Harshness and lack of love for ourselves, seeing only our weaknesses and distortions, our negative karma. An incapacity to recognize signs warning us that a negative action we are about to commit will lead to serious problems. A lack of willpower and determination to take ourselves in hand and assume our responsibilities. Refusal to know and respect Divine Laws.

KEY

A key symbolizes a capacity to have access to resources, to a lifestyle, objects, people, atmospheres and ambiances, etc. It is also a symbol of destiny allowing us to open or lock spaces, usually in order to protect what is there; hence there is the idea of security, exclusivity and privilege in the symbolism of a key. Through its elongated form, it is a symbol of emissivity, activation, materialization and manifestation. Having or receiving a key is a sign of abundance, access to potential or resources that are still dormant or latent. A key can lead to the solution of a problem, to a new step or phase. The *key point* or the *key factor* is the most important, essential point or factor.

⊕ Gives access to spaces where there are beautiful ambiances, resources, knowledge. Opening onto as yet unexplored regions of our conscience. A symbol of intimacy, privilege, destiny, expansion, change, depending on the context. Announces the beginning or end of a particular phase.

⊖ Difficulty having access to resources. Limitation, period of closure, blockage, exclusion. Announces a difficult stage. Loss of privileges and confidence. Discord, disagreement. Restriction, difficulty restoring order, problems with the law. Difficult destiny. Difficulties related to expansion or intimacy.

KISS *cf. Embrace*

KITCHEN

A kitchen is a symbol of preparation of resources for ourselves and others. It is the place where we prepare our nourishment on the physical and emotional levels. It contains the necessary tools and equipment for the transformation of food resources. The kind of food found there, and the way we prepare it, gives an indication of the way we nourish ourselves, the way we look after ourselves, and renew and replenish our vital energy.

⊕ Preparation of healthy, living, well-balanced food for body, mind and soul. Abundant resources and facility to transform them.

Preparation of nourishing, nurturing energy with love, conscience, and devotion. Gratitude and sharing. A sense of sacred ritual in the preparation of meals. Understanding that we become what we eat.

⊖ Problems related to food, or to the way we prepare our physical resources. Exaggerated perfectionism in the preparation of meals; or, indifference and carelessness in matters of nutrition. Food imbalances. Unconscious of the metaphysical and spiritual dimension of food; ignorance of the fact that we become what we eat. Lack of devotion, generosity, and spirit of sharing. Lack of understanding of the sacred meaning of food, and the importance of preparing it with love and gratitude. Non-respect for cycles and stages. Nourishing ourselves on junk- or fast-food, modified, artificial foodstuffs with little or no nutritional value. Difficulty or incapacity to adequately prepare what we need to nourish ourselves and our loved ones, or to renew whatever we need to in order to manifest ourselves.

KITE

A kite represents a state of conscience related to the air, to thoughts on the symbolic level. It indicates an apprenticeship and a capacity to keep thoughts on a high, elevated level and then to master them right down into the world of action and matter as kites are held by a string (or strings) on ground level. A feeling of space and liberty, an abstract dimension emanates from this activity, which gives rise to a feeling of calm, great joy and wonder.

A kite is essentially used as a toy, but it can also serve aerial photography, meteorology, rescue work and location, as well as broadcasting and transmission.

⊕ Apprenticeship and capacity to elevate our thoughts, to lighten up and feel free. Connection with our inner child. Seeking a global vision and understanding of a situation.

⊖ Difficulty elevating our thoughts, our point of view; or, a tendency to over-seek such elevation in order to flee reality. A need to get away from it all, for adventure and conquest to compensate for our frustrations and repression. A feeling of disconnection, of being lost on the thought level. Difficulty seeing the overall picture and understanding the global nature of a situation. Thoughts that are too down-to-earth. *Heavy* mentality or mindset. Intellectual conflicts. A feeling of superiority. Resistance to incarnate and accept our earthly existence.

KNEE

The knee is the joint that allows us to bend our leg. Hence it represents flexibility and suppleness in the way we advance. As it is constituted of three bones, it also concerns our structure and way of constructing our life. Since the kneeling position is often associated with prayer and interiorization, it is also related to the great principles of inner life: submission, acceptance and receptivity. Conscious submission to God, to the Divine Source within us and in all things, results in inner peace, a capacity to accept events in life, and stability in our daily life. It is important to know that in a dream, just as in reality, we shouldn't kneel in submission before another person, even if he holds a high position representing spiritual or earthly power. We should only ever kneel before the Divine, before God.

⊕ Suppleness and flexibility in our structure and in the way we advance and construct ourselves. Submission to what is right. A great capacity of acceptance, adaptation and adjustment.

⊖ Rigidity and lack of inner and outer flexibility. Rebellion, insubordination to what is right; or, submission to what is not right, idolatry. Difficulty adapting, adjusting in action. Non-acceptance, pride. Difficulty remaining upright, difficulty advancing.

KNEEL, TO

Depending on the context in a dream or concrete reality, the act of kneeling represents either a state of prayer, interiorization, receptivity and humility; or, a state of subjection, servility, dejection, or resignation. This symbol may indicate that it is time for us to submit to a situation; or, a tendency of ours to submit to unfair, incorrect people, conditions or terms, to venerate concepts that are detrimental to our evolution, to give in to authority naively or excessively. It may also signify a tendency to give our decisional power to others; to allow ourselves to be dominated; or, to glorify things that should not be glorified.

⊕ A state of prayer, receptivity and submission to Divine Laws and Will. Acceptance of our life-program without rebellion. Receptivity to the messages, signs and information transmitted from Up Above. A capacity to obey Divine Order and Cosmic Intelligence with great humility and deep respect. The end of inner violence and wars caused by insubordination and rebellion. A state of peace, serenity and harmony.

⊖ A tendency to allow ourselves to be dominated by others, by imposing forces that manifest a sense of superiority. Refusal to kneel before the Divine indicates the presence of memories of rebellion and insubordination as well as not understanding the importance of submitting to Divine Laws and Divine Will.

KNIFE

Given its elongated form, a knife is a symbol of emissivity. It represents a state of conscience of power, division, separation, protection in case of danger, and a force of decision, rigor and justice. In a negative context, it may appear as a dangerous, aggressive, sharp, cutting, threatening, or criminal element. Since we use it with our hands, it also relates to the capacity to give and receive, the way we manifest, express our opinions, our choices.

⊕ Right, correct emissivity, and application of justice with love, rigor and wisdom. Feelings of strength, power and protection. The capacity to say *yes* or *no* when giving and receiving, to divide and separate with discernment.

⊖ A sharp, cutting, threatening attitude. Application of justice with severity, harshness, and too much emissivity. Abuse of power. Using threats to impose our point of view. Aggressive separation. Revengeful spirit. Possessiveness. An extremist, dangerous character on the relationship level, and in giving and receiving. Cuts off favorable links. The law of the jungle, survival of the fittest, where might is right.

L

LABYRINTH *cf. Maze*

LACK

A lack represents a state or situation where a necessary, useful, or important element is absent. A lack may be found on the material, emotional, mental, or spiritual levels; e.g. a lack of food, water, love, being listened to, confidence, trust, courage, concentration, vigilance, preparation, patience, wisdom, compassion, joy, etc. Generally speaking, a lack is felt as a feeling of inner emptiness; or, as an outer shortage. The fact of feeling a lack indicates that we haven't yet developed within ourselves the lacking element, quality, strength, or ability; or, the capacity to remedy whatever this lack engenders. Lacks or limiting situations may be experienced following personal, relational, and/or professional failures that were caused by erroneous behavior or choices made in our present or previous lives. It is essential to know that a lack is an invitation to make the effort to search and activate within ourselves whatever will satisfy and fulfill it. Hence, by working on impatience, we develop patience; by transforming our fears, we activate courage; by practicing the art of discretion, we develop our listening skills, etc.

Lack always goes hand in hand with excess. It is a question of balance. Hence a lack of *joie de vivre* indicates an accumulation of sadness, an overly serious character that feels burdened and heavy, having lost its lightheartedness. A lack of space may reveal a tendency to clutter up with useless, superfluous things, to keep relics of the past out of emotional attachment and nostalgia; it may also be the result of an accumulation of all sorts of things just in case they might be needed, which simultaneously reveals a lack of confidence and trust in life. A lack of concentration goes hand in hand with a lack of interiorization, both of which indicate a way of functioning that is excessively exteriorized, too dispersed, over-active on the social, collective level. A lack of confidence shows a tendency to mistrust, which fills the person with insecurity regarding both himself and others.

An experience of lack can also become a source of all sorts of dependencies, or lead a person to excessive consumption in compensation. For example, a lack of love often engenders affective dependencies; a lack of food, an exaggerated accumulation of food reserves.

Lacks offer us the opportunity to recognize and acknowledge the fact that we need to work within ourselves to revive and re-establish the link with our divine nature, to heal our wounds, to *fill up* directly at the Source, instead of seeking to superficially compensate on the outside. It is essential to do an in-depth symbolic, metaphysical analysis of our lacks because they reveal the mechanisms of the way we function, our intentions, our motivations, and our hidden, unconscious memories.

We can also live an experience of lack in dream reality; we may have a dream where we are unable to get to a particular place because we lack the means of transport; or, find ourselves facing a problem and not have the necessary knowledge or competence to solve it. All sorts of situations involving lacks can be shown to us in dreams, and their symbolic analysis leads to important understanding and information about our evolution.

⊕ Allows us to become aware of what we lack, what aspects of ourselves we need to work on to overcome the lacks manifested, and transform what causes them. An opportunity to restore balance and equilibrium to the discrepancies that exist within us. Purification and transcendence of memories marked by experiences of lack. Deep, global understanding that lacks are an invitation to develop our latent potential, as well as the qualities, virtues, and capacities that lie dormant within us.

⊖ A tendency to identify with different lacks, to dramatize them, and submit to them as a victim. A lack of understanding of the mechanisms of behavioral functions and dynamics that create situations and feelings of lack. Ignorance of the Laws that govern balance and equilibrium on all levels of Creation. An incapacity to recognize that a lack always accompanies an excess; that each state of lack reveals a discrepancy, an imbalance, a dysfunction within ourselves, which eventually leads to envy, jealousy, competitiveness, and multiple dependencies. Inner emptiness, unease, ill-being. Refusal to work on ourselves to transform the forces that maintain a lack, that limit our autonomy, evolution, opening and expansion of our conscience. Persistence in wanting to satisfy and fulfill lacks only superficially, on the outside. Flight, escapism into all sorts of illusions.

LAKE

A lake is a stretch of water surrounded by land. On a symbolic level, a lake signifies the emotional world (water) related to matter and physical action (land, earth). When its water and banks are clean and accessible, a lake can become a place for leisure, relaxation, renewal and replenishment in nature, a place suitable for swimming, bathing, water games and sports, etc. Hence, it also symbolizes a capacity to exchange, share, and nourish ourselves on the emotional and social levels.

⊕ A stable, renewing, nourishing emotional world. A capacity to purify ourselves both on the inside and on the outside, to be at ease and in harmony with our feelings and emotions, and to share our emotional riches with others. A conscious use of water and affective, emotional potential. Responsible behavior that respects nature and the environment.

⊖ A disturbed, unstable, polluted, emotional world. Difficulty living, nourishing, purifying, and balancing our affective level. Disrespectful behavior toward nature, water pollution, destruction of aquatic flora and fauna, which represent our emotional and instinctual worlds.

LAMP, LIGHT, A

Thanks to the light (*cf. also* this term) it diffuses, a lamp or manmade light allows us to see better, to better discern a situation on the concrete level. Consequently, on the metaphysical level, a lamp or light is a symbol of light or lighting that helps activate clarity of conscience, understanding, lucidity. A lamp may also help to create a warm, reassuring, elevating ambiance on the conscience level.

⊕ A capacity to enlighten ourselves, to discern better, to see more clearly, to facilitate deep understanding of a situation. Elevating ambiance. A reassuring, comforting, confidence-filled source of energy. Discovery and revelation of what was occulted in the darkness, in the unconscious. Favors global vision, lucidity, and awareness imbued with confidence.

⊖ Faulty, weak, or an absence of lamps or lights may indicate problems and difficulties seeing clearly, understanding, and discerning; on the contrary, an excess of light, clarity, or intensity may be a sign of over-confidence, hyperactivity; or, denote an incapacity to rest, go within and interiorize because afraid to visit our inner world. Artificial, superficial dynamics. A tendency to exaggerate to compensate for lacks or to camouflage our insecurity. An absence of global vision, lucidity, clarity, and knowledge. Obscured conscience, locked up in the darkness of ignorance. Sad, dark, shadowy, lifeless soul-states and ambiances, without natural light. Gloominess, obscurity.

LANDSCAPE

Symbolically speaking, the diversity of landscapes represents our different soul-states, our ways of being and perceiving the external world according to what we are experiencing on the inside. Without realizing, we constantly project ourselves through our way of appreciating or not appreciating a place, environment, surrounding landscape. One person may find a landscape magnificent, whereas another will feel ill-at-ease there. Like everything, the feeling of attraction, well-being, unease or aversion we feel toward a landscape is the result of resonance we have with the different elements comprising it. Hence, if we use symbolic language to analyze its key elements, we can better understand why a landscape affects us in such a way. Moreover, the outer world helps us become aware of our inner landscapes, and, rather than passively submitting to our soul-states (moods), we can live them with more global understanding and an enlightened conscience. Whether it is a case of landscapes seen in concrete reality, represented in paintings, or seen in dreams, the procedure for symbolic analysis is the same. Even apparently insignificant elements will add nuances to their interpretation. Generally speaking, everything that attracts our attention in any landscape indicates that, on a certain level of our conscious or unconscious being, we resonate with what is represented there.

⊕ Awareness that landscapes reveal our soul-states, express our inner radiance, what we are, and what we are experiencing deep within ourselves on the personal and/or collective levels at a particular moment in time – e.g. when we observe the scenery on a journey in either concrete reality or in a dream –, or in general – the landscape, the physical environment, in which we live or work, etc. There are landscapes which inspire beauty, harmony, serenity, calm, rest, well-being, balance, equilibrium, peace, which engender an opening, an expansion of conscience, an elevation of our soul and spirit, which create contemplative, meditative dynamics, a feeling of belonging, integration and fusion. An intact, natural, unpolluted landscape denotes, among other things, respect for the environment, an ecological conscience.

⊖ Disharmonious or devastated landscapes, which emit heavy, somber, polluted energies, indicate the presence of problems, difficult soul-states on the personal and/or collective levels. May reveal our inner and outer limitations, the disorder, pollution, confusion, desolation, destruction that we create and experience in our inner world. An unhealthy physical, mental, and spiritual environment. Reflection of a desert-like soul, an arid, anti-life, destructive or hyperactive mind and spirit. Landscapes revealing the discrepancies and lack of synchrony that exist between the different levels of our being, the perturbations of our inner climate. A lack of harmony or discernment. Contemplation of what is not right without doing anything about it, without wanting to change it.

LASER

The term laser is an acronym for ***Light Amplification by Stimulated Emission of Radiations***. On the physical level, it indicates a generator of light waves, emitting very fine, concentrated, powerful rays. Today, lasers are used in the fields of medicine, technology, industry, and the army.

On the metaphysical level, a laser represents a person's inherent capacity to channel and concentrate divine light and vital energy with great accuracy in order to create, heal, evolve, or defend. It symbolizes the tremendous power of the mind and spirit, capable of focusing the energy of our willpower with a specific, well-determined, resolute intention. The luminous effect and phenomenon of a laser are comparable with the way sound is amplified by speakers. A weak light signal can be perceived, picked up (like a voice by a microphone), transformed and re-directed with increased intensity (comparable to sound from an amplifier). A laser represents the multiplying effect produced by the human mind and spirit when stimulated, when inspired to emit luminous radiance, radiations and emanations *via* its great powers of concentration. Through its elongated form, it symbolizes the masculine principle and emissivity, and its infinite, intangible aspect associates it with an immaterial, spiritual dimension, beyond earthly time and space. Hence a laser is a great symbol of inherently emissive spiritual power that is capable of transcending parallel dimensions and realities. The more concentrated we are, the more powerful our spirit becomes, and the more capable of traveling in the multi-dimensions of the Universe.

⊕ Concentration, amplification, and focusing of the light of the mind, spirit and vital energy. Great potential of understanding, healing, defense, and evolution through the activation and emission of divine light. Radiance focused on qualities and virtues. A capacity for accuracy, precision, and concentration in order to attain specific aims and objectives. Ability to focus our will, the power of our mind and spirit, our emissivity and our intention on the essential, on the achievement of noble aims and objectives, the materialization of altruistic works, which serve evolution. Powerful, unlimited energy.

⊖ Powerful emissivity and focused energy with a malevolent, aggressive, harmful, destructive intention. Concentration of the power of the mind, spirit and vital energy on negative objectives and projects. Extremist dynamics. An incapacity to focus our intention, willpower, and concentration to activate our potential and achieve our objectives.

LAW COURT *cf.* ***Court of Law***

LAWN

A lawn represents the vegetable world and so, symbolically, the level of our feelings and emotions. Given the fact that it is used as ground cover, it is also closely related to the earth element, which represents the world of action and materiality. A lawn does not grow naturally; it is an artificial development created by man, and it requires regular care in order to remain beautiful, thick and well-mown. Hence a lawn also symbolizes structuring, organization, regularity, orderliness and neatness. It is associated with the heart chakra on the emotional, affective level due to its color, green. The state of the lawn manifests how we look after beautiful feelings and how we take care of love within ourselves and regarding others. A beautiful lawn emanates well-being, harmony, beauty and esthetics. It may also indicate a search for artificial, superficial beauty as well as a need to look good to be socially acknowledged.

⊕ A well cared for lawn, without using chemical products that are harmful for the environment, reflects the emanation of beautiful qualities on the intimate and social levels; and in particular a capacity to have and harmonize lovely feelings, order, a sense of organization, involvement, cleanliness, beauty and esthetics both on the inside and on the outside. Good discipline to maintain the beautiful aspects of a place, qualities that are emanated by its aura. A well-groomed person, rigorous, meticulous on the personal and social levels. Induces calm, serenity. Creates a healthy, gentle, supple energy to relax and find renewal in the heart of an active life in matter.

⊖ An unkempt lawn represents negligence, neglect, lack of rigor, order, discipline, structure, harmony and esthetics on the personal and social levels. Exaggerated, artificial upkeep confers a snobbish aspect, which reveals a conscience based on appearances, superficial outer beauty, an arrogant, materialistic, polluting state of mind on the level of relationships and concrete. A neglected lawn may also indicate anti-social energy, a lack of love, altruism and respect for others. It indicates difficulty managing our emotions in society.

LAWSUIT, TRIAL

A lawsuit or trial is litigation brought before a court of law (*cf. also* this term) for jurisdiction. Symbolically it represents a problem as to whether our deeds, our actions, are right or not. It is supposed to provide an answer or render judgment to solve the discord between two or more parties in difficulty or conflict. Both a concrete or dream experience of a trial or lawsuit reveals aspects of ourselves that live in a state of duality and discord. It indicates that certain parts of us have called, or are calling, upon the law, because within ourselves, it is impossible to find grounds for agreement, to re-establish harmony in the way we function.

Some people need to go through the experience of a lawsuit and trial because their behavior has gone so far beyond the limit that they have to be judged and eventually condemned for their wrong, unjust actions. In other cases, we might apparently be wrongly accused. In such a case, the real or dreamed lawsuit or trial helps us understand a message from Up Above, which serves to develop our wisdom when confronted with difficult situations; or, to settle karmas contracted in this life or previous lives. It is sometimes surprising to see how, in precisely what way, Divine Justice is activated in our life. Terrestrial laws have their place, of course, but above all, there are also Cosmic Laws – even if we aren't aware of them – whose application takes priority over human laws. It is through infringement of these Cosmic Laws that we engender imbalanced, complicated, conflicting conditions of life that may lead to lawsuits and trials. That is why it is vital to know and respect these Laws that govern all Creation; breaking these Laws causes what are called *karmic bills and debts*. Knowledge of Cosmic or Divine Laws allows us to better understand all situations that seem unfair when only considered from the perspective of terrestrial laws, along with belief in only one life, belief that this life is our one and only chance, our one and only existence. This is true as much for a person's destiny on the individual level as for the destiny of a whole group of people, or even a whole population or civilization, on the collective level. Hence, a government, a ministry, a military unit, a business company, or a bank, etc. may find themselves confronted with Divine Justice and involved in collective lawsuits and trials, for example, when there are accusations of war crimes, genocide, political corruption, embezzlement, misappropriation of public funds, disrespect for human rights, etc.

⊕ Awareness that the conflicting situation that we experience on the outside is the materialization of conflicts, discord, and dualities that we bear within us, often unknown to ourselves, in the form of memories of unjust actions recorded in our unconscious that are part and parcel of our karmic *luggage* (*cf.* this term). An opportunity to question ourselves on the image and understanding we have of Law and Justice. Motivation to work on ourselves to become aware of our inner conflicts. A tribunal of our conscience. Introspection. Self-questioning. Deep reflection and symbolic analysis of the inner and outer circumstances that led to the lawsuit or trial. A capacity to accept the sometimes unexpected and surprising ways Divine Justice manifests in our and other people's lives. An ability to recognize our errors, to re-educate our rebellious parts, which refuse to respect Cosmic Laws, and act in harmony with Divine Order. Revelation of the deep, profound nature of litigation, access to the keys, the essential elements needed to solve it. A capacity to evaluate a situation from all angles and to render a fair judgment. An attitude that favors dialogue and mediation, rather than confrontation and clashes. A capacity to accept a verdict even when it seems unfair from a human law point of view. Integration of a new vision of Justice and the Law. Understanding the pre-eminence of Divine Justice over human justice. A capacity to discern what is right and fair from an elevated point of view, which eliminates all doubt, exonerates, clears, proves innocent. Fair, equitable, impartial judgment. Winning the lawsuit, being proven right at the trial. A state of grace.

⊖ Problems related to justice on the personal or collective levels. An incapacity to see and admit our errors and distortions. Refusal to accept responsibility for our erroneous, wrong deeds, and their consequences. A lack of understanding of the karmic aspects of Justice, of the continuity of causes and consequences from one life to another. Difficulty seeing the causes of our inner conflicts, dealing with them, and applying Divine Justice within ourselves. A period of rebellion, anger, despair, discouragement. A feeling of injustice. Distortion of the truth in the form of false accusations, and/or the production and provision of false evidence and witnesses. Poor, partial, inequitable, immoral, unethical, iniquitous applications of the Divine Laws. Seeking to flee, not wanting to face our responsibilities. A lack of discernment, impartiality, and good will to solve inner and outer dualities, feeling torn, conflict; a tendency to nourish these distortions, to wallow in the role of the victim, to accuse others, and refuse to refer back to ourselves. A tendency to condemn others who think and behave differently. Unfair, excessively authoritarian, rigid, dominant, domineering, crushing behavior that is extremist in the application of justice; or a lax attitude, that lets us be influenced, manipulated, used by others. Criticism. Severe, peremptory, inflexible judgment. Disrespect, a tendency to impose our point of view. Seeking to be right at all costs. A lack of clemency, compassion, wisdom, and global vision. Exploitation, abuse of the law and justice to satisfy sentiments of resentment and a thirst for revenge. An incapacity to forgive and be reconciled. Lack of understanding of the meaning of experimentation in the process of evolution, of the fact that it is normal to make mistakes in order to learn. A quarrelsome, aggressive spirit that seeks to harm, to destroy, that needlessly files lawsuits. Cold application of the law and justice, without forgiveness or pardon. Existential struggle.

LAWYER, ATTORNEY

A lawyer is a professional expert in law, on the collection of laws and social conventions that have been set up for the good of society, its organization and functioning. A lawyer, or attorney, gives legal advice, helps, represents or defends his clients or a cause in court*. He ensures that human manifestations and the realization of a project comply with the law, and therefore has a good aptitude for business, governmental and social responsibilities of all kinds. On the metaphysical level, he represents a capacity to study, understand

and apply justice, defend rights, and decide and do what is right. Moreover, he symbolizes knowledge of and respect for the Divine Laws and their application in daily life, as well as an ability to settle disputes and conflict.

⊕ Discernment and a capacity to evaluate what is right, to understand Justice* and to act while submitting to the Divine Laws. Loyalty. Eloquence, gift for public speaking, oratory skills, business and trade organization. Forthrightness, nobility, uprightness, honesty, integrity, a sense of responsibility, incorruptibility, rigor and respect for the law on both the personal and collective levels. Mediator, diplomat, leader, role model. Seeks truth through logic and reason. Settles conflicts. The study and understanding of Divine Justice, which prevails over earthly justice. (**cf. also* these terms)

⊖ Problems with the forces of justice. Lack of understanding and disrespect for the Divine Laws, for what is right. Abuse of power through acquired legal knowledge; corruption, lies, trickery, scheming. Manipulative, flattering, misleading spirit. Use of justice, power and renown for personal ends. Justice without conscience. Defending injustice for money. Giving in to basic instincts. Agreeing to serve the law of the jungle, which accepts the concept of the survival of the fittest and that might is right, hence a tendency, or even desire, to crush the weak instead of helping them. Authoritarianism. Feeling of superiority, claiming to be an initiate. Lacking uprightness, integrity, honesty. Betraying, instead of defending, the great values of Truth, Justice and Freedom.

LEATHER

As leather comes from animal skin, it symbolizes a person's instinctual needs, which emanate from his aura through aspects of vital energy related to survival on the physical level. Used since the beginning of human life on Earth as protection against the cold and bad weather, over time, leather has become one of the main resources used to make clothes, shoes, bags, belts, tool-cases, and other utilitarian or decorative objects. However, as in the case of long coveted fur, animals have to be killed to obtain this resource. Consequently, any leather or fur object has been imprinted with aggression and man's hunting spirit, as well as memories of the stress, suffering, agony and violent death to which the animal in question was subjected. Fortunately the evolutive stage humanity is going through at the present time is opening our conscience to the sacred dimension of all forms of life, and inspiring us with respect for and protection of the flora, fauna, and the environment in general. This new conscience, which is imprinted with increased wisdom and compassion for animal life, is encouraging a growing number of people to renounce leather products, and prefer clothes, shoes and accessories in natural fibers of vegetable or mineral origin. As well as being peaceful, environmentally friendly resources, such products are noble, long-lasting, and sustainable, and offer our aura a very different radiance that animal skin, leather or fur, which require the sacrifice of animal lives.

⊕ Awareness that leather is animal skin. Conscious renouncement of the use of leather products out of respect for animal life. Evolution of human conscience allowing us to replace an instinctual, combative lifestyle that follows the law of the jungle (survival of the fittest, where might is right) with a pacifist, ecological lifestyle that is in harmony with nature and all of the kingdoms (mineral, vegetable, animal, human, and divine). Receptivity to new, Divinely inspired ways of materialization. Change of mentality and behavior regarding the animal world.

⊖ Attraction for leather clothes and objects indicates conscious or unconscious, instinctual, primitive, machismo, sometimes aggressive, violent conscience and behavior on both personal and social levels. Insensitivity or indifference regarding the fact that the production of leather requires the slaughter of a great many animals. Lack of respect for animal life, the environment and ecological balance. A selfish attitude, emphasis on appearances, superficial luxury and comfort. Connotations of seduction, and in extreme cases, unhealthy sexuality, sado-masochism. Coarse, aggressive, abusive behavior, which reflects complexes of superiority and inferiority, a need to dominate and exploit others. Obstinacy, animosity, and rebellion when confronted with new pacifist, ecological, spiritual currents. An aura that reveals a primitive, little evolved conscience, a person dominated by his instincts and the law of the jungle.

LEFT

The left symbolizes the feminine polarity, receptivity and the inner world. For example, our left leg represents the way we advance on the inside in order to evolve, accomplish a project, and manifest the potential we all bear within ourselves; our left hand is related to the way we accept, receive and give on the inside; our left ear symbolizes receptivity to our inner ear; consequently difficulties regarding this ear indicate a lack of inner listening; in a dream, a person standing on our left represent aspects of our inner selves.

⊕ Receptivity, a capacity to go within and interiorize, to listen deeply and tune into our inner, spiritual, divine dimension.

⊖ Lack of or excessive receptivity, listening, interiorization, meditation, and spirituality. A lack of depth, reflection, and discernment. A tendency to close up, become isolated, reject or flee. Disconnection from our divine, spiritual nature.

LEG

Generally speaking, a leg/legs represent the way we move and advance in action. The left leg symbolizes inner spiritual journeying, the way we advance on the inside before manifesting movement on the outside. The right leg represents the way we enter action, on the concrete, physical level. A symbolic analysis of the state of the legs in concrete reality or featuring as a symbol in a dream, or possible wounds (past or present) on either leg, allows us to understand what we need to change or rectify in our way of advancing, in our capacity for action and manifestation through movement.

⊕ Easy, light, well-coordinated movement and advancing. Capacity to move toward places and planned objectives and goals, to set in motion, go ahead, and accomplish projects on the physical level. Setting in motion the will to take action, concretize, materialize.

⊖ Leg wounds, or a health problem regarding legs, indicate difficulties related to a capacity to advance on the personal, physical level. Limitations and blockages caused by distorted memories regarding advancing and manifestation. Excessive or insufficient will-power. Problems of motivation. Attitude that is over-focused on results.

LETTER (by mail, email)

A letter, whether hand-written and sent by mail, or computer-typed and emailed *via* the Internet, represents a capacity to materialize thoughts and feelings by expressing them in words with the aim of sharing them with others. Letters/emails are written and sent to share news, transmit facts, data and information. A letter/email also conveys regards, wishes, words of encouragement, sympathy, and so on.

Receiving a letter or email indicates to the addressee that he has received a message of some importance and usefulness for his evolution on the personal, professional, or social levels. Consequently, it is important not only to take note of the news and information received on the concrete level, but also to analyze this data symbolically, because we never receive a letter/email at a particular moment, in a given context or circumstances, by pure coincidence. Letters/emails always correspond to what is going on in both the receiver's and sender's inner life respectively, symbolizing specific facets of each. Hence, each letter, each email that we receive or send reveals things about ourselves through their contents and formulation. They are messages to help us become aware of various aspects of ourselves – attitudes, states of conscience, ways of being and behaving, etc. – and hence, when understood in depth, they serve to help us evolve into better people, better souls.

⊕ A capacity to formulate our ideas, thoughts, and feelings in words, and to materialize them through written transmission. Broadcasting and spreading news and data on the personal, professional, or social levels. An exchange of information. Inspires or activates new visions. Transmission or reception of messages that reveal or render official a gesture, act, deed, plan, thought, feeling, or idea. Well-structured communication. A conscious choice of words. Mastery of language. Linguistic and literary talent. Awareness of the symbolism of messages sent and received.

⊖ Difficulty formulating and communicating our thoughts and emotions in writing. Bad news. Broadcasting indiscreet, harmful, disparaging, slanderous words. Expression of malevolent, ill-willed, negative, critical, destructive thoughts. Sending or receiving messages that manifest hypocrisy, dishonesty, or a conformist attitude. An incapacity to express ourselves openly, frankly, and sincerely in a disagreeable, conflicting, or trying situation. Aberrations, errors of judgment. Media manipulation for selfish purposes. Unhappy writings. A lack of positive, constructive inspiration. Contradictions. Controversies. Destructive message.

LEUKEMIA

From the ancient Greek *leukos* (white) and *aima* (blood), the term *leukemia* refers to a type of cancer of the blood, which is characterized by an abnormal proliferation of leukocytes, or white blood cells, in the bone marrow. These cells spread into the blood and infiltrate various organs, disturbing their capacity to function correctly, efficiently. Among those affected, serious infections, hemorrhages, and anemia are very frequent.

White blood cells play an important role in the immune system. They actually defend our organism against the intrusion of viruses, bacteria, and other harmful foreign bodies. Through their color, white, they are symbolically associated with spirituality, and hence represent our spiritual power of prevention and protection through analyzing, stopping and transforming the negative that assails us, on both the inner and outer levels. Whenever the number of white blood cells increases abnormally, it is a sign that a mechanism of overprotection has been set off, either through fear of being invaded or assaulted and aggressed by elements from the outer world, or in reaction to the unconscious forces and memories that have been activated in the person's inner world. These overprotective dynamics can be seen in many different situations in everyday life as well as in the ill person's dreams. Behind every manifested excess, there is always a corresponding hidden lack. Hence a tendency to overprotection indicates the presence of memories related to a lack of protection that engendered all sorts of fear, insecurity, and anxiety.

Since leukemia is closely linked to the blood, that vital liquid that maintains life, it concerns both the world of emotions and feelings, as well as our vital energy, the force of life. When we think of blood, we think of the color red, the color of the 1st chakra which ensures our being well rooted in materiality; we also think of action, the active force, the willpower to materialize, life dynamics in physical, concrete reality. Hence, leukemia may denote difficulties and distortions related to the capacity to materialize, to concretely realize our potential, to accept our life-plan; for example, the dilapidation of vital energy through excessively seeking physical pleasures, a lack of resistance caused by physical and psychological overwork, fleeing responsibilities and social life through a refusal to fully incarnate, to take solid root in our physical body and the world of action, carelessness regarding the consequences of our acts, etc.

Leukemia indicates that the person affected is going through an important opening of his unconscious that brings him face to face with large blocks or reservoirs of negative mental, emotional, and material memories that he isn't able to cope with. It is usually an accumulation – probably over several lives – of feelings of rebellion, anger, and aggression that the person has repressed; the power and force of these accumulated, repressed feelings causes the destructuring of his being, first on the subtle, mental, and emotional levels, then on the material level, in his force of action. Over time, the energies of disharmony, rebellion, and disorder accumulated on the subtle levels condense enough to manifest in the physical body in the form of chaotic, anarchic, uncontrolled cell growth that destroys the person's capacity to materialize in a healthy, well-balanced, right way.

⊕ An opportunity to set about healing conflicting memories that have accumulated over many lives. Intense work on ourselves through self-questioning, awareness, seeking the cause(s), studying resonance. Understanding the fact that seeking healing must not be limited to the physical body, but must also take into account the state of health of the emotional, mental, and spiritual bodies. Acquisition of the necessary spiritual knowledge to alchemize the difficult situation, to succeed in transforming the negative energies and memories. Activation of powers of self-healing. Purification of vital energy. Improvement of the capacity to materialize, to fully realize our potential. Rediscovered feelings of security and protection. Acceptance of our life-plan. development of a deep connection with the Earth, gratitude and acknowledgement for all the life experiences it offers us. Renewed closeness and links with people. A new moral and psychological balance. Restored vitality, force of work and creation. Understanding the deep meaning of life, of existence. Rediscovered *joie de vivre.* The beginning of a new life in matter with a high level of conscience and spirituality.

⊖ A state of rebellion and the deep despair of a person who thinks the whole world is against him. An intense feeling of menace and aggression that provokes a reaction of over-protection. Great emotional and psychological fragility that gradually transforms into physical illness. Discouragement, dejection, despondency, victimization. Existential fear, anguish, and insecurity. Tumultuous emotions. A tendency to excessively fuse with others, to absorb negative energies without knowing how to transform them. Ignorance of the Laws of resonance and karma. A disorderly, chaotic life. Rebellious, anarchic behavior. Memories of lies, calumny, defamation, betrayal, conspiracy. An anti-life attitude.

LICE

Lice (singular: louse) are insects (*cf. also* this term), and as such belong to the animal kingdom, which symbolically represents our instincts and primary needs. As their particularity is to be found on our head, our scalp, lice correspond to instinctual, scattered, insidious thoughts. Head lice prick the skin to feed on our blood; this causes itching, discomfort and distraction, which in turn causes loss of attention and energy on the level of our unconscious thoughts. Symbolically, this means that those forces and aspects of ourselves that feed on distraction, dispersal, and primary needs, feed on and drain our vital energy on the mental level. It is never a coincidence when we find ourselves confronted with a problem of lice: this reveals the presence of attitudes, behavior and a way of functioning that *vampirizes* our vital energy through our thoughts. We want something, and with subtlety, we either grab or disperse the other person's attention so as to get him to go where we want, so as to get what we want. Lice may be very small-scale, minuscule vampires, but their multiplying effect rapidly causes states of dispersal, scattered thoughts, shame and fear, as well as judgmental, critical gossip on the personal and social levels.

As they are tiny and virtually hidden in our hair, lice are difficult to identify, which symbolizes the well camouflaged presence of little, insidious needs that, unknown to us, slip into our conceptual dynamics and our decisions. They are frequently found on children who play on their parents' feelings and manipulate them to get what they want. A female louse lives for a month and can lay as many as a hundred eggs. This symbolizes the fact that those disturbing, perturbing thoughts that isolate us from others have the capacity to multiply rapidly if we aren't careful, if we don't pay attention to them. Similarly, the sticky substance at the root of the hair follicle that keeps the egg on our scalp indicates the difficulty of dislodging, cleansing, and transforming these thoughts. Being polluted by lice prevents children from going to school, which indicates both a need to be careful when in contact with others, and also the need to take the time and necessary means to re-educate our forces that may be, are, or have been parasitized; or, that parasitize.

⊕ Incitement to work on the healing and transformation of thoughts and behavior that engender and maintain parasitic forces. Allow us to become aware of the presence of primary needs and instinctual thoughts that parasitize, vampirize, and disperse vital energy, attention and concentration. Seeking appropriate solutions and remedies to free ourselves of these parasitic forces, to transform the attitudes that resonate with lice characteristics. Understanding that it is necessary to work on the little, insidious needs that disperse us, make us scatterbrained, incapable of correct concentration, that seek to parasitize us or others in order to get what these needs of ours want. Work on the transcendence of personal, selfish needs on the conceptual level. A capacity to achieve better understanding of ourselves through the analysis of the infinitely small. Awakening of discernment. Change of attitude so as to halt the multiplication of negativity in the world of thoughts.

⊖ A tendency to dramatize the presence of lice, to be submerged in shame, fear, guilt and a lack of understanding. An incapacity or refusal to see the connection between the pollution of lice on the outside and its meaning on the inner, symbolic level. Happy to remedy the problem on the outside without changing any of the attitudes or behavior that resonate with lice characteristics, those attitudes and/or behavior that cause the manifestation of lice, that attract them on the physical level. Persisting in nourishing thoughts that are imprinted with little needs that vampirize and exhaust others so as to get what the person wants. A tendency to be scattered and dispersed to satisfy instinctual, egotistical needs, to copy, to multiply distorted thought patterns. A child or adult who, in order to manipulate, becomes weak himself, or weakens others on the intellectual level.

LID

A lid is related to the masculine principle and emissivity because it allows us to cover a container, a receptacle. It serves to protect the contents of a receptacle, to retain and prevent the contents from overflowing, to keep them clean and protected from the air, dust, animals, etc., thereby allowing us to preserve and ensure right, appropriate management of resources. As it hides contents from view, a lid also symbolizes discretion.

⊕ In position, it is a symbol of protection, preservation, good management of resources; or, discretion. Removed, it shows openness, readiness to share, to reveal the contents within the receptacle.

⊖ Absence of a lid may indicate a lax attitude, loss and waste of resources through carelessness, negligence, dispersal; or, a person who over-exposed, over-shared, a person who has too strong a desire to give away, to donate; or, an incapacity to protect contents correctly. A closed, locked lid may indicate a state of reserve, closure, withdrawal due to selfishness, a need to retain and control everything, which incites the person to behave with excessive receptivity or emissivity; it may also indicate forbidden access, or an exaggerated need to keep resources, or our inner riches, hidden and secret. Difficulty circulating, sharing the resources at our disposal. Avidity, greed, avarice, miserliness, and fear of lacking. Tendency to isolate ourselves. Tightly closed or sealed off thoughts, mind and spirit. Imprisonment and stifling of potential.

LIGHT, A *cf.* ***Lamp***

LIGHT, THE

The idea of light is essentially related to the Sun, to Creation, to the manifestation of Life, hence to the idea or concept of knowledge, understanding, conscience, spirit, and existence. Without light, we cannot see and become aware of what has been created. It reveals our field of vision, our level of conscience, and of understanding. Intrinsically associated with the fire element and heat, light has a nourishing, vivifying, enlightening function. It offers us global, distant, multidimensional vision, while enlightening and illuminating our soul, mind and spirit.

Spiritually speaking, the Light comes from the Creator, the Original Source, from God; in astrology, it is emitted by the stars and suns; in cosmology, it is the result of Big Bang. Since the very beginning of our existence on Earth, we humans have evolved thanks to the light and heat rays emitted by the activity of the sun in our solar system. Sunlight and the earth's rotation around its own axis, determine and regulate the diurnal-nocturnal cycles of our planet, the phases of activity and sleep, the seasons, reproduction, growth, the production of hormones, and, generally speaking, our harmonious functioning with natural, cosmic cycles. During the day, the alternation of light also ensures a balance between exteriorization and interiorization, between emissivity and receptivity, activity, exploration, experimentation in matter and the physical world; as well as rest, introspection, contemplation of the inner world and the subtle and metaphysical realities, during the night, in dreams.

However, the often exaggerated use of artificial light in all domains of life today has disturbed the adequate functioning of our inner biological clock as well as our synchronism with natural cycles. Symbolically, the negative aspect of light – e.g. when it serves to allow for excessive prolongation of work, study, research, social activity, entertainment, etc. – indicates an important discrepancy and tendency toward a hyperactive, ever increasingly high-performance, faster, more emissive, extroverted lifestyle. This gradually manifests through states of stress, fatigue, exhaustion, depression and *burn-out*. Continually burning the candle at both ends (i.e. using up our inner flame, our vital energy), we end up in the dark, without any light (the dark night of the soul, a darkened, somber spirit), no matter how intense outer lighting may be.

Nowadays, human consciousness is experiencing a return to the Light, both on the esoteric level, through increased research into spiritual Knowledge and Enlightenment, and on the exoteric level, through scientific research into a better understanding of the human body and the phenomena of our existence. In addition to this, more and more technologies use lasers in very varied domains, including medicine: laser surgery, laser acupuncture, blood treatments with laser beams, etc. More recently, the discovery of *biophotons* (extremely fine light rays emitted on the surface of living tissue, that can now be measured by highly sensitive machinery) has allowed us to understand that exchanges and transmission of information on cell level is carried out by means of light, that this light is found at the base of our conscience, and that the thought process takes place at the speed of light.

This development and stage in human life is a good illustration of the evolution of human conscience. Man now has more and more access to Knowledge from within, his conscience has *lit up*, so to speak; he is becoming more and more spiritual as he integrates the understanding of the multi-dimensions. As he becomes enlightened, he develops a capacity to discern infinitesimal realities, as well as a capacity to perceive the parallel worlds; hence, light, enlightenment, scientific research, and a spiritual quest all join together and open the pathway to a new era of Light. An increasing number of recent concepts, or renewed former ideas, that have permeated our commonly used vocabulary bear witness to this: servant of the Light, warrior of Light, body of Light or Light body, Light healing, even light food products. Such products refer to reduced calorie contents, and while their contribution to our health remains questionable, they nevertheless reflect an underlying desire in Western society to lighten (reduce) our intake of fats and sugars, which goes hand in hand with an increasing desire to become more evolved, enlightened beings, seeking healthier nourishment on all levels.

The perception of light is closely linked to the perception of colors to the functioning of our physical eye, which ensures tri-dimensional vision, and the 3rd eye, that subtle organ of ours that allows us to develop clairvoyance.

Adages and expressions with the word *light* help bring out its close association with the concepts of Knowledge, intelligence, transparency, truth and hope: we *see the light of day* when we are born, or we *see the light* when we understand something, and/or emerge from a difficult, intense, possibly complicated, complex period or task; we *shed light* on something when we add information and knowledge that helps clarify ambiguity or misunderstanding; *a leading light* refers to a person who is usually distinguished, very knowledgeable, and/or skillful, in a particular field; *to see the light at the end of the tunnel* means the end of difficulties is in sight, within grasp, and so we feel hopeful about the outcome.

⊕ A symbol of light, conscience, understanding, knowledge, clarity, lucidity, energy, and vitality. A source of marvel, joy, discovery, revelation, raised awareness. A protective, comforting, consoling energy that brings hope and openings. A representation of the Divine, of Truth, Awakening, birth, a great power or force and abundance of love and wisdom. Charisma, expansion, radiance. Inspiration, elevation potential. An inexhaustible source of energy.

⊖ A difficult, somber, sterile period. Absence of conscience, awareness, knowledge, understanding, discernment, lucidity, global vision, wisdom. A lack of energy, vitality, radiance, motivation. An opaque, ignorant spirit. An incapacity to see, to detect what is hidden, veiled. Discouragement, despair, and, in extreme cases, a suicidal state of mind. Reduced luminosity may indicate a tendency to wish to dissimulate information or to hide things. Difficulty opening up to new understanding, new awareness, and updating our concepts, our vision, and ways of thinking. A lack of optimism in a situation, a tendency to remain in a somber, negative state of mind, where we go round in circles. Excessive light may indicate a tendency to be over emissive; or to let ourselves be easily impressed, blinded by a concept, or situation; or it may reveal that the person is unable to face a situation, to look at it clearly and recognize all of the component elements. Projecting excessive light may mean that we wish to impose our capacity to radiate in order to be acknowledged; or, due to a need to control; or, because of an overly strong desire to know. A lack of light may indicate a tendency to remain limited, ignorant, stagnant, a resistance to evolving, expanding our mind and spirit, to acquiring Knowledge.

LIGHTER

A lighter is related to the fire element and so, symbolically speaking, a capacity to ignite, to awaken vital energy, the power of our spirit that animates our entire being. Easy to transport and use, it offers us the possibility of lighting a fire quickly and safely. It is also very useful in emergencies or life endangering situations.

When analyzed symbolically, we also need to take into consideration its color, shape, size, the material it is made of, the symbols that are depicted on it, as well as the context and way in which it is used.

⊕ Responsible behavior and awareness of the power of the gestures and vital energy that allow us to warm, maintain and save life; or, destroy it. A source of energy used for good. An energy resource that is available when necessary. A capacity to find our way in life's dark, somber situations. A capacity to create warmth. An understanding of the power contained even in little things.

⊖ Irresponsible behavior, waste and exhaustion of vital energy. An ephemeral, short-lived, inner fire. A rebellious spirit that can cause fires and destroy its entourage or nourish distortions. A person who has developed a habit of playing with a lighter, flicking it on and off incessantly, indicates an impulsive, threatening temperament; such a person can easily allow himself to be overcome by dangerous angry moods. An unhealthy energy that continually engenders life-threatening or survival situations. An expensive, gold lighter set with precious stones, engraved with initials, etc., symbolizes material power whereby we seek to impress, to boost our ego, and display our social status. Associated with cigarettes, a lighter often appears as a symbol in games of seduction and abuse of power.

LIGHTNING

Lightning, a flash or bolt of lightning, is a powerful light that comes from a discharge of electricity in the atmosphere during a storm. It is related to fire, air, and water, and symbolically represents an accumulation of tensions as well as great spiritual, mental and emotional power and intensity.

Idiomatic expressions frequently used in popular sayings often correspond to the symbolic meaning. *As fast as lightning* reveals a capacity to manifest very rapidly on the physical and energetic levels; it is generally considered to be positive. *Like a bolt of lightning*, however, refers to fast but extremely sudden manifestation, a completely unexpected surprise or even shock.

The word flash associated with lightning is frequently used to represent a brief, rapid act. *A flash in the pan* refers to something – e.g. a trend, fashion, or news item – that draws our attention, but only for a very short time. *To flash through or into our mind* means to enter our mind for an instant – a thought, an idea, an image, a memory; it may represent sudden understanding or insights, as well as clairvoyance, clairaudience and clairsentience.

A flash back, for example in a film or novel, or simply in our mind, means to return briefly to the past, to a person or people, an event, a moment, a feeling, an emotion, a memory. This too may be a rapid mental or emotional connection which sheds light on something we see, hear, feel, sense, or are undergoing in the present, enlightening us as to its significance, its deeper meaning, and/or its relation to the past, to memories. *To flash a smile at someone* means to smile briefly and brightly at someone, whereas *to flash your money around* is to display your wealth so everyone can see it, to show it off, often in a boastful manner.

Eyes can flash with anger or recognition. This refers to the sudden positive or negative brightening of the eyes in rapid response in a variety of situations.

Similarly the word bolt is frequently used to describe very rapid action as in *to bolt down our food, to bolt across the street,* and *a bolt from the blue* refers to something that happens very suddenly and totally unexpectedly, just like *a bolt of lightning* mentioned above.

⊕ Symbol of the primordial creative fire. Powerful, rapid manifestation. Sudden, surprising understanding or enlightenment. Clarification of conscience. Open-mindedness allowing rapid understanding. Great capacity to let go of tension and regain equilibrium.

⊖ The apparition of threatening, destructive lightning in our dreams or in concrete reality, is a warning that we are not using our creative power in accordance with the Cosmic Laws. Dangerous, destructive use of our spirit's fire and vital energy. Accumulation of anger and aggression. Oppressive thoughts and emotions, full of intense tensions. Over rapid, abrupt manifestation. Impulsive, hot-tempered, irascible character. Need to develop awareness and to transform deep frustrations. Hyperactivity.

LIMOUSINE

Like all cars, a limousine represents a way to advance in social life, to use our energy to go to work, to meet others, or to go home, to regain our intimacy. However, a limousine is more specifically a symbol of wealth, celebrity, success, political and economic power, and great responsibility, because, generally speaking, such a car is most often used by very wealthy people, famous celebrities, or people in very important official jobs. It is also used for special occasions such as a wedding or an inauguration, and may even serve as a *mobile office* for people who have to travel a lot for their job. Usually black with tinted windows that help preserve discretion and anonymity, sometimes bulletproofed when used to transport heads of state, a limousine symbolizes hidden power and wealth, a desire to remain out of sight, protection against eventual threats, or from excessive public curiosity. When it is white, it emanates a different, lighter energy and dynamics. Then it symbolizes a more open, a more accessible spirit, a way of advancing with a spiritual, elevating state of conscience, if it is used in a correct, right, just context.

⊕ A way of advancing of a person who has the capacity to materialize, to help advance major projects, to take on great responsibilities on the collective level. A solemn moment, an important project in progress. An influential person in his field, great notoriety, wealth, and social prestige experienced positively. Large-scale multiplication, materialization force or power of expansion. Symbol related to great people who have marked their era by their example and service to humanity. An initiator of works and businesses dedicated to serve society and the Divine. Depending on the context, may be a sign of confidence, acknowledgement, a high level of conscience, renown, or celebrity experienced in their qualities.

⊖ A sign of megalomania, extravagance, excessive ambition, abuse of power and authority, importance granted to appearances. A need for luxury, and to impress others, our entourage, the crowd. A way of manifesting and advancing in life that indicates an over-sized ego. Activating envy, covetousness and jealousy in other people. Feelings of superiority or a complex of inferiority regarding rich and famous people. May be related to a person who thinks he is incapable of taking on major responsibilities; or, who refuses and rejects expansion, wealth and power. A tendency to let ourselves be manipulated by our desire for glory and prestige. Someone who doesn't feel acknowledged, who, in his ardent desire or yearning for wealth and celebrity, *feeds* on news items about celebrities. Wealth and riches poorly, thoughtlessly used, without conscience. A lack of altruism and openness to others.

LION

A lion is a carnivorous mammal, often called *the king of the animals* because his mane makes him look like the sun, *the king of the sky.* His very powerful muscles and fearsome jaws make the lion a symbol of great instinctual force and power. Lions live in a group, called a *pride,* which calls to mind their proud bearing, their majestic, dignified posture, as well as a certain disdain. The main role of the dominant lion is to protect his pride from other lion prides. However, lions are sociable animals that have developed more elaborate means of vocal and body communication than other felines. Furthermore, lions have a great capacity of adaptation and can live in very different habitats. References to lions or images of lions very frequently feature in symbolism. Traditionally, a lion represents bravery, courage, fearlessness, power and strength, resistance, integrity, nobility, and patience as well as majesty, protection, leadership and justice. It is often looked upon as a protective guardian and a safeguard for power, and through its dominant energy, it is also considered as an emblem of supremacy and domination.

⊕ A symbol of power, strength, authority, force, justice, protection, nobility, majesty related to our vital and instinctual energy. A capacity to assert ourselves with courage, to express ourselves with wisdom. Bravery. Courage. Daring. Dauntlessness. Endurance. Leadership. Great adaptability. Leader qualities, an ability to take on high responsibilities. A royal attitude. A noble mind and spirit. A calm personality that masters instinctive impulses and knows how to act with patience, moderation, and diplomacy in difficult, conflicting situations.

⊖ A person with megalomaniac tendencies and dominant, aggressive, unfair, lazy behavior that enslaves or subjugates others, requiring their obedience and total submission. The negative symbolism could also indicate a lack of courage, bravery, and strength of commitment, of involvement, as well as an incapacity to take on major responsibilities, to face and deal with difficult situations, to protect ourselves or others in a context of domination or abuse of power. Feelings of superiority and inferiority. A need to be acknowledged and admired. Seeking power, strength, wealth and celebrity. Abusive use of strength, force and power that could go as far as murder to satisfy selfish, egotistical desires. Avidity. Vanity. Pride.

LIQUID

The word *liquid* refers to the state of a fluid substance that is capable of flowing. Symbolically, everything liquid refers to the emotional level and feelings. To understand the exact symbolic meaning of a liquid, its composition, degree of fluidity, density, and clarity have to be taken into consideration, as well as the place and context in which it is found.

For example: clean, clear, fresh spring water symbolizes pure feelings, vitality, transparency, and a capacity for purification. Another example: natural orange juice is associated with healthy nourishment and sweetness since it contains natural sugar, and its important contribution of vitamin C and calcium relate it symbolically to the immune system; moreover, its color, orange, associates it with the 2nd chakra.

These examples show how observation of the liquid's degree of fluidity, viscosity, density, or clarity, as well as its properties, gives precise indications as to the quality, authenticity, and state of purity of the emotions that dwell in us. Likewise, when we analyze a liquid, we should also take time to observe the container. A liquid embraces the form of the receptacle that delimits, controls and masters it, which is why it also indicates adaptability, flexibility, and receptivity. For a correct interpretation, we also need to take into account the state of the receptacle. Pure water poured into a dirty, deformed, rusty, old, or ugly container will have a different meaning than water poured into a beautiful, clean, harmonious, transparent container. Hence, depending on the context, the state of a liquid indicates different emotions. For example, if the liquid is enclosed in a receptacle, it may indicate emotional retention, or a reserved, introverted character. If it is moving and flows freely and gaily like a stream, it may indicate a person's dynamism, joy, lightheartedness. If it is at rest, still, in a pleasant, tranquil place, it may represent receptivity, calm, and serenity. If it is rather heavy, viscous, slimy and stagnant, it indicates passivity, inertia, and a marsh-like, bog-like, mired state of emotions. In the case of a substance passing from a liquid state to a gaseous or solid state, e.g. when water turns into ice or steam, depending on the context, this indicates changes in our soul-states or conscience: the transformation of emotions through the power of thought when the liquid becomes a gas; or, the condensing of emotional energies, which end up in material form when the liquid becomes solid.

⊕ Positive emotional potential in the case of vital, useful, beneficial, nutritional, therapeutic, purifying liquid(s). Dynamism, flexibility, adaptability, if the liquid is light, fluid, and in motion. Receptivity. A capacity to contain and master emotions. A capacity to change soul-state(s) and conscience symbolized by fusing, condensing, liquefying, or evaporating, as the case may be. A relaxing comforting, consoling, enveloping, healing effect, e.g. in the case of a warm, therapeutic bath or massage oil.

⊖ Manifestation of negative, destructive emotions in the case of unhealthy, polluting, harmful, toxic, dangerous liquid(s). A state of emotional passivity and inertia. Difficulty changing, transforming soul-states (moods) and conscience. Problems with emotional adaptation.

LISTEN, TO

Listening is a state of receptivity during which we receive information that comes from within ourselves, from others, and from the parallel worlds. It is essential to listen before being emissive because if we are not receptive, we cannot have a deep understanding of people or situations, nor can we catch subtle intentions or innuendos. Consequently we are not able to manifest and act right, correctly, with the aim of developing qualities and virtues, while respecting synchronicity, Divine timing, as well as our and other people's life programs. Whether we are aware of it or not, the entire Universe is based on altruism. Everything that exists is interconnected, interdependent. We need one another to live and evolve. As we gradually learn to listen and understand in depth, we become more lucid, and our clairaudience (*cf. also* this term) is developed. We are then able to hear beyond words, beyond sounds, to perceive the subtle atmospheres and ambiances that exist in our environment. The faculty of clairaudience helps us become more conscious, more aware, and allows us to anticipate the development of situations, and to discern what is right for our evolution and that of others. Not listening is one of the main reasons for misactions (*cf.* this term), which lead to more or less serious karmas.

⊕ Receptivity to what is going on within ourselves, and in others, as well as in our environment. Favors deep understanding of what we, and others, are going through. Connection with Heaven, with other levels of existence and understanding of messages received from these dimensions *via* signs and symbols. Discernment and right action.

⊖ In general, a lack of listening goes hand in hand with a lack of receptivity and excessive emissivity. It can also indicate distorted receptivity or withdrawal, the presence of forces and memories that prevent us from truly listening to ourselves and others, from reading signs sent to us by Heaven, and from maintaining an elevated conscience. When we allow ourselves to become absorbed by our fears, insecurities, material, and personal needs, we become too self-centered, and this prevents us from listening to, being attentive and attuned to others. Such a state of mind, such a state of conscience, pushes us to act selfishly, egotistically, and very emissively, without any thought for other people's well-being.

Listening becomes negative when it serves curiosity, or when we listen to music, discussions, and programs that are harmful for the evolution of our soul, such as those containing criticism, negative judgments, aggressive atmospheres and ambiances, etc. This creates an accumulation of information and negative forces that, sooner or later, materialize in concrete situations. For right, correct listening, we need to discern both the positive and negative aspects of the context, and understand what our senses perceive. It is important to know that we can nourish the negative in ourselves simply by listening, without saying or doing anything. If we hear or observe negative things in a concrete situation or dream, and we are disturbed, bothered, or upset, this means that we have resonance with whatever causes our reaction(s). The fact of not intervening to stop the process, pretending it is harmless, while knowing that what is occurring is not right, indicates that we allow the negative we are observing to continue to thrive and to upset our life. We cannot, and need not, always act on the physical level every time we hear negative things, but it is important to take a stand on the inside, and not support the attitudes and behavior observed on the energy level. Thus, while understanding the other person's situation, we ensure we do not repeat the same behavior either consciously or unconsciously.

LITTLE *cf.* ***Small***

LIVING-ROOM (sitting-room)

A living-room is a room that represents our intimate structure regarding social relations because it is where we receive our friends, converse, and relax as a family, watch television, listen to music, or curl up and read a book, etc. It is a place to share family and social life, to exchange news and information, to be receptive when relating to others, when communicating and transmitting ideas to be reflected on and discussed. The living-room is the main social area in the home and family intimacy. It represents our way of interacting, communicating and exchanging with others.

⊕ Harmonious, well-structured family and social intimacy. Receptivity regarding others on the social level, discovery of new ideas, exchange of information, pleasure sharing. Favors relationships, encounters. Indicates a greater degree of intimacy with guests. Harmonious, interesting social relationships. Gatherings, get-togethers, sharing values and principles.

⊖ Problems related to the structure of family and social intimacy. A person who places too much or not enough importance on family and social life, who doesn't have harmonious family and friend relationships. Relational and family problems. Distanced loved ones. Memories of problematic, difficult gatherings and get-togethers. An anti-social, isolated person; or, someone who is too social, even extravagant.

LIZARD

As an animal species, the lizard represents aspects of our vital energy, our instinctual nature. Belonging to the reptile family, it symbolizes old, ancient, even pre-historic primary needs, and a down-to-earth lifestyle that is greatly attached to matter, since lizards mostly move along the ground. The great variety of lizards that exists on Earth, e.g. chameleons, geckos, iguanas, varans (monitor lizards), as well as the complexity of their characteristics, bears witness to the great adaptability of this species. Although most frequently found in tropical or desert regions, some live at altitudes as high as 5000m, and many are often to be found basking in sunny spots all over the world.

There are diurnal and nocturnal lizards, some of which are capable of digging into the ground, and others of gliding through the air thanks to skin membranes situated along their body. Their size varies from a few centimeters to a few meters. Most lizards have horny skin with folds forming a scaly shield that facilitates the absorption of solar energy, which is necessary for their survival. Autonomy (capacity to release their tail if caught by a predator) and camouflage (*via* the color of their carapace) represent their principle means of defense. They mostly feed on insects and hence contribute toward the reduction of the ravaging insect population. Depending on their natural habitat, some lizard species also feed on fruit, algae, or small animals, but they may also feed on other lizards.

According to the characteristics present in a dream, a lizard may symbolize part of our vital energy that is capable of adapting to the environment, to cold or warm ambiances, and of balancing our energy. It may also indicate a way of looking, observing, and seeing that is very down-to-earth, over-materialistic, with all sorts of needs. The lizard's capacity for camouflage represents a form of discretion, patience, humility; or, possibly excessive timidity, shyness; as well as latent energy that waits before suddenly attacking, a sneaky, perverted aspect of ourselves that is related to our vital energy, i.e. to our needs.

⊕ Great adaptability to the constant transformations in concrete, physical living conditions as well as metaphysical realities, to ambiances and subtle energies. Discretion, diplomacy, patience, waiting for the right moment to intervene, and knowing how to avoid being noticed when it is not appropriate. Protection against invasions of insects, energies that are too animalistic, too scattered, too dispersed.

⊖ Difficulty adapting to changing conditions on the physical level, adjusting to different atmospheres and ambiances. A sneaky, chameleon mind and spirit, someone who changes his energy to attack and obtain what he wants; or, a shy, timid, introverted person who hides in order to flee situations and people due to fear or an inability to assert himself. May indicate someone who is afraid of change; or, on the contrary, someone who easily changes his mind, his opinion, his soul-state (mood), who is inconsistent. Tendency to nourish ourselves on primitive, scattered, non-evolutive energies. Lifestyle that is over focused on matter; or, marked by laziness, inertia, and a lack of motivation. Absence of love and warm feelings and sentiments, emotional harshness, emotional coldness.

LOG

A log is a piece of wood (*cf. also* this term) that serves to feed a fire. It is a resource that comes from the vegetable kingdom, which symbolizes the emotional level; it is also related to the earth element and hence our actions. Symbolically, a wooden log serves to warm us on the level of love and it brings us a feeling of well-being. In addition to creating a warm, lively, joyful, pleasant, bright atmosphere and ambiance, a log nourishes a fire, which symbolically, provides us with light, thereby allowing us to see and understand better. Contemplating a log fire crackling and glowing in the hearth is soothing, peaceful, and favors contemplation, interiorization, going within to encounter ourselves in our inner depths.

⊕ Reservoir of energy available to warm our intimacy. A capacity to create well-being, a beautiful atmosphere, and warm energy.

⊖ A lack of logs, a shortage of heating wood indicates insufficient resources to warm us on the emotional and physical level. An incapacity to create a warm, welcoming atmosphere. Wasting logs, e.g. when we overheat a house, reveals inner coldness, fear of feeling cold, a lack of warmth in the family and on the intimate level; or, people who tend to force others, to have too much energy and warmth.

LOTTERY

A lottery mainly depends on the illusion of believing that we can attain material wealth and happiness quickly, without any effort. It is not automatically negative to play in a lottery, but it is essential to do so with awareness, conscience, discernment, and detachment, knowing that it is Up Above that decides who the winner(s) shall be depending on each person's life plan. Otherwise, we stimulate materialistic needs and attitudes, which create all sorts of problems and dependencies.

Some lotteries are generous and give all or a large percentage of their gains to charitable associations and good works; there are also government-, state-run lotteries, which help to finance public works and welfare.

It is important to know that winning the lottery in a dream does not necessarily mean that we are also going to win it in concrete reality. It may simply indicate that we are about to win or have won power, force, energy and capacity to materialize our projects, that we are experimenting the state of conscience of material success and abundance. Such a dream may show us that destiny is favorable, thanks to merits we have accumulated in this life and/or in previous lives. After such a dream, we feel very prosperous on the inside, very dynamic, and full of possibilities; we feel intuitively lucky to win, to succeed, and to gain access to new resources.

⊕ A lucky, easy period of fortunate opportunities. A hopeful, prosperous, successful, victorious, joyful, happy state of conscience. Using winnings for a second chance. A providential means to raise funds and pool resources. Using resources and material power in conformity with Divine Laws, to serve good, with an intention to evolve in a right, well-balanced manner. Allows financial help for government projects, public works, charities, altruistic, humanitarian projects. Awareness that monetary wealth is a great responsibility, indicating an inner learning program, an inner apprenticeship. Winning a lottery is never a coincidence, but always pre-planned, pre-ordained for the destiny of those concerned.

⊖ An unlucky period, a lack of opportunities. States of conscience dominated by avidity, greed, envy, covetousness, seeking easy victory and glory. Deep dissatisfaction, a desire to change our life without having to make any effort or work on ourselves. Stimulation of a materialistic, selfish attitude toward life. Encouragement of illusion and dependency on gambling. Increased negative karma due to poor use of important lottery winnings because the person has neither the necessary conscience nor wisdom to manage abundance in accordance with Cosmic Laws. Winning the lottery may be part of the life plan of a person who will use the wealth received to experiment *via* distortions: a feeling of superiority, over-confidence, pride, arrogance, snobbery, power games, manipulation, speculation, exaggerated investments with illusory objectives, waste, over-consumerism, and worldly pleasures. A large amount of money won rapidly, without any preparation on how to manage the consequences, may reactivate memories of greed, and fear of losing it all; it may also trigger an obsession of always wanting to force destiny, to win again so as to feel secure, thereby opening the doorway to a dependency on gaming/gambling, as well as covetousness, and jealousy of others. Certain problems and difficulties on the emotional and relational levels that stem from the envy, hypocrisy, dishonesty, and/or trickery of people who frequent the winner, and who would like to take advantage of his sudden wealth.

LUGGAGE

On the physical level, luggage contains what a person needs to take when traveling. Symbolically, it represents useful, practical things, personal resources, and the knowledge needed for exploring and experimenting other zones of conscience, other dimensions of life. It also symbolizes the sum of positive and negative thoughts, emotions, actions, experiences, abilities, and memories accumulated and inscribed in our soul over the course of many lives, which are also referred to as *karmic luggage**.

⊕ Knowing how to be satisfied with essential, truly useful, necessary luggage indicates a capacity to make good use of resources, and to be well organized on business trips, travelling, and moving house. Potential that confirms a capacity to make decisions and get projects off the ground, ability to make good use of positive karmic luggage, and the necessary willpower to transform the negative karmic luggage that manifests in the process. Finding it easy to travel with our conscience.

⊖ A lack or loss of luggage indicates insufficient knowledge or resources to carry out projects. An incapacity to manage our personal means, to organize trips, learning experiences, and to explore new regions, new aspects, and states of conscience. Surplus luggage reveals too many needs. The person is burdened, encumbered, slowed down, hampered, and limited by numerous memories stemming from his present life, or from his past lives, and these memories prevent his advancing, and are detrimental to his evolution. A person who carries his karmic luggage from one life to the next, who resists liberating himself from it; or, who refuses to do conscious work on cleansing, transforming and transcending it.

Karmic luggage* refers to the numerous, usually negative thoughts, emotions and deeds (*mis-thoughts, mis-emotions* and *misactions* (*cf.* this term), known as karma, that a person accumulates during the course of his many lives, and continues to bring with him into his present and future life/lives until he learns to cleanse, transform and transcend them, until he manages to settle any karmic debts he may have incurred. (*cf. also* **Karma; Memory**)

LUNG

Human beings breathe thanks to two lungs (the right and left lungs), each of which is made up of several lobes. Air, inhaled through the nose or mouth, first penetrates the trachea (windpipe), and then arrives in the main bronchi – right and left. These large bronchi divide into many smaller bronchiole. At the base of each bronchiole, there are a cluster of little bags called alveoli, where gaseous exchanges with our blood take place: the inhaled air provides oxygen (O_2) for the blood; the exhaled air allows the rejection of carbon dioxide (CO_2). Hence, lungs help purify the blood, while favoring its circulation. Furthermore, lungs also play an essential role in helping the brain function well, since our brain needs a considerable amount of oxygen.

The metaphysical role of lungs and their symbolic meaning are closely related to the symbolic meaning of air (the world of thoughts), the brain (the intellect), and blood (vital energy). On the metaphysical level, lungs represent a true place of exchange, transformation, and recycling of emotions engendered and maintained by our thoughts. The fact that our heart is situated between the lungs shows that love and inspired motivation help transform distorted, harmful thoughts and emotions. On the metaphysical level, a cycle of integration and elimination of thoughts and emotions corresponds to the movement of inhalation and exhalation. This dynamic, that is essential for life, ensures the perpetual cycle of deaths and rebirths on all levels of our being: physically with anatomical and cell functions, but also on the emotional and intellectual levels. Indeed, through lung activity, breathing allows the transformation and alchemy of negative energies and influences in order to ensure balance and harmony in all of our being.

⊕ Ability to renew vital energy, and to filter, transform, and purify emerging thoughts and emotions. Conscious use of the regenerating, invigorating power of our lungs through breathing. Someone who knows how to stimulate and motivate himself, who consciously uses his discernment and powers of reflection, motivation and decision. Feelings of deliverance, liberty, expansion and plenitude. A capacity to accept what occurs and let go when confronted with whatever we cannot change. Capacity to transform thoughts that engender negative emotions, moods, soul-states. Open-mindedness, integration of new, fairer concepts, and a healthier lifestyle. Work on ourselves allowing us to develop greater sensitivity as well as the determination to free ourselves from our bad habits and all sorts of dependencies.

⊖ Lung deficiency or illnesses indicating difficulties transforming negative thoughts and emotions. Unsatisfied, unquenched affective needs, repression, frustration. Suffocating thoughts on the affective level, possessiveness. Difficulty transforming old concepts and opening up to and understanding new ideas; resistance to change. Destructive hyper-sensitivity. Poor state of health; healthy, well-balanced functioning hampered by thoughts and emotions that nourish various forms of dependency, as well as a need to please and be loved. Susceptibility, complaining attitude. Someone who retains, plays roles, and consciously or unconsciously hides his true intentions. Difficulty asserting ourselves, taking our place, expressing our thoughts and emotions, manifesting our potential. An introverted, morose, sad, despondent, pessimistic character. Tendency to bear a grudge, to be resentful, proud, vengeful, and find it difficult to forgive. Complacency regarding harmful, self-destructive, dangerous habits. Someone who is easily influenced and may be manipulated; or, who may easily influence and manipulate others. Blocked breathing, a tendency to brood over unhealthy thoughts, to go around in circles, and to become introverted. Bad attitudes and living habits that prevent us from using our full breathing, vital, and emotional potential. A lack of lucidity and understanding on certain levels, nourishing vague or insensitive thoughts. Someone who is disloyal to his principles, who acts according to what others want; or, who rebels and impulsively explodes after retention over a very long period of time. Fears, anxieties, doubts, lack of faith in our life plan, in the fact that everything exists to help us evolve by inciting us to develop qualities and virtues. Tendency to want to control everything, to hold on to our privileges, past glories and everything we have attained. A heavy, encumbered conscience.

M

MAGIC, MAGICIAN

Doing magic symbolically represents using Divine Powers to create, to achieve transformation and transubstantiation. Magic symbolizes the highest levels of conscience in the materialization process, and the fact that everything is possible on the Divine Level. It is not the fruit of our imagination, but rather the representation of the capacity of our human mind to surpass form, to transcend our limits, and create manifestations of life all around us, in both the metaphysical and physical levels. Without knowing or understanding the significance and impact of our capacity for *magic*, we are all *magicians* because we constantly create the reality we live and experiment in, through our thoughts, feelings, emotions, and intentions. Whenever these creations conform to Divine Law and Order, the term white magic is used; and in the contrary case, black magic and witchcraft.

Even though magic is mainly a source of entertainment, by using illusion and special effects, it awakens memories in us where this power may have been exerted. In a dream or concrete reality, magic practiced in a negative context, or with distorted intentions, represents power-seeking, a need to be acknowledged, a need to impress, manipulate, influence, to take others in, to fool them. A true magician is an initiate who never uses his powers to boast, show off, entertain crowds and satisfy their curiosity. Neither does he serve any monetary or political power in the sole interest of becoming rich in matter.

Interest in magic indicates that the person is open to the metaphysical, spiritual dimension of life, that he wants to understand the mysteries of Creation, to go beyond a lifestyle limited to ordinary conscience. However, this requires considerable work on our karmic *luggage* (*cf.* this term) and unconscious memories in order to be able to transcend doses of negativity, and hence raise ourselves up and evolve, and not regress and fall.

Being afraid of magic, believing ourselves to be the victim of magic in concrete reality or in a dream, indicates that we have memories of wrongly used spiritual powers, which have deeply marked our soul. However, we can only be subjected to its effects if we resonate with these practices, have already done or experienced the same thing in this life or previous lives, and if, consciously or unconsciously, we fear the Law of return, the application of Divine Justice.

⊕ Capacity to develop or use Divine Powers in their purest state, to create something generally considered impossible to achieve. Skill surpassing all forms of conventional limits, while respecting the Divine Laws. Capacity to transform negativity. Someone who has attained a very high level of evolution on the spiritual and metaphysical levels, and who uses his capacities and powers with altruistic intention, to do good. Evokes mystery. Create a sense of marvel. Opens our conscience to Divine Power, miracles, and the mysteries of Creation.

⊖ Conscious practice of magic with the aim of affecting others, harming or destroying them, seeking to acquire earthly, terrestrial powers. Knowledge of magic deliberately used to satisfy selfish, egotistical needs. Black magic engendered by negative thoughts, malevolent intentions. Ignorance of the demonic power of black magic and the karmic consequences it engenders in the person who has recourse to it. Charlatanism. Need to be acknowledged, to impress, to create illusion. Someone who does not seek to transform himself or to evolve. Non respect for the Divine Laws.

MAIL *cf.* ***Letter, email***

MAKE-UP

As make-up usually concerns the embellishment of the face, its expression, or modification of its features, it symbolizes a capacity to manifest, communicate, and transform our soul-states. It reveals our general mood and personality. When a woman wears make-up, she usually does so to highlight the most beautiful parts of her face; or, to hide her flaws and imperfections. Whether applied in the right way or not, make-up accentuates the wearer's facial features and radiance. Whenever make-up is used to modify a part of the face or body, it is important to be aware of our intention, as well as the result we want to obtain when we apply it, in order to evaluate whether the energy we emanate is right, inspiring, and part of our integrity.

It is interesting to note that not only does the verb *to make up* mean to apply cosmetics (*cf. also* this term) or stage make-up, but it also means to invent, to devise a fiction, or falsehood ("*You made that up!*"), as in *to make up an excuse*, or to make up a story; and also *to make up for* means to compensate for; hence the importance of analyzing the underlying intention.

Choosing to use make-up is never a question of pure coincidence: there is always a link between the part of our face (or body) we choose to apply make-up to, and its symbolic representation. The choice of color is also an element to be taken into consideration, as is the intensity of the make-up applied. For example, when people use too much black eye shadow and eyeliner, this reveals that their vision of life and of themselves is somber and sad, and that, often unconsciously, they want to show everyone that they aren't well. Exaggeration and unsightly, ungraceful aspects always indicate the presence of a problem, a superficial, materialistic conscience, or an intention to seduce.

⊕ If make-up is well-balanced, simple, harmonious, discreet, using natural, healthy, environmentally-friendly products, it symbolizes beauty, grace, refinement, esthetics, metamorphosis, transfiguration, regeneration, eternal youth, and radiance *via* discreet, outer enhancement of inner qualities.

⊖ In its distorted aspects, make-up symbolizes seduction for personal motives, superficiality, materialism, focus on outer beauty and appearances, a tendency to play a role, to lack authenticity. It may also be related to fear of growing old, lack of self-acknowledgement, and constantly seeking to be liked, loved, noticed by others; or, hiding behind a mask, behind appearances.

MALL, SHOPPING CENTER

Given the huge quantity of goods from many different countries, malls (or shopping centers) represent abundance and access to resources, goods, and products created by people all over the world. Generally speaking, not only do we encounter a great variety of stores in malls, but there is also a variety of places to eat, which favors social encounters and exchanges. On the subtle level, among other things, malls constitute places of sharing and mutual help on the professional level, places of great concentration of physical, emotional, mental, and spiritual energies of different kinds and qualities. People who frequent shopping malls are immersed in mixtures of energies, which influence them, depending on their sensitivity, level of conscience, and the resonance they have with these energies. From a positive point of view, the reigning atmosphere and ambiance denote a feeling of great abundance, recognition and acknowledgement of other people's work worldwide; from a negative point of view, a tendency to compulsive buying, over-consumerism, compensatory behavior, and a conscience that is limited to the material dimension of life.

⊕ Access to great abundance. Facilitates business, commercial transactions, exchanges with others. Positive energy in giving and receiving. A capacity to consume wisely, moderately, and responsibly. Good management of resources without waste or useless purchases. Awareness of the impact of over-consumerism on the environment. An altruistic spirit. Feelings of gratitude for all the products available and recognition of the services rendered by the retailers, and all those who contribute to the manufacture of the products, who are sometimes subjected to very difficult conditions. Awareness that material goods are temporal and educational; understanding that all of the stages related to the creation and use of goods reveal how people experiment matter, how our conscience evolves through the different processes of materialization. Appreciation of other people's work, of what matter contributes to the development of human qualities and virtues. Transcendence of artificial needs. Development of a consumer mentality and spirit that respects man and the environment, and favors right, well-balanced, fair use of resources on all levels. A pleasant, agreeable atmosphere in which to make choices, and respond to our fundamental needs.

⊖ Materialism. Over-consumerism. Waste of resources. Compulsive buying. Offering products that create and nourish ephemeral values and artificial needs, such as a need to please, to conform and behave like everyone else, to be in fashion. Superficial, hyperactive, materialistic behavior. A lack of kindness, consideration, authenticity, of an altruistic, humanitarian, ecological conscience. Atmospheres, ambiances, and exchanges of low vibration energy; energy *vampirism.* Excessive visual and aural stimulation, which drains and disperses vital energy. Dizziness, exhilaration, mental and emotional intoxication. Fatigue, exhaustion caused by an awakening of conscious or unconscious memories, related to poor use of resources; or, unsatisfied, unfulfilled needs. May awaken memories of poverty, limitation, exploitation, slavery, situations of survival. Deep insecurity. Fear of lacking. Egotism. Avarice, greed, and/or miserliness. A mind and spirit solely focused on money, monetary profit, and an accumulation of material goods and valuables. An indifferent person who lets himself be controlled by his needs and instincts, and who takes everything for granted. Lack of discernment, wisdom, global vision. Disrespect for the human condition and the environment. A lack of understanding that life is interactive, that we are all interrelated, interconnected.

MAN, A (male, masculine)

On the symbolic level, a man represents the manifestation of the masculine polarity, emissivity, and action dynamics through which he concretely realizes his potential for creation and materialization. This principle refers to all of his behavior, attitudes, activities, actions and deeds.

As well as being used to refer to an individual adult male, a woman's complement, the term *man* is also used to designate the human race, humanity, mankind. While the use of *man* or *mankind* as a general term to describe the human race (in preference to humanity or human beings), is common usage, it may nevertheless reveal a social, or personal integration and maintenance of old, former, erroneous concepts of male domination (and its various abuses) as well as machismo tendencies, and priority given to the intellect and masculine emissivity.

Whenever a woman dreams of a man, or when she particularly notices a man's attitude in concrete reality, that man reflects certain aspects of her inner masculine polarity, certain facets and attitudes of her inner man. Whether we are a man or a woman, seeing a man in a dream, gives us information about our masculine polarity, informs us about the way we manifest in concrete reality. Seeing several men relates to our collective dynamic, the way we function socially, the concrete expression of our emissivity and behavior, the way we act and react. Man as representative of the masculine principle also symbolizes the spirit and is complementary to woman, who represents the feminine principle, receptivity, as well as matter and the original matrix or womb; their union, their fusion, allows us to create, materialize, and give life.

⊕ A force of action, willpower to manifest, concretize, materialize, expand, and evolve in matter and form. Blossoming and flourishing, self-fulfillment in the world of action, in the world of concrete logic. Right use of the qualities and characteristics of the masculine polarity: application of justice, wisdom, global vision, intellect, authority, a capacity to advance, a decisive mind and spirit, self-assertion, application of logic, the gift of understanding, materialization power, the characteristic of protecting and providing for the family, self-fulfillment and a sense of achievement through work, management of conflicts, dangerous situations and dynamics. Acceptance and respect for the Divine Hierarchy in Nature, awareness of our place in the Universe. Responsibility for ourselves and other species. Development of altruism. Clemency, kindness, doing good. Protector and defender of what is right. Seeking well-balanced polarities, respect and love for the feminine principle, for woman.

⊖ Distorted manifestations of the masculine polarity in both men and women. An over-emissive, hyperactive person, who abuses his power; or, who is over-focused on material results and concrete logic. Lack of love, sensitivity, inner vision. A feeling of superiority, thinking we can do what we like, misusing power and strength to dominate, abuse, impose, control, and wanting to be right at all costs. Rude, uncouth, boorish, coarse behavior, a combative attitude, a lack of empathy. Authoritarianism, acting and materializing negatively, solely in search of profit, with no thought or concern for people in general, for the human and humane aspect of things. An over-instinctive person, focused only on physical sexuality, and sometimes bestiality when taken to extremes. Selfishness, egotism, jealousy, possessiveness. Imbalanced polarities, complete rejection of our feminine side and its associated qualities. A lack of gentleness, receptivity, incapacity to express emotions. Not taking the needs of our inner world into account. Lacking initiative, energy, dynamism, involvement, commitment, concrete logic, practicality, power and strength for materialization and self-fulfillment. Not managing to manifest our potential. A tendency to let ourselves be dominated, put down. A lethargic, sluggish, lazy, too naïve, too nice, too sensitive attitude. A lack of self-assertion, an incapacity to say no and to ask for justice for ourselves (e.g. at work), or for our family. A lack of spirituality, listening, connection with the Divine.

MANAGING DIRECTOR *cf. Boss*

MANTRA

Mantra is a Sanskrit term composed of *manas*, meaning arm or tool of the spirit, and the suffix *tra*, meaning protection; hence the usual definition as protection of the spirit. A mantra is a condensed formula, consisting of a sound, or series of sounds, that follow a certain rhythm and that are repeated many times. The goal of a mantra is to discipline the mind and spirit, to teach the practitioner to concentrate on his objectives, to focus his vital energy, to develop his willpower, and to channel rational or discursive mental activity toward higher states of conscience and understanding. Its virtues, combined with the intention and concentration of the person reciting the mantra, are truly beneficial and are a considerable help toward activating the development of qualities and virtues, while facilitating divine inspiration and access to the spiritual level. Reciting mantras also favors development of right, just, qualitative receptivity and emissivity. Furthermore, a mantra is good help for meditation, which opens our conscience and our unconscious. Regular practice leads to physical and spiritual benefits, and allows us to regain calm, peace, and harmony on the level of our mind, spirit, emotions, and actions. Mantra recitation, chanting and/or singing may be carried out during meditation, prayer, and/or a sacred ritual; or, in the very heart of our daily activities. Like meditation, mantra recitation also renews and replenishes our energy on all levels.

Seeing or hearing ourselves recite a mantra – no matter the tradition, provided it is right and just – indicates that we are seeking to integrate the qualities represented by the mantra in question, that we are carrying out inner work, seeking rigor, concentration, and discipline on the spiritual and decisional levels. It may also be used when seeking understanding or answers to all sorts of questions. It is useful to know that we can repeat a question like a mantra, and hence trigger dreams, signs, inspirations, and visions that will lead us to or give us the answer.

⊕ A means of spiritual and multi-dimensional connection, integration and communication. Communion with the Divine, glorification of His Name and what He represents. Facilitates concentration of the mind and spirit as well as access to superior states of conscience. Focuses on the intention. Strengthens willpower on all levels. Helps us acquire purity of intention, apply metaphysical knowledge, and transform negative attitudes. Develops spiritual powers and extra-sensorial capacities (clairaudience, clairvoyance, clairsentience); favors access to dreams and signs. Raises our vibratory level. Activates ancestral knowledge and wisdom. Helps us find answers to our questions. Favors the transmission of information between the spiritual worlds and the material level. Helps restore balance between receptivity and emissivity, helps unify the masculine and feminine principles, intuition and the intellect, the earthly, terrestrial self and the Divine Self. Facilitates detachment and development of global awareness, global conscience. Trains our capacity to manifest divinely in matter. A state of prayer, meditation, interiorization and inner harmonization.

⊖ Reciting a mantra with an impure, distorted intention may reveal a search for spiritual power in order to satisfy the needs and aspirations of our ego, to control our own destiny or that of others. It may denote eloquence oriented toward obtaining personal benefits and use of knowledge solely for material objectives and goals; or, deep insecurities, lacks, fears. May trigger spiritual extremism, idolatry, rigidity, isolation, rejection of matter, flight/escapism from experimentation in concrete reality. May be related to a lack of concentration and spiritual intensity. Dispersed, scattered mind and spirit. Superficial mantra recitation. Difficulty going within, interiorizing, meditating, and fusing our masculine and feminine polarities. False spiritual values. Hypocrisy.

MAP, ROADMAP

Roadmaps represent knowledge of roads, and a capacity to orient ourselves, and plan appropriate itineraries to get to our destination, both in concrete, physical reality as well as in the subtle, metaphysical levels. Maps facilitate journeys and travel plans, and help us to situate ourselves in unknown territory. A roadmap can give a good indication of the route to follow or avoid, the direction to take, and the inner places we may visit.

⊕ An overall view of already existing highways, roads and paths, or those to come. Helps orientation, route planning, and distance evaluation. Information as to the quality of roads, and the services and resources available. A capacity to explore and discover new regions in the outer and/or inner world. An ability to find resources, services. A capacity to guide others. A spirit of synthesis, global vision. Inner knowledge of different worlds and the paths leading to and through them.

⊖ Difficulty or incapacity to orient ourselves, to find our way; or, excessive analysis and reflection to decide which road, which path, to take. A lack of confidence, fear of getting lost. An error of judgment regarding which road to follow. Dependence on outer indications. An incapacity to trust our intuition, our inner voice, to find the right road, the right path. Erroneous, or incomplete road information. Insufficient knowledge of road symbols, or difficulty interpreting them correctly. A limited spirit due to an incapacity to have an overall view, lacking global vision. Fear of traveling, of taking unknown roads and paths, of experimenting expansion.

MARRIAGE

Marriage is a symbol of loving union, creative fusion of the two complementary principles, the masculine and the feminine. On the metaphysical level, marriage means that, on the inside, within himself, a person harmoniously fuses his emissive masculine polarity and his receptive feminine polarity on all levels of his being, thereby enabling him to rediscover his Divine completion, his unity with the Divine Source, and to experience Love, Wisdom, and Divine Materialization.

On the human level, marriage designates the decision of two people who love each other to unite their destiny, share their lives, support and respect each other, and evolve together to realize their creative potential by founding a family and/or materializing projects in common. For a marriage to succeed and lead to lasting happiness, it is essential that the spouses are in harmony, in affinity on all levels of their being (spiritual, intellectual, emotional, and physical), and that their main aim is to evolve together by learning to become better people, better souls. When human marriage is the result of a conscious choice that takes into account the respective life plan and affinities of each of the spouses, as well as the life mission that they have in common, then their union becomes the grounds for an extraordinary spiritual path, allowing them to experiment and concretely materialize the marriage of spirit and matter, and to live and experience happiness on Earth.

However, if the marriage is mainly based on physical attraction, on material considerations and projects, and there is a lack of communication and affinity between the spouses, a lack of spiritual conscience, aims and goals in common, then, sooner or later, the relationship will disintegrate. Indeed, divergences between spouses engender multiple tensions as well as great difficulties on all levels. This may then manifest in the dilution of each spouse's fundamental values and principles, more and more discrepancy in their day-to-day functioning, where each person withdraws into his *bubble* with his habits and personal interests, excluding the other, and hence gradually developing the living dynamics of a couple where, in actual fact, each person is alone.

⊕ A loving union based on commitment, fidelity, loyalty, and mutual trust and respect. A happy, harmonious, well-balanced, stable marriage that engenders happiness, *joie de vivre*, plenitude, self-confidence, and favors the fulfillment of both spouses on all levels. A haven of renewal, replenishment, creative inspiration, inner and outer peace. Reciprocal support, comfort and consolation, and protection in both good and bad times. Understanding the other person's need for solitude, for periods when he needs to be alone to be able to meditate, to call himself and his life, his work, his attitudes and emotions, etc., into question, to replenish his energies and healthily renew himself on the individual and relational levels. Spouses who mutually encourage and support each other in the realization of their life plan, the manifestation of their potential, the materialization of their shared works, humanitarian projects, or their altruistic life mission. A capacity to communicate, exchange ideas, make decisions, and learn from each another. A sense of responsibility, commitment, mutual respect. Legal and moral structures that allow for fusion and sharing on all levels. Encounter of our twin soul, spiritual fusion. Conscious inner unification of the masculine and feminine principles. Marriage of both the inner and outer couple. Experiencing complementarity in daily life, in the heart of the family, in the realization of personal, professional, or social projects. Evolving in contact with others, which allows the experimentation of Divine Love and Wisdom. Union with ourselves, with our spouse, and with God. A harmonious, flourishing, intimate, sexual love life that inspires and multiplies creative energy. Allows for a man and a woman to found a family, provide security for it, materialize projects based on altruistic values and principles. Family spirit, a well-balanced intimate, private, and social life.

⊖ An unhappy marriage due to emotional, sentimental, affective problems and difficulties on the intimate level. An incapacity to truly communicate, a lack of affinities, presence and listening to the other person, a lack of interest in what the other person is and what he is going through, what he is experiencing in his life on various levels. An incapacity, or refusal, to express our feelings, to show our love. A lack of true love, of sincere, deep respect. Difficult karmas and memories regarding love, marriage, fusion of polarities. Superficial commitment based on personal, selfish interests. A calculated marriage entered into under the influence of passion, to satisfy the expectations of our entourage, merely to do like others; or to flee solitude, to ensure financial security, etc. Infidelity, absence of loyalty. Considerable, even great imbalance between private and social life. A tendency to play roles, to pretend, so as to project the image of a happy marriage. Emotional, affective, and/or material dependency. Fear of losing the other. Possessiveness, jealousy, dangerous passion. Games of power and manipulation. Verbal and physical violence. Frequent quarrels and rows. Difficulties related to sexuality, tenderness, gentleness. An unhappy, neglected, absent intimate life; or one based on the satisfactions of basic instincts with unhealthy, perverted, violent sexuality. A tendency to take the presence of the other person for granted, to make no effort to evolve as a couple. Difficulty finding balance between our two polarities both within ourselves and in our couple. Attraction of spouses who manifest serious discrepancies between emissivity and receptivity; e.g. a very emissive, machismo type man who attracts an overly receptive, submissive, dependent woman; or, an overly emissive woman who attracts a man who is too submissive, who doesn't assert himself. Total absence of spirituality in our individual life, or in the life of our couple, in our marriage.

MASSAGE

Massage is related to a person's ability to take care of himself and others. Although there are numerous methods of massage today, their global objectives are relaxation, relief from tension, restoration and renewal of the body, mind, and spirit through the liberation of tension, stress, and general fatigue. Massage re-harmonizes vital energy and the nervous system, and stimulates lymphatic circulation that detoxifies the body. It also helps soothe and relieve negative soul-states, and calms mental hyperactivity.

Since massage is mainly done by hand, it is associated with the capacity to give and receive well-being. Massage bears an emissive, creative dynamic, which translates as a capacity to liberate stagnant energies and transform negative energies. But it also bears a dynamic of receptivity and welcome, as much for the person receiving the massage as for the person who gives it. Indeed, to reach a state of deep well-being, the receiver must be able to open up and let go so as to welcome the benefits of a massage, while the masseur has to be receptive in order to detect the zones of imbalance and tension, along with their accompanying psychological states. The masseur's receptivity guides his movements and allows him to intuitively apply the right pressure in the right place. During a massage, an alchemical process occurs between the giver and receiver since the effect of the massage goes beyond the physical body and is felt in the more subtle bodies. Hence both people are affected by the mind, spirit, and soul state of each other, of their level of conscience, the qualities of their thoughts, emotions, and intention.

In fact, intention plays an essential role in the quality of the massage that is given. While we are giving a massage, if our mind starts to wander from one thing to another, and we cannot concentrate on what we are doing, the value of the massage is diminished. Whenever we give a massage, we should always be wholly present and receptive; we should listen deeply and tune in to what the person is going through on all levels of his being. A person who decides to give a massage should be able to act with pure intention, and know how to fuse energetically with the receiver in the right way, like a parent taking care of his child, otherwise the masseur won't be able to help or treat the receiver in any depth; he could even harm him.

A massage carried out with purity of intention, authentic spiritual conscience, and respect for Divine Laws, is definitely a better quality massage than a massage given with an ordinary conscience, divided attention, and dubious motivation. The latter, whether conscious or unconscious, tends to nourish distortions both in the masseur and the receiver. It is important to know that in this field too, encounters and attractions always follow the Law of resonance: it is never a coincidence that we are massaged by a particular masseur. And in the case where we feel our vital energy is being *vampirized* during a massage, it is a sign revealing to us that this is not the right person to help us, and that we too have aspects and behavior that take other people's energies.

Massage can also be part of a couple's intimacy. It allows the couple to discover the happiness and joy of divine pleasures, provided, of course, that it is carried out with love, tenderness, respect, and in accordance with the principle of fidelity. Furthermore, in family life, massage is beneficial and favorable for the health and well-being of the children, as well as the parent-child relationship.

⊕ A means of relaxation and renewal. Helps physical and metaphysical regeneration, and, in some cases, healing. Favors improved well-being through the re-harmonization of body, soul, and spirit. Helps balance masculine and feminine polarities. Increases receptivity, sensitivity, intuition, and inner listening. Helps appease and soothe an over-intense, over-impulsive force of action and emissivity. Awareness that a massage is not limited to touching the other person's physical body, but is accompanied by energy exchanges and transfers between the subtle bodies of masseur and receiver. An understanding of the importance of respect for the other person, and giving a massage with pure, altruistic intention, and right motivation. Development of the gift of self. A capacity to care for and treat ourselves, and others. Allows us to practice giving and receiving unconditionally. Awareness of the importance of giving a massage in a calm, pleasant, harmonious atmosphere, with a state of mind that emanates serenity and inner peace. A capacity to transform negative, disharmonious energies perceived during the massage.

⊖ An incapacity to massage ourselves, or others, and/or difficulty receiving a massage may indicate problems regarding touching, being touched, and intimacy, following traumatic experiences or physical abuse, which profoundly marked and hurt the person; this may also denote great de-polarization, great imbalance, between the masculine principle and emissive potential on the one hand, and the feminine principle and receptive potential on the other. Refusal or resistance regarding massage sometimes reveals feelings of aversion and rejection, power games, or psychological manipulation. Whenever we enjoy massage, but don't grant ourselves the time either to give a massage or to be massaged, this means we are too busy in matter, too absorbed by action dynamics. We may also have both the time and means, but not grant ourselves the benefits of a massage simply out of laziness, inertia, lassitude, or a lack of willpower to look after and take care of ourselves. There is also the case of idle people, who constantly seek superficial, physical pleasures as a means to temporarily fulfill their emotional, affective lacks, their inner void; or, to satisfy their needs and desire for sensuality, seduction, and infidelity. In certain massage contexts, people, consciously or unconsciously, stimulate their sexual desires, vanity, pride, memories, and tendencies toward licentiousness and prostitution. A tendency to fuse without discernment on the energy level. Problems with authenticity and identity. Energy vampirism. Practicing as a professional masseur only to make money, without an altruistic conscience, without a sincere wish to contribute to our fellowman's well-being.

MASTURBATION

Masturbation represents a state of conscience that relates to the sexual dimension of our vital energy, as well as the need for love, affection, relaxation, and well-being. When the act of masturbation is carried out with an elevated conscience and right intention, as well as procuring pleasure and relaxation on the physical level, it allows us to attain a state of inner exaltation through the fusion of the two complementary polarities everyone has. Whether we experience this act alone, or as a couple, masturbation favors the apprenticeship of the mastery of our sexual impulses and instinctive needs. However, associated with the use of unhealthy fantasies, masturbation may engender profound imbalance on the emotional, psychological, and mental levels, nourish distorted affective relationship memories, and harm, or even destroy, our capacity to truly love.

As it is an act that mainly concerns our hands, masturbation also relates to our capacity to give and to receive on the intimate level, our capacity to touch and take care of ourselves without fear, inhibition, guilt, or reproach.

Masturbation also allows the evacuation of surplus vital energy, and hence the re-establishment of inner balance when sexual needs manifest too intensely, particularly during adolescence. Nevertheless, it is important not to use this act as a vent or outlet to satisfy affective lacks, perverse sexual desires, or to indulge in any fantasies related to idealized, idolized, inaccessible people. Masturbation as a sacred act and spiritual meditation allows us to gradually elevate our vibration level, as well as our state of conscience, and it teaches us to unite our human self to our Divine Self, in other words, to marry spirit and matter, respectively represented by our vital energy and our physical body. Whenever we are not in a couple relationship, instead of projecting our thoughts and desires onto another person, it is better to imagine or think of a beautiful symbol such as a mountain, river, flower, or any other harmonious landscape or image. If alone, without a loving companion, such mental imagery sets us free from our affective dependencies while simultaneously creating beautiful states of conscience linked to sexuality. Of course, we may imagine our companion and make love to him or her *virtually* with pure thoughts of unconditional love, but it is important not to fantasize about people who are not our love-partner. Masturbation while thinking of a beautiful, pure image, or our beloved companion, helps to improve the circulation of our vital energy, and channels our instincts and sexual needs in a right, healthy way, associating sexuality with elevating beauty and purity and feelings of love.

In the Western world, limited vision and an erroneous understanding of the body and sexuality, widespread in certain religions, led to masturbation being very much repressed for several centuries. Today, it is recognized as a normal, healthy, natural, sexual activity, whether experienced alone or in a couple, provided it is carried out in conditions which favor interiorization and respect our intimacy, allowing us better self-knowledge and self-command or mastery.

⊕ A means to relax and restore balance and equilibrium by helping our vital, sexual energy circulate. Allows us to acquire better knowledge of ourselves, our body, and the pleasures it allows us to experience on the physical and subtle levels. Improves the perception of the circulation of vital energy in the chakras and along the meridians. Offers an opportunity to meditate spiritually while practicing mastery of our instinctual needs and sexual impulses. The positive aspect is to be found mainly in the awareness and purity of the intention with which the act of masturbation is accomplished. Allows us to awaken the potential contained in our vital, sexual energy in a right, just, qualitative manner, and to experience the sublime pleasures of intimacy with ourselves in harmony with our Divine nature. Favors preparation for the sexual act, and the fusion of the complementary polarities in both the inner and the outer couple. A sacred moment of love and tenderness for ourselves, as well as exaltation and communion with ourselves.

⊖ Waste of vital, sexual energy. Subservience or enslavement to coarse, boorish, instinctual needs, and unhealthy, perverse sexual impulses. Multiples fantasies: seduction, infidelity, libertinage, voyeurism, possession, sexual abuse, rape. Dishonest, impure, distorted intentions engendering karma with serious, far-reaching consequences. Attitudes and behavior that create and maintain difficult affective memories, as well as an incapacity to love in a right, healthy manner. Seeking only physical pleasure and the satisfaction of carnal desires. A lack of principles, values, and spiritual life. Ignoring the sacred aspect of the body and sexuality. An imbalanced, unhealthy intimate life. An incapacity to love ourselves, and others, deeply and authentically. Difficult, superficial love relationships.

MATTER

Matter is subtle energy of different degrees of density in movement. Although it is perceived as dense and compact by the physical senses, research and discoveries in quantum physics have proved that, in actual fact, matter is constituted of minuscule particles that are in constant, perpetual movement in accordance with certain laws. Matter also symbolizes the power of the receptive feminine principle, which, through its fusion with the masculine principle, allows subtle energy to condense and crystallize in perceptible forms in the physical time-space dimension. However, it is essential to integrate the fact that matter is illusionary and temporal, and that its role is solely educational. Its existence is related to the fact that human beings live with a limited conscience of their body and the physical level. This limitation, which is not a permanent state, but rather the result of choice, allows us to experiment tri-dimensional time and space, as well as duality, the complementary existence of our two polarities: positive and negative, masculine and feminine, good and evil. On a higher level of conscience this limitation does not exist. Beyond the vibratory frequencies that human beings can perceive with their body's physical senses, on the metaphysical, quantum level, matter is a field of pure energy which humans can connect with, perceive, and influence through the power of their mind and spirit, and by developing their subtle senses and a universal conscience.

⊕ Development of a universal conscience and deep understanding of the creative power of the mind and spirit, and the educational role of matter. Awareness that work in and on matter leads to self-discovery and self-fulfillment through the development of qualities, virtues, and spiritual powers. Understanding the interconnection between conscience, spirit, and matter. Awareness of the creative power that mind and spirit can exert on subtle, original energy through focused intention and knowledge of the Cosmic Laws. Development of spiritual will-power, and study of these Laws to learn how to materialize divinely, how to spiritualize matter, how to evolve consciously. Study of resonance and symbolic language, which allows us to understand how the microcosm, man functions as a reflection of the macrocosm, the Universe. A capacity to recognize the existence within ourselves of the different kingdoms (mineral, vegetable, animal, human, and divine), and dimensions (physical and metaphysical) as different levels of conscience. Understanding that we human-beings create our own experimentations, our own reality of life. Work on ourselves to develop our conscience, our subtle perception, focused intention, transcendence of illusion and matter. Development of a capacity to move from the concrete to the abstract, and the abstract to the concrete. Conscious, altruistic use of matter to help our fellowman, to contribute to the evolution of the whole, to raise ourselves up through service. Existential quest to discover the cause, the source, the beginning. Respect for Divine Laws. A great initiate.

⊖ Ignorance of the fact that matter is an illusion, and that it plays a temporary, educational role. Materialistic philosophy that creates attachment to matter, and favors the development of a spirit of rivalry, opposition, competition, possession, as well as behavior and feelings that divide, separate, and render dependent, such as egotism, envy, jealousy, avidity, avarice, miserliness, vanity, a search for glory and material wealth, existential insecurity and fears, subservience or enslavement to matter, corruption. Disrespect for the Divine Laws. Lacking spirituality. Atheism. An over-rational, limited, arid mind condemned to sterility. Corrupt materialization. A lifestyle where intention and motivation are focused on the satisfaction of physical pleasures, and personal, selfish needs. A lack of understanding that everything that exists is mutually and continuously interconnected and influenced. Absence of global understanding, and universal, altruistic conscience. Impressed by matter and living solely for matter.

MAUVE

Mauve symbolizes unity, spirituality, the subtle, metaphysical worlds, creativity, intuition, magic, mystery, the dimension of dreams, visions, prayer, and meditation. It is a mixture of red, which represents materialization, incarnation, vitality, and action in the physical world, and blue, which symbolizes communication, the creative power of words, of language. The vibration of mauve is the coronal chakra, the energy center situated at the top of our head, through which the spirit is incarnated in us to act in matter, to realize projects.

If the color tone is dull, or the dream context or situation negative, it indicates discrepancy between matter and spirituality, memories where we opposed God. In a positive context, mauve and its nuances also indicate calm, serenity, a return to peacefulness, like the flowers (symbol of beautiful feelings and sentiments) that designate it – violets, lilacs, lavender –, and may restore balance and equilibrium to people who are very active in matter. In art, this color transmits spiritual visions of artists whose great sensitivity connects them to the subtle levels. Hence, right, harmonious integration of red and mauve symbolizes the marriage of spirit and matter.

⊕ A mind and spirit that is receptive to subtle, divine levels, to God. Intuition. Spirituality. Creativity. Sensitivity. Gentleness. Goodness. Capacity to nourish beautiful sentiments and to transpose feminine qualities to matter. Global, universal Knowledge and understanding. Communicates the magic and mystery of life in the multi-dimensions. A feeling of unity with Creation. Serenity. Harmony.

⊖ Absence of receptivity and opening onto the metaphysical dimensions. A very materialistic conscience that doesn't accept the existence of subtle, parallel worlds. Atheism or religious extremism. A lack of intuition, sensitivity, and creativity. Difficulty manifesting gentleness, goodness, qualities and beautiful sentiments in general.

Discrepancy between matter and spirituality, either through rejection of spirituality, or through rejection of matter in the name of spirituality.

MAZE, LABYRINTH

A maze or labyrinth refers to a complicated network of paths or passages, above or below ground, that it is difficult to get out of, or to find the center. Symbolically it represents an inextricable situation, a very difficult enigma, a challenge to surpass ourselves, to re-discover our center, and get to know the winding, complex functioning of our being. It also symbolizes a capacity to unravel, to unblock a deadlock situation, an impasse, or complex, unclear, abstract dynamics.

⊕ An ability to feel at ease in enigmatic situations and when faced with life's mysteries. A taste for research, discovery, adventure. End of a period of impasses, blockages, and difficulties. A capacity for in-depth analysis and reflection, a spirit of synthesis. A capacity to advance, to find our way in difficult circumstances, to get out of an impasse, a dead end. Development of patience, perseverance, commitment. Hope. Happy longevity.

⊖ Impasse, dead end. Confusion, distorted, warped mind and spirit. A feeling of being lost, blocked. Difficulty finding our way, understanding a complex, confused situation. A convoluted period, a slowing up of our life-plan.

MEAT

The word meat designates animal flesh we eat. The animal kingdom represents instinctual vital energy, functioning focused on the satisfaction of primary needs, maintenance of survival programming. Consequently, on the metaphysical, symbolic levels, eating meat, and the type of meat consumed, indicates how we nourish and maintain the instinctual aspects of our being, and what we need to transcend regarding these aspects. Whenever we eat meat, we don't only ingest animal flesh, but on the metaphysical level, and in terms of conscience, we also assimilate the state of conscience and subtle energy emanated by the animal's behavior, life and death. Generally speaking, a more instinctual, aggressive functioning is awakened and stimulated in the person who eats meat. Moreover, taking into consideration the conditions pertaining to mass breeding, most of the time, animal flesh is impregnated with the effects of an unhealthy, stressful, unnatural life, and very often, a violent death.

Furthermore, digesting meat requires more energy, which is then unavailable for other functions, for the development of our spiritual potential. Giving up a meat-based diet greatly contributes to and favors more peaceful, peaceable behavior.

It is possible to be a vegetarian and receive dreams wherein we see ourselves eat meat. This indicates that we haven't yet re-educated, transformed, and transcended all of the aspects of ourselves that have been conditioned and are used to functioning with instinctual, survival dynamics. If the type of meat is specified in the dream, then an analysis of its characteristics will inform us more specifically as to the behavior and states of conscience we need to rectify in our life; e.g. eating fish, an animal related to water, hence symbolically related to the emotional world, indicates how we try to satisfy our affective, emotional needs. *We become what we think, just as we become what we eat.*

⊕ Awareness of the importance and influence of our diet in our spiritual evolution. Gradual orientation toward meat alternatives. Conscious of the fact that nowadays we no longer need to kill to eat, and that eating meat means we feed on and nourish ourselves on corpses/carcasses, hence degraded energy with very low vibratory frequency, contrary to the Principles of vitality and Life. Work on ourselves to transcend the aspects of ourselves that are too instinctual, over-focused on the satisfaction of our primary needs, parts of us that still function according to survival dynamics, even though our outer reality is not a question of sheer survival. Cleansing memories of aggression, predator/prey, of a hunter who kills animals for survival or for pleasure.

⊖ Someone who is avid for meat, who ignores or avoids thinking about the fact that meat comes from a corpse, a dead animal, and who doesn't understand that he also ingests the vibratory state and level of conscience of the animal, its lifestyle, and suffering at the time of death, and that this affects the person's behavior as a human-being. A lack of understanding of what meat represents in terms of conscience and memories recorded within us, on our soul. Tendency not to think about or not to want to think about the fact that consuming meat means that a living creature is destroyed for us to eat, and that this necessarily entails karmic consequences that we will have to face one day. Ignorance of the impact of food in man's evolution and spiritual development. Someone who eats without conscience or discernment regarding the instinctual, aggressive behavior and energies of the animal whose flesh he is ingesting. Lack of will to work on ourselves so as to cleanse our survival programming and memories; lack of desire and will to transcend the hunter state of mind, predator/prey dynamics, the law of the jungle, survival of the fittest. Rudimentary, meat-based nourishment, imprinted with aggressive energy that lacks refinement and sensitivity.

MECHANIC

Generally speaking, the job of mechanic designates a capacity to invent machines, to direct their construction, assembly, maintenance, and repair. Symbolically, it represents a state of conscience related to a potential of materialization, construction, structuring, maintenance, reparation, use and handling of matter. It also implies the development and use of logic, understanding, strength, power, adaptation, and ingenuity. It is an important job in the world of action where it is most often exercised by the masculine polarity.

⊕ Specialist knowledge allowing the construction, assembly, maintenance, and repair of machines and vehicles on the physical level, in the world of action. A logical mind and spirit. Accuracy, precision. Discernment. Lucidity. Mental powers. Ingenuity. Intuition. Understanding the Laws that ensure structural coherency, compatibility, and solidity. A great capacity to materialize with the four elements. Awareness that the job we do in the material world has its corresponding *match* in the immaterial world.

⊖ An incapacity or difficulty to build, structure, maintain, or repair on the material level, in the world of action. A lack of knowledge, know-how, accuracy, precision, discernment, and logic to materialize with the four elements. An overly down-to-earth, matter-of-fact, materialistic conscience that lacks spirituality. Boorish, coarse, rough behavior, lacking in grace, subtlety, refinement, sensitivity, and depth. Refusal to acknowledge and respect the existence of the Divine, of a Higher, Superior Power, God, or whatever name we wish to use. An over-rational mind that wants to control and repair everything according to how he sees and understands things. Emissivity that sometimes manifests in a violent, brutal manner. A job exercised with a machismo attitude.

MEDICATION

A substance or preparation, made from chemical or biological components, administered with a view to treating or preventing an illness, or restoring, rectifying and modifying organic functions. Symbolically, a medical drug represents a state of conscience related to a desire to heal, relieve, repair, or solve a health problem *via* exterior means. It may also symbolize Grace, Divine help to regain our health.

⊕ Helps to heal. May represent a second chance, Divine Grace, healing, or miraculous assistance. Understanding the fact that health blockages and problems are engendered by negative memories and behavior. Incites us to reflect upon the cause of physical and metaphysical ill-being, illnesses, and dysfunctions.

⊖ Seeking facility, rapid healing, without calling the illness into question and reflecting on its causes, not consciously participating in our recovery, not making any effort to heal deeply by changing erroneous attitudes and behavior; an unhealthy, imbalanced lifestyle. May also refer to a person who refuses medication, who does not want to receive assistance, who does not wish to have recourse to exterior remedies, to the detriment of their health. A false, erroneous understanding of healing, a tendency to believe it can only be achieved through exterior means and/or intervention limited to the physical body. Ignorance of the fact that true healing is a process that takes place mainly within, on the inner level, that it progresses from the causal level toward the level of consequences. A lack of understanding of body language, the signs and signals our body emits to indicate that there is a problem. A risk of addiction and medical drug dependence, that can go as far as intoxication, poisoning, through ignorance of the contra-indications, or through indifference regarding the side-effects. Recourse to medication because of insecurities, discouragement, or a lack of healthier, natural and/or spiritual alternatives. Relentless, intensive use of medical means to prolong life. Administrating or taking of new medication without really knowing the long-term effects and consequences. Medicine without conscience.

MEDITATE, MEDITATION

The act of meditating is related to a state of conscience of interiorization, introspection, inner listening, contemplation, self-encounter, and deep reflection on Life and Creation in general. Regular meditation allows us to calm our mind, to better manage the stress and tensions of daily life, and to attain a state of serenity and inner peace. It leads to better knowledge of ourselves and others, and favors the evolution of our conscience as well as the development of global, multi-dimensional vision, and a causal understanding of different incidents, events, and manifestations of life and existence. Meditation is also an effective means to renew, regenerate, and re-harmonize ourselves on all levels. It helps toward awakening unconscious memories, and a gradual reactivation of psychic and spiritual capacities, thanks to the development of our subtle senses, called paranormal or extra-sensorial. It is also a tool to help perceive the multi-dimensions. In a meditative state, we can have visions, receive revelations, answers to our questions, solutions to our problems. However, it is important to become familiar with symbolic language and the interpretation of signs, because the messages obtained in meditation always come to us in the form of symbols or feelings.

⊕ Helps us discover and integrate Knowledge, improve ourselves, and solve the enigmas of Life. An important tool for anyone on a spiritual journey. Helps develop psychic, mediumnic capacities, spiritual powers, multi-dimensional perception, and access to the parallel worlds. Allows us to go down into our unconscious, visit the memories contained therein, and hence deepen the understanding and study of our life experiences. Helps reprogram our beliefs, our thought patterns, our mental and spiritual concepts. Facilitates contact with our own and others' souls, as well as communication with Cosmic Intelligence, with God. Helps us gain access to the causal level and Divine thought. Reactivates innate Wisdom and Knowledge, and gradually leads us to Enlightenment. Favors the rise of the kundalini and the harmonization of the masculine and feminine polarities. Procures feelings of well-being, serenity, inner peace, plenitude, light-heartedness and elevation. Helps us master stress and remain calm, confident, well-centered and focused in all circumstances. Activates our powers of alchemy, our capacity to transform negative energies into positive energies and to understand the educational role of evil, wrong-doing, what hurts.

⊖ Difficulty interiorizing, a lack of discipline to find time to meditate, fear of accessing the unconscious levels of our being. A negative attitude regarding meditation, refusal to recognize and acknowledge its usefulness and effectiveness without even trying it. Seeking the fastest, most sensory, anesthetizing, easy means to reach illusory serenity and nirvana; fleeing responsibilities, all sorts of dependencies. Materialistic, rational, atheist mind that denies the existence of the Divine, of subtle realities, of psychic, mediumnic capacities; or, on the contrary, spends too much time meditating so as to flee problems and physical reality. Subjection to excessive, exhausting periods of meditation in the context of religious extremism. Difficulty accepting the fact of being incarnated, of living in a material body. Cultivating a feeling of superiority and spiritual pride through meditation. Using meditation with selfish intentions, with the aim of acquiring spiritual powers. Imposing meditation with brusque, sharp willpower and destructive authority.

MEMORY

Memory is an organic, psychological function that allows us to record, preserve, and restitute the information we have accumulated. Memory constitutes our ability to remember, to mentally reconstitute the past for ourselves. It participates in our identity, intelligence, and affectivity, because it allows us to store what we perceive and record through our 5 senses (hearing, sight, smell, taste, touch), which are entrance doors permitting access to information coming from both the outside and the inside, such as pain or pleasure.

The specialized areas of our brain: associative, sensitive, gustatory, visual, auditory, and olfactory constantly recognize, analyze, and deal with information conveyed through our senses. This sensorial, sensitive memory sets our tastes, preferences, and our search for sensation. Our conscious memories represent a tiny, minuscule part of our global memory, the majority of which remains hidden behind the veil of unconsciousness. This veil separates what we know about ourselves from what we have forgotten, repressed, frozen, buried, stored away, left waiting, dormant, or half awake. Even if we don't know about all these memories, they are still present in us and affect us in many ways depending on the category they belong to. Indeed, the unconscious memories contained in our soul, or *personal computer*, are also connected to collective memory, i.e. to all that exists in the Universe. They can be identified under the following categories:

Unconscious personal memories. Lodged directly underneath the veil, in the unconscious part called the subconscious, these memories are nearest the conscious level;

Memories concerning all of the elements of our life from life in the womb till today. They represent our ***deep** personal unconscious*;

Unconscious family memories transmitted by our family and ancestors;

Unconscious ethnic memories accumulated by our race or ethnic group, containing all the events it has experienced;

Unconscious collective memories accumulated by the whole of Mankind, as well as all of the archetypes (the knowledge and meaning of all symbols);

And finally, the *unconscious organic memories* contained in the history of Life from its origin.

Since we have existed, just like a living computer, we have recorded in our soul all of our positive and negative memories. Our behavior and attitudes are the result of our evolution, which occurs in accordance with our memories. Memories manifest in different forms according to the Law of resonance, always revealing certain known or unknown aspects, facets, and characteristics of ourselves. Our memories reveal who we have become, and who we were in all of our lives. They represent the numerous influences we experienced, and they warn us of what we could become if we do not transform the negative that dwells in us into a positive, constructive force. Simultaneously they connect us with everything that exists in the Universe. They are our multi-dimensional, karmic *luggage* (*cf.* this term), as well as the most secret memories we have kept encoded in our deepest depths.

In our dreams as well as in concrete reality, we constantly visit our memories. Often coded, we need to know symbolic language and apply the Law of resonance and the principle of the mirror effect to be able to *read,* decode, and understand them. When we begin to work on our memories, becoming aware of them, purifying, transforming, and liberating them, we are first of all put in touch with our personal and family memories. As we gradually evolve, Cosmic Intelligence orchestrates learning experiences, apprenticeships, encounters, and life scenarios for us that lead us to work on collective, ethnic memories. Our personal life program is often an integral part of a program for collective evolution, which may concern a more or less large group of people in a social, cultural, economic, political, humanitarian organization context, on a regional, national, or international scale.

Understanding the fact that we are a collection of data and memories that communicate with each other as well as with everything that exists, allows us to better perceive the multi-dimensions we visit in our dreams, as well as the magic of synchronicity and coincidences that manifest in our daily life. We always attract, on all levels, what we are, what resonates with our memories.

⊕ The recording of positive and negative experiences in our soul, in the *hard drive* of our personal inner computer. A capacity to reprogram ourselves, to work deeply on ourselves, cleansing negative memories, and activating positive ones. A good memory, a great capacity for memorization. An accumulation of a large number of positive, pleasant, constructive memories throughout the course of our numerous lives. Ways of thinking, doing, behaving, being, living that engender beautiful memories, positive resonance, pleasant consequences and *harvests*, i.e reaping beautiful results from what we sowed. Understanding that Memory, or the Universal Library (Daath) contains the entire collection of individual, collective, planetary, and cosmic experimentations and events, on all levels and in all dimensions of Creation. An ability to understand how important it is to know the constitution and functioning of human and universal conscience, the Cosmic Laws, especially those that govern resonance, karma, and reincarnation, as well as symbolic language, in order to be able to cleanse, transform, reprogram, liberate, and transcend negative memories, and activate positive memories when necessary.

⊖ A person submerged in negative memories, or who constantly nourishes them, thereby accumulating in his present life all sorts of tensions, difficulties, and blockages, which are added to those of his previous lives. Problems of memory and deep understanding, which manifest in various forms of forgetfulness, oversights, memory lapses, partial, temporary, or total amnesia, Alzheimer's disease, etc. A lack of understanding of conscious and unconscious memories related to negative, limiting, prejudicial states of conscience, thoughts, emotions, deeds, experimentation, and life experiences that a person has accumulated during the course of his lives, which constitute his karmic *luggage*. Refusal to work on ourselves to cleanse, transform, and transcend these memories so as to be able to continue to evolve. Resistance or refusal to take responsibility for the consequences of past experiences; not wanting to understand or accept that we always reap what we have sown in this life or in our past lives. The involutive life dynamic of an old soul that goes round and round in circles from one life to the next, continuing to weigh himself down, remain stuck, crystallizing in the same negative patterns. Nostalgia, a tendency to live in the past; or, to project ourselves into an imaginary future.

MENSTRUATION (monthly period)

Menstruation (or monthly period) is the most visible manifestation of a woman's menstrual cycle. In the absence of pregnancy, menstruation consists of the disintegration of the functional layer of the endometrium (the inner wall of the uterus), which is periodically discharged through a more or less abundant loss of blood through the vagina. Hence, menstruation corresponds to a period of purification and deep transformation of vital energy and creative power. On the metaphysical level, menstruation indicates that this purification is being carried out on all levels (physical, emotional, intellectual, and spiritual). Menstruation favors the regulation of a woman's emissivity and masculine polarity. The sudden decrease in hormones during menstruation allows a woman to become more sensitive to subtle energies; she can then better incarnate feminine qualities: love, receptivity, gentleness, welcoming, nurturing energy, etc. Hence, each month, the menstrual period reminds a woman of the deep, sacred meaning of being born a woman. Painful periods are a sign that the woman is setting herself free from blocks of unconscious memories that resist purification and transformation. In the case of amenorrhea, which isn't the result of pregnancy or the menopause, analysis of the organ or cause responsible for the absence of menstruation will determine the symbolic explanation.

⊕ Physical and metaphysical purification. Regulates the hormonal cycle, renews vital energy, harmonizes the masculine and feminine polarities. A period of transformation, renewal, deep cleansing. Periodic regeneration which reflects fecundity. Helps women become more receptive and develop, integrate, and manifest feminine qualities. A period of interiorization, of being in touch with our sensitivity, our feminine nature. Purification of memories from this and other lives.

⊖ Problems resulting from an incapacity to purify and renew ourselves, to maintain fecundity. Negative temper or mood due to an accumulation of tension, anger, things left unsaid, badly managed hypersensitivity, old distorted memories. Imbalance and discrepancy between the feminine and masculine polarities. Excessive emissivity. Overly masculine, emissive, active energy on the personal, professional, and social levels. Difficulty incarnating and manifesting feminine qualities. Absence of femininity; or, feminine energy that is too harsh, lacking gentleness, softness, and a capacity to listen and welcome. Difficulty going within, interiorizing, resting, and favorably renewing ourselves. A tendency to want to control everything, to believe ourselves to be indispensable. Great loss of vital energy in the case of particularly abundant menstruation. Refusal to accept changes that arise, or modifications programmed in accordance with our Life-Plan.

MIGRAINE *cf. Headache*

MILK

Milk symbolizes our first emotional, vital nourishment. Its white color relates it to spirituality, to prime nourishment at the beginning of life, of a project or situation. This liquid, secreted by a woman's (and female mammals') mammary glands, is a very rich food that ensures young children's nutritional needs in the initial and early stages of their experimentation on Earth. A symbol of purity, divine gift of self, primary energy, milk represents childhood and beginnings in every domain. Breast milk, which is nutritionally complete, well-balanced, and available at any time, ensures regular growth as well as the development of solid immune defenses during the breastfeeding period. Thanks to her milk, a mother can nourish her child on her own substance, her own vital energy, and hence transmit to him her love, wisdom, qualities and values. After breastfeeding comes weaning, when a mother teaches her child to nourish himself without breastfeeding, to discover other foods, other sources of nutrition, other energies than hers. The transmission of experience and experimenting is then added to instinct. By diversifying her child's nourishment, a mother favors her child's gradual independence from her.

It is important to know that animal milk is not suitable for human beings unless transformed into yoghurt or cheese. Cow's milk, for example, can cause allergies and weaken the immune system, among other things. Consequently animal milk is not recommendable in a healthy diet, even though the industrial world that promotes it claims the contrary. Milk made out of rice, almonds, quinoa, oat, coconut, hemp, etc. can be recommended. Such milk is related to healthy emotional nourishment, taking into account whether it is organic and analyzing the nutritional characteristics of each element.

⊕ The first, complete source of nutrition from a physical and spiritual point of view. Transmission of maternal love and fundamental human values. Altruism. Gift of self. Devotion. Emotional purity. Favorable to development on all levels. Ensures the constitution of a strong, solid immune system as well as regular growth.

⊖ Problems regarding fundamental nourishment. An incapacity to nourish the beginning of life, a project, a situation. Lack of love, altruism, and gift of self. Ignorance of the detrimental effects of animal milk and its incompatibility with human beings.

MINERAL

The mineral kingdom is a symbol of natural resources that allow us to solidify, structure, and fashion matter to construct and edify our intentions, objectives and projects. It is related to the very deep layers of our unconscious where memories of actions we committed in our multiple terrestrial incarnations are inscribed, along with memories related to the origins of the Earth.

The mineral kingdom is alive, receptive, radiant, and invigorating. However, compared with the vegetable, animal, human, and divine kingdoms, it has a primary, condensed conscience whose very slow vibration is not perceptible to our physical senses. Since human beings bear all 5 kingdoms within them in the form of states of conscience, they also have the capacity to resonate with each kingdom and all of its comprising elements. This explains the attraction we can feel for certain stones or rock formations, both in concrete reality, or when they appear in our dreams. Such an attraction indicates that we are connected to, that we resonate with corresponding unconscious memories.

⊕ Discovery and/or extraction of great inner potential, of a reservoir of natural resources allowing us to solidify, fashion, and construct our life, and materialize our projects. An inner force of transformation, alchemy, and intensive work. A capacity to condense, crystallize, or combine and ally energies to shape, attain, accomplish, concretize our aims and objectives. Access to the deep layers of the personal and collective unconscious to purify, transform, and recycle the distorted memories contained therein. Conscious work on our inner mineral kingdom. Recycling old forms of action. Discovery of treasures, minerals, metals, and precious gems in the depths of our inner subsoil, and the wise, altruistic use of the forces and powers of materialization they represent.

⊖ Distorted states of conscience related to ancient, former actions and/or materializations dating from this life or previous lives. Difficulty solidifying, constructing our life, accomplishing our projects. A boorish, too down-to-earth, matter-of-fact person who lacks spiritual conscience and global understanding of life, and the different kingdoms (mineral, vegetable, animal, human, divine) that represent it. Presence of old memories that the person refuses to cleanse, to recycle, which prevents him from renewing his life. Resistance to demolishing ancient foundations and structures that have become unhealthy and obsolete. Rigid, fossilized, hard-to-access memories. A rigid, overly cold; or, overly intense person, who is ebullient, effusive, and/or ardent, fervent, impassioned and/or seething in his inner depths. An overly slow process of transformation. Difficulty materializing due to a lack of resources, lack of funds.

MIRROR

The word mirror comes from the Latin verbs *mirare* meaning to look closely at, to observe, and *mirari* meaning to admire, to wonder at, or contemplate in order to evaluate what we see. Generally speaking a mirror designates an object made from metallic-plated glass, or any other shining or polished surface that reflects the light, and reflects the image of whatever object is placed in front of it. Symbolically, a mirror indicates a state of conscience that reveals what is hidden or veiled. The fact of its reflecting an inverted image allows us to see things, others, and ourselves from a different angle, and hence discover aspects, facets, soul states (moods), qualities, faults and flaws we aren't used to seeing. The conscious use of the *mirror effect* (by which our whole environment, everything and everyone we attract and resonate with, is our *mirror*, a reflection of parts, of aspects of ourselves) allows an in-depth observation and perception of who we are, what is going on within and around us, and what we need to concentrate our inner work on.

⊕ A capacity to see ourselves in depth, and to study our soul-states, as well as the image we offer the outside world. Self-knowledge. Authenticity. Detailed vision. Discovery of the different angles of a situation or person. Allows us to see the hidden aspects of ourselves, our aura, what we emanate. An access door to the unconscious. Can induce mediumnic, psychic states. Helps estheticism, and favors the maintenance, the upkeep of beauty, well-being, and self-esteem.

⊖ A person who is over-focused on appearances and the outer beauty of people, things, and himself. A lack of depth, a superficial, narcissistic attitude, vanity, the need to please and seduce; or, on the extreme contrary, when a mirror is rejected, or a person refuses to use one, it may be a case of a lack of self-esteem, guilt, a lack of self-acknowledgement; or, self-rejection. It may also denote a tendency to deform reality, to have a limited vision of ourselves, and others, or an incapacity to be authentic. A lack of understanding of the mirror effect and the Law of resonance, which teaches us that others represent facets of ourselves.

MISACTION

Misaction is our translation of the French expression 'acte manqué' and it encompasses the idea of a slip-up, a mishap, a mistake, a blunder, an oversight, forgetting to do what we'd intended to do, a lapsus, an act of omission, any act or non-action that is not right, that is not divinely harmonious.

MISCARRIAGE, ABORTION

A miscarriage is a natural or accidental interruption of pregnancy, sometimes referred to as involuntary or spontaneous abortion (*cf.* below: **Abort, abortion** (voluntary). Just as human beings give birth to flesh and blood human beings on the physical level, they are also fertile on the symbolic level. Hence in our dreams, children symbolize a new future, a new apprenticeship, or indeed a new part of ourselves that is about to materialize. We may also be shown events, projects and creations in the making, which, like children, are signs of our fecundity. However, when the process of materialization of renewal, whatever it may be, is halted by a miscarriage, this means that, for the moment, the person is incapable of concretizing and manifesting new energies. Developing awareness and inner work are then necessary to rectify certain behavior.

A miscarriage may be a sign that either the person has taken whatever he is in the process of materializing too lightly, or that he does not desire its realization enough. Thus, losing a child or failing to accomplish a project will oblige this person to be more conscious of his responsibilities when he undertakes a project, when he creates, and it will help him to materialize divinely. A miscarriage may also highlight problems related to the two polarities – masculine and feminine – present in every human being, which are expressed by the two forces of creation: emissivity and receptivity. Finally, in other cases, a miscarriage may turn out to be positive. It indicates that the person has stopped a process of materialization that was not right, or that did not include favorable conditions for its accomplishment. In this case, a miscarriage is divine protection, a second chance that prevents the person from undergoing a difficult situation.

The verb *to miscarry* is also used to mean failure to achieve an intended purpose: e.g. a plan that miscarried means it went awry; it didn't work out as intended.

⊕ Protection, liberation, prevents wrong materialization. A sign that favorable conditions for materialization are not present. A period of reflection on life, calling into question values and principles. An opportunity to rectify and help our behavior evolve. A period of change, reorganization, inner work. Awareness of the importance of life and of the responsibilities we have when creating works.

⊖ A problem of infertility. An incapacity to create, materialize, finalize or complete our projects. An irresponsible person, whose attitude and behavior provoke the failure of his undertakings. The presence of forces and memories which oppose the process of materialization, which harm works that have been started, projects in the making; forces and memories which do not respect life or Divine values and principles. Unconscious rejection of works we have created. Loss, emptiness, death, suffering, grief, mourning. Deep disappointment, lack of motivation to advance, pessimism, brooding thoughts, limitation. Anger, revolt, a lack of understanding of the meaning of an ordeal.

Abort, Abortion (voluntary)

To abort means to reconsider a project and terminate it before its materialization. In some cases, abortion also represents the fact of putting an end to life processes through fear, lack of confidence, through selfishness, immaturity, disrespect; or, through understanding that it is wiser to wait for more appropriate conditions for giving birth to a child or materializing a project. It is a decision to recycle a creative impulse, an idea, a situation, a relationship; or to destroy our own vital potential, what we could become, our future. It is a very personal decision that may be right or wrong according to each particular case and the symbols presented in the dream or experienced in concrete reality.

The verb *to abort* is also used to mean to terminate something prematurely: e.g. *Due to mechanical problems, the rocket launch had to be aborted.* It is frequently used in reference to a military operation that has to be aborted for various reasons.

⊕ A capacity to reconsider a project before its materialization and to decide, to accept to terminate it. An understanding of the energy of life, that everything in the Universe is recycled and transformed, that nothing is ever lost, that that soul will come back at the right moment, or it will reincarnate through another mother. Self-study and self-questioning to help take the necessary steps so that such an experimentation need not be repeated.

⊖ Resistance to giving birth to a child, a project, a relationship in the world of matter. Difficulties materializing, completing projects because of egoism, selfishness, fear, or lack of confidence.

Immaturity, lack of respect toward life, the creation of heavy karmas of rejection, abandonment, failure. Strict-, or narrow-minded in the case of an extreme situation, e.g. in the case of rape resulting in pregnancy.

MISERLINESS

Miserliness corresponds to an excessive desire to have and accumulate goods because of a need to possess. At the root of this distorted behavior are memories of loss, considerable lack, and deep, existential insecurity. A miser hoards in order to feel safe and secure, and he sometimes deprives himself of essential things in life through fear of lack, of not having enough. However, miserliness is not limited to the material level. It is also encountered on the emotional level: we can be miserly with our love and feelings; also intellectually and spiritually, we can accumulate great quantities of knowledge, skills and capacities, and refuse to share them, to let others benefit from them. Miserliness is one of the seven distortions, or major vices, along with anger, vanity, pride, laziness, greed, and lust.

⊕ Work on healing memories of lack, loss, and insecurity accumulated over lives. Becoming aware that riches and true security are to be found on the inside, that there is no external guarantee, or means of ensuring we can keep accumulated possessions, whereas nothing or no one can take from us the qualities, virtues, strengths, wisdom, and knowledge developed, acquired, and integrated in our being. Understanding that money and matter have temporal, educational functions in life.

⊖ A compulsive desire to accumulate and possess. Artificial, illusory prosperity. Excessive egotism and materialism. Inner insecurity, lack, and emptiness. Absence of spiritual values and principles. Existential struggle, a vision of life based on false principles. Abuse of and emphasis on earthly power. Possessiveness and incapacity to be detached from matter and to share. Blockage, indifference, coldness, and poverty on all levels. Poor use of resources. Lack of wisdom, love, compassion. Absence of human warmth, incapacity to express our feelings. Proud, insatiable, mean attitudes. Opposed to altruistic achievements.

MONASTERY

A monastery represents a place of spiritual seeking and research, interiorization, contemplation and adoration of the Divine, of God; a place of meditation, devotion, prayer, development of a sense of community and sharing. It may be a place where we consecrate part or all of our life to rebuilding ourselves on the inside, and working on memories of excess and abuse that have been accumulated over several lives; a place where we seek a relationship with our inner divine self. It may also symbolize an old, former, even ancient structure of spiritual seeking, flight from matter, retreat from the outer world due to existential fear, discouragement regarding the state of the world; or, after deep wounds or traumas. The voluntary isolation provided by a monastery may also be a way to flee an affective, emotional, love life, the possibility of conceiving a child and the responsibilities related to family and professional life. (This does not exclude a form of monastic family, nor the fact that certain monastic tasks resemble trades and professions in the outside world). Moreover the choice of living in a monastery may denote profound egocentricity, focused on the satisfaction of selfish, egotistical needs for peace and quiet, solitude, mental tranquility. It may also be the result of erroneous spiritual knowledge.

⊕ Refuge to rebuild ourselves on the inside, to know ourselves on the human and spiritual levels. Facilitates interiorization, meditation, prayer, elevation of conscience, communion with the Divine, with God. Spiritual synergy. Great rigor in the application of the Divine Principles. Development of a sense of sacredness and ritual. Favors work on the mastery of our needs, unconditional service, submission, and devotion. Detachment from matter, privileges, personal ambition, worldly pleasures. Chastity. Peaceful community life led in all simplicity, with respect for rules and regulations, discipline, a sense of sharing, as well as harmonious exchanges. A sense of organization, work, hospitality, helping the poor.

⊖ Escapism. Isolation. Religious extremism. Rigid spirituality. Problems regarding the emotional level, life as a couple, family, children. Difficulty or fear of involvement in matter, of assuming responsibilities. Lack of *joie de vivre*, spontaneity. De-polarization, imbalance between emissivity and receptivity, incapacity to fuse the masculine and feminine principles. Repression or rejection of sexuality; or, on the contrary, distorted satisfaction of sexual needs, assuaging instinctual instincts. Disobedience and denial of the Divine Principles.

MONEY

Money, whether in the form of coins, bills or notes, checks, or bank cards, is a socially accepted means of payment in the commercial exchange of goods and services. On the metaphysical level, it is a form of energy that allows us to satisfy our needs and materialize our intentions, ideas, aims, goals, objectives, projects and plans. Our relationship with money, how we earn it, use it, and share it reveals the values and principles that dwell in us. The positive or negative symbolism depends on the intention with which we use it.

⊕ A source of energy for materializing and exchanging with others used wisely and intelligently. A person responsible for resources, who manages and administers well. Honesty. A right, fair, upright administrator. Power of materialization. Period of abundance and well-deserved prosperity. Understanding that matter is temporal and educational, and that money is merely a means that allows us to interact with others, and to work on ourselves to evolve. Material and spiritual abundance. Right, true values such as generosity, altruism, sharing, and respect for the Divine Laws.

⊖ A lack of money indicates a period of limitation on the material level so as to incite us to reflect on the way we materialize and manage our resources, on the quality of our projects, exchanges with others, and our relationships. Exaggerated spending, waste, superficiality, ensnared in a world of consumerism that continually creates false needs. Over-materialistic mentality, avidity for monetary wealth, avarice (greed) and/or miserliness, envy. Poor understanding of the role of money. Identifying with goods and possessions, as well as with the power of money. Superiority and inferiority complexes. Power struggle, corrupted spirit, illegally acquired fortunes (*dirty*, *black*, *laundered* money). Fear of money, fear of having it and then losing it. Detachment from and rejection of money in the name of spirituality. A person who does not understand the educational role of matter and money in the evolution of the human soul and spirit.

MONK

The term monk, from the Greek *monachos*, meaning single, solitary, unique, generally refers to a man who leads a monastic life. Originally, the term meant *he who lives alone, isolated.* Later, the term was, and still is, also used to designate a person living life in a fraternity, i.e. among a group of men who choose to live in retreat from the material world, in a spiritual community, in a monastery.

A monk represents a state of conscience of deep, spiritual interiorization, and sometimes withdrawal, excessive isolation, flight from personal and social responsibilities. When positive, the monk memories we bear within represent high levels of conscience related to a spiritual quest where Divine Laws and Principles come first, and where we learn to be detached from matter. They also symbolize a period of retreat, where a person prefers to be alone to reflect on his life, take stock of his situation, examine where his choices may be leading him, in order to acquire more global spiritual vision and discover the meaning of existence. He can then devote himself to cleansing his distorted memories related to the satisfaction of multiple needs and all sorts of abuses.

However, contrary to certain beliefs, the very disciplined, restrictive life of a monk (or nun, the female counterpart) is not the be all and end all of a soul's spiritual path; it is only a stage on a spiritual path. A person experimenting monastic life, especially in traditional religious contexts, deprived of deep metaphysical knowledge, will continue his evolutive apprenticeship in matter in a future incarnation, by living in a couple, creating a family that he will have to look after responsibly. In this relational, family life experience, the former monk will be able to learn how to marry spirit and matter, to consciously invest his creative powers in right, useful, individual, and collective materializations, in accordance with Divine Laws.

Seeing a monk in a dream indicates that the dreamer is on a deep spiritual path. Although monastic life leads a person to develop unconditional love, serenity, and inner peace, as well as beautiful rigor and an intense spiritual life, allowing him to carry out great inner cleansing, this choice of life may also reveal negative aspects and states of conscience such as: the rejection of responsibilities (family and others), fear of commitment in matter, distancing ourselves or fleeing from everything that could stimulate our needs and upset us in our quest for the absolute; hence a refusal to experiment materialization in concrete life. It may also denote extremism through a lack of Knowledge, great intolerance induced by a feeling of superiority and the conviction of being in possession of *the one and only* truth, as well as self-centeredness, egotism, hidden behind a façade of altruism.

⊕ Access to high levels of conscience through prayer, meditation, silence, and detachment from matter. Apprenticeship of the transcendence of needs and lacks with the aim of materializing divinely on all levels. Deep work on ourselves, allowing us to purify and transform karmic memories related to distorted desires and needs. Development of a sense of the sacred, compassion, unconditional love, devotion and service to others, to our fellowman. Seeking global vision, deep understanding of masculine and feminine polarities. A preparatory stage for the divine marriage of a man and a woman, of spirit and matter. A great capacity for concentration; the study of dreams and signs. A state of deep receptivity allowing us to receive inspiration from Up Above. Mystical experiences. Revelations, visions.

⊖ States of conscience of voluntary isolation, rigidity, religious extremism. Sectarianism. Fleeing material, love, and family life. Repressing emotional, affective desires and the needs of the body. Selfish, egotistical celibacy. Fear of facing life. Difficulty raising our conscience in matter. An incapacity to be completely and totally open and receptive. Total abstinence on the sexual level engendering great frustration, possibly leading to disorders on the physical level (pedophilia, homosexuality). Ignorance of the benefits of life as a spiritual couple, of inner and outer marriage. Limited experimentation due to discrepancies within a person, between spirit and matter, between the masculine polarity and the feminine polarity, between Heaven and Earth. Non-integration of concepts that favor the blossoming and fulfillment of life on both the material and spiritual levels; in particular, the idea that evil is educational, and that matter is grounds, terrain, soil for human experimentation.

MOON, THE

The Moon is the Earth's only natural satellite. As a star that reflects the light of the Sun, it is a symbol of receptivity, interiorization, subtle, intuitive perception, rest, contemplation, renewal and replenishment; whereas the Sun symbolizes emissivity, exteriorization, diurnal activity, and the masculine principle. Visible mostly at night, the Moon symbolizes the inner world, the hidden, unknown, mystical, magical aspect, as well as the feminine principle. Lunar cycles and attraction engender the daily movement of the tides and influence the bio-rhythm and growth stages, development, evolution, and manifestation of the vegetable, animal, and human kingdoms. The Moon is also related to the concept of time, to the definition of cycles, since its rotation around the Earth and its relationship with the Sun define the 12 months of the year.

⊕ Receptivity to the inner world, to the causal level, to spirituality, and the Divine. Mystical influence, sensitivity. A capacity to detect hidden Wisdom, to tune into and lend an ear to the messages of the Universe, to understand and fuse with the emotional world, and prepare the process of materialization by respecting the cycles, the rules, and the natural laws of the universe. A period of calm, rest, and sleep. Renewal, replenishment, meditation, interiorization, dreams, visions, astral voyages. Nocturnal enlightenment and perception, a capacity to see in the dark, to discern hidden aspects.

⊖ Difficulty being receptive to the inner world, to the Divine, to Knowledge and hidden Wisdom; or, a tendency to let ourselves be pervaded by somber, negative influences, to be dominated by instinctive impulses. Negative mystic influence; subjected to lunar cycles. Hyper-sensitivity. A dreamy attitude. Isolation, withdrawal. Conscious or unconscious flight, escapism. Affective instability, vulnerability, fragility. Fearing the light of day. Insomnia. Excessive emotionalism. Dominant instincts. Disconnection and flight from earthly reality. Difficulty becoming active, acting, and materializing. Autism. Dropping out, losing touch with reality. Depression. Solitude. Suicidal tendencies.

MOSQUITO

As a flying insect, living near stagnant or swampy, marshy waters, on the one hand, mosquitoes belong to the animal kingdom – hence representing aspects of our instinctual energy and primary needs – and, on the other hand, to the worlds of air (thoughts) and water (emotions). Generally speaking, a mosquito is perceived negatively due to its bites that lead to temporary unpleasant consequences (itching, inflammation, infection), or transmit certain diseases. It symbolizes hurtful, wounding thoughts, a mental attitude that stimulates by pricking, *biting*, stinging. As it is the female that pricks people's or animals' skin to feed on blood (symbolically, vital energy), this indicates an overly emissive, even aggressive aspect of a person's feminine polarity, that drains or *vampirizes* other people's energy because of thoughts that are over-focused on material results and the satisfaction of his needs. Furthermore, the incessant buzzing emitted when flying disturbs interiorization, preventing a return to inner calm, rest, or refreshing sleep.

⊕ Awareness of the need to work on ourselves to master our instinctual needs, to transform aggressive emotional and intellectual forces that have harmful consequences. Capacity to remain calm, centered, focused, concentrated, even in agitated, annoying, disconcerting, disorganized atmospheres and ambiances, with people who emanate a prickly, aggressive, hurtful attitude. Capacity to favorably stimulate vital energy and a creative force on the emotional and intellectual levels. Incitement to develop patience and tolerance.

⊖ Aggressive hyperactivity induced by whirling, ill-intentioned, instinctual thoughts that have the capacity to multiply rapidly. An over-active intellect or stinging, *biting* thoughts that *vampirize* others to satisfy our instinctual needs. An intensely irritable, annoying attitude that forces. Tendency to nourish negative emotional and mental attitudes that could lead to serious consequences on the individual and collective levels. Incapacity to go within, to interiorize and restore inner calm. Stagnation or loss of vital energy caused by our own or other people's thoughts and behavior. Source of infection and inflammation that weaken our health and may engender serious, even fatal diseases.

MOTHER

Mother is related to the feminine polarity, the inner world and inner action. She represents maternal love, nourishing, nutritional energy, gentleness, sensitivity, intuitive understanding and wisdom, the emotional level, initial education and capacity to prepare a child, a project, a structure, nourishment on all levels. United with a father to conceive life, she represents the feminine dimension of God, the matrix- or womb-Force of Creation that is indispensable for materialization, giving birth, construction of the physical body of the child to come in the heart of her own body. Not only does a mother nourish her child physically, but she also nourishes him emotionally, affectively, with gentleness and consolation, which is of prime importance at the beginning of life; she infuses her child with love, and teaches him the essential values for being happy and living in harmony with his environment. The emotional force and inherent *heart* or loving wisdom that characterize a mother are inherent in the feminine principle that everyone, man or woman, has within. Hence, a mother represents the way we take care of ourselves and others, or a project. She also inspires listening, devotion, altruism, Universal Love. A woman who radiates these great maternal qualities incarnates the principle of *universal mother*, and she will have a beneficial effect on everyone who comes in contact with her.

A mother, or the person who holds this position, has a great influence on the construction, the edification of a person. For some people, she may be – or may have been – the source of painful, difficult experiences. Hence, a cold, rigid, authoritarian, possessive, etc., mother is a mirror reflection of aspects we need to work on to become a better parental example ourselves, whether we actually become a parent or not. As a mother is the quintessence of the feminine principle, we all have to transcend some more or less distorted traits of our feminine side. While working on our difficult relationship with our mother, it is possible that we won't see any concrete results for our efforts. However, through images related to our mother received in our dreams, we may know the state of gradual transformation of our own erroneous, abusive, wrong, unjust behavior. The same holds true for our relationship with our father, which relates more to the masculine principle of our being, emissivity and action in the outer world.

⊕ Symbolizes the general characteristics of our inner world and our feminine polarity regarding the maternal aspect: maternal love, receptivity, interiorization, listening, gift of self, gentleness, loving kindness, consideration, comfort and consolation, confidence, encouragement, well-being. Fertility, fecundity, and a capacity to give birth to life, a project, a concept, behavior, etc. A capacity to raise, educate, and encourage learning, apprenticeship, to transmit and teach values and feelings, as well as the fundamental principles and behavior of life. A sense of responsibility and duty on all levels. In a dream, a mother may symbolize the beginning of something that is important for the dreamer's evolution; or, an aspect of the dreamer that is being developed on the inside, on the inner level.

⊖ Distorted manifestation of the characteristics of a mother and feminine qualities in general; a lack of love, receptivity, listening, gentleness, devotion, patience, loving kindness, consideration, comfort and consolation, a capacity to encourage, to take care of, bring up, and educate a child, or a project. Possessive, over-protective, excessively controlling, invasive, stifling, suffocating, castrating behavior, which restrains, or hinders, and even prevents the development of autonomy in our own or other people's children. May denote a person who seeks to render his children, works, or other people dependent on him through an unconscious thirst for power, love, or through insecurity. A negligent, irresponsible, self-centered mother, who does not do her duty by her children, who lacks presence, listening, devotion, and the gift of self. An over-emissive dynamic of functioning that is too focused on social life; a lack of privacy and intimacy. Serious imbalance and discrepancy between the feminine and masculine polarities. Fertility problems. An incapacity to procreate, to bring a pregnancy to term, to engender favorable conditions and ambiances for the manifestation of life, for the realization of a project. Multiple difficulties related to the emotional world and the mother principle on the physical, spiritual, and universal levels. An incapacity to appropriately nourish our children, our works, our creations, through selfishness, self-centeredness, emotional coldness, and a lack of maternal love. Conscious and unconscious memories marked by affective lacks, due to negligence, indifference, and situations where rejection by our mother was experienced; or, on the contrary, where we were the one who rejected the other person. A tendency to project our own fears, insecurities, disappointments, frustrations and expectations on our children and entourage.

MOTOR *cf.* ***Engine***

MOTORWAY *cf.* ***Highway***

MOUNTAIN

A mountain represents an elevation of conscience in relation to matter. It teaches us that we need to try hard, to strive, and make efforts in life in order to raise ourselves up, to attain our inner summits. The higher we raise ourselves, the more concrete manifestations of life lose their dense, condensed character, and the more unified our vision becomes.

Symbolically, for those who reach its summit, a mountain procures a feeling of light-heartedness, completion, fulfillment, and global vision of life on Earth. It also makes it easier to feel closer to God, to a Superior Power, and leads a person toward self-knowledge and knowledge of the superior qualities of the soul. If coming down a mountain is harmonious, joyful, and serene, the descent then symbolizes willpower and a capacity to enter the world of action, the world of matter, and therein incarnate the wisdom and global vision acquired on the mountain top, and also to realize, to concretize the inspirations received and implement the decisions made during the upward climb, the elevation.

⊕ Offers an elevated point of view, which allows us to see things differently, to attain global, unifying vision and understanding. Spiritual elevation in relation to matter, or descent into matter to experiment our acquired, elevated wisdom. Stability. Solidity. Power. A capacity to conceptualize and prepare the materialization of our aspirations, aims, objectives, or new projects. Favors contemplation, interiorization, meditation, a quest for self-discovery. A feeling of completion, fulfillment, accomplishment. Alleviates the responsibilities of the physical world, and the heaviness of matter. A state of mind and spirit of grandeur and success. A source of inspiration, revelation, teaching. A place of renewal and replenishment, introspection and initiation in the solitude of great heights. Feeling closer, or becoming closer to, and communing with the Divine. Spiritual rebirth. Return to the Light.

Climbing a mountain: A need and the will to become detached from matter, to elevate our mind, spirit, and conscience, to look at things and life from an elevated point of view. Seeking causality, a global vision. Desire to attain an elevated goal, an ideal, and to understand and integrate the multi-dimensions.

Attaining the summit: A capacity to persevere and surpass ourselves. Reward after great effort. Feelings of success, satisfaction, and victory. Attainment of high levels of conscience. Access to Knowledge.

Coming down a mountain: Indicates that the person is ready to act, to begin a new stage of materialization after deep reflection. A capacity to fuse meditative, contemplative states of conscience with the concrete world. A capacity to maintain our spiritual conscience while becoming involved and fully incarnating in matter. An ability to materialize in a right, just manner, in accordance with Divine Laws, and to make healthy, well-thought-out decisions.

Snowy mountain: A capacity to face cold regions, both on the outside and on the inside, to transcend our frozen feelings thanks to an elevated conscience. High, meditative, contemplative states. Access to important emotional and spiritual resources.

Alone on a mountain: A feeling of unity and fusion with the Divine. A period of reflection, introspection, self-questioning. Revelations. Spiritual communication. Global, unifying vision and understanding that allows us to solve the enigmas of life. A capacity to marry spirit and matter. A mystical, initiatic experience. Discovery of the link that unites us to everything that exists. A certitude that everything is possible. An understanding of our place, role, and function in life. Activation of Divine Power within us. A capacity to sense the Divine Harmony that is reflected in the beauty and natural order of things.

⊖ Difficulty raising ourselves up, being detached from matter; or, incarnating and being fully involved in concrete action. Heaviness, inertia. A lack of spirituality, of global vision. Excessive behavior of a person who wants to impress others, to raise himself up socially at all costs, who seeks renown, power, and glory, and is ready to do whatever it takes to achieve this. May also indicate a person who is shy and retiring, who flees social life, and is too much of a hermit.

At the foot of a mountain, feeling incapable, or afraid of ascending it: Difficulty surmounting an obstacle through a lack of courage, willpower, determination, strength, perseverance, and confidence in our potential. May also indicate that a person has limited vision, that the summit (the aim, goal, or objective) seems inaccessible, that he is bogged down in matter, and afraid to detach himself from it, to set himself free; or, he refuses a different vision of life that would disturb him in his well-settled, material comfort, and his safe, reassuring living routine.

At the top and not wanting to descend: May represent an unsociable, hermit aspect, flight from matter and social life, fear of manifesting in concrete reality; or, it may denote a feeling of superiority, a desire to remain above the world, above everyone so as to be in control, or to dominate.

An exaggerated desire and drive to climb mountains: A person who activates and nourishes his feelings of superiority, his search for power and domination. Indicates a great need for elevation, global vision that the person tries to attain on the outside because he doesn't know how to raise himself up on the inside, in his inner world, on the level of his conscience, mind, and spirit. May also indicate that a person is sated or has had a surfeit of matter and social life that he seeks to flee; or, someone who continually sets himself challenges to prove his endurance, his potential for performance, exploits, feats, in order to impress his entourage.

A dangerous, impetuous ascension: A need to experience strong sensations. Imprudence in our objectives and projects. Bad use of vital energy (extreme sport). A tendency to want to force destiny, to follow paths that are not recommended, and embark on dangerous routes.

Giving up before reaching the summit: A lack of willpower, rigor, preparation, and discipline. Heaviness. Inertia. Laziness. Some parts of the person prevent him from being detached from matter and following his spiritual elevation. Fear of the unknown and of change. Presence of inner limitations and resistance. Difficulty applying the great principles and spiritual teachings in our daily life. Feelings of guilt, failure, and inferiority. Multiple needs that impede and hinder the accomplishment of high aspirations.

Disliking snowy mountains: Indicates the presence of frozen emotions, conscious or unconscious cold behavior, which creates unease, ill-being, and prevents a person from attaining high levels of conscience.

Living alone in the mountains and feeling isolated: A rigid person who feels alone in the world. A tendency to isolate ourselves, to be cut off from our emotions, to flee others, to reject social life, and the world of matter and action. May also be a sign of spiritual extremism, and denote a person who experiences great discrepancy between spirit and matter.

MOURNING

The word *mourning* refers to the pain, affliction and sadness felt on the death of a person we were close to or shared a lot of affinities with, or of a much loved pet, or the loss of something or other that we were very attached to, that meant a lot to us. Mourning also indicates the inner process of gradually letting go of the deceased person or lost object. This process usually involves four successive stages: denial, anger, sadness, and acceptance. When mourning is healthily experienced as a transformation phase, a period of change and renewal, it becomes a contributing factor to our evolution. Acceptance of the end of a cycle and adaptation to a new reality offer an opportunity for rebirth, not only to the departed, but also to those experiencing this departure. Mourning necessarily goes hand in hand with deep questioning on the meaning of life and death. In most cases, it brings people closer and allows them to express and liberate long repressed emotions. The wish to understand the phenomenon of death often triggers the beginning of a spiritual path. As understanding is gradually acquired, the mourner reorganizes and restructures his life, and continues to evolve in a new way.

⊕ Period of interiorization and questioning on the meaning of life and death. Intense phase of both inner and outer transformations and changes during which old patterns also have to die. Work on awareness, consciousness and open-mindedness that allows us to accept, let go and ultimately transcend our loss. Spiritual growth. Deep existential reflections on life, death and rebirth. Understanding that on the metaphysical level, death does not exist, that our spirit continues its existence, and that the end of one form of life is simply the beginning of another.

⊖ Period of regrets and resistance to change. Feelings of loss, imbalance, abandonment and solitude. Deep pain and sorrow, depression, discouragement, distress, despair. Difficulty adapting and letting go. Denial, refusal to accept a new reality. Lack of understanding of death, difficulty accepting it as a stage, a passageway to another existential dimension. Lack of vital energy and motivation to face life that goes on, tendency to let ourselves go, thoughts of committing suicide.

MOUTH

The mouth is both an entrance and exit, an opening that links the inside of a person to the outside. Its symbolism is quite complex. It is a symbol of receptivity due to the fact that it receives solid and liquid nourishment from the outer world. It is a symbol of emissivity through its participation in the process of verbal (speech) and sonorous (singing) expression. It is a symbol of love and tenderness since it allows us to kiss. It is a symbol of purification as it allows us to evacuate waste air when we exhale through the mouth, to spit out whatever obstructs our throat, and vomit up whatever the body rejects in order to remain healthy or whenever it is ill. The fact that the mouth is a permanently wet environment – at least when the body is healthy – symbolically links it to the emotional level. This interconnection manifests very clearly when we begin to salivate when we think about, smell, or see food we like.

The state and hygiene of our mouth also indicates how we behave when faced with vital, instinctual needs, how we nourish ourselves. The way a person takes care of his mouth and uses it for eating, expressing himself, and manifesting his feelings reveals a lot of things about his character, temperament, degree of sensitivity and level of conscience. For example, a person who eats calmly in silence, with a feeling of gratitude for the food he is eating, who chews his mouthful consciously because he knows the first step toward healthy digestion takes place in the mouth, is not only going to absorb the nutritional value contained in the food, but also the subtle, prânic energy it conveys.

⊕ Conscious use of the mouth for nourishment, expression, communication and manifestation of our thoughts and feelings in a healthy, well-balanced, harmonious way. Good oral hygiene. A capacity to ingest, digest, assimilate and integrate resources and energies that are good for our development, and the ability to consciously evacuate harmful, detrimental elements.

⊖ Problems related to the mouth's functions and capacity to nourish ourselves: ingestion of unhealthy food, the habit of eating too quickly, avidly, with no conscience or gratitude; insatiable needs; problems concerning digestion, assimilation and integration; poor oral hygiene; a tendency to talk too much, to shout, criticize, gossip, use bad, vulgar or impoverished language; difficulty expressing our feelings, love, emotional lacks and needs. Using our mouth to seduce, e.g. wearing loud, provocative lipstick.

MOVIE, MOVIE THEATRE *cf. Cinema*

MOVING HOUSE

Moving house represents a state of conscience related to change, renewal, adaptability, a capacity to transform our inner and outer world, and to re-organize our life.

⊕ The end of a cycle of experimentation and the beginning of a new one. Allows us to move on to another stage, to discover new things, aspects and parts of ourselves that we didn't know. A large factor of evolution, renewal. Opening of conscience. A period of deep transformation, mutation, metamorphosis. Detachment from what is known. An opportunity to do great cleansing in our life, to set ourselves free of old patterns, to recycle old energies. Creation of new intimacy.

⊖ Difficulty moving can indicate resistance to change, fear of the unknown, immobility, paralysis, crystallization in the status quo, attachment to old behavioral patterns and habits, static structures, rigid, materialistic memories related to cultural heritage and patrimony. A lack of flexibility. Difficulty adapting, accepting change, moving on. A symbol of separation, loss, bankruptcy, poverty, misery. A lack of longevity. Instability. Moving hastily, in a rush, may indicate a tendency to flee unpleasant, problematic situations instead of solving them. It may also indicate a need to find shelter, to protect ourselves from danger.

MUSCLE

Muscles are tissues that are excitable by nerves, which allow movement. There are different types of muscles. *Skeletal muscles* affect our exterior movements, and symbolize the strength and power to advance, willpower, motivation, and courage as well as the vigor of our structure since they are attached to our bones. When we want something, we activate these muscles and our energy to obtain it (e.g. extending our arm to take something). As for *smooth muscles*, their function is to transport different substances in the organism, such as blood through veins and blood vessels; food through the digestive tube; air through the bronchial tubes; urine through the urinary system, etc. These muscles, which contract slowly and involuntarily, are not consciously controllable. Nevertheless, their specific action bears witness to an intelligent force at work on the unconscious level to maintain balance in our body.

The red color of muscles calls to mind the color of blood and the 1st chakra, which symbolizes a capacity to act on matter, thanks to our vital energy, and our incarnation in a physical body.

⊕ Strength, power, and structure on the level of willpower. Vigor. A force of manifestation. Well-employed motivation. Correct, right use of the power of our mind to advance. Suppleness. Harmonious movement. A capacity to concentrate our vital energy, to become active in order to obtain our objectives, to materialize. A capacity of expansion. Right action. Courage and bravery.

⊖ Excess or lack of willpower, vigor, motivation, concentration and determination to manifest, to get up and act. An incapacity to master our strength, our intensity. Tensions. Stress. Rigidity. Inertia. Inaction, immobility. A lack of courage and bravery to face life, and take ourselves in hand. Unconscious negative intention and willpower that need to be rectified.

MUTISM *cf.* ***Dumbness, Mutism***

MYOPIA *cf.* ***Short-sightedness***

N

NAIL (finger, toe)

Nails are the product of the extreme keratinization (accumulation of a particular protein) of the layers of horny skin at the tips of human, and certain animals', fingers and toes. In humans, nails are a way of protecting the fingertips by ensuring a function of densification and solidification, thereby allowing the hand to take, give, receive, and manipulate with precision and solidity; as for the foot, nails reinforce the toes so as to ensure correct walking, advancing, stabilization, and adaptation to all sorts of terrain.

In addition to protecting finger and toe extremities, nails serve to scratch ourselves (e.g. to relieve an itch), to scratch the soil, to scratch or scrape an object in the context of work (e.g. when cleaning, gardening, tinkering), or, in some cases, to scratch others to defend ourselves. Generally speaking, our nails connect us to our instinctual, animal dimension. Hence the use we make of them, their aspect, as well as the importance and attention we give them, reveals the way we use our instinctual capacities and our innate survival programming.

In their negative aspect, nails remind us of animal claws, especially when used to be aggressive and to hurt. Their negative usage denotes a brutish, coarse temperament, that lacks sensitivity, delicacy, finesse, and meticulousness. Whenever a person pays excessive attention to his nails, by spending too much time on manicure and pedicure treatments, varnishing and decorating his nails, or regularly visiting beauty salons, it denotes a superficial attitude, a lack of authenticity and depth, as well as a desire to seduce, a need to please on the outside, through his appearance. Of course, manicures and pedicures have their rightful place and help toward self-esteem, the manifestation of beauty, of delicacy and finesse when they serve to ensure the health and hygiene of our hands and feet, or when they are given to people who are ill, confined to bed, handicapped, and who are not able to take care of their own nails.

⊕ Beautiful, well cared for, clean, harmonious, well cut, healthy nails reflect healthy, well-balanced vitality, sensitivity, delicacy, authenticity, estheticism, an artistic sense, and natural beauty. A good capacity for protection, solidification, and densification regarding dexterity, giving and receiving, when fingernails; agility and stability in walking and advancing, when toenails. A person who uses his nails to discreetly scratch himself to relieve itching, or to disperse tensions related to stagnant energy. Manicure and pedicure carried out with right intention, to ensure hand and foot health and hygiene.

⊖ Generally speaking, a tendency to have long nails and spend a lot of time looking after them, or having them looked after, varnishing them, decorating them, highlighting them with noticeable colors and decorations indicates that the person maintains his feline, animal, instinctual nature, and seeks to seduce, to please, to attract attention in order to impress others. Moreover, over long nails get in the way when using our fingers and hands, preventing us from materializing correctly, from being fully involved *hands on* in a concrete task or physical action, as too preoccupied with our nails, not wanting to break them, spoil their varnish, etc. Superficiality, attachment to ephemeral values, lacking authenticity and depth. Seductive, provocative behavior, a desire to bewitch others through seduction and passion. Tiger/tigress energy, seeking to hang on to others, to objects, because of memories where unfulfilled primary needs, survival dynamics, as well as existential lack and fear have been recorded, inciting the person to react with impulsivity, possessiveness, and brutality. Overlong nails on a woman may indicate overconfidence, aggression, and emissivity; on a man, they are a sign of negligence, disconnection, or de-polarization, excessive femininity, a lack of self-confidence, difficulty being self-responsible.

Long, sharp, pointed nails indicate the presence of conscious or unconscious memories and forces imprinted with aggression, wild, animal-like, brutish behavior, that lacks sensitivity, delicacy, gentleness, refinement, precision. A tendency to manifest too instinctively, aggressively, in an overly sharp, cutting, fussy manner. A feeling of superiority and a complex of inferiority. May indicate an overly independent, difficult to approach spirit, who, under the influence of unhealed wounds *shows his claws* in order to protect himself, by keeping others at a distance, thereby hoping not to experience the same hurt(s).

Dirty, unkempt, or broken nails denote negligence, a lack of hygiene and cleanliness in the way we look after and take care of ourselves, as well as in our contacts and exchanges with others. They also indicate the presence of memories and forces that incite us to give up, let go, despair, disconnect, due to multiple, unconscious, negative needs.

Too thin, fragile, brittle nails that break easily indicate health problems, a lack of vitality, and, symbolically, difficulty protecting ourselves when doing things, in activities that involve dexterity, when fingernails; and advancing, when toenails. This state of nails reveals that the person is too focused on materialization, work, doing things; or, that he feels he has been flayed by life, by ordeals, and has become incapable of looking after and taking care of himself and/or others; or, that he refuses to do so, preferring to remain in the role of victim.

Ingrown nails are quite a common, painful problem, which mostly affects the big toe; it denotes a feeling of withdrawal into ourselves, selfishness, guilt, or regret regarding choices we have made or a direction we have taken. Like the thumb, the big toe is related to willpower, altruism, and power; hence, the pain caused by an ingrown nail should incite us to question the way we use our willpower and capacity to advance, the way we make decisions and choices.

Biting nails indicates behavior imprinted with insecurity, nervousness, anxiety, obsessive attitudes, a lack of confidence, fear of not achieving our objectives, aims, goals. Bitten nails often reflect a feeling of shame and fear of being judged by others, because they reveal that the person has problems, that he is fragile and lacks inner stability.

NECK

The neck symbolizes the link between the intellectual and the emotional levels, and a capacity to communicate. It brings suppleness and flexibility to the thought level, and participates in body mobility. It allows us to move our head to the right, left, up and down, and to see what is going on around us; hence it is also a symbol of help toward discernment.

⊕ Supple, flexible connection and fluid, harmonious communication between the world of thoughts and the world of emotions. A capacity to look around, orient ourselves, and choose a direction in our surroundings.

⊖ Problems connecting and communicating between the intellectual and emotional levels. Rigidity, difficulty with discernment, orientation and direction. De-structured functioning. A haughty, arrogant attitude.

NEED(S)

A need designates a state or feeling that may or may not be conscious. We can distinguish between: primary needs that are natural, vital, instinctive and indispensable for survival, such as the need for air, water, food, light, heat, shelter, defecating, urinating (biological needs) as well as the need to move, create and procreate; secondary needs, stemming from social life which, although not natural, represent requirements to be able to function and materialize the creative potential we incarnate, such as the need for clothes, accommodation, vehicles, tools, materials, electricity, etc.; imaginary, superfluous needs induced by advertisements and a consumer lifestyle, which are actually desires and wants, an expression of our will to have, to possess. Hence, a desire for food may be the result of a feeling of hunger stemming from a need to eat, but the food habits people have developed are very often the result of adopted, conditioned desires rather than real, innate needs. Likewise, the desire to drink should not be confused with a feeling of thirst, and even less so with our body's need for water. We frequently desire what we do not need. Our desires often render us insatiable, whereas when we satisfy a true need, for instance when we drink water because we are thirsty, we naturally reach a state of satisfaction.

A need is often associated with a feeling of lack, discomfort or privation, which triggers an intense desire to satisfy or to make this need go away so as to feel better. In a symbolic analysis of needs that are felt either in concrete reality or in dreams, it is important to discern whether satisfaction of them is beneficial for our evolution, on the contrary, if these needs are inspired by distorted thoughts, emotions, intentions and behavior, which hinder our evolution, keeping us under the influence of an ordinary conscience and a limited vision of life. A spiritual path leads us to carry out great work on our various needs in order to transcend them and develop an altruistic, universal conscience.

⊕ A capacity to recognize essential, useful needs that are good for the evolution of the soul and conscience, for our health, as well as a capacity to renounce satisfying those which are detrimental. Conscious work on ourselves so as to achieve mastery of our instincts and various impulses stemming from our physical, emotional, and intellectual bodies. Liberation and transcendence of imaginary needs and conditioned, inculcated desires, behavior and dependencies, which incite consumerism and a will to accumulate futile, useless possessions. Detachment from matter, an understanding of its illusory, temporal character. Conscious work on *low frequency* memories, emotions, thoughts and attitudes which encourage attachment to matter, possessiveness, envy and undiscerning satisfaction of our desires. Seeking true, spiritual values that lead to Wisdom and Universal Conscience.

⊖ A lack of discernment and wisdom when satisfying needs. A person who lets himself be dominated by his instinctual, animal impulse, who is a slave to his needs and desires. A lifestyle that leads to misery, poverty, ruin and degeneration. A lack of understanding of the impact of conscious or unconscious, distorted memories and the subtle, psychological dynamics that engender and maintain imaginary needs as well as numerous desires on the emotional and mind levels. A lack of willpower to work on ourselves, to tidy up and cleanse our needs, to learn to master our desires, dependencies, our consumer, compensatory habits. An incapacity to recognize and satisfy essential needs. May also indicate a tendency to ignore or repress vital, natural needs, to forbid all desire, all pleasure. An extremely austere, rigorous, ascetic lifestyle. Religious indoctrination which makes a person feel guilty if he listens to his needs and allows himself the joys and pleasures of life.

NEGATIVITY, THE NEGATIVE

Negativity and the negative aspect of things is a dynamic that is essential to understand on a spiritual path. The field of electricity helps to better explain and integrate its importance since an electric current – symbolically, vital energy – requires both its positive and negative poles in order to flow and circulate. In life, the negative sometimes appears through an apparently unfair, unjust situation, which incites us to reflect and improve our discernment, or to change certain aspects of ourselves, our way of thinking, of seeing things, of acting so as to rectify them.

We have to learn to manage our own negativity and be able to face others' by considering it to be an educational force that helps us evolve. When we don't understand that the negativity we encounter is a force organized by the Guides of the parallel worlds to help us grow and evolve, we criticize and feel bothered, annoyed, upset, ill-at-ease, and we manifest either more or less total passivity toward it; or, constant opposition, which engenders multiple complications. We limit ourselves to an emotional evaluation of the situation, only seeing the distorted aspect, wanting to resist and fight it, rather than accept it and transform its corresponding resonance within us. A person who only sees the negative aspect of events, remains focused on himself, on his emotions and needs, instead of opening up to what is actually occurring and living the present moment. His personal, selfish needs and limited understanding take over, and he loses global vision of the situation, as well as a capacity to find solutions.

Whenever a situation perceived as negative involves more than one person, excessive concentration on ourselves, our thoughts, emotions, and vision of things, may indicate refusal to come in contact with others, resistance to communication, sharing, educating, or negotiating to come to mutual agreement. Such an attitude engenders blockages, great frustration, which, in extreme cases, may lead to violence, aggression, even war. A person on a spiritual path uses all annoying, irritating, upsetting, negative contexts or events to analyze his feelings and emotions, and to cleanse his memories. He has integrated the idea that evil is educational, that it stimulates the development of conscience and teaches us how to transform negativity, evil, into good.

In virtually every positive aspect of our life, we can find a negative facet to improve, transform, or balance, and in every ordeal we experience, there is positivity (positive aspects) that serves our evolution. In its broadest sense, negativity or evil serves good. We all experiment states of conscience that engender the negative, although at the time, we think it is right. This is the educational, evolutive effect of illusion. By experimenting with the negative, and then reaping its fruits and consequences, in the short or long term, we re-orient ourselves toward good. Hence, each of us acquires the experience and wisdom that will incite us to choose good.

Generally speaking, it is the way we see a situation that renders it exclusively negative. We are all capable of transcending the negative by working on ourselves and freeing ourselves from erroneous concepts that maintain a mind and spirit of limitation, separation, opposition, combat. Once we realize and do this, while we continue our lives, the negative is no longer seen as an element to be fought, but rather to be transformed. By recognizing and acknowledging the resonance we have with the negative or evil, we develop better knowledge of ourselves. We then know what we need to change in ourselves in order to evolve, to blossom and flourish, and to attain the highest levels of purity and wisdom. Thus negativity is an evolutive, experimental force that allows those of us who study it to discover our distortions and to engender the necessary motivation to transcend them.

⊕ Understanding and integrating the fact that negativity, the negative, is an experimental, complementary element to positivity, the positive, and that it has an evolutive, educational function, that eventually, ultimately leads to good. Work on ourselves to change our vision of negativity. A person who constantly, consciously trains himself to see the positive aspects of every difficult, annoying, upsetting, or trying situation and event, thereby developing a capacity to maintain his enthusiasm, *joie de vivre*, hope, and optimism in all circumstances. Right, just attitude and behavior in ambiguous situations. An ability to accept what is and to live the present moment. Great receptivity and compassion. Understanding the meaning of ordeals, of personal and/or collective difficulties. Integration of the concept of Divine Justice, a capacity to use the negative wisely. Someone who rightly respects other people's limits and rhythm of evolution, who focuses on the positive, while remaining aware of the negative. Understanding the fact that long cycles are sometimes necessary before seeing the negative transformed in ourselves, others, or in a country. Understanding that illusion is educational, that what we may think is right, is not always so. Study of the highest level of Knowledge, leading to right understanding of the positive and the negative, of good and evil. An ability to raise our conscience above these concepts and maintain a global, multi-dimensional vision of events and life in general.

⊖ A person who doesn't understand the lessons his life teaches him, who doesn't recognize his resonance with the negative, the fact that everything that annoys, bothers, and upsets him on the outside, reveals the presence of similar memories and forces within him. Ignorance of the experimental, educational, evolutive role of negativity, of the Law of resonance and the Principle of complementarity. A lack of spirituality, compassion, global vision. Difficulty perceiving and materializing the positive. Negative attitudes and expectations leading from varying degrees of melancholy, sadness, weakness, ill-being, uneasiness, insecurity, existential anguish, despair, and/or depression to mental illnesses, including paranoia or megalomania. A tendency to focus our mind on the negative, to continually dwell on morbid, toxic thoughts, thereby creating somber, depressive soul states within and around us. A fatalist who paralyzes his vital energy and annihilates all motivation, all enthusiasm, and poisons his living environment by his attitude, words and deeds. Passivity, lethargy, inertia, induced by a very negative vision of things. Absence of *joie de vivre*, moroseness, wallowing in negativity, in cold, sterile atmospheres and ambiances. Rigidity and harshness toward ourselves and others. A negative influence on others. An accumulation of frustrations, criticism, heavy, harmful energies. An aggressive, offensive, combative attitude regarding negativity and everything that annoys, bothers, upsets us. Anger, perpetual revolt and rebellion directed toward others, even toward the whole world. An ill-intentioned, manipulating personality, that tries to make others feel guilty. Becoming locked into, stuck in negativity through egotism. Feelings of superiority and inferiority. Pride, arrogance, ingratitude. Making poor choices, refusing to learn, to change our vision of things, our way of thinking and behaving.

NIGHT

Night designates the darkness into which part of the Earth is plunged every day, when, owing to its self-rotation, the Earth ends up facing away from the Sun. Consequently, night represents a lack and absence of light and heat, an incapacity to see, to recognize, to discern clearly, hence symbolizing the absence of Direct Knowledge and deep understanding. From a positive point of view, night symbolizes a need for intimacy, rest, and warm, comforting, welcoming sentiments. The characteristics of night incite us to return to our house or apartment, to the family home, to retreat into our inner world; they inspire us to draw on our inner potential, to seek the solar force, the light, warmth, radiance and Knowledge we bear within ourselves. We succeed in doing so thanks to receptivity and the feminine principle, other aspects also symbolized by the night, which allow us to perceive on the inner, metaphysical levels.

Furthermore, night symbolizes the unconscious, and a capacity to connect with it, thanks to sleep and dreams. It facilitates interiorization, reflection, introspection, meditation, inner preparation, gestation, and general transformation of life. Since the majority of activities in the outer world are stopped, or at least, considerably slowed down or decreased during the night, people can renew and replenish themselves on the inner level, and integrate the experiences of the day, before returning to their daily life the following day. The difference between night and day can also be felt on the energy level: at night, generally speaking, the atmosphere and ambiance is calmer, more tranquil, peaceful, silent; dense, physical energies calm down, and fall asleep, while the subtle, spiritual energies awaken and become active. At night, the activities and vibrations of the different kingdoms – mineral, vegetable, animal, human and spiritual – are not the same as in the daytime, and these vibratory differences, which continually influence us, are perceptible to those who have developed their subtle, metaphysical senses.

⊕ A period of calm, interiorization, reflection, meditation, awareness. Rest, restorative sleep, regeneration. Integration and assimilation of the day's experiences. Visiting the inner world, the metaphysical levels, the parallel dimensions, and the memories lodged in our unconscious. Favorable dynamics for the cleansing of unconscious memories. Activity, apprenticeship, and evolution in dream reality. Visions and revelations allowing us to understand the mysteries of life. Preparation for future actions, the beginning of new stages, gestation of the future in the subtle levels. An atmosphere that is favorable to receptivity, perception of subtle realities, and communion with the Divine. Direct access to Knowledge.

⊖ Fear of nocturnal darkness, or being alone at night may be the result of fears, resistance, or refusal to visit our inner world, to discover what is hidden behind the veil of the unconscious, to become aware of metaphysical realities. A tendency to regularly work late into the night indicates excessive emissivity, a hyperactive lifestyle, difficulty being receptive, interiorizing, relaxing, detaching from matter to renew, and replenish ourselves, to *recharge our batteries* on all levels, and to be inspired by the world of the spirit. A lack of rest, calm, silence, and of spiritual conscience and life. Problems of discernment, blurred vision, understanding limited by ignorance or a lack of knowledge. Disorientation. Anguish, anxiety, fear, discomfort when light is lacking. A feeling of being alone and abandoned in the dark. An impression of being watched, persecuted, or haunted. A lack of understanding of the fact that the sensations, impressions, and emotions felt during the night are caused by an opening of the unconscious and an encounter with the forces contained therein. Ignorance of the Law of resonance. The dark night of the soul. Experiencing a difficult initiation. Revelation of negative aspects and accumulations of negative memories that we bear within ourselves, which, if not transformed, prepare future trials and ordeals; they may explain certain cases of insomnia, or a tendency to have nightmares.

NORTH

The North is one of the four cardinal points allowing orientation on a map. From a negative aspect, it is often associated with a climate or region where cold, snow, and ice prevail, where vegetation is rare or virtually non-existent; hence, symbolically representing a lack of human warmth, an absence of love, soul-states marked by coldness and sterility, preventing life from unfurling, manifesting. To correctly analyze its meaning in a dream, or in concrete reality, the general context must be taken into consideration, because it could be the north of a hot country, for example; in this case, this would be more related to direction rather than information linked to climate.

North is the cardinal point we seek when we need to situate ourselves geographically. In the sky, we seek the North Star, and both ancient and modern orientation systems (compasses, maps, GPS or Sat-Navs, etc.) align with the magnetic North, which confers on this cardinal point the attribute of detecting direction, providing a structural point to calculate distances, as well as longitudes and latitudes. Thus, it serves as guidance to help us find our way, or to indicate which direction we should take.

⊕ Allows us to orient ourselves, find out where we are, find our way again, both literally and figuratively, and helps us find our way back to our country of origin; or, an ability to feel good in cold situations, to know how to transcend them, to know how to study, analyze, and understand memories and contexts that manifest emotional coldness, an absence of love and human warmth. Good planning on all levels. An ability to keep calm (mentally and physically) in all circumstances, even when our usual bearings, our landmarks, guidelines, reference points disappear. May be related to the capacity to remain connected to the Cosmic dimension, to let ourselves be guided by Heaven throughout our multiple travels, voyages, incarnations on Earth.

⊖ A disoriented person, with no guidelines, no reference points, no bearings, lost in both the outer world and in his own inner world; or, it may indicate emotional coldness, a lack of human warmth and love, difficulty materializing our potential on account of a hostile living environment. A muddled, mixed-up, obscure, direction-less life. Instability. Incoherence. Confusion, feeling lost. Complete disorganization. Loss of good sense and global vision. Swimming against the tide. A lack of spirituality, intuition, inner bearings, guidelines, getting lost in abstraction.

NOSE

A nose represents a capacity to smell, and therefore, by extension, clairsentience: the capacity to sense deeply and perceive with subtlety, on both the physical and metaphysical levels. It is symbolically related to the world of air – thoughts – and our inferior mentality; the latter governs our intellect regarding our instincts. The nose and sense of smell are related to the 1st chakra, to the roots of our vital energy, our primary needs, and the animal dimension of our being.

A nose allows air to pass through and into the lungs, which are a center of transformation and purification of thoughts (air), and vital energy (blood). Moreover, it contributes to phonation, hence communication. It also refers to man's survival instinct: just as animals sniff one another to *get to know each other,* so too do we humans sense and feel our environment and perceive our entourage through odors.

Metaphysically, a nose represents a capacity to sense and feel in our interior world; i.e. to *smell, to sniff out* and so know our soul-states and inner ambiances, as well as to do likewise in the outer world, in our surrounding environment. Due to its position at the base of our center forehead, the nose is related to our intuition, to our premonition and understanding of different situations, people and things. In a dream, if we feel attracted to someone only because of his smell, this could indicate that we are under the influence of very basic instincts.

In dreams or concrete reality, the context in which we notice a nose, or its particular characteristics, informs us of its symbolic meaning. For instance, *a nose with very large nostrils* symbolizes a very instinctive person, who is nourished by what he feels and senses, who seeks too much to find out and know, who will *stick his nose into everything, a nosey parker,* because he is too curious, worried, anxious, or in search of sensations on the level of his basic instincts.

A red, blotchy nose may indicate a problem of alcoholism, hence affective, emotional dependency; a health problem related to poor circulation, symbolically reveals the presence of obstacles or hindrances to the good circulation of our vital energy (symbolized by blood).

A turned-up nose may call to mind a haughty, cunning, pert, mischievous, or impish soul.

A blocked nose hindering breathing may indicate difficulty managing our thoughts and emotions, constriction on the intimate or social level, a major discrepancy due to hypersensitivity, or an incapacity to manage all we feel and sense in our entourage and environment. If the left nostril is blocked, the reason will be emotional and related to the inner world; if it is the right, the blockage will be more to do with the way we feel and sense the outer world, the level of concrete action.

A nose bleed indicates that the person is going through events which cause him to lose his vital energy; or, that he is tired of feeling and sensing his environment or his own over-intense inner ambiances.

A congested or runny nose due to a cold or allergens reveals a surplus or overflow of feelings, an incapacity to transform all that we have perceived over a certain length of time.

A broken nose indicates a need to change our olfactory perceptions and our deep, instinctual structure, so as not to be attracted to or impressed by just any odor or ambiance, by everything and anything that activates and nourishes our primary needs and basic instincts.

⊕ A capacity to feel and sense deeply, to perceive *via* our sense of smell and our clairsentience. A capacity to instinctively know, to sense and anticipate soul-states, thoughts and intentions. Power of our inferior mentality to capture and wisely manage odors, scents, ambiances, as well as people's subtle, instinctual conduct. Mastery of our basic instincts and primary needs. A great force of intuitive discernment. A well-developed, natural sense of justice.

The gift of premonition. Deep, conscious breathing, which favors the integration of thoughts on the emotional and physical levels of our being. Understanding the importance of establishing rules and making informed, well thought out choices as regards desires, wishes, and instinctual needs.

⊖ Excessive focus on instincts and primary needs. Seeking strong olfactory sensations. Excited by penetrating, coarse, brute, animal smells. May indicate a lack of capacity to sense and smell, a blockage of olfactory potential through fear of using this sense, or through puritanism. Dynamics of a person who uses his inferior mentality either for survival, or who lives according to the law of the jungle (survival of the fittest) and so seeks to satisfy his basic instincts. A lack of intuitive discernment. An under-developed or corrupt sense of justice. Absence of rules, rigor, and values to incite a person to learn mastery of his instinctual desires.

NOURISHMENT *cf. Food*

NUDITY

Nudity symbolizes a state of conscience related to intimacy, purity, natural simplicity, authenticity, recognition and acknowledgement of who we are, feeling good in ourselves, well-being. Nudity renders the physical body wholly and completely visible to ourselves and others, without camouflage or enhancement. Nudity reveals our good points, our qualities, as well as our flaws, faults and distortions.

Depending on the environment and circumstances, nudity can be appropriate or inappropriate, and have a positive or negative symbolic significance. For example, seeing ourselves naked in a public place in a dream may denote a feeling of shame, inferiority, a discrepancy, or incapacity to manifest socially; or, it may indicate an extrovert way of behaving, an exaggerated desire to be intimate and fuse with others to satisfy our affective, emotional needs and lacks. Similarly, from a negative perspective, nudity may also indicate an excessive need for love, recognition and acknowledgement; e.g. in the context of nudist resorts, where it very often reveals a tendency to exhibitionism and voyeurism, a desire for attention, rather than a true desire for naturalism. Seeking sensations to fulfill his affective deficiencies, the nudist *democratizes* his conscious or unconscious needs for intimacy and sexuality through the means of collective nudity. As well as trivializing the intimate dimension of nudity, the nudist movement is also an expression of marginality and rebellion.

⊕ A capacity to accept and like our body as it is. An expression of the intimate, natural relationship we have with ourselves. Apprenticeship and evolution through the study of the body. Authenticity with ourselves and others in right, appropriate circumstances or context. Favors intimate relationships, fusion between a man and a woman. Respect for our and others' intimacy. Well-being. Liberty. Humility. Allows us to feel we belong to the Whole, the Great All. Return to original purity and simplicity. Communion with nature.

⊖ Problems related to intimacy and authenticity. A person with complexes, who feels ashamed and inferior, who has difficulty manifesting naturally, in his natural state. May also indicate extrovert behavior, indicating a need to please, to seduce, in order to feel loved, acknowledged and appreciated; or, on the contrary, it may denote very introverted behavior, with feelings of unhealthy embarrassment, shyness, and excessive modesty toward the naked body, owing to an erroneous, rigid, puritanical, or abusive education. An introverted, withdrawn attitude. Problems of esteem, respect, confidence and trust. A tendency to fuse excessively on the social, collective level. A lack of intimacy. Enslavement and subjugation to bodily appearance. A lack or excess of self-esteem.

NUMBER

Not only do numbers allow us to evaluate and compare quantities or size, but also to order, organize, and manage elements through numbering. Often written with the help of one or several digits, numbers interact through operations settled by slide-rule.

Numbers are concepts mainly used by mathematical sciences and they are the basis of all arithmetic calculations and all operations referring to a quantity or denoting proportions. There is also the *Golden number or ratio,* which defines the rules for identical, invariable proportions between two dimensions or figures; its value = 1,618. This number, also called divine proportion, is synonymous with harmonious beauty, symmetry, balance, perfection and agreement between the different parts of a whole. Its omnipresence in all Creation, in natural, life sciences, in the human body, in the DNA, or in the arts, such as painting, architecture, or music, can only be the fruit of a superior Intelligence and Knowledge, which is Divine. Indeed, the Universe is a logical, multi-dimensional, perfectly structured, mathematical whole, whose elements interact in precise order, which reveals the states of conscience at the basis of the process of materialization.

On the symbolic and metaphysical level, each number has a specific meaning, which goes back to its deep nature and the origin of Knowledge. Each *doorway* or *portal* bears a specific energy and corresponds to a state of conscience. Here are a few examples:

By definition, **1** is the number that represents a person (I); it signifies the beginning, setting in motion, willpower, self-assertion, etc.; and also Divine Will, Unity – Unity of the Great All, of the Divine, of God.

2 multiplies unity. It represents our polarities (masculine and feminine), relations with another person, the couple. From a positive point of view, it refers to harmony, well-balanced polarities; from a negative point of view, it refers to duality, opposition, or problems between our masculine and feminine polarities.

3 = the principle of construction related to polarities (masculine and feminine) because when two people unite, they can create a project, and in the case of couples, they can conceive and procreate a child. In the case of associations, enterprises and so on, two people/ partners/ teams/ groups/ associated companies, etc. can create a project(s), various works.

4 = the power of manifestation, the square, rectangle, structure, the house that the family (3) build for themselves, and so on.

Symbolically, numbers allow us to evaluate ourselves, to measure our efforts and to call ourselves into question so as to be able to rectify ourselves on both the material and spiritual levels. They also represent a capacity to understand ourselves, to organize ourselves, and put things into order both on the inside and on the outside. The symbolic importance of numbers is recognized in all initiatic teachings; for example, initiatic numerology based on the 72 Angels of The Traditional Study of Angels, which attributes a number, representing a superior Field of Conscience, to each Angel.

⊕ Allows inner and outer evaluation, structuring and understanding of states of conscience related to our materialization and functioning. Allows us to analyze, compare, organize, put in order, and be precise, accurate, exact. The study of the mechanisms of the Universe, of Divine Architecture. Understanding the fact that everything in the Universe is mathematical, that a number represents more than a quantity or material dynamic. Allows us to rectify, be precise, and synchronize. Search for excellence, efficiency, right, upright, honest productivity.

⊖ Outer and inner difficulty evaluating, structuring, organizing, managing, and understanding the relation and correlation between things. Someone who is focused solely on the material, quantitative dimensions. A lack of understanding of the symbolic meaning of numbers and their spiritual origin. A lack of logic and capacity for the abstract; or, an overly logical, rational, rigid mind and spirit. Science without conscience. Cold appreciation of people and things, a lack of love, wisdom, flexibility, and spirituality. A complex of inferiority or superiority depending on loss or gain. A lack of inner order. An imprecise, inaccurate, complicated, inefficient, overly bohemian person, who lacks structure.

NURSE

People who do this job represent parts of our being that have acquired a capacity to look after and take care of those parts of ourselves that are ill, injured, wounded, in distress, as symbolized by a nurse's patients. This profession is also a symbol of loving kindness, consideration, gentleness, as well as a humanitarian mission in collaboration with and supervised by a doctor who has more complex, deeper knowledge of the most appropriate treatment for the illness. It is also related to health prevention, education, training, supervision and management.

⊕ Help and support to heal ill parts of ourselves. Care, kindness, gentleness, a sense of altruism. Management, planning and administration of care and treatment. A capacity to work calmly and serenely, to manage high tensions, to transform negative energies, and to maintain mastery in difficult, trying, demanding, or unexpected situations. Great humane qualities. Understanding that illness, ill-being, and what hurts have an educational function. Sense of organization, efficiency.

⊖ An incapacity or difficulty to take care of ourselves and others when ill, unwell or suffering from ill-being. A lack of gentleness, humanism, compassion and love while doing this job. Medicine without conscience, a loss of the sacred aspect in acts of caring and healing. Coldness, indifference, insensitivity, working mechanically, out of duty, or only through a need to earn our living. A limited mind and spirit, a very down-to-earth mentality and conscience, ignorance of the spiritual aspects of healing, trusting only exterior, outer medication, care and remedies. Difficulty transforming the negative energy, which causes the illness on the outside, and regaining balance and harmony on the inside. An incapacity to manage tension, stress. A tendency to cut ourselves off from our feelings, senses and humanity. A feeling of superiority, haughty, arrogant behavior, severity, cruelty, an anti-life attitude; or, a feeling of inferiority before doctors, a tendency to compete with them, to criticize and judge them.

NUTRIENTS, NUTRITION *cf.* ***Food***

O

OBESITY

Obesity is an excessive, abnormal accumulation of body fat that is bad for our health. It may manifest in a person whose state of conscience is inhabited by lack. To fulfill his lacks, needs, and/or material, affective, or even intellectual insecurities, the person eats excessively and compulsively beyond any feelings of hunger. An obese person has instinctual survival behavior, which responds to an extreme need for vitality. Driven by great insecurity and fear of lacking, he tends to stock up on the inside and he represses his emotions. As his affective, emotional level is generally his most fragile level, and also the most powerful to create compulsion, it is often filled with repressed or frozen negative emotions, and the resulting ill-being is the root cause of obesity. Such great insecurity may come from experience in this life, but also from experiences in past lives. Thus, in a more or less distant past, the person may not have known how to use the abundance he had at his disposal in a right, just manner. Over time, his multiple exaggerations create excess in his conscience, which then materializes on the concrete level through overweight.

Seeing ourselves as bulimic in a dream when we do not suffer from a weight problem, announces that our conscience is setting up a concrete program of obesity, which will materialize sooner or later if we don't work on the memories of fear of lacking that have accumulated in our conscience over time. Obesity is a blockage of vital energy. It denotes our incapacity to transform our life experiences.

Some ancient traditions glorified a form of obesity since it was a sign of abundance in periods of famine and starvation. Hence some statues to be prayed to are presented with an obese belly because it was a sign of abundance, and indirectly, good harvests. This is also related to profound lacks and deep insecurities on all levels.

⊕ Healing of abuse and/or becoming aware of memories of lack or exaggeration in this life or others so as to transform them. Profound questioning of our general lifestyle, of what we *eat,* how we nourish ourselves, on all levels (physical, emotional, intellectual, spiritual). Study of our affective and relational behavior. Seeking evolution, carrying out rigorous work on ourselves to discipline and re-educate ourselves and regain our original willpower. Regained health and fitness of body, mind and spirit, through sport and general physical activity. Seeking to surpass and improve our quality of life.

⊖ A person who abuses, exaggerates and nourishes himself badly on different levels (physical, emotional, intellectual, spiritual). A burdened, encumbered soul that becomes heavier and heavier, ill, absorbed by matter, by unmastered instinctual needs, as well as memories of lack and deep insecurity inscribed in the unconscious. A false source of pleasure and satisfaction. A feeling of guilt caused by the absence of willpower, discipline and rigor. A person who is a slave to his instincts, desires and impulses. A person who is too down-to-earth, lacking in spirituality, in high, elevated objectives and goals; or, false spiritual concepts based on past lacks. (*cf. also* **Bulimia; Weight Gain**)

OBSCURITY, DARKNESS

On the concrete level, obscurity designates the absence of light, and figuratively, symbolically, it denotes a lack of clarity and understanding, an incapacity to see and to discern; or, positively, a good time to rest, interiorize, reflect, question ourselves, and be introspective. As light is a symbol of knowledge, of an enlightened mind and spirit, as well as an awakened conscience, absence of light represents ignorance, a dark, gloomy spirit, an obscured conscience; or, a visit to the unconscious, to our hidden aspects. Fear of obscurity (or its appearance in a dream) indicates that the person is becoming conscious of certain somber, dark aspects of himself, of certain negative memories of his soul that he has to face for his fear to disappear. In a dream, the appearance of darkness plus a negative feeling or an unfavorable atmosphere and ambiance indicates that there is a deficiency on the level of clarity, understanding and knowledge in ideas, emotions and manifestations. It may also refer to a difficulty reaching an agreement in an ambiguous situation, which seems to be confused, impenetrable and unintelligible.

⊕ Facilitates interiorization, referring back to ourselves, self-questioning and reflection. A period of rest, calm, meditation. Time devoted to intimacy and our intimate life. Favors an encounter with our unconscious and work on the memories revealed therein. Activation of the subtle senses.

⊖ A lack of lucidity, discernment, understanding, knowledge. Erroneous perception. Blocked intuition. Mental opacity. Ambivalence. Confusion. A tendency to get lost in abstraction. Awakens fears, anxiety, insecurity. Depression. The dark night of the soul. A dark, malevolent spirit that seeks to manipulate, to obscure truth, and hide its intentions or deeds.

OBSTACLE

An obstacle is a blockage, a limitation a person is confronted with, that leads him to slow down his advancing, or even bringing him to a complete halt. It may be bypassed or avoided, but it always symbolizes difficulties that need to be understood for them to disappear from our path. An obstacle never manifests by coincidence, and must always lead us to call ourselves and our attitudes into question, to reflect deeply on its possible causes (karmas) and reasons (lessons) for it. The limitation engendered thereby provides us with an opportunity to take time to go within and interiorize regarding the situation. Whenever it is a symbol of protection, the obstacle allows us to develop better vigilance and foresight in our actions, and it reinforces our sense of responsibility.

In cases where a person cannot manage to understand the deep meaning of an obstacle, he may feel frustrated, outraged; or, he may tend to flee it, to seek shelter, renounce or give up so as to escape the efforts required to overcome or circumvent it. Thus, as well as being limited, the person creates multiple karmas by wishing to avoid the challenges or ordeals life has put in his path to allow him to surpass himself, to activate his potential and evolve. It is necessary to integrate the fact that our past experimentations have constructed our present life, and that the barriers that get in our way also come from our past. There is a teaching hidden behind every obstacle that becomes a springboard for our evolution if we are capable of accepting it and understanding its educational and evolutive role.

An obstacle may also announce a poor choice or decision regarding a project or specific, concrete situation. If we have set ourselves a goal and several events block us, it could be an indication that we need to change direction, and review the choice, decision, or goal we had envisaged.

⊕ May indicate the end of a difficult situation, release from an impasse; or, indicate that it is necessary to stop, to go within and reflect on the causes that materialized the obstacle. Invites us to refer back to ourselves, to call our behavior and way of functioning into question, and to analyze the symbolic meaning of the nature of the obstacle. Understanding the fact that an obstacle may indicate the necessity to repair errors, to settle karmic debts. Acceptance and resilience when confronted with obstacles and difficulties. Favors the development of our willpower, perseverance, and courage in the face of ordeals and initiations. Capacity to be detached from the concrete aspect of the obstacle and understand the deep cause that engendered it. A preventive, protective sign warning us that we are about to embark in the wrong direction; or, that we have made a poor decision or choice.

⊖ A period of blockages and discrepancies that lead to a feeling of inhibition, slowing down, or the impossibility to realize our aims and objectives. May be a sign that the person facing the obstacle has an unconscious that is overloaded with negative experimentations that prevent events in his life from proceeding smoothly, easily. Lack of synchronicity. In some cases, the obstacle may reveal inner resistance to evolving. Discouragement, giving up. Tendency to force and struggle against destiny in order to get what we want. Accumulation of frustration and anger through a lack of understanding of the meaning of an ordeal.

OCEAN *(cf. also* ***Sea****)*

An ocean is related to the water element, and hence to the emotional, sentimental level. Through its vast extent, great depth, and the immense quantity of water it contains, it symbolizes a reservoir of collective memories and emotional energies, both conscious when what happens is on its surface and/or only as deep as the naked eye can see, and unconscious when what is found is deep down, and can only be discovered by diving and exploring the deep, vast underwater and ocean bed with adequate equipment and training.

Whenever an ocean manifests in a dream or is related to a concrete event, it always implies global, collective, multiplying involvement, affecting a great number of aspects and parts of ourselves, while maintaining its power at all times, in all circumstances, both concretely and in terms of conscience. On the other hand, a situation related to a small quantity of water, such as drinking or spilling a glass of water, a puddle we absentmindedly step into, etc., refer more to an individual emotional level, to a rapid event that has only a small-scale impact.

The concrete and symbolic importance of the oceans for life on Earth also comes from the fact that their water contains salt, such an indispensable element for the functioning of the human body that it was nicknamed *white gold.* Moreover, oceans are the natural habitat for a very rich, diversified flora and fauna, which undeniably play an important role in the ecological balance and equilibrium of our planet, while also serving as food resources, as vast territories of exploration, study, and discovery, reservoirs of natural and historical riches of all sorts (salt, oil, shipwrecks, sunken treasure, ancient lands and flooded civilizations, etc.). Given its immensity, the ocean also represents the resources it contains and the deep memories associated with it; it represents the guardian of the force of life and the emotional, collective riches of mankind.

However, this reservoir of resources has been and continues to be dangerously put at risk through excessive exploitation and the deadly pollution suffered by seas and oceans as a consequence of the numerous, thoughtless, risky, irresponsible human activities, such as oil spills and discarded waste.

It is interesting to reflect on the fact that there are now whole islands of plastic covering incredibly vast areas, such as the floating carpet of garbage drifting along the Californian coasts, which has a surface area of 18 million km^2, is 10 meters thick, and weighs an estimated 125 million tons. Yet these alarming figures only represent part of the plastic waste found in oceans. Scientists estimate that 70% of it sinks and is deposited on the various strata of the sea and ocean beds, where it buries all life forms, destroying the flora and causing the death of uncountable species of maritime fauna. According to a study carried out by the United Nations, there are as many as 18 000 pieces of plastic per km^2. This state of things is tangible proof that it is vitally urgent for man to become aware of the impact his way of thinking, acting, and living actually has on his living environment. Indeed, the pollution of our living environment is the materialization of the pollution we have created in our inner world: in our mental world, through erroneous, destructive thoughts; in our emotional world, through negative, devastating emotions that cause us to make harmful decisions and commit distorted acts that are anti-life and anti the natural balance of the physical world.

⊕ A great power and force on the emotional level (water). Discovery of the immense emotional potential man has both on an individual and collective scale. A capacity to engender and manifest beautiful, powerful emotions on the collective level. A great life force that has the capacity to purify, regenerate and transform our conscience and soul. Awareness that the various forms of resources found in the ocean symbolically represent the great emotional and vital resources we all have within ourselves, that we need to learn to use in a right, altruistic manner respecting all other life forms that contribute to the natural balance of our planet. Awareness of the effect accumulated, collective, emotional energies and memories have had on the personal and planetary levels since the beginning of time. A capacity to visit and explore the depths of our unconscious and face the memories therein. Emotional mastery and stability as well as a great capacity for unconditional love, which allows us to feel at ease even in deep, tumultuous waters, in intense, trying emotional situations, ordeals, atmospheres and ambiances.

⊖ Problems related to the force, power and immensity of the personal and collective emotional unconscious. An encounter with negative emotional forces that have been inscribed within for a very long time. Awakening and overflow of our emotional volcano. Destructive power caused by an opening of the reservoir of these memories. Difficulty or resistance to visit deep, unconscious memories. Instability, storms, tsunamis caused by instinctive, violent, tumultuous, devastating emotions. May indicate an encounter with an emotional predator, may be a warning of a destructive assault on the affective, sentimental, emotional level. Depression. Sadness. Extreme affective dependence. A lack of love. Repression of emotions in the unconscious. Difficulty purifying and regenerating ourselves, liberating the accumulated pressure in our emotional depths. A reckless person who heads off on adventure to visit his emotions unprepared, not knowing what to expect, ignoring what may await him.

ODOR

The nose is the organ that allows us to capture odors. Man's sense of smell enables him to physically sense or feel through his inferior mentality and to instinctively understand his environment. The world of air – symbolically, the world of thoughts – is intimately related to odors as it is the air that transports and brings them to us. There is a close relationship between the odors we capture and our capacity to understand. Human beings only know an infinitesimal part of their olfactory system, of their capacity to perceive and understand their lives and environment through odors. Without even realizing it, a person thinks according to what he smells, senses and feels.

Odors are not perceived in the same way, or on the same level by everyone. The more incarnated and active a person is in his 1st chakras, the more easily he smells odors on the physical level. The perception of odors also depends on a person's life program and level of conscience. Hence, people who are more *airy*, more intellectual, less incarnated in the physical dimension, may be less aware of dense, intense smells. Others find very powerful smells difficult, and may feel bothered, put out, or even de-stabilized by them. Such differences are explained by each person's lifestyle, fields of interest and activity. A spiritual person, who thinks and meditates a lot, lives more in the spiritual world and in his higher, superior level mentality than in the material world. His cerebral activity and capacity to think, sense and feel are essentially absorbed by his constantly seeking detachment from matter, transcendence of his instinctual needs and desires that are inspired by his emotional body and his lower, inferior, more instinctual mentality. Such a lifestyle diminishes a person's sense of smell on the physical level and activates his subtle olfactory sense, clairsentience, whereas a person who functions in a more instinctive way, who constantly seeks to satisfy his multiple needs and desires, develops more his perception of the concrete, dense odors of the material world.

The ultimate aim regarding our sense of smell is to have at our disposal our full olfactory capacities both on the physical and metaphysical levels; to be capable of smelling concrete odors as well as capturing subtle odors, without being dependent, bothered or de-stabilized. Contrary to what we might imagine, the more we evolve spiritually, the more capable we become of incarnating in depth. Indeed, a spiritual path helps transform the discrepancies that exist between our different bodies (physical, emotional, mental and spiritual), and allows us to live fully and harmoniously on all levels. We then rediscover clairsentience, the innate intelligence of odors, which becomes so refined that we manage to understand the multiple information provided by our olfactory system, while responsibly seeing to our vital needs. We become aware that odors reveal to us ways of being, manifesting, functioning, living and existing on various levels. Through odors and our sense of smell, we capture atmospheres and ambiances; we sense, we perceive if we are welcome, if a person likes us and desires our presence or not, etc.

Disagreeable, negative odors may indicate danger or incompatibility with a person or situation. We ourselves may also emit a bad smell, which tells us that we are out of synchrony with what is right and luminous. Through smells, we can detect a lot of information emerging on both the conscious and unconscious levels. We know that animals mainly define each other by their sense of smell. In his instinctive dimension, man, consciously or unconsciously, functions in the same way. Physical attraction, sensuality, and sexual attraction are based on smell. Likewise, when we feel an affinity with someone on the affective, intimate level, it is because the combination and fusion of our basic, fundamental odors is harmonious; otherwise, we wouldn't be attracted, we wouldn't *feel* or *sense* the other person. Feeling affinities with another person means we like similar things, that we share similar tastes, that we are connected to the same egregores (*cf.* this term) of thought and emotion; in a way, we human beings function like animal species that follow the same program.

Although we have gradually neglected our sense of smell in order to develop and function more with our senses of sight and hearing, the language of odors and our olfactory perceptions constantly influence and condition us, whether we are aware of it or not. This is clear from certain popular sayings such as *to have flair,* or *to smell a rat,* which refer to having good instincts, good intuition, and a sense of suspicion.

⊕ A capacity to capture and smell odors consciously, to discern ambiances, affinities and resonance. Conscious, right use of instincts and intuition. A great force of receptivity and subtle olfactory perception. Development of clairsentience, of a capacity to sense, to have an intuition about people, situations and events. An ability to transcend negative odors, not to be bothered or destabilized by them. A capacity to understand the symbolic, multidimensional meaning of odors, to read and interpret the messages and information they convey. A person emanating pleasant smells, elevating perfumes, who inspires beautiful sentiments, creates lovely atmospheres and ambiances, inhales life with joy and awareness. Work on ourselves to master our instinctual needs, our animal dimension, to purge, purify and refine our senses. Activation of innate intelligence, of hidden wisdom. Lucidity. Discernment. Revelatory perception. A capacity to sense, to feel attractions, affinities, and disturbances without contravening our principles and values, without breaking Divine Laws.

⊖ Problems regarding our capacity to sense and feel, to perceive instinctively and intuitively. A hypersensitive person, who is easily bothered and destabilized by the smells he perceives, who doesn't know the Law of resonance, or who refuses to apply this Law. A person with a puritanical, extremist attitude who wants to avoid unpleasant odors at all costs without working on himself to learn to transcend them. May indicate a person who resists incarnating fully, who rejects the physical senses and perceptions they provide, preferring to take refuge in an imbalanced spiritual lifestyle or flee into a religious order. Or, on the contrary, it may also indicate an excessively instinctual person, who lives in a conscience that is more animal than human, mainly focused on the satisfaction of his primary needs and sexual impulses, nourishing all sorts of dependencies, abuse and distortions. Coarse, boorish, perverse, unprincipled behavior. A very materialistic, predatory mind and spirit, that uses its intuition to manipulate others, who functions according to the Law of the jungle, where it is case of survival of the fittest.

OFFICE (at the workplace), **STUDY** (in the home)

An office, the workplace, is a symbol of intellectual work, research, study, creativity, development of concepts, planning, project management and materialization. It also represents a place where we exteriorize our capacities and talents on a personal or collective level. A study or home office symbolizes studies, learning, apprenticeship, and sharing knowledge, as well as management and materialization on the personal, family level, since it is also the place where official household and family documents are dealt with and stored. The atmosphere that reigns in the study or office, as well as the decor, furniture, light and colors need to be taken into consideration in a symbolic analysis of the situation. The aspect of an office or study is a general reflection of the occupant's state of mind, spirit, conscience and way of working.

⊕ Mental strength and intellectual fertility, capacities of concentration, reflection, creativity, inspiration, formulation and development of ideas, project conception. Work discipline, a sense of responsibility, commitment, motivation, dedication. A large, spacious, bright, clean and tidy office or study, that is harmoniously and pleasantly furnished and decorated, reflects a well-structured, organized, efficient, creative, inspired mind at work and in the management of household affairs.

⊖ Difficulty relating to work and concentration. Overload or incapacity to work. A person who is too busy in matter and lacks organization and structure. A dark, cluttered, dusty, dirty, smoky office or study reflects a similar state of mind. Difficulties in organizing, planning, structuring, incapacity to define priorities, to self-impose a work discipline. Piles of files waiting to be dealt with indicate either an overload of work; or, inefficiency, laziness, lack of motivation, irresponsibility.

OIL, PETROLEUM

Petroleum, more commonly known as oil, is a great symbol of energy resource both positively and negatively. In the middle of the 1900s, it became the primary source of energy in the world, which it still is today even though its decline has been announced. Oil is considered to be a dense, condensed energy because a small volume produces a great quantity of energy. Its liquid and organic density make it a source of transformation and development that offers multiple possibilities. Oil /petroleum is omnipresent in our lives today, and can be found in fuels, plastics, lubricants, textiles and other synthetic products, cosmetics, medication, etc. This polyvalence has created a dependence that exists in all spheres of our life. Symbolically speaking, oil represents an immense energy potential, which can be activated in the worlds of actions and emotions.

As well as being a source of energy, prosperity, and material expansion, oil has become an important political and economic issue, because it confers a certain power on the countries that control it. It is one of the great present and future challenges for mankind. Firstly because its use causes serious environmental problems worldwide, problems which symbolically represent pollution of a person on all levels; and also, because it is a source of non-renewable energy, which concretely and symbolically means that if we abuse the resources we have at our disposal, one day, they will run out.

Oil forms deep down in the soil, in organic matter subjected to great pressure and high temperatures. Its transformation took millions of years, or analogically, in terms of human lives, innumerable incarnations. Symbolically, oil represents the burial and decomposition of our memories, and our former, ancient, physical, instinctual, and emotional actions that have accumulated in the depths of the collective unconscious. Its black color reinforces the symbolism of very ancient memories buried in the unconscious, representing occulted aspects of people, events, and things. Oil also symbolizes the result of the recycling and transformation of these memories, following great inner work of our spirit's fire during the course of our numerous lives. It may also indicate powerful negative energy forces, hidden deep within us, which haven't yet been exploited; or, on the contrary, which have been over-exploited, causing the desolation and exhaustion of our inner and outer environment.

On the symbolic level, the exploitation of an oil well means that we are working to extract our energy resources engendered by the alchemical transformation of memories stemming from our ancient, former actions and emotions. This long inner work is demanding and intense, and for it to be positive, its aim must be noble and right for the whole of the planet.

When oil gushes forth on the surface of the earth, it may represent a major release of unblocked memories, which burst or gush into our conscience, as well as the emergence of a powerful emotional potential for positive or negative materialization, as the case may be. Hence, oil has a considerable effect on our vital energy, our warmth, our capacity to create. It may also indicate an excess of crude, materialistic energy, a force ready to do anything in order to make profit, as well as a *prehistoric* state of conscience in the material conception and accomplishment of our projects.

⊕ Powerful energy of materialization, action, wealth, abundance, and prosperity. Great energy potential that confers a capacity to galvanize, energize, transform, create, and advance more rapidly and easily. An ability to make good use of memories accumulated throughout the course of many lives. Recycling and intense purification work in the depths of our unconscious. Inner and outer transformation that allows us to awaken old memories, to cleanse and reprogram them. Judicial use and sharing of resources. Energy efficiency. A search for alternative, cleaner energy resources. A conscience that has respect for the environment, and that understands that oil is just a step in the course of human evolution, and that one day it will be replaced by something else.

⊖ An overly dense, polluting, destructive source of physical and emotional energy. Non-respect for the environment and the stability of the planet. A lack of long-term vision, indifference regarding the effects on both the human and environmental levels. Waste of resources, which creates imbalance, pollution, and poverty. Abuse of power in the disposal and distribution of energy resources. Exploitation of natural resources with an excessively materialistic attitude, without any scruples or conscience. Selfish satisfaction of ambitions for success and expansion without any thought for others. Use of energy as a means of pressure, blackmail, bribery, boycotting, manipulation, and domination in order to acquire material wealth and profit, political and economic power. A source of conflict, war, social, political and economic interference. Malevolent intentions, destructive mind and spirit. Corruption, extortion. Overconsumption. Seeking luxury and artificial pleasures. Material dependence. Absence of spiritual conscience, ignorance of the Cosmic Laws, not knowing that we always reap what we sow.

Oil leak; oil spill: Absence of mastery, or loss of control, over-dense, concrete energies, as well as forces of materialization stemming from ancient memories, provoking catastrophes in our environment, and in our life in general. Such a leak indicates an awakening of old, negative, unconscious memories, and the emergence of the destructive forces contained within them. A symbolic analysis of the context wherein the leak or spillage occurs will reveal what region of our being is affected (car: our way of advancing toward others; central heating: our capacity to maintain a warm, loving, atmosphere in the home, in our intimate life; oil tanker spillage in the sea: an incapacity to manage and to transform the instinctual, emotional *luggage* (*cf.* this term) accumulated in our unconscious, leading to destruction on the level of the mineral, vegetable, animal, and human kingdoms.

OLD AGE, GROWING OLD

Growing old, i.e. advancing in age, is part of the life cycle, the evolution cycles of everything that exists, from living beings to objects and things. It is a normal, natural cycle that man has no influence on. Aging can even be dreaded by people who are very attached to their physical aspect, their fitness and material well-being. However, on the contrary, old age should be as beautiful a period in life as all the others. Ideally, it's a time when we assess and take stock of our life and transmit our knowledge, experience, and a taste for spiritual evolution to the younger generations. In traditional societies, the elderly were considered to be sages, living libraries, *treasures* of knowledge, experience and good advice. They were often models of wisdom, maturity, right, fair judgment, global vision, compassion, patience, indulgence, spiritual values, and material detachment. They inspired and helped the other generations in their apprenticeship, development, and journey through life.

However, in our modern societies, many old people have lost this inspiring, educational role. Nowadays, the elderly, who may often have had a tough life marked by material lacks and too many responsibilities during their youth, are partly dazed and dizzied by the prosperity they experience in their present old age, and also lost because they don't know what to do with all the time they now have at their disposal. Consciously or unconsciously, to compensate and make up for what they weren't able to experience and live when they were young, many of them tend to become dispersed in all sorts of activities (e.g. card games, bingo, television series, and all sorts of entertainment and distraction). They prefer to seek pleasure and are stimulated by these entertaining, distracting pastimes which are not very evolutive, rather than work on edifying their souls. Furthermore, the knowledge of life that the elderly have is neglected because of the pervading moral values of a consumer society that is more focused on matter, youth, health, etc., than on the inner world. Many people refuse to accept the aging process and resort to extreme means such as plastic surgery, spending huge sums of money to erase the traces of life from their body (the physical envelope and terrestrial vehicle which serves the spirit to experiment matter), and from their face (the reflection of their soul-states).

The more evolved and experienced people are, the more wisdom they acquire with age. Growing old beautifully, gracefully, is to evolve with our body, beautiful on the inside and beautiful on the outside; it's to be proud of the traces and marks life has bestowed on us, because they speak of us, tell our story, so to speak, since we traced them during the course of our experimentations. Aging should always be synonymous with becoming a model of interiorization, wisdom, knowledge, generosity, altruism, and reparation of distorted experiences of our present life so as to better prepare our next incarnation. Only by living our old age positively, by fully accepting it, can we ensure happy longevity on all levels.

⊕ A symbol of maturity, acquired and integrated knowledge, wisdom, and feeling eternally young at heart. Acceptance of all the cycles of life on Earth. Someone who grows old serenely, living fully, in all consciousness of this stage in life. An open-minded person whose inspiring advice makes him a natural leader. Mediator, conciliator. An example of wisdom, a model, a guide, and an example of life to be followed. Diffuser of acquired knowledge. An expert in human relations. A patriarch or matriarch respected by all the family. Detachment from the physical aspect, from appearances and the need to be admired for physical beauty, focus on inner beauty, moral values, and principles of wisdom. A generally healthy lifestyle that favors the maintenance of the elderly person's well-being. Well-balanced, good management of time. Likes helping and being involved in the family and on the social level. Voluntary work, altruism. Right preparation for the future. Someone who devotes himself to his spiritual evolution, who communicates with the Divine, with God, through prayer and meditation. Happy longevity.

⊖ Doesn't understand the meaning of the cycles of life. An overly materialistic conscience. Refusing signs of old age in our appearance; fear of growing old, fear of death. Thinking that age entitles us to all sorts of privileges and prerogatives. A lack of wisdom and love, a person who has become embittered because of not understanding the meaning of the ordeals of his life, and who superficially compares his life with others'. A sour, grumpy, bad-tempered person. A plaintive, doleful attitude; someone who misses the past, remains attached to it, is nostalgic about *the good old times,* who disconnects from the present, lets himself go, feels useless, has no goal. Someone who is no longer young at heart, who maintains old patterns, dated, obsolete thoughts. Refusal to evolve, to renew ourselves, to adapt to change. A lack of opening to new ideas; regression. Degradation of physical and intellectual capacities (loss of memory and concentration). Infantilization, global disinterest. Degenerative diseases. Sluggishness, idleness, sedentary life, despondency, discouragement, depression, isolation. Loss of the joy of life owing to a refusal to accept the loss of vitality. Cast aside in hospitals and abandoned by family. Solitude, a life that is empty of meaning. A superficial person who becomes scattered and dispersed in illusory activities, who wastes his time in futilities instead of taking stock of his life. Someone who seeks to forget his suffering and still raw, unrepaired moral wounds as well as his memories. Lack of spiritual development, of self-questioning, of wanting to know ourselves in depth, of an inner quest.

ORANGE (color)

The color orange is the result of a mixture of red (action, willpower, hyperactivity, or lack of vitality) and yellow (confidence, radiance, overconfidence, or an egotistical attitude). Hence, its symbolic meaning is closely linked to the fusion and marriage of these two colors, and is mainly related to the satisfaction of vital needs and seeking purity in emissivity, the pleasure of the senses and sexuality. It is a warm color, characterizing the 2nd chakra or energy center situated just above the belly button, which governs vital needs and the sexual dimension of vital energy, as well as the capacity to harmoniously fuse both the masculine and feminine polarities in a love relationship and in the act of procreation when it is accomplished with right, pure intention. The color orange is also associated with spiritual life: it symbolizes compassion and the transcendence of sexuality and instinctual needs.

Since orange is one of the colors that most attracts our attention, it is used to indicate a need for vigilance and prudence in our personal needs so that we do not hurt anyone because of our needs. It is to be found, among other things, in traffic lights, warning lights, or road workmen's protective clothes.

The choice of orange for personal clothes denotes a need for renewal, a necessity to *recharge our batteries*, renew our force, vigor, and confidence in order to regain our vitality, our dynamism, energy balance and natural radiance. When we feel the need to wear an orange top, it is the chakras and organs situated on this level that are in need of the vibratory frequency of this color. If we are inspired to wear an orange scarf, it is the throat chakra that is seeking purity and healthy radiance or emanation regarding needs; when it's on the hand level, the meaning of orange needs to be analyzed in correlation with the symbolism of hands; in the case of an orange hat, we need to seek the link with the head and the world of thoughts, etc.

Furthermore, a color may also attract us on the food level. If it's orange-colored fruit (oranges, mandarines, apricots, peaches, etc.), the symbolism is more to do with a need for purity, for vitality on the emotional level, a need for gentleness, affection, fluidity, light-heartedness, as well as receptivity, because these fruits contain a lot of water, juice and sugar, and they are generally round-shaped, therefore more enveloping, consoling, and fertile like a mother's womb or breast.

The same analytical process needs to be applied to understand a need for the color orange (or any other color) in all domains of life: an orange car, orange walls, chair, bed-linen, lamp, dish, etc.

⊕ A right, just attitude toward our vital needs. Great sensorial vitality that comes from the vigor and force of action of red, combined with the warm, bright, solar radiance and full confidence of yellow. Material and sensorial abundance. Divine pleasures, purity, transcendence of instinctual sexuality and emotional, affective dependencies. A healthy, regenerating sexuality. Fertility, reproductive, procreative force or power. A harmonious couple relationship. A well-balanced life. Conscious work on ourselves to transform impulses and excessive or harmful needs. Good digestion, a capacity to transform, to do alchemy.

⊖ Difficulty, or an incapacity, to harmoniously express and manage our material and sensorial needs, desires, and pleasures. Overflowing vitality and emotions, excessive pleasures; or, on the contrary, a lack of vitality, pleasure, and radiance. Problems resulting from a rejection of sexuality; or, sexual excesses. Games of seduction, licentiousness, lust, debauchery; or, frigidity, puritanism, emotional coldness and repression. An incapacity to transcend our instinctual sexual needs. Brutish, coarse, animal-like behavior. A spiritual life that lacks purity, authenticity, harmony and balance. Taking excessive advantage of life, not measuring our acts; or, on the contrary, not managing to rejoice and be happy about beautiful moments; rigidity. A difficult adolescence, or a dissatisfied adult who behaves like an eternal teenager.

ORPHAN

An orphan is an under 18-year-old child, whose biological parents have died, or who has been abandoned. In developed countries, orphans usually live in orphanages or foster homes, whereas in the majority of the world, especially in emerging countries, orphans very often become homeless. An orphan is symbolically related to memories of abandonment, rejection, negligence, solitude, vulnerability, fragility, poverty, and lacks on all levels. It evokes the feeling of being lost, without protection, love, support, or resources to grow up, learn and develop healthily. The image of an orphan often inspires pity, unease, discomfort; or, a feeling of impotency, or guilt depending on the resonance we have with the situation.

Not having a parental model, an orphan will need to develop attitudes and behavior allowing him to create new references, new bearings for himself. His inner program requires him to reinforce himself and to transform those aspects of his being that may have pushed him to abandon, ignore, or neglect his own children in numerous lives. Whenever Cosmic Intelligence plans such a program, it is to lead the person to feel and experience what he subjected other souls to during the course of his experimentations. Simultaneously, this allows him to repair his errors and learn lessons from his erroneous behavior.

To better understand this kind of ordeal, it is necessary to remind ourselves that each person's program is elaborated in accordance with his past lives, according to the karma he engendered, and the qualities he has to develop. It is not a coincidence or a matter of chance that a person finds himself an orphan; in another life, he may have been too collective, too social, not granting any importance to family, to love, to the presence and protection children need. Consequently, he abandoned his children, who are his most beautiful works, and, consciously or unconsciously, caused people to suffer on the personal, family, or collective level.

Symbolically speaking, visiting orphan memories also evokes an encounter with attitudes and memories marked by a lack of responsibility, altruism, and compassion. Hence, a person who is an orphan has to learn to take good care of what he has begun, of what is small, in the process of becoming, and that needs support, accompaniment, attention and love to be able to grow and develop.

⊕ Transcendence of memories of abandonment, rejection, irresponsibility, emotional, affective lacks, the feeling of being all alone, lost, vulnerable. Develops independence, a spirit of improvisation, of making do, as well as the strength, courage, and bravery to face difficulties, to assert and re-construct ourselves. Reparation and settlement of karmic debts. Acceptance of our life program, knowing it was conceived to serve our evolution. A capacity to forgive, open our heart, heal our wounds. Learning to appreciate family life, and to develop a sense of responsibility. Integration of the concepts of a universal family and parents, of a Heavenly Mother and Father. Someone who receives a second chance through adoptive/foster or spiritual parents, Divine Grace.

⊖ Memories of abandonment, rejection, irresponsibility, emotional, affective, and parental deficiencies. A feeling of solitude, of uprootedness, not belonging, not having our place, being undesired, unwanted, the *spare part.* Isolation, vulnerability, fragility, desolation, despair. A state of survival and struggle to find our place, to earn our right to exist. Anger, disconnection, dropping out, itinerancy, a difficult life. Emotional, affective dependency, seeking to please, prepared to do anything so as to be tolerated, accepted, loved, appreciated. Not understanding the Law of reincarnation and karmic consequences, the fact that we always reap what we sow. A lack of spirituality, anger toward God, due to a lack of understanding of our life plan, and the way in which Divine Justice manifests.

OSTEOPOROSIS *cf. Bone*

OSTRICH

The only bird that is unable to fly; the ostrich symbolizes a state of conscience related to our instinctual thoughts, thoughts that are really down to earth. It also represents instinctual parts of our conscience that are rapid, strong and enduring because this bird can run so fast it has no predators, not even lions. An ostrich represents great inner force that can take action to find subsistence, overcome obstacles, and protect itself. Another particularity of this symbol is that although it has a great need for water, it is afraid of water and prefers sand or dust baths. This reveals aspects of our thoughts (down to earth and fast) that simultaneously feel a tremendous need for love along with fear of receiving it, hence preferring the dust of memories or former actions and habits rather than beautiful emotions. That is one of the reasons why the ostrich is associated with aspects of truly down to earth thoughts. As ostriches are polygamous, they also symbolize instability and infidelity on the emotional level. Their eyes are bigger than their brain, which represents a lack of intelligence in the way they see and think. The expression *to bury your head in the sand* as ostriches do, indicates there are parts in us that refuse to face reality, that prefer to remain in ignorance and not to know, which is similar to fleeing and one of the ostrich's great capacities is to run away fast when in fear of danger.

⊕ Rapidity, strength, speed on the level of physical thoughts. Good auditory and visual perception in action. Great inner force capable of taking action to find subsistence, to overcome obstacles and to protect ourselves.

⊖ Thoughts that are too down to earth and flee rapidly. Little developed intelligence. Feeling of superiority. Overdeveloped sense of curiosity. Arid thoughts. Excessive will power. Problems in love, infidelity, multiple relationships on the thought level. Difficulty raising our point of view, difficulty understanding. Fear of reality. Ignorance. Tendency to flee, to run away. Force of thought without conscience, which can be aggressive and fearsome.

OVEN *cf. Stove*

OVERWEIGHT *cf. Weight gain*

OVERWORK, BURN-OUT

Overwork is defined as an excess of physical and/or intellectual activities that engenders health problems on both the physical and metaphysical levels. This exhaustion, which is the result of repeated or prolonged stress, reveals a need to please, to be loved and acknowledged, a deep feeling of insecurity and fear of failure or criticism. It is also the consequence of an accumulation of negative memories where we were too busy in matter, pushed by needs for high performance and perfectionism. As well as reflecting a materialistic philosophy, this great fatigue also shows a tendency to wish to force Destiny.

Overwork materializes first of all on the thought and emotion levels, when we brood over the same negative ideas and repeatedly create emotional drama. It also manifests on the spiritual level; e.g. in a person who is on a spiritual path without respecting Divine Laws, who uses his mediumnity (psychic powers) without ensuring purity of intention, or who suddenly experiences a totally unexpected opening of the unconscious, without being prepared for it, without having solid structures at his disposal, without any authentic spiritual teaching allowing him to evolve healthily, in all security, understanding that the main reason for our existence is to develop Qualities, Virtues, and Powers in their Purest state.

The feeling of being overworked may be caused by an excess of information, deep cares and worries that we can no longer *digest* and manage. If we don't acquire a global, multi-dimensional understanding of our state, if we cannot be detached as regards our responsibilities, or if we don't work on mastery of our obsessive behavior, they can lead us to depression or *burn-out*.

On the metaphysical level, feeling overworked corresponds to a search for answers to existential questions (even though we may not actually be aware of this), which shake us to our very foundations and cause us to lose our bearings. Hence, we experience disintegration, a crumbling of our mental structures, an upheaval of our value system, and we feel a void, a feeling of failure or helplessness regarding our physical, emotional, mental, and spiritual resources. We devote so much time, willpower, and energy to realizing an ideal or reaching a goal that we end up *burning both ends of the candle*, and become exhausted and ill. Sometimes, people turn to stopgap, anesthetizing measures such as alcohol, drugs, overconsumption of medication, with which they try to calm their distorted forces and impulses that lead them to unhealthy, destructive behavior. In extreme cases, deep inner emptiness, and feelings of despair and helplessness can lead a person to commit suicide.

Feeling overworked is a frequent phenomenon among devoted perfectionists who, due to their wanting to do things too well, wanting to realize their objectives and goals at all costs, upset the balance of their life and destabilize it. Such behavior may also reveal a tendency to flee or avoid a situation by working too much. It also indicates a lack of self-confidence that pushes a person to compensate by taking on more and more work commitments so as to prove his value to others, to satisfy his need for recognition and acknowledgement, and material success. Hence, such a person gives priority to his ego, to appearances, to concrete results; he finds it difficult to delegate, and bases himself on the quantitative aspect of his achievements at work rather than on the Qualities and Virtues he can develop by working in the perspective of spiritual evolution. His struggle results in great mental and physical fatigue; his vital energy plummets; his thoughts become incoherent; he loses motivation and becomes totally discouraged. He no longer has the strength to continue at this pace, to transcend a situation that now seems insurmountable, and he lets himself go, he gives up. These states of conscience lead to exhaustion, and total loss of the ability to function; they lead to *burn-out*.

⊕ A serious warning that a change in behavior is necessary, that it is high time to take a step back, to allow ourselves a moment of reflection to question our lifestyle, our priorities, what is or is not essential, and to open up to new perspectives, while continuing to enjoy our work and activities in general. A favorable period for re-organizing ourselves, going within, interiorizing to discover the deep meaning of work, i.e. the development of Qualities and Virtues and Powers in their purest state. Understanding the fact that overwork results in an over-materialistic conscience, a lifestyle that is over-focused on action, on doing, on emissivity, activity and over-dictated by a need to please, to be loved and acknowledged. Announces an opening of the unconscious, the necessity to deep cleanse our concepts, principles, values, and memories. Indicates that our inner computer has become saturated with undigested, misunderstood, untranscended information. Someone who decides to take himself in hand and to re-balance his life.

⊖ A tendency to overwork and exhaust ourselves due to an imbalanced lifestyle where we work excessively, and with an over-materialistic conscience, focused entirely on obtaining results; or, an exaggerated tendency to devote ourselves to others in order to please, to be loved and acknowledged, while neglecting our own vital needs. An excessive person who exaggerates and does too much in order to appear efficient, rapid, and better than others, due to a need for high performance and perfectionism. A lack of discernment, an erroneous understanding of work, of commitment, service and devotion. A tendency to want to force Destiny. A lack of spirituality and Knowledge to understand the multi-dimensions of life and the educational, experimental role of ordeals, including overwork and burn-out.

OXYGEN

Like all gases, oxygen is symbolically related to the element air and to the world of thoughts. It is essential for all life on Earth, whether plant, animal, or human. In the absence of oxygen our physical body can only survive for a few minutes. Oxygen, sometimes referred to as *Vitamin O*, is a major source of nutritional energy. Indeed, the majority of energy (approx. 90%) used by our body comes from oxygen assimilated by our lungs and skin. This form of assimilation of vital energy is what is commonly meant by the word *prâna*. When breathing, oxygen and prâna are indivisibly linked: when we inhale, the energy conveyed by oxygen reaches our lungs, which surround the heart center, and harmonize the functions of the inferior and superior chakras. The important correlation that exists between the mental level and oxygen is clearly manifested by the fact that our mind calms down when our breathing is regular. The oxygen we breathe is transported *via* our blood to nourish all of our cells, and 80% of the oxygen we assimilate heads toward our brain. Our system is also capable of absorbing oxygen directly from food. Water, for instance, is composed of 85% oxygen; certain fruits contain as much as 90% water; carbohydrates contain approximately 50% oxygen; and proteins, approx. 25%.

The fact that human beings cannot live without oxygen, and that it plays such a considerable nutritional role, symbolically reveals the importance of cultivating qualitative, elevated thoughts, and of nourishing ourselves with healthy, vivifying food. Thus, we ensure that our entire being works well on all levels. It is interesting to know that as well as its essential role for the good, healthy functioning of the physical body, oxygen also conveys metaphysical information, a fact that is little known in modern science.

⊕ Awareness of the essential, vital role of oxygen for life on Earth, of its participation in the materialization of life, and the manifestation of spirit in matter. A regenerating force for our physical and subtle bodies. Ability to vivify our spirit, to render it euphoric, to revitalize life in general. A source of nutritional energy, of vitality, of prâna. Behavior that respects the quality of the air, and the world of vegetation, which produces oxygen. Positive thoughts, nourishing pure, right intention on both the emotional and action levels.

⊖ Negative thoughts and behavior that pollute the air, atmospheres and ambiances, as well as the environment, drain vital energy, create sterility within and around us, suffocate and asphyxiate us, engender illness and death. Blocked, superficial, insufficient breathing. Inhaling foul, waste air, which leads to a lack of oxygen, a loss of vitality and conscience. Incomplete exhalation, which indicates a tendency to retain and repress our thoughts and emotions. Traumas, accumulations of serious emotional and psychological blockages, which limit, restrain and prevent life from unfurling and expanding. Behavior that prevents others from thinking and from manifesting their potential.

Choking indicates that we are in touch with negative thoughts and energies that are hostile to life; that through resonance, a subject of conversation, a way of nourishing ourselves, an exterior event or context, has activated in our unconscious difficult memories that prevent us from breathing, take our breath away and leave us breathless.

Feeling dizzy due to too much oxygen may indicate too many negative thoughts, hyperactive energies; or, excessive aspiration, desire, yearning for beautiful thoughts and energies to make up for, to compensate for memories of lack. May also denote a tendency either for us to impose, or for others to impose ideas on us, in an extreme manner.

Altitude sickness – also known as acute mountain sickness (AMS) – is a pathological effect of high altitude on humans, caused by acute exposure to low partial oxygen pressure at high altitude. In a dream, this would symbolize that there are negative memories related to elevation regarding matter, that such memories prevent the dreamer from elevating his conscience.

P

PAIL *cf.* ***Bucket***

PANTS *cf.* ***Trousers***

PARADISE

The word paradise, of Persian origin, and found in both Hebrew (*pardès*) and Greek (*paradeisos*), designates an orchard surrounded by walls, corresponding to the Garden of Eden described in the Bible, in the Book of Genesis. This orchard offers the image of an ever green garden, where nature is generous, and the rich vegetation eternally in flower. It is a place where precious stones, beautiful gems abound, where the animals and other kingdoms live together in peace. The Tree of Life is always to be found in the center; its skyward, heavenward growth, symbolizes perpetual regeneration, constant, divine materialization, and victory over death. In the Middle Ages, this garden of delights, separated from the rest of the world by a wall of fire or water, became a symbol of virginity, monastic life and ideal insularity.

Although the landscape of paradise varies from one culture to another, since time immemorial, all known religions to mankind contain the idea of paradise in one form or another: *a field of reeds* in the Egyptian tradition, *Walhalla* for the Vikings, *Amer* for the Japanese, the *Elysian Fields* for the Romans. In Judeo-Christian tradition, Paradise, or the Garden of Eden, is an important concept presented at the beginning of the Bible, in the Book of Genesis, as a resting place where the souls of the righteous enjoy eternal bliss after death. It is associated with the vision of *Celestial Jersualem*, the place of eternal union with the Angels before God's throne, to be found in Heaven.

The universal quest to rediscover this paradisiacal garden expresses the nostalgia of lost innocence, the search for a pure, beautiful, harmonious, peaceful world, free from the multiple manifestations of evil: flaws, faults, weaknesses, temptations, vices, sins, ill-being, illness, misfortune, suffering, and death. Aspiring to reintegrate paradise expresses a desire to surpass the human condition and rediscover Divinity. Symbolically, paradise symbolizes a state of very elevated, spiritual conscience, thanks to which a person may attain fulfillment by transcending his ego, and fusing with his Divine Self.

The idea of paradise is closely linked to that of free will and the choice to do good or evil. In the Christian religion, finding ourselves in paradise after death on Earth is presented as Divine reward for the person who was righteous and just, and behaved correctly. It is God's promise to all of us who walk the path of Qualities, Virtues, and Divine Powers, continually seeking to improve and perfect ourselves. It is also a state of being, of spiritual accomplishment, which may be achieved on Earth through right, noble living, that ensures happiness, peace, prosperity, bliss.

In the Christian religion, there are 2 paradises: earthly paradise and heavenly paradise. Earthly paradise is the place created by God in the likeness of Heavenly paradise, where Adam and Eve, and their descendants, were to live. However, in order to preserve the paradisiacal state on Earth, man was not to give in to temptation, nor begin experimenting in matter by disobeying Divine Law and Order. Having done so, he lost the state of conscience and vibratory level that allowed him to remain in that sacred place. From then on, he's had to regain his right of access to this state of being through spiritual work that liberates him from his imprisonment in matter.

As for Heavenly paradise, it is used as a synonym for Heaven, God and the Angels and the *chosen ones*' dwelling place; the opposite of hell, a place or state of punishment and deprivation, where, after death on Earth, the souls of fallen humans end up; the souls of those who chose to be separated from God in their lifetimes, thereby excluding Love, Light, Wisdom, happiness, and Eternal Life from their existence.

Moreover, the expression *artificial paradise* refers to often desperate people, who try to escape their unhappy lives, their daily hell, by taking refuge in drug consumption (narcotics, sleeping-pills, although the latter may sometimes temporarily be a useful crutch). In French, a tax haven is referred to as *tax or fiscal paradise* (*un paradis fiscal*). As a place where little or no tax is paid, it reveals a state of conscience where seeking a paradisiacal life is closely related to monetary riches and the pleasures such wealth can buy. Both terms indicate cases of erroneous, illusory understanding of what *paradise* truly means: i.e. a state of conscience that allows us to know the harmony and beauty of Creation and to feel at home in it.

⊕ An ability to understand that we mustn't seek paradise on the outside, or live in expectation of going there after death, but rather that it represents a state of conscience that we can all attain, right here where we are, if we rediscover our original conscience, our Divine nature, by developing Qualities, Virtues, and Powers in their purest state. Feelings of divine happiness, felicity, plenitude, fulfillment. Evolutive success on both the material and spiritual levels. A state of soul, spirit, mind, and conscience felt when working intensely, with right motivation and intention, to achieve an altruistic project serving to improve the destiny of mankind, to favor evolution in harmony with Divine Law and Order. Someone who has accumulated numerous merits and who reaps what he has sown. Consolation after efforts. Experiencing beauty, abundance, harmony, and peace on all levels. A good, righteous soul. An elevation of conscience, fusion with the Divine Self, Enlightenment.

⊖ A false image and erroneous understanding of paradise. A tendency to seek it on the outside in illusory values and appearances. Seeking facility, escapism, flight in artificial paradises (drugs, alcohol, lust, gambling, etc.). All sorts of excess, abuse, and dependencies. An illusory life. False belief regarding life after death: i.e. believing paradise is our due; or, that in order to deserve paradise, we have to live in a very puritanical, severe, rigid way, forbidding ourselves all joy and pleasure. Extremism and religious fanaticism. Ignorance of Divine Justice and Structures in the elaboration of our life's goals. A lack of authentic faith and spirituality. Discouragement, disconnection, dropping out, despair, atheism. An incapacity to believe in a Superior Power, Will, Justice, and Order.

PARENT(S) *cf. **Father; Mother***

PARK, TO

Parking is related to rest and the need to take a break, or to a moment of transition related to a person's driving force, his capacity to advance, and his way of behaving socially. Parking allows a person time to take a step back, to think, to communicate, before going on to his next objective. It may also indicate that a person is in a stationary state, that he no longer knows what to do; or, that he is no longer motivated to advance and be involved in social life.

⊕ Rest, pause, *intermission*, transition time related to a person's driving force and capacity to go forward socially, as well as a place that helps protect this energy so that, with his mind at rest, a person can then go on to the next *service point*. A feeling of having reached our destination, of having accomplished our duty, done what had to be done, and completed a stage. Allows us to reflect on our direction, our destination, and to make decisions. A period of reflection on the way we advance and behave on the social level.

⊖ Limitation, a lack of motivation, a stationary state, lethargy, inertia, or being bogged down and stuck, related to our driving force that allows us to advance in society. A feeling of being immobilized, halted, restricted. Blockage, an incapacity to go ahead on the social level. Difficulty finding our direction, establishing objectives and goals. Laziness, dropping out, disconnecting, a feeling of lacking resources, of being incapable of advancing toward our social objectives, aims, and goals.

PASSPORT

A passport is an official identity document issued by a country's administration to allow its citizens to travel abroad. Today it is mainly used to control entries into different territories. Symbolically, a passport defines the affinities and broad outlines of our identity and culture, our character and lifestyle according to which country it represents. It symbolizes the authorization given by Up Above, by Heaven, to visit and travel in different countries on Earth in physical reality, as well as exploring our inner *countries* (beginning with our blockages and capacities related to the + and the – of our native country) with our metaphysical identity; the aim being to one day develop the qualities of all countries and to transcend their weaknesses and distortions. Indeed, by working on the integration of our different peoples and inner countries, we gradually become universal citizens, and we feel love and compassion for all of the populations, for everyone on Earth.

If, in a dream, a person has a universal passport, that means that he has carried out deep purification work on himself, that he has integrated the Divine Laws, fused Spirit and matter within himself, and has therefore attained the level of evolution required to travel in his conscience into other dimensions, to visit the parallel worlds, or other people's souls. Such a person works toward an altruistic, humanitarian mission, and often disposes of several passports and nationalities, or special status, allowing him to travel easily in the different countries of the physical and metaphysical worlds.

In a dream, it is possible to see ourselves owning a passport representing a different country from the one we are affiliated with in concrete reality. This information indicates our state of conscience regarding the situation presented in the dream. If we see ourselves with a Canadian passport, for example, and the general atmosphere is positive, beautiful, harmonious (the passport is clean, correct, in order; the attitude is relaxed, confident, etc.), it means that in terms of states of soul, mind and spirit, we have the qualities that characterize this country within us. In this case, these would be, among others, the soul, mind and spirit states engendered by vast open spaces, humanism, altruism, heart values, peace and harmony between different cultures and nationalities, abundance, natural simplicity and authenticity in daily life, flexibility and a capacity for adaptation.

If, in a dream, a passport cannot be clearly identified (i.e. if the name of the country it belongs to isn't legible), we analyze all the other available details, such as its color, size, logo, condition, which, in the passport context, are all symbols that need to be related to identity and a capacity to travel from one country to another.

Just like in concrete reality, in a dream, we can see ourselves refused access to a country, a world, a place, or egregore (*cf.* this term), because we haven't got the necessary travel documents (passport, visa, or others), symbolically speaking, we do not have the necessary, required qualities. Difficulty obtaining a passport, entering a country, staying there, or leaving it, represents the materialization of limits and blockages on the expansion level of our soul. Such difficulties indicate that the dreamer needs to think about the positive and negative aspects of the country concerned, and reflect on the reasons given for refusal. E.g. in a dream, or concrete reality, not being able to travel to Canada would indicate that the person needs to work on the development of qualities and the transformation of the weaknesses of his inner Canada; on the positive and negative resonance he has with this country, this egregore, in terms of conscience, attitude, and behavior.

⊕ A capacity to travel and discover different countries either concretely or in terms of states of conscience. Easy access to multiple egregores, ways of thinking and living. Conscious identification with the qualities of the country the passport represents, as well as work on ourselves to transcend its distortions. Expansion of conscience. Access to the collective conscience. Openness regarding the world, the Universe. Ease changing state of conscience, adapting. Universal citizen. A spirit of adventure, discovery, of being an eternal student. Someone who prepares and organizes his travels in accordance with Divine Laws and Principles, flowing synchronicity, and respecting the borders of countries on Earth as well as those in the parallel worlds. Confidence, feelings of protection, abundance, expansion, accomplishment. Awareness that obtaining or being refused a passport corresponds to the application of Divine Justice.

⊖ An incapacity or difficulty traveling and discovering different countries, either concretely or in terms of states of conscience. Problems gaining access and adapting to a country. Limited freedom of movement and expansion of conscience. Feelings of restriction, imprisonment, isolation, solitude, abandonment, rejection. Racism, a lack of openness regarding the world, regarding others. A closed, withdrawn, limited mind and spirit. Discrepancies between our inner aspirations and the circumstances of life on the outside. Problems with customs, collective exchanges, justice. Non-respect of physical and metaphysical boundaries, conveyed, among other things, by illegal activities such as trafficking false or stolen passports. A tendency to force in order to obtain what we want on the social and collective level. Abuse of power and authority. A person who believes he is above everyone and everything else; memories of megalomania. Disrespect of Universal laws, leading to the loss of Divine Protection while travelling. Problems related to the distortions of the country the passport represents. Someone who resists or refuses to work on his memories of limitation, not wanting to make any effort to develop the qualities that would allow him contact with other worlds, other cultures, and other ways of thinking. Seeking illusory paradises, worldly pleasures. Life dynamics constituted of continual travelling in order to flee problems, dissatisfaction, frustrations, responsibilities. A lack of stability, of intimacy. Unhealthy curiosity, conscience solely oriented toward the material aspects and values of life. Disconnection from our origins.

PAST, THE

Study of the past allows us to better understand how we have become who we are at the present time, and how choices, events, experimentations, learning experiences and apprenticeships along the way have contributed to our development. Knowledge of the past allows us to integrate the lessons learned from poor decisions and errors committed, to rectify the thoughts and emotions that engendered them so as not to repeat them. It also allows us to integrate into the present the positive, constructive elements of the past, and to transmit them to the future generations. By purifying and transforming past memories, we favorably influence, not only our present life, but also, simultaneously, events and lives to come.

The past designates what was, i.e. all of the events, as well as their associated memories and emotions, which occurred in bygone space and time. The past is defined as all the stages and cycles already undergone; the thoughts, emotions, and experimentations already experienced. It is related to the present as memory, and it influences both the present and the future, whether we are aware of it or not. In a way, as long as we haven't transformed the memories of the past, they remain present, alive, a collection of latent, more or less dormant, anaesthetized, repressed, forgotten forces, which, through resonance, may be activated, positively or negatively, as soon as the necessary constellation of circumstances is provided. These memories are inscribed in what is called the unconscious and the subconscious.

⊕ Improvement of ourselves, our life, and our destiny thanks to knowledge and transcendence of the past. Acquisition of wisdom, of deeper understanding and a more global vision of life, thanks to experience and apprenticeships in the past. Awareness of the importance of the memories we bear within and the influence they have on our life and our future. Revelation of essential elements related to the past of this or other lives. Return to the original Source, to ancestral Wisdom. A visit to the archives of our soul, to memories recorded in the Cosmic Library (Daath). Awareness of the importance of the present moment, and of the role each person plays in Creation. Understanding the concept of good and evil, and its role in the evolution of our conscience. Rectification of errors committed in the past. A capacity to teach what we have learned. Happy memories.

⊖ Negative memories that are difficult to cleanse and transform. Phobia or old trauma, which create blockages and keep us imprisoned in the past. An accumulation of useless, cumbersome memories, which prevent us from living the present moment well, and creating space for the new. A tendency to flee our past, to reproduce the same old, distorted patterns, to accumulate frustration, rancor, negativity, dependence. A tendency not to learn from experience. Attachment to the status quo, to dislike recalling and remembering the past, calling ourselves into question, reflecting on our history, or working on ourselves in order to improve, to evolve. Fixation on past memories, for example in the case of a bereaved person who cannot get over the death of a loved one. Nostalgia. An incapacity to come to terms with ourselves, to reconcile with our past, or with other people. Memory problems. A tendency to forget, difficulty remembering, Alzheimer's disease. Difficulty living in the present, acknowledging the progress we have made since the past and getting on with our future.

PATH

The symbolism of the word *path* is related to a capacity to advance in a chosen direction, or to follow an indication to reach a destination, to complete a stage in our evolution. The path to be followed in the inner world goes hand in hand with a spiritual journey on the inside, and involves the notions of effort, discovery, adaptation, choice of direction, apprenticeship, evolution, and culmination. Hence, the path we choose to walk leads us to situations, people, and events that we need to experience in order to progress and attain the level of understanding and conscience that corresponds to the next stage in our development. The path we choose is never a coincidence, just as finding ourselves on a path where we are obliged to make our way around obstacles, or even forced to make several detours because it is in a bad state, blocked, flooded, or collapsed under the effects of a landslide, is never a coincidence either. Whatever we experience on a path reveals certain aspects of ourselves, our soul-state, our spirit, as well as the kind of thoughts and reflections that dwell in us at the time we find ourselves on the path in question. The destination and goal we are heading for, as well as our intention and motivation for choosing a particular path, are also essential for a correct, complete interpretation of its symbolic meaning.

⊕ Allows us to advance easily. A capacity to follow an indicated path easily and confidently. A conscious choice of the path we want to walk (*cf. also* this term), and understanding that it simultaneously corresponds to an inner journey. A capacity to recognize signs and warnings transmitted by the state of the path, situations, events, or obstacles encountered along it. Conscious journeying through the different stages of our individual life path, knowing that on the global, universal scale, it is an integral part of the Path of Destiny.

⊖ Difficulty advancing toward our goals; or, a refusal to follow the path indicated, to journey with wisdom, conscience, and vigilance. Obstacles, blockages, pitfalls, detours, limitations, going astray. A tendency to always take the same path for fear of getting lost, through insecurity when faced with the unknown; or, so as not to have to leave our comfort zone, our usual routine. Advancing in a forced, stubborn, obstinate way so as to attain our target at all costs. A lack of understanding that the outer path corresponds to an inner journey, and that, above all, walking our life path serves the development of qualities and virtues and the evolution of our conscience.

PEARL

Due to its gradual construction, a pearl symbolizes alchemy, the capacity to transform the negative into positive. Whenever a foreign substance enters the oyster's shell, the oyster sets in motion great transformation work to assimilate rather than reject the intrusive substance. Hence, a pearl symbolizes great wisdom as well as a capacity to transcend the negative, to use the power of vital energy to transform a perturbing, annoying, upsetting element into something beautiful, harmonious and precious. The expression *a rare pearl* designates certain people who manifest exceptional qualities, or great value and appreciation for certain works of art. The work of an oyster, and the pearl itself, are great initiatic symbols because through love and wisdom, we human beings must continually transform our negative aspects and turn them into qualities, or, symbolically speaking, *pearls*.

⊕ Capacity to transform, to metamorphose any difficult, conflicting, negative situation into a positive one, through great work of transcendence and inner alchemy. Opportunity to practice forgiveness, reconciliation, and create harmony and beauty. Someone who likes and seeks purity, improvement, refinement in what he accomplishes. Great initiate, who develops his ability to materialize divinely. Behavior, actions, decisions that express a high level of conscience, wisdom, and altruistic love. Understanding that every difficult situation is a unique opportunity for improvement, transformation, transcendence. Great quality final results that manifest the process of evolution.

⊖ Incapacity to transform the negative into positive, to alchemize disturbing situations, to transcend ordeals. Difficulty materializing divinely. May be related to a superficial, very materialistic person, focused on the outer aspects of people and things. Incapacity to appreciate inner and outer work for their true value. Tendency to wish to steal or grasp purity and beauty only to destroy or sully them. May also indicate over-perfectionist, over-puritanical dynamics; or, reveal someone who thinks he is pure but who isn't, who seeks to seduce, or who believes he has a right to do whatever he wants to obtain his personal ends. Rejection of the negative, of everything imperfect. A lack of understanding of good and evil, of the educational role that the negative plays in the process of evolution. Superficial behavior, focused on appearances. Fear of change, of being disturbed in our usual routine and comfort.

PENCIL

Through its elongated form, a pencil is a symbol of emissivity related to the creative potential on the intellectual and emotional levels. It represents the capacity to put down on paper, hence to exteriorize, communicate, and materialize ideas, thoughts, inspirations, feelings. Moreover, when it has an integrated eraser, it symbolizes a capacity to rectify, correct, and/or erase aspects and elements that are not right. As for coloring pencils, the color(s) in question, as well as the kind of drawing they are associated with, also need to be analyzed.

⊕ A capacity to activate and make right, qualitative use of our masculine, emissive polarity to express the creative potential within ourselves. A capacity to communicate and materialize our ideas and inspirations clearly and precisely, to elaborate our thoughts, and share our knowledge. A capacity for planning, organizing, and materializing. An artistic gift that nourishes and elevates the soul. A talent for communication, writing, and drawing.

⊖ Difficulty or incapacity to materialize, to exteriorize our ideas, soul-states, thoughts, and emotions; or, blocked or distorted emissivity and creativity. A lack of inspiration, dynamism, planning, structure, and rigor. Manifestation of erroneous, negative, destructive concepts. A tendency to flee materialization. Distorted expression of artistic talent.

PENIS

A penis is a symbol of masculinity, emissivity, virility, the creative force of life, sexuality, and purification. Its symbolic meaning in dreams depends on the context. When it is in erection, it represents the search or need for love and affection, desire, a wish for fusion, expansion, and self-fulfillment. In dreams, as much for men as for women, it may also indicate a desire to procreate or begin a project in matter.

A penis is a fundamental symbol referred to by numerous phallic, emissive symbols, such as a banana, a corncob, a cucumber, a stick, an obelisk, etc. Any symbol that has a slender, elongated form with a rounded or pointed end will relate to the masculine force and may suggest sexuality. If it is not in erection, it may denote a rest period, interiorization, abstinence or mastery of passion, of sexual impulses and desires, of the emissive, creative force; or, a lack of emissivity, a problem with virility, or difficulties with the masculine principle of creative power. This changeable dynamic of the penis, which also serves to urinate, hence emotional purification (as urine is liquid, it is a symbol related to the emotional level), expresses different soul-states related to the expression of love, needs and the creative force that we all have within.

⊕ Symbolizes the masculine polarity, emissivity, virility, vigor, vital energy, creative power and man's intimacy; also represents a capacity to materialize projects or human life with love and wisdom, as well as a capacity to purify ourselves on the emotional level. Self-assertion and fulfillment. Right emissivity. Mastery and transcendence of sexuality. A healthy, radiant, well-balanced, harmonious sexuality that leads to joy, happiness and Divine pleasures. Awakening of the kundalini.

⊖ Problems related to intimacy and sexuality. Impulsive desires, primitive, obsessive needs. A lack of love and tenderness. Difficulty purifying ourselves on the emotional, intimate levels. May also indicate a lack of emissivity, impotency on the physical level because the person lives too much in his head, is too cerebral, over-focused on the world of thoughts; or, too absorbed in his world or social life, to the detriment of his intimate life. Difficulty maintaining a stable, right, well-balanced relationship. An incapacity to fuse with the other person in true love. A lack of mastery, of wisdom. Sexual abuse and waste. Hyperactivity or inactivity. An incapacity or difficulty to provide the necessary energy for the materialization of projects. Sterility; or, extreme fertility, fecundity, multiplying and creating without conscience or love. Megalomaniac, machismo behavior; or, behavior that lacks masculine assertion. Aggression, coarseness, boorishness. Seeing a woman with a penis in a dream indicates excessive emissivity in the dreamer's creative force, and, simultaneously, a lack of receptivity.

PHILANTHROPIST *cf.* ***Benefactor***

PHONE BOOK *cf.* ***Telephone Directory***

PHOTOGRAPHY

When we take photographs, we seek to remember and preserve beautiful moments of life, and, generally speaking, people, things, situations and events that inspire us and that are important for us. Thanks to photographs we can rediscover, analyze and study the states of conscience experienced. As well as helping us deepen our understanding and enlarge our vision of things, they are also a source of inspiration and of unforgettable, long-lasting sentimental memories imprinted in our mind and heart, stored in our personal hard drive. It is very beneficial to encourage children and teenagers to take photographs because, like adults, they learn to look more deeply at people, objects, events, and life.

⊕ Contributes toward developing deep vision and understanding, creativity, the sense of observation. Helps us recognize atmospheres and ambiances, moods, states of soul and conscience, affinities. Inspires us to look differently at ourselves, others, objects, situations and events in life. Facilitates the creation of beautiful memories we can recall at a later date. Helps in the search for identity; helps to build a feeling of belonging. Allows us to work on ourselves by applying the Law of resonance.

⊖ Nostalgia for the past, a tendency to live in our memories, to retain and preserve futilities, a desire to capture atmospheres and ambiances in order to fulfill a void and inner lacks. Difficulty becoming detached, letting go; possessiveness. Fear of lacking something, taking photographs out of curiosity. Indiscretion, voyeurism, sensationalism, superficiality. Seeking renown, celebrity (paparazzi syndrome). Negative vision, tendency to focus on sensations, tragedies, misery in the world, incapable of seeing goodness and beauty.

PLANTS, VEGETATION

Any form of plant life, or vegetation, represents a state of conscience related to emotions and feelings because it is mostly composed of water. However, this state of conscience is the manifestation of more concrete, more permanent feelings, than those related to liquids, because plants are more compact and stable than liquids.

For plant life to grow and mature, it needs earth, air, water, and sunlight. A parallel may be drawn with feelings and emotions that deepen and intensify when they are nourished with beautiful thoughts, intentions, and motivation, which allow them to materialize, take root, and grow.

The fact that plants transform carbonic gas into oxygen, symbolizes a form of alchemy on the level of emotional thoughts, transforming negative thoughts into positive thoughts, just as love can transform war, conflict and tension into peace. Furthermore, if the plant has medicinal virtues, a healing element is added to its symbolism. The plant or vegetation species, the soil and country it grows in, its needs for water and sunlight, etc., are further indications as to the specificity of the feelings in question.

⊕ Stable emotions and feelings that grow and increase in accordance with actions (earth), emotions (water), thoughts (air), and state of mind and spirit (fire). Easy, kind, loving, well-intentioned, emotional growth, engendered by love, wisdom, consolation, gentleness, delicacy. An important emotional capacity and force, favoring regeneration, multiplication, and proliferation. A source of inspiration. Alchemical power, a capacity to transform negative thoughts into positive thoughts. Inspires life, beauty, light-heartedness, and simplicity.

⊖ Unstable, fragile, vulnerable, ephemeral, harmful, distorted, invasive, suffocating feelings. Emotional, affective dependency. Difficulty regenerating, renewing ourselves. An incapacity to carry out alchemy on the emotional level, to transform negative feelings into positive ones, to transform aggressive soul-states into states of gentleness, emotional, sentimental, affective stability, serenity, and peace.

PLATE

A plate is an accessory that is used to receive food. Symbolically it represents receptivity to nourishing, regenerative resources as well as the way we nourish ourselves, and consequently how we nourish others.

A broken plate in a dream or in concrete reality indicates the presence of forces that prevent us from being receptive to regenerative resources. For its symbolic interpretation, we also analyze the characteristics of the plate, such as its shape, size, color, where it comes from or the substance it is made of, because all of these aspects provide complementary indications.

⊕ Receptivity to resources and the way in which we nourish ourselves and others; or, the way we are nourished by others.

⊖ Problem of receptivity to resources and the way in which we nourish ourselves and others; or, the way we are nourished by others. A lack or excess of food, abuse, bulimia, anorexia.

PLAY, TO (game)

Play, playing, and games are a symbol of pleasure, joy, fun, relaxation, and learning. Play is the principal activity and source of learning for a child. Motivation and brain activity are more intense, and integration much more efficient, when learning is joyful. Playful activities and games also help adults re-discover their inner child, and its associated states of conscience: spontaneity, the joy of experimenting, discovery, creativity, learning, sharing, light-heartedness, natural simplicity, and relaxation through pleasure and fun.

⊕ A capacity to recognize and appreciate play as an element of renewal, replenishment, relaxation, learning, education, and sharing. Awareness of the importance of the quality of the game played, and analysis of the capacities, powers, and positive aspects it stimulates and develops. Understanding that each type of game solicits specific qualities and abilities, and that it is important to remain conscious during the game so as to maintain a right, natural, joyful, spontaneous attitude no matter the outcome.

⊖ Play can be extremely harmful when it nourishes the player's mind and soul with violence, aggressive, destructive behavior, and attitudes of rivalry, competition and combat, as do a great number of video games and toys (*cf. also* this term) representing weapons and war figurines. Such games connect the player to fields of conscience and egregores (*cf.* this term) of violent energies, which leads to the manifestation of aggressive behavior, as well as a tendency to become obsessed with the result, to play only to win. Some virtual games can plunge players deep into an imaginary world, in which they become so completely absorbed that they lose all interest in daily life, sometimes even to the extent of becoming dysfunctional in the concrete world. Unfortunately ignorance of the harmful effects of video games is still widespread in our society, which tends to brush over and trivialize these dangers in favor of commercial and financial profit. These games constitute considerable sources of negativity for the children, teenagers, and adults who play them. Seeing ourselves play a violent video game in a dream means that we nourish and reinforce violence in ourselves.

Likewise, games that create a dependency while giving the player the illusion that he can control his destiny are also very harmful. These include gambling and all the games on offer in casinos, as well as the lottery and betting on races, etc. Very often, people who play these kinds of games have a limited, distorted vision of the serious consequences they lead to, both for themselves and their families. These kinds of games reveal a great desire for power; or, deep, material, and existential insecurity, from which the person tries to magically escape by betting on chance, hoping to outwit and thwart his destiny, his life-plan.

Games can also serve as evasion when we don't want to become seriously involved, such as games of seduction or playing a role. Such games show a tendency not to want to commit ourselves, to be responsible, to think about the consequences of our actions and learn lessons from our choices.

Finally, there is also difficulty or an incapacity to play, to participate spontaneously and joyfully in children's games, for example. This may indicate an over-serious attitude to life, being encumbered by problems and bogged down in daily routine; or, it may indicate egoism, a tendency toward materialism, impatience, a lack of imagination, spontaneity, and *joie de vivre*; a lack of understanding of the creative, educational, therapeutic, constructive, evolutive function of play, playing, and positive games.

PLUMBER

A plumber usually repairs or installs domestic or industrial sanitary systems (piping and taps in bathrooms, toilets, kitchens, drain systems, waterworks, aqueducts, as well as heating systems based on water). Symbolically, this job is related to the development, adjustment, and maintenance of emotional resources, inner purification, ensuring the evacuation and drainage of polluted, negative emotions, as well as the free circulation of positive, healthy, favorable, emotional energies. In concrete reality or in a dream, if a plumber works in a person's home, it refers to the personal and family level, whereas if he intervenes in a large structure, such as a street, store, hotel, airport, etc., it refers to the collective level.

The initial sanitary installations prior to all constructions ensure the maintenance of hygiene, comfort, and respect for everyone's intimacy, so as to harmonize people's biological needs with their family, social, and professional lives. Likewise, to function in a healthy, well-balanced way, our inner world requires the same conditions of cleanliness and hygiene, discretion and comfort. Hence a plumber's actions have a direct impact on our health and general well-being. A good way to understand in depth the symbolic and metaphysical importance of a plumber's job, on the individual and collective levels, is to think of the inconvenience, the discomfort, and ill-being we experience when confronted with a burst pipe, a blocked toilet, a leak due to a broken pipe; or, on a larger scale, to imagine the millions of people living in shantytowns and slums with no sanitary installations to ensure hygiene, biological needs or respect for each person's intimacy.

⊕ A capacity to repair or improve the potential access to emotional resources, purification systems, evacuation and liberation of waste energies on the physical and emotional levels. A capacity to meet and provide for the needs of our physical body, to facilitate purification and to nourish our actions with more love and affection. Efficient reparation of structures related to the use of emotional and sanitary resources on both inner and outer levels. An ability to ensure good hygiene, healthy, comfortable living conditions that respect everyone's intimacy. Development of individual and collective capacities to install new inner and outer structures to allow rapid, easy access to water, i.e. emotions, symbolically speaking. Installation of a heating system (if hydraulic), which allows us to regulate our inner ambiances, render them warmer, and hence more loving, more welcoming. Liberation of emotional blockages, retention and repression (e.g. rancor, resentment, anger, sadness, grief, vengeance).

⊖ An incapacity to change, repair, or install new emotional resources and/or new systems of purification and evacuation. A lack of inner and outer hygiene on a personal or collective level, according to the given situation. Difficulty purifying ourselves, facing and dealing with emotional blockages or affective excess, or overflow, which can lead to retention or waste of emotions, resources of love and affection.

POLICE

The police force is an institution whose role consists in ensuring the security of people and material goods by enforcing law and order. In dreams and in concrete reality, the police are necessary to face up to the negative and prevent it from expanding on both the personal and collective levels. They are a symbol of protection, security, authority, order, rigor, the law, ethics, and justice. If, in a dream, the police act incoherently or inappropriately, this indicates that there is behavior that needs to be rectified on the level of the dreamer's inner justice.

⊕ Symbol of security, protection, authority, justice and rigor. Capacity to ensure order and stability, to enforce the law and protect social harmony. A sense of justice, duty, and devotion to society, a trustworthy, rigorous person. Exemplary moral, ethical behavior. Ability to stop – in dreams and/or concrete reality – our delinquent forces, our rebellious parts that disorganize our well-being and our personality, thereby avoiding the manifestation of these forces in misactions (*cf.* this term), in criminal acts in concrete reality. An honest, incorruptible, upright person of integrity who has a positive influence on the principles and values of a society. Understanding Divine Justice, karma, and the Law of reincarnation.

⊖ Problems related to justice, security, protection, order, respect for the law; or, lack of assertion on the level of justice, hence allowing wrong (evil) to continue to proliferate. A coarse, brutish, aggressive, manipulating force; a feeling of superiority. Someone who abuses the power conferred on him by his job as a policeman, who sets a bad example, who believes himself to be above the law. Machismo attitude. Law of the jungle, which promotes survival of the fittest, and agrees that might is right. Criminal disguised as a law enforcer. A corrupt, rebellious delinquent person who creates disorder and acts against both earthly, terrestrial laws and Divine Laws. Someone who seeks to enforce justice within himself, but is too severe. Destructuring of humane, human values.

POLLUTION

Generally speaking, pollution designates the degradation of the eco-system. However, it is essential to know that before manifesting concretely in the air, water, or soil, and creating serious damage to the environment, to human, animal, and vegetable life, pollution first occurs on the metaphysical and causal level, in our inner world, on the level of the thoughts, concepts, values, sentiments, feelings and emotions that we engender and maintain. The physical consequences that we are experiencing today (climatic upheaval, the problem of the ozone layer, the manifestation of new illnesses, etc.) are simply the reflection of immense quantities of memories and distorted actions, accumulated on the individual, personal and collective, social levels, throughout the course of our numerous lives. Just as the magnificent places on Earth symbolize the beautiful qualities, values, strengths, and virtues that human beings bear within themselves in terms of conscience, so too does pollution in its various forms represent the materialization of our erroneous thoughts, emotions and actions.

Symbolically, air pollution (smog, harmful clouds of gas, the presence of dangerous viruses in the air, etc.) corresponds to polluting thoughts and ways of thinking that are bad for our health and destroy equilibrium and harmony on the individual and collective levels.

Water pollution denotes the massive presence of negative, destabilizing, destructive emotions, which act like poison on people's emotional, affective level, with repercussions right down into the physical level (e.g. the dumping of solid and liquid waste products into various waters; the constant increase in waste water, and simultaneously, the reduction of drinking water; shipwrecks of cargo boats transporting products that are harmful, toxic for the flora, fauna, and man; oil rig catastrophes, oil slicks, huge floating islands of plastic, etc.).

As for soil pollution, symbolically related to the earth element and concrete action, it is the materialized form of distorted, wrong, unfair, abusive actions, in the way we humans use the earth and its resources (waste buried in the ground, ever-increasing large quantities of abandoned waste due to over-production, excessive consumerism, and waste).

Furthermore, with the continued development of technology, and increasing artificial needs, new forms of pollution have appeared: electro-magnetic, radio-active, sound and light pollution, etc. These all reflect the growing imbalance in how we use our potential of emissivity and receptivity.

Space is also affected by pollution: damaged satellites, risks of collision, disturbed atmosphere, increasing threats for the Earth. However, through this aspect, we can also see the interest human beings have in extra-terrestrial worlds, our aspiration to know, discover and explore the multiple dimensions of the Universe, the parallel worlds, and the causal level of Creation. Nevertheless, if we don't want to create collective, planetary karmas, with very serious consequences, we must take care to be suitably prepared for this, with a spiritual conscience and pure, right intention.

Generally speaking, all forms of pollution are the result, the consequence of experimentations carried out through ignorance, indifference, carelessness, greed, avidity, egoism, and rebellion, while not respecting Divine Laws and Order. Such attitudes destroy happy longevity and hamper well-balanced, harmonious evolution. Moreover, those who cause pollution will necessarily have to go through a re-educational, learning process established by the consequences of their acts. *We always reap what we sow, just as we become what we think.*

⊕ Individual and collective awareness allowing for a change of attitude, behavior, and polluting lifestyles. Capacity to understand the multi-dimensionality of pollution. Awakening of conscience and the will to learn from our mistakes, to recycle, to transform polluting aspects of ourselves, and work on our distorted memories related to pollution on different levels. Return to harmony, peace, well-being, and equilibrium between our inner and outer environment. Development of a new way of thinking and living, that pollutes as little as possible and respects the natural balance, the living environment of the different kingdoms, and planetary environment on the whole. Participation in the elaboration and realization of projects aiming to cleanse and decontaminate heavily polluted regions, and preserve the natural state of other zones. Awareness of the fact that everything we observe in physical reality also exists within us on the metaphysical level, and that we always reap what we sow.

⊖ Problems resulting from an accumulation of heavy, polluting, degrading memories. No respect for the environment and natural balance due to carelessness, negligence, laziness, indifference, cowardice, ignorance, a lack of awareness, conscience, global and long-term vision. Harmful, polluting, malevolent, sick states of soul, mind and spirit that exert a negative influence. Collective memories full of destructive forces. Egotistical, self-centered, megalomaniac behavior. Refusal to learn from our mistakes and experiences. Lack of purity, order, and harmony on the inside, which is reflected in a polluting lifestyle on the outside. A large degree of inner and/or outer pollution that can trigger great ordeals, provoke deep self-questioning, and activate a very difficult life plan if the person or persons concerned do not undertake deep self-questioning and change their ways of living, thinking, behaving, and doing.

PORT

A port is situated on the banks of a river, làrge lake, or beside the sea; its main role is to welcome boats and ships, allow them to load/unload their cargo, replenish and renew their resources, carry out repair work, as well as favoring the transfer of passengers and travelers. Linking the water and earth elements, a port symbolizes the way emotions and feelings manifest in exchanges, and the dynamics of giving and receiving in the world of concrete action. It is also closely related to the symbolic, metaphysical meaning of a boat (*cf. also* this term), which represents emotional, sentimental, affective stability and advancing.

A port also denotes a major collective dimension given the fact that it shelters or welcomes a great number of boats, people, and goods. It is generally associated with major departures and travelling across the seas and oceans, as well as cruises, which allow us to visit islands and/or specific coastlines. As both a concrete and symbolic link between earth and water, it may be considered a passageway between emotions leading to concrete actions; or, conversely, between actions that engender emotional reactions. It is also a zone of intensive energy exchanges through the constant giving and receiving that takes place between the people working in the port, on the boats, the passengers, and the transported goods. Hence, it facilitates access to the supplies and provisions of the resources needed to manifest ourselves, and helps toward collective emotional communication, as well as the broadening of our horizon through visiting other countries, either concretely, or in terms of conscience. Finally, it represents the way we protect the transit of our resources, and our capacity to exchange with others on all levels, because a port is always strategically important.

⊕ A place of transit, passing through, a passageway, a place of travel and adventure, allowing us to discover new parts of ourselves on the physical and emotional levels. A capacity to welcome our ability to advance on the emotional level (boats), and to ensure the necessary corrections, rectifications, and reparation. A symbol of protection, shelter, refuge, renewal of resources, consolation, and stability regarding emotional excesses and overflow (e.g. when a boat arrives into port after navigating in rough seas). A capacity to exchange resources and emotions harmoniously with others, to experiment and integrate right, qualitative giving and receiving on the individual and collective levels. A warm, welcoming, open mind and spirit. Facilitates the passage of emotions toward the physical level, and our passing from the physical level to the emotional level.

⊖ Difficulty exchanging resources on both the concrete and emotional levels. Distorted, erroneous experimentations, related to giving and receiving on the collective level; a lack of altruism. A cold, calculating, withdrawn mind and spirit, closed off from others and the world. A lack of welcome, of human warmth. A hideout, lair, or den for bandits, pirates, illegal activities (smuggling, drug-, weapon-, and even people- trafficking). Scheming, intrigue, non-respect of laws and customs, abuse of power, corrupt administrative and political structures. Blocked horizons. Flight dynamics. Integration problems. Poor organization on the collective level. Difficult transforming (repairing) our capacity to advance on the emotional level (boat). A place of excessive control, rigid rules, a tendency to over-protect ourselves; or, a lack of protection, shelter, refuge, and emotional stability.

POSITIVE

The word positive defines perception of that which is good, right, valuable, appreciative, acceptable, in all domains. What is considered positive is very relative and depends on our level of conscience and Knowledge. In mathematical, numerical, and electrical polarities, as well as in many other fields of activity, positive is a qualifying adjective that is considered in conjunction with negative (*cf. also* this term).

On the symbolic level, positive refers to qualities, a person's beautiful forces, powers, energy, expansion, and light; negative refers to distortions, dark forces, difficulties. It is important, however, to remember that while the negative is opposed to the positive, it is also complementary, and has an educational and evolutive value. These two poles balance each other to create the dynamics of the Universe: they are the very basis of evolution.

⊕ All Qualities and Virtues in general. Seeking Knowledge, Love, advancing toward the Light. Expansion, power of natural, creative, constructive evolution. Hope, the will to accept and follow the natural movement of things, to rediscover equilibrium, equity. Everything that favors a person's evolution, everything that allows him to follow his program harmoniously and correctly.

⊖ Exaggerated, false positivism, over-confidence, excessive naivety, and a tendency to deny the negative; or, not to want to recognize and acknowledge the positive, educational, evolutive aspects of a negative situation. An incapacity to evaluate with discernment, fairness, and accuracy what is good, right, qualitative, favorable. A tendency to dramatize, to nourish and maintain the negative instead of learning to transform it into something positive, to transcend it. Excessively perfectionist behavior and rigidity so as to appear perfect; puritanism. Taken to extremes, conscious rejection of the positive in order to do harm. Everything that harms a person's evolution, everything that hampers and hinders the harmonious, right accomplishment of his program.

POVERTY

Poverty is the absence of abundance, a state of lack, which does not only manifest on the material level. Indeed, we can also experience poverty in our emotional world, on the intellectual level, have a poor spiritual life, have and maintain poverty in our conscience. In a society that is oriented toward excessive consumption of resources and the accumulation of material goods (consumerism and materialism), people in an ordinary conscience usually consider themselves to be poor when they haven't got the financial means to buy everything they want, when they cannot satisfy all their desires, all the artificial needs created by advertisements, the media, the lifestyles of the rich and famous. In this case, their poverty isn't really situated on the material level, because usually these people have all they need to live: food, shelter, clothes, an income, access to education and professional training, as well as to health and social services, etc. It's more a case of emotional, intellectual, or spiritual poverty that they try to flee or fulfill by creating habits of excessive consumerism and a lifestyle focused on illusory values and artificial paradises.

It is important to understand that it is never the result of coincidence or injustice when a person finds himself experiencing poverty, perhaps even barely surviving, lacking almost all essentials. In order to understand the very difficult living conditions whole populations experience in different countries of our planet, we have to consider them from a global point of view and take into account Cosmic Laws, especially the Law of karma, which stipulates that we always reap what we sow; the Law of reincarnation that explains that our soul and spirit evolve through numerous lives in accordance with all that we do, all that we experiment, sow and reap in each of those lives; the Law of resonance, whereby we attract the life situation and living conditions that resonate with all that we are and all that we have created throughout our multiple lives, in the + as well as the –; the Principle of Divine Justice, which is absolute and applies to each and every one of us, without exception; the temporal dimension of matter, and the educational role of evil, wrong-doing, what hurts, which allows us to experiment matter in time and space, and helps us learn from our errors, weaknesses, and faults.

Even though we can denounce the obvious, external causes of poverty which manifest individually or collectively in physical reality (e.g. exploitation, slavery, egotism, waste of resources, all sorts of abuse of power, etc.), considered from a causal, multi-dimensional point of view, poverty is always a consequence that stems from and is the result of non-respect for Cosmic Laws over a long period of time, sometimes several lives. It is the materialization of a major accumulation of negative karmas, misactions (*cf.* this term), wrong, abusive, unjust behavior and attitudes that cause a person or whole populations to experience the Law of return, the boomerang effect of their own wrongs. The principle that we always reap what we sow is a very revealing perspective from which to consider a person experimenting from one life to another; sometimes wandering far from the path of Divine Order, hence creating lives of extreme difficulty, privation, limitations that Cosmic Intelligence has to orchestrate to incite him to rectify his behavior and use universal abundance in a right, fair, altruistic manner.

The educational function of poverty consists in stimulating a person, shaking him up, deeply transforming and, reforming him. It is a tool for motivation, inspiration, and constructive creativity. Poverty is a non-natural state that needs to be surmounted and overcome. We can manage to overcome it by activating the Qualities, Virtues and Divine Powers that lie dormant within each and every one of us. As well as exercising an educational, evolutive role on many levels, the experience of poverty simultaneously contributes to the settlement of accumulated karmic debts.

Before poverty manifests in physical reality, it is first of all inscribed on the metaphysical level, in the subtle levels, in our mind and spirit, and in the memories we record in our soul. It is essential to know that every time we misuse abundance and the resources we have at our disposal, each time we are jealous and envy, manipulate, deceive or waste, we impoverish our soul, which is naturally rich. Simultaneously, our individual conscience strays further and further from, disconnects more and more from, and may even sever connection with, the Laws and Principles that govern permanent access to universal abundance. Hence, through our thoughts and actions, we prepare subtle energy molds or patterns, through which poverty materializes in our concrete reality. Consequently, anyone who wants to avoid or overcome poverty should carry out conscious work on himself to transform everything that resonates with the notion of poverty in his thoughts, emotions, behavior and acts. This is how he will transcend poverty, first of all in his conscience, and although living in poverty on the outside, on the material level, he will manifest a soul-state of great wealth and a spirit of abundance.

An accumulation of tension, dissatisfaction, insecurity, as well as a fear of lack, memories of shortage and struggle for survival, can hinder, hamper, and block the manifestation of abundance in different domains of a person's life. Furthermore, in principle, the presence of material wealth in a person's life does not mean that he is perfect, or that he knows how to use his wealth well, right, qualitatively. Everything depends on his intention, his conscience, on the way he uses his prosperity. Cosmic Intelligence may orchestrate success and material wealth in a person's life-plan to allow him to experiment the power of action in matter, to provide him with opportunities to learn how to use resources on the personal and collective levels the right way, justly, fairly, altruistically. Usually, many lives are necessary to accomplish this apprenticeship on a vast scale. If the person chooses to use these resources and the power they confer to harm others, to cause damage, to sow suffering and destruction, sooner or later, in the same life or an ulterior reincarnation, he will have to take responsibility for his attitudes and behavior, and undergo life programs of poverty. The greater the multiplying effect his distorted, unjust acts have, leading to massive consequences on the collective level, (e.g. a politician, member of parliament or president of a country who misused his country's wealth on any or many levels), the more difficult his future experience of poverty will be.

Poverty can also be experienced in dream reality while being well off, prosperous, or even very rich in concrete reality. Sometimes, Cosmic Intelligence sends dreams of poverty to someone who lives a life of abundance but doesn't truly appreciate it, who dilapidates his resources in various excesses, luxury, and waste without any conscience, scruples or remorse. In such cases, dreams of poverty are warnings, calls to order, to give the person an opportunity to correct and rectify his lifestyle. He is shown in dreams what he is in the process of creating in the subtle levels, and what he will have to live concretely if he doesn't change. If he does not understand the message, these dreams will trigger in him great insecurities regarding losing his material abundance, and that is why he may want to accumulate it even more instead of changing his behavior and cleansing his memories; it is in fact a vicious circle.

However, the opposite is also possible: a person who lives in material poverty may receive dreams where he is rich. In this case, when positive, these are encouraging dreams wherein Cosmic Intelligence reveals to him the wealth and abundance he is creating in his inner world thanks to his efforts, to the transformation of his memories, and the settlement of his karmic debts, which, in a virtuous circle, will one day materialize in concrete abundance; or, if negative, they may be dreams whereby the dreamer is shown that he submits to his outer poverty, feeling like, considering himself a victim. Instead of working on himself, he tends to take refuge in fantasies of imaginary wealth and riches. For an accurate interpretation, it is necessary to take into consideration all of the elements contained in the dream in question.

⊕ A life-program of limitation forcing the person to become detached from matter, to appreciate and use the resources present in his life with conscience, to develop true values on the human and spiritual levels. A period of raising awareness, of rectification and reparation. A capacity to consider poverty not as a cause, but as a consequence engendered by a lack of wisdom in the use of resources in this life, or in previous ones. An ordeal that helps us grow and see life differently when it is well-lived. A capacity to accept our destiny and difficulties without protest or rebellion, to develop the courage, motivation, and right, vivifying force of action to do our best each day, while remaining honest and upright, maintaining our integrity. Integration of the educational role of poverty. The willpower to develop the Qualities, Virtues and Divine Powers that transform poverty and quite naturally attract abundance. An intense period of spiritual evolution. Acquisition of a new vision of prosperity, a universal understanding of what true wealth is. Discovery of the true meaning of life.

⊖ A period of despair, disconnection, dropping out, victimization, possibly going as far as suicide. Wallowing in self-pity. Vagrancy. Letting ourselves fall into complete despondency. De-vitalization, loss of the will to live, to evolve and become a better person, giving up, letting ourselves go. Loss of self-esteem and self-confidence. Feelings of failure, rebellion, anger, injustice. A lack of understanding of the meaning of trials and ordeals. Refusal to take responsibility for ourselves, to make any effort to improve and get out of our situation. A state of survival. A tendency to believe that we are entitled to everything, to take for granted that society owes us everything. A critical, envious, jealous spirit. Forcing destiny. An incapacity to manage resources and materialize in a right, fair, just manner. Conscious or unconscious theft. Ready to prostitute and enslave ourselves to become rich. A lack of understanding of our life scenario; that difficulties come from misactions also committed in other lives, that they are karmic consequences. Refusal to correct our behavior, to repair and settle our karmic debts. Desiring wealth and riches without working, without making any effort. An illusory, evasive life, lacking commitment. A mental attitude that maintains poverty and limitations. A lack of motivation to work on ourselves so as to transform the forces and memories that nourish and engender poverty. Unhealthy living environment. Total absence of hygiene.

PRAYER, TO PRAY

A prayer is an individual or collective dialogue between a person and his Creator, in words, song, or in silence. There are different types of prayer: those where we implore for ourselves; those where we intercede for another person; those where we confess our flaws, faults, weaknesses, errors on all levels; or those where we express our gratitude.

Man uses prayer to contact superior levels, so as to communicate with the Source, with the Divine, with God, with Cosmic Intelligence, whatever name is used. Through prayer, he asks for help, healing, or even a miracle. According to the depth and intensity of his beliefs, consciously or unconsciously, he asserts his will to act and live spiritually, in harmony with the Divine Laws that govern the manifestation of Life on all levels.

Most religions offer their believers ready-made prayers for different occasions and life situations, with specific rituals for each. However, we don't need to belong to an established religion to pray, to live a spiritual life, to believe in a Superior Power. Sometimes a person takes refuge in silence, contemplation, meditation to feel fusion with the Divine, and to experience a great feeling of Unity. Such a meditative state, such inner listening, favors openness, receptivity; it welcomes the heavenly Hierarchies and facilitates connection and communion with the Divine. Prayer helps re-align body and spirit, develop spiritual gifts and powers, experience deep mystical states such as beatitude, felicity and grace. Many great spiritual Masters received their Teachings during these deep interiorizations.

Today, a great number of people have turned away from some of institutionalized religions for several reasons: because these institutions have become fossilized, stuck in old structures and belief patterns; because they abused their power; or, manifest serious tendencies toward extremism; or, because they offer an apocalyptic vision of things. Currently, a new spiritual conscience, a new way of praying, is emerging and manifesting. More and more people are finding their own path, developing renewed, living faith, as a result of their direct personal experience with the Divine, thereby liberating themselves from religious dogma and indoctrination.

Generally, when we pray, we are either in a state of gratitude and acknowledgement, great joy, heavenly grace; or, in deep disposition to work on ourselves to improve and become a better soul. Prayer may also be inner research into Knowledge and an understanding of our experiences, of what we are going through. We use prayer when we go through difficult, problematic situations, such as a separation, mourning, dismissal from our job; or, to ask for support, consolation, guidance. Some people pray simply to talk to someone. There are people who think prayer is abstract, and remains without answers. However, the more we understand that human beings function like living computers, able to connect to God or the Cosmic Computer at any time, the more we realize the power of spiritual Communication. It allows us to receive answers that are coded in symbolic language, in dreams, through daily signs, as well as through the subtle senses of clairaudience, clairvoyance and clairsentience.

The aim of meditation and religious rituals is to live every second of life like a prayer, in a spiritual conscience that connects Man with the Divine, and allows him to make each of his daily gestures sacred, to marry Spirit and matter. The spiritual practice of prayer is a sacred act of communication with God, that we apply each and every second of our existence, as well as each time we need an indication, a direction. It is a very concrete experience and guides us like an inner *GPS* or *SatNav*.

⊕ Communication and communion with the Divine. Request for help, support, guidance. Seeking Knowledge and deep, global, multi-dimensional understanding. Allows us to receive Teachings and to acquire spiritual autonomy. Improves self-knowledge. Encounter with the Divine Self. Interiorization, contemplation, inner listening, a conversation with our soul, with God *via* symbolic language. Facilitates re-centering, re-focusing, inner reinforcement and reconstruction, the development of humility, receptivity, respect for the Heavenly Hierarchies. Favors access to elevated levels of conscience, as well as the experience of powerful, revealing, mystical states on all levels. Detachment from a lifestyle that is over-focused on matter, on doing and having. Work on the transcendence of our needs, and on spiritual willpower to be right at all times, and to learn to act in matter with a spiritual conscience. Favors the recognition, acknowledgement, and integration of Values, Qualities, Virtues, and Universal Principles. Right use of spiritual Powers. The study and understanding of our life plan. Helps to enter into contact with the deep, profound essence of everything that exists in the Universe, to visit and study the parallel worlds. Conscious, active participation in the Divine Plan.

⊖ Prayers guided by selfish, egotistical motivation, a desire to see our personal wants and needs granted by Heaven. Someone who refuses to pray because he doesn't believe in the Divine. Superficial prayers, requests and wishes, over-focused on matter. A lack of willpower, concentration, rigor, and depth in our intentions; or, fear of asking, of bothering the Divine. Someone who doesn't pray because he doesn't feel worthy of Divine Love; or, because he lacks faith; or, who prays for others out of a need to be loved; or, out of fear; or, because he ignores the meaning of ordeals. De-responsibilization, unaccountability (*passing the buck*) through prayer. Neediness, impoverishment, and deep lack of gratitude and a sense of the sacred. An attitude of superiority and over-confidence. Abuse of power, seeking to control destiny and other people's lives. A charlatan, false spirituality. Religious extremism, someone who prays for destructive ends, with evil intentions, that connect him to negative forces, whether he is aware of this or not.

PREGNANCY

On the symbolic level, pregnancy represents starting off a new project, new materialization. It may also announce the coming of a child, or great changes on the level of our personality, entry into a new stage in life, preparation for rebirth.

⊕ Fertility and receptivity on the metaphysical and physical levels. A capacity to conceive, plan, gestate, and materialize a new life, a new project. Blossoming, feelings of love, happiness, plenitude, fulfillment, accomplishment. A state of fusion with the work (child or project) in question. Apprenticeship of patience, inner listening, respect for stages and natural cycles. A feeling of having achieved our mission, our life plan. Consecration of our works to God.

⊖ An incapacity to conceive a child, or to materialize projects, reveals a lack of receptivity, an infertile, sterile state due to arid emotions, a lack of love, patience, perseverance, self-confidence, and fear of not being up to standard. This state of conscience can also result from overly strong emissivity on both the mental and physical levels, excessive willpower, hyperactivity in matter, a selfish, superficial attitude that over-focuses on appearances. Material and emotional dependencies. Relationship problems, and the illusion that having a child can repair or save a marriage. A complaining, plaintive attitude that creates a heavy atmosphere. Corrupt materializations; or, self-destruction of a project by unconscious, distorted forces and powers that we bear within. Seeking love and acknowledgement through the accomplishment of projects.

In a dream, *a man who is pregnant* symbolizes that the person wants to materialize too much on the physical level, in the world of actions; it is also linked to a person who tends to be self-sufficient and to rely only on himself.

PRIEST

A priest is a representative of a religious community authorized to conduct religious services and rituals. In the Catholic Church, priests are invested with the power to say Mass and administer the sacraments. Symbolically, a priest is an example of spiritual vocation, consecration and commitment because he dedicates and devotes his life to serve God and his fellowmen. He is also a referential authority as he represents the moral and spiritual values of a religion and fulfills the role of guide, advisor, important model, and link between God and man. In addition to his religious function, he also has the task of looking after his community, supporting the ill, the suffering, the underprivileged, the rejected and abandoned; to inspire faith, hope, and the foundations of spiritual life, as well as the courage to face up to and willingly accept our destiny.

Nowadays the role of a priest is held in lower esteem than in past centuries due to numerous abuses of all sorts that were committed throughout history by the different representatives of the clergy and the Church. This has turned a large number of people away from institutionalized religion, and has incited them to seek a more authentic, more autonomous spiritual life, independent from established religious structures, institutions, orders and dogma. Today, the birth of a new spiritual conscience on Earth has contributed to considerable change in people's attitude to religion. The Church and priests have lost a lot of their influence on the spiritual, political, and social levels. A priest's role is now more restricted and more focused on religious, community and humanitarian aid.

⊕ A great quest for God. Authentic religious vocation and commitment. Gift of self. Dedication and devotion. A life of service. The will to devote our life to God and our fellowman. Capacity to transmit true spiritual and moral values through example. Deep desire to help the poor, the underprivileged, the sick, lost, drifting, abandoned souls. Confident, unshakeable faith. Mystical experiences of communion and fusion with God. Visions. Revelations. Ability to help others discover their spiritual potential, their connection with God. Altruistic, unconditional, universal Love. Kindness. Goodwill. Compassion. Tolerance. Deep understanding of the human soul. Capacity to console, listen to, and unconditionally support. Gift of oratory, mediation and preaching. Humble, responsible, authentic missionary spirit that puts into practice the values and principles preached. High level of morality. Conscious choice to live a life of voluntary simplicity. Great capacity to be detached from matter. Transcendence of sexuality and instinctual needs.

⊖ Puritanical, strict, rigid, desiccating, sectarian, extremist religious behavior. Someone who, consciously or unconsciously, idolizes hierarchy, who is on a quest for personal power in the Name of God. Seeking recognition, acknowledgement, prestige, and glory on the personal, social, and spiritual levels. Superficial, spiritual commitment. Incapacity to make the gift of self, to truly and authentically serve and help our fellowman. Need for human love. Repression of affective, emotional and sexual needs, which pushes the person to compensate by all sorts of unhealthy, perverted thoughts, behavior and outlets. Lack of humility and simplicity. Spiritual pride. Feelings of superiority. Hypocrisy. Religious charlatan. Manipulator of conscience. Abuse of power, of authority. Malevolent, ill-willed, dominating, despotic, tyrannical spirit that imposes his faith and ideas, and is ready to do anything to achieve his ends. Lack of opening toward other religions and spiritual currents. Serious discrepancies between words and acts, between the spirit and behavior in matter. Lack of true spiritual knowledge. Ignorance of the parallel worlds. Demonic spirit that hides behind appearances.

PRISON, IMPRISONMENT

Prison represents a deprivation of liberty following a presumed serious criminal offence. Imprisonment can be in a physical place, usually a custom-built building; or, it may be question of an inner prison: imprisonment experienced on the physical level (e.g. when we are prisoner of a handicapped body); on the soul level (when we feel paralyzed by overwhelming, oppressive soul states); or on the mind and spirit level (in the case of a mental handicap or false beliefs). In order to understand prison symbolism in depth, we need to know that no matter what level the deprivation of liberty occurs on, it is always a consequence that manifests after one, or several, serious offenses against Cosmic Laws and Principles, or repeated disrespect, sometimes over many lives, for the same Laws and Principles. Human justice offers many examples of verdicts contrary to what both the accused and the defense had imagined based on earthly laws. From a universal, multi-dimensional perspective, such cases are explained by the role of karma and the application of Divine Justice. Even when it appears unjust, and even in those cases of judicial errors from a human law perspective, imprisonment always corresponds to the settlement of karmic debts, to a reparation of injustices committed in the past, in this life or in a previous one. Divine Justice is absolute, and to understand it, we need to know that we always reap what we sow. Even the greatest criminals and wrong-doers who think they are protected, all-powerful, and above the law because they have managed to corrupt earthly justice, they too will have to face Divine Justice one day.

Prison as a place of incarceration has several functions. Its principal function is to temporarily deprive a person who has committed a serious offense of his liberty, with the aim of leading him to reflect on his acts, acknowledge and regret his errors, and rectify his behavior so as not to repeat the same errors once released. By limiting his capacity of movement and action, on the physical level, Up Above confines a person to a restricted space on the outside to help him expand his inner world. Prison also plays a dissuasive role, acting as a deterrent, by arousing fear of being sent there, or of returning, thus inciting people not to commit crimes. It also plays a role of protection by locking up criminals to prevent them from causing harm.

Seeing ourselves in prison in a dream should be considered as a warning, telling us that our behavior, our way of thinking, our intentions, do not conform to Cosmic Laws. The aim of dream-experienced imprisonment is to call upon the dreamer to reflect deeply and symbolically analyze his dream experience so as to become aware of whatever in his attitude and behavior is not right and requires rectification. Otherwise, sooner or later in concrete reality, he will attract situations that correspondent to his unjust, incorrect, wrong behavior and deeds, which could take on serious proportions. It is important to know, that through symbolic language, dreams show us what is in preparation or in the process of materializing. They allow us to recognize what we need to change in our way of thinking and living, so as to avoid attracting difficult, trying situations through resonance.

⊕ A period of limitation allowing intensive work on ourselves and the re-education of rebellious, delinquent forces that ignore or refuse to respect Cosmic Laws. Deep self-questioning. A capacity to acknowledge our errors and wrongs. Humility. An ability to understand the role and impact of personal and collective karma, to realize that injustice does not exist, that we always reap what we sow in this life or previous lives. A beneficial period of introspection, reflection on our life, values, and priorities. An intense phase of inner transformation, renewal, rebirth. Development of the gift of forgiveness. A capacity to isolate destructive tendencies that are dangerous for ourselves and others, and to transform them. Capable of recognizing and acknowledging a superior, Divine verdict in any imprisonment, and an opportunity for the prisoner to rectify whatever in his way of being and behaving is harmful for his own evolution and the evolution of his family and entourage. End of a difficult cycle that helps toward the development of conscience and the liberation of our soul and spirit. It may also be a sacrifice by a great initiate who was warned in a dream about the purpose of his unfair imprisonment, that it will play an inspiring role on the collective level.

⊖ Serious problems with the Law, an erroneous sense of Justice, ignorance of Divine Laws and Justice. Imprisonment lived as an injustice, a limitation, which engenders anger, rebellion, aggression, frustration, the feeling of being a victim. May be related to a person who lacks clemency toward himself, who judges himself too harshly, imposes severe restrictions on himself, whose inner justice is too rigid, who withdraws into himself, creating his own inner prison to punish himself. Dynamics of repression, isolation, self-punishment, self-sabotage, and self-destruction. A rebellious tendency not to worry about the consequences of our acts, to be casual, nonchalant and flippant, even in prison, or despite the risk of being sent to prison. A person who is incapable of recognizing, transforming, and re-educating his distorted, unjust, destructive parts; or, who refuses to do so. Not wanting to admit our wrongs, claiming to be a victim, and always blaming other people or society. A vengeful spirit that functions according to the Law of the jungle, an eye for an eye, a tooth for a tooth.

PROSTITUTION, PROSTITUTE

From the Latin verb *prostituere* (place in front, show, display), the term to prostitute oneself was very quickly used in a context where sexual intercourse was offered in return for payment. The term prostitute designates a person who puts himself forward, exposes himself to view, displaying himself to his potential customer. The word prostitution, unlike other, more vulgar terms, is the most neutral term used for this today.

In the history of humanity, the development of the phenomenon of prostitution is closely related to the image of woman (as a slave, an object of exchange, whore, concubine, mistress, escort, call-girl), and the way man treated, and continues to treat, the feminine principle, and all it represents: love, fusion, the power of conception, gestation, forming and materializing, fertility, the maternal aspect, the nourishing womb, receptivity, sensitivity, intuition, and a capacity to perceive on the subtle levels. The fact that today prostitution doesn't only concern adult women and men, but also young, teenage girls and boys, and even, children, on a vast scale, is a telling sign clearly revealing that our materialistic societies have serious value and moral problems. The situation is made worse by the fact that prostitution, both heterosexual and homosexual, almost always goes hand in hand with drug consumption and trafficking, as well as organized crime.

Although usually associated with sexual activities, prostitution is a dynamic that doesn't only concern the physical body. Every time we put illusory, material values to the forefront, thereby shaking and gradually destroying the fusion between spirit, soul, and body, creating ever greater discrepancies and malfunctions, we exert a form of prostitution. No matter what level prostitution occurs on, it represents a violation of the sacred aspect of life and an infringement of the Divine Laws that govern it. We may also symbolically prostitute ourselves on the soul level, e.g. when we give in to temptation, betray our humanity, use our conscience and integrity for profit, and corrupt our mind and spirit.

On the symbolic level, prostitution represents a state of conscience where we are ready to do anything for carnal pleasure, matter, money, or physical survival. It denotes a state of moral poverty, degradation of human and spiritual values, the destruction of the sacred aspect of love, and an incapacity to fuse with the other person in a respectful, responsible manner, with the aim of creating right projects. The sexual act of prostitution aims solely to satisfy instinctual needs, seeking primitive, superficial sensations. Like animals, contact is limited to the physical body; there is no thought for the other person's well-being, nor any interest in what is going on in their mind and soul before, during, or after the sexual act.

The context of prostitution is associated with all sorts of distortions, discrepancies, and illusions. People who get involved on this path often have great needs on the material and affective levels, profound insecurities, and intense suffering. Not knowing Cosmic Laws, especially the Law of resonance, the Law of karma, and the Principle of Divine Justice, they often consider themselves victims of circumstances. They don't know that by seeking an easy way to subsist, and by renouncing any direction or route involving effort to remain on the path of Qualities and Virtues, they betray the sacred aspect of life, simultaneously manifesting a lack of faith and spiritual life, the consequence of which is the gradual engendering of, a context of life of prostitution, inner suffering, and emotional, sentimental, affective emptiness.

⊕ Awareness of the extreme aspects of someone who is prepared to do anything to superficially satisfy his emotional, affective, sexual, and material needs. Understanding that prostitution is a consequence that doesn't only concern the physical level, but also a person's deep, profound intention, and the way he seeks to fulfill his needs in general. Work on ourselves to rectify a way of life that only engenders misery, desolation, sorrow, discouragement, and resignation on the personal, intimate level. Work on individual and collective memories of exploitation, subjugation, domination, and discrimination. A capacity to free ourselves from the role of victim. Cleansing and transcendence of memories, forces, and patterns of behavior, which, through resonance, lead a person to contexts of prostitution. Profound self-questioning and the will to change paths, to improve our life. Rediscovery of the sacred, Divine aspect of sexuality. The willpower to correct degraded values and principles, and to develop Qualities and Virtues. Transcendence of memories of exploitation, slavery, lust, depravation, sexual abuse, selfishness and self-centeredness, allowing a person to rediscover a sense of the sacred, to recognize and acknowledge his Divine nature, and respect his body as the temple of his spirit. The fact that prostitution has attained an alarming level worldwide has triggered widespread awareness and incitement to reflect on the deep causes that produce it. A search for solutions and healing. Integration of a better understanding of the principles and values of a couple and of true love.

⊖ Someone who is prepared to do anything to satisfy his lack of money, his instinctive impulses, and his primary needs; or, who grants too much importance to success, to the power of money, and the material aspect of life, people, and things. Someone who lets himself be exploited, dominated, and abused by others. Someone, who, instead of working on himself to learn how to manage and heal his distortions regarding sexuality, chooses to frequent prostitutes to satisfy his sexual fantasies and impulses, his basic instincts, his animal nature; or, conversely, it may be someone who uses his charm and natural beauty to get rich, or to lead a bright, glittery life of worldly pleasure, and in order to do so, uses seduction, manipulation, bribery, and sexual dependency (concubine, mistress, escort service, call-girl). Great material insecurity associated with a lack of love and wisdom, which leads a person to seek happiness in an illusory way. A truly desperate person, who, when faced with the crushing weight of his problems, cannot see any other way out than to prostitute himself, to let himself be enticed into decadence. A lack of respect regarding sexuality and the other person's intimate life. Ignorance of the fact that what we do to others, we also do to ourselves, and that we always reap what we sow. Moral and human decadence, normalizing prostitution without understanding the inner and outer suffering it engenders. A loss of the sacred meaning of love and the relationship between a man and a woman. Disconnection from Divine Principles. Infringement of both human laws and Divine Laws. Unhealthy attitudes and behavior that create difficult, emotional, sentimental, affective karma, destroy a person's capacity to truly love, and distance the possibility of ever encountering the love of our life. A lack of understanding of karmic consequences, which are the result of abuse committed in this life or previous lives. Addiction and sexual dependencies, often combined with drug addiction. Emotional, affective emptiness. Male and female slavery, subjugation, illegal, clandestine trafficking of children, young girls and boys in many countries all over the world. Sexual tourism. Camouflaged, disguised prostitution, taking on all sorts of appearances in the atmosphere and ambiance of the artificial paradises of certain holiday complexes.

PSYCHIATRIST

A psychiatrist is a doctor who diagnoses, treats, and tries to prevent mental illnesses, psychological troubles and emotional disorders. He helps people who present psychiatric problems not to disconnect or *crack up*, or commit harmful acts that are dangerous for themselves or others. While practicing his profession, ideally, a psychiatrist will use symbolic language to analyze his patients' symptoms, behavior, living context, as well as their dreams. This manner of proceeding allows him to explore in depth his patients' inner life and better understand the discrepancies they experience regarding the outside world. Symbolic analysis helps decode the mechanisms of unconscious functioning within them, and gives access to important revelations of their personality, while gradually leading them toward true psychological and spiritual autonomy.

A psychiatrist may prescribe medication, which will temporarily appease his patient's psychological problems, so as to help him in his therapy, or to avoid more serious malfunctioning on the physical level, in concrete reality. However, complete healing requires encountering the memories recorded in the unconscious that are the root cause of the manifested troubles. As long as those memories have not been transformed and liberated, the psychiatric treatments, over-focused on medication rather than genuine psycho-therapeutic care of the patient, will only provide superficial results, which are unsatisfactory long term. Today, thanks to the recognition of the close link between the body, soul, and spirit, an increasing number of psychiatrists and other health practitioners are changing their approach and work methods. Generally speaking, a great opening of conscience and a better disposition to admit man's multi-dimensional nature can be seen among all those who work in healing. These changes on the conscience level, which go hand in hand with the numerous discoveries made by quantum science and medicine, are shifting the focus of healing research from the symptom, or consequential level, to the causal level. This shows that we have begun to integrate the fact that health problems first manifest as disharmony and dissonance on the subtle levels, on the soul and spirit levels, before materializing in the form of symptoms, illnesses, disease, on the physical level.

In terms of conscience, a psychiatrist symbolizes in us, a part of us that is capable of treating the most serious psychiatric problems, and of facilitating their treatment through the understanding and cleansing of memories. He also represents a capacity to detect anxieties, anguish, depression, a propensity to commit suicide, schizophrenia, dissociative identity disorder (otherwise known as multiple personality disorder), etc., and he can treat them in great depth by understanding their origin. When presented negatively, a psychiatrist may reveal a part of us that is over rational, that lacks spirituality, love, devotion, and metaphysical knowledge, thereby preventing him from studying the cause of behavior and memories that engender mental and psychological pathologies. Of course, when a person is seriously affected by mental illness, it is difficult to begin a path of personal development that will lead to rapid results. Often, a lengthy re-education in trust and confidence is necessary, during which the psychiatrist helps his patient to transform the personal and social malfunctioning he has inscribed in his unconscious over many, many lives. A person suffering from serious mental problems is very often a very old soul whose inner computer needs to be completely reformatted.

⊕ A capacity to heal on the psychological and emotional levels. Help for treating, relieving, or controlling mental illnesses and affective problems. Temporary relief, which avoids escalation, worsening of the patient's state. In-depth work through the symbolic study and analysis of the causes. Understanding how the human conscience works, the prevalence of unconscious memories and the phenomenon of resonance. Helps transform destructive behavior in others and in ourselves. A period of rest, renewal, revitalization, recovery, and inner re-organization. Important revelations, awakening awareness. Re-adjustment of discrepancies. End of a difficult stage. Existential questioning. Courage and willpower to delve into the unconscious to discover the secrets and mysteries of our being. Re-connection with inner wisdom. Development of intuition and knowledge. A capacity to be compassionate, patient, and persevering to help the soul, body, mind and spirit regain balance and equilibrium, to heal and to evolve.

⊖ Great difficulty treating, controlling, or healing ourselves on the psychological and affective levels. A lack of knowledge and understanding to adequately analyze and evaluate distorted behavior and discrepancies. An incapacity to activate our self-healing potential through self-study and self-knowledge. Refusal to call ourselves into question. Not wanting to work on ourselves to transform the dissonance between our soul, body, mind and spirit, to master discrepancies, to heal dependencies. A lack of inner dialogue; or, too much inner dialogue. A tendency to flee our inner world for fear of what it might reveal; or, on the contrary, a tendency to plunge too powerfully and ardently into the unconscious, or to rely on erroneous concepts. Problems of egocentricity, narcissism, or megalomania. Rebellious behavior on the personal and social levels. Personality problems stemming from memories of this life or previous incarnations. A lack of understanding of the fact that our soul functions like a living computer, which, stores the totality of all the experiences of all our numerous lives. A way of proceeding that serves to satisfy the needs of our ego, thereby worsening the problem, rather than favoring healing. A person who lacks humility, who is not ready to acknowledge the mirror effect his patients reflect back to him, who is not ready or capable of applying the Law of resonance, nor of accepting the fact that his patients reveal aspects of himself. Inappropriate care. Treatment limited to numbing the symptoms and masking the true causes of health problems. Irresponsible prescription of medication. Medicine without conscience, without global vision, which does not take into account the metaphysical and spiritual levels, or man's multi-dimensional nature. A person who relies too much on the results obtained through medication, who refuses to open up to alternative, metaphysical, spiritual methods through a lack of knowledge, conscience and faith. Seeking healing too rapidly, too superficially, only through medication, without questioning errors, without wanting to understand the causes. Difficulty trusting and exchanging with specialists, experts, who could help us find the appropriate tools to aid the healing process.

PSYCHOLOGIST

The word *psyche* in Greek means the soul, and so psychology means *the science of the psyche, the soul.* A psychologist intervenes in all domains of society (health, education, work, sport, etc.) in order to help people maintain or improve their well-being and psychological health, develop their potential, or favor social integration. By helping patients get to know themselves better, a psychologist helps them discover the causes and consequences of their behavior and attitudes, thereby allowing them to improve their lives on all levels. A psychologist plays an important role of listening to his patients; he is their confidant, their friend, their moral support, and their advisor who helps find answers to their problems, all at the same time. Ideally, a psychologist will use the analysis of dreams and signs to understand the mechanisms of unconscious functioning in each patient to lead each of them toward the development of awareness, and access to important revelations of their personality, while gradually leading them toward true psychological and spiritual autonomy. In all cases, at all times, a psychologist will practice his profession with the intention of developing qualities, such as receptivity and altruism. He will also be aware that, on a certain level, to a certain extent, his patients are a reflection of aspects of himself, and that the work he does with them is simultaneously work he carries out on himself.

⊕ Represents our capacity for in-depth study of our behavior, soul-states, attitudes, conscience, feelings and sentiments so as to regain well-being. Provides conscious and unconscious psychological assistance. Helps improve our life. Favors introspection, dialogue, self-questioning, reflection on our behavior and deeds, as well as those of others, so as to understand how we function, our lifestyle, our relationships, our environment. A capacity to delve into our unconscious and analyze causal life *via* dreams, signs and symbolic language. An ability to modify our old, former thought patterns, living habits and customs, and establish new ones. Helps in the search for balance, equilibrium, and stability. Provides consolation and support at painful, emotionally difficult times. Inspires humanist values and principles. Allows the discovery of spirituality, of a more global, universal dimension of life, of existence. Favors the development of friendship through trust. A discreet, compassionate, responsible person who doesn't judge us and whom we can trust.

⊖ Difficulty or refusal to settle problems related to our behavior, soul-states, attitudes on the psychological and affective levels. May indicate a lack of receptivity, of knowledge of ourselves and others. Difficulty trusting and opening up to others. A tendency to want to analyze coldly, critically, too intellectually; or, in an extreme case, to want to dominate or influence negatively with erroneous concepts. A person who thinks he is wise and evolved, but who is not. A lack of or limited understanding of the metaphysical dimension of problems that are actually the manifestation of consequences, the true causes of which sometimes go back to other lives. Over-rational dynamics on the psychological level. A lack of spirituality. Someone who does not refer back to himself, does not apply the mirror effect. A lack of understanding of the Law of resonance whereby others, the external world, the situations we go through, reveal aspects and parts of ourselves. A lack of altruism. A feeling of superiority. Discrepancy between the advice we give as a psychologist and the life we lead.

PURCHASE, A

A purchase is the acquisition of goods or a service in exchange for a monetary contribution. It is important to reflect on the way we consume and what we consume, because what we buy reflects who we are, and symbolically denotes the use we make of our energy (here represented by money); it indicates those areas of our life to which we grant importance, as well as what we are becoming, and how we materialize our potential. In a dream, just as in concrete reality, the type of service or goods acquired is also an indication of what resource(s) we integrate on the metaphysical level, because if we become what we think and what we eat, we also become what we buy. Furthermore, we have to develop our conscience and sense of responsibility, both related to the act of buying. We should ask ourselves if our intended purchase is right, useful or superfluous, whether it is a fair trade product, and whether the company or manufacturing firm that produces it embodies and conveys beautiful values, etc.

⊕ A wise, well-thought-out, discerning choice of consumption and acquisition of goods or services. Exchange dynamics that allow us to learn to be right, fair, and honest. A feeling of satisfaction and well-being when our purchases are well-founded and carried out in full awareness and conscience. Power to materialize. A feeling of abundance. Reaping the fruit of our labor. A capacity to meet our needs and those of our family, and provide for all our necessities. Purchases carried out with an altruistic aim, and with a conscience that favors autonomy on the material and spiritual levels, that respects human and animal life, and the environment. Understanding that what we buy has an impact on people's lives all over the world.

⊖ Problems regarding the way we materialize and develop. Using energy and money for superfluous, useless, superficial things. Difficult or impossible access to resources due to memories of waste, excess, and abuse. Difficulty managing our resources, achieving our goals, providing for our vital needs. Compulsive behavior of over-consumerism, and an accumulation of all sorts of goods. Miserliness, fear of spending, hoarding.

Q

QUANTITY

Quantity is related to concepts of addition, subtraction, multiplication or division of the element in question, and generally speaking, to the management and repartition of abundance, and the equity of resources (e.g. small, medium, or large quantities of any substance: food, drinks, snow, rain, water, ice, cars, bicycles, horses, flies, sunshine, etc.). It may indicate fair, excessive, or insufficient dosage; or, denote a level of intensity in terms of states of conscience and energies to be managed. For example, seeing ourselves confronted with a lion in a dream may be an intense experience in relation to the strength of assertion and power. However, if we have to face 100 lions, the effect of the experience and state of conscience represented would be considerably more powerful in either a positive, or extremely dangerous, destructive context.

⊕ Announces great abundance, and/or right and fair repartition of resources. May indicate a capacity, or necessity, to evaluate our level of involvement in, or commitment to a situation. Favors an understanding of what we have to decide and what we have to do. Ability to increase and multiply resources, to manage them well and to share them equitably.

⊖ Problems manifesting an incapacity to materialize, multiply, evaluate, manage, share, and divide the available quantities fairly and impartially, and to use them altruistically. Dynamics of lack and deep insecurity. Difficulty mastering the physical, emotional, intellectual, or spiritual intensity represented by the quantity in question. Bad use of wealth and riches, which sooner or later leads to lacks, and difficult karmas, for this life or a future life. A person who privileges quantity at the expense of quality, who materializes without conscience, without respecting Divine Laws.

QUARREL *cf. Dispute*

R

RABBIT

A domestic rabbit is a non-aggressive, vegetarian mammal. It symbolizes part of our vital energy related to pacifism, sweetness, gentleness, tenderness, naïve innocence of childhood, which usually makes the rabbit a favorite with children.

Given its very rapid proliferation, it is mostly associated with sexuality, repetitive satisfaction of instinctual needs, and the multiplication of materializations. Two well-known examples show these aspects well: the magazine cover of the men's magazine *Playboy* with its rabbit (bunny) emblem; and Easter Bunny, the rabbit that distributes and hides many colored, fresh, sugar, or chocolate eggs. This symbolizes a positive capacity to produce sweetness; or, an intense capacity for manifestation and production, used to satisfy expectations and fulfill deficiencies of sweetness, gentleness, and enchantment, as well as hyperactive behavior, through which we try to obtain what we want rapidly.

In its wild state, a rabbit (or hare) is essentially prey in the food chain. Hence it manifests great survival instincts, which incite it to make the least noise possible. Having to be continually on its guard regarding its predators keeps it in a state of constant nervousness. It is particularly active at dawn and dusk, both times of day when it is more difficult to be spotted.

A rabbit constantly needs to nibble and eat. This characteristic stems from its deep nature and takes concrete form in its front teeth (incisors), which never stop growing.

At birth, a rabbit is blind and naked (furless), well-hidden in its burrow. It is rarely aggressive, and only ever toward other males. Normally, it quickly submits to the strongest because of its extreme sensitivity regarding predators.

These characteristics confer on rabbits the following negative aspects: easy, vulnerable prey; nudity and blindness at birth expressing fragility and a lack of vision, discernment, and clarity; a fearful, timid character that is an incitement to hide and remain as unnoticed as possible, symbolically indicating exaggerated discretion, possibly developing into morbid shyness or timidity; excessive sexual activity and proliferation, denoting a need to please and be loved; mainly nocturnal life dynamics, symbolically linking it to what is hidden, masked, invisible, unknown, or unconscious.

⊕ A symbol of fertility, proliferation, and rapid growth. A great multiplying force related to vital, sexual energy, allowing us to create a big family; or, to materialize numerous projects in a pacific, peace-loving altruistic state of mind. Mastery and transcendence of impulsive sexuality and thoughtless, uncontrolled reproduction. Sweetness, gentleness, tenderness. Innocence. Delicacy. A calm mentality, a non-aggressive temperament, also revealed by its vegetarian diet. Agility and rapidity in situations that require such qualities. A capacity to avoid snares and to make our way despite difficulties and/or aggressive people.

⊖ Solely instinctual, impulsive, naïve, and excessive sexuality, with no thought for the consequences. Intimate, sexual relations that nourish basic instincts, seeking power, and an overly materialistic spirit. Waste of vital, sexual energy, licentiousness, infidelity, lust, prostitution. Excessively seeking to satisfy primary needs. Seduction games to satisfy emotional, sentimental, affective lacks, and a need to please, to be admired and desired. Sterile conscience, manifested in a difficulty to create projects and/or an incapacity to procreate, infertility. A tendency to multiply projects without any awareness or conscience; or to engender a lot of children without taking responsibility for them, without wanting to look after and take care of them. Irresponsibility. Multiplication of works due to insecurity in order to reassure ourselves and fulfill inner emptiness. Fear when confronted with aggressive people, who emanate predator energy. A tendency to let ourselves be easily tricked, fooled, abused, dominated. Submission to what is not right through vulnerability, a lack of self-assertion, or naivety. Perverse, vulgar, coarse behavior. A lack of sweetness, gentleness, affection. Bulimia.

RACE, ETHNIC GROUPS

Among humans, a race designates a group of people, who, on account of immutable hereditary characteristics, consider themselves, or are considered, different from other groups. The idea of race comprises subjective and social elements, as well as apparent characteristics, usually immediately visible, such as skin color, shape of face and distinctive features, hair type, etc.

On the symbolic level, our belonging to a particular race or ethnic group defines the broad outline of our Life-plan regarding ethnic, social and cultural influences that we are to experience and experiment. The aim of our life on Earth is to integrate the qualities and transcend the distortions of all populations, all races and ethnic groups that exist. In the course of our evolutive journey, we are called to develop a global, universal conscience, a mind and spirit that are open to all cultures, a capacity to look at life and all of its facets with a unifying regard, expressing Divine Wisdom and Love. A symbolic analysis of the egregore (*cf.* this term) of each race, along with all of its historical memories and cultural characteristics, allows us to know ourselves in greater depth, and to better understand and fulfill our own life program.

Each race has its + and its –, none is better or superior to another: they all offer opportunities for learning and experimentation, thereby allowing us to improve and perfect our respective strengths and qualities. All races are governed by the same Divine Laws and the aim of their evolution is to develop Qualities, Virtues, and Powers in their purest state. By experimenting life in different human races during our various incarnations, we get to know and learn to integrate the qualities of each, and at the same time, to transcend our weaknesses and distortions. Hence, we gradually develop an altruistic, universal, multi-dimensional, Divine conscience.

⊕ Understanding the fact that each human being bears every race, every population, every country, every world (on earth and in the parallel dimensions) and every kingdom (mineral, vegetable, animal, human, and spiritual) within himself in terms of conscience. Feelings of unity, universality, belonging to a cosmic, planetary family. Development of altruism, fraternity, and transcendence of all negative aspects related to different races. Great wealth of varied knowledge. A capacity for adaptation to everyone no matter their race or origin. A state of inner and outer peace in regard to our and others' racial origin.

⊖ A racist person who seeks to dominate, to categorize according to exterior criteria, who believes he is superior or inferior, who is afraid of other people's differences. Narrow-minded, sectarian, intolerant. Discrimination. Exploitation. Slavery. Problems regarding feelings of belonging and identity. Belief that there are superior and inferior races. Arrogant, snobbish, egotistical, megalomaniac behavior. Non-respect and unfair, unequal treatment of different races. Absence of universal feeling, of unifying, global vision. Ignorance of the fact that from one life to another, we pass from one race to another, in order to integrate the whole ensemble of human qualities. A lack of understanding that, from a cosmic point of view, there is no racial difference, that all manifestations of life are governed by the same Laws. Limited conscience. Absence of love and wisdom.

RAIN

Rain is a natural climatic phenomenon that is essential for the distribution of water on Earth. It is symbolically related to the world of emotions and feelings, to the distribution of emotional resources without which life dries up and dies, just as nature perishes when water is rare or absent. Generally speaking, rain is related to the collective emotional level since it falls on more or less widespread regions, unlike artificial sprinklers and watering systems, which are either for individual usage (e.g. flower and vegetable gardens, paddling pools), or for an area (e.g. a public park, a farmer's fields).

Soft, pleasant, refreshing rain usually has a calming, soothing effect that incites contemplation, meditation, interiorization and rest. It favors the growth and harmonious flourishing of our emotional world, the purification of our thoughts, atmospheres and ambiances, as well as the renewal of nature and life in general, both in our inner world and in the outer world. Rain is a symbol of life and survival, as desert regions bear witness to so well. We, who live in regions with abundant, annual precipitation, become aware of this each time a prolonged dry period causes gardens and fields to dry up and awaken fears of the loss of crops, cattle, and the risk of shortages on various levels. When rain falls from the sky, vivifying nature, it represents Divine Grace.

If rain affects us negatively, if it makes us sad, melancholic or morose, it's because it plunges our spirit into conscious or unconscious memories marked by difficult emotional experiences, that made us cry, caused us pain, sorrow, grief, suffering. The way in which rain affects us in concrete reality reveals our capacity to manage our feelings and emotions in our affective, sentimental life. The same goes for dreams about rain. After a dream wherein we experienced an unpleasant, disagreeable rainy situation, (for instance, where it rained heavily and we felt lonely and abandoned), the following day, we won't feel well even though, on waking, it may be a beautiful, sunny day outside. We will still be affected by the emotional energies we were immersed in during the night, and unless we consciously transform them, we will continue to feel their effect, and be subjected to their influence.

Whenever rain is unfavorably presented in a dream, or in concrete reality, it manifests imbalance on the emotional level: cold, freezing rain denotes emotional coldness; torrential rain indicates a fallout and overflow of emotions that were too long retained and accumulated; several days, weeks, or even months, of non-stop, intense rain causing all sorts of dangers including floods, landslides, risks of drowning, loss of life and goods, indicates that considerable quantities of distorted, destructive, emotional energies are in the process of materializing on the collective level.

⊕ A source of emotional energy that is essential for life. Renewal, revitalization, regeneration, vivification. A capacity to begin again in a right, harmonious, well-balanced way. Affective, sentimental conditions which are favorable for growth, flourishing, and the manifestation of abundance. Refreshment, cleansing and purification of soul-states and ambiances. Rebirth of our inner child. Renewed *joie de vivre* and creative power on all levels.

⊖ Triggers souls-states burdened with sadness, nostalgia, melancholy, moroseness. Painful emotional memories that cause us to shed tears and even weep. Tumultuous emotions. Risk of being ship-wrecked, submerged, and drowned in torment and passion. Sentimental overflow as well as being overwhelmed and bogged down by emotions. Affective dependencies. Solitude. Drought, poverty, or emotional coldness. Difficulty engendering and nourishing beautiful, healthy, harmonious feelings and sentiments. Sentimental, relational problems. Attitudes and behavior that create emptiness all around us, as well as a flooded, or deserted inner state. A lack of love, gentleness, and vivifying emotional energy.

RAINBOW

A rainbow is an optical, meteorological phenomenon, which renders visible the continuous spectrum of daylight whenever the sun shines through rain. Consequently it is related to the fire element, which symbolizes the spirit and light, and the water element, which symbolizes emotions and feelings. Its seven colors represent the luminous vibratory frequencies of the seven chakras. Intangible but visible, a rainbow represents a Heavenly manifestation, a bridge between Heaven and Earth, a path and a link between the world here below and the world Up Above. It is associated with beauty, magic, enchantment, mystery, and the power of Creation. Its appearance makes the child in us rejoice and marvel and we can feel the presence of the Divine in the heart of existence.

⊕ A sign of spiritual re-connection and inspiration or the right decision to make. Exalts the conscience and inspires beauty and harmony. Reconciliation and communication with the Divine. Feelings of joy, wonder, and gratitude toward Heaven. Powerful, spiritual emotion.

⊖ A lack of spiritual conscience and connection with the Divine. A sign from Heaven telling us we are on the wrong path. Someone who trivializes the sacred aspect of life and who lacks receptivity to manifest beauty. An over-rational mind of a person who thinks he is above everything and who trivializes the manifestations and powers of Nature. A confused, joyless, colorless, light-less life. Duality, rift, discrepancy causing melancholy and sadness on the spiritual level.

RAT

Since it belongs to the animal kingdom, a rat represents aspects of our vital energy related to instinctual needs. As a rodent that feeds on whatever it finds, including human waste, and that can be aggressive when hungry or threatened, it symbolizes an instinctive force that is capable of engendering negative emotions, such as constant anxiety and insecurity, as well as greed and a fear of lacking resources for survival. Such emotional states plunder our vital energy and literally *gnaw on* and *eat away* all our energy. A rat's reproductive cycle is very brief, which symbolizes the fact that the negative aspects it represents risk multiplying at top speed if we don't deal with them.

This animal is also known to have transmitted many illnesses and diseases in the past; it contributed to the wide-scale spreading of epidemics such as the plague, which indicates a negative potential that can rapidly grow beyond all control. Rats can endanger crops and their harvests; in other words, the forces rats represent can cause us to lose our inner abundance, our rich, noble feelings and sentiments. The expression *the rat race* refers to a hectic, exhausting, unremitting, competitive routine, activity or lifestyle, which is usually associated with a pressured, urban, working life spent trying to get ahead, where there is little or no time for contemplation and self-renewal, and little or no place for selflessness, altruism, kindness, consideration, generosity, etc. The rat is also related to a complex of inferiority through the repugnance and rejection inspired by its ugliness. Furthermore, its size and agility enable it to infiltrate almost everywhere, without being noticed, thereby denoting sly, sneaky aspects and hidden intentions. Hence the figurative use of the verb *to rat on* meaning to divulge secret information, to betray someone's trust. Likewise *to smell a rat* means to suspect dishonest, foul behavior. The fact that when searching for food, a rat rummages through anything and everything, and is content to even eat garbage, symbolizes forces that feed unhealthily on just about anything, hence favoring the multiplication of distortions as well as dispersal on the social level.

A more positive aspect of this animal is the fact that it helps eliminate waste products. Without the presence of brown rats that feed on waste found in urban sewage systems, these systems would be continually blocked up. From this point of view, a rat represents an element of recycling and environmental self-regulation, corresponding to an urban lifestyle marked by over-consumerism and, as yet, a poorly developed ecological conscience. Symbolically, this aspect reveals the existence of an animal, instinctive potential in human-beings, that helps us transform our inner waste, and purify congestion and blockages caused by our multiple activities related to matter, work, our social life, leisure, etc. It is a potential for transformation and natural recycling, but it is also a potential for intelligence and instinctual agility. It is interesting to note that rats are very frequently used in laboratory research on behavior and to test medical treatments destined for human use. Consequently they also represent part of our animal, instinctual nature that, together with our intelligent forces and inner doctors, pharmacists and scientists, helps us develop positive behavioral patterns and improve our self-healing capacity.

⊕ Transcendence of greed and behavior based or focused on instinctual needs that feed on anything at all on the personal and social levels. Incitement to work on feelings of insecurity, fear, and anxiety that nibble and gnaw and eat away our vital energy. A capacity to instinctively adapt to any situation, to any circumstances and to survive in extreme conditions. A potential for transformation, recycling inner waste, negative, unhealthy energies contained in our memories, or in our relations with others. An indication of the necessity to undertake purification work, inner cleansing; or, may be used to help improve our self-healing when positively submitted to medical testing by scientists in laboratories.

⊖ Greedy, selfish, avid, acquisitive behavior, based and focused on coarse, instinctual needs; or, may indicate that we feel dominated, diminished, and insecure, either because of lacks, or because we find ourselves struggling for survival, barely living on subsistence level. The presence of fears that gnaw and eat away our vital energy, that destroy inner resources, the potential we bear within. An inferiority complex that nourishes a tendency to be content with leftovers, with the crumbs from others' tables, with what others discard. Conscious or unconscious memories marked by existential anguish and anxiety, and fear of lacking. An unclean, neglected person who spreads negative, unhealthy energies, and even illnesses. A lack of generosity, a refusal to share. A sly, sneaky spirit that spreads malevolent, harmful intentions and actions.

REAR *cf.* ***Back***

RECYCLING

The word recycling indicates that something is introduced into a new cycle. In our daily life, this term is generally associated with recuperation, sorting, and re-use after transformation of waste products and used materials, such as plastic, paper, glass, metal, biodegradable or compostable substances, etc., as well as professional training. However, recycling does not only apply to the physical, concrete level and the outer world. It also takes place in our inner world, on the level of our thoughts, emotions, conditioning, beliefs, knowledge, concepts, and working structures, as well as in all of our conscious and unconscious memories.

Among those of us who live in an ordinary conscience, who only take into account the outer world and the physical level, the numerous, continual recycling processes go unnoticed. A person unconsciously perceives a thought, an emotion, an atmosphere or ambiance, integrates and assimilates it, is influenced by it, and more or less transformed; then he shares the result, the product of his inner recycling, with his entourage through the way he communicates, exchanges, acts and is. This is how the process of evolution, the gradual acquisition and transmission of knowledge and experience occurs. However, inner recycling work may be experienced more consciously and actively when we train ourselves to live with global vision, and when we've acquired the necessary metaphysical, spiritual knowledge to understand the multi-dimensions of existence and the workings of our conscience. We then become aware of and feel those moments when an inspiration occurs, when we perceive a thought, a soul-state, or when an emotion has been activated. And instead of unconsciously reacting or being subjected to their influence, we observe the effect they have on us and we are able to choose how to act, or not act, much more consciously.

Just as our thoughts, ideas, inspirations, and emotions are dealt with, worked on and used in accordance with the level of conscience, and degree of knowledge, wisdom, and mastery we have attained, so too is our emotional, intellectual and spiritual waste. Thus, recycling on the metaphysical level takes place in the same way as recycling in the physical dimension: the more evolved a person is, the more responsible he feels for the waste he produces and its recycling, the more he strives to avoid all production and accumulation of useless waste. Recycling on the physical and metaphysical levels is just as much part of the creative process of life and a person's evolution as of Life and Evolution on the cosmic scale. Everything that exists undergoes perpetual transformation.

Whenever recycling appears as a symbol in a dream, it reveals the way the dreamer manages his inner and outer resources, the use he makes of his knowledge, skills, gifts and talents, his feelings, his time, whether he lives in harmony or disharmony with himself, his entourage, the environment and nature in general. Such a dream may reveal a process of re-education is taking place in the dreamer's inner world, whereby he is learning to use resources in a right, just, qualitative way, and to develop a lifestyle that respects the environment and renounces all forms of waste. Of course, a dream concerning recycling may also have a negative symbolic tendency. For example, there could be a scene where the dreamer is confronted with mountains of garbage that prevent his advancing. Such a dream would be an important warning that he really shouldn't take lightly. Indeed, it would reveal that the person has accumulated huge quantities of all sorts of garbage and waste in his inner world, and that he has long refused to deal with their recycling. If he doesn't do the necessary work to transform these mountains of garbage on the metaphysical level; they could easily materialize in one form or another in his concrete reality: for instance, by his being exposed to life in a very polluted region with no recycling nor any garbage collection, or next to a dumping zone, or, in extreme cases, reincarnation in a very poor country where, for mere survival reasons, the dreamer would have to rummage through mountains of garbage to find the wherewithal to simply exist.

⊕ Awareness of the importance of recycling waste on all levels, in both the inner and outer worlds. Re-education of behavior and lifestyles so as to put a stop to over-consumerism, waste of resources, and pollution of the environment. A great capacity to transform all sorts of energy waste and recreate new resources thanks to knowledge and experience recorded in our memories during the course of this life and previous lives. A sense of duty. Accountability. Respect and protection of the environment. Global, long-term vision. Right, fair, altruistic use of resources in our personal life, as well as on a collective, planetary scale. Willingness to learn from past errors and to rectify attitudes and behavior so as not to repeat them. Reparation through awareness, becoming conscious of erroneous waste. Activation of the alchemical power of recycling on all levels: transformation, transmutation, transsubstantiation, renewal, rebirth.

⊖ Refusal to acknowledge the necessity for recycling through ignorance, indifference, or laziness. Waste of resources, a thoughtless accumulation of garbage, and an aggravation of pollution, both on the outside and on the inside. Poor management of available resources. A person who congests, blocks, and pollutes his life and others' with all sorts of waste. An incapacity to sort through life experiences, to assimilate their lessons, to recycle and transform the residue. The presence of difficult memories that obstruct and impede access to a new stage in life. Encumbered by old concepts, outdated patterns of behavior and functioning. Stagnation, fear of change, fear of renewal. Resistance to letting people, things, situations go. Nostalgia, a tendency to hang on to the past. An incapacity to transcend the negative that has accumulated in and around us. A lack of short-, medium-, and long-term vision. A lack of understanding of the fact that we always reap what we sow. If we compare waste recycling with weeding a garden, we understand how essential it is to set ourselves free of outer and inner waste, garbage and weeds as they manifest, so as to avoid their becoming completely invasive, thereby rendering good, right growth and all fruitful harvesting impossible.

RED

The color red is related to the 1st chakra, situated at the base of our spine. It represents the vital energy that animates us, incarnation on the physical level, willpower, motivation, and the force of action, materialization, achievement, as well as the power of love. The color of fire, red symbolizes both vivifying, stimulating warmth as well as destructive fire. It also represents personal aspirations, wants, needs, and desires regarding the body and matter, and all that may seduce a person on this level. From a negative point of view, red represents danger, violent death, war, hatred, anger, passionate love, temptation that makes us deviate from the right path, and shame. It is no coincidence that the colors red and black are combined to represent the demonic, diabolic aspects of a person who is ready to do anything to satisfy selfish, egotistical needs and desires.

⊕ A force of materialization, incarnation, achievement, stimulation, or motivation. Love, life, vitality. Transcendence of basic instincts, selfish, egotistical needs. Well-mastered vital energy. Good use of resources. A capacity to set things in motion and be active, to materialize our projects, satisfy our vital needs. A person we can rely on. Great willpower and capacity to work, to be involved. A noble, royal spirit that uses its power, strength and force correctly, in the right way.

⊖ An over-materialistic attitude; or, difficulty incarnating and materializing. A lack of or too much willpower, vitality, dynamism, enthusiasm; or, loss of energy due to being dispersed, scattered, excessive seeking of physical pleasures. A need to be noticed and acknowledged (very bright, flamboyant red clothes, accessories, decor, etc.). An excessive, bad-tempered, angry, violent character. Abuse of power, domination, war, hatred, demonic behavior. Problems related to vital energy. Fragility regarding physical and psychological resistance. Devouring passion, unhealthy eroticism, possessiveness, jealousy. Appropriation of people and resources. Atheism.

REFRIGERATOR (fridge)

A refrigerator, more commonly called a fridge, allows us to preserve and safeguard food and other substances for a certain length of time by keeping them cool. Hence it symbolizes a capacity for good management and protection of available resources while taking into account the conditions and circumstances that manifest both on the outside as well as on the inside.

⊕ A capacity to preserve and manage an abundance of resources so as to use them when needed, at the appropriate time. A possibility of always having resources available, of organizing their use efficiently, and of planning to replenish them in view of short- or medium term, foreseeable needs. A generous, altruistic spirit that foresees, plans, and prepares food reserves in order to share them with his entourage and those in need.

⊖ Problems resulting from poor management and preservation of available resources through negligence, laziness, lethargy, or indifference; or, a tendency to keep excessive quantities of food reserves through fear of lacking food, or to satisfy obsessive, unhealthy hunger, which reveals the presence of memories of shortages, poverty, and deficiencies on the physical and emotional levels. Problems of dependencies, bulimia and/or anorexia, uncontrollable needs of excess, abuse, or waste of resources. Emotional coldness that halts, paralyzes, freezes a person's means, his capacity to master an overly hot, passionate temperament, a very intense character with excessive, hyperactive behavior, which destroys abundance of resources on all levels.

REMUNERATION *cf.* ***Salary***

RESTAURANT

A restaurant represents a state of conscience that is animated by the joyful desire of nourishing others in a social context. It is also related to the pleasure of being in society, of experiencing and experimenting multiple ambiances, as well as sharing a meal with friends, family members, or work colleagues, without having to do the cooking ourselves. Moreover, the existence of restaurants facilitates daily life when we lead a very active professional life or whenever we travel. We are also given an opportunity to get to know other culinary traditions thanks to the multitude of ethnic restaurants found in most countries. Not only do they offer a range of the immensely varied food customs that exist on this planet, but they also serve their food in the typical decor and ambiance of their native country.

A restaurant is also a symbol of service and provision of different food resources as well as the culinary knowledge, skills and talents needed for their preparation. Whether we are conscious of it or not, whenever we eat in a restaurant, not only do we nourish our physical body, but we also nourish ourselves on the emotional, intellectual, and even spiritual levels, through the different ambiances, discussions, etc., that co-exist there. All of these aspects need to be taken into consideration when we analyze a restaurant symbolically. There is also a great energy and vibratory difference between a restaurant that mainly offers meals that are meat or animal based, another that only serves fast food, or one that specializes in health food and vegetarian cuisine, that works with an altruistic, ecological conscience.

⊕ A capacity to nourish ourselves and others on the social level. Seeking ambiances and atmospheres, inspiration, new ideas. An ability to be at ease in a great variety of ambiances and contexts. The pleasure of having a meal in other people's company, and discussing various topics, that are interesting and inspiring on all levels. A place to meet, share, and reunite with friends, family and/or colleagues. An ability to assemble people around beautiful values. Feelings of abundance, wealth, expansion, and belonging. A capacity to savor pleasures of the physical and subtle senses. Helps develop a sense of service, giving, receiving, and sharing resources. Gratitude for those who prepare and serve us meals. Conscious efforts to offer a nourishing, nurturing energy that is healthy and well-balanced on the collective level, in a warm, welcoming, pleasant, harmonious atmosphere. Allows us to develop culinary art, which others can enjoy and benefit from. Discovery of the culinary art of different countries and traditions. Awareness of the sacred dimension of food, gratitude and thanks for the Divine abundance represented by it. Conscious choice of ways to nourish ourselves on the social level, of the restaurants we frequent, while taking into account the nutritional quality of the meals, as well as the energy emitted by the general atmosphere, the decor, welcome, quality of service, and the impact on the environment, by, for example, avoiding frequenting restaurants that produce huge daily amounts of plastic waste and other polluting material. Mastery of instinctual, compulsive food habits and needs. Development of Divine pleasures.

⊖ Difficulty or incapacity to nourish ourselves and others on the social level. Seeking worldly pleasures. Superficial social encounters that lack depth, meaning, and true values. A waste of time and energy as a result of frequent eating out. Problems on the intimate level. Excessive search for social contact in order to flee solitude, ill-being, affective, sentimental, emotional deficiencies. Social, worldly bulimia. Enjoying being served, haughty, arrogant, artificial social behavior. Focus on culinary reputation, the financial aspect, the satisfaction of instinctual, sensual needs. Epicureanism. A tendency to nourish ourselves socially on distorted energies, to frequent unhealthy, boorish, unrefined atmospheres and ambiances, to feed on dependencies, abuse, and all sorts of excesses. Waste of resources. Fast food. Junk food. Neglect and destruction of our health through indifference, ignorance, and a lack of conscience. Pollution of the environment. An impoverished conscience *vis-à-vis* the impact on the environment of food choices and habits, as well as working conditions in the restaurant and food industry throughout the world. A lack of understanding of the symbolic meaning of a dirty, unhealthy restaurant, which indicates unclean, harmful nourishment on the physical and metaphysical levels.

RIGHT, RIGHT-HAND-SIDE

The right, or right-hand-side, is related to the masculine polarity, emissivity, action, and the outer worlds. Everything that is on the right in a dream indicates a link with concrete reality, whereas the left is related to the world and action on the inner level.

⊕ Dynamics related to outer action on a personal or social level. Movement or energy of emissivity, exteriorization, and concrete manifestation.

⊖ A problem related to outer action, emissivity, exteriorization on a personal or social level.

RING, A

A ring is a piece of jewelry we place on our finger. When it is an engagement or wedding ring, it symbolizes union, fusion between the masculine and feminine principles. To correctly interpret its symbolic meaning, it is necessary to take into account its shape, color, the materials it is made of, the context in which it is worn, etc. This allows us to know the wearer's state of conscience. Generally speaking, jewelry symbolically represents an alliance, or a fusion with a way of being, loving, thinking, as well as the main aspect of the personality of those who wear it, and those who created it, and it also reveals an aspect of the person who offers it. A ring is also a symbol of loyalty, fidelity, and obedience to someone or something we admire, respect, look up to, would like to resemble, whose values and principles we would like to embody; or, on the contrary, it may represent admiration for and fidelity toward a rebellious attitude; or, superficiality, over-materialistic ways of being and thinking.

⊕ A symbol of union, alliance, fusion and fidelity. Deep commitment to a person, a cause, or way of thinking. Announces a new union or its preparation. A conscious choice and knowledge of the symbolic meaning of both the ring(s) we wear and the finger(s) we wear it on.

An engagement ring: Serious, conscious commitment to the person who offers it, to his being and lifestyle, his way of thinking and behaving.

⊖ Unconscious use of rings for adornment, for appearances, to bedeck ourselves and impress others. Union, fusion, commitment, or dependence to what or whom is not right for us, not right for our evolution. A deep need for love and fusion. Emotional dependency on a person, people, or things. Superficiality. Ignorance of the represented symbolism. A need to flaunt material wealth by wearing rings and jewelry. A ring may also represent an alliance with negative forces, commitment to a doctrine that serves earthly power, a sectarian philosophy, an elitist mindset.

Wearing a ring on every finger indicates extreme attachment to matter and to people, a very materialistic conscience, which multiplies alliances and harmful influences, and limits the person to a very superficial, down-to-earth lifestyle.

Regarding an engagement ring: Refusal of an engagement ring may indicate a difficulty to commit, to be faithful, and to respect our commitments, a problem in the couple's relationship.

Desiring a gaudy ring or one with a large, expensive gem: reveals a materialistic, superficial mind, a need to be acknowledged, admired; an attachment to matter; commitment based on material wealth and prestige.

RIVER

Given the fact that it belongs to the water element, a river refers to the world of feelings, sentiments, and emotions. Fed by the rain, melting snow and glaciers, as well as by springs and numerous tributaries, symbolically, it represents all of the states of conscience of our emotional world. Its clear or muddy, calm or tumultuous waters speak of our soul-state (mood) and the quality of our emotions in different situations or at different times and moments of our life. Its capacity to flow in accordance with the topology of places symbolizes our emotional adaptability and malleability when faced with various circumstances in life. Dams formed by leaves, branches, or other obstacles may slow its flow, just as obstacles sometimes get in the way and hinder our capacity to advance. Its bed may dry up; or, on the contrary, rise up and burst its banks, causing more or less serious flooding, just like our emotional climate, which can manifest aridity or overflowing, devastating emotions. Furthermore, when a smaller river joins a larger one, symbolically, this indicates that, through the quality of our personal emotions, we, either positively or negatively, nourish and influence reservoirs of collective emotions..

In a positive context, the symbolism of a river evokes calm, regenerating, soothing states of conscience. It also embodies purity because it springs from a natural environment. A picture or photo of a river suggests vivifying, stimulating emotions, freedom, plenitude, and clear, limpid intentions, which call to mind the freshness and curiosity of childhood. In a negative context, it indicates blockages in our advancing, periods of stagnation, aridity in our feelings, tumultuous emotional overflow and outbursts; or, if the water is polluted by different agents, it symbolizes the degradation and destabilization of our emotional world.

⊕ Natural, spontaneous, renewing, soothing emotions that are continually, flowingly, fluidly renewed. A well-structured emotional force that adapts to whatever direction Up Above has planned in accordance with our life plan. A feeling of liberty, natural advancing, purification, supple, joyful, serene, innocent renewal on the emotional level. Awakening, blossoming, flourishing and thriving feelings and sentiments regarding our inner child. Capacity to manifest positive emotions and feelings that can be of healthy assistance, comfort, consolation and solace for other people's affective, emotional thirst.

⊖ A tendency to let ourselves be invaded or destroyed by accumulated, repressed, unexpressed, blocked emotions; or, by sudden emotional outbursts and overflow; or, emotional poverty, arid sentiments. Absence of motivation. Rigidity. An anxious, anguished person; or, someone who feels emotionally polluted. Difficulty experiencing a feeling of freedom, a natural flow on the affective level. A lack of spontaneity, joy, and possibilities of renewal. Difficulty feeling and expressing positive, vivifying, stimulating emotions. An incapacity to nourish our affective life, to manifest our feelings in our acts. Sorrow that is so deep it seems never-ending. Feeling as though we are going round in circles in our emotional, affective life, of being in an impasse.

ROAD BLOCK *cf. Dam*

ROAD

Unlike the terms path and lane, which refer to less elaborated, usually quite simple, often narrow access routes, that are not available to all type of vehicles, the word road designates a generally comfortable, quite large access route in good condition to ensure easy, safe, quite fast displacement of a large number of various vehicles. Roads allow us to travel and advance easily, as much on the individual as the collective level. (*cf. also* **Highway**)

The state of the roads we take in concrete reality, or in our dreams, as well as those we encounter and experience in transit, reflect parts of ourselves, the state of our advancing and manifestation *routes*. Roads reveal to us how our thoughts, ideas, emotions, and intentions travel, and what kind of inner traffic dynamics they create. Beautiful, clear, well-equipped, wide roads in good condition reveal inner and outer traveling that is carried out in harmony, serenity, and synchronicity. On the other hand, blocked, jammed, congested roads in poor condition, along with the manifestation of obstacles, accidents, bad weather conditions, etc., indicate accumulations of memories preventing us from advancing. Such roads and difficulties have been created by forces that wanted to advance too quickly; or, that lacked motivation, thereby engendering major discrepancies between the way we function in our inner world and what we display in the outside world. They may also indicate a lack of synchronicity caused by a hasty or badly organized departure.

To take to the road allows us to begin a new stage in our life, and opens up new opportunities that will help us develop our autonomy and independence. Each road we travel opens up a new horizon for us, simultaneously enlarging our potential for expansion. Traffic fluidity, rapidity, and security reveal how we advance on the road of our life, the path of our destiny. Are we receptive enough? Do we listen enough to others, or to our inner voice so as to intuitively know what is the right road for us, when to take it, and with whom we should take it? Or, do we tend to rush headlong along the road, or disperse ourselves, rushing around in all directions, without any precise aim other than fleeing life, others, ourselves? Are we easily confused when we travel, or do we remain well-centered, well-focused on the essential?

⊕ Clear roads, in good condition symbolize ease and facility when traveling and advancing, synchronicity in events, in stages as we proceed. A feeling of freedom, discovery, renewal. A great capacity to adapt, to change, when it is necessary to try a new way, to take an unknown route or road. The willpower to go ahead, to move toward our objectives and goals. A spirit of adventure. An ability to maintain a positive attitude, motivation, enthusiasm, and hope, even when we encounter obstacles *en route*, on our path. Someone who isn't easily knocked off his stride, or confused, who trusts Up Above, who recognizes and acknowledges that it is Up Above that guides us through signs and dreams, and who has the wisdom to submit to this guidance.

⊖ Roads in poor condition denote difficulties related to advancing and traveling, going places, in order to manifest, to achieve our objectives, materialize projects; or, to expand. Difficulty determining an objective or goal, and setting out to achieve it. A lack of motivation, enthusiasm, courage, and willpower to advance, or to try new roads, new routes. Absence of a spirit of adventure, of discovery; or, someone who has too much willpower, whose desire to advance is too strong, and hence may cause accidents, difficulties in his advancing, in the achievement of his objectives and goals. Missed opportunities, misactions (*cf.* this term), stagnant projects, heaviness, retention, repression. Hindrances, obstacles, or limitations on the outside, which reveal blockages on the inside, on the inner level. Someone who is stuck in routine, who always takes the same route, travels the same roads, due to insecurity regarding what is new, fear of change, of the unknown, and of getting lost; or, due to inertia, laziness and lassitude.

ROCK, STONE

As an element representing the mineral kingdom, rock or stone, is symbolically related to the earth element and the world of action on the physical level. Constituted of an amalgam of several minerals, the different sorts and size of rocks, of rock strata and formations, represent the solid, physical, and material structure of the Earth. Memories of the creation of our planet are recorded in rocks, in those found on the surface of the earth as well as those hidden in its depths, or in the seas and oceans. A study of the earth's crust and its various layers, and the composition of the rocks, vegetable, animal, and human traces that are contained therein and make up these layers, allows us to know the evolution of the Earth, the climate changes it has been through, the movement of its waters, the varieties of vegetable and animal species that existed on it, as well as the development of man. This study, analysis, exploration and discovery work can also be carried out in terms of conscience, by exploring our inner earth, the different layers of our unconscious. Our unconscious harbors all the recordings of all our memories related to our lives on Earth, which constitute the foundations of our personality. By working in depth on our unconscious memories, we gradually discover our inner *rocks* and *rock formations,* in the form of very old, ancient, crystallized, hardened, solidified blocks. In their positive aspects, they reveal to us the solid, stable, harmonious, right structures of our being, hence the positive idiom *as steady as a rock*, used to describe someone who is always dependable and steadfast. In their negative aspects, they reveal the distorted constitution of our being, and the way in which our first experimentations in earthly matter have concretely fashioned and shaped our future, our evolution. The negative aspect of behavior and attitudes that have eroded and weakened our foundations and structure can be found in the expression used to indicate that a relationship is in serious danger of breaking up, when we say, *their marriage is on the rocks.*

In a dream, *walking over rocks* means that either the person is well grounded, very solid and stable in the way he advances in life; or, it may relate to a person who is too down to earth, too materialistic, who is *heavy*, who lacks spirituality, whose behavior, attitude, and way of being is based solely on matter.

An attraction to rocks in concrete reality (e.g. visiting caves, collecting stones while walking/hiking or traveling, professions related to geology, paleontology, etc.), indicates that the person, consciously or unconsciously, wants to know his profound structure, the detailed composition of his inner earth; the *stones*, *rocks*, and *minerals* he has generated during the course of his lives through his actions, gestures, behavior, and materializations. At the same time, it is powerful initiatic work that step by step, will lead him to transform his *ordinary stones* into *precious stones,* i.e. symbolically speaking, into qualities, virtues, and powers in their purest state, and, eventually, thanks to his efforts and perseverance, lead him to find the *philosopher's stone.* If the interest in rocks includes water, vegetation, and the animal world, then the symbolic meaning will also involve the person's emotional level and his instinctual vital energy.

⊕ Visiting deep memories of our unconscious related to our former actions; or, the discovery of as yet unknown potential regarding our structure, the constitution of our conscience on the concrete, physical level. Powers of stability, solidity, resistance, and endurance. Initiatic, alchemical work thanks to which we can succeed in transforming those parts of ourselves that resonate with dark, unattractive, coarse, brute rock into beautiful, luminous, harmonious, inspiring *precious stones* that are pleasant to look at, to feel, and to live with. Study of ourselves, of our fundamental structure, of our original constitution.

⊖ Problems resulting from blocks of solidified, hardened, fossilized memories related to very old, ancient actions, behavior, and ways of materializing that weigh heavily on the person's unconscious, simultaneously keeping him limited to a state of conscience that is too down-to-earth, that prevents him from lightening up, and raising himself up. Structural difficulties, a lack of solidity, stability, resistance, and foundations. An accumulation and condensing of misactions (*cf.* this term). A hardened, uncommunicative person who shows very few emotions. A somber, heavy, stagnant, threatening, inner mineral world. A lack of light, transparency, and transforming, liberating movement. A mind and spirit that are over-focused on material values, an absence of spiritual conscience. Attitudes and behavior that resonate with coarse, brute rock, preventing the transformation of *ordinary stones* into *precious stones* in a person's inner earth. A period of de-structuring, fragility, and de-stabilization. Difficulties materializing and creating on solid, original foundations. May denote a person who lacks anchorage, who isn't grounded, who hasn't got enough inner solidity, and who seeks it by granting excessive value to outer rocks and stones; e.g. through collecting and/or accumulating precious stones, jewelry, nostalgic memories, souvenirs, and all sorts of stone objects, as well as excessive attraction to rock formations, such as found in caves, rocks, mountains, etc.

ROCKET

A rocket is a symbol of force, emissivity, and power of elevation allowing the discovery of new spaces, new parts of ourselves on the physical, intellectual, and spiritual levels. It indicates a very advanced level of study, research, and inner work, as well as great potential of evolution regarding new ways of thinking and acting. It is also a symbol of the journey and expansion of conscience that lead mankind to discover and gradually understand the Universe, the parallel worlds, the infinitely great, and ultimately, God.

⊕ Forces of elevation, evolution, research, and discovery on the intellectual and spiritual levels allowing the materialization of great projects. Power to raise ourselves up, self-elevation. Beautiful emissivity. Opening and expansion of conscience. Wish to learn and evolve. Beginning of a great spiritual journey. Gradual discovery of the parallel worlds, of different spaces of conscience. Understanding that everyone has his place and mission in the Cosmic Order. Humility in the face of the greatness of the Universe and Creation.

⊖ Difficulties regarding the capacity of elevation, discovery of new spaces of conscience on the mental and spiritual levels, and the materialization of great projects; or, someone who seeks to flee; or, in extreme cases, autism and mental illnesses. Elevation that is limited to the rational, intellectual level that lacks spirituality. Excessive emissivity. Tendency to force, to want to discover the mysteries of life at all costs. Great potential of elevation used egotistically, to impress others, to position ourselves above others. Seeking material possessions and conquests.

ROOF

As the highest point of a building or house, a roof is symbolically associated with the head, the structure of the world of thoughts, decisions, and authority, according to the place, type and shape of building, as well as its reliability in all circumstances. It is also a symbol of protection, related to thoughts, which, on the structural level, ensure well-being and order in the family, social, cultural, political field, etc., depending on the roof context. If it is the roof of a family or individual's home, it will be related to thoughts and a capacity to protect the intimacy of private, personal life. In the case of the roof of a factory, or administrative office building, the symbolism will refer to the way we work, manage, produce, and function on the professional, social, collective levels.

On the metaphysical, symbolic levels, roof problems are related to the emotional level (e.g. when there are water infiltrations), or reveal a deficiency on the level of structure and protection, when there are inner emotional, affective upsets; or, regarding situations of excessive, emotional coldness or warmth.

⊕ The structure of the world of thoughts, of the way of conceiving, protecting, making the right decisions concerning an intimate or social place. Stability, solidity regarding authority, decisional aspects, the capacity to supervise a dwelling. On the structural level, provides global vision of the place the roof covers.

⊖ Problems with structure on the thought level regarding an intimate or social place. Difficulty conceiving, protecting, supervising our physical or inner dwelling place. Problems making decisions, problems with authority, related to a place, a covered, roofed building. Difficulty understanding, a lack of global vision of what goes on in a place. Limited structural and intellectual framework or constitution, which is either too rigid or too lax, fragile, contaminated, permeated by physical and emotional weather conditions.

Water leakage in a roof: Indicates emotional difficulties in our way of thinking regarding the place affected. A tendency to let ourselves become emotionally de-structured on the thought level, in our way of making decisions, in supervising a place.

Badly insulated roof: A tendency to retain, problems regarding ventilation, the circulation of heat and cold on the thought level regarding a place, or its function. (E.g. the symbolism of a school roof would refer to our capacity to learn and to teach; a hospital roof, healing; a church roof; spiritual concepts, etc.)

ROOM, A

A room, most often situated in a building or house, is related to our inner world and the structure of our conscious and unconscious internal functioning. When we dream of a room, we are visiting our behavior, our acts and deeds related to activities that took place in this room. It is important to know what goes on in a room to know which attitudes to encourage or which to change or purify. All of the various composed words, such as bedroom, living-room, dining-room, bathroom, storeroom, etc., reveal dynamics related to each place. Similarly a classroom, meeting-room, boardroom, waiting-room, or reception room relate to behavioral dynamics, interaction with others, on the collective level.

⊕ A functional, harmonious, social, personal or intimate structure. Allows us to relate to others and to experience beautiful exchanges, lovely inspiring moments. Conviviality, sharing, friendship. Capacity to organize social exchanges. Facility to be warm, welcoming, and easy social contact. A feeling of personal or social expansion, accessibility to collective, family, or personal, intimate resources.

⊖ Difficulty creating or having harmonious, well-structured social, personal or intimate connections. Problems organizing events, social or personal encounters. Imbalanced life caused by affective dependencies, an exaggerated need for social or personal relationships; or, an anti-social, marginal, extremely shy attitude, refusal to be with others and to fraternize, to share. Collective disorder, irresponsibility, incapacity to be organized in social life or society. Isolation, relationship problems, choosing to remain apart, always on the sidelines.

ROPE

A rope is a long, flexible, resistant object made of intertwined or plaited threads. It is used to attach, secure, hang, bind, link or decorate. Symbolically, it represents a more or less strong, solid link, relationship, support, attachment. It also includes the idea of security.

⊕ A capacity to link, assemble, gather, and support with flexibility or strength. Secures and supports in difficult, dangerous circumstances. Idea of a strong link, a strong relationship.

⊖ A lack of attachment, stability, solidity, and support; or, a tendency to become excessively attached to others, to situations; and/or to want to attach others. In the case of a very tightly stretched rope: lack of flexibility, excessive attachment, possessive force that retains and limits. Dependency, overly intense, fusional or too close relationship, suffocation, knotted, complicated, dangerous links. Symbol of humiliation and brutality in the context of imprisonment, slavery, and torture. Destructive force when used to hang ourselves or others.

ROW *cf.* ***Dispute***

RUBBISH BIN *cf.* ***Garbage bin***

RUBBISH *cf.* ***Garbage***

RUN, RUNNING

The action of running allows for faster individual displacement and advancing than walking. It generally indicates that the person is in a hurry; or, that he has a lot of willpower and good motivation to advance and act in matter, to reach a destination, to achieve an objective, or to materialize a project. As for the sport of running, it reveals a large dose of determination, willpower, and emissivity. We never choose a sport or activity by chance: they always reveal some of the person's inner dynamics; what he is experiencing in his inner world.

⊕ Motivation and a capacity to advance rapidly to achieve our objectives. Development of qualities such as: willpower, perseverance, endurance, courage, discipline, rigor, concentration. Abundance of vital energy, momentum. Feelings of victory, success. A powerful mental force to materialize our projects.

⊖ Excessive willpower. Hyperactive behavior. A tendency to force in order to achieve our objectives more quickly, to wish to precipitate destiny; or, on the contrary, a lack of willpower, dynamism, and motivation, preventing the person from advancing with a certain zest and vivacity. Competitive spirit. Need to compare ourselves to others, and to surpass them. Attention exaggeratedly fixated on the result. Seeking personal glory, renown. Waste of energy. Lack of synchronicity. Willpower used in action to flee because of fear.

S

SALARY (wages, remuneration)

A salary represents condensed energy that is usually attributed to us in the form of money hence it concerns the dynamics of giving and receiving. Contrary to what some spiritual people believe, being remunerated for our work is not negative in itself. There is no question of scorning a salary or money, nor of rejecting them in the name of an ideal of purity, and detachment from matter. It is, however, sometimes necessary to review and re-educate our attitudes rather than renounce a salary or remuneration, which represent resources allowing us to materialize our creative potential in our daily life. It is always the way we do things and what motivates us to do them, our intention, that counts, that is essential.

A salary, symbol of an exchange of energies, of evaluation and/or acknowledgement of work accomplished, of mutual help and thanks, provides the person who receives it with the possibility to construct his life with his family, to build his dreams in matter, and to satisfy his fundamental needs in order to experience greater or lesser abundance in this life on Earth.

⊕ A symbol of reward, merit, gratitude, appreciation, acknowledgement. Understanding that a salary is a form of condensed energy, a resource allowing us to satisfy our fundamental, basic needs (shelter, food, warmth, etc.), and to materialize our potential, concretize our projects, and fulfill our Life plan. Right, fair payment for services rendered or work accomplished. Sentiments of achievement, fulfillment, self-worth, expansion, and satisfaction with what we have accomplished. Learning to give and receive fairly, honestly. Realization of the fact that material security and a feeling of well-being and confidence in the present and in the future are not dependent on our salary.

⊖ Difficulty accepting or having to pay a salary, provide remuneration. Financial insecurities, fear of lacking money, resources; or, fear of abundance because afraid of losing it again. Feelings of frustration, of being exploited because we don't receive the salary we reckon we deserve. Seeking recognition, admiration, and appreciation thanks to a large salary. A materialistic person, whose self-identify is based on his salary, his purchasing power, and consumerism, on the image and influence his salary provides him with;.or, someone who only works out of material interest. A period of limitation, precarity, poverty, due to karmic consequences. May refer to someone who has an erroneous spiritual vision, which leads him to believe it is unworthy to work for a salary, for money.

SALT

Salt, which is generally white, comes either from minerals (ancient dried up lakes), or from the evaporation of seawater. It is used as a nutritional, taste additive in food. Given its capacity to retain water, to fuse with this element, salt plays an important role in the preservation of foodstuffs and also in salting roads in winter.

In the human body, salt allows the activation of the nervous influx, muscle contraction, and water retention.

Originating in the mineral kingdom, salt is therefore symbolically associated with the deep layers of the unconscious, to very old, ancient action memories. Its particular relationship with water makes it a symbol of a person's emotional regulation (water softener), and the dissolution of frozen memories (ice, snow). It is also a symbol of purification, preservation of resources, modifier of primary savors, intensification of the appreciation of resources, and a potential for dissolution. It also symbolizes the activation of our willpower and capacity to materialize (conduction of the nervous influx, muscle contraction). Its color, usually white, refers to a spiritual aspect, to the force of spirit which transforms. If it is a different color, then we refer to the symbolic meaning of whatever color it is.

⊕ Helps purification, transformation, regulation of our physical and emotional potential. Allows us to protect resources. Enhanced, increased appreciation of resources.

⊖ An excessive person who is *over-purifying*, too puritanical. Emotional blockages; hinders good management of our energy flux. Difficulty managing our inner, emotional balance. Someone who seeks to contain, to retain because of lacks and/or insecurities. Rigidity, control, imposing our will, a dry, arid attitude. May create emotional overflow; or affective lacks, energy leaks, fatigue, aridity. Excessive willpower. Puritanical spiritual attitude.

SAND

Sand belongs to both the mineral kingdom and the earth element, so it represents the world of memories related to action and materialization. A grain of sand symbolizes one element of a whole, of a unity; hence, in terms of conscience, a capacity to be one, complete, unique element, while also being part of a greater Whole, constituted of a multitude of tiny parts. Sand is also a very supple material that is malleable, that adapts and shapes itself to its environment, thereby seeking stability and balance. Grains of sand are light enough to be transported by wind and water, and hence modify the landscape by forming beaches and dunes, leveling soils, etc. Their formation, which comes from the disaggregation and erosion of bigger pebbles and stones, alters, transforms, and helps structures and contours such as hills and mountains evolve. Sand has numerous uses and applications, notably serving to filter water (sea, beaches, riverbeds), to resist and protect (sand dikes to avoid flooding), and as greatly sought after building material for masonry, in foundries, as raw material for glass, as an abrasive, etc.

Sand has given rise to several, symbolically interesting expressions: e.g. *to be built on sand* meaning enterprises or projects that do not have solid foundations and risk failure; *to bury, hide, or have our head in the sand* meaning to refuse to think about an unpleasant situation, hoping that it will improve so that we will not have to deal with it; *building sandcastles in the air* meaning daydreaming, having projects and plans that will never materialize. Also *quicksand* – deep, wet sand into which anything heavy readily sinks – symbolically meaning a concrete action and/or emotional situation that is dangerous and difficult to get out of; being easily and rapidly, possibly fatally, bogged down due to an accumulation of multiple emotions in matter, in action.

⊕ Old, ancient memories related to the world of action that come apart, form again, and are gradually transformed, creating new forms, new structures. Very old elements representing particles of our ways of functioning, behaving, doing. Reflects patience in the cleansing process of our old memories. Allows us to link, build, protect; inspires altruism. Adaptability, malleability, flexibility, lightness on the action level. Helps reflection on how time modifies and continually transforms life and things. Understanding the role of the infinitely small. Capacity to assemble multiple little parts harmoniously, to be one with all the elements that we are composed of and surrounded by. Search for stability, equilibrium, fusion. Ability to gradually filter what needs to be purified. Delicacy and refinement on the action level. Capacity to go from the collective to the individual, to undo, to take apart.

⊖ Problems related to old, ancient memories related to action. Lack of structure; a period of de-structuring, disorganization, dispersal on the material level. Becoming bogged down in matter; someone who is too down-to-earth. Unconscious difficulties regarding outdated concepts, old foundations. Difficulty assembling parts of ourselves harmoniously, and fusing them. Lack of adaptability, flexibility; or, someone who is too flexible, too pliable or weak on the action level. Not understanding evolution, the power of time that transforms all things and modifies life to create new situations and more evolved worlds.

SATNAV *cf. GPS*

SAUCEPAN

Like all containers, a saucepan is a symbol of receptivity. Mainly used to cook, re-heat, or temporarily preserve food, it represents a capacity to receive, prepare, and transform solid and liquid food resources to nourish ourselves and others. As it usually contains hot food, it is also related to the fire element, and hence to the creative power of the spirit, vital energy, and when it contains liquids, to emotions and feelings.

⊕ Receptivity. A capacity to prepare and transform a person's food or energy resources; an indication of how we nourish ourselves. An abundance of food and/or energy resources. Sharing the food we have with others. Generosity. Altruism. Simplicity. Beautiful norms of hygiene, qualitative food preparation and spiritual nourishment.

⊖ Difficulty receiving, transforming, and preparing resources; or, a lack of food resources. An incapacity to nourish ourselves, or others. Preparation of unattractive, unappetizing dishes, symbolizing insipid, indigestible spiritual nourishment. Insecurity regarding resources, fear of lacking, avidity, selfishness, or waste. An over-intense, exaggerated transformation energy, as in the case of a burned saucepan bottom.

SCAR

A scar symbolizes a capacity to repair, the healing process of a wound on the physical, emotional, psychological, mental or spiritual levels. It is also a symbol of inner transformation and developing awareness as it generally represents a fragile, vulnerable zone. Given the fact that it remains visible on the skin and sensitive to touch, it is a permanent reminder of the wound incurred, the mark of a painful experience, the memory of which has not fully healed, or is in the process of healing, as the case may be. It indicates an apprenticeship – a learning experience – a person has undergone through experimenting evil, wrong-doing, what hurts in one way or another. It also symbolizes an innate faculty to heal and renew ourselves when confronted with aggression and possible manifestations of evil. A scar indicates a capacity to continue to advance in spite of the marks and traces life may have in store for us.

⊕ Capacity for healing, regeneration, repairing, transformation and evolution. A capacity to integrate the lesson of the experience that led to the scar. Apprenticeship of the fact that all wounds or negative experiences lead to greater understanding of ourselves and of good and evil.

⊖ A wound which manifests difficulty healing or a scar which remains sensitive and painful indicate problems related to the power of healing and regeneration, the capacity to renew, repair, evolve and continue our spiritual journey despite the ordeals and hardships experienced. A state of fragility, vulnerability. Incomplete healing. Suffering, an accumulation of violence, of intense difficulties. A tendency to focus on bad memories. Self-pity. An incapacity to forgive, which prevents the activation of the power of self-healing.

SCHOOL REPORT

A school report is a document that is periodically issued by school administration in order to inform pupils' parents of the progress their children have achieved in their school work, the marks they have obtained in various subjects, as well as their general behavior. It also serves to warn parents when there is a risk of failure or when a pupil regularly misbehaves or perturbs the class. In a dream, a school report reveals aspects related to the dreamer's apprenticeship and development. It indicates what stage he has reached in his apprenticeship and evolution, in the construction of his future.

⊕ When a school report contains good marks and positive remarks, it represents encouragement to persevere in our efforts to learn. Not only do we receive congratulations and encouragement from teachers on the horizontal level, but also from Up Above, from Heaven.

⊖ A negative school report indicates learning and behavioral problems; it incites us to take stock of, assess and clarify our situation, and correct our attitude and way of working so as not to have to repeat the same life lessons, the same difficult learning experiences. Learning difficulties which result in a discrepancy between theory and application. Failure through lack of involvement and application, lack of effort.

SCHOOL

A school is an establishment dedicated to learning and teaching. Symbolically, it represents our potential and capacity to learn and to teach. Furthermore, it is important to know, understand, and fully integrate the fact that we are always simultaneously a teacher and a student; we all learn and teach and learn from each other all the time. Life is a school, a continuous learning process to help us evolve and become better people, better souls.

⊕ Apprenticeship favoring the emergence of what exists potentially in us. Beautiful motivation to learn or to teach. Importance of analyzing the symbolism of the subject we are studying or teaching, for example, when we see ourselves in a dream in a Math, French, English, sewing, woodwork, cookery, or other class, we analyze the respective subjects.

⊖ Difficulties and blockages related to learning or teaching. Problem integrating new knowledge. Lack of motivation to learn, discover, or share knowledge with others. Blockages that limit the future and destiny. When we experience difficulty learning, we should remember that each new step, every new project, always begins with a learning process, an apprenticeship. It is important to integrate a love of discovery, in small things as much as in big things.

SCHOOLBAG *cf. Bag*

SCISSORS

A symbol of emissivity through their length and double blades, scissors allow us the capacity to adjust, rectify, separate and cut precisely and accurately. They allow us to remove what is superfluous or useless in the accomplishment of a project or relationship with others. Scissors are a useful instrument in the process of creation, structuring and materialization.

⊕ Manifestation of creativity and a capacity to materialize. The faculty to adjust, rectify, separate, cut precisely and clearly. Refined taste. Equity, fairness. Freed from past, useless, or harmful ties.

⊖ A sharp, dualist, aggressive, cutting attitude, which creates ruptures and divisions. Separatism. Problems regarding a capacity to create, re-adjust or rectify a situation, to separate fairly and justly. Hurtful dynamics, distancing, and rejection. Cuts links with parts of ourselves and others. Problems with refinement.

SEA

The sea is related to the water element and symbolizes the power of love, emotions and feelings, as well as the affective strengths and weaknesses human beings have developed. The depths of the sea, and the oceans, represent the emotional unconscious, the whole collection of affective memories inscribed in the depths of our being and in all humanity. Whenever we explore the depths of the sea in a dream or in concrete reality, symbolically we enter into contact with old, ancient emotional memories; we discover the relics, ruins, and experiences of shipwrecks or treasures buried deep in our common affective unconscious.

The sea is also a great regenerating force, which recycles, vivifies, transforms, and liberates our affective potential and our emotional tensions. A walk along the seashore or a boat-ride on the ocean sets off a powerful process of deep thought and reflection, awareness and questioning of our life. As our physical body is made up of more than 70% water, contact with the sea creates a very powerful regenerating movement on all levels of our being.

⊕ A visit to the collective emotional unconscious and the transformation of memories therein. Regeneration, well-being, vivification via the emotional world. Purifying, self-cleansing forces of body and soul. Helps us reflect, question and implement changes in our life.

⊖ Problems regarding the emotional conscious and unconscious. Difficulty regenerating, vivifying, and transforming ourselves on the affective, sentimental, emotional level. Unstable, agitated, tumultuous, stormy, perturbing emotions creating affective, sentimental torment and *shipwrecks* in our life. A tendency to retain our affective needs, thereby engendering powerful destructive forces within ourselves. May indicate an incapacity to master anger, aggression, excessive, compulsive behavior. Difficult, troubled sentimental, affective relationships, revealing problems related to love in general. A collective emotional unconscious encumbered with negative memories that have accumulated over many lives, which manifest in both the inner and outer worlds in the form of tsunamis and serious affective de-stabilization.

SEED

Symbolically a seed is a state of conscience that represents potential, the beginning of materialization, of accomplishment, a life force related to a project or situation that has the capacity to develop and take shape, if offered favorable conditions for its growth, its evolution. It is a collection of forces that remain dormant until the right time comes to awaken and expanse in the form of a project or new evolution program. It also contains the notion of multiplication and expansion, because when a seed is sown, it results in a production that then engenders other seeds. It also symbolizes perseverance, resistance, adaptability and the wisdom to wait for the right moment to reveal itself; a seed can remain latent for a long time, until the ideal conditions for its germination and growth come along. Generally speaking, a seed represents great potential and a state of conscience which have yet to be activated.

⊕ A latent force with the power to create life, works, a project, a new stage in life. A capacity to wait for the right time, the opportune moment to develop and help a thought, idea, feeling, or project to grow. A faculty to protect inherent potential until ideal conditions are present.

⊖ Negative potential that can come into being if given the required conditions to develop. An announcement that a negative situation has been sown. Non-use of existing beautiful capacities or beautiful potential. A tendency to go too fast, not to respect the cycles and stages of materialization. Sterility, an incapacity to create life or ensure the healthy growth of a project. Destruction of life.

SEWER, SEWERAGE SYSTEM (drain)

A sewer (sewerage system or drain) is a symbol of collective purification that allows the circulation and evacuation of what needs to be cleansed, purified, and transformed in us, on both a personal and collective level. As sewers are underground, they are related to memories lodged in the subconscious and the deeper unconscious.

⊕ Depending on the quantity of sewers we see and their location in a dream or in a concrete situation, they symbolize cleansing and liberation on a personal and collective level, an intense process of inner purification, a renewal of the unconscious through the alchemical transformation of karmas.

⊖ Blocked, broken sewers or drains and the resulting damage indicate a state of conscience that engendered serious blockages and retention of unhealthy memories. When it is a home sewer, it refers to blockages and retention of unhealthy memories on the personal level, whereas problems in a town sewerage system refer to the collective level. Feeling of inner stagnation. Accumulation on both the personal and collective levels of heavy, cumbersome, embarrassing situations where we feel mired, bogged down, stuck. Difficulty evacuating and positively transforming social negativity. Accumulation of all sorts of excesses. Difficult, painful cleansing. A tendency to retain negative karmas. Individual and collective social pollution.

Note: In dreams, seeing sewers or drains repeatedly, or in great quantity, in negative contexts is a warning that the accumulated blockages, those feelings of being bogged down, may materialize in the form of an illness. It is time to transform the negative, to cleanse our memories.

SHARK

The shark, a fish that lives in all of the world's oceans except the Antarctic, is a very ancient animal that existed long before dinosaurs. Hence it represents instinctual, emotional energy as well as very old, ancient primary needs on the collective level. Although sharks rarely attack man (and often, by mistake), they have a bad reputation because shark attacks can awaken feelings of fear, threat, powerlessness, and terror of falling prey, of being a victim. As sharks only predator is man through overfishing, they are referred to as *king of the ocean*, and thereby associated with a symbol of power, strength, and instinctual, emotional power. Their role in the sea is similar to lions on dry land. Sharks eliminate sick fishes, genetically deficient animals, corpses; they play the role of organic purifiers that are necessary for the balance of the marine ecosystem. Shark energy is usually pacific energy that knows how to establish and keep order if necessary *via* the strength and force conferred by its size, powerful action, and vivacity.

Symbolically, a shark indicates the presence of instinctual, emotional forces that can manifest aggressively and pitilessly, that inspire fear of being attacked, thereby inducing predator/helpless victim dynamics. Sharks are rather discreet animals that only need to rise to the surface to breathe; they represent hidden emotional forces that are activated in the depths of our individual and collective unconscious. The coldness of shark energy is related to their living in warm waters to compensate for their lack of inner warmth. This is because emotional coldness related to power, control, implacable will, fearless force that can become aggressive, hurtful, destructive, and act without any emotion, engenders a need for outer warmth.

Sharks have a highly developed sense of smell. This is related to the first chakras and the satisfaction of primary vital needs, good instinctual intuition and an excellent sensorial capacity to perceive, conquer and dominate their environment. Sharks also have mobile, independent jaws full of several rows of teeth, which are renewed throughout their life. They often lose teeth when attacking and eating. As soon as teeth fall out, they are replaced by others from the next row. Solidly rooted in fibrous tissue, they straighten up toward the outside when a shark opens its mouth, which allows sharks to bite more efficiently. Symbolically, this reveals a way of functioning on the structural level, where instinctual needs are constantly manifested and push us to attack and dominate like a dictator; someone who abuses his power and the resources at his disposal in order to maintain his domination in front of other people.

As a symbol in a dream, if the shark is mastered and positive, it represents great potential for power, as well as great powers of assertion on the instinctual, emotional levels.

⊕ Capacity to use great emotional power combined with powerful, instinctual vital energy, without aggression. Capacity to stay calm and fearless in any environment. Instinctual, emotional sovereignty, with no domination and no predation. Ability to keep order and balance through mastery of emotions and instincts. Capacity to detect, recognize, purify, and transform our own distorted, dangerous attitudes that can attack and dominate with extreme coldness and selfishness. Great vital energy that helps us act in the right way, and to react quickly in dangerous, conflictual situations.

⊖ Abuse of power. Desire to dominate, to feel superior, to impose our strength and power on the instinctual, emotional levels. Ferocity, sudden, searing, impulsive, aggressive force. Egotistical, destructive, predatory emotions. Someone who never thinks of others, who always gives priority to his own wishes, ambitions, and personal needs, treating others as obstacles to be eliminated. Hard, brutal temperament that has no love, feelings, or compassion for those weaker. Supports the law of the jungle, survival of the fittest. A person who attacks, eliminates, casts aside or dismisses coldly and unscrupulously, without any thought of the consequences for other people, in order to get rich, to satisfy his instincts; or, someone who is afraid, who lets himself be emotionally dominated by ill-intentioned, unfair, arid, aggressive authority. Vulnerability and incapacity to assert ourselves when faced with people who misuse and abuse power.

SHOE

Shoes protect our feet and keep them from being hurt; they facilitate walking, moving around and advancing in all sorts of situations, provided that they are comfortable and adapted to the type of ground and climate. Symbolically, shoes represent the reinforcement of our capacity to advance to manifest and realize our potential in the different domains of life. The energy emanated by the shoes, their appearance, heel height, material they are made of, color, and general state all give us more specific indications as to the way we advance in life.

On the symbolic level, each pair of shoes reveals a state of conscience. For instance, high-heeled shoes raise the body above the ground, creating a sensation, a feeling of elevation, albeit superficial. An attraction for high heels indicates the usually unconscious need, for recognition and acknowledgement, for greater height, and either a complex of superiority or inferiority as the case may be. A heel that is too high automatically has a negative connotation since regularly wearing such heels creates back problems and may be dangerous. Dreaming of wearing high heels invites us to work on these negative aspects. A high heel that breaks, either in concrete reality or in a dream, indicates that our way of walking in life and the confidence we had up until the breakage has been shaken: we find ourselves de-stabilized, thrown out of kilter, imbalanced, and the old force that helped us advance superficially has been broken. Certain past attitudes and activities have now become superfluous; there is no longer any reason for them to exist.

Taking off our shoes to walk barefoot, for example, in summer, on a beach by the sea, or at dawn on dew-covered grass, indicates a period of relaxation, a moment of intimacy with ourselves, fusion with nature, a state of conscience of light-heartedness, freedom, non-conformity, non-consumerism, of simple, joyful life. Walking barefoot helps us be well incarnated, feel the power of the earth element, and it activates a feeling of gratitude for existing and being able to experience and experiment life on Earth. From a negative point of view, walking barefoot may indicate a frivolous, irresponsible attitude, laziness, a lack of endurance in action; or, a state of survival, an incapacity to manifest on the social level.

⊕ Represents our way of advancing, our personal motivation, our endurance to attain our objectives, our goals on the personal, professional, and social levels. Provides information about our willpower, our intention in action. A person with right motivation, who is well organized, well-structured, responsible, reliable, animated by a beautiful inner force, who is trustworthy and dependable. Foresight and prudence in the way we move and advance. Protection of our capacity to advance to realize our objectives, to attain our goals. Easy advancing. A capacity to advance in all circumstances, to overcome obstacles encountered on the way.

⊖ Difficulties or lack of personal endurance in the way we advance to realize our personal, professional, and social objectives. Instability in our advancing; or, hyperactivity, wanting to advance too quickly in life, without respecting each stage. May indicate a complex of superiority, over-confidence, a superficial, egotistical attitude, a need for appearances, a desire to seduce in order to reach our goals; or, may denote someone who is negligent or remiss, who lacks dynamism and self-confidence, who has an inferiority complex regarding personal advancing.

Shoes that are too tight, too small: reveal an inferiority complex, an inhibited person, who limits his potential for manifestation, his capacity for advancing, moving, progressing pleasantly, comfortably.

Shoes that are too big: denote a feeling of superiority in personal advancing; the person would like to be bigger, advance more quickly. Buying shoes that are too big, e.g. for children, claiming that they will last them longer, may indicate fear of lacking resources, not being able to replace shoes they have grown out of with new ones which respect the child's growth rate.

Too pointy shoes: indicate a person with a sharp personality, who is ambitious, opportunist, and doesn't hesitate, either consciously or unconsciously, to go where he wishes to go.

Dirty shoes in poor repair: are a sign of letting things go, of negligence and neglect in the way we advance, a lack of attention, refinement, structure and organization because we don't take time to clean them and/or have them mended; or, they may denote an overly materialistic person, with a discrepancy between his intimate and social life, who doesn't look after himself enough.

Wearing someone else's shoes: reveals a person's tendency to live through other people's stories, to be envious, jealous, to experiment life by walking, advancing like someone else, evolving through other people's success or resources.

Having to go barefoot because destitute: May denote a state of extreme poverty, great limitations for advancing in life on the personal and social levels. On the symbolic level, indicates that the person is confronting the consequences of his misactions (*cf.* this term), his negative attitudes and behavior through which he made poor use of his resources, manifesting and advancing in an unfair, wrong manner in other lives, and possibly in this life too; hence he is now reaping what he sowed. A lack of shoes also reveals difficulty or an incapacity to manifest on the social level.

Leather shoes: generally speaking, indicate a conscious or unconscious way of advancing under the influence of over-instinctual needs, since leather comes from the animal world.

A great number of pairs of shoes: indicates hyperactivity, ambitious dynamics, a lack of certainty and security; or a tendency to be scattered and dispersed under the influence of a multitude of forces and needs that push the person to advance on the personal and social levels in order to satisfy his needs to please, to seduce, to be admired, acknowledged, loved, and successful. An excessive quantity of shoes indicates too many different personalities in the way we advance socially.

SHOPPING CENTER *cf. Mall*

SHORT-SIGHTEDNESS (Myopia)

Short-sightedness (myopia) is an incapacity to have a clear, correctly focused, unclouded vision of distant objects. Symbolically, this indicates that the short-sighted person has difficulty discerning, having precise, long-term, global vision. Myopic eyesight problems are the result of being excessively self-centered and self-focused over a long period. A shortsighted person tends to live in insecurity, fearing the future, lacking self-confidence and spontaneity to go ahead. On the personality level, this may lead to hindering or delaying the development of leadership qualities; or, on the contrary, it may incite us to develop over-confidence, too great a leadership force, in order to compensate for a lack of vision, ideal, aim, mission in life.

Myopia, shortsightedness, represents a learning program that obliges a person to concentrate on what is close to him, so as to rebuild his foundations, to correct and rectify his behavior, and any emissivity, exteriorization, and expansion that has taken up too much space in this life, or even in several of his past lives. Hence, his visual limitation incites him to re-construct his connection with his inner world, to develop humility, to practice *referring back to himself,* to learn to appreciate the present moment, and acknowledge the importance of small, tiny things, close at hand, instead of always looking into the far distance. Myopia may also be the result of a person granting too much importance to others, to social life, to the outer world, which confuses and blurs his perception and vision of himself, causing discrepancies between his functioning and behavior and the values of his inner world. Finally, myopia may indicate an ego problem, excessive self-confidence, an overestimation of our worth, a tendency to consider ourselves as the center of the world, believing the world revolves around us.

⊕ The healing of or work on memories related to being too self-centered, lacking global vision and social discernment, as well as either a lack or an excess of self-confidence. Allows us to do deeper, more in-depth study. Incites us to develop humility, capacities, and a regular habit of referring back to ourselves, the willpower to rectify memories of superiority and inferiority, ego-problems, and the feeling of insecurity regarding others. Helps us review our mental, emotional, thought, and behavioral patterns, and rebuild our foundations, live in the present moment, no longer waste, and give social life its rightful place.

⊖ Excessive self-centeredness, over-confidence, a feeling of superiority; or, a lack of self-confidence, an inferiority complex, existential fear, a tendency to disconnect from social life and remain alone and withdrawn. Anguish, anxiety, insecurity hindering our capacity to advance, to manifest in the outer world. Selfishness, egoism, a megalomaniac spirit, someone who lacks receptivity, listening skills, and openness to others. Problems of discernment and lucidity. A tendency to let ourselves be impressed, or to impress others; or, a wild, hermit spirit. A lack of global vision, an overall view.

SHOULDER

Shoulders represent a state of conscience related to general support, moral support, consolation, and tenderness. They also symbolize a capacity to understand in depth the inherent responsibilities of life. Since shoulders are prolonged by arms and hands, they participate in gestures of giving and receiving. As the roots of our arms, they constitute the beginning of a capacity to make, shape, form and produce, which is then materialized by our hands.

Straight, well-balanced, relaxed shoulders reflect good physical and mental health; they ensure correct posture, deep breathing and the correct functioning of the solar plexus. With its numerous joints, the shoulder is also the most mobile part of the body. Symbolically this aspect represents flexibility and adaptability when faced with needs for support, consolation, and tenderness. The way a person holds his shoulders also indicates the way he accepts the events of life. Hence, rounded shoulders reveal a tendency to withdraw into ourselves and consider life events as burdensome and hard-to-bear. Straight, upright bearing, with an open chest and relaxed shoulders, emanates well-being, lightness and ease in exchanges with others, a healthy, well-balanced radiance. However, straight posture may also be exaggerated, and if so, it reveals rigidity, a superiority complex, a need to please, and a competitive, rivalrous spirit. An extremely straight posture is often found in military environments where it is considered, both positively and negatively, as a sign of strength, discipline, obedience to authority, and unshakeable solidity in the face of danger.

⊕ General and moral support. Protection. Consolation. Tenderness. Kindness. Mutual help. Altruism. Loyalty. Uprightness. Acceptance of responsibilities. A force of involvement. Ease in exchanges. Solidity. Courage. Flexibility and adaptability when facing life's challenges. Shoulder posture offers revelations of the power and memories related to giving and receiving.

⊖ A lack of uprightness, capacity for moral support, solidity. An inability to console, support, take on responsibilities, to face and cope with life. Pride, arrogance. Feelings of superiority and inferiority. Overwork, a tendency to force in order to be acknowledged and loved. Difficulty helping, sharing, giving and receiving unconditionally. A state of heaviness. Laziness. Inertia. Inconstancy. Difficulty becoming involved, committed. Ingratitude. Lack of generosity. Incomprehension of the meaning of ordeals. Combative attitude.

SINK *cf. Washbasin*

SISTER

Given her proximity in our personal life, a sister symbolizes an important part of us; she is a mirror of our feminine polarity, of our receptivity, and our inner world and inner action. She represents sensitive help, support, consolation, trust, and the capacity to listen in depth and influence atmospheres and ambiances by her mere presence, often at important moments in our life. A sister is also the complement of our mother, our source of nourishment and love on all levels, and like our brother, we can count on her in the good and bad times of our life. When family bonds are right and constructive, they are sources of altruism and very evolved, unconditional love, help and support.

On the symbolic level, a sister indicates inner behavioral dynamics related to memories of our present life and our past lives. To better understand the symbolism related to the presence of a sister in a dream, we need to ask ourselves what she represents for us in terms of qualities and strengths, when she is shown in a positive context, and in terms of distortions, flaws and weaknesses, when shown in a negative context.

In various circumstances, when we wish to recognize, establish and/or encourage qualitative sisterliness – e.g. in the context of friendships, religious/spiritual communities, extended family relationships – terms such as sisterhood, sorority, soul-sister, etc., tend to be used. In official contexts, potential sister bonds are acknowledged by terms such as sister-in-law, half- or step-sister. Whenever these bonds grow into deep, true sisterly relationships, then the people concerned usually prefer to use the term sister, thereby indicating the existence of a good, qualitative relationship that goes deeper than any official status.

⊕ Deep, harmonious family or friendly relationships; mutual help and unconditional love, devotion, sense of service, sense of family and fair sharing, sisterly, altruistic support. A trusting, well-balanced, authentic affective relationship; deep, sincere exchanges. A spirit that encourages people to get together, to maintain family relationships and friendships. May be a replacement or complementary symbol for the mother as regards support and affection.

⊖ Difficult affective memories and relationships regarding family and/or friends; or, jealousy, envy, rivalry, comparison, affective competition. Invasive, overflowing, imposing, manipulating, dominant attitude; or, rejection, emotional coldness, indifference, bitterness, feelings of betrayal or revenge, quarrels, conflicts. Emotional blockages, lack of support, mutual help, kindness, devotion, and sisterly spirit. An incapacity to help and love unconditionally.

Half- or Step-sister: Using the term half- or step-sister is never really positive because it denotes dynamics of repulsion, setting aside, relational and emotional problems regarding the family, an attitude of separation, a lack of sisterhood, fusion, trust in the other person, and/or non-acceptance of the remarriage of a parent or loved one, difficulty renewing, starting our life afresh, and making deep, sincere friends. It indicates a tendency to exclude the other person due to very old, deep, unhealed affective wounds. It is a term that nourishes conflict, comparison, lack of love, acknowledgement, support and attention, and its use may create flagrant injustices. Whenever we love the other person deeply, even though biologically speaking she is only partially our sister, we don't use these terms because we always consider her as our soul-sister.

SITTING-ROOM *cf.* ***Living-room***

SKELETON

The skeleton is the body's framework, its structure, the bone system that supports it, and it is related to body functions. Symbolically, bones are related to the mineral kingdom, which represents a very deep part of the unconscious, where very old, ancient memories regarding the world of action have been recorded. Hence this structure represents the fundamental concepts on which we have built our life, our relationships, enterprises, materializations, and actions in matter. From birth, our skeleton is constituted in accordance with how we lived in our past lives, and all of its elements are brought together in accordance with our life plan. An analysis of our skeleton reveals the positive structural forces as well as the weaknesses and injuries stemming from our behavior, ways of being and doing that have been inscribed in our memories and deposited in our unconscious. It should therefore call us to deep introspection on our way of being and behaving, on a problem of stiffness, for example. Skeletal muscles engender movement by acting on our tendons, which, in turn, exert traction on our bones, and symbolize the will to act, the way we move, and our flexibility *versus* our inflexibility. The bones of the skeleton and the muscles attached to it work in coordination so as to allow the body to function, to move, to take action; they also reveal the power to advance, the willpower and motivation established in the structure of our being.

The skeleton is also a symbol that may indicate illness, serious danger, or death on the structural level.

⊕ Solid structure, a good framework, positive structural strength and power indicating a person's foundation and way of behaving rest on right concepts and values. Someone who constructs his life with love, wisdom, integrity, flexibility. A lifestyle that ensures healthy mobility, a good capacity to be active, to materialize on the physical level. Ability to recognize warnings and potential danger in the symptoms and problems affecting the skeleton; an invitation to reflect on our way of being and behaving, on our physical actions.

⊖ Problems related to our structure, our framework, our foundation and our mode of behavior and action. May announce a death, a major illness, the end of a life cycle; or, indicate that a situation will end badly. A destructive mind and spirit, an unhealthy, morbid, anti-life attitude that causes the death of relationships or projects. Difficulty manifesting, materializing. Either extreme rigidity or complete laxity. Unconscious weaknesses and injuries that sooner or later set off deep de-structuring to incite the person affected to re-construct himself differently. An extremist attitude that is destructive rather than constructive. Also symbolizes negative memories in our structure that have not been solved and come back as a reminder.

SKIN

Skin is an organ composed of several layers of tissue, forming a protective envelope, a container, allowing vital energy to circulate and organs to function within the physical body. When it is healthy, it has a great regenerating, healing capacity. Through its suppleness and resistance, it protects organs, hence ensuring their good functioning and cohesion. It may be endangered by external elements, which, symbolically speaking, represent resonance we have with these elements on the inner level, in our conscious or unconscious memories. Skin participates in the perception of our environment through physical touch, and on the subtle level, through psychometry (extrasensory perception) and clairsentience.

Skin reveals who we are and expresses our states of deep well-being or ill-being, mainly regarding our emotions. Essentially related to sensitivity, to a search for tenderness, gentleness, harmony, and love, our skin is the mirror of who we really are, our authenticity, and our soul-states engendered by what we are experiencing on the inside and on the outside, according to our memories and resonance. For example, healthy skin represents a healthy, calm person who is in harmony, who has beautiful memories and resonance. On the other hand, if we are in disharmony and imbalance, experiencing states of stress, tension, and dissatisfaction that trigger physical, emotional, or mental hyperactivity, we may develop skin problems such as redness, itchy patches, acne, eczema, psoriasis, etc.

As for the color of our skin, it relates, positively or negatively, with whatever the history, culture, and mentality of the race or ethnic group represents, generally or specifically, depending on the case.

⊕ Soft, smooth, well-hydrated, radiant skin symbolizes beautiful sensitivity on the emotional level, a pure, harmonious soul-state, transparency, and receptivity. There is a popular expression in French – *être bien dans sa peau – to feel good in your skin,* which denotes a well-balanced, serene, benevolent person, who emanates love, inner peace, *joie de vivre,* and beautiful radiance on all levels. A great capacity to heal, to transmute energies and negative memories, to regenerate life in general. An intense emotional, affective force. Emotional mastery. Beautiful, noble feelings and sentiments that reveal the light, the brightness of the soul. A delicate, refined inner life. Skin that reflects vitality, good health, beauty, calm, serenity, and well-being on all levels.

⊖ Thick, rough skin indicates a primary, very down-to-earth, little developed state of conscience. Problematic, dull, grey-tinged, dry skin reflects emotional difficulties and/or relational problems, a lack of love, an incapacity or difficulty transforming our own emotions and negative thoughts, or those of others, perceived through clairsentience. May indicate someone who creates barriers, who diminishes himself; or who grants too much importance to what other people think. Hypersensitivity, emotional hyperactivity, an overload of tension and stress. Problems with intimacy, a tendency to be either too social or antisocial. May indicate over-protection; or, conversely, a lack of protection, a need to keep others at a distance; or, too open to others, due to a lack of self-knowledge and self-respect. A lack of clemency toward ourselves and others. Inner vulnerability, fragility, problems related to the first chakras, someone who isn't incarnated enough; or, who is too incarnated, too down-to-earth, lacking spirituality.

All skin ailments are generally related to affectivity, on the personal and social levels, to a person's sensitivity regarding his memories and environment.

Acne: Problems related to soul-states, to an incapacity to transform the negative, to a lack of love for ourselves and others, to the fact of granting too much importance to what other people think of us. May also be caused by eruptions of anger, the emergence of unconscious repressions, frustration, irritation, resentment, as well as memories of rejection, fear, shame, a lack of self-esteem, insecurity, and multiple needs.

Rashes and itching: The person is going through strong inner tension, caused by what he perceives both in the outside world and in himself, which creates powerful openings of the unconscious within him. Difficulty managing stress, hyperactivity, problems stemming from deep memories.

Cracked, split skin: This indicates a lack of deep love, the feeling of being split, torn between several choices.

Bruises: Someone who has been hurt, mistreated, who is struggling for survival, fighting with himself; or, who lets others beat him, who self-punishes by banging into things, by being too harsh or too lax with himself, or in his actions.

Burned skin, burns: Too lively, too intensive, and/or excessive vital energy; may also denote a person who is unable to defend himself, who gets *burned* by others because of his hypersensitivity.

Deeply cut skin: Deep memories of aggression and violence, an unhealthy, problematic environment. The presence of extreme tensions and dominating forces that incite a person to attack, to cut, to divide. Hypersensitivity and incapacity to defend ourselves.

SKY, HEAVEN, THE HEAVENS, UP ABOVE

Generally speaking the word *sky* designates space as seen from the Earth, the vault where, from our planet, we can observe other parts of the universe and the celestial bodies that inhabit it. The sky is related to the world of air, and therefore to the world of thoughts, and also to spirituality, to the spirit, and the multi-dimensionality of life, and all that exists. Referred to as Heaven, it forms a complementary dyad with our planet: Heaven and Earth. In this case, Earth symbolizes the physical world, and Heaven, the heavens, or Up Above, represents the metaphysical world, the causal world, the spiritual level. Symbolically speaking, it also represents the masculine principle, the spirit that fecundates and animates matter, the feminine principle, symbolized by the Earth. The sky or heaven is also associated with the concepts of: the universe, the cosmos, vastness, infinity, eternity, immortality, perfection, the absolute, lightness, freedom, elevation, expansion, totality, the global nature of all that exists. Finally, it is a symbol and mirror of ambiances as its color and appearance depend on the atmosphere: a cloudless, bright sunny, blue day sky inspires a completely different ambiance than a heavy, cloudy, grey, night sky or indeed a stormy, electric sky. Likewise, a night sky with shining stars, a full moon or aurora borealis, creates quite a different ambiance from a completely dark, black sky that seems rather worrying, threatening, and possibly oppressive.

⊕ *A bright, blue sky* represents beautiful thoughts and ambiances full of immensity, lightness, elevation, spiritual opening, and enlarged awareness and conscience. A capacity to access what is beyond the earthly world. An interest in the universe, infinite space, and the other physical and metaphysical dimensions and worlds. A taste for exploration. A thirst for knowledge, understanding and discovery. Feelings of infinity and eternity. Humility and gratitude in the face of Creation, of the Divine.

A cloudy sky in a context that is calm, quiet, and serene symbolizes a state of interiorization and introspection, calm, peaceful thoughts, and a mind that, drawing on renewed resources within, is renewing and replenishing itself.

A stormy sky: It is important to know that even a stormy sky may be positive if our soul-states and the general symbolism of the situation are right. If this is the case, then such a sky would indicate great intensity on the thought, mind or spirit level, an activation of our force and power to manifest our inner nature in a particular situation. In certain circumstances, a stormy sky symbolizes a powerful stand taken on the mind and spirit level.

⊖ *A cloudy, overcast sky in a context where the ambiance is dull, sad, downcast* indicates limitations on the thought level, a lack of our spirit's expressivity, of global vision, of universal consciousness, of opening onto other dimensions and realities; a darkened, somber mentality; too down-to-earth, heavy-hearted, encumbered, burdened soul-states weighed down with feelings of sadness, nostalgia, and discouragement. May indicate an absence of spirituality, a deeply atheistic spirit that rejects all belief in a Superior Intelligence as creative principle.

A dark, black, threatening, stormy sky may indicate the presence of heavy, possibly oppressive, ambiances full of negative, unkind, mean thoughts, and a harmful, destructive spirit. Difficulty raising ourselves up and elevating our thoughts. Inertia, a very down-to-earth state of conscience, heaviness. A limited, blocked horizon.

SLAVERY

Slavery represents a state of conscience of great suffering, humiliation, domination, fear, limitation, exploitation, and submission to what is unjust. It is control over our original right to exist and express our potential for life and creativity. Slavery symbolizes imprisonment of conscience, soul, spirit, mind and body; deprivation of freedom to decide, choose, exercise free will, live freely and autonomously, and realize our potential.

⊕ Awareness that slavery is a serious distortion and injustice that leads to heavy karmic consequences. Capacity to put an end to a state of slavery and resume our place with dignity. Respect for other people's liberty and autonomy. Understanding the Law of karma that we always reap what we sow. Gift of forgiveness. Development of the will to live in harmony with Divine Law and Order.

⊖ Soul-states and memories of captivity, bondage, submission, great restrictions and limitations. Extreme dependency. Loss of freedom and autonomy. Exploiting others by abusing of our influence, authority, power and strength.

SLEEP

Being in a state of sleep allows the immobilized, physical body to recuperate after its earthly activities, while the spirit and soul continue their apprenticeship in the world of dreams. During dreams, they travel in the multiple metaphysical dimensions where time and space are unlimited. Sleep also gives us access to Knowledge. Sleeping can be considered as active inner meditation, as a period of interiorization, wherein we assimilate experiences we have had and where we prepare the following stage of our evolution.

Simultaneously, sleep is both a period of renewal and exploration. While the physical body rests, the metaphysical body (our spatial vehicle) travels.

⊕ Period of inactivity, immobility, regeneration, renewal of the physical body in earthly reality and, simultaneously, a period of activity, apprenticeship, and evolution of the subtle bodies in the metaphysical realities.

⊖ A state of unconsciousness, of laziness and heaviness that prevents us from seeing the depth of life, from perceiving the multidimensionality of our being. Hyperactivity, excessive emissivity and exaggeration in action causing insomnia. Vision limited to the material dimension. Latent, dormant, unawakened conscience and potential. Difficulty facing problems, tendency to take refuge in sleep, to flee concrete reality, life in matter, in the material dimension.

SLIMMING *cf.* ***Weight loss***

SMALL, LITTLE

Small, or little, is a qualifying adjective that generally describes a size, dimension, or quantity that is inferior to the average, as well as power, importance, or intensity that is considered to be weak. Small (or little) can be used to qualify an object, a project, an animal, a person, or inner notions such as feelings. It is always relative to an implicit norm or given context. It is on evaluating this context, as well as our feelings toward what is small, that we can apply positive or negative symbolism. Small (or little) also refers to what hasn't yet reached maturity (e.g. a child), what can expand (e.g. a company), what can improve or still develop (e.g. an effort, idea or concept). It indicates that a person, situation, or project is in the process of development, growth, or construction. However, this word is also used to indicate an inferiority complex, a feeling of weakness, a state of vulnerability, fragility. Examples reflecting this particular symbolic meaning that are frequently encountered in dreams are:

clothes or shoes that are too small, a small, puny, or stunted tree, tiny objects, or very small, undersized people, including dwarves, etc.

Small may be used and implied or inferred pejoratively when it is attributed to a person, object, idea, or anything else, with the intention of belittling, scorning, humiliating and showing contempt, as for example when we refer to a person (or people) as *small fry* (originally referring to tiny fish caught but then thrown back into the sea because too small to eat), or *birdbrain*. Spoken in a haughty, condescending, disdainful, pitying tone, these words can be very hurtful. The word small is also often used by people who minimize and trivialize, not wanting to acknowledge the full extent or impact of a problem, a situation, or indeed their own worth or qualities; or, mixed feelings, duality regarding the monetary value of something as in *It cost a small fortune.* There is also the expression *a big fish in a small pond* referring to someone who wields power and is important but in a context of little importance, or locally, and not on a wider, more global scale. However, there is also the positive English expression: *good things/the best gifts come in small packages*; and its Spanish equivalent: *the best perfume comes in a small bottle.* These expressions acknowledge the power of *smallness*, of concentration, of being well-focused.

⊕ Represents what is in the process of development, has a capacity for growth, or offers a potential for expansion. It symbolizes the child, freshness, fragility, vulnerability, simplicity, renewal. It invites us to respect natural rhythm and cycles, to recognize a state that requires time to grow, to take shape, to unfurl, to learn. Work on the transcendence of feelings of inferiority. Knowledge of the Law of resonance and the Law of karma, providing global understanding and helping us accept a situation where we feel diminished, looked down on, debased. Confidence and trust in Divine Justice. An ability to evaluate correctly, fairly, justly, without comparison or discrimination. Awareness that everyone and everything has their place in the Great Whole, belongs to the Great All. A capacity to see the infinitely big in the infinitely small, the macrocosm in the microcosm, and the Divine in everything that exists. May indicate the beginning of a project, a situation.

⊖ Displays feelings of inferiority (a garment, a bicycle, a chair, etc., that is too small). However, small may also convey feelings of superiority (e.g. when we see others as smaller than us), or indicate that we grant little importance to an object, person, an idea, etc., by saying, for instance, "Oh, it's just *a little something* I picked up," about a gift, thereby denoting a lack of care and depth; similarly *small talk* refers to unimportant, superficial conversation; to be *small-minded* is to be petty and narrow-minded, lacking openness, tolerance and expansion. In a dream, if we see one or several elements that are smaller than they normally are in concrete reality, depending on their symbolic meaning, they may indicate the presence of discrepancies in the dreamer's capacity of perception, soul-states engendered by poor self-esteem, feelings of inferiority, jealousy, fragility, discomfort, neglect, impotency, a need for attention, or all sorts of lacks, desires, and expectations. A small space indicates a restricted, limited, inner and/or outer environment. Feeling small also indicates having lost touch with the Divine, withdrawal into ourselves, isolation in a particular place, a restricted world both on the inside and on the outside, a limited conscience, and an incapacity to understand that we have to work on ourselves to open up, overcome these states, manifest our grandeur, unfurl our potential, experiment expansion on all levels.

SMELL(S), SENSE OF SMELL *(cf. also **Odor**)*

SMOKE

Smoke is a cloud of solid particles emitted by a fire or mechanical heating. It is related to the air and fire elements. On the metaphysical level, it may represent dense, negative energies indicating real danger, or it may indicate the presence of energies of positive transformation and transmutation. It may also symbolize tumultuous, sometimes destructive forces and thoughts that cloud our vision, prevent advancing, or that have the power to pollute, suffocate, choke or burn our entourage and others.

⊕ May be a warning of hidden danger; may indicate the presence of negative thoughts and energies, or a great, positive force of transformation, of transmutation.

⊖ Dangerous, harmful, destructive thoughts, ambiance and energy that prevent us from breathing, seeing clearly, advancing and evolving.

SMOKE, TO (cigarette, cigar, etc.)

The act of smoking corresponds to a dependency related to the world of air symbolizing thoughts. Smoking is related to a search for artificial relaxation, independency, freedom, a need to escape, to momentarily get away from cares and worries and stress. It is also related to a false image of virility and seductive, mysterious femininity, as well as being a means to appease hunger pangs so as to remain slim and satisfy social criteria for what constitutes beauty and desirability. It is also related to a rebellious spirit who imposes his presence and his confusion onto others. Although there are still a large number of smokers on the planet, numerous advertising and health campaigns in favor of smoke-free living spaces, at work, in leisure and social activities, developed over the last few years, as well as various forms of assistance offered to smokers to help free them from their dependency on nicotine, bear witness to the evolution of conscience in this domain.

⊕ Awareness that smoking is an act that pollutes our thoughts and the surrounding air, and confuses our life and other people's too. Giving up smoking represents an end of confusion, of a rebellious period. Awareness and healing work on sick thoughts and a disposition to die in order to defend very down-to-earth ideas, wrong, unnatural concepts. Someone who smokes to gain artificial relaxation so as to avoid destructive tendencies, or over-stressful behavior that could create major difficulties for the person or his entourage.

⊖ A confused, rebellious spirit. Polluting, destructive thoughts, artificial relaxation. A lack of discernment. Poor choice. An easily influenced or very critical, intolerant person. Egoism hidden behind an attitude of superiority. Self-destruction through over-confidence in wrong ideas. Identification with unhealthy patterns and behavior. A false ambiance of abundance. Seeking elevation to escape reality. Dropping out. Seeking mental confusion to cover up, cloud over and blur unconscious lacks and fears. Despair.

SNAKE

As it is an animal, a snake represents certain aspects of our instinctual vital energy. Since it crawls along the ground, its symbolism is closely related to the earth element and to the world of action in matter. Its elongated form, which recalls the male sex organ, the penis, refers to the masculine principle and emissivity. Its cold blood obliges it to regularly seek out sunny places to capture the heat of the sun. On the symbolic level, from a negative point of view, the coldness of its blood and the need for solar energy represent emotional coldness and the absence of inner life dynamics to radiate, enlighten, and warm the person and his entourage. Associated with the distorted use of masculine aspects, this characteristic leads to a selfish person who uses his power of emissivity and action to control and dominate others in order to satisfy his own instincts, his primary needs, his personal and sexual pleasures and desires. A snake is also a predator that knows how to remain calm, discreet, immobile, hidden and well camouflaged in its environment, waiting for the right moment to catch its prey. This behavior associates it with slyness and hypocrisy, just as its forked tongue evokes duality in the way we communicate.

Other snake features are the fact that it is deaf and it finds its way by using its sense of smell as well as its tongue, its sense of taste. This symbolizes difficulty in being receptive and listening to the needs and advice of our entourage, as well as a tendency to advance solely focused on our own tastes, moods, desires, and needs, thereby feeding on others, on the energy level. Moreover, when a snake moves, its head precedes the rest of its body. Symbolically, this indicates an obsession with our thoughts, which forces our other levels (emotional and physical) to follow. This results in very sly, insidious behavioral dynamics to get what we want.

In religious tradition, the snake symbolizes the tempter that puts people to the test, confronting them with the choice of behaving in accordance with superior realities, i.e. respecting them and obeying the Divine Laws that govern them, or acting according to instinctual impulses and personal desires, without worrying about the possible individual or collective consequences their choices and acts may lead to.

On the energy level, the image of a snake curled around the base of our spine is associated with *kundalini*, our vital energy potential that we have to learn to awaken and raise up through the superior energy centers (the chakras) so as to activate their respective creative potential. This work aims to develop each chakra's corresponding qualities, virtues, talents and powers, and when we do it correctly, with right, just intention and motivation, we transform the distorted aspects of the snake within ourselves and we learn to transcend its negative symbolism on both the individual and collective levels. Its powerful instinctual vital force will then manifest great powers for materializing concrete, altruistic objectives, that the person will carry out with uprightness, integrity, authenticity, and true, enlightened communication. Symbolically, it represents a person who seeks to raise his conscience to attain enlightenment. In such a person, the energy of the *kundalini* – which refers to the transcendence of the snake symbolism – rises along the vertical axis to reach the brain in order to enlighten the superior centers of conscience, thereby allowing him to discover the multi-dimensions of his being, instead of using his potential only on the horizontal level, in physical action, and the illusory, ephemeral values and attractions of matter.

The fact that a lot of people are afraid of snakes in concrete reality represents conscious and unconscious, metaphysical and spiritual fear of succumbing to the temptation of losing themselves in instinctual, carnal pleasures, of deviating from Divine Order and the Divine Plan, and then having to face the consequences, often throughout several lives.

⊕ A person who works on himself with right intention and just motivation so as to transcend the instinctual, vital, sexual force symbolized by the snake. Mastery of instincts and needs. Strength of character, inner stability, absence of fear. A great capacity to create in matter, to be active, and to manifest in accordance with Cosmic Laws. A good capacity to go within, to interiorize. Well developed subtle perception. Inner power and creative potential serving the collective good and the Divine. Full use of the creative energy potential contained in each of the chakras and their corresponding levels of conscience. A capacity to align our personal will with Divine Will when making decisions and manifesting. A capacity to understand the dark forces (demons and the devil), and recognize and anticipate their scheming. Development and manifestation of the qualities of a true, authentic, radiant leader who expresses himself with diplomacy, discretion, right authority, knowing how and when to use hidden Wisdom.

⊖ Someone who uses his vital, instinctual force with excessively powerful intensity and who over-focuses on matter and the satisfaction of primary, sexual needs. Attitudes and behavior that are excessively aimed at the power and pleasures of the senses; or, a tendency to let ourselves be dominated, to unresistingly submit to abusive people seeking to satisfy their multiple desires at other people's expense. A way of life and behavior that drains and vampirizes other people's vital energy. Problems with obsession, egoism, servility to basic instincts. Manipulating, sly attitudes, using all sorts of strategies to achieve our ends. Excess or lack of emissivity, respectively engendering either too great a willpower and desire to materialize; or, a difficulty materializing because the person is not incarnated enough; his creative or inner snake – his *kundalini* –is still asleep at the root of his being, resulting in a lack of power to act and achieve his concrete objectives and projects. Problems related to sexuality, conscious or unconscious memories of sexual abuse, sexual impotency, frigidity, repression and rejection of sexuality, or lust and sexual debauchery. Emotional coldness toward ourselves and our entourage, a tendency to live too much in our head, in the world of thoughts, and neglect our physical and emotional needs. A lack of receptivity, an incapacity to listen to others and to our own inner voice. False communication, a hypocritical, sly mind and spirit, two-tongued (like the snake's forked tongue). A lack of human warmth, an incapacity to generate and express authentic, deep, heartwarming emotions. Possessiveness, hypocrisy, manipulation, attitudes that subtly strangle the other person on the metaphysical or energy levels. Someone who serves demonic forces by creating all sorts of temptations to harm and debase others.

SNOW

Snow is a common symbol in dreams and it represents frozen emotions, atmospheres and ambiances of coldness on the relational, emotional, sentimental, affective levels. However, from a positive point of view, it stimulates human warmth, encourages a spirit of welcome, and interiorization. It reinforces a person to help him face situations of emotional coldness at any time; and if it is pure, immaculate, white snow, it conveys freshness of conscience, purity, and spirituality.

A detailed analysis of its formation reveals its symbolic depth. It begins in altitude in the form of very fine water droplets high up in the air in the form of a cloud; when the temperature is sufficiently cold, the air crystallizes the droplets through condensation, using microscopic impurities (dust particles, smoke, and others) as support. Studies have shown that even bacteria present in the air are found in the formation of snow crystals. These crystals agglutinate to form heavier crystals, which, thanks to gravity, fall and lie on the ground. The phenomena accompanying the formation of snow as well as the effects it produces, allow us to draw an analogy with the processes that take place in our inner climate: certain levels of conscience and ways of thinking engender emotions, soul-states, and actions that chill, harden, and pollute our environment, our air, our water, and our inner lands (countries), while others produce a warm, welcoming atmosphere and ambiance, that reflects love and inner purity. Knowing that on average a snowflake is constituted of 1 particle of water for 10 particles of air, we understand the importance of our thoughts and their positive or negative action on our emotions.

The fact of maintaining a permanently cold environment on the inside creates a certain sterility that affects the whole of our being, our evolution, and our actions, just as the earth, lacking warmth, remains intact under snow, but becomes sterile, incapable of producing life, of letting vegetation grow. Hence, on the thought and emotional levels, coldness and rigidity freeze our potential, our possibilities of manifestation and development on all levels. Sometimes, a person even manages to block, reject, or destroy all gentleness within himself, and so feels ill-at-ease regarding the warmth, gentleness, tenderness and love that others manifest toward him. Such people find it difficult to create and maintain deep, healthy, affective, affectionate relationships, because they reject on the outside what they are incapable of feeling on the inside.

People who have accumulated a lot of coldness in themselves are often afraid of snow. They fear it or flee it, because the resonance this element creates in them brings them back to and reflects their inner landscape or climate, their mentality, their temperament, their frozen heart. Snow represents the outer manifestation of the lack of love and human warmth that dwells within them, and which is unbearable for them. Conversely, there are people who are greatly attracted by snow, by extreme cold, northern, isolated, sparsely populated regions, where hostile living conditions reign. Such an attraction for snow may indicate positive or negative resonance with this element. The resonance is positive in cases when the snow and the cold, stimulating and vivifying on the outside, lead the person to seek and create in his interior (whether in his home or in his conscience) warm, welcoming, comforting, soothing living conditions and ambiances. On the contrary, the resonance is negative if the attraction for snow limits the person to a mainly survival-instinct way of functioning. Indeed, this scarcely evolutive lifestyle greatly limits the development of the immense potential that dwells in every human being.

It is important to know that incarnations in cold countries, that remain snow-covered for a large part of the year, or in cultural and family contexts marked by emotional coldness, serve to incite the person to work on his own memories and attitudes of coldness in order to transcend them and liberate the potential kept imprisoned, *snow-* or *ice-bound*, so to speak. The manifestation of problems related to cold and heat represent an essential aspect in the development of a soul, who is thus called upon to successively visit his memories and learn to activate, contain, or retract vital energy, as necessary.

Snow storms, blizzards, gusts, and flurries that prevent or reduce visibility represent cold thoughts and emotions that have become so uncontrollable that the person loses his sense of direction, discernment, and judgment. Also, just as snow hinders traffic, creates mounds, drifts, and snow-banks that obstruct roads, trap pedestrians, cause accidents, and, in the worst cases, avalanches, so too does a person create *snowbanks,* difficult, freezing cold, chilly barriers in his relationships, causing catastrophic situations for himself and others when he is cold, lacking in love, warmth, ardor, and positive dynamics on the relational level. As snow can damage buildings and electrical installations, similarly a person with frozen emotions risks damaging his structure and his vital energy, that intelligent energy that allows him to move, think, and feel warmly.

However, snow has numerous positive aspects too. Its crystals, which form magnificent shapes of extraordinary beauty, harmony, and perfection, are proof of this. They symbolize the materialization of beautiful thoughts and feelings, thanks to which we can create and maintain harmony, serenity, and well-being, even in cold ambiances and difficult circumstances. In addition to this, the magical, fairylike beauty of snow-white landscapes inspires purity, serenity, contemplation, introspection, calm, rest, silence, and inner listening. The arrival of snow is always welcomed with joy and wonderment or awe by children; in adults, it also favors the expression of their inner child, as well as a capacity to discover and experience life with an open heart, full of warmth, joy, and love. Finally, snow has inspired the development of many activities through which people of all ages may stimulate, vivify, and manifest their inner fire, their vital energy, their conviviality, creativity, and multiple gifts and talents: playing in the snow, tobogganing, sliding, winter sports, snow and ice sculpture, dog-sleighing, ice-fishing, etc.

Snow also plays a role in insulating and protecting the soil against burns caused by intense cold. Moreover, it allows the vegetation (symbolically, our feelings and emotions) and animals (symbolically, our instinctual vital energy) to live in accordance with nature and its cycles, respecting a phase of rest and necessary hibernation after an active period. Snow melting in spring rehydrates the air and the earth, thereby ensuring gradual provision of water, essential for the rebirth of vegetation and life in general.

⊕ A symbol of immaculate purity and magical, fairylike, majestic beauty, which exalts the soul, elevates the spirit, activates human warmth, and invites us to enjoy contemplation, meditation, inner listening, introspection, rest, and communion with the Divine. Favors the manifestation of a spirit of conviviality, fraternity, mutual help. A capacity to be at ease in cold atmospheres, ambiances and climates, in contexts of frozen emotions. An ability to transcend the coldness of thoughts and emotions engendered by ourselves or others. Encourages spiritual work and the elevation of conscience. Favors renewal and replenishment of the soul. Exerts a stimulating, purifying, transforming effect. Soothes ardor, passion, impulsivity. Refreshes and purifies the mental level. Increases receptivity and the perception of the inner world and the subtle levels. Trains a person to develop a great capacity for adaptation and survival in all circumstances on the one hand, and his capacity to love, and show human warmth, gentleness, compassion, helpfulness, and altruism, on the other.

⊖ Emotional coldness, a lack of human warmth. Relational, emotional and affective problems resulting from a rigid, stiff, frozen mind and spirit, manifesting a closed, hardened heart. A lack of love, compassion, tolerance, flexibility and adaptability. Repression of tenderness, gentleness, heartfelt impulses. Isolation. Indifference. Emotional blockages. Difficulty expressing our feelings. Disappointment, unhealed emotional, sentimental, affective wounds, hurts, that prevent us from opening our heart and loving truly, deeply, unconditionally. A tendency to nourish affective dependency, fear, limitation, and possessiveness. Difficulty letting go, mastering our desire to control everything: e.g. on the emotional level, when confronted with relationships and contexts of great coldness; or, on the contrary, emotional overflow and outbursts; and also on the concrete level, when a snowstorm or great accumulation of snow hinders our intentions, prevents us from going out, circulating, advancing, realizing our projects. Multiple fears engendered or reactivated by snow: fear of accidents, fear of being held snowbound in our home, in our car, or physically in a deep snowdrift; or, anxiety. May also concern the behavior of someone who defies the snow and cold, who launches into extreme experimentations to prove to himself and others his capacity for endurance, his tenacity, courage, bravery, and his capacity to survive in a hostile environment.

SOFA *cf.* ***Couch, sofa***

SOLDIER

Soldiers together make up an army, which is an experienced force of intervention that serves the Nation. A soldier's principal mission is to protect his country and its people in the case of conflict, but it is also his duty to assist in the case of natural catastrophes or other circumstances. In many countries, under the auspices of the United Nations, soldiers perform a deterrent, peacekeeping role to maintain law and order, and consequently avoid the emergence or continuation of serious problems or conflicts. These peacekeepers are recognizable by their blue helmets, and are sometimes referred to as the *Blue Boys Action Squad* or *Blue Berets.*

Soldiers are subjected to rigorous discipline, training, rules and regulations. They are very organized and well structured. They are under obligation to keep secret all knowledge they may have concerning any facts or information related to their job. A soldier can develop a lot of qualities regarding order, discipline, obedience, rigor, and respect for hierarchy.

People, especially those on a spiritual path, are often under the impression that armies should not exist, but just as soldiers exist on Earth, so too do they exist in the parallel worlds, where they have an important duty of protection and conflict management. Soldiers in the parallel worlds are instructed in the Knowledge of good and evil, and trained to apply Cosmic Laws and ensure Divine Order runs smoothly and correctly.

⊕ A force of protection, defense, order, structure, and discipline, whose aim is to aid and assist society in the case of conflict or wide-scale catastrophe. Humanitarian aid. Work that controls and manages negative forces that are developing or are already active. Respects hierarchy, obeys orders. Application of rules and regulations and maintenance of security, peace and harmony among different races, cultures, religions, and mentalities. Protection of the civilian population. Humane treatment of the wounded and prisoners. Protects social structures, human rights, the circulation of resources and abundance. A capacity to adapt. Great capacity to manage political, ethnic, religious, or social tensions and conflicts. Allows the development of global vision, a sense of duty, loyalty, right, fair, just responsibilities, team spirit, mutual help, solidarity, and altruistic cooperation.

⊖ A person who abuses power, does not respect the law, manifests overly emissive, dominant, extremist, destructive forces. A machismo spirit that only believes in force and violence. A lack of discipline, rigor, order, respect for hierarchy; or, rigidity, an exaggerated sense of duty, a vengeful, aggressive, impulsive spirit, a violent character, coldness, a conflicting spirit. Insubordination, disobedience, desertion. A lack of love, gentleness, clemency, flexibility, and wisdom. Obedience without conscience. A lack of understanding of the role of a military army, which is to protect and prevent evil from becoming organized, developing, becoming stronger, being reinforced, and destroying the human experimentation of good. Authoritarianism. An incapacity to solve a conflict. A lack of diplomacy. Curtailing, restricting, or running roughshod over individual rights. Inhumane behavior, mistreatment and abuse of the civilian population, the wounded, and prisoners.

SOUTH

The word south originally comes from the Saxon word *sund,* which designates the sun. And today the sun (radiance, knowledge, etc.) and warmth or heat (consolation, love, etc.) is associated with this word, depending on the context; for example, for many people, the South evokes vacations in the sun, the beach, the sea, and exoticism, as a temporary change, as well as getting away from emotional coldness, resting, and renewing our energies on all levels. A south-facing house (a person's intimacy) benefits from the sun all day long, and the south wind is generally warm and dry (warm, loving thoughts, without any excess of emotionalism).

This cardinal point refers to orientation, a direction to follow, or a position and idea of territory, border, delimitation, or division. The presence of this symbol in a dream allows us to *map* part(s) of ourselves, to indicate a path or route to follow, a general direction, or a division. In a geo-political context, it may refer to poor countries, i.e. symbolically speaking, emerging, developing parts of ourselves. The South designates what is at the base or bottom of a map. It reveals the warmest parts of our being, since it is related to the first chakras, whose energy is particularly active and intense, which, taken to extremes, may engender over-passionate, impulsive, irrational, thoughtless behavior. However, in a context that involves the South Pole, it may symbolically indicate that we are visiting very cold, isolated areas of our inner Earth.

On an earthly global scale, the South, generally speaking, represents countries whose first chakras are the most open, that's why very intense, solidly incarnated, warm, open populations that manifest great *joie de vivre* are found there. The intensity of the sun in southern countries leads to their inhabitants' more extrovert, exteriorized dynamics, and radiance. However, in their negative aspects, these people manifest a lot of passion, laziness, tensions, a tendency toward abuse, excess, anger, violence, and also more illnesses related to sexuality such as AIDS. Moreover, in several Southern countries, earthly riches, especially metals and fossil energies are to be found, but they are often mined by Northern countries. Hence the South may represent a tendency to be dominated, manipulated, and exploited for resources; a tendency to experiment and experience corruption, power struggles, and extremism.

⊕ Orientation, direction toward heat, warmth, sunny places, comfort and consolation; or, toward the discovery of new territories, new resources. Symbol of beautiful emotions, abundant resources to nourish ourselves on all levels. A period of rest, renewal, replenishment, reflection, far from daily obligations and duties. Pleasures and *joie de vivre*. Discovering and visiting of new parts of ourselves. Activation of the first chakras, of energy, of the vital force within us. Light, regeneration. A favorable period for exteriorization.

⊖ Excessive search for heat, warmth, sunshine; or, related to the deepest, coldest aspects in our way of being and manifesting. A tendency to laxity, to let ourselves go and become lazy, seeking facility, fleeing or refusing responsibilities. A lifestyle dominated by extroversion, social dynamics, going out, *la dolce vita*, an easy life, seeking sensual and worldly pleasures, deliberately forgetting all our cares and worries. Escapism/Flight from reality and daily obligations into artificial paradises. An excess of heat or cold; too much light; or, a lack of light. An overly intense, or desiccated, and desiccating spirit. Arid behavior. Difficulty renewing and replenishing ourselves.

SOW, TO

The concept of sowing indicates the way we construct our life, the way in which we prepare the different stages, which will lead us to abundance on all levels. When we sow, we are active; we are involved in preparing the future so that one day we may reap the fruit of our efforts. Agriculture, farming gives us in-depth teaching of the principles of abundance, patience, conscientious work that, sooner or later, will engender the results planned by Providence. Farmers submit to the laws of nature and have to accept what resources Up Above provides. It is the same for all of us in our work, because numerous imponderables may perturb our *harvest*. It is important to remember that we always reap what we sow, in this life or another. That is why we sometimes reap difficulties, even though we don't think we deserve them. In the universal education of the soul, the principle of merit is absolute; it is not based on one life but rather on the whole collection of our multiple lives: we are the creators of our happiness and unhappiness.

Sowing symbolizes that we are ready to commit ourselves to a new project, to make an effort, to be patient, and allow the time necessary for all the phases of evolution. Since most seeds are sown in the ground, they represent the first stage of materialization as well as the potentiality of beautiful resources or energies in our concrete world, which are in the process of preparation or realization. Sowing also acts on the energy level, because each time we think, communicate or interact with someone, we sow a certain vibration, a seed of knowledge, which, one day, will become concrete, and be transformed into projects, new realities, etc. Ultimately, we are all farmers, and it is no coincidence that this activity was one of the first professions in the world. It is important in to sow beautiful states of conscience, beautiful initiatives, in order to reap beautiful works. It is also essential to know that, in a dream, when we see a positive sowing stage, it means that a project is beginning, and that it will take some time before it materializes concretely in our life.

⊕ Patience, wisdom, discernment, great capacity for work, preparation, production, expansion, materialization. A period of fertility and fecundity, a feeling of abundance, certitude that anything can happen, confidence. Seeking growth and development. Capacity to germinate ideas, projects, new realities right down into concrete reality. An innovator, someone who consciously participates in every stage of the concretization of his destiny. Well-balanced management of resources. Respect for the natural cycles, for human evolution. Noble sentiments and a capacity to live in inspiring ambiances. Respect for Divine Norms.

⊖ Sterility, infertility, poverty, impatience, poor harvests; an ambitious, materialistic person who wants too much, who tries to force nature by not respecting natural cycles, who is hyperactive and seeks to obtain results too fast. Excessive emissivity in projects we wish to set in motion, a tendency to want to skip stages. Material limitations. Difficulty realizing our projects, producing, constructing, and having access to abundance. Poor initiatives, a lack of wisdom and discernment in our choice of projects. Someone who multiples without discernment, without conscience, and who creates harmful works, thereby engendering karmic debts. Someone who only seeks expansion and profit; who is prepared to materialize anything at all for gain. May also indicate fear of abundance, of reaping the fruit of our labor, due to memories of insecurity and failure.

SPACESHIP

A spaceship allows us to travel in the Universe, into unknown spaces very far from the Earth. Symbolically, it designates access to parallel worlds that are more evolved on the thought and spirit levels. It is a symbol that refers to the spiritual level as it allows us to raise ourselves up to very high levels, very quickly, and it also refers to the physical level since it brings very advanced knowledge back to Earth. Traveling in a spaceship allows us to experience states of conscience that lead us to the discovery of other spaces and dimensions of ourselves, and of life and existence in general. It opens our conscience, brings us new spiritual, conceptual, physical and metaphysical knowledge. It helps us discover new worlds, new lands, to foresee and prepare the future by testing space-related inventions that will one day serve us all.

A person who dreams of spaceships is *avant-garde*, a pioneer in the evolution of conscience. The extra-terrestrial energies he visits and frequents when he leaves planet Earth in his dreams create powerful openings in his conscience and, just like a speceship crew, lead him to develop the motivation, energy, capacity, discipline, rigor, and determination to always go further on his spiritual path and in his discoveries on the mind and spirit level.

Negatively, we could get lost in the immensity of space and become disconnected from earthly reality; in other words, we could *have our head in the clouds* and be too *airy,* too ethereal. In a dream, a person may see extra-terrestrials aboard a spaceship coming to kidnap him, which could be a very disturbing experience. However, it is important to understand that good or bad extra-terrestrials do not merely belong to a fantasy world of science fiction; they are actually very real aspects of a human being; they are symbolic representations of forces that dwell in him. Whenever these forces are extremists on the spiritual level, and/or on the level of knowledge and self-discovery, they may manifest in the form of malevolent, aggressive extra-terrestrials. The day after a dream like this, the person may tend to want to impose his beliefs about other worlds, and inwardly criticize everything he considers either not sufficiently, or not at all, spiritual or evolved, thereby believing himself to be superior to others. Hence the importance of referring back to ourselves to interpret symbols correctly, because whatever we experience in dreams or concrete reality, whatever happens to us, whatever life experiences we attract, all represent ourselves because because of our resonance with them, and everything that exists in the Universe also exists within ourselves in terms of conscience.

We may also see ourselves in a dream in the middle of spaceship battles and hence experience conflicts on the spirit level, the very source of human potential. This kind of dream is frequent among people who haven't yet activated their power of materialization, who live more virtually than concretely, and so face their inner wars and conflicts with others in this way.

⊕ Capacity of our mind and spirit to travel and discover other physical and metaphysical dimensions, other states of conscience, to visit different realities on the personal and collective levels. Exploration of unknown zones of our conscience. Expansion of conscience. Ability to be detached from the terrestrial, material level and its limitations; discovery of the infinite possibilities of the mind, spirit, and conscience, and their capacity to travel throughout the Universe. Activation of a scientific mind on the physical and metaphysical levels, of the motivation to seek, to know and to understand. Knowledge of science and the higher worlds. Open-mindedness allowing us to view events from a distance, to have a more elevated, evolved vision that remains modest and humble before the immensity of the Universe. Connection with the parallel worlds, spiritual guides, the Divine, God, or Cosmic Intelligence (whatever name we prefer), with the origin of Creation; mystical experiences.

⊖ Difficulty opening onto new dimensions, mind-traveling to discover other physical and metaphysical realities, experiencing different states of conscience, visiting the depths of our unconscious; or someone who is too down-to-earth, too focused on the material, terrestrial level; or, someone who tends to flee his responsibilities in concrete reality, whose head is too much in the clouds, who is too spiritual. A haughty mind or spirit, a feeling of superiority regarding others on the intellectual and/or spiritual levels. Discrepancy regarding everyday life. A person with great spiritual potential and a capacity to raise his conscience, but who is stuck or mired in serious blockages, in aspects that weigh down on, break, or destroy his ability to awaken and raise himself up in order to evolve. Open-mindedness that is hampered and slowed down because the person isn't ready, isn't sufficiently trained to envisage new concepts, other worlds and realities. Power-seeking and desire to visit the parallel worlds only for egocentric, selfish purposes. Inner wars and struggles among our different levels. Spiritual and conceptual extremism. Atheism, an overly rational mind and spirit.

SPIDER

Spiders, which belong to the arachnid family as do dust mite and scorpions, possess hooks or fangs that inject venom. They use these to paralyze and liquefy their prey. They also possess silk-producing glands, which they use to spin webs to entrap and bind their victims. All known spider species are predators and feed exclusively on live prey that they hunt by entrapping them in their webs, or, in the case of larger prey, by hiding to watch for their arrival and then attacking at the right moment.

Fear of spiders is one of the most widespread phobias because spider behavior symbolically represents the worst subtle or furtive attitudes a person can manifest in order to get what he wants: entrapping, binding, possessing, acting cruelly, satisfying his primary instincts through others , and feeding on others energetically and emotionally.

So as not to lose their prey, spiders reel it in, entwine and attach it; then, using their hooks, inject the prey with venom so as to liquefy it, because spiders feed exclusively on liquids. On a symbolic and metaphysical level, this represents a person who, through his attitudes, usurps and feeds on other people's emotions and vital energy.

Of course, spiders have their place and function in nature and its balance. They play an important role in the regulation of insect populations, which can have a very destructive effect if allowed to multiply uncontrolled. In terms of conscience and on the symbolic level, this indicates that the instinctive, cunning, patient, vigilant, and very efficient energy spiders represent, prevents a person from becoming too dispersed in his multiple needs to the detriment of his projects. Although spiders inspire fear in a lot of people, they are renowned for the beauty and solidity of their webs. They are masters of the art of spinning and weaving, and they carry out their art with astonishing patience, determination, and perfection. The silk they produce is very elastic and extremely resistant, which symbolizes the capacity to create a network and establish connections that are flexible, adaptable, strong, and long-lasting.

⊕ Great inner force that transcends possessive energy, cruelty, restraint, spitefulness and malevolence. Capacity to adapt and regulate when confronted with scattered, negative energies. Transcendence of deep anxieties.

⊖ Memories and negative forces related to possessiveness, domination, restraint, spite and malevolence. A person who feeds on other people's vital energy, who empties them of their energy, and who manipulates to get what he wants. Memories related to behavior that creates deep anxieties. Scheming, intrigue, lies. Paralyzed by phobias and fear. It is important to remember the Law of Resonance, which says that we always attract what we are. Hence the difficulties and ordeals we experience indicate which conscious or unconscious aspects of our being we need to work on.

SPINE, SPINAL COLUMN (backbone)

The spine, spinal column, or backbone is a symbol of structure. It represents the central pillar of our body, the axis that links us to Heaven and Earth. It also supports our head, hence our brain, our capacity to think. As it is situated in the back, it is also related to the past. Often associated with the image of a snake straightening up – a symbol of vital energy rising up through our spine –, it also represents our capacity to transcend the instinctual aspects of our life force, our animal nature, to direct and use our creative potential in a thoughtful, well-organized, right manner that seeks to develop qualities and virtues rather than satisfy primary needs and desires.

⊕ When it is in good condition, it symbolizes a solid, supple, reliable inner structure, indicating that memories of the past have been transformed and transcended. Uprightness, integrity, solidity, stability, flexibility, loyalty to values and Divine Principles. Transcendence of instinctual, vital energy, allowing us to activate the superior centers of conscience. De-structuring period that may be difficult and intense, but which serves to undo what is no longer in harmony with our original structure; its rectification ultimately leads to positive, harmonious, right structure.

⊖ Problems regarding the spine reveal difficulties related to a person's fundamental structure regarding his past, as a result of distorted values and principles that he has lived by for a very long time, possibly for several lives. Someone who has difficulty transforming and transcending his instinctual, animal, primary forces and attitudes. Over-emissive behavior that lacks receptivity on the structural level; or an overly receptive attitude that lacks emissivity, assertion of ourselves, our principles and values. Lack of uprightness, integrity, solidity, and flexibility.

SPIRIT

The spirit is related to the fire element as Primordial Fire, and whenever it is spelled with a capital letter, Spirit is symbolically defined as the Original Source, or Cosmic Intelligence. Spelled with a lower case *s*, it represents the human spirit, the vital energy that animates our body and soul. A human-being can be compared to a living computer, and our soul represents the hard drive, the space containing all of our memories and past experimentations; while our spirit symbolizes the electricity, the energy that makes it work in accordance with programs based on recorded memories and corresponding to our life-plan. Hence, the Spirit/spirit acts like electricity and animates memories in accordance with programs that have to be experienced; it is also the Energy of God, the Supreme Intelligence that we all have within. The existential aim of we human-beings is to evolve thanks to our experimentations and to succeed in manifesting our divine energy, nature and potential. To do so, we need to transcend our instinctual needs, transform our unconscious memories, and fuse our individual spirit with the Universal Spirit.

⊕ Energy, vital forces, Pure Intelligence. Encounter with our primordial fire. Reflection and research to understand the role and function of the human spirit. Powerful, mystical experiences allowing us to understand the existence of the Universal Spirit and its multiple facets in the form of individual spirits through which the Energy of Life animates and activates everything that exists. Study of our creative forces.

⊖ Difficulty understanding the role of the Spirit/spirit and accepting the presence of a Superior Intelligence in the physical and metaphysical manifestations of Life. Problems with our vital energy and forces. A person that is disconnected. Atheism. Destructive inner fire, spirit.

SPIRITUALITY

Spirituality (from the Latin word *spiritus*, meaning spirit) is the study of the spirit, of the nature of the soul, of a person's inner life. Through spirituality, a person walks a spiritual path that leads him to open up to several currents of thought regarding the Divine so as to find the path that suits him to evolve. No matter what name we give to God, the aim of spirituality is to develop Qualities, Virtues, and Divine Powers, to study, understand, and gain access to the metaphysical capacities that are innate in all of us. Spiritual knowledge and powers allow us to know ourselves better and to understand in depth the meaning of our experimentations, as well as the situations and events that manifest in our life. To rediscover our spiritual powers, we have to cleanse our unconscious, transform the distorted memories we have accumulated throughout our multiple lives, which prevent us from fully experiencing our potential.

Spirituality designates the quest for meaning, hope, awakening, expansion of conscience, and ultimately, the fusion of spirit and matter. It includes the initiatic processes, rituals, and personal evolution work that we can accomplish through different methods and techniques which vary from one culture, one tradition to another. It is an intense transformation process that gradually leads us to spiritual autonomy. However, spirituality is not only that; to be spiritual is first of all learning to be receptive, to listen to what we feel and sense, our intuition, our inner voice, and to communicate with the Divine through meditation and prayer. Often, spirituality is considered a value or lifestyle that is incompatible with everyday life. This belief denotes an erroneous understanding of what spirituality really is: a means to incarnate, to embody spirit in matter so as to be able to experiment and experience it in accordance with Divine Laws, Values, and Principles; otherwise, we risk sinking into and getting bogged down, mired, imprisoned in matter, enslaved by it. The person who lives his spirituality in his daily life continually practices fusing spirit and matter in the various situations and events life offers him. In the beginning, the integration of spirituality on the material level may be difficult to conceive and live. For a certain length of time, we may feel torn between the negative forces contained in our unconscious memories, which often date back to past lives, and our desire to be and do what is right, to attain high levels of conscience, and altruism. Through the analysis of dreams and signs, with the help of symbolic language and the application of Divine Laws, we learn to know ourselves better, to adjust, to communicate with our soul, to gradually understand how our spirit and conscience work.

A spiritual person seeks to know the true meaning of life, the hidden meaning behind everything. All along his path, he works to achieve in-depth understanding, without rejecting the grounds for experimentation offered by matter. At the same time, he is aware of the fact that evil is educational, that it plays an evolutive role in the heart of the Great Whole.

In dreams, spirituality is represented by universal Forces, such as God, or accepted symbols, such as an Angel, White Light, a Deity, a sage, priest, monk, nun, guru, shaman, etc. It may also be a member of our family, a friend, a teacher who is known to be spiritual, or a child in all its purity, dressed all in white, etc. The environment, context, and general atmosphere of the dream will let the dreamer know if his spirituality is pure, luminous, solid, profound, authentic, right; or, on the contrary, if it is dark, extremist, superficial, based on false beliefs, etc. For instance, seeing a member of a religious order exhorting his congregation or followers to vengeance would reveal fanaticism, whereas seeing a sage meditate or prone non-violence would indicate right spirituality.

⊕ Allows us to acquire better knowledge of ourselves by developing receptivity, intuition, inner listening, communion with God, meditation and prayer. A spiritual path that involves the cleansing and purification of the unconscious, of memories of negative experimentation and experiences recorded in this life and in previous lives, as well as the rectification and transformation of erroneous ways of thinking and behaving. Spiritual experimentation, mystical experiences, metaphysical studies and research gradually leading to true Knowledge, Wisdom, unconditional Love, multi-dimensional understanding, and a unified conscience. Work on ourselves to develop Qualities, Virtues, and Divine Powers in order to become a better person. Study of dreams, signs, and the deep meaning of our life, of our existence on Earth. Discovery of the parallel worlds, metaphysics *via* meditation, dreams, signs, and symbolic language. Development of clairvoyance, clairaudience, and clairsentience. Understanding the true meaning of spirituality, which is to be found in the marriage of the spirit and matter in the heart of our daily life. An open, fraternal, altruistic, universal spirit. Study of spiritual currents of thought, integration of the meaning of sacredness. Apprenticeship of spiritual practices (meditation, interiorization, prayer, rituals, mantras, yoga, etc.) to unify body, soul, mind, and spirit, and maintain contact with the Divine within ourselves and in all things. Belief in God, in the Divine, in Cosmic Intelligence that is right and full of love, in the Creator, no matter what Name we give Him. Study of initiatic science. Understanding Hidden Wisdom. A great initiate who has developed the capacity to raise the veil to gain access to Knowledge.

⊖ Problems related to the study of the spirit, to self-analysis and self-knowledge, to the metaphysical dimension of life. Fear of knowing ourselves in depth, lack of faith and confidence in our Divine nature. Negative representations and ideas that don't give priority to Divine Qualities and Virtues. Fleeing reality, over-abstract research, lacking a concrete dimension. Someone who is confused, lost, has no faith or beliefs; or, who is an extremist in his search for spirituality and spiritual research, who imposes his point of view and forces others to think and believe as he does. An overly materialistic, puritanical, or megalomaniac attitude, a tendency to believe we are superior because of our spiritual knowledge. Superficial spirituality, based on appearances, on form. Atheism. Religious fanaticism, sectarianism, abuse of spiritual power. Manipulation of other people's conscience and beliefs. Diffusion of erroneous spiritual concepts. Charlatanism, someone who abuses people's good faith. Difficult experimentations caused by the absence of motivation, rigor, and discipline.

SPOON

The symbolic meaning of a spoon is related to giving and receiving, to our capacity to nourish ourselves and others on both the physical and emotional levels since we usually use it to eat liquid food, or mixtures of solids and liquids. Its rounded, hollow shape makes it a symbol of receptivity too. Safe and easy to handle, it is an appropriate utensil for young children, both to feed them and for them to learn to feed themselves. Used for measuring purposes in the preparation of meals as well as for serving purposes, a spoon allows us to compose, mix, stir and share food/nutritional resources.

⊕ Receptivity, a capacity to prepare, measure out, mix, and stir, share, give and receive physical and emotional nourishment. Safe apprenticeship regarding nourishment.

⊖ Difficulty receiving and giving, preparing and sharing nutritional resources on the physical and emotional levels. A tendency to overeat and force others to overeat on the physical and emotional levels. A lack of receptivity. Problems regarding the apprenticeship of food. Bulimic or anorexic tendencies.

SPORT

Sport represents a state of conscience related to action, willpower, dynamism, and motivation. It allows us to develop focus, concentration, and discipline in our objectives of life. It inspires victory and success. It leads to physical and mental fitness, and self-esteem when our intention is right and not focused on competition, but rather on developing, improving, and surpassing ourselves. It favors conscious or unconscious liberation of accumulated tension, stress, and negative forces.

Sport should be part of a well-balanced life, focused on a healthy mind in a healthy body. Sport allows us to discipline the mind, activate it, and train it to follow our life objectives. Practiced with wisdom, without exaggeration, it is a healthy way to have fun, renew and replenish our energies, and relax on the physical, emotional and intellectual levels, as well as to be in contact with ourselves and nature, as the case may be.

On the symbolic level, each sport has its own particularity: e.g. swimming stimulates the swimmer to develop ease, strength, and suppleness or flexibility on the emotional level because it concerns the water element; running, hiking, or walking trains the soul regarding the willpower to advance, to attain objectives and goals; hence someone who lacks willpower to get up and go, to move forward, to advance, may rediscover these capacities, and a person who has too much willpower learns to channel it, to dose it more correctly. All sport helps to liberate the mind and spirit, vital energy, accumulations of tension and problems. Sport can be practiced as active meditation, when we take care to have right intention and motivation, and we renounce competitive and comparative attitudes.

⊕ Allows us to activate and develop willpower, perseverance, discipline, endurance, leadership, concentration, courage, bravery. Transformation, transcendence of negative forces, elimination of stress, depression, and hyperactivity. Development of mental forces, flexibility. Activation of receptivity (the feminine principle) and emissivity (the masculine principle). Practicing sport without competition, with good team spirit, coordination, mutual help, solidarity, fraternity. Dynamizes vital energy, awakens the sleepy, the lazy. Procures self-esteem, *joie de vivre*, a feeling of liberty and accomplishment. Consciously and unconsciously reinforces good, positive, authentic values and principles of life. Engenders great willpower for advancing and self-fulfillment.

⊖ Either lack or excess of willpower, perseverance, discipline, endurance, leadership, and courage. Excessive competitive spirit, exaggerated training, overwork. Pushing ourselves to the extreme through a need for recognition and acknowledgement. Complexes of superiority and/or inferiority. Lack of confidence, self-esteem, and respect for others. Laziness, disconnection, dropping out, letting ourselves go. Seeking emotions and strong sensations so as to feel more alive or to fill inner emptiness. Egotism, absence of team spirit, boasting, pride. A clannish spirit that separates, divides, compares, and judges only according to results, performance. Seeking to win at all costs, over-confidence. Rigidity, extremism. Sporting activity serving to express and give free rein to our aggression rather than transforming it. Appearances. A will to control. Basing everything on the physical, on brute force, a lack of refinement.

SPOUSE, LIFE PARTNER (husband, wife)

Our spouse or life partner represents aspects of our inner man or woman, of our emissivity, our masculine principle, or our receptivity, our feminine principle. It is a very important symbol of fusion on the couple-relationship level as well as the materialization of our intimate life. Our spouse or life partner reveals a considerable part of ourselves, and the resonances we have with him/her in his/her qualities as well as in his/her distortions. Our spouse is the person we should be able to fuse with on all levels. It is important to understand that before we can experience this fusion on the outer level, we first need to achieve it on the inside, with our two polarities, with our inner couple. The goal of the union between a man and a woman is to attain the highest levels of conscience, love and wisdom, to experiment their divine nature and the Creative Force of Life in fusion with the other person.

The term life partner usually refers to couples who share their life without being officially married and may also represent a certain reserve regarding commitment and total fusion with the other person. Some people simply use the word partner, a term usually employed in the business world. This may represent a fusion mainly on the material level. If, at a mature age, people refer to their girlfriend or boyfriend, this represents a relationship that lacks depth and real fusion, true sacredness.

⊕ Fusion in love and wisdom. Peace and marital harmony. Revelations regarding a shared life, or projects to be carried out together. A capacity to create an atmosphere and ambiance of great well-being, divine pleasures in the intimate life. An energizing, vivifying, inspiring sexual relationship. Unification of the spouses' potential of emissivity and receptivity. Development of an ability to sense and know if a person is a suitable spouse-to-be, or not.

⊖ Relationship problems. Difficulty finding an appropriate spouse. An incapacity to create a harmonious, peaceful marital life, which leads to well-being. A tendency to take life as a couple, our couple relationship, lightly; reticence to commit on all levels. Memories of infidelity, betrayal, and rejection. Emotional, affective wounds, traumatizing experiences on the loving, intimate, sexual level. Selfishness and self-centeredness, which prevent correct, right fusion between a man and a woman. An incapacity to see what is wrong on the masculine and feminine polarity level in ourselves. A lack of understanding that the outer couple is always a reflection of the capacity or incapacity to harmonize and fuse these two principles within ourselves, and that to experience and live a beautiful couple relationship on the outside, we must first purify memories related to former love experiences.

SPRING (the season)

Spring represents re-birth, the beginning of a new stage in life, a new cycle of activity, creativity, experimentation, apprenticeship and learning. It bears new energies; fecundity; it is the season of love, and the launching of new projects because everything is favorable to development and growth. In Nature, it is the time when the sap rises in the trees, seeds germinate, vegetation grows again, and animals come out of the torpor of winter and hibernation to take up their active life again, their migrations, etc.

⊕ Awakening, rebirth, renewal, new departures, second wind. Vitality, dynamism, renewed, increased energy, growth, development, expansion, evolution. Fecundity on all levels. A favorable period for amorous encounters, the blossoming of beautiful feelings and sentiments in relationships. Propitious energy to prepare and launch new projects, new creations. The start of a new stage accompanied by childlike qualities: freshness, spontaneity, enthusiasm, natural curiosity, light-heartedness, *joie de vivre*, eternal youth. Harmonious transition from an introverted phase to an extrovert phase, from a period of retreat, isolation, withdrawal, and/or emotional coldness toward a new opening onto the outside world, social life, and interaction with others.

⊖ Difficulty regenerating, renewing ourselves, being reborn, beginning a new cycle of apprenticeship, of experimentation, of growth, of expansion. Seeking rapid, superficial growth and expansion; or, difficulty emerging from inertia, torpor, and passivity; difficulty welcoming life. A period of sterility, stagnation, failure. May be related to artificial, frivolous, libertine behavior. Superficial encounters and exchanges. A tendency to want to force stages and natural cycles. Impatience, intolerance, refusal to adapt. Sadness, heaviness, apathy, discouragement. A lack of vitality, dynamism, flexibility, suppleness, spontaneity, light-heartedness, *joie de vivre*, confidence and trust in life. An incapacity to engender beautiful feelings and sentiments.

SQUARE

A square is a regular four-sided polygon, i.e. its four sides are of equal length and its four angles are right angles. The first representations of a square date back to prehistoric times. Along with the circle, it is one of the most studied geometric figures since Antiquity. Like all geometric forms, a square represents a fundamental, archetypal concept. In a dream, geometric forms announce a new apprenticeship, and like the first numbers, they indicate the very first stages of materialization. A square represents well-balanced structure, solidity, and stability. Starting with a square base structures the movement of expansion both horizontally and vertically. It may also be associated with the four natural elements (fire, air, water, and earth), with the four cardinal points (north, south, east, and west), as well as the four seasons. Hence it is a symbol of structure of the elements of the Earth and matter. It is also a symbol of limitation; figuratively speaking, a person is described as *a square* when he is too rigid, lacks flexibility and open-mindedness and tends to be restrictively conservative. On the other hand, to *square* things with someone means to settle things, to set things straight, to resolve any issues there might have been.

⊕ The beginning of materialization, a solid, well-structured, stable construction. Regularity, uniformity, balance. May also indicate rigor, precision and exactitude on the level of thoughts, words and deeds. Also symbolizes a positive framework.

⊖ Problems related to the structure and the initial phase of a construction. A lack of stability, balance, and regularity. Limitation due to a lack of creativity and open-mindedness. Coldness, a drastic attitude. Square-minded, rigid ideas. A lack of flexibility and adaptability.

STAIRS, STAIRWAY

Symbolize a capacity to gain access to another stage/phase, to move from one level to another by going up or down. Ascending stairs represents a dynamic of elevation toward the world of thoughts, the causal, divine world, or toward a more global vision of a situation experienced, which we may observe from a more elevated level of conscience. Descending stairs represents incarnation, entering action. A stairway leading below ground level, to a basement or into the depths of the earth, indicates that we have access to memories lodged in our unconscious (symbolized by the basement), or that we are able to visit regions of our inner landscape, various levels of our unconscious where our oldest memories have been recorded. According to how far down we go, we may penetrate what is preparing to emerge.

⊕ *Going up* stairs symbolizes our conscience rising into the world of thoughts, toward global vision and understanding that includes cause and consequence. Access to high levels of conscience. Symbolically we rise toward Heaven; hence we accede to the causal world, which is a source of very important information for our soul. Integration of new knowledge that offers better understanding of people and life in general. *Seeing ourselves go down* a stairway represents entry into the world of action, material experimentation, a capacity to incarnate our potential. *Seeing ourselves go below ground level,* down into the earth announces the discovery of new areas of our unconscious. (*cf. also* **Step**(s))

⊖ *Difficulty rising* onto the thought level and gaining access to the causal world. May indicate a will to rise in order to flee physical reality and the world of consequences; or, *difficulty incarnating* and entering action to materialize our potential, and to visit areas of our subconscious and unconscious. Problems of superiority and inferiority.

STAMMER *cf.* ***Stutter***

STATION (train/bus/coach)

A station is a place where trains or buses arrive and depart. It comprises various installations for multiple functions, including the arrival and/or departure of travelers toward a destination, the loading and unloading of goods and luggage, indicating that the person sends, receives, or transports collective and individual resource; the relative security of traveling by train or bus reveals a capacity to ensure our safety during collective transport. A station is an important individual and social symbol related to our capacity to travel on the earth level. It also represents an ability to circulate resources in the collectivity, and hence visit and discover other aspects of ourselves, other inner countries and regions. A station also evokes personal and social change, a passage from one stage to another on the action level.

A large city station often evokes a similar state of conscience to an airport, the major difference being the connection with overland means of travel, hence its relationship with the concrete world of action. (An airport is related to the air element, which is symbolically related to the world of thoughts, ideas, and concepts.)

Of course, for a correct interpretation of a station in a dream, as for all symbols, all of its details, such as its location (in a city, in the countryside, in the mountains, etc., above or below ground level, even in space), its importance (local, intercity, international), the reigning atmosphere, etc., must be added to the equation.

⊕ Point of departure or arrival for a greater or smaller life change on the action level; or passage from one stage to another on the personal and social levels. Desire to change our life; or, searching for a new direction on the level of social action. Harmony while traveling and advancing on the collective scale. Facility for traveling and discovery. Guidance toward a new destination on the action level. Opening of conscience regarding our own inner regions.

⊖ An incapacity or difficulty to bring about a change in our life, to move from one stage to another on the action and social levels. Blockages, limitations, an impasse; or, someone who seeks to flee his life plan. Lack of orientation, direction. Disorientation related to the multiple choices to be made to direct our life. Absence of synchronicity. Tendency to want to force change. Blocked horizons. Fear of evolving and changing.

STEP(S), STAIRS

A stair-step, a step or rung on a step-ladder, a step up onto another level, onto a landing, any step or stairway in fact symbolizes a capacity to step or go up, to raise ourselves up toward the causal world or seek a more global vision, better understanding. A step downward represents our descending into the world of action, our will to incarnate so as to materialize and concretize our ideas. When the steps or stairs go down into a cellar, basement, or any underground place, they symbolize a descent toward memories lodged in our subconscious and the different layers of our unconscious.

A doorstep symbolizes a capacity to go from an outer, social state of conscience to an inner, intimate one, from outside to inside; a staircase symbolizes a capacity to go from one state of conscience to another (as represented by each floor) while respecting the necessary stages. The figure of speech *step by step* is a good expression for gradual progress, respecting each stage, whether on the personal, professional or spiritual level.

⊕ A capacity to raise ourselves up as regards matter, to attain a more advanced, more global, more causal level of understanding; or, the will to descend into the concrete world, to become active and take action to fulfill ourselves, to materialize projects, to put into practice what was understood. Possibility to explore the unconscious and the subconscious, to encounter memories that are ready to be unveiled, and to discover resources we didn't know we had. (*cf. also* **Stairs, stairway**)

To climb the steps of a podium with humility, with right bearing: Victory. Great success, recognition and acknowledgement on the social level.

⊖ *Rushing up steps or stairs*: fleeing matter and the concrete level. *Climbing the steps of a podium with too much confidence and/or arrogance*: a feeling of superiority, seeking power and glory. *Difficulty climbing steps or stairs*: a lack of motivation or a tendency to force success, elevation; difficulty considering events from a causal level; an accumulation of intellectual, emotional, and/or spiritual heaviness. *Over rapid, rushed, precipitated descent of steps*: fleeing the causal or spiritual world; the person is too attracted to matter and the world of action. *Not wanting to descend*: a lack of humility, resistance, fear, or lack of willpower to become active and take action to materialize, or to visit unconscious memories.

STICK

Symbol of emissivity and power, a stick represents a state of conscience of authority, support, strength, power, taking charge of a situation, advancing, effort, defense in case of danger; or, dynamics of attack, domination, subjugating others; or, rebellion and discontentment.

⊕ Symbol of power, justice, authority, assertion, strength and courage. Support, assistance, and protection in difficult moments or situations. Force that helps set ourselves in motion, take action, advance. Capacity to master our strength and force and be an enlightened leader. Beautiful, right, just emissivity.

⊖ Abusive or unjust, wrong use of force, power, and authority. Memories of aggression and destruction; or, on the contrary, resignation, impotency, lack of strength and courage to assert ourselves, defend ourselves, or act when protection is needed. Threatening, repressive, tyrannical, dictator behavior. A spirit of rebellion, of attack. An offensive, aggressive, belligerent, warlike attitude. Assuming the role of victim or ill-treated, abused person. Excessive, unbounded emissivity.

STIFF NECK, TORTICOLIS

A stiff neck, medically referred to as *torticolis*, a term which comes from the Latin words: *tortus* (twisted) and *collum* (neck). It consists in a painful contraction of the neck muscles. Muscles symbolize a capacity to be active, to take action, motivation, and the willpower to manifest. Since a stiff neck hampers head movements, it is symbolically related to the level of thoughts, decisions, and authority regarding our capacity to act concretely. Before manifesting as a concrete, physical, muscular contraction or tightness, a stiff neck or torticolis is metaphysically engendered by tensions and rigidity in our mental world. It may also be an indication of hyperactive behavior, difficulty granting ourselves time to rest, a tendency to be scattered and dispersed, either due to looking in all directions to make sure we act well; or, because we are influenced by multiple needs and desires. It may also reveal unhealthy curiosity, libertine, licentious thoughts, a lack of fidelity.

A person who creates too many discrepancies between what he thinks on the one hand, and what he decides and does on the other, who often displays behavior that oscillates between rigidity and immobility, laxity and dispersal. Hence, when he finds himself in a situation where his mental rigidity prevents his energy from flowing freely in action, a stiff neck occurs to show him the level on which the malfunction is situated. Someone who exerts too tense, too rigid authority may also find himself immobilized by a stiff neck indicating his lack of flexibility. However, the other extreme, i.e. a tendency to laxity and dispersal, leading a person to continually change direction, and move his head and neck too much, also engenders situations that are conducive to a stiff neck. Hampering the freedom of movement and direction of the head, a stiff neck forces the person to re-center, to refocus his energy and scattered thoughts, to learn to look and think in a right, just, qualitative manner, without rigidity or dispersal, with right flexibility.

⊕ Incites us to reflect on our tendency to be dispersed, hyperactive, over-focused on our needs; or, too rigid both on the mental level as well as in behavior and actions. Helps us understand the need to have a supple, flexible mind and spirit while remaining well-centered and focused in action. Awareness of a lack of flexibility on the level of decisions, which are dictated by fears, or reflect overly rigid authority and ways of thinking. Acceptance of our limitations. Favors the apprenticeship of discernment, integrity, right orientation, fidelity to Divine Principles. Incites us to work on ourselves to rectify discrepancies between our thoughts, emotions, and concrete action, to cleanse distortions and blockages recorded in our unconscious. Allows us to re-center, to take care of ourselves, to liberate inner tensions so as to attain a state of serenity that we will then emanate and communicate on the outside too.

⊖ Process of decision-making tinged by multiple needs and desires; or, influenced by rigidity, fears, anxieties, insecurity. Libertine behavior, infidelity, or limitation caused by mental rigidity and a lack of discernment, which prevents the person from evolving with panoramic, global vision and opening toward others as well as unknown parts of himself. Hyperactivity, dispersal, scatterbrained in action; or, someone who is too concentrated, too focused on results. Excessive willpower to make things advance; or, immobility. Difficulty communicating, being open and adopting the right vision of the outside world, of our entourage. Difficulty orienting ourselves, finding which direction to take, as well as communicating our intentions in the right way. Limited vision or excessively puritanical. Lack of love, gentleness, flexibility for those parts of ourselves or others that we find difficult to accept. Lack of understanding of accumulated discrepancies between our thoughts, our feeling/emotions (since the neck is the passageway between the head and the heart) and actions. Communication problem between the metaphysical (thoughts, emotions) and physical (actions) worlds.

STING, BITE, PRICK, A

A sting, bite, or prick is a little wound caused by a very pointed instrument, the sting or bite of an insect, the thorn of a plant, as well as the stinging feeling felt on our skin after the application of certain, strong medical substances. It is fundamentally a symbol of intense emissivity, serving to defend or nourish ourselves, as in the case of certain insects (bee, wasp, mosquito, etc.), to protect ourselves like certain plants (roses, thistle, cactus, etc.), or to disinfect and heal as the stinging effect of certain medical substances, including the pricking of medical injections. We may also prick ourselves involuntarily, for example, when sewing or doing handiwork.

In order to understand the symbolic, metaphysical meaning of a sting, bite, or prick, we need to establish a link between its origin, the part of the body that is affected, the beneficial or harmful effects it produces, and what we were doing or thinking about at the time of the sting or prick. For example, if we prick a finger of our right hand while mending clothes because we were in a hurry to finish and move on to do something else, we look at the symbolism of the hand and finger concerned, as well as of sewing and clothes. We also make the link with impatience and a tendency to over-focus on matter, on all that we think we have to do, not taking time to concentrate calmly on one task at a time and doing each task as an active meditation.

If the prick comes from a plant, e.g. a rose we want to pick, we question ourselves as to our intention at the moment of cutting, or putting it into a vase: why and where did we pick or buy it? Who is it for? What was our mind and soul state when we were picking, buying, or putting it into a vase? Was it really the right, appropriate moment to offer a flower, a rose? What were our expectations, our motivation in offering it? What does the intended receiver represent for us? What color is it? By reflecting on the answers to all of these questions, we do great conscience or awareness-raising work on the inner level, thanks to which we will be able to detect the pricking, stinging attitude or intention we emanated in this situation regarding ourselves and/or others, as the case may be. We then recognize the manifestation of the Law of resonance in the concrete, physical prick, sting, or bite, and the immediate return of karma that we created: we prick or sting others with our intention, our mental or emotional energy, and we ourselves instantaneously feel the effect, the consequence on the physical level.

In some countries, it is insect stings or bites that bother people during certain periods of the year. Depending on their intensity, they may even be a source of infection and illness/disease with more or less serious consequences on the health and hygiene level. Moreover, the physical and metaphysical marks, scars, and after-effects they leave are inscribed and accumulate in the personal and collective memories of the individuals affected, thereby engendering, on the mental and emotional levels, a fear of insects, a fear of traveling in certain countries at certain times of the year, etc. In order not to get stuck in this kind of negative thought or emotion, it is important to understand that stinging, biting insects symbolically represent parts of ourselves that use their instinctual force to bite and sting, to bother and annoy others on the thought level (if the insect in question can fly).

Consciously or unconsciously, we all can engender pricking, stinging, biting vibrations that have the power to create tension, ill-being, outbursts of anger, or conflicting situations. Sometimes a mosquito bite can become quite a considerable trigger element, leading the bitten person to exaggeratedly aggressive behavior. This is due to the fact that, within the person, the bite awakened a block of memories of aggression, possibly accumulated and repressed over several lives, while secretly nourishing feelings and sentiments of rancor, resentment, bitterness, and revenge. Hence, a short visit to a mosquito-infested region may suffice to cause the memory reservoir to overflow and activate these long retained, repressed forces. Some people may then truly manifest vengeful behavior, and fiercely swat at and strive to kill every single mosquito that goes by. However, such behavior doesn't help them settle their fundamental problem, because mosquitoes only serve as scapegoats, while their aggressive force, although expressed, has not yet been transformed.

It is essential to understand that whatever bothers us, whatever we seek to fight or kill on the outside, always reflects aspects and parts of ourselves that we reject or wish to eliminate from our life, from ourselves. That biting mosquito may be a particularly annoying boss or work colleague, a former friend turned enemy, an irritating, bothersome neighbor, etc. Understanding that an insect bite or sting represents a state of conscience that manifests through dominating or hurtful emissivity, we can work to transform these forces and memories, which, through resonance, attract into our lives, *pricking, stinging, biting* people, elements, and events. We then consider all forms of pricks, stings, or bites as a stimulation of our physical and metaphysical immune system, which is then fortified and better able to face certain harmful circumstances. On the subtle levels, we are continually exposed to pricking, stinging, biting energies, coming from other people's distorted thoughts and emotions. However, these can only affect us if we resonate with them. This means that when we work on transforming our own negative resonance with stings, pricks, and bites, we are no longer sensitive and receptive to their effects.

However, a prick or sting may also be the result of right intention and have positive effects: e.g. in the medical context when a vein is pricked for a blood sample or donation, or when our vein, skin, or muscle is pricked and injected with medical substances to help cure us or alleviate intense pain; it's the same for acupuncture; and similarly, the stinging effect of certain antiseptic substances to deep cleanse a wound to help it heal. Of course, when we prick a human being or animal to insert a syringe full of harmful substances, such a gesture creates negative karma for which, one day, the person will have to take responsibility, one way or another. Similarly, the pricking of needles associated with drug addiction belongs to the negative aspects of this verb.

⊕ An ability to sublimate and transcend aggression, and a feeling or sentiment of revenge that may be felt in annoying, trying situations, where we may be stung, pricked, or bitten concretely, physically, or more subtly, on the metaphysical level. Development of endurance, tolerance, resistance, and detachment in the face of irritations that annoy, bother, and hurt us. A capacity to remain serene, calm, peaceful in the face of negativity, to understand it and transform it by applying the Law of resonance.

The prick of a medical injection: Allows the injection of a liquid (emotion) substance into the physical body to heal, cure, or attenuate pain caused by a wound, injury, or illness/disease. May help us overcome a difficulty, transform the negative, and offer us a second chance.

Insect bite or sting: Causes us to react and incites us to consciously work on ourselves to improve our character and master critical, aggressive, stinging, pricking, biting forces and minor needs or discontentments of our own; or, those we encounter on the concrete, emotional, or mental levels of others, in different personal, professional, or social contexts.

⊖ A tendency to sting, prick, or bite others on the energy level, with our thoughts and emotions; or, to be stung, pricked, or bitten, to have our vital energy in relationships and unhealthy dynamics *vampirized*, without understanding that this is the result of karmic consequences. Awakening and activation of memories where we have accumulated feelings and sentiments of aggression, violence, revenge, intolerance, impatience, fear or anxiety and anguish; an attitude of flight, choosing not to expose ourselves to situations that could trigger the forces contained in these memories in order to avoid having to call ourselves into question and work on ourselves. Harsh, critical, hurtful, intolerant forces that don't respect others, that impose their point of view, their way of doing things.

The prick of a medical injection: Fear of syringes and the pain caused by the prick, which may indicate a person's resistance to healing, to getting better, his not accepting to make the necessary efforts to improve his state, to help himself heal or be cured; or, it may indicate the presence of memories where the person recorded great suffering, an experience of martyrdom, as well as intense emotions of fear and fright that caused him to flee or lose consciousness; or, on the other hand, excessive, unhealthy use of syringes to inject drugs (narcotics), which are the unhealthy emotions a person anesthetizes himself with, when confronted with the same, very great suffering. A lack of receptivity and inner and outer listening. An encounter with parts of ourselves that are too emissive, symbolically represented by the person who administers the injection, his attitude, behavior, voice, way of speaking, moving, etc.

Insect bite or sting: A tendency to impose ourselves on the relational and social levels with a stinging, pricking, biting, annoying, irritating energy that seeks to control and dominate others through constant criticism. Confrontation with very emissive forces, needs, or instinctual discontentment, that cause dispersal, a lack of concentration, and nourish themselves aggressively on just about anything, where any pretext serves to nourish such forces in us.

STOMACH (abdomen, belly, tummy)

The stomach, abdomen, belly or tummy region, is the place where the digestive, purifying, transformational functions of the body are concentrated. This is also where the 2nd chakra is situated, just above the navel. It is related to our vital needs, sexuality, and sensual pleasures. Hence the stomach (abdomen, belly, tummy) is related to everything concerning our needs, our instincts, as well as material and sensorial abundance.

It also houses the womb. Before coming into this world, a human-being develops in his mother's womb, in the amniotic liquid, symbolizing the world of emotions and sensitivity. With all of its power of creation and transformation, the stomach (abdomen, belly, tummy) is therefore symbolically related to emotions; and it is sometimes called the *second brain* or the *emotional brain.* Whenever we feel a positive emotion, (love, joy), or a negative one (fear, anxiety), physical manifestations of these emotions are experienced in this region.

The abdomen is an alchemical crucible (or cauldron), a zone of creation, digestion, and transmutation of life's experiences.

⊕ Capacity to digest, transform, assimilate, integrate nourishing resources, and the experiences of life on the physical and metaphysical levels. Alchemical power. Emotional intelligence. An ability to purify and master instinctual, emotional, sentimental, affective needs. A great force of love that creates ambiances, taste, sensation, fulfillment. Fertility, fecundity, giving birth. A capacity to manage material and sensorial abundance. Divine pleasures.

⊖ Incapacity to assimilate well, to digest, transform and integrate nourishing resources. Emotional force oriented toward the satisfaction of selfish needs, seeking only personal pleasure, and/or power. A conscience that is overly instinctual, animal-like, focused on survival, on the satisfaction of crude, primary needs. Envy, jealousy, continually comparing ourselves with others and maintaining a competitive spirit. Nervousness, unpleasantness, annoyance, upset. Difficulty accepting a situation, understanding it in depth. Incapacity to go within, to interiorize to understand the meaning of an ordeal. Perception limited to the world of consequences. Tumultuous emotions, affective, emotional dependency, fear of loss or lack, conscious or unconscious possessiveness, emotional imbalance, all of which engender digestion problems of all sorts, including overweight, and even going as far as tumors, cancer. Repressed needs, blockages, retention, heaviness. Sterility, difficulty conceiving.

STONE *cf.* ***Rock*** ; *cf.* ***Mineral***

STORAGE DEPOT *cf.* ***Warehouse***

STORM

On the physical level, a storm is a violent, atmospheric disturbance, characterized by electrical phenomena (lightning, thunder), often accompanied by rain and wind. In nature, a storm occurs when, on days of great heat, warm air loaded with humidity rises and, high in the sky, encounters a cold layer of clouds, whose water particles have a different electrical charge. Their encounter creates tension, pressure differences, cloud and air (thoughts) movements, which bang and collide into each other, producing the electrical phenomena of thunder and lightning. They symbolize an over-emissive expression of the force of our spirit, as well as heavy, tense thoughts and emotions.

This natural weather manifestation corresponds symbolically, and principally, to tensions accumulated on the level of our mind, spirit, and willpower, which engender and maintain thoughts, causing our emotional level (heat, humidity) to over-heat. People who resonate with stormy weather in their inner world and climate, generally notice that they tend to be more impulsive, tense, clumsy, nervous, agitated, annoyed, impatient, bad-tempered and angry before a storm, and once the storm is over, they feel liberated, relieved, purified, cleared, just like the air, sky, and the weather on the outside.

Furthermore, the expression, *There's a storm brewing* is used both for outer, physical weather conditions, and to indicate that an individual, relational, or family atmosphere is full of tension, things left unsaid, frustration, retained anger, and could explode at any moment. There is a clear analogy between the natural processes that prepare a storm and those that operate in our inner climate.

The clouds that accompany a storm are often dark grey or black, indicating that we nourish negative, aggressive thoughts and emotions, causing disharmony, instability, clashes, tension, unease, and ill-being. This produces electricity, which on being discharged, engenders bad temper and a bad mood, outbursts of impatience, fits of anger, rows, verbal, and even physical, violence.

A storm may also be announced and occur in our dreams. A symbolic analysis of the details of the turbulence and its surrounding elements, enables us to grasp the kind of thoughts, emotions, and attitudes we need to keep an eye on and rectify, so as not to be the cause of a stormy situation in our daily life, in our family, couple, at work, etc., the following day. Sometimes, in a dream, after experiencing a storm, followed by good weather – the proverbial *calm after the storm*, the re-establishment of balance and equilibrium – on waking, we may feel liberated from the accumulated tension, the dark, heavy soul states that were weighing us down, crushing us. Such a dream experience may indeed help us purify and transform negative memories, frozen emotions, aggressive energies that have been retained for quite some time. This kind of dream is good proof that what we do at night in the subtle levels of our being always manifests, one way or another, in physical reality.

Storms may also be a sign of reaction, powerful affirmation and assertion, indicating a need to channel and evacuate accumulated tension so as to regain natural order and balance.

⊕ Allows for the liberation and evacuation of tension accumulated in our mind, spirit, thoughts, emotions, and conscious and unconscious memories. A great energetic, stimulating, vivifying force. Powerful assertion, liberation of tensions both in inner and outer nature, allowing the resolution of conflicts, the rediscovery of balance, the re-establishment of harmony and right order. Helps us de-compress, purify our soul states, rediscover or regain serenity, harmony, balance, the calm after the storm. Study of our resonance with storms and their corresponding symbolism. Conscious work on ourselves to transform the stormy atmospheres and ambiances on the inside, within ourselves, as well as in our relationships on the outside.

⊖ Difficulties related to stormy, angry, impulsive, accumulated tensions on both the conscious and unconscious levels. An overheated, reactive, aggressive mind and spirit. Violent, brutal, destructive behavior. A tendency toward excessiveness, immoderation. Insubordination, rebellion, disobedience, a lack of respect, listening and obedience. Hyperactivity, over-intense, too electrifying, electrocuting vital energy, that can burst out without any warning. Explosive impulsivity. Moroseness, negativity, somber, muddled, confused thoughts and emotions, full of frustrations, rancor, resentment, aggression, radicalism, and violence. An incapacity to understand the correspondence and resonance that exists between what we are going through on the inside, and the ordeals and stormy situations that we create and attract on the outside. Difficulty doing alchemy, transforming the negative into positive.

STOVE (cooker, hob, oven)

A device conceived to produce heat to allow the transformation, cooking or warming of food resources. As well as the hotplates (the hob) on which we set saucepans, a stove (or cooker) is usually also equipped with an oven, which represents the feminine principle, a capacity to receive, to contain. Through the heat it produces, a stove symbolizes love, and through the fire element that generates heat by means of electricity, gas, or wood, it is also a symbol of vital energy, of the power of our spirit that is capable of transforming, transubstantiating, fusing, and creating through alchemy.

⊕ Capacity to act as a source of heat and nourishing energy. Ability to transform nourishing, nutritional resources for ourselves and others with love and the power of vital energy. Great receptivity, generosity, helpfulness, and capacity for work. Capacity for alchemical transformation, transubstantiation. Kind, considerate, loving maternal or paternal spirit.

⊖ Incapacity or difficulty transforming nourishing resources due to a lack of heat, love, receptivity, generosity, and commitment, involvement. Problems with food, tendency to overeat as well as to impose food on others to impress them, to prove our worth, to be loved; or, lack of food resources for ourselves and others. Tendency to burn resources through distraction, negligence, carelessness; or, through excessive, over-emissive energy. Lack of loving kindness, consideration, and interest in looking after ourselves and others, in satisfying nutritional needs. A deficient maternal or paternal spirit. May be related to bulimia and/or anorexia.

STRESS

Stress is generally defined as a state of chronic physical and psychological tension that is perceived as negative, dangerous, or insurmountable by the sufferer. The stressed person finds it difficult to manage the pressure sometimes engendered by his multiple activities and responsibilities. Contrary to popular belief, there aren't two types of stress – positive/negative – because stress is never beneficial for the conscience.

Stress is mainly determined by the desire for concrete, material results, and such desire diminishes or excludes the real meaning of our life experiences, which consists in developing qualities and virtues. A state of stress also reveals that the sufferer lacks self-confidence, lacks confidence in his capacity to overcome the events with which he is confronted. Stress manifests in anxiety, fear, frustration, and fluctuation of vital energy, motivation and our driving force, our force for advancing; it induces an inhibition of action and/or a dissimulation of the person's reactions. Stress prevents a person from fulfilling himself completely, divinely.

Three types of causes may provoke states of stress: rapid change (positive or negative); threats or dangers we encounter (whether objectively founded or not); our impression (whether justified or not) of having to react rapidly in a situation.

If no action takes place, if nothing is done, if nothing is undertaken, then the risk of suffering from stress is considerably increased. The person refrains from acting by attenuating the intensity of his action, or by imposing limits that force the action to remain incomplete. Often, he goes further and calls a complete halt to his action, replacing it with immobility. Sometimes too, the person seeks to dissimulate his reactions: he forces himself to remain expressionless, or to eliminate the intensity of his reactions. This is when we can speak of inadequate management of pressure. When stress is experienced continually or repeatedly, it increases states of fear and anxiety, leading to fatigue, exhaustion, withdrawal, depression, and *burn-out*, increasingly limiting the affected person's potential, and gradually leading to his disengagement, his withdrawal from people, from the world. In other cases, a stressed person transposes to another state of conscience and regains calm, e.g. by listening to music, or by thinking about a positive person or situation; such behavior represents an intermediary stage of evolution, because the feeling of stress ceases, but the true cause, what triggered it, has not been settled or transformed, and consequently, it will return.

It is often change, novelty, the unknown, incertitude, frustrations and conflicts – all of which are challenging opportunities to surpass ourselves – that engender stress; hence our incapacity to organize our schedule adequately, by prioritizing our responsibilities according to their importance. A person may experience stress when he self-imposes high standards of performance, when he puts a lot of pressure on himself in order to be acknowledged, to please, and to be loved. Likewise when he has difficulty seeing and accepting reality as it is, constantly wanting to change it, and control the people and situations around him – even unconsciously – by forcing things, and not respecting the natural laws and everyone's personal rhythm. Whenever a person experiences stress, he often feels he should protect himself from something; he is in a kind of continual survival mode, focused on his ego and his needs that have become obsessive. Stress also influences our thoughts, emotions, and actions. Our thoughts may become confused, muddled, and/or obsessive; our emotions become too intense and agitated; and our actions, tainted with fear and rigidity. A person, who is capable of recognizing and admitting his errors is less subjected to stress.

A stressed person has erroneous beliefs that limit him in his materialization. His system of values is deformed or distorted since it is solely based on material success. Symbolically, stress is essentially ignorance of the fact that the sole purpose for our being here on Earth is not to obtain results at all costs (to the point of losing our health); it is to develop Qualities, Virtues, and Divine Powers, so as to improve ourselves and become better souls.

⊕ Indicates the need to do inner cleansing and transformation work on frustrations, discontentment, possessiveness, and the need for results and control. Incites us to better manage our tendency toward perfectionism. An apprenticeship of letting go, of developing a capacity to let go while remaining responsible and involved, committed, together with clear awareness that everything that happens to us is there to help us evolve. An indication of the fears, worries, anxieties, lacks, and insecurities that we have within ourselves. A necessary period for introspection, for calling ourselves into question, followed by the cleansing of accumulated memories and beliefs, as well as the rectification of erroneous behavior. A time of reflection, re-organization, and changes to be undertaken in our life to rediscover balance and harmony. Visiting the unconscious and the memories harbored therein. An invitation to embark on a spiritual path, to seek a different way of living. Leading to a new understanding of existence, of life. A motivating force that allows us to meet challenges, whatever they may be.

⊖ A state of high alert and survival, lack of letting go, a need to control everything. Difficulty managing change, novelty, the unknown, incertitude, frustrations, and conflicts. Difficulty adapting. Rigidity. Fears, anxieties, tensions, and cares. Mistrust, multiple worries. Muddled, confused, obsessive thoughts. Intense, agitated emotions. A lack of calm, not granting ourselves time to reflect, time to understand. Fatigue, withdrawal into our fears, disengagement or withdrawal on the social level. Immobilization, paralysis of our vital energy. Deeply disturbed. A dissatisfied perfectionist. Someone who is over-focused on matter and high performance, and thereby suffering from too much self-imposed pressure. An overly materialistic, limiting philosophy and lifestyle. Absence of spirituality. Difficulty accepting reality as it is, and recognizing our own errors. Flight or attack. An incapacity to understand our life program. A lack of faith in the Divine as well as in our own capacities.

STRIKE (related to work)

In the context of work, a strike represents the choice and the right not to work, not to put up with unfair conditions on the professional and social levels. A strike, which is when workers stop working, becomes necessary when bosses or companies exploit workers. It is declared when talks and common sense no longer lead to a solution. It is a means used to indicate deep discord concerning work and to ensure workers' rights and liberties are respected.

A strike may also relate to a person who is never content with his job, who exploits the system, always wanting more, demanding too many personal privileges and benefits. When a strike appears as a symbol in a dream, depending on the context, it indicates either too many demands regarding the job and the employer; or, a situation that requires taking a stand and the courage to say no to what is not right or fair on the work level.

⊕ May announce the end of a strike, of a major problem at work; or, indicate a capacity to assert ourselves in a peaceful way and refuse unfair conditions in the field of work. A period of questioning and readjustment to norms and ways of working. Help to develop awareness that the work each person does on the collective level allows us all to fulfill ourselves individually.

⊖ A period of rebellion, extreme demands, and perpetual dissatisfaction on the work level. A tendency to let ourselves be influenced and give in to the pressure of excessive protesters. An attitude that paralyzes other people's evolution. Multiple criticisms on the personal and collective levels. A complicated, egocentric person who only thinks of his own needs. A lack of global vision and understanding of the world of work. A person who exploits the democratic system. A lack of submission, insubordination. Ready to do anything to achieve our goals. Laziness, a mindset where the law of the least effort rules. Feeling of superiority.

STUDY, A *cf.* ***Office***

STUTTER, STAMMER

A stutter or stammer is a speech problem which is manifested by a spasmodic repetition of a syllable or an involuntary halt in speech rhythm. It denotes a state of hesitation, of inner confusion as well as a lack of self-esteem preventing the person from expressing himself and communicating with ease and fluency. Stuttering is caused by a lack of self-confidence and a deep feeling of inferiority. Having this kind of difficulty indicates that in another life the person greatly mocked others, bullied and prevented people from expressing and manifesting themselves. Stuttering is also related to games of power and dominating behavior wherein people deliberately leave things unfinished, intentionally keeping up a hesitant, indecisive attitude in order to have power over others and keep them waiting, hoping. An accumulation of this kind of behavior may create such karma that one day the person has to experience a limitation of his own capacity to express himself in order to understand the suffering he inflicted on others.

⊕ Work on healing memories related to a lack of self-confidence and self-esteem, a feeling of inferiority, hesitation, mockery, and discrepancies between body, mind, and spirit. Developing patience, perseverance, and humility. Detachment from other people's regard and judgment. Liberation from a feeling of guilt.

⊖ Isolation and introversion through a lack of self-assurance, self-confidence, and self-esteem. Inferiority complex. Shyness, feelings of stress and guilt. Hesitation and fear of communicating or manifesting because of awkward, halting speech. Blockages, limitations, and difficulties on relationship and social levels.

SUBWAY

A subway is a means of public transport that circulates on subterranean, underground, or aerial, overhead rails, without passing any other means of transport. It reflects a desire to protect the environment by centralizing means of displacement, hence economizing energy resources.

It allows us direct, rapid access to different places, for work, study, exchanging with others, materializing projects, etc. Consequently it represents multiple possibilities for changing direction, orientation regarding action and advancing in different domains of life.

Traveling by subway, either in concrete reality or in a dream, symbolically represents an encounter with both individual and collective unconscious memories. It reveals to passengers the unconscious motivations they have at the heart of their projects and intense, multiple activities, as well a large number of positive and negative attitudes and behavior that they have accumulated during the course of their different lives.

Whenever a subway circulates on ground level, its symbolism resembles that of a train, and it reveals how its passengers behave and act consciously in life. Whenever it is suspended overhead in the air, its symbolism refers to the mental, thought level, our way of thinking.

On awakening after a dream containing subway scenarios, we may feel burdened, heavy-hearted; or, scattered and dispersed, because we have visited memories and sometimes contradictory, multiple forces and influences, that travel and manifest simultaneously in our unconscious. They reveal parts of ourselves that go in different directions, each with its own ideas, projects, aims and objectives. In concrete reality, we encounter all sorts of people in the subway. Some subway travelers are very busy in matter and use the subway to get to work; others are very selfish and tend only to think of themselves; some are homeless; others drug addicts, suicidal, or more or less violent delinquents; but there are also members of the police force; shoppers of all sorts; tourists, people of all ages and nationalities, taking the subway to visit places of cultural and/or historic interest, etc. It is important to know that the people encountered represent more or less conscious aspects of ourselves. Seeing them in a dream, or observing them in concrete reality activates the resonance we have with them, often without our realizing.

A subway is an extraordinary meeting place of diverse culture and information that can help our evolution if we know how to integrate and master the resonance activated in us. Traveling by subway incites us to become more universal, to learn to healthily, calmly and serenely manage social intermingling on all levels, and not to let ourselves be led to nourish misanthropic, selfish, egotistical feelings and sentiments.

⊕ A great capacity to manifest socially and rapidly. An emerging, vivifying, very inspiring force to concretize and materialize. Stimulation of our will to become active, to set to work. Dynamism on the social level, on the action and advancing level, to materialize our life. Mastery of the forces of materialization on both the conscious and unconscious levels. Expansion of our conscience regarding our deep memories. Openness to others and discovery of new influences and possibilities. Acceptance, tolerance, and compassion for others. A capacity to manage multiple possibilities, while remaining focused on the aims and objectives to be attained. A sense of organization. Easy access to the collective unconscious while protected and advancing fluidly.

⊖ An awakening of scattered, dispersed, overflowing, delinquent, destructive forces and memories. Feelings of heavy-heartedness, insecurity, anxiety, or even anguish, when exposed to unconscious, collective energies. Intolerance, indifference, extreme individualism. Hyperactivity, excessive action, movement, materialization. Someone who is too down-to-earth, stifled, restrained, blocked, and closed in or imprisoned by matter. Difficulty making choices when confronted with the multiple opportunities and possibilities offered on the personal and social levels. An incapacity to get in touch with, to contact our unconscious memories related to materiality, advancing on the social level and in the world of action in general. A tendency toward schizophrenia due to the multitude of influences and directions.

SUGAR

Sugar is a food substance extracted from sugar cane or sugar beet. Its sweet, pleasant taste has made it into a product that is consumed daily in most countries. Symbolically, sugar is related to affective aspects since it procures sweetness and consolation; this substance allows us to instantaneously feel a stimulating, vivifying energy, emotional and affective abundance, a feeling of well-being and motivation, that gives us energy to advance and manifest. This source of energy rapidly stimulates the body, which immediately uses it to become active.

It is common knowledge that we all need to know how to master our sugar consumption, because, medium or long term, it is dangerous for our physical health and balance; it may lead to pathologies such as diabetes or cardio-vascular diseases; indeed, excess sugar is transformed into fat and stocked in our fat reserves, little by little creating obesity. Linked to affective aspects, sugar reveals dependency on the emotional, sentimental, affective level, a need to be loved, acknowledged and appreciated by others, and society in general. It also reveals a passionate aspect, emotional torments; or, a desire for performance, stimulation, and sensations. Sugar is negative when a person takes it to fulfill his inner lacks.

⊕ A source of stimulation, motivation, vivification, affectivity. A feeling of being rewarded. Affective abundance, sweetness, consolation, well-being. A choice of well-dosed, natural sugar indicating a desire for healthy, well-balanced nourishment. Work on the level of emotional, sentimental, affective needs. Stimulating energy that allows us to manifest rapidly.

⊖ Seeking stimulation, motivation to activate ourselves superficially, high performance willpower, too much rapid energy, hyperactivity; or, someone who forbids himself sweetness, pleasure, even when it's a question of good, natural, unrefined sugar in moderate quantities. Emotional, affective deficiencies, the person wants to satisfy his inner lacks, his desire for sensations, by using something on the outside (sugar); or, a rigid person who doesn't give himself the right to fulfill his emotional, affective needs, such as sweetness, gentleness, consolation, support, attention, rewards, and who seeks them on the outside. Coldness leading to an absence of inner softness, sweetness, gentleness, that we seek to fulfill by eating sugar. Bulimia, obesity. Emotional, affective dependency, sadness, passion, leading to a need for, or rejection of, sugar. Poor nourishment, erroneous use of resources, excesses, waste of energy; or, a lack of energy to manifest.

SUICIDE

Suicide represents the intentional end of a life on Earth. This death, however, is neither natural nor right, and through this act, the person who commits suicide expresses a total, definitive refusal of his life-plan: he does not want to do the work that is necessary for his evolution and this attitude causes him deep despair, discrepancy, and negative karma which leads him into dark, somber, very difficult regions. A person who takes his own life does so in the hope of setting himself free from his limitations, his blockages, and great inner suffering; it is the ultimate action of fleeing and attempting to escape, but it does not liberate him at all. On the contrary, the person is automatically transferred into worlds that represent his inner state, where anger, violence, and desolation exist; his stay in this other dimension is far from easy because his thirst for a better world hasn't been quenched.

If, from an early age, we were to receive metaphysical teaching regarding suicide, we would understand that this act denotes a refusal to learn, to evolve, which leads to very serious consequences after death and for subsequent lives. This understanding would put the brakes on such a destructive impulse and the person would opt for another choice: the choice of consciously working on his ill-being, his feelings of frustration and limitation. Knowing what awaits suicides in the next world helps us understand the importance of empathy, compassion, and respect for these suffering, suicidal people.

Committing suicide in a dream reveals very deep despair and indicates that we bear the seeds of self-destruction. Likewise, seeing another person kill himself in a dream, or even being confronted with a real-life suicide, indicates that we have to discover and analyze that part of ourselves that is totally discouraged, that wants to give up completely and self-destruct. It is also possible to visit the soul of another person in a dream so as to be able to help him in concrete reality. If this is the case, if we haven't been otherwise authorized by Up Above, we shouldn't tell him about the dream we received; we should simply surround him with a lot of love and kindness, talk to him, while deeply listening, offering him a very attentive ear. Hopefully such compassionate sharing will help teach him what suicide really is, either directly, or by subtly integrating an example of the suicide of someone we know, or a newspaper article telling the story of someone who was contemplating suicide, etc. to give him a sign that he bears this dangerous tendency within himself. Proceeding like this is more likely to awaken his interest and curiosity. Through the story we share, we will inform him about how the person's soul found itself in the parallel worlds, in the grips of great difficulties such as those mentioned above. It's a question of openly discussing the subject with a certain detachment so that he doesn't guess it may be him we are talking about, and yet with enough intensity to make an impression and help him understand the metaphysical consequences of suicide. If it is possible or appropriate, we could direct the conversation as if we were telling a child a story, or even read extracts from this entry.

Seen or experienced in a dream, suicide may indicate the intention of the person we dreamed of or our own intention to commit the act; or, it may announce the imminent death of the person we've dreamed of; or, that sooner or later, his life program is headed toward more suffering.

In concrete reality, many souls here on Earth today commit this crime against themselves; they cause their loved ones great suffering and transmit all of their failure, despair, sadness and desolation to them. Behind this act that cries out in pain and distress lies hidden a lack of values and principles, a life that is over-focused on matter, comparison, envy and social success, a rebellious aspect, as well as self-destructive forces that have accumulated in the soul for numerous lives. A suicidal person is an old soul whose inner computer is overloaded with negative memories, failures, frustrations, sorrow, a lack of self-confidence and self-esteem. When we lose our taste for life, we lose the taste for learning, making efforts, evolving. Suicide also denotes a lack of faith, of spirituality, of an authentic, transforming spiritual journey. The person doesn't want to exist any longer because he no longer wants to suffer; he no longer wants to have to strive and struggle.

Suicide is such a serious, brutal, decisive, deadly act in a person's life that it is important to examine in detail the reasons for and the consequences of this act. It results from a lack of understanding of the meaning of ordeals and it leads to very serious consequences for the soul, because after a suicide, our soul doesn't head off for vacations on the beach. Quite the contrary. It finds itself alone, or with other beings who have committed this act, in a parallel world, in desolate landscapes and dark, sad, terrifying places that correspond to his inner states. Although the film *What Dreams*

May Come presents this theme in a rather romanticized way, it is, nevertheless, an interesting example of what a suicided soul experiences. The film shows that once the act has been committed, the person remains in the state of conscience that drove him to this act. For a certain length of time, he may be confused, have doubts and fears, and undergo all sorts of negative, demanding, trying situations. His loved ones also live in confusion, not only because of their resonance, but also because the person who committed suicide may try to communicate with them. In this case, it is vital to invite him to concentrate on his inner work, to detach himself from Earth so as to be able to continue his spiritual path. He committed an act; now he has to accept responsibility for it and learn whatever lessons it teaches him.

On dying, most people are welcomed by the souls of recently deceased loved ones, who haven't yet reincarnated, or, by guides who take on the symbolic form of people they know so as to reassure them; for people who commit suicide, it's different. They are met by guide-therapists who are full of unconditional love and compassion, who fully understand the Principle of Divine Justice. These guides take charge of the suicide victims like doctors and therapists; or, when required, like policemen would do so on Earth when their suffering is too destructive, to help them face it before pursuing their apprenticeship in their next reincarnation on Earth.

When confronted with suicide, we must de-dramatize this wrong without trivializing this act which engenders serious consequences. It's the same as any other field wherein we commit a misaction (*cf.* this term), in order to fully realize what we've done and to rectify it, we have to reap what we've sown. The person who commits suicide will come back to Earth, where he will have to cleanse his memories; and not only will he have to live, to experience the difficulties he attempted to flee, but also those he engendered through this act; e.g. he may be confronted with the suicide of a member of his family, find himself alone, orphaned, devastated so as to help him recognize and acknowledge the value of life, to understand the importance of family, and to learn what suicide puts near and dear ones through.

If a member of our family commits suicide, it means we are connected to the egregore (*cf.* this term) of suicide. This event, along with all of the consequences it entails, teaches everyone something. In such a situation, we need to work on detachment, on freeing ourselves from feelings of guilt, and cleanse our own memories related to this event. It is good to remind ourselves that there are guides in the parallel worlds that are perfectly qualified to give the suicide victim all the appropriate help and care he needs. It is wise to let his soul go, not to seek contact with him, to trust Up Above, and work on our own hurt, our own wounds.

Usually, whenever we remain stable after the suicide of a loved one, it means we are at the last stage of a cycle engendered in another life. We are in the process of finalizing the healing of wounds and hurt related to former difficulties, such as lack of hope, perseverance, wisdom, and faith in the existence of a Divine Power. Once we have succeeded in cleansing these memories, instead of experiencing negative feelings of despair, grief, remorse, or guilt, we simply feel compassion and empathy, and we go on living serenely, accepting the other person's program.

Suicidal people's dreams reveal a lot of darkness and great inner tension. They believe their life has no meaning any more; they can no longer see the positive side; they feel all alone, limited, and may have the feeling of permanently falling; their state, which is primarily depressed, prevents them from seeing the light at the end of the tunnel. They suffer greatly, and even though this suffering may also be physical, it is mostly to be found in the soul, on the level of accumulated memories that haven't been understood.

There would probably be fewer suicides if people knew the impact of the *Laws of resonance, reincarnation, and karma*. Hopeless people suffering from despair would consider the ordeals they have to go through differently if they understood that life is not a question of chance and coincidence. The more we evolve spiritually, the more conscious we become that life and death are sacred and that we shouldn't play with them. Understanding these Divine Laws changes our perception of life and we no longer feel sad or grieved when a negative event occurs. In the case of suicide, we must remember that the soul of the person who committed suicide will continue its evolution. One day, it will reincarnate and be able to purify itself over time; and, like every other soul, one day, it will reach the Light. We understand that everyone reaps what he sows, that the

Earth is a School where we are called upon to develop Qualities, Virtues and Powers in their purest state. Although suicide is very difficult and bears heavy consequences, it nevertheless remains a personal experimentation and learning experience through which the person ultimately discovers the deep, sacred meaning of Life. Evil is always educational and it serves Good.

To you who are feeling desperate and contemplating suicide: *If Heaven has guided you to read this text, it is to prevent you from committing suicide, from killing yourself; it is to tell you that you are capable of taking a step toward the Light. Go and talk to someone, find a therapist or someone who, for you, represents compassion and wisdom.* ***Ask for help****. Talk openly about your dark thoughts because you are not the only one to have them. It will help you to open the valves of your unconscious, which is full of fears, desires for a different life, anger, and sadness. And as final advice,* ***ask God to help you****. Repeat this prayer over and over again, like a mantra: "God, I need help, please help me!" Do this, take this step, cry your heart out and you will see, Heaven will answer you through a dream, a sign, an event, or a person. Don't expect all of your problems to be solved by the stroke of a magic wand. Seek only the slightest, tiniest ray of sunlight that will lighten your soul and restore hope to enable you to begin solving your problems, one by one. Refer back to yourself; rebuild yourself, one stone, one brick, one step at a time.*

⊕ Understanding that suicide engenders serious consequences after death, sometimes for several lives; that this act doesn't solve anything. Difficulties that incite us to call ourselves into question, to rediscover our courage and rebuild ourselves. Ability to deal with a situation of suicide with understanding, love and compassion, hence setting in motion liberation work of a difficult karmic cycle. Reinforcement and increased activation of faith, Knowledge and Communication with the Divine. Time to meditate, go within and pray for ourselves if we have suicidal thoughts; or to better help someone else who is suicidal. May become the trigger element of a spiritual path, a quest for Knowledge, an awakening of conscience regarding parallel worlds. The willpower to carry out deep inner work, to undertake the cleansing of our unconscious, of the hurt, the wounds, memories, forces, and beliefs that inspire the idea that suicide could be a solution. Favorable time for sharing with someone we trust. An opportunity to raise awareness in others, to help them toward an in-depth understanding of the different Cosmic Laws and the consequences of suicide. Hope, promise of renewal in the next life, a second chance that allows the soul of a person who committed suicide to repair his act through an intense, difficult life and numerous examinations of his conscience.

⊖ Distress, despair, great sadness. Suffering caused by an accumulation of negative memories, such as frustrations, failures, dissatisfaction, having been extremely demanding of ourselves and others. A person who believes he is all alone in this world. Closing in on ourselves, lack of communication; the person shuts himself off from others and becomes isolated and mired in his negative soul states, in darkness, in the depths of despair. Ignorance of Cosmic Laws and the inherent consequences of suicide in this life and the following. Ignoring the rigor of Divine Laws; *we always reap what we sow.* False beliefs; believing suicide will put an end to all our suffering. Lack of love, faith, spirituality. Separation from the Divine, a lack of confidence in ourselves and in the Universe, in Life. A burdened mind and spirit, a conscience that is too focused on the material dimensions and value of life. A dead-end, a blind alley, no way out, depression, mental illness. Seeking to control everything. Loss of our bearings in everyday life. Going from one experience to another without understanding the aim of our existence, the reason for living. Hyperactivity. Lack of understanding of the meaning of ordeals. Someone who forces destiny, who refuses his life plan, who is prepared to do anything at all to escape suffering, who doesn't want to understand and accept it as part of himself that he needs to transform in order to evolve. Fleeing reality and difficulties. Fear of the future. A lack of global vision, difficulty projecting ourselves into the future and seeing the light at the end of the tunnel. Weak-minded, demonic spirit; satanic pact. Self-destructive force and ultimate flight, escapism. Negative influence on others. Seeking to make others feel guilty. Egocentric, stubborn, rebellious spirit.

SUMMER

Summer represents a vast state of conscience, which encompasses several symbolic aspects. It is the period of the year when we benefit from maximum natural heat and sunlight. Many people take their vacations then, enjoy being outdoors for leisure or sport activities, meeting up and sharing with friends, or relaxing, resting, renewing their energy and finding replenishment in nature, savoring the sweetness and happiness and lightheartedness of life. People spend more time outdoors, wear light clothes and feel freer.

Summer also symbolizes an abundance of resources, because lots of fruit and vegetables grow in this season when heat and light favor plant growth and ripening. It is also an intense period on the emotional, relationship levels as the production of hormones stimulated by the sun favors activity of the first chakras: being rooted in the physical body and the world of action; encounters, sharing and marriage of the two complementary polarities, the yin and the yang, male and female, man and woman; the expression and manifestation of ourselves on the social, collective level.

Summer, with its longer days allowing us to make the most of sunlight, has an anti-depressor effect. It induces states of joy, well-being, and a desire to celebrate life. The fact of being more easily in contact with people around us and more sensitive to our surroundings favors the development of a larger conscience and wider vision of things.

On the other hand, however, excessive heat combined with a shortage or lack of water creates devastating droughts which destroy the vegetable world, set off fires, induce risks of dehydration, and increase the level of air pollution. Symbolically these phenomena correspond to states of conscience related to over-intensive, destructive energy, crushing willpower, or behavior that destroys happiness through lassitude, dissatisfaction, heavy-heartedness, laziness or inertia.

In certain regions of the planet, summer manifests as extreme drought, torrential rains, tornadoes or cyclones. Such manifestations symbolize states of conscience dominated by ardent, over-intense, tumultuous, conflicting or devastating emotions.

⊕ Warm feelings. Vacations. Rest. Well-being. Intense, fecund life. A feeling of lightheartedness. Sharing. Leisure. Anti-depressor effect. Renewal, regeneration. Optimism. Radiance. Sweet living. Clear understanding.

⊖ Sweltering, crushing atmosphere. Burning energy. Drought. Dehydration. Overheated, overwhelming, oppressive, stifling emotions. A person who seeks to please, seduce and be loved at all costs. Excess, abuse, or lacks on the affective, emotional level. Disorderly and seductive emotions, excessive passion. Difficulty expanding and radiating harmoniously. Heaviness. A lack of motivation, willpower, strength. Laxity. Negligence. Inertia. Apathy. Laziness. Difficulty to motivate ourselves, act, breathe. Arid mentality. Incendiary, destructive behavior. Crop loss.

SUN, THE

The Sun is the central star of our solar system. It is related to the fire element, and symbolically represents our life energy, our warm radiant aspect, our force of light. A parallel can be drawn between the physical dynamics of the sun and the very many celestial objects, from the planet to interplanetary dust layers, from natural satellites, asteroids, comets, etc. that orbit around it, and the metaphysical, symbolic level whereby the sun's divine aspect, its dynamic as a representation of God that enlivens, enlightens, inspires, and illuminates all Creation is illustrated. Since time began, the Sun has always been related to the Divine. Its imposing physical mass reflects the sheer immensity and multi-dimensional force that the sun symbolically represents in us. Without the Sun, life as we know it wouldn't have developed on Earth. It is interesting to note the astronomy and astrology symbol of the Sun, which is a circle with a point in its center. This symbol is also used to represent the 3rd eye, the eye of God that sees everything, the marriage of spirit (the point) and matter (the circle), as well as Mikaël, the Archangel, associated with the Sun, whose name in Hebrew means *like God.*

The sun represents the source of energy that sustains life, allows it to renew itself, and to become concrete. It also relates to our capacity to radiate beautiful energy of light, life, and solace. It also symbolizes the masculine polarity and the emissivity of our being. It is a great symbol illustrating the capacity to see clearly, to evolve in the Light of Knowledge and Truth, to attain Enlightenment. It may also express Divine radiance through us to manifest right, just power, and our seeking to be like God. Regarding earthly, terrestrial life, the Sun's emissive dynamic is complementary to the Moon, which symbolizes receptivity and the feminine principle. As the Sun provides us with light and day, when it rises in the morning, it is related to setting things in motion, becoming active, materialization, activation of new beginnings, a fresh start, and to the end of a cycle when it sets in the evening. In the past, the sun served as a natural alarm clock, and hence has maintained the symbolism of awakening to a new conscience, to new experimentations.

⊕ Symbol of energy, life, heat, creative fire, confidence, emissivity; representing Divine radiance in ourselves, or God is all His Glory and Power. Source of heat, light, clarity, understanding. Vitality, intensity. Supreme Love and Wisdom. Awakening, activation, stimulation, motor of the earthly, terrestrial universe. Essential element in the creation of climates in both our outer and inner worlds. Allows the renewal and concretization of life and natural cycles.

⊖ Someone who is too emissive, too intense and passionate, hyperactive, egocentric, megalomaniac, who seeks to radiate and dazzle too much, whose intensity, whose excessive force of action and emissivity *burn* other people, his entourage, and himself; or, someone who lacks vitality, the will to act, to undertake projects, to manifest because *burned out,* exhausted, feeling as arid and desiccated as a desert. Over-concentration of energy, lack of mastery, tendency to blaze forth, shoot ahead, cut corners, skip stages on all levels: physical, intellectual, emotional, and spiritual. Darkness, obscurity, cold, conscious or unconscious death; or, when there is no notion that the sun is absent, an incapacity to see and understand what is happening. Destructive energy.

SWEEPING BRUSH, BROOM

A sweeping brush, or broom, is mostly used to sweep up dust, crumbs, litter, waste, or refuse from the floor or ground. Hence it represents a capacity to keep our environment clean and tidy regarding the world of action and the way we advance. So a sweeping brush (broom) is a symbol of inner and outer cleansing and purification that facilitates manifestation and advancing. Its elongated form makes it a symbol of emissivity, hence activating (or not activating) our capacity to cleanse and purify in our active life.

⊕ Ability and willpower to clean up before moving on to a new stage. Someone who likes cleanliness, tidiness, an orderly, well-organized space, who has a sense of responsibility, duty, and rigor, who fully commits to putting things in order, ensuring they are clean, tidy, and right. Capacity to clear up a living or work space and free it from accumulated dirt so as to ensure clean, orderly manifestation. Potential for cleansing and transcending memories of past actions. Rediscovered, renewed well-being *via* outer cleaning, which symbolically represents simultaneous inner cleansing. Deep understanding of the cleaning ritual.

⊖ Difficulty cleaning dust, residue, rubble resulting from former actions; difficulty tidying up our vital personal space or workplace. Lack of willpower to clean and sweep up when necessary; or, exaggerated inner or outer cleaning. Obsessive need to sweep up, purify, and keep things tidy and clean. Tendency to go rapidly from one action to another without thinking about or dealing with the cleaning, recycling, and transformation of residual energies. Accumulation of misactions (*cf.* this term) regarding lack of hygiene, dirt, disorder and untidiness, which gradually engenders blockages, limitations, or illness. Lack of understanding that the cleaning we do in the outer world corresponds to simultaneous purification on the inside, in our inner world.

SWEETS *cf. Candy*

SWIMMING

Since swimming is an activity that takes place in water, it is symbolically related to the world of emotions and feelings. Unlike diving, especially deep-sea diving, where we explore deep water, including the sea and ocean beds, hence, emotional memories lodged in the different layers of the unconscious, swimming concerns more conscious and subconscious emotions. This is because part of the body always remains out of the water, while the rest of the body moves just below the surface; in addition to this, breathing is done naturally outside the water. Swimming leads us to be at ease and to advance confidently on the emotional level. A good swimmer also knows how to deal with waves and turbulent water, without fear of going under, sinking, or drowning. Swimming is also related to an ability to make efforts; it favors perseverance, endurance, vigor, courage, while being beneficial for our general, overall health.

Someone who hasn't learned to swim because of fear of water indicates that he is afraid of encountering his conscious or unconscious emotions. The way we swim reveals how we advance and manifest when we *plunge* into our personal emotions, when we swim alone; or, when we *soak* or *bathe* in collective emotions, every time we swim in the presence of others, in water frequented by the public. If swimming is practiced as a performance or competitive sport, it indicates that the swimmer confronts the world of feelings and emotions with a competitive, comparative spirit. He wants to prove to himself, and others, what he is capable of in order to be acknowledged, admired, and loved. Whenever we practice swimming peacefully, it allows us to simultaneously carry out inner work on our emotions and soul states. This work takes place even when we don't know the symbolic meaning of this activity. That's why we always feel refreshed, renewed, regenerated, and purified after swimming.

For an adequate interpretation of a dream or concrete situation related to swimming, the circumstances in which the activity takes place, and the emotional state of the swimmer need to be considered. For example, if he is swimming peacefully, with a feeling of serenity and inner peace in the calm waters of a lake, it reveals emotional stability and a capacity to fuse with his entourage, his environment. On the contrary, however, if he is in rough seas, we may deduce the fact that he is experiencing great disturbances on the emotional level, because swimming in a difficult sea indicates that the person is lost in his personal and collective emotional, affective memories. The movement of the waves brings to the surface, old memories deeply buried in the depths of his collective emotional unconscious (symbolized by the sea). A person swept away by currents indicates that he has completely lost control, and that a great emotional force seized and took hold of him. This is not entirely negative if the swimmer manages to survive this ordeal, which would indicate that he knows how to face his emotionally disconcerting, disturbing memories and forces.

⊕ Develops motivation, courage, endurance, and perseverance to learn to act, advance, and manifest on the emotional level. Willpower and determination to make efforts to get to know and master our emotional, affective level, so as to attain our objectives, and achieve balance and well-being, both on the inside and on the outside. Allows us to refresh ourselves, relax, liberate our tensions, stress, and fatigue. Favors renewal of our energies, regeneration, purification, detachment from difficulties and frustrations. Develops inner listening, reactivates intuition, and easy fusion with the environment. Beneficial activity for re-harmonization on all three levels of our being (body, head, and heart; physical, mental, and emotional) since it allows us to develop graceful, harmonious physical movements while simultaneously carrying out inner work on our emotions, favoring relaxation and letting go on the mental, intellectual level. Practiced with conscience, with awareness of its symbolic, metaphysical meaning, swimming is a precious tool to train ourselves in the management and mastery of our emotions.

⊖ Difficulty advancing, manifesting, making efforts on the emotional level; or, someone who is submerged in his emotions, exhausted, afflicted, desperate, melancholic. Emotional instability, turbulence, and affective storms. A lack of force, motivation, courage, perseverance, endurance, willpower, and determination to confront our or other people's emotions, to work on ourselves so as to transform, purify, liberate, master, and transcend them; or, excessive willpower, stubbornness and obstinacy on the emotional level. A troubled, muddled, confusing period, where the person forces himself on the emotional, affective level to motivate himself, to hold good in an unfavorable, or even harmful, situation concerning his physical and psychological health, so as to attain material objectives and goals, to succeed, be successful, to make it to the top of his career. A tendency to approach emotions with a spirit of competition and comparison; an overly intellectual, dry, rigid, harsh attitude. Emotional deficiencies, dependencies, obsessions. An incapacity to let ourselves be carried, rocked, caressed by the water, by the waves coming in and going out, by gentle feelings of tenderness and love. Obstinacy in swimming against the tide, exhausting ourselves, hurting and injuring ourselves, destroying ourselves by fighting against the waves, the tide of life, instead of letting go and swimming with the natural flow, accepting change, detachment, metamorphoses, and inevitable, necessary mutations. Seeking strong sensations and extreme experiences, revealing suicidal tendencies, for example when swimming in perilous conditions (cold, polluted water, infested with dangerous animals, enormous waves, storms, etc.).

SWIMMING POOL

As a delimited space filled with water, used to refresh and renew ourselves, to relax, swim, or play in, depending on its size, a swimming pool is related to the world of receptivity, feelings and emotions, as well as the soul states and behavior displayed by its users. It also refers to the collective, family and friends levels since it is usually used by numerous people, especially in the case of public swimming pools. Thus it also symbolizes our emotional and corporal capacity to behave and exchange in a friendly, respectful, polite, prudent, and responsible manner when we are in a context of close, intimate proximity with others, given the fact that all we wear is a swimsuit, and that we are physically quite close to other swimmers, especially when a swimming pool is popular and frequented by a lot of people.

In a symbolic analysis of a concrete or dream situation with a swimming pool, it is important to remember that all of the people in the pool represent known or unknown parts of ourselves, and that the situation reveals how the energy, emotional, and behavioral dynamics of these parts of us act and exchange on the collective and social levels. For a detailed interpretation, the other elements related to the swimming pool need to be taken into consideration: the quality and temperature of the water; the concentration of chemical additives, or not; its size, color(s), the general atmosphere and ambiance; the surrounding decor; the place where it is to be found – in nature, outdoors, in a town or city, indoors, in a leisure center, spa, medical center, etc.

The positive, multiplying effects of a swimming pool are clearly revealed when we observe its benefits on children: as soon as going to the pool is mentioned, their usual reaction is delight, enthusiasm, excitement, and exaltation. This also reveals how much children need to express and share their joy, pleasure, and spontaneity by moving and playing in this element. Moreover, the adults who accompany them notice the same effects on themselves if they let their inner child take part in their games, which also helps them liberate accumulated stress and tension.

Furthermore, whenever a swimming pool serves in the apprenticeship and training of the art of swimming, its symbolic, metaphysical meaning is related to the practice of discipline, perseverance, endurance, and the mastery of emotional forces.

⊕ Great potential for emotional receptivity. Allows contact with and relaxation on the emotional level, renewal, refreshment, vivification of the soul, body, mind, and spirit. Procures a feeling of purification, liberation, relieves stress and tension. Favors light-heartedness, calm, a return to peacefulness, feeling soothed and renewed, eternal youth. Procures consolation. May have a stimulating effect on motivation and willpower. Offers an opportunity to learn friendly, polite, prudent, responsible interaction and exchange on the emotional level in a collective context (public swimming-pool), or social and family context (private pool, or one that is restricted to a group of people). A place for playing, joy, laughter, childlike pleasure. Facilitates social, friendly, emotional communication.

⊖ A lack of emotional, sentimental, affective receptivity, of a capacity to relax, to experience convivial states of being. Emotional emptiness on the personal and social levels if the pool is empty; emotional coldness on the relational level if the water is cold or frozen in winter. May indicate an excessive, hyperactive, burning, aggressive temperament on the emotional, relational levels if the water is too hot. Someone who doesn't like going to the swimming pool because he has difficult interacting and communicating with others in a collective, social context involving the emotional level. Antisocial behavior. An incapacity to share with others in close intimacy. Embarrassment, shyness, shame, not wanting to be seen in a swimsuit, a complex of inferiority; or, on the contrary, a feeling of superiority, seeking admiration, seduction. Voyeurism or puritanism, attitudes that nourish our basic instincts or that repress them. Behavior that reveals emotional, affective dependency, possessiveness, envy, jealousy, infidelity, affective excesses, licentiousness. A competitive spirit.

SWORD

Through its elongated form, a sword is a symbol of emissivity related to the masculine principle. From a positive point of view, it represents justice, discernment, power, authority and, in certain circumstances, loyalty. It is also associated with notions of nobility, uprightness, integrity, bravery, and a quest for truth. As it is an ancient weapon that is no longer, or very rarely, used in contemporary combat, it symbolizes wars and battles of the past. It is mostly displayed as a symbol of justice, as a force that is capable of clearly, unquestionably, separating good from evil.

⊕ Right, just use of power and justice. Capacity to discern good from evil. Power strength, agility, bravery. Uprightness, integrity, nobility of mind and spirit. Seeking truth. Loyalty to Divine Principles. Incorruptibility. Memories related to force, to power, developed in the past.

⊖ May symbolize a very emissive, sharply, abruptly decisive person as regards justice, and also in word and deed; or indicate difficulty asserting ourselves with right, firm, just authority. Abuse of power. Tendency to forcefully impose power and authority. Aggressive, fighting, vindictive, provocative spirit. Tyrant, dictator. Presence of memories marked by poor use of power and force in the past. Haughty, arrogant, over-confident attitude; dominating, conqueror behavior. Lack of discernment. False nobility and lack of loyalty to Divine Principles. Arms trafficking, instigator of personal and/or collective wars. Bearer of contradictions. Criminal ideas. Excessive rationality; judging others. Complexes of superiority and inferiority.

SYMBOL (symbolism, symbolic language)

A symbol is something that represents key information, and is the very basis of universal language, metaphysical and spiritual language, serving to understand dreams, signs, matter, the elements, behavior, events, everything that exists. It is directly related to the archetypal structure, the original essence of a person, an object, an idea, a concept, a word, a sound, a character, a way of thinking and acting.

Symbols interconnect and form networks and varied, interactive systems because they are the representation of values and principles that can be presented sometimes as an image or metaphor. Generally speaking, the positive or negative value of a symbol depends on the context in which it appears, as well as its relationship with the other elements present. The positive aspects of a symbol are defined by criteria of qualities and virtues, such as beauty, order, harmony, etc., while their negative aspects are the representation of distortions and weaknesses, such as disharmony, disorganization, violence, etc.

In a dream, the association of elements, the composition of scenarios, and the events that follow sometimes seem disorganized or incoherent, which often makes it difficult to understand the message and information conveyed by the dream. That is why a correct analysis and interpretation of dreams is only possible with thorough knowledge of symbolic language. Indeed, symbolic language allows us to decode with mathematical precision and accuracy and to understand the correlations between different symbols, the dynamics of attraction and repulsion that are at work in a situation experienced either in a dream or in concrete reality.

Symbolism is the fundamental language used by Cosmic Intelligence to express Itself, to communicate and transmit information and Knowledge throughout Creation. It is also the language of conscience, and in our human dimension, the means by which our unconscious communicates with our conscious level. For those people who function with a conscience that is limited to a physical, material perception of things, of life, this communication takes place without their realizing, and consequently, without their understanding it. However, although this universal language goes beyond cultural limitations, even someone with a more evolved conscience tends to use it very subjectively since his interpretations are tinged by his personal experience and all of the conscious and unconscious memories he has recorded throughout his multiple lives. That is why it is essential to combine the study of symbolic language with intense cleansing and transformation work on our memories to ensure the most authentic, true dream, sign and symbol interpretation. Moreover, to find our way in the symbolic world, it is necessary to develop discernment, inner listening and intuition, to apply the right meaning, and find the right balance between emissivity and receptivity. In addition to this, we also need to be capable of applying the Laws of resonance and karma, and of referring back to ourselves instead of projecting the ambiance, events, behavior and deeds of the characters seen in our dreams onto the outer world.

If the symbols are logotypes (e.g. numeric, alphabetical, road or mystical signs) they represent quantity and/or structural, relational, communicative, directional, or divine concepts, as the case may be. Hence, depending on the context, the number 2 refers to relationship(s) with another person, with others; or, the couple. 2, like any other number, may also indicate quantity, or refer to a date or number that is important for us. If 2 is shown to be important in the workplace, then we make the following equation: 2 + workplace = relationship with others in our job, and in the way we work.

Since each symbol represents a state of conscience, this kind of equation to interpret a dream or concrete situation can be formed not only for numbers, but also for everything that exists on Earth, everything that surrounds us physically and energetically. After making a list of all of the symbolic elements present in a given situation, we explore their positive and negative meanings, and then relate them all to one another, thereby defining the global equation, which will provide us with the information, teaching, or revealed message.

Symbols that appear in our dreams also reveal to us the learning program, the apprenticeships that are either underway in our inner computer, or that are about to be activated. It is important to know that these programs always correspond to our life plan, to what our soul has chosen to experience and experiment in our present life for the good of our evolution; simultaneously, they have been conceived in accordance with the positive and negative karmas we created during the course of our past lives.

⊕ Generally speaking, each time a symbol appears in an appropriate manner, in the right place, at the right time, in a positive, right context, and it is beautiful, intact, inspiring, luminous, well-proportioned, etc., we take its positive essence into consideration. Capacity to understand that everything is symbolic, that everything that exists represents a state of conscience. Ability to discern symbols, signs, and contexts that represent Qualities, Virtues, and Divine Powers in a true, authentic way. Study of symbolic language and its integration into our way of living. Development of the capacity to observe, read, listen, and communicate in symbols.

Seeing a positive abstract or unknown symbol: indicates the beginning of something, of a quest or a discovery.

⊖ Generally speaking, each time a symbol appears in a distorted manner, in the wrong place, at the wrong time, is imperfect, dull, dark, inappropriate or unsuitable in its context, etc., to analyze and interpret it, we have to take its negative aspects into consideration. The negative aspects of a symbol may indicate a complicated, over-intellectual, too rational-minded person; or, reveal erroneous behavior that is prejudicial in all respects. We also need to bear in mind that a symbol or context may seem positive, whereas it is not; hence the importance of analyzing and interpreting each symbol and concrete or dream situation with discernment and integrity, by observing the purity of our intention, as well as the atmosphere and ambiance, to ensure our ego doesn't take over in order to nourish distorted needs.

Seeing an abstract or unknown negative symbol: indicates the beginning of very negative, even demonic forces and influences.

SYRINGE

A syringe is mainly a medical instrument used to inject or withdraw liquid substances into, or from, a patient's body. Used in medicine, a syringe symbolizes healing, a capacity to administer medication deeply and accurately. It is therefore related to healing through great work on the emotional (liquid) level, and on our vital energy (blood). Through the needle and its very fine, hollow tip, it denotes an emissive aspect, great precision, and access to difficult places; the tube symbolizes receptivity, because it can contain a gas or liquid for an injection; or, a blood sample for various analyses. A syringe also helps to nourish a sick/ill person, who is physically incapable of nourishing himself.

Through its capacity to penetrate deeply, a syringe may sometimes reveal excessive emissivity, an intrusive, pricking attitude, and a dangerous, or self-destructive tendency (as in the case of people addicted to hard drugs). Dreaming of injecting something into ourselves using a syringe indicates that the product to be injected is being deeply inscribed in us, right into our vital energy, favoring either healing or harm depending on the substance injected.

⊕ An ability to inject substances to help deep, accurate, precise healing, including in regions that are difficult to reach. A capacity to withdraw samples for analyses, which will help toward an understanding of the health problem(s). Purification, work, strengthening, reinforcing, and/or nourishing the physical body with vital energy. Pain relief.

⊖ Someone whose energy is too *stinging or pricking* in his desire to heal others or himself. A harmful emissive force, that has an excessive desire to heal; or, that doesn't want to heal, because, consciously or unconsciously, the person is afraid of illness, pain, accidents, and death. Difficulty healing deeply and being accurate, precise, right in the way we heal. An awakening of memories that trigger deep fears: loss of energy, wounds, injuries, pain, etc. Resistance to deep analysis, to being receptive to our vital energy, to studying and healing it. Fear of intrusion of our intimacy. Intrusive, imposing dynamics, caused by insecurity. Fear of not succeeding in dispensing healing treatment, or pain relief. Science, knowledge without conscience, love, or wisdom. Injection of harmful, destructive substances. A state of conscience of an executioner.

T

TABLE

The symbolism of a table is essentially related to sharing resources and transmitting and exchanging knowledge and information, since we sit at a table to eat, talk, communicate, discuss various matters, study, or work. An analysis of its function, place, size, material it is made of, and its general aspect, allows us to develop important awareness regarding the way we share and exchange.

A dining table is a social symbol of rituals and sharing. Hence it represents who we are through the food we eat and the way we eat (alone, with others, in a calm atmosphere, talking and chatting, listening to the radio, in front of the television, reading, on the computer, regularly receiving and sending text messages on our mobile phone, or working). To further refine the interpretation of the related elements, we can also consider what is to be found on the table. For example, the dishes, plates and glasses: are they new or chipped, colorful or dull, made of china or a coarser material, etc? And the food: is it abundant or frugal, refined or very basic, healthy or unhealthy, beautifully, invitingly, lovingly presented or not?

A conference-, office-, or work-table evokes the way we realize a project, exchange information, discuss and make decisions to sign a contract.

The aspect of a table may also be studied in metaphysical terms: a solid, steady, stable table symbolizes a feeling of solid incarnation in sharing; a reliable attitude that can be counted on; resistant, steady and robust, even in difficult situations on the exchange level; on the other hand, a wobbly table reflects instability, weakness, irresponsibility, a lack of structure and/or reliability in sharing and exchanges.

The material a table is made of may also be taken into consideration in its symbolic + and – aspects: a wooden table links the symbolism of knowledge and construction of values, and hence reflects a desire to construct well, to materialize well; a glass table indicates a desire for transparency, authenticity, or purity; or, may be a sign of fragility, an indication that the person finds it difficult to be reliable, authentic, sincere; a metal table reflects a certain solidity, endurance, resistance, a capacity to withstand degrees of tension; or, it may indicate exchanges marked by harshness, rigidity, a boorish, rough attitude, a lack of warmth, depending on the context.

In addition, the people sitting at the table, the atmosphere and ambiance emanating from the subjects discussed there may also be studied. Also, depending on the task, are the work tools in order and tidily arranged or not? Generally speaking, the more attention we pay to detail, the more accurate and precise the symbolic conclusion of the word studied, and hence what it reveals about ourselves.

⊕ A symbol of sharing, exchanges, conviviality, fraternity. Favors communication, beautiful encounters, trusting conversations, confidences, an opening of the heart. A family spirit; or, a spirit of work, meetings, decision-making. Altruism. Preparation, organization. Community, family, fraternal dynamics, warm, joyful, festive atmosphere and ambiance.

⊖ Difficulty related to sharing, exchanges, conviviality, trust, fraternity. Problems with communication, planning, management, manifesting during meetings and discussions held around a table. A lack of altruism, listening, openness, and receptivity toward others. Absence of cooperative, community, family, or team spirit, as the case may be.

TASTE (sense of)

Among the 5 senses, taste is the sense that allows us to perceive flavors and choose food according to our preferences or nutritional needs. Moreover, the sense of taste is closely related to the sense of smell (*cf. also* this term). Taste buds, almost exclusively found on the tongue, distinguish 5 main flavors: bitter, sweet, salty, sour, and spicy, as well as their combinations, which may mean hundreds of others. Taste orients our choices, decisions, and helps guide us in our intuitive senses and feelings.

Generally speaking, we appreciate the flavor of healthy food. Nevertheless, everyone's taste is conditioned by individual and family values and memories (incurred from conception), as well as the socio-cultural context in which we live. Desire or distaste for a particular flavor sometimes stems from a conscious or unconscious emotional imbalance. Hence, a flavor may be perceived as pleasant or unpleasant depending on the affective memory with which it is associated. For example, we may have an aversion to particular food related to an unpleasant event that, although we may have forgotten it, we haven't yet *digested* it because it is recorded in our unconscious; or we may feel attracted to a particular type of food that reminds us of something pleasant and happy. However, we sometimes discover new, unknown food flavors that, much to our surprise, we instantly like and enjoy; in this case, it may be as a result of memories of our having already acquired this taste in past lives. Rather than saying we don't like particular food, we should really say that we aren't used to it.

On the symbolic level, a person may choose sweet food to calm inner tension, i.e. to fulfill affective deficiencies, a great lack of sweet gentleness, softness and kindness that has been repressed in the unconscious, to compensate for feelings of rejection, inferiority, disappointment, fear, rigidity; or, to satisfy a need for expansion; or, a desire to do things without making any effort. An exaggerated preference for salty food reveals a need for control and power, a tendency to be repressive, to repress a lack, a feeling of lack, a feeling of restriction, limitation; or, it may be related to contradiction. Too great an attraction for fatty food indicates a state of heaviness, a very down-to-earth, materialistic mind and spirit, as well as a lack of self-esteem, a need to protect ourselves, a tendency to gluttony, laxity, letting ourselves go, dropping out, lack of willpower, and indifference regarding our health. When we feel like eating something spicy, symbolically, we need stimulation, our life lacks spice. However, since spicy food prickles our tongue and palate, and when very spicy may seem to set our mouth on fire, then, symbolically, this may reveal the fact that we nourish fiery, fierce, prickly ideas that could hurt others, leading to heated, hurtful remarks, for example, or over-passionate or extremist attitudes. From a negative point of view, a taste for bitterness reveals that we nourish ourselves on embittered feelings for a person or a situation;

a·pronounced taste for sour food indicates sadness, bitterness, discontent, frustration, and a complaining, plaintive attitude.

Taste can also reveal a need to be loved, desired, and acknowledged by certain members of our entourage. For example, we may accept flavors that actually repel us (alcohol, cigarettes, etc.) and even end up dependent on them, merely because our wanting to belong to a group led us to conform to the group behavior. In such a case, we wish to relieve or anesthetize our anxiety, we wish to calm our emotional dependencies, compensate for our fear of solitude, our lack of confidence in ourselves and in our personal values.

From a positive point of view, taste symbolizes *joie de vivre*. If we have *a taste for life,* we display enthusiasm, dynamism, ardor, and healthy curiosity for all aspects of life. We are able to savor daily experiences with refinement and subtlety, without continually seeking superficial, unhealthy sensations. We are open-minded and easily *taste* new experiences in different domains. Figuratively speaking, *good taste* refers to elegance and grace often sought and developed but also innate, a capacity to embellish our environment with refinement in decor, fashion, the arts, clothing, and indeed everything that can improve our quality of life and help us evolve. From a negative point of view, creating and/or nourishing refined fashion tastes may encourage behavioral patterns and attitudes of exclusivity, luxury, pretentiousness, solely materialistic perspectives based on appearances, a desire to please, to be admired, etc.

In concrete or dream reality, seeing a person or an animal rapidly devouring food, without taking time to taste and savor it, symbolically shows excess, avidity, greed, impatience, and hides a desire for limitless possession. Such a person behaves in a coarse, boorish, unrefined, gluttonous manner, without savoring his food, without appreciating its taste. He leaves the table with a bulging, distended stomach because he overate and is incapable of feeling true satiety when his hunger has been satisfied.

Tastes may be changed and re-programmed by the establishment of new habits that we consciously repeat so as to deeply anchor or ingrain them within ourselves. Healthy nourishment reprograms a person's tastes in depth, and it is good for his health on all levels. Food that is deficient in nutrients inscribes an imbalance in the person's desires, leading him to greedily desire rich, fatty, sugar and salt filled food, as well as luxury, power, and sensuality, etc., in order to compensate for his lacks on different levels. Our tastes are directly related to our conscious and unconscious memories and needs, and in order to evolve spiritually, it is essential to learn to manage them well, to transform and transcend them.

⊕ Well-developed, well-balanced, harmonious taste on all levels. A capacity to feel, to sense and let ourselves be guided toward what is good, healthy and favorable for our development, our evolution. Sensitive, intuitive understanding of what is beneficial and what is harmful. *Joie de vivre*, enthusiasm, open-mindedness, a healthy disposition to taste new things, to discover the unknown. A capacity to overcome the aversion we may have for certain tastes we personally find unpleasant. Discernment to identify healthy food, right principles and values. Taste experiences that activate the multiple dimensions of our intelligence. Expansive, mystical, pleasant dynamics. Divine Pleasures.

⊖ Hedonism. Desire for enjoyment and pleasure solely on the material level, using taste focused on the satisfaction of instinctual, primary, coarse needs, which obstructs well-being and health on all levels. Puritanism, extremism, or being complicated regarding taste, regarding what we like and what we don't like. Someone who, through despair and disconnection, or who is extremist in his way of thinking, feeling, behaving, living, has lost his *joie de vivre*, who no longer has a taste for good food, who no longer savors life. Rebellion, stubbornness, selfishness, pretention. Rejection, aversion, refusal to taste what is new, to experiment the unknown. A lack of refinement. Affective, emotional problems, dependencies, possessiveness, a need to fulfill deficiencies on various levels. Someone who has to go through unpleasant experiences and taste what he subjected others to, in this life or in previous lives; difficult karmas. Refusal to cleanse and transform our conscious and unconscious memories. Living under the influence of our inner animal forces, perverted, unhealthy desires.

TATTOO

A tattoo is a design or image that is drawn on the body by means of injections permanently introducing dyes under the skin; it can also be applied non-permanently with no effect or a more gentle effect on the skin. It generally symbolizes something that is important for the person who chooses to have it, and it defines, rather intensely, sometimes emissively, his personality and what he wishes to be. On the unconscious level, tattoos reveal hidden aspects of the person's experience, memories of his previous lives, facets of his being, his resonances with positive or negative forces, depending on the kind of tattoo.

Many people don't realize that the negative symbols they have tattooed onto their bodies represent accumulated memories and forces related to violence, aggression, ego problems, complexes of superiority or inferiority, relentlessness, cruelty and abuse of power. Also, a tattoo represents identification with a still hidden or unconscious aspect of the soul. If the image is very negative, even demonic, the bearer of such a tattoo, either consciously or unconsciously, connects with egregores (*cf.* this term) of respective forces in the subtle levels and risks seeing such forces materialize in his life; or, it may lead him to become what the tattoo on his skin expresses. People who choose symbols representing evil as their tattoo reveal their resonance with these forces. In their unconscious, such people usually have memories filled with frustration, aggression, rebellion, egotistical brutality, and they are either obsessed with, or they have to repress the desire to dominate or annihilate others.

In some cultures, like Japan, large areas of the body, especially women's, are tattooed and considered as living works of art. In other circles, for example in prisons, in the army, or certain secret societies, the tattooed images and symbols relate to the rank and experiences the person underwent. Nowadays, an increasing number of young people are attracted by this art and multiply body tattoos, thereby revealing the strengths and weaknesses that dwell in them.

⊕ Positive, unexaggerated, subtle ornamentation that inspires beauty, a search for harmony, right action, the development of qualities and virtues. Exteriorization of a wish, a life goal. Conscious choice of a tattoo and understanding of its symbolic meaning and the resonance we have with the tattooed image. Deep reflection on the tattoo, and inner work to transcend the reasons and needs that led us to have it done.

⊖ Concrete expression of the forces and memories of a rebellious, hurt, or disillusioned soul. An identity crisis, a need to identify with the negative in order to defend and protect ourselves from the negative, from our conscious or unconscious fears. Seeking admiration, a need to feel superior, to believe ourselves to be stronger than others, to be powerful. The will to dominate, to abuse the weak; or, to demean, abase, and make a fool of ourselves because of an inferiority complex. Someone who nourishes and manifests unhealthy, dangerous thoughts, who isn't aware that violence engendered on the metaphysical level engenders violence on the physical level. A confused, troubled, pessimistic, or overly materialistic mind and spirit. Affective, or other level, dependency. Behavior of a wounded soul who has lost his faith and hides behind muscles and aggressive attitudes. An overly emissive person who seeks to prove his virility, strength, and power. A machismo attitude, a need to be acknowledged as well as to incite fear to better dominate. A lack of discernment and love for ourselves and others; indifference regarding long-term consequences; someone prepared to wear a symbol on his body without knowing about its destructive impact on his soul, mind, spirit, and life; ignorance of the fact that certain substances used to color the skin have proved to be carcinogenic. Lack of symbolic knowledge and the metaphysical dimension of the tattoo. May denote a person who's been possessed.

TAX, TAXATION

A tax is an obligatory contribution levied on the income of people living on the same territory. It is a symbol of concrete, altruistic participation, help, and financial contribution, and is considered as a primary means for a country to maintain the structure and functioning of operations in the multiple domains of daily life (education, health, social assistance, infrastructures, economy, politics, culture, etc.). It is also used to develop projects, invest in research, reimburse public debt, and also external debt, when necessary. Taxation requires that each person contributes to the autonomy and evolution of his country, according to his resources. Even though tax may be a very controversial issue in concrete reality, in its profound symbolic aspect, it represents a manifestation of altruism, a willingness to share resources and awareness of collective responsibility toward a common patrimony.

⊕ An altruistic contribution to help the collectivity. Participation in the collective destiny. A multiplying factor of individual generosity, which allows a country to develop its multiple potentialities in the service of the common good. Global vision. A capacity to materialize on a large scale thanks to a concentration of active energy. Understanding the fact that financial resources and money are forms of energy that allow us to materialize projects, to experiment and create in matter. A fair, just, honest, upright, kind, caring person who understands the necessity to be concretely involved, and who realizes the beneficial effects of his altruism. Integration of the fact that the way a country's government or leader manages and uses tax on the collective level reflects inner values in accordance with the universal principle that what is on the outside reflects what is on the inside, just as what is below reflects what is Up Above. Allows a country to decrease its debt; metaphysically, partial reparation of a collective karmic debt. Understanding the fact that the tax system represents concrete and symbolic power that is a part of ourselves, and that we need to learn to give, to entrust this power with wisdom and discernment on the individual level, to learn to manage and use our resources, our force of action and creative power not only with a materialistic conscience and short-term vision, but also with a universal, altruistic conscience and long-term, global vision.

⊖ A selfish, egotistical person who only thinks of his own interests, lacks altruism, generosity, and collective, global vision. A rebellious spirit that refuses to acknowledge the necessity of sharing resources, the importance of financially contributing to the good functioning of our country's structures; or, someone who gives too much, who causes an imbalance in his personal resources by wanting to satisfy other people's needs, requests, and expectations. Insubordination in the face of authority. Dishonesty. A system that has been corrupted by abuse of power on the financial, political, and economic levels. Tax evasion, fraud. Criminal behavior. A person who unscrupulously withdraws money that belongs to his country in order to enrich himself by taking advantage of tax paradises; a tendency to think he is above the law, above others, to nourish a feeling of superiority regarding society and the masses. On the other hand, however, quite on the contrary, a person may feel an intense feeling of discouragement in the face of the world, a deep inferiority complex, which incites him to let himself go, to live off society, which also shows extreme laziness and a tendency to let himself be taken care of by a structure of help and assistance.

TAXI

Generally speaking, a taxi is an individual means of transport, driven by a chauffeur, available to anyone who wishes to travel or get somewhere (usually short or medium distance) when he cannot use his usual personal vehicles (bicycle, car, etc.), or other means of transport. It represents dynamics of occasional transit, regarding a capacity to advance and manifest on the personal, professional, or social levels, in particular situations, or in emergencies.

Less personal and intimate than a car, a taxi symbolizes a dimension of service, assistance, and social support. Compared with public transport services (bus, tram, train, subway) with predetermined itineraries, a taxi is very efficient, because it allows us to get to the required destination more rapidly and more directly, especially when the taxi-driver knows the best way to get there. As a substitute for public transport, taxis are usually found in densely populated areas, such as large towns and cities, all over the world, which makes a taxi a collective symbol, easily recognized by its color or other distinctive signs, such as a logo or light. In poorer countries, a taxi may serve to transport several unrelated passengers, and hence becomes a means of public transport.

Taxi rides, which are usually of short or medium duration, are a commercial transaction where money is paid in exchange for transport. The cost represents an energy value related to the time and distance of the journey. The fare and our reaction to it, depending on whether we think it is fair or exorbitant, gives us indications as to the value we grant our social advancing, in time and space, regarding a particular action.

Symbolically, we are both the passenger and the driver, and neither can be dissociated from the vehicle. As a passenger, we choose the destination, but we often don't know the way. Generally speaking, the driver decides the itinerary and ensures our safety by respecting the Highway Code. Hence, a taxi represents the provisional, temporary state of conscience that dwells in us when we head toward a usually important activity (generally speaking we do not take a taxi for ordinary, everyday activities), as well as the ambiance experienced during the ride. In a dream or concrete reality, it is important to note the interaction between the passenger and the taxi-driver, the trusting or mistrustful atmosphere, the conversation, silence, or sound of the radio, the driver's courtesy toward other road users, his knowledge of the area, of the itinerary, etc. Is the taxi-driver polite, cordial, friendly, honest, calm; or, agitated, irritated, annoyed, angry, upset, stressed, impolite, dishonest, etc.? The condition or state of the taxi also informs us of our way of advancing in society when we help or accompany others. Is the taxi comfortable, spacious, luxurious; or old, shabby, dirty, smoky, etc.?

Unlike a car that we own, which reveals the way we advance toward others on the personal, intimate level, a taxi represents a more temporary state of conscience that reveals a particular moment of the day, or a period in our life. It may also be our profession. The work we do in the outside world always corresponds to an inner work program. Being a taxi-driver reveals that the person's life plan provides learning situations regarding service, assistance, manifesting, or materializing an intention more rapidly and in a right, just, qualitative way.

The fact that customers are driven adds the notion of power to the idea of service. Furthermore, a person who takes a taxi can devote his time to doing things: thinking, centering, inner focusing, as well as preparation for what awaits him at his destination, observing what he sees during the journey, or communicating personal or work-related messages by phone, text messaging, the Internet, etc. Depending on the context and type of activity, the fact of taking a taxi in a dream or concrete reality, indicates the meaning and importance of our priorities related to our social occupations, and shows us the possibilities we have at our disposal when, occasionally or regularly, we let someone else do the driving. If we are a taxi-driver, the symbolism relates to the attention and consideration we grant the customer, who is simultaneously part of ourselves.

⊕ A capacity to be organized, structured, and to manifest efficiently, to easily make our way toward our aims, objectives, goals, to ensure the realization and materialization of our social initiatives and manifestations. An ability to have recourse to a practical, reliable, efficient, rapid means of transport to get from one place to another in a high-priority, urgent, or emergency situation, regarding our personal, professional, or social advancing. Occasional assistance in our evolution when we are short of other means of advancing, of transport. Letting go and trusting others to guide, to do the driving.

⊖ A hyperactive, agitated person, who lives a stressful, whirlwind social or professional life, and who uses taxis to satisfy his need to advance at all costs; a lazy person, or someone who is submerged in fears (e.g. fear of driving), and who therefore finds his capacity for personal, social, and/or professional advancing is limited; or, someone who lets himself be driven to nourish his ego and to give himself a sense of importance. Lifestyle that is over-focused on material and social aims, a tendency to always want to go faster. Difficulty finding a taxi when needed may reveal an incapacity, or resistance, to obtaining assistance and support to be able to move, travel, get around in urgent, emergency situations, due to the presence of inner forces that block a person's progression and the realization of his objectives and aims. Delay, lack of synchronicity in social advancing. Reticence to letting ourselves be driven by others, a lack of confidence in their skills, refusal to let go of control. Refusal to make the effort to advance with a collective conscience. Abuse related to the power of being able to drive someone, others. Someone who, through resonance, attracts a dishonest taxi-driver, who betrays his customer's trust and good faith by, for example, lengthening the journey to earn more money; or, who behaves impolitely, roughly, or even aggressively; or, haughty, arrogant, disrespectful behavior of the person who is being driven, who thinks he can behave as he likes because he is paying for the service. Feelings of superiority and a complex of inferiority.

TEACH, TO

Teaching allows us to transmit knowledge to other people and to pass it on from one generation to another. Without teaching, evolution would not be possible. The transmission of acquired knowledge enriches and enlarges our conscience and allows our mind and spirit to manifest its potential by developing new concepts, ideas, and understanding. Teaching also relates to broadcasting knowledge as well as ensuring its longevity. It is important to teach with beautiful thoughts and emotions, because while we transmit teachings, we simultaneously transmit all that we are. If, while we are teaching mechanics, for example, we are angry or confused, the students will tend to reproduce our behavior, our way of being, when they do mechanics. Likewise, an arrogant teacher will inspire the same kind of behavior in his students.

⊕ A capacity to transmit knowledge and to learn from others while teaching them. Sharing what we are, putting into practice acquired experience and skills. Awareness that while we are a teacher, we remain an eternal student. A capacity to teach with devotion, love, wisdom, discernment, and right authority. A well-balanced person on all levels.

⊖ Incapacity or difficulty transmitting knowledge. Spreading erroneous information and knowledge. An irresponsible person, who teaches without having the necessary qualities or skills. Seeking social renown and acknowledgement. A haughty, arrogant, know-it-all attitude. False teacher. Teaching dangerous concepts that engender collective misactions (*cf.* this term), confusion, and problems. Complexes of superiority and inferiority. An exaggerated tendency to dissect and analyze, which prevents understanding. A lack of love, patience, and pedagogy. Ignorance. Intolerance. Discrimination. Sectarian spirit. An abuse of authority and power when teaching.

TEACHER

In a dream, any teacher – primary, junior/senior high school, university professor, technical, art, music, sewing, cooking, sports, special needs, etc., – represents our capacity to teach others and ourselves, the various skills and competence pertaining to whatever aspect is indicated and our capacity to learn, to develop the Qualities, Virtues and Pure Powers to be found therein. A senior high school teacher and university professor symbolize a state of conscience related to the transmission of knowledge and knowhow at a higher level than primary teaching. Such teachers are specialists in particular fields and their opinions and advice are generally acknowledged and respected.

Seeing a senior high school teacher or university professor symbol in a dream indicates that the dreamer is experimenting his capacity to teach at an advanced level; or, that he is in a deep learning stage seeking advanced knowledge. It is important to know that no matter what studies we may have done, no matter what degrees, diplomas, or certificates we may have obtained, no matter how many skills or experience we may have accumulated, we always remain simultaneously both a teacher and a student. A true teacher (at any level) knows that he is an eternal student. Hence, simultaneously and continually, he cultivates his love of teaching and learning. This double requirement of teaching and learning implies the development of inner and outer rigor and wisdom. Hence a teacher's behavior, and especially his capacity to instill discipline and exert right, fair, good authority over his students reveals the way he manages those parts of himself in his inner world that fulfill both the teacher's role and the role of an apprentice, the role of a learner, which is symbolized by students in the concrete world.

A teacher must be an inspiring example not only through his professional competence but also through the human, humane values he manifests, such as: integrity, authenticity, honesty, self-knowledge, wisdom, understanding, altruistic love, kindness and consideration toward students. He must be able to recognize the priorities of the different learning stages. Moreover, he needs to be able to constantly motivate himself and his students, maintaining the wish to learn and develop a sense of responsibility and duty, determination to make whatever efforts are required on the way, receptivity to new concepts, and readiness to call into question all he has learned so as to favor evolution on all levels. An excellent teacher who accomplishes his mission adequately must also be a good communicator, able to make complex ideas and concepts understandable, and to update old, former knowledge.

⊕ Ability to teach and transmit knowledge. Application of right, loving authority, based on the example of authenticity and integrity that we are capable of offering. Creator of atmosphere and ambiance that favor joyful learning, while also ensuring a disciplined work-attitude, and serious, attentive, motivated involvement. Love for studying, learning; eternal student. Open-mindedness, tolerance and respect for all cultures, all teaching, currents of thought and lifestyles. Capacity to create positive, constructive learning dynamics. Good, patient, understanding, dedicated pedagogue, motivated by altruistic love, who rejoices in his ability to contribute to other people's development. Capacity to listen not only to the words expressed by pupils and students, but also to what their souls communicate through their choice of words, their facial expression, body language, and behavior in general. Ability to settle conflict and relational problems. Sense of organization and order. Efficient use of time. Global, long-term vision. Understanding that everything we learn in concrete reality must essentially serve to develop Qualities, Virtues, and Powers in their purest form. Awareness of the fact that the subjects and subject matter that interest us indicate the orientation of our inner research and study, and reveal a deep wish to know, understand, and learn, as well as being an indication of our inner research and study to help the evolution of our soul, mind, and spirit. Capacity to understand and teach the interaction of cause and consequence.

⊖ A haughty, arrogant, conceited person, who finds it difficult to transmit his knowledge because he is too closed on the mental level and doesn't manage to create human, personal contact with his students, who cannot move them, touch their souls, or awaken their interest; or, lack of confidence to share, to teach what we know; or, lack of motivation or knowledge to do so. Someone who seeks to dominate and abase others, abuses his power, imposes his point of view. A narcissistic person who shows off his knowledge so as to feel important, acknowledged, loved. Teaching erroneous knowledge and concepts. Professional incompetence. Lack of the pedagogical and human qualities required to be a good teacher. Rigidity. Impatience. Feeling of superiority or inferiority regarding teaching. Arrogant attitude. Lack of devotion, dedication, wisdom, altruistic love. Problems of communication, leadership, diplomacy. Overly authoritarian, even tyrannical behavior that demands exaggerated levels of discipline and performance; or, absence of authority and discipline. Bad example.

TEAR(S)

Tears are secreted by the eyes and are related to the world of emotions because they are liquid. Sadness, joy, and many other soul-states (moods) may be accompanied by tears to relieve, liberate, express difficulties, pain, fears, dramatization, or a surplus of poorly managed emotions. Tears also play an important role cleansing and protecting the eyes. To correctly interpret their symbolic, positive or negative, meaning, the context of the scene experienced needs to be taken into consideration.

⊕ Someone who experiences his emotions and accepts them without repressing or retaining them. Authenticity and sensitivity as regards feelings. Expression of joy, exaltation, gratitude; or, fragility, disappointment, sadness, distress, etc. Helps purify the body and soul, freeing us from tension and often long accumulated memories of pain and suffering. Evacuation of repressed emotions without shame, restraint, or shyness. Protection and cleansing of our eyes, our vision of events and people, and a capacity to induce reconstructive, repairing emotions.

⊖ May denote a hyper-sensitive, excessively emotional person, who cries at the slightest opportunity; or, fear, pain, profound sadness and disorganization, despair; or, on the contrary, someone who finds it difficult to give in to his feelings, to express his emotions. Shyness, timidity, or excessive modesty, which can block emotional liberation. Using tears to manipulate and make other people feel guilty in order to get what we want. Tendency to exaggerate, dramatize, complain, whine, and feel sorry for ourselves. Erroneous, unhealthy upbringing that conditions a person to believe that tears are a sign of weakness and vulnerability. Harsh, demanding behavior that wants to be irreproachable, thereby preventing the person's true emotional nature from blossoming, flourishing. Someone who lives in a state of affective aridity, not wanting to admit his feelings due to rigidity or unconscious fear of facing his deep nature, who he truly is. Tears accompanying a laughing fit and unhealthy, exaggerated humor, manifesting an excessive need to laugh in order to compensate for habitual, over-serious behavior or to liberate excessive tension.

TEENAGE *cf. Adolescence*

TELEPHONE DIRECTORY

A telephone directory is an annually updated public collection of data containing information such as the names, addresses, telephone numbers, profession, and other information concerning people or businesses established in a particular area. It represents a capacity to structure ourselves, to organize ourselves efficiently so as to facilitate research, contact, communication, and the creation of links and exchanges on the individual, collective, professional, cultural, and social levels. Symbolically, the data in a telephone directory reveals information about ourselves, and the people we seek or consult in a particular context reflect aspects of ourselves that we need to rediscover and reactivate in order to get information, services, assistance, etc. Being listed in a telephone directory indicates an opening onto society, a great broadcasting capacity, making available to the public what we are, the services and experience, skills and knowledge that we can offer. It may also be featured in a dream to show us that it is important to contact a particular person or business.

⊕ Efficient structuring and organization, allowing rapid access to useful, necessary information in order to concretely accomplish our objectives, materialize our intentions, carry out our projects. Facilitates the creation of contacts, exchanges, communication and cooperation between private people, companies, organizations and all kinds of institutions, in all fields. Allows us to broadcast and to let ourselves be known on the personal, social, and professional levels. May be connected to an important contact we need to make.

⊖ Difficulty establishing contacts, finding the information and person/people needed to materialize our projects correctly. A tendency to being scattered, dispersed, to getting lost in details or in useless information. Disorientation. Distraction. Lack of organization and structure. Neglecting to update our database, our contacts. Difficulty ordering and managing multiple information. Wasting time. Loss of energy. Inaccessibility to personal or professional resources.

TELEPHONE

A telephone is a means of communication that symbolizes our capacity to communicate with others from a distance. It allows us to practice receptivity (the feminine principle) through listening, and emissivity (the masculine principle) when speaking; these two aspects form the essential basis of communication. It is just as important to know how to listen well, to receive, as to know how to emit, to speak. If a telephone is out of order, whether in concrete reality or in a dream, a problem of communication, of receptivity and emissivity can be deduced.

Whenever we phone someone in a dream, it is possible that we are not conversing solely with a part of ourselves, but that we are truly in contact with the soul of the person on the other end of the line. What is said in the conversation must always be logical, related to the other person, and analyzed using symbolic language, even if the message refers to a concrete situation in our daily life.

Via a telephone call in a dream, we can also receive surprising revelations about the other person or obtain important information about a situation. It is even possible to speak to deceased people. If the message is coherent, plausible, and logical as regards the person on the phone, the situation in question, or a subject mentioned, then, generally speaking, the person we are talking to really is present, in connection with our soul. However, unless our interlocutor is very open and receptive, he is very rarely aware of this conversation, during which he may reveal veiled or hidden information that he wouldn't be able to share in concrete reality.

⊕ A capacity to communicate with parts of ourselves, or soul-to-soul with others. A great ability to listen, analyze, and understand. A capacity to tune into, perceive, and decode the deep, symbolic meaning of words, as well as the true intention and ambiance conveyed by the sound vibration of the voice. Capacity for clairaudience and clairsentience. An ability to listen lovingly and wisely to what the other person thinks and shares, knowing he represents a part of ourselves, that he reveals aspects of our own being to us. Understanding both the physical and metaphysical aspects on the communication level. An apprenticeship of right, well-polarized communication, maintaining well-balanced receptivity and emissivity.

⊖ Difficulties related to communication with ourselves, or with other people's soul. A lack of deep listening, not taking the time to analyze the true meaning of a conversation, to understand the deep meaning behind words. Multiple dependencies that result in an exaggerated need to call others to put an end to our boredom, to fulfill our lacks, to satisfy our curiosity, to relieve our worries. A tendency to telephone often and for a lengthy period of time. Fear or apprehension regarding what we may hear, what the other person may think of us. A lack of understanding of the fact that others represent parts of ourselves, that they reveal the positive and negative resonance and affinities we have with them. A lack of spiritual Knowledge. Excessive or insufficient receptivity and emissivity. A tendency to want to control the communication, to impose our point of view, our ideas, our emotions, to want to be right at all costs, thereby preventing things from being settled, or progressing and improving. A lack of inner communication engendering an excessive need to communicate with the outside. Multiple dependencies that result in a lack, or an exaggerated wish to communicate with others.

TELEVISION

A television is a collection of techniques destined to emit and receive audiovisual sequences called programs (including films and commercials). The contents of these programs may be described analogically, and they can be transmitted through radio-electric waves or cabled network. The device to display the images and diffuse the sounds of a program is called a television set, or, quite simply the television, TV or *telly*. Invented at the beginning of the 20th century, the television is part of most people's daily lives. From a simple cathode-ray tube to a plasma screen, television has greatly evolved. Today it is interactive and auto tactile, and offers us a glimpse of the technological advances the future holds in store for us.

On the metaphysical level, television represents both our potential for emissivity (because it diffuses programs conceived by human beings) and our potential for receptivity (since we usually watch TV sitting or even lying down, hence in a relaxed, receptive state). The very principle of television is emission/reception, and thus it represents an interactive dynamic common to all human beings.

Apart from this interactivity, television also has an important collective dimension: thanks to the television, we have permanent access to worldwide information. The programs broadcast allow us to connect with the rest of humanity, and also, metaphysically, to our inner world, aspects of ourselves that come from multiple, worldwide countries. Hence television constitutes a privileged tool to visit different levels of man's conscience and unconscious.

That's why, despite often superficial contents, the television remains an important educational tool thanks to which we learn to better understand how certain mentalities, egregores (*cf.* this term), and states of conscience work.

In a dream, a television represents our capacity to visit our conscious memories, or our positive and negative unconscious potential; in some dreams, it may be a direct access to concrete information regarding the collective level, to what is happening or in preparation on Earth. These revelations then represent a real form of clairvoyance.

Since everything that exists on the outside is an integral part of our global being, through the news and programs broadcast, television reveals the tendencies, influences, and programs taking place in the individual and collective conscience and unconscious. TV also concerns communication and shows us what is broadcast within ourselves, whenever it is related to us because we see situations and familiar symbols, or because we are directly involved in the scenario presented on the screen; the positive information corresponds to developing or acquired qualities of ours; and the negative information corresponds to distortions we need to work on.

Provided that television is used as a means of physical and metaphysical apprenticeship, it is positive. Unfortunately, many people spend too much time passively watching it, letting themselves be pervaded by useless, false, dull, negative, destructive information, without analyzing it with discernment and multi-dimensional understanding. When television is used without discernment it has a harmful effect, especially on children. According to numerous studies, television plunges children into a state that is close to hypnosis; it favors obesity (lack of exercise, snacking, advertising for rich food often lacking in nutrients); it disturbs sleep; bridles the imagination (children's capacity for imagination is de-structured); it prevents them from concentrating on concrete, daily reality (excessive stimulation that can lead to attention deficit); and makes them violent (their brain reacts as though they were exposed to real-life situations, hence they get used to violence and reproduce it without emotions). Most people who watch TV with an ordinary, horizontal conscience show mental and spiritual laziness. Without realizing, they refuse to recognize themselves in what they see on the screen and appreciate this opportunity to evolve by applying the Law of resonance. By training ourselves to always refer back to ourselves, to discover aspects of ourselves in everything we watch, we develop a capacity to be constantly in direct touch with our personal and the collective unconscious, and to evaluate a situation with the Wisdom of our Divine Self. People don't understand that replying only instinctively and without conscience to negative words, situations, and acts (witnessed on TV or in concrete reality) reveals the presence of distorted memories. This kind of behavior stimulates future actions and erroneous behavior and hinders the development of discernment of good and evil. For many people, television is a means to compensate for a dull, trivial life that lacks depth, values and true qualities; they seek refuge in a virtual, illusory world.

⊕ Diffusion of information, and educational, evolutive messages. Someone who practices applying the Law of resonance while watching TV so as to get to know himself better and to better understand the scenario of his own and other people's lives. A capacity to be receptive, to listen to ourselves and others, to have access to new, veiled or unknown information about ourselves and the collectivity. Study and understanding of what is happening in our inner and outer world. Warns us of what is going to happen or the probabilities of what may happen. Shows the present, past, and future. Helps open the horizon, develop discernment, and acquire a metaphysical and multi-dimensional vision. Helps develop an analytical, concise mind and spirit, as well as a social, global, universal conscience.

⊖ Difficulty or incapacity to have access to news about our conscience or our personal and collective unconscious; or, someone who is too much in search of information, who greedily nourishes himself on the social level through a need for power or a lack of activity, who is easily influenced, dependent, and naive, who absorbs all sorts of information without discernment or awareness. Someone who watches television without referring back to himself, who doesn't apply the Law of resonance, and who doesn't reflect on the correlations between what he sees on the screen and what he experiences in his own life. A lack of understanding of the scenario of our life because of a lack of self-knowledge. A tendency to let ourselves be impressed and to give our power to others without any discernment. Someone who flees concrete reality and lives through the stories he watches on TV, who gets lost in the memories and resonance awakened by overconsumption of television programs. Egocentricity, lack of global vision, withdrawal into ourselves. Problems engendered by the diffusion of negative messages that are unconstructive for humanity. A lack of receptivity and/or emissivity.

TENSION *cf. Stress*

TERRORISM

Terrorism is an extremist movement, which has increased in strength, power and intensity over the last few years. The aim of terrorists is to create a climate of insecurity, to exert pressure on governments in order to defend their ideas, their ideology of the world, and thereby influence and impose their doctrine on the collective level, on the greatest number possible.

Terrorists are often people who display a lot of intensity and convictions on the social and/or religious level; they are people who have nourished feelings of revenge, which have fashioned extremist thought systems, pushing them to use force to support, spread, and broadcast their message. These very dangerous people, filled with hatred, anger, and frustration, are capable of anything to achieve their ends. Whenever a person in search of spirituality mixes good and evil to the point where he can no longer tell the difference between what is right and what is not, he may then be led to act out of desperation, and hence commit ignoble acts of violence in the name of God or of his convictions regarding social justice. The determination and extremism that dwell in terrorists push them to commit destructive acts often affecting the collectivity. Terrorists want to destroy what they don't accept, what they don't understand, what they don't agree with, and they organize themselves in groups to materialize acts of violence, hatred, cruelty.

In a dream, in terms of conscience, terrorist dynamics may manifest in us when we visit concrete forces and unconscious memories related to rebellion, revenge, hatred, violence, and aggression, when we defend an opinion or cause which is dear to our heart, too intensely and relentlessly, because we believe our ideas, our cause, is the only way possible for us and/ or others. In such cases, we try to impose our point of view, and if we act out of frustration and anger to spread and broadcast what we believe in, then our words and gestures become destructive weapons pointed at our near and dear ones, our fellowmen, and ourselves. Our little inner terrorist may also appear when we feel that a person isn't right, and we want to change his mind; we force, we insist, we impose, believing we are helping him. Our behavior becomes extremist and does not respect the other person's level of conscience, or his rhythm of evolution, which will, in fact, only serve to delay him, hold him back on his spiritual path, or in his understanding of our ideas, even causing him to reject and/or fight them himself.

In order to transcend such states of terrorism and extremism that many people experience at the beginning of their spiritual path, we need to understand that the Earth is a School, and that its inhabitants are at different levels of apprenticeship, in different classes, so to speak. Some people are still in kindergarten, while others are in higher, more advanced classes, but all of us, absolutely every single person, is in his rightful place in this School of Life.

⊕ Someone who understands that not only does violence engender violence, but that it also destroys positive conscience, mutual help, trust and confidence, love and wisdom, on the individual and collective levels. Awareness of forces and memories that have terrorist tendencies, on a small or large scale. Understanding that it is neither wise nor beneficial to impose our point of view to awaken others and to push them to evolve at our rhythm, according to our conceptions. Acceptance of the fact that all change comes from healthy, right education, that it sometimes takes time, sometimes a long time, before a new stage materializes. Acquisition of a multi-dimensional vision of politics thanks to an interaction of Universal Laws; understanding the correlation between cause and consequence, of the fact that we always reap what we sow. Transcendence of aggression, intolerance, radicalism, and destructive forces in ourselves. Development of respect for others, treating them right, with compassion and understanding. Referring back to ourselves as soon as we are annoyed, bothered, put out, upset. Application of the Law of resonance, an ability to recognize how Divine Justice manifests through human justice. Arrest and imprisonment of terrorists, trials, application of human justice to ensure the protection of society.

⊖ An extremist person who imposes his point of view, his way of thinking, and who uses force to do so, on a small or large scale. A dominating person, who abuses power; or, who, after subjecting others to such acts in this life or in previous lives, experiences the Law of return by finding himself a victim of terrorist acts. A tendency to let ourselves be abused, terrorized; or, to want to seek revenge, to direct our anger and frustration onto others, to deny our own errors, to seek scapegoats onto whom we can project our feelings of annoyance and hatred. Refusal to call ourselves into question, irresponsibility, intolerance, fanaticism. Dreams and/or concrete situations revealing the fact that the person is visiting memories that are identical to what he reproaches others with. A lack of understanding of the Cosmic Laws of resonance, karma, and reincarnation, as well as of the fact that Divine Justice is absolute, and that it manifests in our life, not only in accordance with acts committed in our present life, but also taking into account all that we have thought and done in all of our lives. A megalomaniac, who takes himself for God or his executor; who believes himself to be above Divine Laws, a messenger invested by God with a mission giving him the right to judge and condemn others, who is convinced his acts are right, when in actual fact he accomplishes a demonic mission, a mission that uses and engenders evil, wrong-doing, hurts. A savior attitude, believing ourselves to be upholders of the law, and hence arbitrarily using authority, force and power, instead of educating people's conscience, mind, and spirit with love, wisdom, compassion, and tolerance. Rebellious, disobedient forces, that refuse to recognize, acknowledge, and respect Divine Laws; or, that interpret and apply them for their own ends. Someone who ignores the fact that through his destructive acts committed in the outside world, he unconsciously tries to liberate what bothers, annoys, disturbs, upsets him in his inner world. A lack of understanding of the fact that evil is educational, and that we always reap what we sow. Imprisonment, trials, tumultuous ideologies. A puritanical, haughty attitude. A complex of superiority. Megalomania.

THIGH

The thigh refers to our intimacy as it is situated near the genitals and is also a part of our body that is not often on show. As a considerable muscular part of the leg, the thigh also represents strength in the way we walk and advance in life. It is also a symbol of seduction in both a positive or negative way, of sensuality, sensitivity, and of intimate relationships.

⊕ Opening and revelation on the intimate level, sensuality, sensitivity. Power or strength to undertake and advance. Mastery of basic instincts.

⊖ A tendency to reveal too much of our intimacy; or, to be too prudish. A lack or excess of strength and support in advancing. Charm and seduction for personal gain; or, to impress others. Provocatively seeking sensual pleasure. Lack of love, of personal attention, or difficulty in intimate relationships.

THUMB

The thumb is the first finger (*cf. also* this term) of a human hand; it is the thickest finger and is made of two phalanges (digital bones), and is opposable to the other fingers. It is an essential finger as it allows us to grip objects, hence allowing hand actions. Symbolically, it represents Divine Power and Love, altruism, mutual aid, support, dedication and devotion in giving and receiving, in our capacity to make, manufacture, construct, and manifest.

⊕ Related to an altruistic, dedicated person who enjoys helping and supporting others, who gives and receives with a spiritual conscience, who tries to manifest Divine Power and Love in every gesture. Related to courage, to protection, given its enveloping, protective effect of our other fingers when we close our fist.

⊖ Difficulties regarding altruism, mutual aid, support, dedication, devotion, and protection. Excessive will. Seeking to control. Abuse of power. Megalomania. Powerful anger expressed when giving and receiving, in the way we materialize. Idleness. Clumsiness.

TIE, A (necktie)

A tie is a symbol that is related to virility. Its shape, like an arrow pointing downward toward the genitals, reinforces a masculine dynamic of assertion and emissivity on the material level. It is often worn in the context of work, and by people who give prime importance to materiality, business, and the conception and materialization of projects. It can also be compared to a rope tied with a slipknot or noose, which obliges the wearer to obey matter, like an animal on a leash. Today, as in the past, it is a global symbol of a fashion associated with material success, both for well-known personalities as well as people in the business world, particularly those in positions of responsibility.

⊕ Adaptation. Respect for mentalities: wearing a tie indicates the choice of following social convention so as not to disturb others in the workplace or create pointless difficulties or conflicts in our environment. We can wear a tie because socially obliged to do so while fully understanding its symbolism.

⊖ Artificial search for power, renown, success, imposing presence, and authority. Subjugated by matter, by social recognition. A person who is attached to society life and stuck in social conventions. Abuse of power. Materialism. Feelings of superiority and inferiority. Playing a role which nourishes our need for appearances, a feeling of being important and powerful, the illusion of having a privileged position. Distorted, unjust emissivity. Male chauvinism. Conformity. A feeling of strangulation. Hiding and repressing our true personality behind appearances.

TIGER

Tigers are solitary, carnivorous animals, which mainly live in Asian territories. This animal is considered to be the largest wild feline in the world. It does not like to share its territory, especially with other males, and its wild, solitary nature distinguishes it from the lion, which is a more sociable animal that lives in a permanent pride of lions, composed of females and cubs, wherein the dominant male has total power over the *harem*. The male tiger possesses territory that includes two or three domains reserved for females. Tigers are hunters, bloodthirsty predators, whereas male lions only hunt exceptionally in order to protect the pride from intrusions of other lions in their territory. It is interesting to notice the difference between these two felines and compare their social behavior with human behavior, where we regularly encounter evolved, more gregarious types of behavior and other more solitary, *untamed* types. A tiger has a much more negative connotation because of its reputation as a night-hunter, which makes it a symbol of dangerous instinctual force on the unconscious level. It is also known to attack man and there are numerous famous cases of man-eating tigers; e.g. the *man-eating tigress of Champawat* (eventually shot and killed in 1907) attacked and killed over 435 people in eight years.

From a positive symbolic point of view, a tiger represents great instinctual force, which protects its possessions and territory, and is capable of facing powerful emotional energies, because tigers are excellent, long-distance swimmers. Its anti-social, solitary nature symbolizes a strong tendency to reject others in a savage, ferocious manner in order to dominate and satisfy personal needs, as well as a lack of altruism. Such flaws are typical of a self-centered person, who is ready to do whatever it takes to get what he wants, even if it means attacking like a thief in the night. A tiger's tendency to reject its cubs, to use female tigers only to satisfy its sexual needs, to attack only the weaker and younger, reinforces the negative symbolism of this animal, which, on the human level, can be found in a person who abuses his power and is megalomaniac, violent, irresponsible, greedy, anti-social, dominant and domineering. A tiger spots or detects its prey by sight and hearing, rarely using its sense of smell, which shows that it is solely focused on its own concerns and has such confidence in its strength and power that it doesn't need to use its sense of smell to protect itself as the majority of animals do.

⊕ Great physical, instinctual strength and power. Ability to face powerful, intense emotions, and major conflicts, fearlessly, calmly and serenely. Sense of protection of territory and possessions. Exceptional force of survival. Capacity to remain alone with ourselves without fear, anxiety, or need for others. Transcendence of abuse of power, aggression, dominance, megalomaniac, violent, irresponsible, abusive, greedy, anti-social tendencies. Ability to manage aggressive forces arising from our unconscious.

⊖ Symbol of aggression, violence, domination, excessive force and strength, the law of the jungle (every man for himself, survival of the fittest, where might is right). Tendency to attack those weaker than us; or, on the contrary, to let ourselves be dominated, abused, attacked without protesting, without having recourse to justice and the law for fear of reprisals. Ready to do anything to get what we want, to kill, assault, rape, abuse others, etc. Predator, bloodthirsty hunter. A person who is dominated by his instincts; dangerous, even criminal behavior. Someone who commits crimes with absolutely no remorse or guilt. An anti-social, over-solitary loner. Aggression related to very powerful, unsatisfied needs. Extremely worrying, threatening, devastating, raw power. An irresponsible, coarse, brutal, self-centered person, who only thinks of himself. Total lack of altruism. Not wanting to look after and care for others, our works, our family. No feelings of love or wisdom; a person who is completely focused only on his needs; sexual aggression.

TIRE (GB: tyre)

As an essential element of the wheel of a vehicle (car, motorbike, bicycle, airplane, etc.), a tire is related to the cycle of advancing and to the way we move around. It ensures different functions such as adherence to the ground, shock and vibration absorption, thereby facilitating a vehicle's movements. Consequently a tire is a symbol associated with the way we advance and move, as well as our motivation and enthusiasm as we move around. The fact that it is filled with air (or another gas) connects it to the air element, symbolically speaking, the world of thoughts, while its contact with the road associates it with the earth element, the world of action.

Symbolically, it represents a capacity to have very concrete, stable thoughts, which serve our advancing in life, ensuring solid anchorage in action. It also designates the necessary flexibility to absorb the shocks we may receive or feel when manifesting. In terms of states of conscience, it indicates a certain capacity to adapt, and withstand initiations and the less comfortable aspects of life, without losing our ability to advance and evolve with stability and steadfastness.

By adhering to the ground, fixed to an axis, a tire allows a vehicle to ensure good road-holding abilities and safe braking. Hence it expresses a capacity to be in contact with matter and the concrete world, while maintaining mastery of the direction we wish to go in.

⊕ Flexibility, motivation, and harmony in concrete thoughts, which allow adequate, right, qualitative advancing and create an active driving force. A capacity for adaptation, adherence, and progression in all types of terrain or situations. A capacity to resist the tensions and obstacles life presents us with during our manifestations. A capacity to follow the direction of our choosing, respecting the time needed for each stage so as to succeed in materializing, concretizing it positively.

⊖ Difficulties related to our capacity to advance, motivate ourselves, materialize and concretize our ideas, our projects. A lack of flexibility to adapt to an environment, a situation. Fear of committing ourselves and being involved in action, in advancing on the personal or social level. Absence of dynamism to manifest.

Deflated tires indicate a lack of motivation, a state of fatigue on the thought level, negligence, sluggishness, nonchalance, laziness;

or, overly materialistic dynamics, that are too heavy and affect our road-holding ability, our capacity to advance, possibly constituting a danger, when we have to brake or take a corner. Difficulty adapting to the unexpected, unforeseen events or situations, heading toward a new objective, a new goal, choosing another direction to advance. Behavior that provokes rapid, uneven tire wear, indicating on the symbolic level that the person is tired of advancing socially, collectively.

Symbolically, *over inflated tires* represent a tendency to excessively motivate ourselves and become active on the thought level and in action; such tires express a desire to drive fast, competitively.

Worn tires: Fatigue, exhaustion, a lack of road-holding capacity, difficulty being involved in the world of matter, driving, choosing our direction, concretizing, materializing our aims and objectives. A tendency to want to force advancing, to *wear out* our life, exhaust ourselves by dangerous driving, be being too busy in matter, pursuing social success, or the satisfaction of our needs.

Burst tire: A person who experiences too much intensity, too much pressure, and tension in his active life, and in the materialization of his thoughts. Excessive willpower, a person who forces too much in matter.

Inappropriate tire size and breadth: Indicates different discrepancies such as a complex of superiority, manifested by machismo behavior; or, a tendency to put too much importance on matter and appearances (large wheels with conspicuous, fancy, shiny rims); or, if the tires are too small and inadequate, a complex of inferiority, a lack of self-confidence, or restrained motivation, a limited spirit, not wanting to advance socially.

Old, used tires: Another negative aspect of tires is their impact on the environment. Old tires, abandoned and/or thrown into the dump are not biodegradable. Consequently, they are a source of pollution, and potentially, of difficult-to-extinguish fires, which produce toxic fumes. Hence, symbolically, they represent a state of conscience where a person advances with an old, outdated motivation force, lacking vision and long-term planning, caring little for the consequences of the way he materializes his thoughts.

However, more and more today, as our ecological conscience and care for the environment grows and expands, old tires are being recycled and their traditional re-use has now been extended far beyond a child's makeshift swing, to be used as an alternative fuel source for industries, as shock-absorbing surfacing for recreational and athletic areas and pavements, for collision-reducing barriers, in making shoes and bags, to mention just a few. Such positive recycling of old, used tires symbolizes our capacity to make good use both of our environment and our former ways of advancing.

TOE

Toes help our foot to advance by giving it impetus; hence they symbolize a force of advancing, of movement, progression. As they are to be found at the very extremity of the foot, they are more specifically related to the stability, flexibility, suppleness, and precision of our gait, step, or walk. They also confer agility in certain physical exercises. In addition to this, toes allow us to walk across an unstable surface, to adapt to the different obstacles and variations encountered, and to keep our balance.

As they touch the ground when a person is standing up, toes also represent connection with the earth, a capacity to be rooted in the concrete world.

Furthermore, toes allow us to walk on tiptoe. From a positive point of view, this way of moving represents a person who moves delicately, gently, discreetly, careful not to make noise, not to disturb or waken others. From a negative point of view, it may indicate that a person would like to slip away, sneakily, furtively, to shirk a duty, avoid responsibilities, or slip into a place without drawing attention to himself, without being heard, possibly hiding erroneous, or selfish, self-centered behavior, like being late for personal reasons, for example. It may be related to an uneasy conscience, a feeling of guilt, malevolent intentions; or, on the other hand, denote a feeling of superiority, a need to be above others, an aspiration to be taller, *higher,* in all senses of the word. Little children learning to walk are often observed to walk more frequently on tiptoe than with the sole of their foot wholly on the ground. If this persists, it may denote an airy, more ethereal dynamic, and eventually, a resistance to or difficulty in incarnating fully. Some people maintain this type of gait into adulthood. Moreover, in certain domains, a capacity to walk on the tips of our toes is considered a sign of agility, finesse, grace, elegance, as in the world of dance, for instance. As it is not a natural way of moving around, and is detrimental to the health of our feet – as in the case of classical ballet dancers –, it also has a negative connotation, and indicates a desire for recognition and acknowledgement, conscious or unconscious feelings of pride, arrogance, and superiority.

Toes may also serve as prehensile tools for gripping and materializing when people have lost the use of their hands, whether due to congenital invalidity, an illness, or an accident. Although loss of an arm or hand reflects a serious distortion on the symbolic level, the fact of being able to develop the capacity of our toes to compensate for such a handicap, indicates that the person has worked intensely to reactivate his capacity to manifest, to give and receive, as represented by our hands and arms.

⊕ A force of advancing. Stability, flexibility, suppleness, and precision in our way of advancing. Agility. Facilitates adaptation of the foot to different obstacles and variations of terrain; balance, equilibrium. Connection with the earth, a capacity to be in contact with the concrete world. A delicate, graceful, refined, discreet, gentle gait. A capacity to raise ourselves up to enlarge our field of vision.

⊖ Difficulty advancing. A lack of stability, flexibility, suppleness on unstable surfaces, in unstable areas. Deficient connection with the earth, difficulty being rooted in the concrete world. An incapacity to display delicacy, finesse, discretion, gentleness in our gait, in our walk; or, mistreatment of our toes and general health in order to display false grace and elegance, unnatural, damaging suppleness and agility. A haughty, ambitious person, who nourishes and displays a feeling of superiority to camouflage his inferiority complex, of which he may, or may not, be aware. Ways of walking that indicate a guilty conscience or malevolent intentions.

TOILET

A toilet is a place where a person can urinate, defecate, and generally speaking, relieve himself of the natural excretions of his body. Toilets are a very common, even recurring symbol in dreams for anyone on a spiritual path. A toilet represents a place of inner purification and liberation, both physical and metaphysical, which procures a global feeling of well-being. Whenever the visit to the toilet goes well, when the atmosphere is calm, and the timing is right, and all of the dream elements are in their right place, this indicates that we have liberated ourselves of the negativity absorbed in our conscience on the physical, emotional, intellectual, or spiritual level. This induces a feeling of light-heartedness and renewed vivification. If the conditions are bad, and the toilet is blocked, dirty, or overflowing, it indicates the presence of emotional blockages, and misactions (*cf.* this term) that have been accumulated in our present life, or in previous lives. Having neglected to rectify, purify, and transform them, they remain in our unconscious until the day a trigger event reactivates them, causing them to overflow.

In a dream, the place where a toilet is located is important because it determines the sector or region that we are purifying in our conscience. If it is inside a house or apartment, the process of purification concerns our intimate, private life, our relationship with ourselves and our family. If it is in a more collective place (a restaurant, workplace, train, airport, etc.), it is more to do with our social life, our memories of communication, and our relationships with others, as well as the type of activity we are doing at that particular moment.

In general difficulty eliminating stools, constipation, denotes a tendency to repress retained, negative experiences we haven't understood, which prevents the body from being liberated. Diarrhea is a sign of extreme, radical, or violent rejection of what we have ingested on the physical and metaphysical levels. It indicates an incapacity to correctly digest, assimilate, and eliminate a situation, event, news, etc.; or, refusal to face it. The context as a whole needs to be considered to be able to decode what we need to become aware of and digest.

The difference between a toilet and other purification symbols such as a washbasin, a shower, or bidet, resides in the fact that a toilet is a place that allows the elimination of digestive waste products, the result of the transformation of elements on which we nourished ourselves, on the physical or subtle levels (solid and liquid food, thoughts, emotions, soul-states, attitudes, etc.).

⊕ A capacity to purify ourselves, to renew our inner self in a healthy manner, to liberate ourselves of useless, negative energies and experiences, after becoming aware of them, after digesting, transforming, and transcending them. Cleansing a way of being and doing induced by heavy, negative memories that we have accumulated in our unconscious, and/or in our active life. A feeling of well-being, renewal, light-heartedness. An ability to terminate cycles, to get rid of old patterns that weigh us down, encumber us, making us heavy and constipating us. A new stage of experimentation and regeneration.

A clean toilet: Well-being, a healthy, pleasant atmosphere and ambiance. Easy acceptance of the necessity to regularly cleanse and purify ourselves on all levels of our being. A period of good balance on the intimate level.

⊖ Difficulty cleansing and purifying ourselves on the inside, opening up to a new stage of evolution, renewing our way of thinking and living. An incapacity to face the negative contents of experimentations in our life, to digest them, and consequently put an end to these cycles. Someone who finds it difficult to accept their flaws, to be authentic with themselves. Rigidity, a tendency to repression or overflowing. Retention due to deep insecurities, through fear of lacking and feeling empty. Excessive desire for cleanliness, perfectionism in purification, puritanism. Self-evaluation without compassion and extremist *vis-à-vis* cleansing being carried out. A person who lacks physical or metaphysical hygiene.

A dirty toilet: An unclean, ill-intentioned, negligent, dispersed, over-busy in matter, hyperactive, confused person. Laxity. An irresponsible, bohemian spirit. Ignorance of the importance of inner work, and hence, a lack of willpower to improve ourselves.

An overflowing toilet: An unconscious that is overburdened with negative memories that can no longer be contained. A person who is incapable of transforming the negative stemming from past experiences. Overflowing, too great an accumulation of difficult experiences that we haven't taken the time to digest and evacuate.

A blocked toilet: An overburdened unconscious. Problems manifesting an inner blockage, a lack of understanding of the meaning of ordeals. A symbol of an undigested, unpurified life experience. Indication of the necessity to meditate on the meaning of a difficult experience to unblock the inner situation. A blocked person who has repressed a lot of emotions, behavior, or thoughts. Difficulty letting go of everything that is wrong, harmful, or too much. An accumulation of memories that may be the origin of illnesses of the digestive or elimination system.

TOOTH DECAY, DENTAL CAVITY

Teeth represent the structure of our primary needs and instincts. Tooth decay leading to a dental cavity indicates a lack of wisdom in the way we nourish ourselves or in our general lifestyle. The main reasons for dental cavities are: poor dental hygiene, an excessive consumption of sugar (which indicates lacks of affection and gentleness), smoking (which corresponds to bogged down, confused thoughts), stress (which reveals a state of hyperactivity), and certain illnesses.

⊕ Awareness of behavior that needs to be modified regarding primary needs and instincts. An understanding of the importance of healthy, well-balanced, wise lifestyle and nourishment. Restoring balance in our lifestyle.

⊖ Problems with primary needs and instincts. Lack of conscience and knowledge regarding hygiene and food. Difficulty managing our needs. Structural problems. Abuse, excess. Tendency to be negligent, lazy. Lack of upkeep, maintenance, work on ourselves, and wisdom. Problems of discipline, carelessness, ignorance and not taking proper care of the way we live. Lack of willpower and motivation to change negative habits, always waiting for serious consequences before making the effort required for positive change. Not understanding that a little unresolved difficulty will sooner or later engender a larger one. Satisfied living in an ordinary conscience. Maintaining a cycle of bad habits.

TOOTH, TEETH

The essential purpose of teeth is to eat, bite, and chew, but they also participate in speaking. They represent the structure of our primary needs, and their color, white, represents wisdom in the way we nourish ourselves. The bone part, which is associated with the mineral kingdom, symbolizes connection with forces and memories that dwell in the depths of the unconscious. All our materializations bear the imprint of our inner structure, of what we are, and of what we have been in the past. It is normal to receive dreams about teeth when we begin a spiritual path. Such dreams inform us as to the cleansing that is being done in the deep structure of our being, and reveal changes in our way of nourishing ourselves and reacting to our needs. Teeth problems indicate that we have memories and behavior, ways of being that manifest through a poor, unhealthy diet and habits. Teeth also represent the combative potential of our instinctual force, our capacity to attack by biting to get what we want.

Upper teeth are related to the causal, spiritual world.

Lower teeth are related to the element earth and the material world.

Wearing braces: Indicates that the person is in the process of re-structuring and re-setting his fundamental needs as well as his personality regarding seduction and self-esteem.

A crowned tooth is related to self-esteem, what we emanate when we seek to satisfy and/or are motivated by basic, exterior needs. A crown (which is also applicable as a type of dental restoration) can completely *cap* or encircle a tooth or dental implant when a large cavity threatens the ongoing health of a tooth. In this case, a second chance is given to retrieve self-esteem and a positive way of nourishing ourselves.

The roots are more connected to the unconscious level of our basic inner needs in terms of nourishment. When they are healthy, they reveal a good, healthy way of nourishing ourselves; or, on the contrary, when they are unhealthy, they indicate, both concretely and symbolically, a negative way of nourishing ourselves. They may also indicate aspects of ourselves that tend to hide negative tendencies of our personality regarding the way we nourish ourselves.

⊕ Balance and wisdom in the way we nourish ourselves and satisfy our primary needs. Transcendence of our instincts, the animal forces in us. A healthy foundation and structure. A well-balanced diet and life. Self-confidence. Self-esteem. Harmonious, peaceful communication and self-expression.

⊖ A lack of wisdom, structure, and balance in the way we nourish ourselves and take care of our primary needs. Aggression and combativeness, pugnacity to get what we want. Superficiality. Emphasis on esthetics, appearances. Need to please. Lack of self-esteem. Loss of energy. Deficiency problems. An unhealthy diet and life. Carelessness, thoughtlessness. Abuse. Poverty. Beginning of initiation, de-structuring of the way we act when faced with needs. A sharp, mordant, sarcastic spirit.

TOUCH

Touch is one of the 5 senses of man, animal, and certain plants. It helps in the exploration and discovery of the environment, walking, holding and gripping objects, nutrition, in social, affective, and sexual contacts. It is needed and used in certain professions (medical care, massages, etc.).

Receptors, corpuscles, that are sensitive to touch, are tiny organs that are invisible to the eye and are located in the dermis (skin); each receptor has a specific task of responding to heat, cold, pressure, or pain. In reality, the sense of touch is multi-dimensional; it is linked to the whole of our being: our conscience and unconscious, our strengths, and all of our physical and metaphysical capacities.

Through touch, we can reach and move another person, depending on his degree of sensitivity, his capacity of perception, his receptivity.

Some people, for example, are only touched on the physical level when they are caressed, receive a gift, etc. Others feel gestures more deeply; they are more receptive to other people's emotions, to the intention that motivates an event, a word, a gesture, etc. Such people have developed an extra-sensorial perception of touch that is called clairsentience, and which consists in tuning into and perceiving energy that exists beyond or behind the actual physical situation, through multi-dimensional listening. Through touch, we establish physical contact and an energy exchange with ourselves and others, who represent parts of ourselves too. It allows us to concretely enter the world of action on the physical level. Through touch, contact is established on the one hand with condensed matter, the outside world, and, on the other hand, a person's nervous system, his brain, his mind and spirit, his vital energy and all of the memories he has recorded on his *hard drive* (his soul).

Touching or being touched awakens and reactivates positive or negative memories, which induce the + or – atmosphere of the context wherein the exchange takes place, and affect the way in which we receive the other person's energy and give ours.

On the metaphysical level, the sense of touch shows our capacity to perceive the way we touch others on the level of subtle energies and intention, and the way we ourselves are touched by others. The development of a multi-dimensional conscience helps reactivate clairsentience thanks to which we can feel and sense what is going on beyond the physical body, in the metaphysical levels of our being and in the parallel worlds. Everyone has the capacity to activate his inner clairsentience potential. We can do this if we work on ourselves, with right, pure intention, with the goal of becoming a better soul by transforming our weaknesses, faults, and distorted memories. We will then develop intelligent feeling, extra-sensorial perception, and spiritual autonomy, and be able to materialize our potential divinely and act like an angel on Earth.

⊕ A capacity to explore, discover, tune into, perceive, and have an in-depth understanding of concrete and subtle information. Ability to manifest love, kindness, tenderness, and wisdom through touch. Healthy, pure, renewing, replenishing, loving, sensual, sexual touching. Ability to touch others and to be touched ourselves with right intention, on both the physical and metaphysical levels. A feeling of being alive, well incarnated. Favors the awakening of all the senses, connection with vital energy, the other dimensions of conscience, and the different areas of the unconscious *via* the sense of touch, *via* clairsentience. Good balance between emissivity and receptivity, between giving and receiving, allowing us to heal ourselves and others, to love and act authentically and unconditionally. Appreciation of what is concrete, of work and efforts made. Favors creativity, constructive, evolutive handling of matter, helps develop a healthy relationship with matter, and to marry spirit and matter consciously, respecting Divine Laws. Gratitude for all the experiences life offers us. Harmonious communication between our inner and outer worlds. Allows us to develop and to understand our environment.

⊖ Problems related to touch, to giving and receiving, difficulty touching others and/or ourselves, or being touched physically, emotionally, and/or energetically. Possessiveness, need to control; or, someone who rejects physical contact and his incarnation because of discrepancies between the different levels of his being that he engendered during the course of his lives. A hyper-materialistic person. A lack of love, tenderness, kindness, and wisdom; or, difficulty expressing them. Poverty on the level of receptivity, over-emissive behavior; a lack of sensitivity and subtlety preventing the person from feeling deeply. Someone who uses the sense of touch to selfishly satisfy his instinctive needs, who touches others with a crude, animal state of conscience. Excessive, perverted sensuality and sexuality. Behavior displaying coldness, indifference, aggression, violence, destruction, the law of the jungle. A lack of interest in exploring and discovering life through the sense of touch and developing the gift of clairsentience so as to feel, to sense the multi-dimensions they reveal to us. Ignorance of the educational function of matter and life on Earth. Someone who limits others, prevents them from fulfilling themselves in action. Ingratitude for the concrete world, for the work and the efforts made to create, make, and materialize. Disbelief in the existence of parallel worlds and in everyone's capacity to perceive them by developing his subtle, metaphysical senses.

TOWN *cf. City*

TOY

A toy is an object that is usually for children, and it allows them to learn, discover, experiment and develop certain capacities and abilities through play (*cf. also* this term). Toys allow for the creation of imaginary situations favorable to the exploration of different states of conscience, and different, personal and social, relational dynamics. Mostly used by children, the symbolic meaning of toys is very much related to childhood, and the notion of joy, pleasure, fun, light-heartedness, candor, imagination, fantasy, creativity, exploration and discovery. Toys also contribute toward the gradual development of a child's autonomy, of his capacity to make choices and decisions, to assert himself, to activate and manifest his capacities and potential, to integrate altruistic qualities by learning to share his toys, to exchange and communicate nicely, respectfully with other children and the world around him while playing.

⊕ Conscious choice of positive, beneficial toys that favor learning and give children the desire to experiment, explore, acquire capacities, experience, and knowledge with joy, pleasure and light-heartedness. Development of dexterity, skill, attention, observation, concentration, and patience. Exploration of different states of conscience on the personal, family, and social levels. Construction of identity, personality, character. Development of imagination, creativity, a capacity for deduction, and imitation. Gradual acquisition of autonomy, and altruistic behavior. Facilitates connection with our inner child.

⊖ A lack or excess of toys; or, a negative choice of toys that encourage children to manifest distorted aspects such as competitiveness, comparison, aggression, anger, impatience, vanity, envy, jealousy, etc., leading to behavioral problems, the development of a dysfunctional personality, difficulties learning and experimenting on the personal, relational and social levels. Difficulty acquiring autonomy, manifesting our potential; or, a childish attitude. May be related to multiple lacks and unfulfilled needs that lead to obsessive behavior regarding success, winning; or, fear of losing, fear of failure. Tendency to take refuge in an imaginary world so as to flee harsh reality, a very difficult childhood. Incapacity to marvel, to play joyfully, with pleasure, candor, spontaneity, and light-heartedness. Disconnection from our inner child.

TRAFFIC CONGESTION, TRAFFIC JAM

Traffic congestion represents a limitation, hindrance, obstruction of transport and communication routes on the ground, water, and air levels; hence, it is symbolically related to physical action, emotions, and thoughts. The various terms used such as congestion, bottleneck, gridlock, all denote very well what happens on the inside when we are caught in traffic jams or congestion: our willpower to act and advance, nourished by our emotions and thoughts, finds itself halted, blocked, hampered, and all sorts of emotions and soul states are activated, rise to the surface and emerge, such as impatience, frustration, annoyance, irritation, aggression, anger, fear of arriving late, or missing opportunities, etc.

On the symbolic level, traffic congestion indicates the presence of inner obstructions and blockages on the level of social interaction, in the way we go toward others (ground); on the level of our emotional stability (waterways); and on the level of our thoughts (air). Such blockages are created by too many simultaneous intentions and actions, which prevent us from advancing toward our destination continuously and harmoniously, and from achieving our goals, from accomplishing our projects, one at a time, step by step. Since each excess has a corresponding lack, it is important to reflect not only on excessive attitudes and behavior in the way we function, but also on the lacks felt, consciously or unconsciously, on one level or another, which push us to want too much and to do too much in compensation. As traffic congestion usually affects a large number of people and vehicles, it concerns the collective level; hence, symbolically, lots of parts and aspects of ourselves that all need to learn patience, tolerance, respect for stages, balance between emissivity and receptivity, doing and being (not doing), as well as the cleansing of unconscious memories, that, through resonance, attract and participate in the materialization of congested situations in our concrete life, or in our dreams.

⊕ Awareness that the congestion we encounter on the outside reflects our inner congestion. Reflection on the symbolic and metaphysical meaning of the various sources and situations of congestion we encounter so as to discover what behavior and attitudes we need to change, which distorted memories we need to cleanse and transform in order to liberate these states of limitation, congestion, and blockage on all levels of our being. Work on our fear of being late; or, missing opportunities. Understanding the fact that a traffic jam, or other congestion, that prevents us from advancing or arriving on time at our destination, indicates a lack of synchronicity, discrepancy between our personal priorities and inner dynamics on the one hand, and the priority and rhythm of outer events orchestrated by Up Above, on the other. Integration of the concepts of synchronicity and resonance. Incitement to study in depth, in the light of symbolic language and the Law of resonance, the multidimensional causes that hinder and hamper the realization of our projects, and even our destiny. An opportunity to work on ourselves to develop more patience, tolerance, compassion, calm, serenity, and deep, global understanding of the situations that slow us up, delay and limit us, or even stop us from what we were doing, or intending to do. An ability to use time spent in congested traffic as a period of introspection and renewal in the heart of intense action. Respect and indulgence regarding collective dynamics in the outer world, knowing that they reflect aspects of our inner world.

⊖ Ways of behaving and acting, as well as mind, spirit, and soul states that slow us down, and engender limitations, blockages, and forced halts. Impatience. Intolerance. Annoyance. Irritation. Frustration, anger, aggression. Fear of arriving late, or missing an opportunity. A tendency to want to force life and destiny. Agitation, disharmony, and imbalance that leads to discrepancies and loss of synchronicity with the Divine Plan. Excessive willpower to succeed and attain our objectives and personal ambitions. Insecurities that push us to go ahead. A hyperactive person who grants too much importance to matter and social life, refusing to take time to work on himself so as to cleanse his memories of limitation, and rectify his excessive attitudes.

TRAFFIC *cf. Circulation*

TRAIN

Given its capacity to transport passengers and resources, a train represents a great force of advancing related to the world of action, the conveyance of human or physical resources, on the social and collective level. It also symbolizes new orientations, new directions in life, because it brings us toward other towns, cities, regions, or countries. It usually circulates on two rails fixed to the ground, which, on the one hand, relate it to the symbolism of relationships (number 2), and, on the other hand, stability, firm rooting on the ground. The symbolism of a suspended train is the same except that as it circulates in the air, it relates more to the world of thoughts, and not materialization, as it doesn't touch the ground. As for a monorail train, the idea of willpower in relationships with others becomes more concentrated, more determined.

A train also symbolizes great willpower, a force of determination, solidity, and stability (iron rails) in our life and spiritual path, in our way of advancing. When we look at a train from above, its aerodynamic, longitudinal form recalls that of a snake (or male sex organ), which, metaphysically, confers on it a great emissive force, a linear energy, indicating a direction, a path or route to follow. A locomotive serves to push or pull railroad cars. This term may also refer to a motivating group cheer, which gradually increases in intensity, and is usually led by a cheerleader. In French, this term is used to describe people who are the driving force in a group, meaning people with great energy and lots of leadership to help others, to help projects advance.

In a symbolic analysis of a dream or concrete situation containing a train or a train journey, all of the elements must be considered as parts of ourselves: the type of train, its quality and the services it offers, the place of departure and destination, as well as the places, landscapes, and countries it travels through, inform us as to the influences, the memories, that dwell in us, in terms of states of conscience, and show us our concrete way of advancing collectively during great stages of movement and change in our life. Likewise, the passengers are to be considered as either known or unknown facets of our own being (as the case may be), that the train journey allows us to see; hence enabling us to observe dynamics of functioning, attitude, and behavior. On becoming aware of their presence and by applying the Law of resonance, we discover aspects of our own social, collective dynamics.

A train journey usually requires good planning regarding the destination and the most appropriate itinerary to take to reach it, since, unlike a car journey, it does not allow us to change direction, or to stop at any time. When we travel by train, we are less flexible, since stops are essentially concentrated in collective destinations such as stations in the city center, on the outskirts, or in large towns and villages. Organizing a train journey, especially when long-distance or to another country, requires good inner and outer structuring and organization on the collective level; hence deep reflection on the aim, necessity, and usefulness of the trip.

A train is usually considered to be a comfortable, safe means of transport, that is increasingly popular, especially in countries with a well-developed rail system, so as to avoid and reduce road traffic density, traffic congestion, the fatigue and stress of driving. It also favors social contact and brings people from all origins into close proximity, helps develop an ecological conscience, and a better use of resources and time, as we can work, study, read, exchange, contemplate, meditate, etc., while traveling.

A train journey experienced in a dream very often symbolizes the activation of an important program of advancing with a collective, social dynamic; or, the beginning of a new stage for the dreamer, setting off in a new direction of life and evolution, depending on the context. If we mistake directions when taking the train, it may indicate the need to go back, to reverse a decision regarding direction, because the direction/orientation taken isn't right, is not the most favorable one for the realization of the person's program on the social level. Cosmic Intelligence can orchestrate such an experience to incite the person to reflect, and, eventually, to help him understand that the reason he wants to go on a journey is to escape or flee a difficult situation, rather than apply himself to finding a solution on the spot. Furthermore, mistaking trains, or arriving late for a train, may indicate that certain parts of the person refuse to change or go in the chosen direction. It also indicates a lack of willpower and conviction to change socially.

⊕ A great force to start off personal or social projects. A capacity to physically and metaphysically transport and convey useful, necessary resources. Someone who chooses to change his life on the social level by taking the right path. A new direction, allowing the re-orientation of our life, as well as expansion on the inner and outer levels. Total confidence in Destiny, a great capacity to adapt to unexpected changes, to compromise and accept the unexpected (delays, obstacles preventing the train from circulating, accidents, etc.). A capacity to advance rapidly (direct, fast trains), but also to recognize and acknowledge the importance of advancing in stages (train changes in the course of a journey, an itinerary). Powerful emissive potential, allowing us to be active on the collective level. Great motivation, and motivating leadership capacities, setting projects in motion, helping them advance, establishing business links, or facilitating social encounters. A multiplying aspect, given by the great variety of possibilities of encounters, exchanges, discoveries, etc., symbolized by the passengers and human and material resources found aboard a train. A person who is sure of himself, with good social intuition, knowing how to listen to his inner voice to take the right train, the right direction. Great determination to act, to take a direction and follow it to the end. Reliability, punctuality. A capacity to attain our collective objectives in the world of matter, an ability to organize important encounters, meetings. Awareness that synchronicity, or the absence of synchronicity, is always managed and organized, orchestrated, by Cosmic Intelligence. Altruism. Respect for the environment. Collective, multi-dimensional conscience. Feelings of inner and outer liberty and expansion.

⊖ An over-emissive person, who forces to set a project in motion, to make it advance, to set up social encounters; or, on the contrary, a person who lacks motivation, leadership, the driving force to advance collectively, who tends to *miss the train* (i.e. to miss positive opportunities on the social level), or to take the wrong train or direction. A limited, blocked person who would like to change his life, take a new direction, but who doesn't dare do so. Poor, wrong choice, wrong direction in life. Excessive willpower; or, a lack of willpower to be active on the social level. Difficulty attaining our objectives in the concrete world, an incapacity to travel, to transport and convey resources, to organize important events. Problems with social orientation. Resistance when it becomes necessary to change direction. A tendency to flee responsibilities. A feeling of solitude and insecurity, fears, apprehensions. Discrepancies between personal and social life. A lack of altruism, and environmental awareness and conscience.

TRASHCAN *cf.* ***Garbage bin***

TRAVEL

Traveling means going to visit new regions, new countries, discover other cultures, mentalities, lifestyles, to enter into contact with other egregores (*cf.* this term). Whenever we travel, not only do we go toward another place, but we also change state(s) of conscience within ourselves. Symbolically, traveling means undertaking the exploration of certain aspects of ourselves, certain zones of our unconscious. Indeed, the regions we visit all represent parts of ourselves that we know to varying degrees or not at all; often, we visit places we have never or rarely explored. Our choice of destination is not a coincidence. Whether a trip is for pleasure or business or any other reason, it always corresponds to what we need to discover about ourselves, or what we need to deepen our knowledge of. A symbolic analysis of the qualities and weaknesses of the places we travel to, study of the positive and negative resonance, attraction, or annoyances experienced are indications of what we need to become aware of, or cleanse and transform in our conscious and unconscious memories, by going beyond the frontiers of the known, to gradually become a universal traveler, capable of feeling well, comfortable, at home everywhere.

In order to have a pleasant, positive, constructive travel experience, it is essential to develop the capacity of adaptation, flexibility of mind and spirit, the will to call ourselves into question and not to be prejudiced. It is also important to know and respect the effects of the Law of synchronicity. Hence, when we wish to go traveling, it is recommended to ask for signs and dreams to find out if the timing is right, if it is the right way, the right destination, if it is good for our evolution. Thus we learn to prepare travel plans first of all on the metaphysical level before realizing them on the physical level. Proceeding like this, there is less risk of our heading off on travels that go against our life plan, which will lead to harmful consequences and problematic situations.

However, even when our travel plans have been confirmed by dreams and signs, and their preparation and departure is problem-free, our trip may turn out to be initiatic, and confront us with unconscious memories, or distorted aspects of ourselves through trying situations encountered en route. We need to be able to accept this as part of our learning and evolution program, and not project onto others whatever annoyances and bothersome things happen.

In a dream, a perturbed, problematic journey or trip may indicate difficulties adapting to change, exploring our inner world. A trip dedicated to superficiality, where we rejoice in artificial pleasures, and indulge in laziness indicates that we have superficial attitudes and behavior within us, that we lack authenticity and depth regarding knowledge of our inner self, an incapacity to face our memories related to what others think of us, as well as frivolous or worldly appearances.

We can travel without going anywhere physically speaking, for example, in our mind, in our imagination, and in our sleep thanks to our subtle bodies and our capacity to dream. Indeed, in our dreams, we can travel in the parallel worlds, the multi-dimensions of life. The metaphysical places and regions we visit at night in dream reality engender in us all sorts of states of conscience, and allow us to discover and learn a lot about ourselves, just the same as traveling to different countries in physical reality. We also *travel* when we converse with someone, depending on our level of conscience and according to the resonance we have with him, our mind travels in his inner world and visits his soul states, intentions, and conscious and unconscious intentions that emanate from him like a new country to be discovered. On integrating the multi-dimensionality of our capacity to travel, we realize that our life, and all existence is a continual journey leading us from discovery to discovery, even when, physically, we remain in the same place.

By traveling with the awareness that everything we encounter and discover represents parts of ourselves, we quickly get to know ourselves in depth, to get out of crystallized habits, surpass our limits, our own borders and frontiers until one day there aren't any left. In spite of the multiplicity that manifests everywhere, we are then capable of deep feelings of harmonious unity.

⊕ The will to discover other realities, cultures, mentalities, lifestyles, worlds. A great capacity of adaptation, flexibility, and supple-mindedness. Awareness that when we travel in the outside world, we simultaneously travel in our inner world, that we always resonate with everything we visit and discover, both in the qualities and in the distortions, in the + and the –. Experiencing initiatic journeys in full consciousness, knowing they are an invitation to encounter and transcend memories lodged in our unconscious, to go beyond known horizons, to overcome our limitations. Someone who travels with the aim of widening his vision, conscience, knowledge, understanding and perception of the world. Development of tolerance, non-judgment, respect for others, a feeling of fraternity, of belonging to a planetary family. Integration of the fact that everything we visit and discover represents parts of ourselves. A capacity to globally evaluate the situations and events that turn up during the course of our lives and to understand them in depth. Transcendence of outer and inner borders. Someone who prepares his travels while taking into account signs and synchronicity, asking for guidance in his dreams, so as to ensure his motivation, destination, and time chosen to travel are right. Someone who consciously trains himself to become a universal traveler, to develop and manifest Divine Qualities and Virtues everywhere he goes, and to transcend human distortions and weaknesses.

⊖ Resistance to traveling, difficulty leaving our daily routine, our known environment, adapting to change, to what's new, to a different way of being and living; or, someone who travels superficially, being dispersed in a multitude of activities, wasting resources, all to escape his daily routine or to flee his responsibilities; or, who refuses to face his conscious and unconscious memories, to cleanse and transform them. A feeling of emptiness in spite of numerous trips because of a lack of anchorage and centering. An absence of principles and true values allowing us to have a well founded, solid, stable inner life. A limited, stubborn spirit, intolerance, prejudice, rejection of what is different, unknown. A tendency to criticize others, their lifestyle, their habits, to always compare them with our own criteria, to project onto them and the outer world whatever bothers us, the obstacles, negative situations and incidents we are confronted with on our travels. Refusal to refer back to ourselves, to apply the Law of resonance. Blocked horizon, a lack of global vision and understanding of the multi-dimensionality of traveling. A harsh, sterile evaluation of other cultures and mentalities. Anti-social behavior, preferring to travel alone, in a bubble, a tendency to isolate ourselves, to travel in order to flee difficulties rather than face them. A bohemian lifestyle, a nomadic life without conscience, fear of creating links, putting down roots, selfishness and self-centeredness. Ignorance of the fact that our whole life is a journey, that our spirit continually moves around, that, mostly unknown to us, we ceaselessly tune into the metaphysical energies of other travelers, just as we are also influenced by what emanates from those travelers who move through our daily life in one way or another. An incapacity to accept others as they are.

TREASURE

The word treasure usually calls to mind an image of a collection of material riches (coins, jewelry, gems, medals, statues, vases, works of art, etc.) that were once buried, hidden, or stowed away somewhere in the outside world. However, treasure may also refer to discreet, inner riches that we may or may not be aware of, such as an accumulation of gifts and talents, merits, good deeds, etc., which correspond to great inner work and spiritual evolution that manifests in qualities, virtues, and high moral values.

The idea of treasure is often associated with pirates and treasure hunts, legends and myths that talk about mysterious, lost, veiled, secret treasures hidden and/or buried in secret places, protected by people, animals, or objects with supernatural powers and such like. Stories about treasure have always awakened curiosity, a spirit of adventure, discovery, and exploration in us, and nourished our imagination, dreams, illusions, as well as all sorts of sentiments, feelings, and deeds that are far from noble, such as: envy, covetousness, avidity, greed, ambition, betrayal, violence, murder.

Attraction to books and films about treasure indicates that the person is either on a quest, seeking to discover or re-discover resources that will help him materialize his wishes, dreams, and/or projects; or, that he feels nostalgic about treasure he has already possessed in the form of wealth, resources, knowledge, or influence that he lost after poor use of them. Reading a story or watching a film about seeking and finding treasure nourishes, mostly unconsciously, parts of himself that regret the past. Simultaneously, through the different aspects of the characters and storyline, the person integrates on his soul-level the lessons he needs to learn. Furthermore, a symbolic analysis of a treasure story and the resonance we have with it, and the resulting newly developed awareness, allows us to do very evolutive inner work. The same holds true for an attraction to the game called *treasure hunt* frequently organized at children's parties, and for adults in the context of club get-togethers for example, where the players, the treasure hunters advance from post to post by solving clues and enigmas. They often feel as though they have to find their way through a maze, before reaching the final post. The first person or team to have successfully solved all of the enigmas finds and claims the reward, the treasure. The fun is in the quest, in solving the enigmas, understanding and following the messages and signs. The game is positive when it is played in a spirit of fun and the treasure offered is simply a symbolic gesture. It is negative when the theme and clues are of instinctual, crude, boorish taste, awakening and appealing to our basic instincts, when the game is taken too seriously, creating ill-temper, competitiveness, jealousy, covetousness, poor loser dynamics and other distortions, and when it is played solely to win material treasure. Such a game, like many others, owes its variety and popularity to the fact that it symbolizes man's life quest and evolutive path to develop qualities, virtues, and powers in their purest form, which are divine treasures for our life on all levels.

We may also receive dreams wherein we seek or find treasure. Whenever we discover positive treasure in a dream, and when the context, atmosphere, ambiance and all of the related elements are appropriate, luminous, in their right place, it indicates that the dreamer is rediscovering within himself how to use the creative power of his spirit, or resources allowing him to concretize his life in a right, just, altruistic way. It may be a sign that from now on, the dreamer will be able to reap what he sowed in other lives. However, it is essential to understand that such a dream does not necessarily mean that we are going to find treasure or material wealth in concrete reality.

If the dream has a negative tendency, it shows the dreamer the source, the root cause of his erroneous behavior, the reasons for the limitations, restrictions, and lack of resources he may currently be experiencing in concrete reality. In this case, it is important for the dreamer to be able to consider such revelations as the discovery of essential treasure thanks to which he will be able to purify, liberate, and transcend the forces, attitudes, and behavior that block the manifestation of his Divine potential, his true treasure, which for each of us is revealed in the discovery of the inner riches of our soul.

⊕ A symbol of the discovery of riches, wealth, abundance, and aspiration to rediscover and/or regain hidden, forgotten, lost or veiled potential, knowledge, resources, gifts and talents so as to make good use of them. Using found treasure with discernment and an altruistic conscience; sense of sharing, mutual aid, generosity, and solidarity. A person who discovers treasure in his inner and/or outer world, after great purification and transformation work on his distorted forces and memories. Understanding that the attraction treasure exerts on us reveals positive and negative resonance within us. Spirit of discovery, adventure, and exploration to regain the true treasures of Life: Knowledge, Love, Wisdom, and Qualities, Virtues, and Divine Powers in their purest state. Courage, integrity, honesty, loyalty, incorruptibility. Capacity to understand the deep, multi-dimensional, symbolic meaning of hidden or rediscovered treasure.

⊖ Someone who discovers resources that have been accumulated in suspicious, illegal contexts, that were stolen, usurped, etc., and seizes them for himself; or, seeking treasure because of envy, covetousness, avidity, greed, a desire to be rich, aspiring to celebrity and renown at all costs. Tendency to live in illusion, in an unreal, imaginary world; to flee concrete reality and daily responsibilities; to spend our life seeking fortune, glory, prestige, power, control, superiority, and material possessions; to hunt for treasure on the outside, without understanding that we first have to find it on the inside, within ourselves. Materialistic spirit, that only thinks of getting rich, who is ready to do anything to achieve his ends.

Manipulation, cheating, betrayal, corruption, violence. Absence of knowledge of symbolism and resonance. Non respect for other people's lives, defying human and Divine Laws. All sorts of dependencies. Someone who, consciously or unconsciously, lives with feelings of nostalgia regarding the existence of hidden inner treasure that he cannot gain access to, without knowing what to do, how to rediscover it, without understanding that in actual fact, he is seeking Qualities, Virtues, and Powers in their purest state.

TREE

In almost every culture in the world, trees occupy concrete spaces as well as having important symbolic meaning. As it lives for many, many years, a tree symbolizes the forces of Life, the capacity to materialize, construct, and develop. This is also why its image is chosen as a symbol on the mystical and spiritual levels when we speak of *The Tree of Life*.

Like everything in the Universe, a tree follows cycles. In winter, its sap descends into its roots. In spring, its vital energy rises back up into the trunk and branches giving birth to leaves, flowers and fruit. This gradual growth attains its maturity in summer. In the fall, it yields its fruit and sheds its leaves as it prepares for another winter period.

On the symbolic level, a tree's cycles represent the wisdom of gradual evolution. The winter stage corresponds to a concentration of conscience, energy, and effort regarding work on our unconscious through meditation, interiorization and introspection. The spring stage corresponds to rebirth, renewal, reactivation of our vital energy, and the emergence of beautiful feelings, symbolized by the leaves and flowers. The summer stage is one of maturity when a person materializes his projects, represented by fruit. It is a period of expansion when we unfurl and spread the wings of the potential we bear within.

A tree is an extraordinary symbol to represent gradual growth and development on the physical, emotional, intellectual, and spiritual levels. It begins as a tiny seed that grows into a big, strong, solid, stable, upright being. It produces other seeds, symbolically speaking, other children. It settles in one place just like a person in his home, and it works like a real factory, producing all the elements it is made up of, as well as offering all it produces, all it is. It transforms pollution and participates in the creation of oxygen that is essential for life on Earth. All by itself, a tree represents a truly altruistic society because it freely offers shelter and food to a multitude of species, including man.

Regarding human beings, tree roots symbolize our anchorage or roots in concrete life, on the level of materiality. But they also symbolize the work we do on the level of our unconscious, which helps us construct ourselves solidly so as to grow upright with beautiful thoughts, beautiful feelings, and consequently to materialize beautiful works. Its trunk represents uprightness, integrity, solid legs and spine; the crown constituted of branches, leaves, and fruit, symbolizes our head, hair, and brain; its general appearance represents the energy we emit, our aura, our radiance, our blossoming, and our fulfillment.

When our inner tree is solid, healthy and blooming, it produces fruit that we can share with others. Through its link between Heaven and Earth, it communicates Knowledge to us, helps us rediscover our original roots, and be confident in taking responsibility for the experience of materiality.

⊕ A sound, healthy tree represents a great capacity for materialization, wisdom, and development. A feeling of having roots, well-being and happiness there where we are. Anchorage to Earth, and, at the same time, connection with Heaven. Inner and outer construction. Respect for cycles, for gradual, harmonious development. Capacity to simultaneously tune into and receive Earth energies as well as influences from Heaven. Generosity, sharing, altruism. Knowledge. Great vitality.

⊖ A sick, leafless, dried up, felled (etc.) tree represents a lack of roots and great difficulty materializing ideas and projects. An unstable period of important deconstruction. Lack of vitality and energy to manifest and materialize. Destructive period. Lack of motivation and intensity to construct our life. Poor connection with Heaven and Earth. Lack of knowledge and wisdom. Difficulty having beautiful feelings, being generous and altruistic. Non-respect for cycles.

TRIAL *cf. Lawsuit*

TROUSERS (pants)

Trousers are an item of clothing related to the masculine principle, to emissivity, self-assertion, and authority. They also symbolize aspects of our aura: the energy we emanate in the way we advance and manifest in action, in our social, professional, and private lives. The popular expression *to wear the pants* is a metaphor meaning to be the one who commands, who makes the decisions. This image is a good illustration of the dynamics of authority and self-assertion associated with wearing trousers. The style, shape, color, length, and quality of material used, the context in which trousers are worn, as well as the make, the brand name, constitute a collection of characteristics that help us come to an accurate understanding of the symbolic meaning of trousers in either a concrete situation or as a dream element.

⊕ Capacity to assert ourselves, to make decisions, and take action with right, just, well-balanced emissivity (as a man or woman). Leadership, authority. Protection while advancing, in action. Trousers that may be considered positive (regarding style, color, material, etc.), worn in a context that heightens and elevates a person's image and the aura he emanates.

⊖ Excessive emissivity, over-masculine behavior, over-authoritarian attitude, need to control, to impose our decisions and way of advancing on the personal, social, and professional levels; or, on the contrary, blocked, oppressed, repressed emissivity, which leads to difficulty asserting ourselves, making decisions, taking action. Dirty, torn, faded, over-tight trousers, or style of trousers that denotes an intention to seduce, provoke, and/or attract attention, are a negative attribution to the wearer's image and radiance.

TRUCK (GB: LORRY)

A truck or lorry is a vehicle that is generally used to transport goods and products for the collectivity. As an earth-based means of transport, it represents the way we conduct ourselves on the action level whenever we relate to others in order to provide them with resources. It also symbolizes the way we behave at work, in business, in commerce, in associations and partnerships of a collective nature. With a transport potential, size, weight, power and force for advancing that is greater than a car, learning to drive a truck is more demanding and skillful, and requires increased vigilance and prudence. A truck represents an emissive aspect that is more collective than a car, which makes it a powerful symbol of the way we conduct our life. However this power is limited to certain routes and times, because trucks are not allowed to circulate on all roads at all times. If, for example, we see ourselves driving along a road forbidden to trucks, this indicates that we force too much in our projects, in the way we do business. For a deep understanding of the symbolism of a particular truck, its color, general condition, state of cleanliness, the type of goods it transports, the energy of the driver, the context in which it is used, etc., should also be analyzed.

⊕ A great capacity to advance on the collective level. Willpower, strength and power in relationships, business, and exchanges with others. Abundant resources. A sense of altruism and service to society. Ardor, power, courage in social involvement.

⊖ Distorted advancing and manifestation on the collective level. Excessive emissivity, over-confidence, a feeling of invincibility, over-strong willpower in action, a tendency to take up too much space. Impulsive, destructive brute force, which imposes on others and defies destiny. A materialistic attitude which considers transport and commerce solely as means to make money. A complex of superiority or inferiority. A lack of willpower, feeling crushed by collective needs. Great insecurity concerning resources and the materialization of projects.

TSUNAMI

A tsunami is related to the ocean which represents an immense reservoir of conscious (when related to the surface) or unconscious (when related to its depths), collective, emotional forces. Given that it usually manifests after an underwater earthquake or following the fall of a meteorite into the sea, the symbolism of a tsunami is connected to both the water and earth elements; hence its connection to the world of emotions, feelings and sentiments related to concrete behavior and way of doing actions.

In a dream, a tsunami may be symbolically set off by different signs from those mentioned above. For instance, we could see our Aunt Julie, and all of a sudden, a tsunami is set in motion in the following image. To understand such a dream, we need to analyze Aunt Julie because since she preceded the tsunami, she is the cause of it. If Aunt Julie is generally sad and depressed because her ex-husband cheated on her, she refers to memories related to relationships of infidelity, trickery, dishonesty, and betrayal. The causes of our *tsunami* may be related to real situations we've been through, or they may come from other lives, which indicate deep memory cleansing on the level of their origin.

Whenever a tsunami is triggered by an earthquake, this means that unconscious emotional forces related to memories of negative actions, in this life or in others, are emerging so as to be understood, cleansed, transformed, and transcended. If no revealing symbol precedes the tsunami, then it is simply related to the encounter of destructive emotional memories that dwell in us. This kind of dream is frequent among people who are depressed, or on a spiritual path, since the latter consciously cleanse their memories through deep work on themselves, or else are subjected to the tidal-wave-tsunami effects of their past actions because it is the time for this in their life program. This kind of situation in a dream is very upsetting and de-stabilizing. So as not to unfurl disturbing, destructive *waves* (extremely destructive actions and/or emotions) in our lives and on the people around us; so as not to create *a storm in a teacup* either (a lot of fuss and agitation for nothing); or to suffer from a *tempest* of confusing, troubling, disturbing thoughts (extreme mental agitation), it is strongly advised to take some time to go within and meditate.

Symbolically, a tsunami is great emotional energy that assembles personal and collective unconscious emotions, which have accumulated over many lives and which can be very destructive. If they aren't well managed, these forces cause serious excessive emotional behavior and destroy our capacity to love, to motivate ourselves, and to renew ourselves and our entourage.

⊕ Awareness of our emotional potential. An opening of the emotional unconscious, of old, former repression, inhibitions. A capacity to manage and channel a great collective emotional force. A warning advising us to keep an eye on our emotions and work on mastery, on cleansing their causes. Vigilance so as not to blunder and commit emotional misactions (*cf.* this term) that could hurt, destabilize, and destroy our entourage, our environment, and ourselves. Deep cleansing of hidden emotions buried deep within us.

⊖ Destructive emotions, emotional overflow, excessive, impulsive behavior. Someone who dramatizes, exaggerates and amplifies anything and everything. Lack of emotional mastery. Difficulty managing openings of the unconscious. Difficulty advancing on a spiritual path due to a lack of spiritual and metaphysical knowledge. Loss of control. Difficulty regaining reason and clear ideas. Someone who gets lost in tumultuous emotions (fear, insecurity, lack of love, aggression, depression, emotional, affective instability, dependencies, etc.).

TUMMY *cf. Stomach*

TUMOR

A tumor is an excess of tissue, which develops when cells of an organism reproduce too rapidly and inappropriately. Hence the formation of this new body tissue indicates a malfunction in cell growth. A tumor may be benign, thereby offering a second chance if considered as a serious alarm signal, setting off deep reconsideration, inciting us to call our lifestyle into question. Or, it may be malignant (cancerous). Cell growth, which represents the beginning of life itself, is affected by an excess of negative emissivity. For a good understanding of its symbolic meaning, we need to analyze the region affected. E.g., if the tumor is on the foot level, it indicates problems in our way of advancing, of being active, taking action, whereas a stomach tumor indicates the development of negative forces and an incapacity to digest difficult experiences.

A brain tumor is related to the mental level, to our way of thinking, deciding, concentrating (too much or not enough), to abuse of power, to excessive emissivity, aridity on the thought level, excessive rationality, to lack of gentleness, lack of interiorization, to our repressing what doesn't suit us. There is a metaphysical cause for each tumor. To obtain more precise details, to facilitate symbolic analysis, we can ask to be enlightened by dreams as to the type(s) of thoughts, emotions, behavior that are the root cause, the origin of the problem, and which we need to rectify to halt such anarchic cell growth, and even favor its disappearance.

The manifestation of a tumor represents the destructuring of part of a person's vital functioning, of his capacity to engender life within himself. It reveals hyperactivity, excessive emissivity, intensive multiplication of certain negative aspects, and possibly an anti-life attitude regarding other cells and parts of himself, which prevents healthy, harmonious regeneration of life.

It is important to know that dreaming we have a tumor isn't necessarily a prediction that we will develop one in our physical body; it's more of a warning that we bear memories and forces that could develop a tumor, and in order to avoid such development, we need to rectify the attitudes and behavior related to what the tumor represents symbolically.

⊕ The will to seek the cause and understanding of the metaphysical and symbolic meaning of a tumor, of its location, and the body function affected by it. Determination to work on ourselves to cleanse the memories, and transform the thoughts, emotions, and behavior that disrupt healthy, right, harmonious cell growth. Openmindedness regarding spiritual, multi-dimensional healing, and the power for self-healing that exists in each and every one of us. Helps us understand the importance of balancing receptivity and emissivity, of regularly meditating, of integrating spirituality in our daily life so as to strengthen our faith and connection with the Source of Life, with the Divine in ourselves and all things. Humility in the face of illness, capacity to accept the ordeal and use it to grow, to evolve. May be a warning of an illness in the making, giving us a chance to anticipate and consult a doctor before it is too late. If physically incurable, it allows the person affected to peacefully prepare the end of his present life on Earth.

⊖ A person whose thoughts, emotions, and behavior engender and maintain negative, over-emissive, sometimes morbid forces, which disrupt healthy cell growth and favor anarchic, disorganized production of harmful cells. Hyperactive, over-rebellious, anarchic forces; or, an overly receptive attitude that absorbs too many unhealthy, morbid, death-bearing forces. Indicates the presence of large blocks of distorted memories, sometimes accumulated and repressed over several lives, which materialize in the form of a malignant, life-threatening tumor. Multiplication of negative mind-, spirit- and soul-states, which hinder the healthy functioning of the organism. Tendency to rebel against our life plan, our evolution program, to want to force Destiny. Anti-life attitudes and sentiments, intense frustration and anger against God. Pride, ambition, excessive willpower, dominating behavior. Lack of deep understanding, refusal to call ourselves into question, continuing to multiply our errors. A lack of understanding of the meaning of ordeals, of illness in general.

TUNNEL

A tunnel represents a capacity to have access to subterranean spaces, and to advance therein in a concentrated, precise, safe way. It also symbolizes a capacity to focus our willpower on traveling without getting dispersed, without scattering our energy and resources. The passageway through a tunnel symbolically denotes a passageway from one state of conscience to another, traveling through certain layers and regions of our unconscious, and the memories found therein. Generally, it is a public passageway, sometimes secret, allowing us to get rapidly from one place to another, one stage to another.

A tunnel and/or underground passageway are usually conceived to facilitate traffic, improve transport of people and goods, for pedestrians, or animals, to safely cross the road, to channel water, etc., all of which add a different angle and depth to its symbolic meaning. Usually, we enter and advance inside the tunnel, symbolically, progressively going through it toward an opening, toward something new, unknown, or toward something that we re-discover. As a safe, underground construction, conceived and built by man, a tunnel symbolizes conscious and unconscious willpower and determination to get to know and master hidden, repressed, forgotten, difficult-to-access parts of ourselves, so as to advance along our evolutive, spiritual, life path. Going through a tunnel may also represent an initiation, in the sense that it leads us to face accumulated memories and forces in our inner soil, our inner territories that we need to transform in order to liberate a passageway toward a new stage in our life path.

On the symbolic level, a dark, narrow, unsafe tunnel may indicate that we are about to enter or go through a difficult period. It may be a period where we have to, or believe we have to, advance in limiting situations, that evoke feelings of fear, insecurity, heaviness, pressure, intimidation, oppression, imposed control, on both the material, physical level, as well as the psychological, emotional, intellectual, or spiritual level. The simple fact of being about to go through a restricted underground passageway may become a trigger element, awakening a more or less large number of unconscious memories or fears, on the one hand, related to the will to advance and face unknown, unimaginable obstacles that could appear en route, or places where we can find negative memories that are hidden, buried, veiled to ensure we do not remember them; and, on the other hand, resistance regarding advancing to discover ourselves in depth, through a lack of willpower, motivation, courage, faith, and self-confidence. A tunnel symbolizes an important state of conscience in dreams, and it may be presented positively or negatively depending on the dream and context shown.

Whenever we find ourselves stuck in a tunnel, it means that we are going through a stage where we are finding it difficult to *see the end of the tunnel;* i.e. we feel closed up in our memories, imprisoned in all sorts of difficulties that encircle us, creating a feeling of *impasse,* and the impression of not being able to make any headway, no longer being able to progress. Given that in a tunnel the air is generally limited and of less good quality, we may also experience a situation where we are afraid of lacking air, oxygen. As the air element symbolizes the thought level, such a reaction indicates a lack of understanding of what is happening to us, an incapacity to maintain hope and confidence, and to engender positive, constructive, regenerating thoughts in the ordeal we are going through.

Finally, in a dream or in a near death experience, a person may find himself in the tunnel of Light. This is generally a powerful transforming experience, which allows the person to have access to Knowledge, encounter the afterlife, causing a deep, deep awakening of conscience, transforming his perception of life and death. It may also be a preparation for death, for the passage of the soul into other dimensions; or an amazing, extraordinary, mystical experience, thanks to which, the person discovers the ultimate aim of evolution: return to the Light, to Knowledge of himself and of the whole Universe.

⊕ Facilitates going from one state of conscience to another, from one stage to another. Helps make going through the unconscious levels easier and faster. Allows us to interiorize deeply, to enter the heart of memories related to action, concentration of our willpower to advance toward a goal and come out improved, more mature, more evolved, after getting through obstacles that may have slowed our advancing. Great force and motivation for advancing. A person emerging from a period of upheaval and inner limitations, who rediscovers the Light after a period of darkness and difficulties. May indicate a great awakening of conscience, a mystical experience that will transform the person; or, it may concern a visit to the soul of a deceased person in a parallel dimension; or, announce that a person is going to die, and so help him prepare his *passageway* to the next world.

⊖ Difficulty or fear of advancing when we have to penetrate the unconscious, make our way through memories related to former actions, or pass from one state of conscience to another, from a known, concrete reality to an unknown reality. A limited person, who lacks willpower and determination to advance; or, who feels forced, obliged to advance. A feeling of being lost, weighed down and burdened by matter and problems related to repressed memories, long forgotten in the depths of our being. A lack of light, understanding, confidence, faith. A concentration of destructive forces. A sensation or feeling of danger, of being exposed, closed in, imprisoned by obscure, hidden, malevolent forces. A blocked or interrupted spiritual or life-path; an incapacity to continue to evolve. Separation between two realities and difficulty joining them. Not believing in the afterlife, a person who is too down-to-earth, too materialistic, lacking spirituality, lacking connection with the Light, with knowledge, not believing that the subtle, metaphysical worlds are as real as the physical world. Fear of dying, apprehensive about passing through the tunnel of Light, of encountering the unknown.

TWIN(S)

The symbolism of twins is associated with the notion of learning to share. Twins first share their mother's womb. After birth, they share their parents' attention, the same living conditions throughout their childhood, the same birthday, etc. Their life program is closely linked, and includes mutually integrating understanding to develop complementarity and altruistic dynamics toward each other, so as to rectify memories of egocentricity recorded in past lives. In the majority of cases, between twins, there is a climate of dominator/dominated, of envy and jealousy, because one is usually more extrovert and emissive than the other; hence twins are also symbolically associated with notions of superiority and inferiority in relationships.

⊕ Symbolizes the apprenticeship of sharing, generosity, mutual aid, reciprocal support, altruism. Allows for the study of soul, spirit, and mind resonance and affinities; understanding and integrating the mirror effect. Development of unconditional fraternal love.

⊖ Reveals work to be done on ourselves regarding difficulty sharing, being generous and altruistic, as well as regarding negative attitudes and behavior such as egoism, egocentricity, envy, jealousy, competitive spirit, exaggerated need for attention and acknowledgement, an incapacity to love unconditionally. Complex of superiority/inferiority. Tendency to want to dominate the other person, or to let ourselves be dominated. Lack of understanding of the mirror effect, of the Law of resonance.

U

UMBRELLA

Symbolically, an umbrella represents a state of conscience that allows us to protect ourselves from emotional showers and downpours, to remain serene, well-centered, well-balanced and stable, even though we have to face very intense emotions. It symbolizes a capacity to shelter ourselves from unpleasant sentiments and soul-states (moods), such as sadness, melancholy, grief, moroseness, discouragement, solitude, emotional coldness, and inner storms. A person who has developed the ability to activate his inner umbrella is not only capable of going through the emotional showers encountered on the subtle level, with equanimity and detachment, but also concrete rain showers and downpours, even when he does not have an umbrella or raincoat to protect him. Such a person emanates beautiful inner weather, *joie de vivre,* lightheartedness, and confidence at all times and in all circumstances, even when damp, wet, or drenched.

⊕ Emotional stability that allows us to feel protected in tumultuous, stormy situations and capable of facing great intensity of sad, negative feelings. Capacity to master our emotions, to exert *an umbrella effect,* to transform unpleasant emotional ambiances, to create good weather in our inner world, on the subtle levels, no matter what the weather is like in the outside world.

⊖ Lack of protection and stability when faced with tumultuous, stormy emotions. Deep resonance with negative feelings (sadness, grief, melancholy, etc.). Fear of bad weather, intense climatic manifestations in both physical reality and on the metaphysical level. Lack of courage, bravery in the face of adversity. Vulnerability, fragility, emotionalism. Limitations; a complicated, critical person who is easily discouraged, afraid of the rain, of emotions, and of being exposed without protection and getting wet.

UNDERGROUND/ SUBTERRANEAN PASSAGE

There are natural underground passages such as those explored by speleologists connecting groups of caves, for example. There are also artificial, manmade underground places and passages such as cellars, crypts, and tunnels. Subterranean constructions and passageways may be used for a variety of purposes; e.g. to serve as a refuge, to allow people to flee from or to support military operations, and many others. Not only are they frequently found in old places such as castles, fortresses, churches, medieval towns and villages, but also in modern cities. The US term *Subway* and the GB term *Underground* refer to their respective underground city railways and underpasses either for cars or pedestrians that are commonplace in most large cities today.

As its name clearly indicates, an underground passage is related to the earth element, i.e. the world of materiality and concrete action in matter. More precisely, it represents an access route to hidden, protected memories kept secret or buried, repressed, and/or forgotten that are to be found in our subconscious and the various layers of our unconscious, which, mostly unknown to us, influence our daily life, our decisions, our future selves, what we will become. A subterranean passage represents an archeological path, a passageway that allows us to enter into contact with memories of ancestral actions, ways of being, behavior and actions in our former lives. Whenever we go underground in terms of conscience it is to be able to work on our unconscious memories. This work is not always done consciously, precisely because it is carried out below the conscious level. However, that doesn't prevent it from being real, considerable, and evolutive. Indeed, such work allows us to rediscover and examine the strata and foundations of who we are so as to cleanse, purify and transform them. These subterranean visits correspond to openings of the unconscious that gradually lead us to an enlarged horizon, an expansion of our conscience, deeper vision and understanding of the multi-dimensions of life.

However, an underground passage may also denote flight dynamics, extreme insecurity, and a tendency to remain alone, isolated from others. Hence, through the image of an underground passage in a dream, we may be shown an attitude of ours that leads us to isolate ourselves from others, to cut ourselves off, to protect ourselves, either because we are frightened or feel so threatened by very old negative actions committed in this life or others that we want to hide; or, because we don't know the Law of resonance and we've suffered so much we want to *go to ground*, to hide away and protect ourselves so as to be able to go on living. It may also reveal an extremist person with apocalyptic tendencies; or, someone who is spiritually very rigid, and has become lost in the meanders of his past that he broods over without any love or compassion for what he was. This symbol may also indicate that the person is too down-to-earth, too focused on matter, who lives with a conscience that is too heavy, too materialistic, that lacks light.

To analyze and understand the symbolic meaning of a subway or underground train in a dream, we need to take into consideration the + and/or – aspects of a train combined with the + and/or – aspects of an underground passage; likewise for a highway tunnel.

⊕ Discovering and visiting our subconscious and unconscious memories related to our past actions. Access to knowledge and secrets buried in the depths of our inner earth, deep down in our own inner underground constructions and passageways. The archeological path of the soul, discovery of old, former behavior in this life and others. An opening of the unconscious that invites us to carry out inner purification work in order to get out of the confusion and impasses present in our life. Someone who seeks to know and transform himself. A good capacity to go within, to interiorize, to observe and analyze our inner world, to accept the emotions, thoughts, and soul-states that arise, to work on ourselves with humility, discretion, and gratitude. Transcendence of ancestral fear of the depths, the dark, the unknown.

⊖ Someone who is lost in the maze or labyrinth of his past, of his subconscious and unconscious memories, who encounters obstacles and blockages without knowing what to do to solve them. A heavy, burdened conscience; a tendency to repression and to cutting ourselves off from others, hiding, afraid to face who we are, all that we have avoided, forgotten, or that we don't yet know. An overly materialistic, too down-to-earth attitude that only considers what is visible, tangible. May denote a person on a spiritual path who is extreme, who wants to get to know himself too fast, without respecting the different stages; or, someone who sees catastrophes everywhere, who flees, who doesn't want to go down into his inner depth; or who is very frightened of a concrete situation. A lack of openness and of light. Unhealthy, obsessive discretion; a tendency to be self-centered and/or antisocial.

UNEMPLOYMENT

The term unemployment is used to designate the state of a person who is out of work because he was dismissed, or voluntarily resigned, or wants to change his job.

Being unemployed means that the person concerned cannot put the fire of his creative potential, capacities and willpower to good use. In spite of his efforts to find another job or activity that corresponds to his potential, skills and creative fire, his spirit remains idle; his motivation, momentum and positive attitude may be used up or worn out, thereby engendering discouragement, pessimism and depression. Unemployment is often associated with poverty, insecurity and in some cases, social exclusion. A person going through such a situation needs to understand that it is not a coincidence because there is no such thing as coincidence. He must not consider himself a victim but should apply the Law of resonance and true Cosmic Intelligence, which always synchronizes life's circumstances and situations as a whole according to what is best for the evolution of our soul. Even if unemployment is rarely desired for many reasons, it still represents the ideal situation to help us take an important evolutive step. A period of unemployment offers us an opportunity to work on ourselves, to call ourselves into question, as well as to develop an understanding of work and the role it plays in our lives.

Whether experienced in concrete reality or in a dream, the context of unemployment needs to be analyzed in depth by the person concerned. He needs to understand the importance of working in matter with the intention of evolving and not with the aim of earning money and accumulating material goods. Unemployment represents a state of conscience wherein the unemployed person's manifestation or the realization of his potential is blocked on the professional and social level. The unemployed person experiences limitations because he has recorded distorted memories related to work; e.g. in another life, he may have been a dreadful boss who only ever thought of his own profits and dismissed his employees unfairly. Consequently, in a later life, he is led to experience difficult work situations, where he in turn loses his job and has problems finding another one. Cosmic Intelligence limits his possibilities of manifestation as well as the materialization of his resources at work so that he may experience what he put others through. Thus he repairs negative karmas while progressing in his understanding of the role of work and of the right attitude in the employer-employee relationship. He eventually understands that in addition to social involvement, work comprises an altruistic dimension, and, above all, it reveals the work that we need to do on ourselves. A person who discovers the sacred meaning of work becomes luminous in all his undertakings and contacts with others.

⊕ Self-questioning. Improvement of our way of working and our social involvement. Cleansing memories that engender unemployment. Developing awareness that allows us to correct and rectify erroneous, unfair behavior and attitudes on the professional and social level. Understanding karma and the fact that an ordeal serves to repair and evolve. A period of transition, renewal, re-orientation, re-education. Work on ourselves. Analysis and study of our experience in the field of work. A capacity to keep our morale high, remain positive, and trust in Up Above, in Heaven. Receptivity and gratitude for proposed help, guidance and opportunities that arise and allow us to improve our situation and change our lifestyle.

⊖ A person who repeatedly experiences professional limitations and unemployment situations without calling himself into question or while always considering himself a victim. Deep insecurity. Existential fear. An identity crisis: the person no longer knows who he is. Feeling or being undervalued, depreciated, discredited. A lack of self-esteem, self-deprecating. Discouragement. Distress. Sadness. Depression. Frustration. Loss of faith. Passive attitude. Stagnation. Inaction. Lethargy. Absence of enthusiasm and willpower to take the necessary steps to find a job. Difficulty finding a job due to a bad attitude. A lack of motivation and objectives. Dropping out. Memories from previous lives that continue to create blockages, preventing the person from realizing his full potential. A tendency to aim either too high or too low. Over-confidence; or, lack of self-confidence. Fear of change. Negative radiance. An incapacity to act or react positively. A rebellious spirit that worsens his situation. A tendency to grant too much importance to social etiquette and to identify with our work.

UNICORN

A unicorn is a legendary creature that looks like a great white horse with one long, single, spiral horn right in the middle of its forehead. This horn has the capacity to neutralize poison. A unicorn symbolizes mastery and transcendence of powerful vital energy, thanks to its resemblance to a horse, and a great capacity to advance with wisdom and spirituality, given the fact that it is white. It evokes a magical, imaginative dimension as well as liberty and purity. Legend has it that only the pure of heart may see and approach it. The power of its horn sets us free from illness, and cleanses water, the emotional level, of all impurity. The positive appearance of a unicorn occurs in the dream of someone who has rediscovered the purity of his heart and intention, who henceforth advances with the powerful energy of vital energy that has been purified of needs.

⊕ Great willpower to advance in a right, just, magical, qualitative manner. Spiritual power, strength and purity, which confers the power to treat, purify and heal. Great liberty acquired by the transcendence of instinctual needs, vital, sexual energy. Using the Primordial Creative Fire and Divine Power with pure intention. Elevation toward greatness and wisdom. Inspiration and confirmation of healing powers that come from the Higher worlds.

⊖ Lack of dynamism and spiritual willpower to advance in a right, just, qualitative manner, to purify ourselves, to treat and heal ourselves or others. Wild, mistrustful behavior, making a person intimidating and difficult to approach in spite of great spiritual potential. Impulsiveness, rejection of others. Poor use of vital and spiritual energy, lust, debauchery. Absence of spirituality; or, seeking spiritual power only to serve coarse, boorish, instinctual needs, perverted desires, and diabolical impulses. Tendency to flee social life, to isolate ourselves, and live like a hermit. Fear of matter. Sterility, incapacity to materialize our spiritual potential. Problems of duality, states of discrepancy between our potential and our mind and spirit, between the aspirations of our soul and our physical needs.

UNITED STATES OF AMERICA, THE

A country that mainly symbolizes expansion, political and economic power, liberty and democracy, as well as cultural and ethnic diversity, the United States is characterized by the fact that people from different countries, nations, races and ethnic groups have succeeded in living together, working together, and forming a union with a democratic mentality, allowing for the emergence of a world super-power. It is considered to be a model of material values and success in every field because it offers everyone, regardless of their origin, the possibility to realize the *American dream*, to prosper and become rich and famous.

Regarding qualities, as a democratic nation, the United States of America inspires the whole world by the great self-confidence they emanate, their powers of large scale organization, realization, and materialization, their sense of practicality and logic, their capacity to prosper, to succeed, their intelligence, their innovative spirit, their sense of family, their hospitality, their respect for values and principles, their sense of justice, liberty, loyalty and duty, their well-balanced life, their faith in God, their deep spirituality, their openness regarding all religions and beliefs, their capacity to live in peace and harmony in a multi-ethnic society, their respect for hierarchy, their victorious spirit, etc.

Since its role as liberating savior, helping end World War II, the United States has been involved as a super power in international politics and economics, and positions itself as protector and re-builder of the world according to democratic values. Since this role is causing more and more difficulties, this country is presently being called upon to change its past image of protectionism, power control, lack of openness and knowledge of the world, over-materialistic vision, attitude of over-confidence and superiority as regards other countries, forgetting that its population originally came from many of those very countries. The major problem of the USA is the fact that its capitalist values taken to extremes, which ignore social needs, have created a serious imbalance between giving and receiving. This attitude also favors the mentality of every man for himself, the survival of the fittest, on both national and international levels. Its worldwide political and economic interventions were less intended to help the development and autonomy of the countries concerned than to seek control, power and enrichment. It is interesting to know that the majority of Americans don't have a passport and don't travel outside their country. The present change of the United States' image is in the process of engendering new planetary dynamics and a re-organization of the axis of world economics, which is developing more and more in the direction of India and China.

⊕ A state of conscience of expansion, abundance, super-power, strength, leadership, justice, rights, liberty, ethnic diversity, creative genius, power of organization, realization, and achievement in matter. Great confidence, natural charisma, force of conviction. Sense of education, practical intelligence. Respect and harmony among the different ethnic groups, feelings of fraternity, solidarity, hospitality. Symbol of the new world, model for the planet. Collective influence and inspiration on the level of values and principles. A country of faith, strong spiritual and/or religious conviction. Great capacities to undertake, begin, set things in motion.

⊖ Seeking and abusing power, control, domination. Extreme conquering, warrior, protectionist spirit. Over-confidence, feeling of superiority. A tendency to impose our ideals and values, to believe ourselves to be above everyone and everything. A lack of tolerance and openness to the world, a stubborn, self-centered spirit. Too much emphasis on glory, celebrity, renown, a tendency to idolatry. Poor use of resources, over-consumerism, malnutrition, pollution, waste, materialistic spirit. Exploiting justice for our own ends. Unfair, inequitable exchanges. Imbalance between giving and receiving. All sorts of exaggeration and excess. Religious extremism and intolerance.

UNKNOWN, THE

The unknown represents what we don't yet know, that is to say what we haven't yet consciously experimented. Generally speaking, the term *unknown* designates the totality of what is not yet known, discovered, unveiled, revealed, experimented. The unknown, of course, is closely related to the unconscious, because we cannot really know something without being aware of it. The development of knowledge goes hand in hand with the evolution of our conscience, because each new discovery leads to awareness, to our becoming conscious of this, and vice versa. Hence, as we experiment, as our conscience evolves, what is unknown gradually becomes known. Consequently, it is essential for us to cultivate an interest in the unknown, a sense of discovery, a taste for adventure, along with willingness, readiness to integrate the new and adapt to change. In our dreams, each time we see people we don't know in the dream, symbolically they represent parts of ourselves that we do not know yet, unknown parts that we discover; the same concept applies in concrete reality.

From both its positive and negative aspects, the unknown, i.e. all that we ignore, that we don't yet know, needs to be encountered, integrated and transcended. The learning process, our apprenticeship of ourselves, of Life, is a process of the gradual unveiling of Knowledge. In fact, Cosmic Intelligence continually activates new data and knowledge in us; the ultimate goal is to allow us to develop the Wisdom to fuse with the Source, with God.

Knowledge of ourselves, of others, of the Whole, the Great All, is a long path or journey, a quest into the heart of the unknown in the immensely big and the infinitely small. The inscription on the Temple of Delphi *Know yourself and you will know the universe* is the perfect expression of the nature of this quest and what is at stake.

⊕ Represents a new stage, the discovery of new facets of ourselves. An incitement to explore, to experiment, to learn and get to know what is new, as well as our latent, hidden, occulted potential, so as to be able to evolve toward another stage. Love for the discovery, study and research into Knowledge that allows us access to the heart of the mysteries of Creation. Exaltation. Healthy, evolutive curiosity.

Understanding and acceptance of the fact that Cosmic Processes are only revealed to us very gradually. A capacity to break out of old patterns and integrate new concepts. Open-mindedness. A period of intense questioning and deep reflection. Development of the faculty of reasoning and synthesis, the superior mind. Expansion of conscience. Receptivity to Divine Inspiration. Confidence and trust in Up Above. Confidence in Cosmic Intelligence, in the existence of a Supreme Being, an Absolute Principle.

⊖ Fear of the unknown, of everything new and unusual that we haven't yet become aware of, or accepted in our consciousness. Difficulty letting go and being detached from what is known, rebuilding our life on new foundations. Erroneous perceptions. Blocked horizons. Phobias. Multiple dependencies that limit us and keep us imprisoned in vicious circles. Difficulty learning, or a lack of motivation to study, experiment, discover and explore. Ignorance, lack of interest in Knowledge. An anesthetized, numbed, lethargic, lazy mind that doesn't want or seek to evolve. Intolerance, conformity, sectarianism. Incomprehension of the educational role of evil, wrong-doing, what hurts. Reticence to advance toward the unknown.

URINATE, TO

To urinate means to cleanse the body of its liquid waste. The act of urination is related to the emotional level, since urine is a liquid. Given the fact that its evacuation is through the genitals, its symbolism also concerns a person's intimacy. Urination represents the purification of accumulated emotions regarding actions carried out in the concrete world. It also concerns our capacity to renew ourselves, to liberate emotional tensions, and to regenerate ourselves through the release of non-desirable substances.

In a dream, the place where a person urinates is important. If the place is appropriate, such as a toilet, and all the surrounding elements are also appropriate, then urination may be interpreted as a beautiful capacity to purify ourselves. However, if the place is inappropriate, then the act of urination is associated with the difficulties and distortions of the unsuitable place in question (bed, armchair, vehicle, classroom, public place, etc.).

⊕ A capacity to purify ourselves, to evacuate negative emotions. An ability to relieve both the physical body and the inner emotional world. Purification of our intimacy, of personal experiences on the affective and emotional levels.

⊖ Difficulty urinating may denote problems purifying ourselves, evacuating negative emotions or memories that we have accumulated and maintain; or, indicate a rebellious, over-emissive, over-extravert spirit. Painful urination expresses considerable negative, emotional energy. A tendency to repress our feelings, to restrain ourselves, to refuse to let go. Problems related to intimacy; uneasiness, or feeling ill-at-ease as a result of blocked, unpurified, untransformed emotions.

V

VAGRANT, TRAMP, HOMELESS

The words vagrant and tramp are used to designate a homeless person. The noun form of the verb *to tramp*, meaning to walk heavily, to plod over long distances, figuratively speaking, includes all the images associated with originally jobless people walking the streets, going from one place to the next in the hope of work as well as today's vagrants and beggars, aimlessly wandering the streets, begging, hoping for a coin or two to buy alcohol, and sleeping in doorways or under bridges using newspapers and cardboard boxes to keep warm through the night. Generally speaking, they suffer from social exclusion and are often referred to as *down-and-outs.* The words tramp and vagrant have mostly been replaced by the less pejorative term, the homeless, even though it does not have exactly the same meaning.

On the symbolic level, vagrancy indicates a state of conscience that is characterized by marginalization, inadaptability, lack of motivation, dropping out, living on the fringe of society, and victimization. When a person consciously chooses to reject established values, structures, institutions, and lifestyle, and turns his back on society to lead a life of vagrancy, homelessness, this indicates a rebellious spirit that refuses the structure, order and laws that are necessary in all forms of social life. This also indicates that the person does not understand that what he rejects on the outside is a reflection of what he bears within, and that he has resonance with whatever it is that bothers him in society. Indeed, society is the materialization of the conscience, ideals, values, qualities and virtues, as well as the weaknesses, faults and distortions of all of its members. Consequently, it is not by dropping out that we can change the face of a society, but rather by becoming consciously involved, participating and contributing to its transformation and evolution, beginning with ourselves.

A vagrant's life can also be the result, the materialization of heavy karmic *luggage* (*cf.* this term) and structural problems in the mind.

In that case, it also indicates an accumulation of memories where, perhaps over several lives, the person recorded negligent, careless behavior, a lack of motivation, laziness, an absence of aims and objectives, a lack of direction, a loss of identity, and disconnection, dropping out on all levels. Such an attitude may be the result of a powerful emotional shock, deep psychological trauma, intense suffering of the soul which renders the person dysfunctional; or, it may come from a tremendous feeling of guilt and helplessness, which pushes the person to inflict a difficult life of vagrancy on himself in punishment. Life as a tramp always indicates the presence of considerable discrepancies on all levels, as well as an incapacity or resistance to rebuilding his life, re-integrating society and consciously working on himself to recognize and activate his potential for creation and evolution.

Whenever the tramp, vagrant, homeless symbol appears in a dream, it reveals a tendency of certain parts of the dreamer to drop out, to become marginalized so as not to face an ordeal, a problematic situation that may be related to a separation, loss of a job, bankruptcy, a death, or lack of acknowledgement in his personal or social life. Not in possession of the tools, knowledge and adequate resources to go through this situation constructively, the person tries to flee it by withdrawing into himself, becoming marginalized and giving up his place and active role in society.

⊕ Becoming aware that dropping out, marginalization and victimization are not the solutions to problems. Willpower to take ourselves in hand and work on ourselves to transform the memories, attitudes and behavior that may incite us to turn our back on society, to want to flee our responsibilities, our karmic debts, life-lessons, and initiations. Development of conscience. Opening of the mind onto the spiritual dimension of existence. Apprenticeship of the Cosmic Laws. Integration of the concepts of karma, resonance and Divine Justice. Understanding the dynamics of cause and consequence. New motivation. Re-orientation of our life through new choices. A positive, constructive state of mind and spirit. Re-insertion in society. Acceptance of our life-plan, our programs of learning and evolution. Recognition of our place and potential to realize our personal destiny and help the collectivity advance. Understanding that everything we live is experimentation, and that errors, misactions (*cf.* this term), and poor past choices can be repaired.

⊖ A feeling of being a victim, marginalized, rejected and abandoned by destiny and human society. Deep suffering. Turmoil. Extreme despair. A feeling of helplessness. A situation of survival. A tragic, miserable fate. Fatalistic spirit. Total lack of motivation when faced with an ordeal. Unfavorable period. Collapse of structures. Moral degradation. Ruin. Absence of a spiritual conscience and knowledge allowing us to understand the karmic dimension of difficult, trying life conditions; a lack of understanding that they are a manifestation of the Law of return, whereby we reap what we sowed in other lives. Refusal to learn from our mistakes. Insubordination, rebellion. Obstruction, blockage of the realization of our superior nature. A lack of direction and objectives. Flight when faced with responsibilities. Absence of common sense and global vision. Feelings of superiority and inferiority. A tendency to compare ourselves with others. Deep envy and jealousy.

VAMPIRE, VAMPIRISM

A vampire is a legendary creature from beyond the grave that feeds on living people's blood in order to withdraw a person's vital energy, his capacity to live. The myth of vampires is centuries old and exists in many cultures. The reason why it has endured and why some people, pushed by dementia, by insanity, wish to become vampires resides in the fact that, consciously or unconsciously, man has always sought to nourish himself on other people's energy. He has always wanted to *suck on* other people's vitality. Energy vampirism is a common occurrence on more or less subtle levels. It is carried out by people who mingle their animal and human energy, and by people who are really intensely connected to obsessive states and passions for their needs. Whenever we wish to satisfy our own needs at other people's expense, unconsciously, we indulge in vampirism. We use, we exploit others, we take advantage of their naivety, their kindness, their resources on various levels; we manipulate them to receive love and attention. We sometimes betray, deceive, or force them to reply to our needs. Nowadays, young people in particular have a tendency to *vampirize* without realizing it. This is due to their evolution program, which is much more collective than that of past generations. They are often raised as *king-children* in families, where restrictions and limits have not been well-structured and clearly established; where a clear, firm *no* is lacking. Hence, these young people express their physical and metaphysical needs very intensely, and all the more so because their symbiotic use of video games, computers, mobile telephones and other technology, maintains their virtual, individual vision of a world where they are allowed everything they want. If we don't give priority to values and principles that are right and just, then material abundance, easy imposition and satisfaction of our wishes, as well as the power to control everything instantly, may create megalomaniac tendencies.

Small-scale vampirism exists in many human relationships, but its most extreme form is to be found in theft, abuse, and rape. The strong, long, pointed, canine teeth that characterize vampires, like the fangs to be found on carnivorous animals, represent both animal and human aspects, behavior focused only on the satisfaction of instinctual needs, desires and impulses. When a vampire is very hungry, it eats without thinking, without altruism, without conscience or awareness. Daylight is harmful to a vampire that lives at night, which explains its dark, somber, hidden aspects, its lack of conscience and Knowledge. This symbolizes unconscious facets of a person's personality, repressed needs and a desire to do whatever it takes to obtain what he wants. Another typical detail associated with vampires is the fact that, during the day, they take shelter, hide, and protect themselves in tombs. This reveals that their behavior and way of living create death in the concrete level, that they are governed by distorted memories, that have been accumulated over the course of several incarnations, which may lead to the death of good and of life.

Understanding, clarity, and truth, represented by the light of day, scare vampires because these qualities prevent them from existing, from appearing, taking shape and manifesting, creating illusion to perpetrate their crimes, their negative behavior. People who maintain vampire attitudes mostly lack faith in the Divine, and live only for the attractions of matter, in search of obsessive sensations, and the satisfaction of their primary needs, linked to affective dependency.

⊕ Cleansing and liberation of obsessive behavior. Work on ourselves to transform and liberate a tendency to compulsively satisfy our primary, instinctual needs. A person who is ready to call himself into question, to analyze his energy exchanges and relationships with others, to study his attitudes and behavior so as to recognize when he seeks to nourish himself emotionally or energetically on other people's vital energy, or to live at other people's expense. Understanding the subtlety of vampirism, extreme dependencies, theft of resources or vital energy on the individual and collective levels. Awareness that dependency engenders physical or metaphysical dramas in life.

⊖ A person who *vampirizes*, manipulates, and is ready to do whatever it may take to satisfy his physical and energetic needs; or, who lets himself be impressed, *vampirized*, sucked empty, who abandons his power to the other person's dark forces. Obsessive, multiple dependencies, passionate drama, tragedy, lack of love that leads to evil. Physical and/or energy theft and abuse. Dangerous, criminal seduction with the aim of satisfying personal, instinctual, vital needs. Demonic, animal-like behavior. Unhealthy intimate relations, insatiable emotional, affective hunger. Sexual abuse, sadomasochism, seeking illusory, coarse, brutish, violent pleasures. Melancholic, depressive, manipulating, thirsty temperament. Abasement of human conscience to animal, instinctual conscience. Uncontrollable, devouring primary needs. Difficulty replenishing ourselves and being emotionally independent. An intelligent person with a somber, dark temperament, lacking in light, who lives more intensely at night than during the day, who hides and makes himself seem mysterious, like a spider weaving its web.

VEGETABLE(S)

Vegetables belong to the vegetable kingdom, which is symbolically related to feelings and emotions. They represent a healthy, natural source of nourishment, of food, that is produced without engendering any violence. Vegetable cultivation and consumption helps develop beautiful qualities: patience, perseverance, respect for cycles of growth and development, confidence in the principles of divine materialization, which teaches us that we reap what we sow, harmony with nature, a sense of responsibility and observation.

⊕ Nourishment that is healthy, living, energizing, light, easy-to-digest and assimilate, creating well-being, dynamism, availability, radiating pleasant peacefulness and a pacific, peace-loving attitude. An abundant food source, produced in harmony with nature along with a non-violent, fair and equitable lifestyle. Organic farming, respectful of the environment.

⊖ Imbalanced nourishment where hardly any or no vegetables are included; or, consumption of withered, de-vitalized vegetables; or, vegetables that have been cultivated in an unhealthy way that is detrimental to the environment, which symbolically indicates a lack of conscience, purity, gentleness, loving kindness, beautiful feelings and sentiments. May denote a person with a fragile constitution, weak resistance, a tendency to tire easily and rapidly become exhausted. A withered, wilted aspect, a lack of life, dynamism, vitality, difficulty asserting ourselves and taking action. A weak, vegetative mind and spirit. A tendency to neglect our health, to seek aggressive nutritional energy, for example, with essentially meat-based meals, which push people to be continually active, inciting them to react impulsively instead of behaving in a calm, composed, thoughtful, serene, peaceable manner. Difficulty materializing in a right, just, qualitative manner. Disrespect for the environment. An extremist attitude in decision-making, consumption and nourishment. A lack of longevity.

VEGETARIANISM

Vegetarianism is a food practice based on a philosophy of life that advocates the consumption of vegetables, and excludes all consumption of animal flesh. Symbolically, everything that belongs to the vegetable kingdom is related to emotions, feelings, and sentiments.

The benefits of a vegetarian diet – a symbol of a healthy, well-balanced life – manifest on all levels. Physically, a vegetarian is usually in better health than the average population. After meals, he feels light and his digestion is rapid, requiring approximately only 3 hours. The vital energy that is blocked by digestion is hence liberated more quickly and gives the person more time to devote himself to other activities. Moreover, a vegetarian diet is favorable to spiritual work: it facilitates meditation, as well as the capacity to dream and remember our dreams. Vegetarian food also helps us have a peaceful character, like herbivores, because when we ingest an animal's flesh, we find ourselves assimilating its energy, its deep behavior, on the unconscious level. Furthermore, non-violence and vegetarianism are intimately connected because a person cannot declare himself to be non-violent and go on exploiting and killing animals.

A vegetarian diet is also the solution to the food problems of our planet. Approximately 70% of the food given to animals destined for consumption comes from cereals that are also suitable for human consumption, such as corn and soya. Furthermore, raising animals for human consumption requires vast quantities of land, water, and other resources that could be used to relieve famine that is rampant in several developing countries. Apart from health benefits, the decision to become vegetarian is often due to a combination of factors in response to the miserable conditions and brutal treatment of animals destined for slaughter, as well as the distorted multi-dimensional reactions this engenders in meat-eating people.

In a dream, being vegetarian indicates that the person is in the process of transcending his animal nature, that he is developing a more spiritual, multi-dimensional conscience, and generally cultivating pacifist attitudes. A dream that highlights negative behavior related to the concept of vegetarianism may reveal to the dreamer that he is suffering from discrepancy and is disconnected from his physical reality, that he is too ethereal, not sufficiently incarnated; or, that his values and principles are extreme, too radical, moralizing and puritanical toward others and society, that he thinks he is superior particularly as regards food, but also in terms of evolution.

⊕ A pacifist, a peace-loving, calm person with an awakened conscience on all levels, who takes care of his health by eating a well-balanced, healthy diet. Understanding and assimilation of the energetic and metaphysical dimensions of the way we nourish ourselves. Development of an ethical, non-violent, ecological, and spiritual conscience, a universal spirit, and a multi-dimensional vision of life. Respect and protection of animal life. Love of nature. An environmental conscience.

⊖ A person with an extremist, haughty, puritanical ideology of life, who entirely or partially keeps himself apart from society, who lives on the fringe, who maintains anger and scorn for those who do not adhere to the principles of vegetarianism; or, someone without conscience or knowledge on the food level, who ridicules vegetarianism either through ignorance or to defend and justify an unhealthy, coarse way of nourishing himself, or who only follows old social patterns. Dropping out of society, a more or less sociable person. Self-assertion through criticism and judgment of others. Impression of superiority, fiercely traditionalist regarding food, ecology and the environment. An imbalanced diet, nutritional deficiencies, a lack of protein and certain vitamins, such as B12. Poor food planning; too lazy to cook. Ignorance or disregard for the physiological requirements necessary for good health. Attitude of rejection of matter and useful technology. A gentle, overly receptive nature that hides memories of all sorts of abuse.

VEGETATION *cf.* ***Plants***

VERANDA *cf.* ***Balcony***

VERTICAL

A vertical line is a straight line, at right-angles to a horizontal (*cf. also* this term) plane, parallel to the direction of gravity indicated by a lead thread, from the sky to the Earth, and vice versa. In contrast with *horizonality*, i.e. a concrete, or materialistic, too down-to-earth approach, verticality indicates a capacity and will to simultaneously explore our depths (downward vertical movement), and the parallel worlds, the different levels in the Hierarchy of Creation (upward vertical movement), through spirituality and receptivity. Verticality induces the idea of a link between causes situated on the metaphysical level and the consequences that manifest on the physical level, which symbolize both an *involutive* movement, incarnation in matter, and *evolutive* movement, spiritualization of matter, thereby unifying the earthly, terrestrial world with the other worlds of Creation. It indicates an elevated point of view, spiritual vision that allows us to see the multi-dimensionality of Life. Seeing and understanding vertically means we have assimilated the Laws that govern the Universe, Divine Justice, and have a causal understanding of life events. It also implies a capacity to be detached from matter, an ability to function with an overall view, with the understanding that everything is mathematically precise and has its rightful place in the Universe, that nothing is the fruit of coincidence. From a negative point of view, verticality may denote a haughty, arrogant attitude, a feeling of superiority, or flight behavior, escapism, discrepancy, or even rejection of matter.

⊕ Symbol of elevation, of evolution, of global, multi-dimensional, universal vision, of access to superior states of conscience; or, the notion of involution (regressing instead of evolving), of incarnation, of descent of the spirit into matter, as the case may be. Awakening and expansion of conscience and development of the capacity to visit the depths, the different layers of the individual and collective unconscious. Capacity to conceive multi-dimensionality, parallel worlds, to understand the link between up above and down below, between the metaphysical and physical worlds; i.e. the union between Heaven and Earth, the connection between the levels of cause and consequence. A feeling of connection with the Great. Whole, with the Source. Integration of Cosmic Laws. Servant of Heaven, who understands and respects Celestial Hierarchy, a universal citizen, uprightness, right, just authority, honesty, integrity, and capacity to materialize divinely.

⊖ Difficulty developing vertical conscience, attaining global, universal, multi-dimensional vision and understanding. Lifestyle limited to the horizontal level, to the world of consequences, solely materialistic vision, difficulty understanding events from a causal point of view. Lack of discernment, spiritual and metaphysical knowledge. Problems incarnating and/or elevating ourselves, discrepancies between the different levels of our being. A bogged down, clogged, mired spirit, blocked horizon. Complexes of superiority and inferiority. A haughty, or too ethereal, abstract attitude. Tendency to judge and criticize others. Absence of flexibility regarding principles, rigidity, intransigency, authoritarianism, radicalism. Lack of spirituality, atheism.

VICTIM

The term victim is used to designate the state or situation of someone who has suffered damage, ill treatment, injustice at the hands of others or as the consequence of an accident, natural disaster, war, etc. However, from a metaphysical, spiritual point of view, in the light of Divine Justice, no true victim exists. According to the Law of resonance, consciously or unconsciously, we always attract what we are, both positively and negatively; and according to the Law of karma, we always reap what we sow. Hence, any situation that causes us suffering should lead us to understand that we ourselves engendered a similar situation in this or another life. Going through it now provides us with an opportunity to learn a lesson about our behavior, to integrate what we subjected others to, and to repair the karma we contracted by behaving as we did. In the case of a natural disaster that usually affects, *victimizes* a large number of people, symbolic analysis helps us understand in depth what kind of thoughts, emotions, attitudes and actions caused the materialization of such an event on a collective scale.

The concept of karma teaches us that misactions (*cf.* this term), errors and injustices can be corrected and repaired through forgiveness, repentance, expiation, transformation of our negative thoughts and emotions, and changing our distorted behavior. Depending on the gravity of the act to be repaired, sometimes, either in a dream or concrete reality, we have to relive an apparently unfair situation similar to what we subjected others to, but this time with the roles inverted: we are now the victim and not the wrong-doer. It is important to know that we cannot be a victim without first having been an aggressor, a wrong-doer. The role of victim is often adopted by people in an ordinary conscience experiencing all sorts of difficulties and ordeals. Instead of calling themselves into question and working on themselves to see, recognize, understand and rectify the aspects of their being that are the true cause of their situation, they are content to complain, to feel sorry for themselves, thus wanting to attract other people's attention and pity and be taken in charge by them, concretely, emotionally, and/or on the energy level. Understanding the karmic dynamics of aggressor/victim helps us develop causal vision, and feel compassion when faced with the multiple learning situations in which life places us in order to allow us to integrate the lessons of our past erroneous deeds, and to repair our negative karmas.

A person who does not believe in reincarnation and Divine Justice, who isn't open to the concept of karma, the Law of return, the effect of resonance, feels like a victim subjected to unfair treatment by others, society, destiny, bad luck, ill-fate. He refuses to acknowledge the fact that he reaps what he has sown, to accept the difficulty or ordeal as an opportunity to rectify errors he committed in the near or distant past. Consequently, he deprives himself of the chance to break out of the vicious circle of being a victim. It is possible to break such a vicious circle once we understand, wholly and completely, with our entire being, that sooner or later, a wrong-doer will have to pay for the negative karma he has created through his deed(s).

⊕ A person who needs help, support, comfort, understanding and justice; a person who becomes aware that he has been caught in wrong-doer/victim dynamics, who decides to work on himself and his life so as to set himself free from this vicious circle. Transcendence of the victim role through deep understanding of the correlation between cause and consequence. Integration of the concepts of karma (*I reap what I sow*), reincarnation, resonance (*I attract what I am, both positively and negatively,*) and Divine Justice (*a verdict or sentence that seems unjust according to human laws, is not unjust if we judge the situation with causal vision, with an understanding of the fact that the person is encountering karma from this or a previous life; Divine Justice is absolute*). Someone who trains himself to always refer back to himself, who has the will to examine his life, to study and check his behavior, attitudes, emotions and thoughts. Understanding the fact that the consequences of our misactions don't necessarily manifest immediately, that the reparation of negative karmas may extend over several lives. Capacity to accept our life plan without complaining, without nourishing feelings of bitterness, anger, rebellion, despair, or revenge. Transformation and liberation of conscious and unconscious aggressor, wrong-doer, and victim memories. End of a difficult karmic cycle; a new positive stage of evolution.

⊖ A person who doesn't understand that he behaved in the same way, did the same thing in the past to now deserve to live that experience as a victim, that he has attracted that situation because he has something to learn from it. A plaintive person, who wallows in the role of victim to attract attention, to be taken in charge of by others, to manipulate them, to make them feel guilty, to control them subtly, emotionally, or psychologically. Tendency to dramatize, exaggerate, and feel sorry for ourselves, to have a negative vision of everything, and to nourish feelings of sadness, bitterness, frustration, limitation, injustice, despair, anger, revenge, as well as pessimism and a fatalistic vision of life. Ignorance of the Divine Laws and concepts of karma, reincarnation, resonance and Divine Justice; or, refusal to acknowledge and accept them. Someone who projects his unhappiness onto others, onto society, onto bad luck, ill-fate, who is incapable of accepting the fact that he reaps what he has sown, that he attracts what he is, on the conscious and unconscious levels of his being. Mired, bogged down in existential torment and struggle. Atheism, difficulty believing in God, in a Higher, Superior Power, no matter what name we choose to use; difficulty understanding that there is a reason for all trials, ordeals, and difficult situations, that they are part of our learning program and serve to settle our karmic debts while favoring our evolution. Incapacity to truly forgive the other person; or, to heartlessly apply human laws without any clemency or compassion for those who suffer. Limited, stubborn spirit that refuses to evolve, to be enlightened by Divine Knowledge and Light.

VISION

Vision is the function that favors the use of the sense of sight. It is the fact of seeing and/or looking at something. The eye perceives light, color, shapes, distance, and movement in the surrounding environment. Vision symbolizes a person's perception, his way of seeing, perceiving, conceiving, and understanding the outer world in relation to his inner world, his choices, and the direction(s) he takes in life. It may also be related to the imaginary perception of unreal objects (hallucinations); or, to a mystical image, a supernatural apparition; and perception of the Divine, of God, of Cosmic Order, through intuition and clairvoyance.

In a dream, it is possible to have a very clear, precise vision of the distance of an object, shapes, shades, colors, clear perception of day or night, of what is taking place on the horizontal or vertical level, etc. The different visual experiences in dreams help us understand that we human beings have a capacity to see multi-dimensionally, to have a global perspective, an overall vision of our choices, discernment regarding what is true or false, clairvoyance, precise focus, lucidity, contemplation from an elevated point of view, good inner lighting, flexibility, open-mindedness, etc. In either a dream or concrete reality, whenever an obstacle obstructs our line of vision, it is important to decode its symbolic meaning, because this obstacle prevents us from seeing the truth.

The word *visionary* refers to someone who has, or thinks he has, supernatural visions; or, a capacity to intuitively anticipate the future, as is sometimes the case with artists, or in a company where a person may conceive, imagine, and engender new ideas, that go beyond normal limits, who sees potential others have not seen. Whenever a person has developed the skill of calmly observing the world around him, contemplating and understanding the essences that constitute the reality observed, and coming to a synthesis, his vision can be said to be a form of receptivity. Receptive observation is very similar to deep listening.

In a dream, we may have vision through our 3rd eye (through the opening of the 6th chakra), which allows us to know our memories as well as our future, to be warned in advance about a future situation, etc. There are also several pathologies related to vision that may be present in dreams, such as short-sightedness, long-sightedness, blindness in one or both eyes, blurred, double, or tunnel vision, obscured vision, black and white vision only, etc. Each specific aspect reveals various limitations regarding a person's perception, his way of seeing, his perspective, and his more or less enlightened knowledge of the inner and outer worlds.

⊕ Allows us to discern true from false, and to receive Knowledge, revelations on all levels. Right perception, helping to warn us in case of danger, or to make the most appropriate decisions. Capacity to see without criticizing or judging negatively. Open-mindedness; understanding multi-dimensions. Allows us to reveal masks and see beyond the form. Favors access to the essence of a person, object, situation, and event. Clairvoyance, opening of our 3rd eye, mystical awakening. Global perspective, perception of unity, contemplation from an elevated point of view, capacity to see beyond the horizon.

Stable, steady mind and spirit that is focused and understands limits as well as possibilities. A sense of synthesis, good understanding. Optimistic, flexible, open, creative, subtle perspective. Ability to penetrate the unconscious. Mystical visions, revelations received in dreams, intuition, great receptivity to the Divine. Guidance that facilitates choices, decisions, and creates a mystical experience of matter. Capacity or talent to read signs. Visionary mind and spirit.

⊖ Difficulty discerning true from false, as well as receiving revelatory visions on all levels. Lack of receptivity, depth, wrong, erroneous perception, poor analysis. Incapacity to perceive true danger. Critical, complicated, too intellectual, too rational, down-to-earth mind and spirit. Closed mind, lack of understanding of multiple dimensions. Blurred vision, ignorance, limited field of vision. Lack of precision and clarity on the level of values and moral principles, vague observation of a given situation, vision that is not right. Hallucinations, distorted perception, illusion, confusion between dream and reality.

A blind person, in dream or in concrete reality, has recorded memories, in this life or past lives, where he made poor use of his vision, had an overly horizontal mindset, lacked depth and appreciation of the values of the heart, lacked inner observation of people and things, was deficient regarding work on himself to advance on his inner path, absence of contact with his soul. Now, through the extreme problem of blindness, he is obliged to look within and develop his inner world, and a new (or renewed), deeper, truer way of seeing.

Short-sightedness: Lack of altruism and opening toward others, egocentricity. A person who is too focused on details, and has difficulty having an overall view of things, lacking global vision in a situation. A person who is extremely fussy about details, who is very pernickety, a dissatisfied perfectionist.

Long-sightedness: Difficulty taking care of details, of himself, and concentrating on simple, modest things. A person who flees and doesn't want to know the root of a problem. Lack of interiorization, someone who is over-focused on the social aspect, the outer world, and superficiality; absence of depth in his way of seeing, looking at and observing things.

Sight in only one eye: Overly specific vision, too concentrated on one thing. Lack of global vision and receptivity in relationships with others. An over-concentrated person who forces others to see things his way, who does not consider other people's points of view; or, who lacks vertical conscience, spiritual vision; or who has a radical way of seeing things; or, a too down-to-earth mind and spirit.

Black and white vision only: A pessimistic, sad, melancholic person. An old, outmoded vision of life. Absence of vitality.

Indistinct vision: Ignorance. Lack of clarity, understanding, extended vision; or, a darkened conscience that schemes and plots. Fear, anxiety, depression, dropping out, disconnection from social norms, lack of vitality.

2D vision, or ill 3rd eye: Lack of depth. Superficiality and incapacity to see beyond the form and understand multi-dimensions, the parallel worlds, dreams, signs, and symbols.

Imbalanced mystical vision or schizophrenia: Someone who confuses good and evil in his conscience. Spiritual knowledge mixed with a need to please, be loved and acknowledged, a desire for renown, etc. Clairvoyance used to serve dark forces, egocentric spiritual vision mixed with personal needs, anger, frustration, envy, jealousy, criticism; or, someone connected to demonic forces that are very dangerous for him and others. Confusion between dreams and reality, poor interpretation of signs and symbols, lack of Knowledge. Megalomania, abuse of power, seeking domination, egocentricity. A person who has forgotten the meaning of life, which consists in developing qualities and virtues, and always acting with love, harmony, and wisdom.

VITAMIN(S)

The word *vitamin,* which contains the Latin word *vita* (life), designates an organic substance that is indispensable, albeit in very small quantities, for the growth and good functioning of the human body, and all living organisms. As the body is incapable of creating and synthesizing vitamins, they have to be obtained in sufficient quantities through food; they may also be taken in liquid or tablet form, when necessary.

Symbolically, vitamins represent a source of vitality, dynamism, stimulation, and reinforcement of our vital energy. Each vitamin has a specific role in the healthy functioning of the organism, and for a good understanding of its metaphysical, symbolic meaning, it is necessary to analyze this role in depth.

There are two sorts of vitamins: hydro-soluble, which dissolve in water, and so are symbolically related to reinforcement on the emotional level; and lipo-soluble, which dissolve in fat, and are thus related to lipids, to the energy dynamic of the human body on the concrete level. Vitamin deficiency has different consequences for the body, and may even lead to serious illness; this is also true in the case of excessive consumption, an overdose of vitamins.

⊕ A capacity to understand the importance of vitamins as indispensable elements for the growth and good functioning of the human body. A person who helps, supports, works toward and maintains his good health, his vital energy, his dynamism, and is prepared to make efforts to maintain the vital, life-activity and capacity for vivification within him, so as to be able to make good, full use of his potential and inner resources.

⊖ A lack of interest or willpower to look after our health, to do whatever is necessary to nourish ourselves in a healthy, well-balanced way; or, someone going through great insecurities on the physical level, who is always afraid of being sick or ill, of lacking vitamins, essential life resources. A tendency to be over-focused on the physical body, and to seek or *boost* vitality *via* the outside to ensure continued emissivity, not understanding the need to interiorize, develop receptivity, and replenish our vital forces on the inside. A lack of understanding of the fact that all health problems stem from the metaphysical level, and are engendered by a person's mind, spirit and conscience, as well as by his unconscious memories. A lifestyle that creates imbalance, deficiencies or excesses, affecting the person in his very foundations, emptying him of his vitality.

VOICE

The voice, a collection of vocal sounds produced by human-beings, is a fundamental characteristic of our identity and the expression of our inner states. Each voice is unique and constitutes one of the major components of verbal or sonorous communication, such as speaking, singing or shouting. Once we know how to listen to a voice, we discover nuances, and sometimes, subtle tonalities, in both the high and low notes as well as in the person's breathing, which reveal the conscious and unconscious intentions of the person speaking or singing.

The voice, emitted in speech or song, is a multi-dimensional instrument, which is simultaneously emissive and intimate because its sound comes from within the body, and the quality of its vibration reveals the depth and purity of a person's soul, state of mind and spirit, and even conscience. Furthermore, a voice can vibrate and transmit its vibratory state through resonance, and hence cause others to vibrate. Thanks to our voice we can be heard, we can express ourselves, and more easily convey a message from our soul, thoughts, or feelings. With our voice, we can reassure, explain, speak, sing, calm, console; or, show authority and assert our presence. From a negative point of view, we can manifest anger, impatience, embarrassment, scorn, etc. By being receptive, by listening to the intonations in a person's voice, we can deeply understand his mood and the emotions he's feeling. Hence, deep listening allows us to discover the speaker's true personality.

With time, the more we develop clairaudience, the better we are able to listen to and hear in depth not only what the person says, but also what he leaves unsaid, his conscious or unconscious, hidden, veiled intentions. This extra-sensorial communication manifests through feelings, images, or signs that occur while the person is speaking, and may come directly from concrete, physical surroundings, or be of a more symbolic, metaphysical order. Advanced spiritual development is necessary for this kind of deep, multi-dimensional listening to be possible without feeling out of phase with ourselves and others. In psychiatric hospitals, patients who hear voices, are often people with great opening on the metaphysical level regarding extra-sensorial perception. However, as they don't know how to cleanse and transform the distorted memories, fears, and anxieties accumulated in their unconscious, their mediumnity (psychic powers) results in confusion and continual interference, which prevents them from living normally, maintaining self-control; it makes them dysfunctional.

We sometimes refer to our *little inner voice, a little voice within*, to explain a mystical experience that manifests in the form of clairaudience, which leaves us with the impression of having heard a voice. We usually attribute this impression, this feeling, to our intuition, or to inspiration coming from another level of our being, from our Divine Self, or from Up Above. The psychic, mediumnic power of clairaudience, i.e. the capacity to *hear* subtle energies that come from our and others' inner selves, is related to the throat chakra, which communicates with our hearing. When we know how to listen to this *little voice*, or these multiple *little voices* coming from all over, when we know how to master them thanks to great spiritual work in ourselves, we then understand their contents, their scope, their precision.

⊕ Symbol of communication, identity, and expression of a person's inner states. Ability to speak, express and assert ourselves, communicate and transmit our messages from the heart with sincerity and wisdom. A clear, sweet, pleasant, harmonious voice. Right expression and words, eloquence used with conscience. Capacity to listen to and hear states of soul, mind, spirit, things left unsaid, true intentions *via* clairaudience, beyond words, sounds and vibrations. A person who is receptive to his little inner voice and listens to it with discernment.

⊖ Problems with communication, elocution, identity, self-expression, and our inner states. Difficulty speaking, expressing ourselves, transmitting a message, asserting ourselves; or, someone who talks too much, who has an unpleasant, strident, harsh voice that may be too loud or too weak. Tendency not to dare express our point of view or our feelings. Unhealthy communication, tinged with manipulation or seduction. Destructive words. Incapacity to hear our *little inner voice* and activate our clairaudience because of over-emissive, hyperactive behavior; or, a lack of receptivity, spirituality, meditation, introspection, in-depth listening. Ignorance of the fact that behind every voice, sound, and tonality, there are intentions and vibrations that express both conscious and unconscious aspects. Dumbness (*cf. also* this term), mutism, caused by karmas engendered in this or other lives, which stems from poor use of the gift of voice.

VOLUNTARY WORK

Voluntary work indicates an altruistic action, an act of service chosen voluntarily and carried out without remuneration. It is generally done within an association or non-profit organization, a labor- or trade-union, or public, community, cultural, environmental (etc.) organization. Voluntary work is also sometimes referred to as beneficience, benefaction or good will. The origin of these words comes from the Latin word *benevolus* , meaning *good will.* Another word sometimes used is philanthropy, which comes from the Greek *philos* meaning "loving" in the sense of benefitting, caring for, nourishing, and *anthropos,* meaning human-being, humankind, humanity. Hence, volunteer work corresponds to one of man's fundamental needs because essentially man, in his essence, is an altruistic being animated and enlivened by the will to serve good and help his neighbor. On the metaphysical level, it represents the capacity to serve, help, offer our time, experience, competence and skills freely, without expecting anything in return, through pure altruism and the desire to participate in a social cause. (*cf. also* **Benefactor**)

⊕ Allows us to develop generosity, selfless service, gift of self, love of our neighbor, a sense of responsibility, a social, humanitarian, universal conscience and vision. Altruism and devotion.

⊖ A person who acts with hidden motives, for his personal interests and with superficial social commitment. Seeking recognition and wanting to be loved. Helping others for personal benefits. Difficulty being truly altruistic, because while helping others, we think too much about ourselves. Excessive volunteer work, e.g. becoming involved to the point of exhaustion and working for several organizations at the same time, indicates a great need for love and acknowledgment. Very often, especially when a person is committed to humanitarian or environmental work, he isn't aware that he is acting to satisfy inner needs, inner lacks.

VOMIT

The fact of vomiting expresses a surfeit, a surplus, owing to the excessive consumption of something harmful for our organism; or, an incapacity to digest a situation, a state of psychological and emotional stress. It is a sign that the person has attained his threshold of tolerance. He cannot take anymore. It is a natural reflex of purification, liberation, and protection of the body, soul, or conscience to expel a surplus of negativity, hence avoiding upsetting bodily functions, general, global malfunctioning; however, vomiting may also occur when a person is exposed to positivity and such high-level, quality energy that he cannot stand it, and because of that he may vomit it up. Generally speaking, vomiting indicates physical and metaphysical incapacity to digest, assimilate, transform, and integrate what we have ingested on the physical, emotional, mental, or spiritual level. Some very sensitive people vomit more easily than others who have donned a thicker shell and developed greater insensitivity.

Seeing ourselves vomit in a dream is a message inviting us to have a look at what in our life indisposes us to the point of making us sick. A study of the symbols surrounding the situation allows us better ability to understand the surplus of negativity – excess, abuse, overwork, overstimulation, etc. –, which needs to be rectified, requires moderation or evacuation of unhealthy contents buried in our cells and in our memories for quite some time. The mechanism of vomiting is similar to a resurgence of memories: the contents of the stomach rise up through the body to be evacuated through the mouth. This means that it is mainly energies absorbed by the mouth that come back out through the mouth. The fact that these contents have not been digested, that they resurface, are *thrown up,* may indicate a link with a trying situation either recently experienced, or very old, e.g. disturbing news or an event that provokes (or provoked) a state of shock, chemotherapy treatments, etc.

This phenomenon of purification *via* vomiting is frequently found, more or less intensely, in pregnant women. The arrival of a child, a powerful energy, that integrates the mother's body, creates a great metaphysical upheaval as well as engendering major changes in the physical body. Hence, the mother experiences purification caused by the vibratory intensity of the child, who seeks to create the best environment possible in which to develop. Through vomiting, the future mother evacuates her surplus negative memories on the physical and metaphysical levels, so as to be more receptive, and better adapted to the processes taking place within her. Among women who find it more difficult to be receptive, who tend to be too emissive, too masculine on the energy level, vomiting may manifest with greater intensity in order to invite them to more intensively, more vigorously activate maternal dynamics and feminine qualities: welcome, receptivity, love, listening, devotion, all that a child needs.

⊕ Elimination, purification, liberation on the physical and/or psychological level of harmful, indigestible elements, which hinder the proper functioning of the organism, harmony between the body, soul, mind and spirit. A force of protection, a power of detoxification, purification work ensuring the health of the body and soul. May be caused by a sudden awakening of negative memories resurfacing from the depths of our unconscious because the time has come to face, cleanse, and transform them. Liberation of inner blockages caused by tension, an accumulation and stagnation of negative energies, difficult-to-digest thoughts and emotions, which the person is incapable of understanding, dealing with, and transforming. Awareness that since vomiting is evacuation through the mouth, it also concerns the way a person communicates, exchanges with others, the way in which a person nourishes himself and others *via* energy transmitted through words, affection, and nutrition on all levels.

⊖ An incapacity to transform negativity, tensions, blockages, trying situations; difficulty managing and dealing with change, or a difficult, chaotic situation. An unhealthy, imbalanced way of nourishing ourselves on the physical and subtle levels, creating all sorts of excess, surplus, surfeit, overwork, blockages, and malfunctioning. Someone who lets himself be invaded, who absorbs anything and everything without protesting, without saying anything, so as not to displease, in order to be liked or loved and accepted. A tendency to repeat the same old patterns, refusal to call ourselves into question. Ignorance of the fact that vomiting also indicates the presence of communication problems: a tendency to tell lies, or to keep quiet in order to please or due to fear; or using words to seduce, manipulate, hurt, or destroy. Bulimic and anorexic tendencies (excessive, immoderate, disproportionate ingestion followed by deliberate vomiting). A lack of discernment and knowledge to correctly dose what we ingest and accumulate on the level of our physical body (solid and liquid food), on the level of our emotional body (feelings and emotions), on the level of our mental body (thoughts, ideas, information, reading), and on the level of our spiritual body (beliefs, spiritual, religious concepts). Overflow, a sudden, intense need to *throw up*, to clear out, to violently reject and free ourselves from what is felt to be polluting, negative, or over-stimulating. Difficulties freeing ourselves step by step, one stage after another, of inner blockages caused by an accumulation of harmful energies and unconscious negative memories.

WAGES *cf.* ***Salary*** *(wages, remuneration)*

WALK, TO

Walking is the most natural way of getting around. It allows us to get from one place to another, to reach a destination, to attain an aim or goal, to visit different states of conscience. It represents our autonomy to move around and our capacity to advance, move forward, and progress as much in our inner world as in the outside world. It also represents our capacity to become active and advance so as to evolve healthily, in a right, qualitative manner, while respecting each step or stage on the way. Sometimes it may also symbolize a time of relaxation, meditation, recuperation and renewal of our resources on all levels.

⊕ A capacity to advance, explore, and visit different states of conscience. Ability to renew ourselves and regenerate on the physical, emotional, mental, or spiritual level according to each dream or concrete situation.

⊖ Difficulty or incapacity to take time to renew ourselves, to analyze ourselves on our spiritual path. A lack of motivation to advance on the inside, to attain the objectives and goals we set ourselves. A tendency to advance with only one idea in mind, when single-mindedness is synonymous with selfishness, as we are only concerned with reaching our personal goal, attaining a result, and therefore no longer receptive either to ourselves or others.

WALL

A wall is a symbol of structure, protection, solidity and foundations; or, limitation. Depending on where it is to be found, its symbolic meaning will be related to our private, intimate life (the walls of a house and the different rooms in it), our professional life (the walls of the office, factory, the workplace), or collective, social, public life (the walls of a public, administrative, cultural office, a school, hospital, station, subway, etc.).

For example, the walls of our sitting-room concern the structure of our intimacy on the family and social levels, since a sitting-room serves to unite the family, receive friends, or find out about the outside world through television, radio, etc. Bathroom walls are related to purification; office walls, to our professional dynamics; hospital walls, to the capacity to take care of, treat, and heal on the collective level; school walls, to our capacity to learn and to teach; etc. Hence, the symbolic meaning of walls is defined by the activity that takes place within its boundaries, the people there, and also by everything that specifically characterizes them: i.e. the material(s) they are made of, their color, and the decoration found on them.

A damaged wall indicates a structural problem, an incapacity to build solidly, or to repair when necessary. The symbolic meaning will also depend on the location of the wall. For instance, a shabby, dirty bedroom wall reveals important structural problems in the way the couple, or bedroom occupant, rests, renews energy on all levels, or in relation to the couple's intimate, love life.

Generally speaking, walls denote our organizational structure on the personal, family, and collective levels. They also incite us to respect space devoted to work, intimacy, discretion, and renewal.

⊕ A capacity to structure ourselves, to build a personal, intimate space for ourselves; to protect ourselves, to define ourselves, or to be respected in our vital, living space by founding ourselves on right principles and values. An ability to healthily retreat and set ourselves limits. Respect for our own sacred space and that of others. Discreet behavior that respects other people's space. A person with a stable, solid, inner and outer structure that emanates a feeling of security and protection.

⊖ Feelings of limitation, imprisonment, that prevent a person from using and expanding his potential and achieving his aims; or, a scattered, dispersed mind or spirit, that is too open to others and the outside world, lacking principles and structure on the intimate level. An inaccessible, withdrawn, over-structured mind and spirit that creates blockages and impasses. Excessively controlling, critical, separatist behavior. A tendency to put up walls on concrete, energy, and metaphysical levels to protect ourselves for fear of being hurt, invaded, overworked. Instability, fragility, insecurity that push a person to close up, withdraw, compartmentalize, and hide from the outer world. A person who is either too secretive, or not secretive or discreet enough. Difficulties and problems due to a person structuring himself and setting himself limits based on erroneous principles. A lack of structure, an incapacity to interiorize, to grant ourselves an intimate, protected space, ensure it is respected and respect it ourselves. Disrespect for the space and intimacy of others.

WALLET (bill-fold, purse, pocket-book)

A wallet is a holder that contains money, usually in the form of bills (hence the term bill-fold), and a person's bank and identity cards. It symbolizes what we are, the resources we have at our disposal, the energy that will allow us to materialize. In the context of a positive dream, a wallet represents the possibility of manifesting our earthly and Divine identity in a right, just, qualitative manner, of concretizing our wishes in outer and inner abundance in accordance with Divine Laws. If the dream or concrete situation is negative (e.g. stolen, lost, or damaged wallet), it could indicate that the person concerned lives in a de-structured way, without resources, without the possibility of materializing concretely, that he is subjected to the effect of memories related to poverty, as well as inner and outer disorganization.

A purse or anything used to contain loose change refers to resources in lesser proportions.

It is also useful to symbolically analyze the details of the wallet or purse: its color(s), design, size, shape, material it is made of (natural, synthetic, or leather), the image(s) depicted on it, its exact contents, etc.

⊕ Security, abundance, stability; good management of and easy access to resources, assertion of our earthly, terrestrial identity. Will to materialize well. Generosity. Right, just use of resources. Cleansing memories related to poverty and lacks.

⊖ Material and identity problems; or someone who is over-focused on matter, on money. Financial insecurity, poor and/or careless management of resources, waste, extravagance, squandering. Abusing or misusing excess, which may engender poverty, dependency, limitation. Avarice, miserliness, greed, covetousness, possessiveness, an excessively materialistic person. May be related to forces that steal, that seek to obtain other people's resources, that want an easy life, with no need to work, no need to make an effort.

WAR

War represents a state of conscience connected to memories of inner conflicts of great intensity. The person lives in a state of inner division and is subjected to rebellion and violent, destructive confrontation among his different, opposing parts. He experiences anger, aggression, lack of flexibility and diplomacy toward others and himself. War also represents parts of ourselves that have excessive willpower to destroy everything in our entourage that bothers us or is contrary to *their* vision of things, *their* way of doing things. It originates in a climate of opposition and incomprehension and indicates an incapacity to settle differences with diplomacy, wisdom and a peaceful, attitude. The memories and state of mind that generate it are often marked with competition, jealousy, vengeance, racism, fanaticism, a total absence of tolerance and altruism, a thirst for power and domination that can go as far as megalomania. Our inner wars materialize in the form of outer wars when the combative forces of conflicting thoughts and emotions have been condensed to the point of no longer being containable within. Hence, to find the means to enable them to exteriorize, they seek an outer trigger, a scapegoat, and war breaks out. This process takes place on both the individual and the collective level. A war between nations indicates the presence of a great number of collective memories that resonate. It only takes one sufficiently powerful, determined mind to cleverly channel these memories to lead people into war.

⊕ A capacity to settle conflicts diplomatically and wisely, even if it is sometimes necessary to have recourse to force and the rigor of Divine Justice. Understanding the causes that engender wars. Development of tolerance and understanding that nothing is yet perfect on Earth. Capacity to remain stable and imperturbable in a hostile environment. Well exercised power and authority. Mastery of needs and forces that desire too much expansion in matter. Diplomat and mediator faculties, capable of harmonizing oppositions and sowing peace.

⊖ Multiple tensions and conflicts on both the inside and the outside. A rebellious, explosive, violent, dominating temperament. Memories marked by conflict, intolerance, aggression, cruelty. A spirit that divides, separates, and destroys; imposing willpower. A tendency to let ourselves be dominated, crushed by others, incapable of defending ourselves. Crushing power, dictatorship, anarchy. Overly severe, despotic application of justice. Abuse of armed forces both on the inside and on the outside, invasion, oppression, genocide.

WARDROBE *cf. Cupboard*

WAREHOUSE

A warehouse represents a capacity to welcome, stock, manage, protect and preserve large quantities of all sorts of resources. It is a temporary place of storage from where the stored goods may also be expedited. Symbolically, a warehouse corresponds to a state of conscience that enables us to store and manage our inner potential and resources with a view to sharing, exchanging, and putting them at the disposal of the collectivity as needs be.

⊕ Great potential for materialization and commercial exchanges. Preservation and protection of resources. A talent for logistics, organization, and management. Fair exchange and sharing of resources.

⊖ Difficulty materializing on a large scale. Poor management of resources; or, an incapacity to preserve and protect them. A tendency to burden ourselves with superfluous, useless goods. An accumulation of reserve stocks through insecurity, through fear of lacking. Fruitless projects. Loss of stored goods and all power of materialization. Problems storing harmful or dangerous products.

W

WARMTH *cf.* ***Heat***

WASH, TO

In a dream or in concrete reality, everything to do with the act of washing (ourselves, others, an object, etc.) represents purification, cleansing. The process doesn't only refer to the physical body or the material level, but also applies to our energy, thoughts, beliefs, emotions, and behavior. For example, washing clothes symbolizes the purification of our aura, of what we emanate on the personal and social levels; doing the washing-up indicates purification of our receptivity to nourishing energies; washing our face symbolizes the purification of our soul-state(s); washing our hands represents cleansing our capacity to give and to receive; cleansing our mouth indicates purification of the way we communicate, love, and nourish ourselves; washing our feet is related to cleansing the way we advance; etc.

⊕ An act of purification, cleansing, restoring order on the conscious or unconscious levels related to what is washed or cleansed. Purification of mind, spirit and soul-states as well as our general emanation and radiance. Aware of the importance of regularly washing and purifying ourselves on both the physical and metaphysical levels. Understanding the symbolic meaning of the act of washing ourselves: what we wash on the outside, in the exterior world, corresponds to a part of ourselves that is simultaneously washed or cleansed on the inside, in our inner world.

⊖ Difficulty related to the capacity to wash and purify ourselves, to cleanse our life, soul, mind, spirit, conscience, in order to renew ourselves, to evolve. An intense feeling of being dirty and polluted on the inside, which leads to carelessness, neglect, letting ourselves go, and manifests through laziness, indifference or negligence regarding our body and our environment; or, which may be linked to a puritanical attitude and an excessive need to wash ourselves or clean our house, our living environment because we lack the necessary tools and knowledge to purify ourselves on the inside, on the emotional, intellectual or spiritual levels. A lack of respect for ourselves and others.

WASHBASIN, SINK

A washbasin is a symbol both of a recipient as well as an outflow. As it is destined to receive water, and is most often found in a bathroom, it relates to emotional receptivity and cleansing, self-purification. Generally speaking, it serves to wash our hands (our capacity to give and to receive), our face (our soul-states), and our teeth (wisdom and solidity of our inner structure, of our basic instincts related to our capacity to nourish ourselves). A washbasin associated with running water, symbolizes our capacity to nourish ourselves emotionally and to purify ourselves thanks to a renewal of feelings and emotions, which helps us get rid of the negative, impure energies we may have absorbed or cultivated. The symbolism of a kitchen sink is related to the state of conscience and manner in which we cleanse and purify ourselves before meals, or while preparing them; the way we cleanse certain foods before eating them, as well as the attitude with which we do the washing-up and generally keep the kitchen clean.

⊕ A symbol of cleansing, purification, refreshment and vivification of our being, our soul-states (moods), our capacity to receive and give resources, and to create. For the symbol to be truly positive, the washbasin or sink and its tap water must be clean, and the outflow of water must be obstacle-free, i.e. the cleansing, nourishing or preparatory emotional energy must circulate freely.

⊖ Difficulty regarding purification, cleansing, nurturing, nourishing emotional energy and receptivity of resources. A dirty washbasin or sink denotes a refusal to wash and purify ourselves. It may indicate the presence of distorted emotional memories and negative soul-states, which prevent a favorable use of our purification and/or nutritional potential, which has negative consequences on our manner of giving, receiving, and manifesting in our intimacy, in our exchanges, as well as our attitude when eating or preparing meals. On the contrary, a tendency to excessive washing of our hands, face or teeth, or a desire for extreme cleanliness in the kitchen, when washing-up or preparing food, indicates a need to please in order to be loved, and is a sign of rigidity, puritanism and extremism; or, it may denote the presence of obsessive-compulsive disorder (OCD). A blocked washbasin or sink reveals difficulty emotionally evacuating our distortions, a tendency to retain our negative emotions.

WASTE PRODUCTS *cf. Garbage*

WATCH *cf. Clock*

WATER

Water is one of the four elements: fire, air, water and earth. It represents the world of feelings and emotions. Like love and feelings, it is an essential source of life and contains unique properties of universal solvent, of receptive, flexible, adaptable, enveloping, comforting power, and has the capacity to cleanse, purify, transform, dilute, nourish, and help grow.

⊕ The quality of the water shows what is being experienced on the emotional level. A source of transformation, life, receptivity, purification, purity, and gentleness. Emotional mastery. A capacity to adapt to all situations and also to dilute what is too concentrated or condensed. Power to renew, replenish and heal.

⊖ Problems relating to the emotional level. Unstable feelings. Affective dependencies. Tumultuous, polluted emotions. Storms, shipwrecks. Emotional overspill, excessive excitability, hyper-emotionalism; or, absence of emotions and feelings. A tendency to over-dilute; or, impossibility to dilute because excessively concentrated or condensed.

WEAKNESS *cf. Flaw*

WEATHER FORECAST, METEOROLOGY

Weather forecasting or meteorology symbolically informs us of our inner climate, i.e. the different soul-states we are experiencing. It tells us about our emotions (represented by water, snow, ice, etc.), our thoughts (represented by winds, atmospheric pressure, tornadoes, etc.), as well as our vital energy (represented by sun, temperatures, the intensity of various elements, etc.). People pay great attention to the weather forecast, partly because, consciously or unconsciously, they are interested in their own inner climate. Consequently, they are happy when good weather is forecast, because they like to feel fine, sunny-tempered, radiant, stable, and warm on the inside, whereas rain can awaken memories of sadness and solitude, just as snow can revive emotional coldness. Moreover, whenever people talk about the weather and temperature, symbolically, they reveal the inner states that dwell in them at that moment.

Since meteorology is a science that predicts the weather and temperature, it also concerns the idea of anticipation and foresight. For example, we may be able to foresee and understand our inner atmospheres, our inner ambiances, from weather information contained in a dream. This symbolism may also concern the collective level, and, for example, show us whether the atmosphere, ambiance, and circumstances are propitious or not for the realization of a project.

⊕ A capacity to analyze and understand our inner ambiances and climates. Such data helps us better manage our thoughts, emotions, vital energy, the power and force of our mind and spirit, as well as our capacity for materialization. A capacity and power of adaptation. An in-depth study and knowledge of the four outer elements (earth, water, air and fire) and what they correspond to on the inside (the physical, emotional, mental and spiritual levels), which helps us acquire mastery on all levels. Gift of foresight. Right perception. Global vision. A possibility to anticipate our personal evolution program, or a collective program, and then make the right, appropriate decisions. A great capacity to analyze and manage multiple sources of information and data.

⊖ Difficulty anticipating and sensing inner atmospheres, ambiances, climates. Inner imbalances corresponding to outer imbalances of the four elements (earth, water, air and fire). A lack of understanding of the natural, evolutive mechanisms of temperature and climate. A need to be in control, an incapacity to simply let go. Difficulty adapting. A feeling of survival, existential fear. A fatalistic, apocalyptic person who lives in expectation of natural catastrophes. A tendency to be over-focused on the outer climate, on what the weather is going to be like. Fear, panic, multiple insecurities, a need to know the weather in advance; or, on the contrary, a lack of foresight and appropriate planning and organization. A lack of confidence in Destiny and the Divine.

WEIGHT GAIN *(cf. also* ***Obesity****)*

Gaining weight over and beyond the normal weight for our physical size represents a state of conscience that is characterized by great unsatisfied needs, considerable repression and inner lacks, which push us to all sorts of nutritional excess and abuse. Consciously or unconsciously, a person who puts on weight always wants more. Not knowing how to recognize nor how to satisfy his physical, emotional, intellectual and spiritual deficiencies in a right, healthy way, the person tries to satisfy his different starving, thirsty parts with the only food he knows. Weight gain may also manifest in someone who eats a normal or even little quantity of physical food. This indicates that such a person represses within himself all that bothers him on the outside; or, that he is incapable of appropriately digesting the huge amount of subtle energy he has absorbed, sometimes over several lives. This energy gradually accumulates and condenses in the person's subtle bodies until its density reaches the point where it materializes in the form of physical weight. An overweight person tends to retain his thoughts and emotions. He doesn't express what he is going through on the inside, and tends to have affective, emotional deficiencies. He stocks negative energies without discernment, without analyzing them, and without knowing how to transform them. It is often a case of a soul that lacks willpower and has accumulated, sometimes over several lives, a whole set of *luggage* (*cf.* this term) filled with frustrations, emotional lacks and needs, without ever trying to master and transcend them by educating and disciplining himself. It may also be shown in a dream that it is related to our negative memories in connection with the animal kingdom, such as the insatiable hunger of a bear or an octopus.

⊕ Development of the will to work on our needs and primary instincts, as well as on our impulsive emotions and thoughts, to learn to manage and transform them. Awareness of the existence of the need for nourishment of our subtle bodies, i.e. our emotional, mental/intellectual, and spiritual bodies. Learning discernment and mastery of our soul-states (moods). Alchemy and transcendence of negative energies and memories of lack. Work on our complex of inferiority, dependencies, the cause of our excesses, the need to please and seduce through physical appearance, or an image of artificial beauty.

⊖ Indication that the person concerned lives under the influence of memories wherein he has inscribed all sorts of excess and abuse; or, that his soul is overburdened with memories of lack, repression, unsatisfied needs, and dependencies. Poor food habits. Being bogged down. Tendency to retain, to keep everything inside ourselves. Fear of shortages, deficiencies, and deprivation. An old soul that has accumulated all kinds of energies, sensations and influences. Lacking the willpower to change, to discipline and educate ourselves, to define clear, right, just limits. Great difficulty managing emotions and tensions. Ignorance of the nutritional needs of our subtle bodies. Lack of knowledge, wisdom, and love. Incapacity to manage the negative, to find balance and harmony. Unhealthy, perverted living habits. Tendency to denigrate ourselves and to trivialize our state and our nutritional problems. Inferiority complex. Trying to hide our feelings and soul-states behind a mask of humor. Seeking to satisfy our needs artificially by nourishing ourselves on the energy level through physical beauty, appearances, celebrity, and the seduction games of public figures featured in the media.

WEIGHT LOSS, SLIMMING

Weight loss may be voluntary or involuntary. It may be a consciously chosen means to rectify poor food habits that have encumbered our body and upset its healthy, well-balanced functioning. As well as having beneficial effects on the general health of our physical body, slimming (or weight loss) also represents a period of inner purification, regeneration, lightening, alleviation, and transformation of our personality, as well as a liberation of our spirit and soul, because poor nutrition always affects all levels of our being. Hence, weight problems are not only engendered by excess, deficiency, or poor quality physical nourishment, they are mainly the result of memories of lacks, possession, affective and material insecurities, as well as multiple untranscended needs. Very often, not knowing the correlation that exists between unconscious memories, instinctive needs, a lack of appropriate nourishment on the emotional, mental and spiritual levels, and nutritional behavior on the physical level, causes people to function through compensation. And what they choose as compensation on the outside resonates on the vibratory level with what they are experiencing on the inside.

Weight loss, even major weight loss, may also occur quite naturally during a period of intense work on ourselves. In this case, it is a physical reflection of the great cleansing work being carried out on the subtle levels, and, with a positive state of mind, it can also be accepted and well lived. However, rapid, excessive weight loss, accompanied by pain and other alarming symptoms may not only indicate great sorrow, deep grief, intense suffering, or lack, but also a serious health problem, or the presence of an undiagnosed illness. It is important to consult a health-care professional.

⊕ A period of cleansing and purification on all levels. Rectification of erroneous food habits or nutritional behavior as well as distorted, harmful needs. Re-balancing and healing of the functions of the physical body. The willpower to work on our vital needs, especially affective needs and material insecurity. Liberation of accumulated heaviness on the soul and spirit levels. Development of rigor and discipline on the nutritional level. Awareness that it is essential to appropriately nourish all of our bodies, physical and subtle, in order to favor the integral, harmonious evolution of our whole being, and avoid imbalance that leads to dysfunction on different levels. Transformation of memories of lack that induce poor nutrition. Improvement of our self-image and self-esteem.

⊖ An exaggerated or obsessive wish to lose weight indicates an excessive desire to correspond to a socially valued image of beauty due to a need to please, a need to be loved and acknowledged. Focus on criteria for physical appearance and beauty that have been decided upon by fashion and society. A lack of self-esteem. An incapacity to acknowledge, love and appreciate ourselves for what we are, for the values and qualities we incarnate. Superficial conscience that nourishes illusion. Deep imbalance between body, mind, spirit and soul. A tendency to be hard, harsh, severe on ourselves and self-impose extreme, radical diets that upset the natural functions of our physical body and cause our soul to suffer. Presence of memories that incite a person to refuse or reject available nutritional abundance and the pleasure of eating. Self-punishing behavior. Rigidity. Poor use of our will-power and motivation. Loss of vital energy. Depression. Eating disorders (*cf. also* **Anorexia; Bulimia**). Suicidal ideas. Ignorance and lack of awareness, knowledge, and resources to nourish ourselves in a correct, well-balanced way on all levels.

WEST

West is a cardinal point situated on the same side as the setting sun. The four cardinal points – North, South, East and West – allow us to situate places and ourselves geographically. Symbolically the 4 cardinal points represent the direction and orientation of our life, possibly indicating a new route, a new destiny. As the sunset announces the passage from day to night, the West (as opposed to the East and the rising sun) represents the end of a cycle, the end of a phase or stage. In terms of state of conscience, it indicates transformation, interiorization, and dying in order to prepare a new cycle.

⊕ End of a cycle, a transition period, or a period of interiorization, of inner transformation thanks to which the person will experience renewal, rebirth, similar to our daily cycle of going to sleep at the end of the day to wake up refreshed, ready for a new day. A capacity to orient our life, a new direction to follow.

⊖ Arrival of a difficult cycle, difficult transition. Difficulty or an incapacity to accept a stage, to go within and interiorize in order to prepare for a new cycle, for renewal, for rebirth. Fatalism, despair. Resistance to evolve, to abandon distorted behavior. A feeling of being lost.

WHALE

A whale represents a collection of instinctual needs related to the emotional level. Through its huge size and corpulence, this marine mammal has great physical strength, hence its capacity to dive to the depths of the ocean. Symbolically, a whale reveals a capacity to immerse ourselves deeply in collective, emotional memories. This powerful potential indicates great emotional capacity and considerable primal needs linked to emotions.

⊕ Great physical strength and powerful vital energy to plunge into the personal and collective unconscious and face emotional memories.

⊖ Considerable needs on the affective level. A tendency to abundantly nourish strong dependencies. An inclination to become burdened with emotions and negative energies related to emotional needs.

WHEEL

A wheel evokes an idea of movement as well as cyclical renewal since it turns around on itself and always returns to the point of departure. It illustrates the fact that human existence is made up of a succession of experimentations, cycles of perfecting ourselves, beginning over and over again, which allow us to increasingly deepen knowledge of ourselves and of the Universe in a continual, evolutive movement.

It also symbolizes continuity, eternal Life, governed by Cosmic Laws, including the Law of reincarnation, which allows us to understand that death is not the end of life, since it is followed by a new birth. Indeed, the permanence of the soul throughout its successive incarnations teaches us that we always reap what we sow according to the Law of karma. Karma leads a soul to experience the consequences of its positive and negative acts, created throughout the course of its experimentations, throughout its numerous lives. Karma engenders periodic returns to negative behavior and attitudes in the course of human destiny in order for us to purify them. Hence it allows a soul to understand the educational role of evil, wrong-doing, what hurts, and to attain Knowledge, thanks to which it can then, in all conscience, refuse to reproduce evil in the course of new experimentation.

On the physical level, a wheel is related to the earth element as it allows the movement of a vehicle along the ground, thereby facilitating advancing and the transport of people and things. On the metaphysical level, it symbolizes ease moving around, with all the conscious and unconscious *luggage* (*cf.* this term) we may carry. Hence it represents a capacity to advance, to materialize our destiny in the course of a dynamic process where everything evolves, where everything – thoughts, emotions, instincts, energies – is in transit, where nothing is permanently set, established, or stuck.

From a negative point of view, a wheel evokes the repetitive character of actions, which reproduce the same errors, and which means we are necessarily confronted with the same problems and difficult, troublesome, annoying situations, often referred to as a vicious cycle. The person has not understood in depth the meaning of ordeals, or the gift of potential evolution they contain. Such a person will find himself experiencing more and more difficult ordeals in order to attain a better understanding of the necessity of undertaking a spiritual path or journey.

⊕ Positive movement and advancing; or, a period to pause, halt, have a break or *intermission*, to rest, and to analyze. A capacity to continue to advance toward the realization, the materialization of our aims and objectives. An ability to concretize our potential, to materialize easily and reliably, thanks to an understanding of the cycles of evolution. Understanding the wheel of karma, the Law of reincarnation, the principle of causality, the correlation between cause and consequence. A capacity to accept our destiny, to follow our life path with wisdom. Development of the will to set ourselves free from the effects and consequences of a negative, limiting, destructive karmic circle.

⊖ Hyperactivity, exaggeration, immoderate, excessive ambition, induced by a desire to go fast, to cut corners, to reach a result considered to be an end in itself (materialistic concept), due to a lack of understanding of our life plan. Or, on the other hand, immobility, passivity, laxity, a period of resistance, involution, deep insecurity because we feel unable to advance. An incapacity to adapt and face ordeals in order to realize our aspirations, attain our objectives. A lack of understanding of the stage we are in. A lack of understanding of the cycles through which life evolves. Ignorance or wrong understanding of the concepts of karma, reincarnation, and causality. A feeling of being alone, lost, immobilized, submerged by an ordeal because of an overburdened unconscious. An excess of perfectionism. Repetitive failure. Prisoner of our ego and our subjugation to matter. A lack of willpower to change and set ourselves free from harmful patterns. Refusal to learn from our errors. Imprisoned in the wheel of karma.

WHITE

As a color, white is the synthesis of all the colors (when we superimpose monochromatic light beams, we obtain white). As the best reflector of life-giving sunlight, white is thus the perfect symbol of the Divine and spirituality, of the light of the spirit, of the highest level of power, love, wisdom, purity, and original innocence. The origin of its symbolism comes from its immaculate aspect. White also symbolizes peace and calm. It is also the color of sperm and breast milk, two essential life elements.

It is interesting to draw an analogy between white and the color condensed matter manifests when exposed to high temperatures. The phenomenon can be observed when watching logs burn in a hearth fire. As it is consumed by fire, wood goes through different colors and the hotter the fire, the whiter the wood becomes. This process is also the origin of the transformation of coal into quartz, although this takes place over a period of several thousand years and represents a hidden alchemical process that takes place in the depths of the earth. The more crystalline, transparent and pure the quartz, the more its transformation is considered complete. On the symbolic level, this means that the more we expose our ego and the unconscious distorted memories that create it (our *coal*) to the purifying power of alchemical fire, the more our true identity, our immaculate divinity (the crystal, and ultimately, the diamond we are) can be revealed.

White also represents abstract, latent, not yet manifest creative power; for example, the white page awaiting a writer, the blank canvas before an artist, a bride's white dress which traditionally manifests her virginity and receptivity to fusion with the masculine principle to create a new life, children, a family.

Etymologically, the word white comes from the Germanic word *blank,* meaning shining bright, clear, stainless, morally pure; its other meaning is naked, a symbol of authenticity.

⊕ Purity, clarity, spirituality, divine power, supreme love and wisdom. Soul-state related to spiritual values and divine principles. Purity of intention, respect for the universal laws and right use of divine powers. Achievement, divine realization. Creator of an atmosphere of peace and freedom.

⊖ White, in various forms – color, light, clothing, decoration, decor, etc. – may have a negative connotation and indicate a context where a person is lost in abstraction. It may also appear in a context of spiritual pride, extremism, religious fanaticism, or abuse of spiritual power. It is often used by false gurus and leaders of sects to dazzle followers, to deform their capacity of discernment, and to camouflage an inversion and perversion of spiritual principles. On the individual level, white may be the dominant color of both the clothes and living-environment of people on a spiritual path who believe they are very evolved, even perfect. Such people often have an over-blown ego, believe they are right, powerful, and masters of various trends of so-called spiritual knowledge, ignorant of or ignoring the heavy karma such an attitude engenders.

WIDOWHOOD

Widowhood is the social and legal state of a person whose spouse has died. This state of change and mutation, whether experienced positively or negatively, is related to the couple, to love, and to the masculine and feminine polarities within each of us. The person whose spouse has died sees a phase of his life come to an end and another begin. When death occurs, a stage has been concluded; it has come to an end in compliance with the natural cycle, in accordance with each person's life plan, in order to make way for new experiences, a new rhythm of life. In dreams, widowhood represents deep, intense change on the affective, relational levels. It indicates a period of acceptance and renewal. However, it may also announce great sorrow, emptiness, solitude, separation, despair, deep insecurity, and disconnection. Whenever this cycle is set in motion and experienced negatively, then the mourner needs to work on his memories of affective dependency, lack, and attachment, as well as his difficulty dealing with solitude, interiorizing, etc. (*cf. also* ***Death***; ***Cemetery***)

⊕ The end of a cycle, a period of great change that sets in motion a new stage of life; announces rebirth, departure toward new horizons, the springtime of a new life. Calling ourselves, our life, our aims, objectives and goals into question; deep reflection, meditation, inner quest. A favorable period for reconstruction, work on ourselves to establish new bases, new foundations.

⊖ Great sorrow, nostalgia, melancholy, emptiness, lack, insecurity, consternation, despair, inner vagrancy; or a materialistic, too down-to-earth attitude, avarice, seeking profit, personal enrichment. Someone visiting his forces and memories of dependency, possessiveness, attachment, egoism; or who unveils repressed, negative attitudes, a sick personality. Lack of faith, of spirituality. Incapacity to believe in life after death, the eternal life of the soul and spirit, the continuity of existence in the parallel worlds, and incarnation. Tendency to withdraw into ourselves, to isolate ourselves socially, to hang onto memories of our life as a couple that is now over. Lack of understanding or non-acceptance of the cycles of Life that serve material, mortal form in order for us to experiment birth, growth, flourishing, composition and decomposition, construction and destruction. Absence of global, multi-dimensional vision, lack of understanding of the process of evolution. Rebellion, repressed or expressed anger, atheism; not wanting to believe in a Higher Power. Tendency to go around in circles, to live in our memories, nostalgia for the past; to be consumed with pain, unable to see the beauty and great potentialities Life continually offers; feeling utterly devastated, a lost soul. The grieving person ignores or totally rejects the complementary polarity that dwells in him.

WIFE *cf.* ***Spouse***

WIG

A wig is a manufactured covering for the head made out of natural or synthetic hair. It is used for various reasons. As it is specifically made to be worn on the head, it is related to ways of thinking. However, it is mainly related to self-esteem or a desire for self-transformation. It is usually used to hide baldness, dirty or unkempt hair; or, in the context of disguise. The fact that it covers or hides our real hair or lack of it, leads to wigs being associated, on the negative level, with a lack of authenticity, difficulty accepting and acknowledging ourselves as we are, a tendency to grant too much importance to our own and others' physical appearances and beauty.

In some cases, a wig may help cancer patients keep up their morale as it allows them to discreetly hide the loss of their hair caused by certain cancer treatments; hence, it helps the person to feel more at ease in a social context, and to re-build himself on the psychological level. In other cases, a wig may support actors' work when actors interpret a role for the theatre or movies; or, it may play a role in children's games, and participate in the disguises chosen for carnival, Halloween, or a masked ball. It contributes to the discovery of new, unknown parts of ourselves.

In many countries (often in former British colonies and Commonwealth countries), members of the legal profession (judges, barristers) are obliged to wear wigs as part of their official dress. This archaic tradition originated in the 17th century when Louis XIV starting wearing a wig out of vanity to cover his baldness. It spread to the courts, where judges and lawyers/barristers wear white wigs as part of their official dress to remove traces of personality and self-identification, to help them embody their role with solemnity and dignity, and honorably dispense the law and judgments as fairly and wisely as humanly possible. However, from a negative point of view, such wigs serve to set members of the legal profession above and apart from the people they represent; they tend to impress people for superficial reasons. The expression *a bigwig* refers to a person who has an important and powerful, often official, position; it is sometimes used pejoratively to refer to a person with an inflated ego. More recently, there has been a tendency to simplify lawyers' official attire and in some countries (e.g. New Zealand) wigs have been phased out and are now only worn for ceremonial occasions.

We need to know the person's aim and intention for using a wig in order to understand whether its symbolic meaning is positive or negative. The form, color, texture, harmonious or disharmonious aspect of the wig, as well as the attitude and energy emanated by the wearer, allow us to know whether its use indicates a lack of authenticity, a complex of inferiority, a tendency to flee from ourselves, a need to play a role or hide our true self by displaying over-positive humor or a false personality; or, a temporary *crutch*. A detailed analysis of all of these elements will determine whether the symbolism is positive or negative.

⊕ Facilitates the healing and transformation work on memories marked by a lack of self-esteem. May help an ill person rebuild his self-image as regards the outside world or himself, thereby helping him avoid depression, discouragement, and/or social isolation. A useful accessory in certain professions, in certain contexts of entertainment and fun. Reveals hidden aspects of the wearer. May serve to inspire, to transmit coded, symbolic messages.

⊖ Lack of authenticity and self-esteem. Tendency to play a role, to dissimulate what we really look like, to hide our true nature. Someone who is over-focused on appearances, on the physical aspect. Seeking to please, to be loved, to be recognized; or, showing off, extravagant behavior. Indiscretion. Artificial attitude. Superiority or inferiority complex. Helps us constitute a mask, a false identity, in order to hide dishonest intentions, ill-will, malevolence, hypocrisy, lies. Lack of purity on the thought level. In extreme cases, it may be related to a person suffering from mental problems, schizophrenia, multiple personalities.

WIND (climate)

The wind is directly related to the air element (the world of thought), and thus symbolizes the forces that animate our thoughts with more or less intensity. Metaphysically, wind creates movement, represents energy variations, evolution, and changes in our way of thinking. It may inspire thoughts, and positively animate our being; or, it may be disturbing, too intense, even destructive, when it blows too strongly. For example, a tornado in a dream reflects turbulent, tumultuous, angry thoughts that may dwell in the dreamer. Wind is a representation of the continual motion of the world of thoughts, which maintains a person's psychological equilibrium.

⊕ Healthy thoughts, inspiring, vivifying, elevating, renewing mental activity. A natural, spontaneous surge. A capacity for evolutive thought, that helps us advance healthily, at the right moment. Intellectual riches. A motivating, multiplying force that helps us transform ourselves, progress, discover new horizons, new currents of thought. Flexibility of the mind and spirit, self-questioning, an opening of conscience. Someone who masters his inner *mind-wind(s)*, who knows how to balance his mental level.

⊖ An unstable, tumultuous, devastating; or, inactive, becalmed mental level. Disturbing, rebellious, turbulent thoughts; a complicated, tormented person. Mental illnesses. May designate intellectual hyperactivity; or denote carelessness, indifference, mental stagnation, refusal to change, evolve, or move on the thought level. Someone who goes around in circles, brooding over and dwelling on the same ideas, who may thus engender tornadoes, destruction on all levels, as the mind, the mental level, influences all levels.

WINDOW

Symbolically a window represents a capacity to see, look at and observe, on both the inner and outer levels. It allows us to look into the intimacy of a structure and see what is happening on the inside; or, to observe social, collective dynamics on the outside in relation to what we are experiencing or feeling on the personal level. It gives us a view of the environment, people, and life in the outside world and, simultaneously, it gives us access to our inner world, to the way we live and function on the personal and/or family level, when it is a window of a private house; or, on the professional and social levels, when it is a public building window, e.g. in an office, workshop, factory, hospital, school, etc.

Windows also let natural light, a symbol of knowledge and understanding, into our home, our life and workspace; symbolically speaking, into various spaces of our inner world. Hence, windows allow us to see things more clearly, with greater discernment and lucidity on both the physical and metaphysical levels. We can be enlightened, awakened, inspired, stimulated, vivified by the light that shines through them and better understand what we are going through, or what is going on. Moreover, whenever a window is open, the incoming air favors good aeration; symbolically, the inner world *breathes* well and thoughts circulate more easily. A window is also a symbol of transparency, authenticity and, sometimes, revelation. It may indicate a person's openness and receptivity to the light, and outer ambiances and stimulation. It also allows us to observe what is going on inside a building, and, in some circumstances, to detect problematic situations or potential danger.

To symbolically analyze a window in a given context, its size, the quality and cleanliness of the windowpane, the presence or absence of curtains, blinds, shutters, or bars, whether it is open or closed, etc., also need to be taken into account.

⊕ Depending on the position of the observer, it allows contemplation and analysis of the outer or inner world, of the surrounding environment, of life and events going on therein, of the ambiance and atmosphere emanated. Facilitates access to the light, clarity, increased global vision and understanding, as well as the refreshment and renewal of the air and thoughts. It also allows foresight, anticipation, and protection against unfavorable climatic conditions on the outside and their corresponding aspects on the inside.

A window with the curtains drawn allows us to indicate a need for intimacy and tranquility; it incites discretion and respect for privacy.

A clear, curtain-less, and/or open window is a sign of open-mindedness, receptivity, transparency, and authenticity. It favors lucidity and discernment in the evaluations of situations and exchanges that take place on both the inner and outer levels.

⊖ *The absence of windows or windows that are always closed, with the curtains drawn* indicate difficulty opening up to and welcoming life, and exchanging with the outer world; or, a lack of interest in social life. The person barricades himself in, shuts himself off from the light, fresh air, and exchanges with others because he is afraid; or, extremely shy, introverted and withdrawn; or, unsociable, rather wild, mistrusting, and/or with hermit tendencies. Veiled vision and lack of transparency, which reveal a state of darkness and obscurity on the inner level. Problems with receptivity to light, to understanding ourselves, others, and life experiences. It may also indicate that the person has something to hide, is involved in shady, forbidden, immoral, illegal, criminal activities.

Broken windows indicate a lack of protection from the coldness and hostility of the climate, and/or general surrounding atmosphere and ambiances.

Dirty windows are a sign of neglect, negligence, lack of cleanliness, poor hygiene, blurred, unclear vision, a lack of lucidity and discernment in our perception of what is going on, both on the inside and on the outside.

Observing others through the window indicates indiscretion and excessive curiosity; someone who spends a lot of time doing this nourishes parts of himself on the energy level that have all sorts of lacks, desires, unhealthy needs. Voyeurism.

WING(S)

Wings are a characteristic feature of certain animals and devices that can raise themselves up, take off and fly through the air. They indicate a light, airy, exalting movement; above all, they are a symbol of lightness, lightening up, soaring, freedom, elevation toward the sublime, surging enthusiasm and impetus for transcending the human condition. Simultaneously related to the world of action, since they are attached to a physical body, and to the world of thoughts as they allow flight through the air, they represent the mind and spirit's capacity to rise up and attain global vision, universal conscience. They also symbolize the power of spiritualization and transfiguration. The expression *to take someone under our wing* adds the symbolism of protection and support given to someone to help him develop and realize his potential. Joy and knowledge can also *give us wings*.

⊕ Indicates energy of soaring flight, elevation and expansion dynamics on the thought and conscience levels. Grants access to global vision, to freedom, and to the causal world. When attached to an Angel or Heavenly Being, wings refer to Divine Powers. In the case of a winged animal, they indicate transcendence of the instincts and characteristics of the animal in question. A luminous, winged lion, for example, would reveal that certain aspects of our instinctual energy have been transcended, which would manifest through greater vital energy, authority, leadership, a greater capacity to make decisions and act, as well as greater power on the thought level.

⊖ Difficulty raising ourselves up, difficulty reaching high levels of conscience due to a lack of spirituality and a too down-to-earth vision of things. Tendency to take refuge in our thoughts, to seek an ethereal state so as to escape the heaviness and slowness of the material level; or, to flee certain fears. Unconcerned, imprudent, rash, superficial, irrational ideas. Seeking artificial paradises, evasion and excessive detachment from the material level. A negative, winged animal, such as a demon or threatening dragon, would indicate that instinctual vital energy is used to satisfy distorted needs; or, to create destruction and evil. The negative symbolism also applies in the case of a very intelligent person who consciously does wrong, who misuses his knowledge, talents and powers.

WINTER

Winter represents a state of conscience which favors and facilitates interiorization, introspection, deep reflection, inner listening, and work on ourselves. The cold, damp and wet, the ice and snow which characterize this season incite us to activate our inner warmth, the fire of our vital energy, the love and tenderness of our heart, and our spiritual strength. The contemplation of snowy landscapes and nature plunged into silence creates a calming, restful effect which helps us feel inner peace and inspires the elevation of our soul and spirit. The winter climate and living conditions also require work on patience, endurance, perseverance, acceptance, and adaptation to the natural outer phenomena and the development of a pleasant, temperate, well-balanced climate in our inner world. During this resting period, not only does nature prepare for renewed life, which becomes visible each Spring, but also a new stage, a new cycle, a new re-birth is prepared within ourselves.

⊕ A capacity to create and maintain a warm, serene, happy, well-balanced inner climate regardless of outer conditions. An aptitude for feeling good, radiating joy, remaining in harmony with ourselves and our entourage in all circumstances. Work on ourselves to transform and transcend memories marked by emotional coldness, lack of love and warmth. Rest, contemplation, interiorization, meditation. Creates a climate of closeness and intimacy. Favors loving moments, making love, the fusion of man and woman. Elevation of conscience allowing us to feel the magic of Life and Divine Light. Deep, mystical, spiritual experiences.

⊖ Emotional coldness, a frozen heart, absence of human warmth, incapacity to express our feelings, congealed, frozen vital energy. Memories of solitude, of lack of love and warmth, of difficulty surviving. A complaining, whining attitude. Difficulty adapting to winter conditions. Withdrawal, loss of dynamism, motivation, cheerfulness and energy. Cold appreciation, criticism, getting lost in abstraction. Absence of joy, moroseness, depression, suicidal tendencies. A taciturn, withdrawn, surly, glum, tough, lifeless spirit. Blockages, limitations, retention. A lack of sensuality, warmth and tenderness in intimate relationships, when making love.

WOMAN

A woman symbolizes a state of conscience related to the characteristics of the feminine principle and receptivity. The masculine and the feminine are inherent in all manifestations of life. Fusion of these two polarities is indispensable for creation, procreation, accomplishment, and evolution. Each human being, whether male or female, bears both principles within him. We are all on Earth to develop and manifest the qualities of the polarity we incarnate. The qualities of the feminine polarity are related to the inner world, receptivity, and the emotional level. Hence, each woman's principle mission in life is to develop qualities that allow her to unfurl and display her femininity. She can then better inspire those around her, such as her husband, her children, friends, colleagues, etc., and with them, help create a harmonious, well-balanced, right, qualitative atmosphere and ambiance on all levels. Feminine qualities influence the way we receive others, our knowledge of how to nourish them with love, confidence, and encouragement, our will to submit to what is right, and our capacity to act with kindness and goodwill. The feminine polarity represents the feminine aspect of God.

Whenever a person dreams of a woman – mother, sister, friend, girlfriend, a little girl, a female stranger, etc. – she reveals aspects of the dreamer's feminine polarity, which exists in both men and women. In the case of a man (the women that appear in his dreams, as well as those he shares his life with, or simply encounters in his daily life, all represent aspects of his inner woman and his emotional world in general.

⊕ Reflection of a person's inner world and emotional level. Incarnation of feminine qualities: love, gentleness, grace, delicacy, sensitivity, compassion, devotion, gift of self, capacity to listen, subtle perception, intuition, psychic capacities, mediumnity. Great force of materialization, creation, and giving form as it is women who give birth to children, and it is within them that the child develops its physical body. Dispenser of nourishing energies on all levels. An important source of inspiration. The heart and motor of a family and intimate life.

⊖ Difficulty manifesting and recognizing feminine qualities. Discrepancy and imbalance between the two principles. Depolarization. May concern either an over-masculine or over-emissive woman, who represses or rejects her femininity, who lacks the capacity to listen, who lacks sensitivity, intuition, and receptivity, who has difficulty expressing love, gentleness, and compassion; or, it may indicate a man who has problems with his feminine polarity, his inner world, and emotional level. Superficial behavior based too much on seduction. An excessive need to please and be loved at all costs. Affective, emotional dependency. Excess or absence of sensitivity. Emotional coldness. A lack of nourishing energy and emotions. Infertility. Weakened potential for creation and materialization. Uninspiring energy for our entourage. May also indicate a person (male or female) who is too feminine, too gentle, too passive, excessively sensitive and receptive, who has difficulty asserting himself, being respected, deciding, taking action, and manifesting his emissivity, willpower, and authority.

WOOD (construction)

Construction wood represents accessibility to resources for building, edifying personal or social projects. Wood is a renewable resource that comes from trees, which are solid, polyvalent representatives of the vegetable kingdom (symbolically the world of feelings and emotions), and a symbol of knowledge, materialization, being well-grounded, well-rooted on the earthly, terrestrial level since tree-roots grow deep in the soil, while simultaneously connecting with Up Above through their branches. Wood also represents abundance of resources and a capacity for noble, sustainable construction.

⊕ A constructive period. Abundance of resources to build and accomplish evolutive projects on the personal and collective levels, while respecting the environment and natural balance. Responsible behavior. Awareness of the vital importance of woods and forests for the survival of man and other forms of life on this planet.

⊖ Impossibility of accomplishing building or renovation projects due to lack of resources, or difficulty procuring them. Unfavorable, limiting period that is harmful or damaging to construction or starting projects. May be related to dynamics of destruction of resources, nature, ecological balance because of indifference, egoism, greed, and abuse of power. Thoughtless, irresponsible deforestation.

WOOL

Through its animal origin, wool is related to the instinctual dimension of vital energy. It is a natural resource that is obtained without having to kill the animal it comes from. Used to protect us from the cold and damp, wool symbolizes protective, comforting warmth. The energy it radiates is calm, soothing, non-aggressive, and reflects softness, gentleness, because fleeced animals (sheep, goats, llamas, etc.) are herbivores with peaceful, tranquil temperaments. For a more detailed, deeper analysis, the use we make of wool (clothing, socks, gloves, hats, blankets, etc.), its color, and the symbolism of the animal it comes from, need to be taken into consideration.

⊕ A source of warmth, protection, comfort and consolation, softness, and gentleness. Worn as clothing, wool expresses a form of simplicity, modesty, and humility in the wearer's aura and energy. Inspires pacifist, peace-loving, warm, tender, affectionate soul-states (moods). A capacity to adapt to cold temperatures, atmospheres and ambiances. Possibility of creating new clothes with previously used wool, which relates it to creativity, dexterity, and non-wasteful energy.

⊖ Lack of warmth, softness, gentleness; or someone whose aura and behavior reflect the flaws, the weaknesses of the animal concerned; e.g. in the case of sheep's wool, a tendency to be too submissive and obedient, possibly even to unjust, wrong authority; or, a lack of submission; a tendency to follow without any discernment; or letting ourselves be abused by others and not saying anything, just like a sheep; stubborn, obstinate, capricious behavior, like a goat, etc. An incapacity to comfort, console and protect others or ourselves from cold ambiances. Lack of modesty or simplicity. Fragility, vulnerability. Excessive frugality.

WORK

Work is a symbol of intellectual, manual, emotional, and spiritual creation, production, conception and realization, materialization, both on the outer and inner levels. Right understanding of work, of our attitude to work, and the role we give it in our individual, professional, and social life depends on our level of conscience. Indeed, work allows us to discover the creative potential of our mind and spirit, through our experimentations in matter, and hence to manifest the Qualities, Virtues, and Divine Powers that dwell in each of us. It is founded on the principle that it is through doing, being involved, committing ourselves to a voluntary or imposed action/activity, that we learn and become competent, accomplished, responsible, and free. Often, people who live in a horizontal conscience, limited to the physical, material world, see work as an unavoidable necessity in answer to their basic, fundamental needs. If the obligation to work to subsist didn't exist, a lot of people would become lazy, nonchalant, and stagnate in their evolution. Indeed, when a person has all he needs at his disposal, is rich on every level, then he needs to be very evolved to continue to work constructively and in a well-balanced way, both on the inside and on the outside. Whenever wealth is limited to the material, financial level, the following phenomenon is frequently observed: either the person continues to work through greed, insecurity, excessive ambition, or megalomania; or, he becomes bogged down, mired in a lifestyle that makes him weak, capricious, vain, inclined to desire and feel he requires just about anything and everything to the point of becoming unhappy and empty.

To understand the symbolic meaning of the work we do in concrete reality, or that is featured in a dream, it is essential to analyze its physical and metaphysical nature, as well as what led us to this activity. In actual fact, the work we do is an essential key to understanding what dwells in us in terms of memories, distortions, or qualities, and to discover what it is in this life that we need to work on metaphysically, on the level of our unconscious. We do not choose a job by chance or coincidence; we could say that it is our job, our work that chooses us, or, differently expressed, it is our memories (conscious and unconscious) that choose our work.

Each job allows us to develop different qualities. Take a nurse and a plumber as examples. A nurse has a program that is more oriented toward healing his memories, care, human devotion, the application of wisdom, caring for, bandaging, *patching up* all sorts of wounds of all shapes and sizes, unconditional service, and the development of universal love. A plumber works more on putting order and structure back in his emotional world (the world of water), on his purification related to his needs, his instincts, and, thanks to his assistance and work, he allows others the possibility of emotional renewal, the cleansing and purification of their bodies and souls.

It is also important to validate inner work, especially when we find ourselves experiencing unemployment (*cf. also* this term), or in a rest period, so as not to feel guilty and undervalue ourselves for not having work, for being limited in our power of action on the physical or social level. It is vital to understand that inner work is the basis of all other forms of work, activity, duty, and responsibility; that everyone in whatever work they do, or position they hold, is both a teacher and a student; that every job, all work, has the same degree of importance in the eyes of Cosmic Intelligence, whence the popular saying, *If a job is worth doing, it is worth doing well,* which expresses the intrinsic value of every task we do. Work allows us to manifest our innate creative potential in a concrete, altruistic way, thanks to the multiple complementary gifts and talents invested in us.

As our conscience gradually awakens and evolves spiritually, we discover the multiple dimensions of work. Its educational, evolutive aspect gives deep meaning to everything we accomplish: by working with the intention of getting to know ourselves deeply, of blossoming, and fulfilling ourselves, our soul feels nourished and our spirit is continually inspired and motivated. By consciously uniting, marrying inner work and outer work, we discover the true meaning of Universal Wisdom, which helps us redefine and deepen our priorities to concentrate on the essential goal of Life.

⊕ Work on ourselves, on our personal and spiritual development by gradually and progressively integrating Qualities, Virtues, and Divine Powers. A person who materializes, concretizes, produces collective resources with the aim of helping, of being of assistance, developing altruism, evolving. Allows us to experiment our innate creative power and capacities, while being useful, helping, serving, surpassing ourselves, so as to grow in maturity and wisdom on the inside. Procures the joy of being alive, of being able to create, experiment, materialize. Satisfaction of a job (task) well done. Awareness allowing us to know ourselves, more truly, in greater depth, to discover our strengths and weaknesses, to continually learn. Develops knowledge, wisdom, practical logic, a capacity for decision-making, for undertaking various tasks, and taking responsibility for what we do, setting ourselves and various projects in motion. An understanding of the spiritual, moral, and material meaning of work. A symbolic study of each person's work (job, trade, profession), allows us to understand its deep meaning, as well as the reason why that person has such a job, does that type of work rather than another. Integration of states of conscience of abundance and confidence. Allows us to receive resources, consideration, to be proud of ourselves. A feeling of expansion. Procures abundance, vital resources. Foresight, protection, security. Stability, strength, power, adaptability. Liberty and truth found through work. Discipline. Motivation. Concentration. Helps develop a sense of justice and right authority. Allows us to cleanse our memories, to settle and repair karmas from this life or others. Understanding our mission, our life plan, through the work carried out as we go through life, as we advance along our Life path.

⊖ Someone who works either too much or not enough on the inner and/or outer level. Excess, abuse, slavery, all sorts of dependencies. Hyperactivity, prisoner of work (workaholic); or, laziness, procrastination. An overly materialistic, too down-to-earth person, who only thinks about money; or, escapism, seeking to flee personal, intimate, inner realities; or, someone who hasn't got his two feet on the ground, who is too disconnected from concrete reality, who thinks Up Above will take care of everything, do everything for him, without his having to make the slightest effort. Someone who only works for material benefits, success, financial security. Need for acknowledgement, seeking to prove our capacity to work, our abilities, to others. Overconfidence, forcing destiny. Insecurity, destabilization, existential anxiety and anguish, fear of lacking. A person who has a limited vision of the world of consequences, who is subjugated, who submits and lets himself be abused, exploited, due to memories where he abused and exploited others in previous lives. Memories of social injustice, abuse of authority. A lack of understanding of the spiritual, multi-dimensional meaning of work, of the evolution of the soul through work.

WRITE, TO

Writing allows us to materialize thoughts. Writing is an emissive act through which we exteriorize our knowledge, experience, and emotions using the creative power of words. Whenever we see ourselves writing in a dream, it means that we are working on getting to know, develop, and manifest our ideas. As a means of communication, writing allows us to share and exchange information as well as transmit knowledge on both the individual and collective level. (*cf. also* **Journalism; Letter**)

⊕ Communicating inspiring, elevating thoughts favoring the development of our conscience. Sharing beautiful sentiments, feelings. Developing and transmitting ideas. Elaborating a project, instruction, inspiration. Broadcasting knowledge on the individual and collective levels.

⊖ Difficulty communicating ideas and elaborating projects. Difficulty expressing thoughts and emotions. Using writing to manipulate, distort truth, to give false information, etc.

Y

YELLOW

Like red and blue, yellow is a primary color. It belongs to the group of warm colors that have a vivifying, energizing, exteriorizing effect. Often compared with the bright, luminous, warm radiance of the sun, it is also the color of the 3rd chakra, situated on the same level as the solar plexus. It symbolizes emissivity, self-confidence, as well as a capacity to diffuse and radiate light, knowledge, enthusiasm, human warmth, a force of manifestation and expansion, on the personal and social levels.

⊕ Divine, solar radiance. A luminous state of being. Authority. Confidence. Optimism. Harmony. Self-fulfillment. Understanding. Human warmth. Force of involvement. Expansion. Divine materialization.

⊖ Authoritarianism and/or over-confidence. Excessive emissivity and expansion. Overflowing enthusiasm, exaggeration. Agitation, rebellion. Artificial radiance. Exalted, exaggerated, excessive behavior. Self-fulfillment with the aim of acquiring prestige, recognition and acknowledgement; or, a lack of radiance, confidence, enthusiasm. Incapacity to activate our potential for emissivity and expansion. Pessimism. Lack of warmth, understanding, as well as inner light, clarity, lucidity.

YOGA

For thousands of years yoga has been an individual or collective spiritual practice of the development of the mind and spirit through physical exercises and breathing. It exists today in a multitude of forms depending on various traditions and their different approaches and methods, but virtually all of which share the following aims: development of receptivity, knowledge and mastery of body, mind, and spirit, awakening of conscience, as well as improvement of sensorial, multi-dimensional perception, thanks to our physical and metaphysical senses, in order to activate our full spiritual potential and attain overall, global well-being, plenitude, fulfillment, self-achievement, *nirvana.* Yoga seeks to unite our physical and metaphysical dimensions, notably by detachment from material needs and through serenity of mind and spirit. Yoga helps us improve our psychic life through active meditation and to rediscover the sacred meaning of our physical body.

Yoga also allows us to re-balance the two complementary polarities of receptivity and emissivity. Moreover, we learn to hear and listen to our inner voice, to be in contact with our feelings and senses, and to accede to the multi-dimensions. Seeing ourselves do yoga in a dream means we are in a deep process of inner, spiritual development, provided that the yoga and dream context are positive, harmonious, fulfilling, and evolutive.

Over the last few years, in order to more easily popularize yoga in social and community centers, in order to make it more accessible to the general public, some teachers have tended to diminish or even hide the spiritual aspect of yoga. Such an approach is not lacking in wisdom for certain social backgrounds. However, it may lead the person to over-develop his ego, to over-focus his attention on physical appearances and esthetic criteria, thereby losing the original, sacred meaning of yoga, i.e. to ensure the unification of body and spirit.

⊕ Allows us to develop receptivity, knowledge and mastery of body, mind, and spirit, subtle perception, contact with the spiritual dimension of our being. Favors fulfillment, well-being, harmony, serenity of mind and spirit, detachment from material goods, unification of our physical and metaphysical dimensions. Active, invigorating meditation that renews our energies on all levels and helps us integrate the sacred meaning of our body as a temple of the mind and spirit; it also helps us balance our receptivity and emissivity, our masculine and feminine polarities. Sets off a deep process of inner, spiritual development and multi-dimensional evolution. Opens a door onto mystical knowledge, favors discernment of good and evil.

⊖ Seeking high performance, a tendency to hide our ego behind a spiritual practice. May denote a person who is too down-to-earth; or, the opposite, whose head is in the clouds and who is too *airy-fairy*, too detached from matter. A bohemian life, lost in our spiritual quest. A tendency to flee matter, to reject the concrete world. Difficulty or incapacity to materialize due to discrepancies between the different parts of our being. A lack of spiritual knowledge and understanding of the symbolic language of dreams, signs and symbols. Difficulty opening our mind, our spirit, our conscience to walk a spiritual path. Over-passive spirituality; or, not involved enough on the concrete level. Difficulty finding harmony within ourselves, fusing the physical and metaphysical, well-balancing our masculine and feminine polarities, our emissivity and our receptivity. Someone who is more focused on the concrete result than on the spiritual intention. Over-seeking physical results and forcing a position or movement without working on our spirituality, on beautiful thoughts and emotions, only seeking esthetic beauty, following a trend. Difficulty accepting our limits and rhythm of evolution, a tendency to become excessively obsessive on the physical and/or spiritual levels. Doing yoga without conscience, or depth, without seeking spiritual improvement. Charlatanism, false yoga teacher, false guru, seeking power over others, domination, celebrity, renown, nourishing ourselves on people's admiration, adulation; false yoga student, prepared to, even preferring to give up his free will to blindly put into practice whatever his teacher says, using yoga as an excuse for refusing self-responsibility.

Z

ZEN

The word *Zen* (a Japanese word meaning meditation) refers to spirituality, to ancestral wisdom concerning meditation, harmony and enlightenment. This Buddhist method was first taught in China, before being introduced into Japan in the 12th century. This word also refers to *zazen*, the seated position chosen by Buddha to meditate. This form of meditation requires determination and the meditator has to master his body (posture) and his mind by means of harmonious breathing. This practice has multiple effects: the meditator feels calm and serene, develops improved concentration and receptivity, increased, better listening capacities, unification of his body, mind and spirit. He also benefits from an opening of conscience and perception of his inner world *via* dreams and self-study. Moreover, meditation allows us to connect with our Divine nature and thus to Universal Conscience, and to become aware of the fact that we belong to the Great Whole. It helps reduce stress, tension and hyperactivity. It helps us become detached from futility, to see our lives in depth, to accept and face great difficulties peacefully.

From a negative point of view, this particular meditation practice is sometimes considered too rigorous, too hard, too rigid. Moreover, a lack of knowledge of symbolic language may make it difficult to interpret the spiritual information received during meditation. Furthermore, seeking to forget self, which is a central aspect of this method, in order to reach a state of emptiness may create discrepancies with matter, and extremism when the practitioner becomes too detached from his body, from his life, his family and friends and the material world. A certain solitude may make the person austere, rigid, with lacks and discrepancies on the emotional, affective level.

⊕ Self-study and self-knowledge through meditation, contemplation, inner listening. Development of receptivity, high states of conscience, spirituality. Discipline, rigor, determination, courage, perseverance and willpower to walk a spiritual path. Allows us to renew ourselves, to enter the alpha waves. Favors openings of conscience *via* the senses. Triggers dreams. Develops great concentration, the ability to elevate our mind, spirit, and conscience, the capacity to be receptive to our deep Self as well as Universal Conscience. A philosophy of life based on serenity, harmony, inner peace. A *zen*, calm, relaxed person who deals with his life peacefully and tranquilly. A capacity to manage high tensions, to remain persevering during initiations. An initiatic life, someone who works to develop the potential of his spirit, and who walks a solitary path toward wisdom.

⊖ Austerity and rigidity in the search for mastery through meditation. Rejection of thoughts, someone who represses his memories, refusing to sort them out, to analyze good and evil. Disconnection between the spirit, mind and body. A dangerous meditational practice that leads people to cut themselves off from the world and all of the pleasures of life. Difficulty accepting unconscious memories that re-surface. Idealization of ourselves, of our ego, camouflaged in a rigorous but misleading spiritual practice. A tendency toward extreme isolation, exaggerated solitude. Outward display of a zen attitude while storms rage on the inside. Someone who experiences discrepancies regarding matter, his couple, or his family due to an over-solitary, anti-social activity. Spiritual extremism, someone who is too contemplative, who doesn't live his concrete life enough, who distances himself from others, lacks sociability, and loses his capacity for true, concrete altruism.

ZOO

A zoo is a public place where visitors can see mostly exotic or rare animals in captivity, or semi-liberty. It is a place of observation and learning, allowing us to better understand the animal world, to study it, and, in some cases, to ensure the protection and survival of endangered species. Symbolically, a zoo represents contact with and the study of numerous aspects of our instinctual needs and behavior, of the animal dimension of our being.

It is a place that greatly attracts children, who often visit a zoo with their family. When we know the Law of resonance and symbolic language, a visit to a zoo may prove to be very revealing, because our preferences and reactions of attraction and repulsion regarding the different animals reveal the relationship we have with our inner animals, how we consider and treat our instincts and vital energy. For a more detailed analysis, the specific symbolism of the animals(s) that attracted our attention needs to be taken into consideration.

From a negative point of view, a zoo is associated with limitation, sequestration, excessive control, imprisonment, poor, even cruel treatment, theft and illegal trafficking of animals, of our vital forces and fundamental needs.

⊕ A place of discovery, observation, learning, education, allowing us to better understand our inner animal world through the observation and study of animals in the outside world. Awareness of the correlations and resonance that exist between animal characteristics and human attitudes and behavior. Contact with a great variety of our fundamental needs and the expression of our animal dimension, revealing how instinctual we are, as well as the instinctual way we behave and act. Facilitates the study and analysis of our sometimes dangerous inner forces, so as to better integrate them and cleanse their wild, instinctual, animal-like, distorted, aggressive, coarse behavior dictated by programs of survival. A capacity to tame, domesticate, educate, and master our vital energy. Access to little known or unknown potential of our inner world, our instinctual needs, and our vital energy. Protection of rare animal forces, symbolizing aspects of our diversity. A determined ability to establish right, rigorous rules for instinctual behavior and have them respected. A person who works in a zoo for love of animals, for what animals are, and what they represent. A capacity to isolate negative forces and energies, to observe, analyze and study them from a distance, so as to be able to understand and transcend them. Conscious work on basic, very intense emissive forces. Awareness that for each animal there is a corresponding symbolism with our human character, with our fundamental behavior, the way we are, the way we behave, the way we act.

⊖ A person who limits, represses, mistreats, or restrains and curbs his animal nature, his instinctual needs, his vital energy. A feeling of being ensnared, caught in a trap, of having great strength, power, and energy within us, of having an immense potential for action and manifestation, but which are pent-up, limited, imprisoned, and cannot be released and set free. May be related to an outburst of vital energy, which, having been long restrained and oppressed, suddenly emerges, bursting forth brutally and violently. Functioning in survival mode; impulsive, wild, anti-social, cruel attitudes. Problems of extreme dependency, of repressed anger, harshness toward ourselves and/or others; or, a tendency to laxity, loss of mobility and power of action. Someone who treats his instinctual needs with indifference, insensitivity, lacking in love and understanding; or, who is a slave to those needs. De-naturalization, unnatural exploitation of life potential. An absence of principles, rules, and healthy, safe structures in the use of vital energy. Non-respect for our own, or others', instinctual nature. Energy retention, rigidity. Conscious and unconscious memories marked by suffering and wounds regarding the manifestation and expression of our vital energy.

HOW TO INTERPRET DREAMS & SIGNS
Kaya
ISBN 978-2-923654-11-9
e-Book version ISBN 978-2-923654-13-3

THE 72 ANGEL CARDS
DREAMS, SIGNS, MEDITATION
Kaya and Christiane Muller
ISBN 978-2-923097-60-2

IN THE LAND OF BLUE SKIES
Gabriell, Kaya and Christiane Muller
ISBN 978-2-923097-65-7

DREAM JOURNAL
BORN UNDER THE STAR OF CHANGE
(200-white-page Notebook,
Other covers available)
ISBN : 978-2-923654-20-1

STUCK IN INSECURITIES: CHANGE YOUR INNER CLIMATE
THE TRADITIONAL STUDY OF ANGELS
AUDIO INTERNATIONAL LECTURE
Kaya and Christiane Muller
ISBN 978-2-922467-26-0

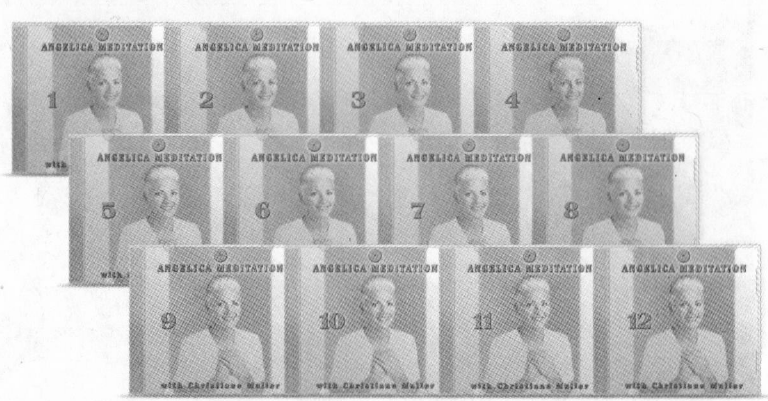

ANGELICA MEDITATION COLLECTION

CD 1: (Angels 72 to 67) ISBN: 978-2-923097-68-8
CD 2: (Angels 66 to 61) ISBN: 978-2-923097-69-5
CD 3: (Angels 60 to 55) ISBN: 978-2-923097-70-1
CD 4: (Angels 54 to 49) ISBN: 978-2-923097-71-8
CD 5: (Angels 48 to 43) ISBN: 978-2-923097-72-5
CD 6: (Angels 42 to 37) ISBN: 978-2-923097-73-2
CD 7: (Angels 36 to 31) ISBN: 978-2-923097-74-9
CD 8: (Angels 30 to 25) ISBN: 978-2-923097-75-6
CD 9: (Angels 24 to 19) ISBN: 978-2-923097-76-3
CD 10: (Angels 18 to 13) ISBN: 978-2-923097-77-0
CD 11: (Angels 12 to 7) ISBN: 978-2-923097-78-7
CD 12: (Angels 6 to 1) ISBN: 978-2-923097-79-4

ANGELICA MUSICA COLLECTION

CD 1: (Angels 72 to 67) ISBN: 978-2-923097-80-0
CD 2: (Angels 66 to 61) ISBN: 978-2-923097-81-7
CD 3: (Angels 60 to 55) ISBN: 978-2-923097-82-4
CD 4: (Angels 54 to 49) ISBN: 978-2-923097-83-1
CD 5: (Angels 48 to 43) ISBN: 978-2-923097-84-8
CD 6: (Angels 42 to 37) ISBN: 978-2-923097-85-5
CD 7: (Angels 36 to 31) ISBN: 978-2-923097-86-2
CD 8: (Angels 30 to 25) ISBN: 978-2-923097-87-9
CD 9: (Angels 24 to 19) ISBN: 978-2-923097-88-6
CD 10: (Angels 18 to 13) ISBN: 978-2-923097-89-3
CD 11: (Angels 12 to 7) ISBN: 978-2-923097-90-9
CD 12: (Angels 6 to 1) ISBN: 978-2-923097-91-6

BORN UNDER THE STAR OF CHANGE
Kaya
Production: Russ DeSalvo, New York, USA
Record Label: Golden Wisdom Records / Airgo Music
Genre: Adult Contemporary / Pop / Inspirational
Format: CD and MP3
# of songs: 13
Item number: 627843159308

ANGELICA MANTRA VOL. 1
ANGELS 1 to 12
Kasara
ISBN 978-2-923654-35-5

ANGELICA MANTRA VOL. 2
ANGELS 13 to 24
Kasara
ISBN 978-2-923654-36-2

ANGELICA MANTRA VOL. 4
ANGELS 37 to 48
Kasara
ISBN 978-2-923654-38-6

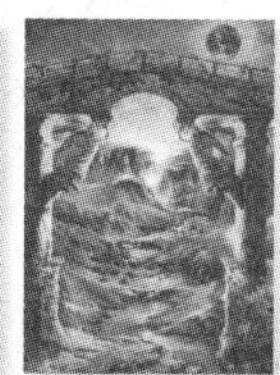

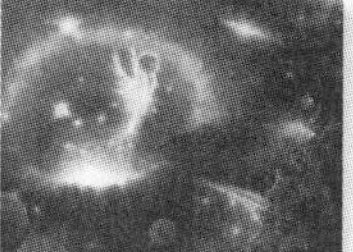

GREETING CARDS EXPOSITION ANGELICA
Artist: Gabriell
A collection of 65 greeting cards

NOTES

NOTES

NOTES

NOTES